mav·er·ick (mav'er-ik), *n* 1. an unbranded steer. Hence [colloq.] 2. a person not labeled as belonging to any one faction, group, etc., who acts independently. 3. one who moves in a different direction than the rest of the herd—often a nonconformist. 4. a person using individual judgment, even when it runs against majority opinion.

Maverick Guides by Robert W. Bone
The Maverick Guide to Hawaii
The Maverick Guide to Australia
The Maverick Guide to New Zealand

The MAVERICK Guide to

Robert W. Bone

1987 EDITION

PELICAN PUBLISHING COMPANY

GRETNA 1987

First edition, May 1977
Second edition, January 1978
Third edition, January 1979
Fourth edition, April 1980
Fifth edition, January 1981
Sixth edition, January 1982
Seventh edition, January 1983
Eighth edition, January 1984
Ninth edition, January 1985
Tenth edition, October 1985
Eleventh edition, January 1987
Second printing, February 1987

ISBN: 0-88289-632-6
ISSN: 0278-6613

For my parents,
ROBERT O. BONE, JUANITA C. BONE.
Also dedicated with special appreciation to
TEMPLE H. FIELDING

Manufactured in the United States of America
Published by Pelican Publishing Company, Inc.
1101 Monroe Street, Gretna, Louisiana 70053

Contents

List of Maps

Preface

Everything in this annual volume represents in one way or another our own experience or opinions. This is not to say that we have personally eaten in every restaurant, slept in all the hotels, and taken every new tour offered over the past 12 months, although we certainly do a lot of that kind of thing. Nevertheless, as the saying goes, "We know the territory."

If you're looking for mistakes, well, we're sure you'll find a few authentic Boners (as well as a couple of bad puns). This is the eleventh edition of the first book in a series of guides to Pacific parts of the world. (The others are *The Maverick Guide to New Zealand* and *The Maverick Guide to Australia*.) For this reason, we would like your help. If you see an error or note a change in any entry since we investigated it, we'd appreciate it tremendously if you would send the information to us in care of the publisher. You may thereby become one of our most critical editors for subsequent editions. (Use the special letter-envelope on the back page, or write us reams in your own envelope.) Incidentally, we try very hard to answer every letter that we receive.

Let it not be said here that you cannot visit Hawaii without a guidebook. Lots of people do. There are plenty of guided tours that begin by strapping you in on the Mainland and that don't let you off the leash again until you're back home. And there are other visitors who say they do not intend to leave the beach (ouch!) for the entire length of their sun-drenched vacation.

There are also many hotel desk clerks and tour guides to direct you to places in which they or their companies have financial interests. You can get along with these recommendations—in the same way that an automobile that is designed to run more smoothly on low-cost regular gasoline gets along only a *little* jerkily when it is fed expensive, high-test fuel instead.

But we want to keep you rolling smoothly *and* economically, while at the same time gently guiding you along adventuresome beaches and byways. There you can find your own individual fun, as we have done, here in the Hawaiian Islands.

Aloha,

BOB AND SARA BONE

Honolulu

P.S. And tell 'em we sent you!

ix

Mahalo a nui loa!

These are the people who helped us the most—not because it was in their interest to do so, or because it was part of their job, but mostly just because they wanted to do so:

Anita Abramson, John Anderson, Bill Bachran, Tony Bartlett, Laura Baumann, Bruce Benson, Ferd Borsch, Buck Buchwach, Joan Cameron, George Chaplin, Hugh Clark, Patti Cook, Jeanne Creamer, Alberta de Jetley, Ron DeLacy, Dave Donnelly, Sheila Donnelly, Hobe Duncan, Sally Edwards, Kani Evans, Jane Evinger, Betty Fay, Marlene Freedman, Victor Givan, Hal Glatzer, Ann Gottlieb, Betty Green, Wayne Harada, Anne Harpham, Jay Hartwell, Tom Horton, Pat Hunter, Sandra Matsukawa Hu, Stephen Hu, Carolyn Imamura, Ron Jett, Carol Johnson, Ben Kalb, Tom Kaser, Ken Kay, Mike Keller, Ed Kennedy, Arnold Kishi, Bob Krauss, Wendy Long, Gerry Lopez, Leonard Lueras, Harry Lyons, Jeanne McKinley, Ken Metzler, Alan Miley, Barbara Morgan, Dan Myers, Gale Myers, David Pager, Sylvia Pager, Donna Raphael, Rick Raphael, Frances Reed, Stephen Reed, Eunice Riedel, Ross Roberts, Ronn Ronck, Rock Rothrock, Stephanie Salazar, Wade Shirkey, David Smollar, Ellen Spielvogel, Lester Spielvogel, Scott Stone, Ed Tanji, Harolyn Tanji, Jan TenBruggencate, Noelani Teves, Spencer Tinker, Polly Theriot, David Tong, Thurston Twigg-Smith, Madge Walls, Janice Wolf, Peter Wolf, Connie Wright, David Yamada, Ron Youngblood, Sanford Zalburg, and especially Frumie Selchen.

THE MAVERICK GUIDE TO HAWAII

1

Why and How
to Use This Book

One evening not long ago, we were at Honolulu Airport waiting for friends who were coming in on a late flight from the Mainland. We held flower *leis*—the traditional welcoming gift of the Islands—to place over our friends' heads once they stepped off the Wiki-Wiki bus carrying them from the plane to the main terminal.

Nearby, an elderly Oriental-Hawaiian woman also waited. She told us she was there to meet her cousin who was returning from a vacation in California. She, too, carried a *lei,* and she wore a bright *muumuu,* that long Hawaiian dress which, for more than a century, has enhanced the beauty of every woman who has ever put it on.

Not far away stood two young, attractive, dark-skinned women dressed in ti-leaf skirts. Employed by a professional greeting service, they held about two dozen leis in their arms. They had been contracted to meet a particular tour group.

After some delay, the first of the buses from the jumbo jet arrived. The tour group soon appeared, and the two hula girls went into their act. The *leis* were dutifully draped over the shoulders of each passenger who was wearing a gummed label of a certain color.

Less than a minute later, the label wearers and the Hawaiian maidens had finished with each other, and they all moved off—the visiting group toward the baggage area and the young women toward a place to change out of their costumes. Other nonaffiliated passengers continued to disembark from the bus.

One Mainlander alighted happily, but immediately let his face fall into an expression of deep disappointment as he watched the two greeter girls disappear into the night.

"Where's mine?" he asked, at first of no one in particular. Then he spotted our friend, the Oriental-Hawaiian: "Don't I get some flowers, too?"

The woman hesitated for only a second. Then she stepped forward and placed the *lei*—the one she had bought for her cousin—around the visitor's neck. She was considerably shorter than the newcomer, so he had to stoop.

"*Aloha!*" she greeted him. The man gave her a smiling kiss on the cheek, straightened up wearing his new *lei,* and then joined the crowd in a search for suitcases, blissfully unaware that anything out of the ordinary had happened.

"What else could I do?" The woman looked at us helplessly. "He seemed so unhappy!"

The vignette at the airport was an illustration of today's Hawaiian contrasts. The once-all-pervading Aloha Spirit may have largely disappeared from the Islands, to be replaced by commercial imitations of its content. Yet the genuine article continues to survive, too, in wonderful and surprising smaller doses.

Our Modus Operandi. *The Maverick Guide to Hawaii* has been carefully constructed mainly for two types of readers: (1) the visitor to Hawaii, and (2) the new resident of the state.

There is a Hawaiian word covering both groups—*malihini* ("molly-*he-knee*"). It means "newcomer" or "stranger," and you'll hear it a lot, usually used in an affectionate way.

To continue the language lesson for a moment, this book is specifically for *akamai* ("ah-kah-*my*") *malihinis*. An *akamai malihini* is a newcomer with a certain amount of savvy. He's a visitor who is not cheap, but who certainly is not interested in throwing money around unnecessarily.

Hawaii no longer just happens to welcome visitors who may casually stop off on its shores. The state reaches out for them. It actively seeks *malihinis*, advertising for them, with all the resulting zealousness that a Madison Avenue campaign implies.

Sure it's got a good product, and a visit to Hawaii should be a lot of fun. But although you will seldom be bothered by rain, the good times can still be dampened. It's the purpose of this guide to make sure they aren't.

Tourism is by far the biggest business in the state, its monetary returns having long ago passed the revenues from the traditional sugar and pineapple industries. And it's likely to remain Number 1 for some time.

But like sugar and pineapple, the growth of the visitor industry in Hawaii has sweet and sour implications.

This book was not written to satisfy, assuage, or coddle those whose profits and livelihood depend on the five-billion-dollar-a-year Hawaiian tourist business. No owners, managers, skippers, drivers, lecturers, maîtres d'hôtel, or any kind of operators—fast-buck or soft-sell—have put out money, friendship, or favors to insert anything into (or keep anything out of) this guide.

Generally speaking, our close friends are not in the tourist industry, and we try to keep it that way. We don't play golf with hotel managers. We don't play poker with restaurateurs. And we don't "play ball" with anyone. With a few exceptions, such as an occasional orientation tour, special inaugural, and the like, which are sometimes extended to legitimate travel writers and press groups, we have paid our own bills for this annual volume. All in all, we think this book is perhaps the cleanest travel guide of its type in the world.

Unlike other guidebook writers, we make our home in Hawaii, and we have lived here for the past 16 years. During that time we have learned that there is no substitute for walking the ground over and over again to maintain an accurate picture of today's vacation conditions.

Therefore it is our earnest belief that the price of this book will save you many times over that investment. And when you meet the poor fellow and his wife who have signed up for two $10 seats on the boat cruise to Pearl Harbor without knowing that the U.S. Navy runs a better one—a *free* one—then we feel sure you'll believe it, too.

The two of us did not grow up in the Hawaiian Islands. But between us we have lived over much of the world—in the South Pacific, in England and Europe, in North and South America, and in the Caribbean. We also have two teen-age offspring—David, who was born in Spain, and Christina, a native New Yorker. When they were youngsters, they were the most sophisticated travelers since Bobby Shafto and Dick Whittington. Today David is in the Navy and Christina is studying drama.

We think our experiences on the move, plus our living the Island life for more than a decade and one-half, have given us special opportunities to realistically assess and appreciate all that we have found in Hawaii.

In addition, Sara (who was born in New Zealand) and the kids all have a smidgen of Polynesian blood wandering through their veins. So again we are tied to Pacific life, the New Zealand Maoris and the native Hawaiians being at least genealogical first cousins.

But probably most important, the male half of this team is a battle-scarred veteran of guidebooks to Europe produced by the late Temple Fielding, whom *Time* dubbed "the archon of U.S. guidebook writers." Under Fielding's intense tutelage, I explored hundreds of European hotels, restaurants, nightclubs, guided tours, and other tourist facilities, as well as toiled at home on Mallorca, where we pounded the manuscripts into the strict form that Fielding demanded.

The Organization. One of the most difficult tasks for any guidebook author is to arrange his book in an easy-to-use pattern. After experimenting with several systems for this volume, we have come up with one we believe is superefficient.

Following chapters on such general subjects as nature and people, we devote the final six chapters individually to the six inhabited islands you may visit in Hawaii. Each "island-chapter" is divided into twelve numbered sections, and each section is devoted to a separate subject about that island. The sections and their numbers remain the same for all six island-chapters:

1. **Around the Island**
2. **The Airport**
3. **Transportation**
4. **The Hotel Scene**
5. **Restaurants and Dining**
6. **Sightseeing**
7. **Guided Tours and Cruises**
8. **Water Sports**
9. **Other Sports**
10. **Shopping**
11. **Nights on the Town**
12. **The Address List**

Once you have become familiar with one of our six island-chapters, you will be acquainted with the order-of-march through the rest of them, too. With the numbers, you'll learn to find something to eat under "5," boat trips under "7," stores under "10," and so forth.

We hope you will read this book before you even leave home. Make some plans on the basis of your homework. Decide which islands you will visit and what you probably will want to do on each. Pick out hotels. If you are considering coming with a group, see how well the itinerary and descriptions given you stack up against what we have reported on in the following pages. Make lists of things you will take with you and of things you may buy in the Islands.

Pick up lots of maps and free travel folders from airline offices and travel agencies. Jot down any changes in prices you have found in this literature.

Finally, long after you have begun to dog-ear this guide during the planning phase, be sure to bring it to Hawaii. As important as it can be in advance preparations, it is as a reference on the scene that the volume will really prove itself.

You will use this book for decisions on the spur of the moment—stores to shop in, for instance, or nightclubs to visit. There are those unexpected changes of plans, like suddenly having to rent a car on the tiny island of Molokai on Sunday night. Whom can you call after the sidewalks are rolled up? How exorbitant will be the rates?

You may notice a plethora of telephone numbers in this guide. They're usually in parentheses following the name of a facility of some sort, and they may at first seem impediments to the smooth reading of the text. However, your eye will soon learn to skip over the little (Tel. 555-1212) *until* the time comes when you need it. *Use* the telephone. Thankfully, everyone in Hawaii speaks English. Pay phones will soon be going up to a quarter a call, but that's still a small investment when you may save a lot on a hotel, restaurant or other facility by calling them first. Private telephones are allowed an unlimited number of local calls. (However, you may be charged 50 cents or more per call from your hotel room, so check that out when you check in.)

Anywhere on any one island all phone calls are local. Only interisland calls are long-distance or toll calls. (Look out; it sometimes costs more to call interisland than it does to dial California!) But for local calls, at any rate, you can use the phone to find out late changes in operating hours or prices, or just to ask for specific directions and distances to help you get someplace.

We feel that although the telephone service is not as dependable as in many areas of the Mainland, it is nonetheless one of the cheapest, most valuable, and most underutilized tourist aids throughout Hawaii.

And from your own home on the Mainland, you can make good use of the "800" series for toll-free calls direct to some Hawaii numbers. Check the appendix for toll-free numbers of Hawaiian hotels and rental-car companies, and don't miss our remarks on these in the Oahu Transportation and Hotels sections (chapter 5, sections 3 and 4).

2

Before You Go
Holo-Holo

When you consider that only a little over 200 years ago there was no way to get to Hawaii at all, it's little less than amazing how accessible the place is today. Now almost anyone who wants to can go *holo-holo* (make the rounds) in all the Islands.

There are four ways to travel to the Fiftieth State, and two of these—private yacht or military transportation—we'll skip. As a practical matter, you have one choice to make: whether to sail or to fly.

By Ship to Honolulu

If you (1) are a sentimentalist, (2) are pretty well-heeled, and (3) have time on your hands, by all means take a luxury liner to Hawaii. It is the most beautiful and traditional way to go.

Sadly, most of us fulfill qualification number one above, but have trouble with either or both of the other two prerequisites. As a matter of bald fact, so few vacationers travel by ship to Hawaii, and so few passenger-carrying vessels call there anymore, that some may think it's a waste of time to discuss them.

One possibility for luxury-lining to Hawaii is with the San Francisco–based **American Hawaii Cruises,** which annually makes a few trans-Pacific crossings to connect with its week-long sailing around the Islands in the 30,000-ton twins *Independence* and *Constitution*. One or the other of the ships occasionally calls at Seattle, San Francisco, and Los Angeles before returning to Honolulu. No 1987 rates have been published at this writing, but we'll guess you could count on a minimum fare of at least $1,000 one way for the trans-Pac portion alone.

We know less about the plans for the newly organized **Aloha Pacific Cruises**, which plans to relaunch the old 563-foot liner, S.S. *Monterey*, in Tacoma, Wash. this year and then sail her to the Islands this summer. (See chapter 5, section 7 for more about both American Hawaii Cruises and Aloha Pacific Cruises.)

One problem for ship lovers is that it is generally not possible to travel simply from one American port to another American port on a foreign ship. This "cabotage" procedure is forbidden by an anachronistic law called the Jones Act, which hasn't changed since the day it was passed in 1896. (It now also applies to airlines.)

However, you may visit Hawaii as part of a cruise to many other ports. And then if you board any ship at a foreign port like Sydney or Auckland, you are certainly permitted to sail to and even disembark at Hawaii. With these possibilities in mind, below are a few cruise lines to consider. But check with your travel agent, too. With the cancelling of many sailings in the Atlantic and the Mediterranean over the past year or two, more cruise ships are expected to ply Pacific waters in the months to come.

The **P&O Lines** has just retired the *Oriana*, which usually showed up in Honolulu on its way to and from the South Pacific. However, P&O's 45,000-ton flagship *Canberra* continues to call in Honolulu and Lahaina on one of its world cruises, usually in October or November.

The P&O-owned **Princess Cruises** has begun operating its *Island Princess* on one round-trip cruise from Los Angeles to New Zealand and Australia via Hawaii. This Love Boat stops at Lahaina and Honolulu on the way Down Under, probably in October, and then returns on the northbound trip from Sydney and Auckland to drop in on Honolulu during April on the way home. In addition, Princess Cruises' flagship, the 45,000-ton *Royal Princess* will cruise from the West Coast on Feb. 14, 1987 to call in Lahaina and Honolulu on the way to the South Pacific.

For the first time, the **Royal Cruise Line** is represented in Hawaii this winter. The *Royal Odyssey* sails from Los Angeles Oct. 24, 1986, and calls at Honolulu on the way to the South Pacific. She will return over the opposite itinerary in late February, 1987. Plans for later in the year are incomplete at our deadline.

Every year for almost the past 10 years, we have heard that the new Seattle-based company **United States Cruises** is about to get underway with the newly refurbished liner *United States*, which hasn't seen sea duty since about 1969. We've just heard it again, and the latest date given for launching its California-to-Hawaii cruises is January, 1988. Tune in next year.

A few European-based cruise ships call at Honolulu from time to time. Liners like the *Rotterdam* and the *Sagafjord,* which leave New York or Florida in January, usually make it through the Caribbean, the Panama Canal, and up to Honolulu by about March.

Royal Viking Line ships stop in Hawaii four or five times a year. The *Royal Viking Star* and the *Royal Viking Sea* may call in Honolulu on the return voyage from the South Pacific early in the year on their way to California. Then the *Royal Viking Sea* usually chooses Honolulu as one port on its annual winter/spring cruise.

Also, the Cunard Line's *Queen Elizabeth 2* generally calls at Honolulu and sometimes at Lahaina or Kailua-Kona on its annual circumnavigation of the globe.

One last possibility, of the very slim kind: How would you like to sail to or from Hawaii as a paying crew member on a genuine sailing ship? A few experienced people can do it, anyway, aboard the *Californian,* the "Official Tallship of California." It's a training vessel for young people which has been going to the Islands in June and then on a few interisland cruises before returning home in August. At this writing, high school and college students, called "cadets" sign on for $1,000, and adults pay $1,800 for the 16-day voyage. Get further details from the **Nautical Heritage Society** at 24532 Del Prado, Dana Point, CA 92629, or phone (714) 661-1001.

And now, most of us will return to the real world.

The Air Ways to Hawaii

Many vacationers who go to Hawaii not only spend too much money while there, but actually lay out more than is necessary to travel to the Islands in the first place.

Some jet there First Class, and we would have to agree that it is a comfortable and pampered way to fly—when you have the dough. There are extra-wide, supersoft seats, plenty of leg and arm space, multicourse gourmet meals with elaborate service, all you can eat and drink. . . . It's living a luxurious Life of Riley at 30,000 feet. But today more travelers are questioning whether flying First Class is really worth the more than 30 percent price difference.

Coach Class. You'll probably save more than $100 off the one-way First Class (F) West Coast–to–Hawaii fare by moving to the narrower seats in the back three-fourths of the airplane. That means flying Coach, also called "Y Class."

For Coach Class fares, you have to give up a few luxuries. The movie on board will cost you about $3 if you want it. There will be no free drinks (you pay a buck or two for those you want), and your meal will be more limited, with little or no choice of food.

Still not enough savings? Okay, beyond that, there are special excursion fares (covering a limited period of time); advance purchase fares (APEX), which may also be set up for a limited time only; and some other temporary discount fares designed to better the airline's competitive position. Remember that the lowest fares will also be "capacity controlled"—that is, they are sold for a certain number of seats on each flight and not for all of the coach section.

Also, you just may find a rock-bottom "standby fare," used to fill up those last few empty seats with passengers willing to go out to the airport with their bags full of clothes and hearts full of hope.

All this is a result of airlines having been deregulated—freed from impositions by the old Civil Aeronautics Board. They now have more freedom to compete, and you may have read about their controversial decisions to drop unpopular, money-losing routes or to charge passengers more per mile for those high-cost, low-load flights.

Happily, the West Coast–to–Hawaii routes (like the New York–to–California ones) are among the most popular and heavily traveled flights in the country. The airlines seem to keep tripping over each other to offer the most attractive deals they possibly can on the Hawaii runs, and sometimes they enter into "fare wars" in an effort capture the lucrative market.

If you aim to get the cheapest possible fare—rather than to choose a particular airline or even a specific date of departure—it is important to find a good travel agent who can instantly come up with the least expensive way for you to make a trip to Hawaii. (More on travel agents later.)

Fare Predictions. All right. For those who insist that we make an attempt to estimate economy airline fares, we'll put on our turban, peer into the crystal jet stream, and make the following (intentionally vague) prognostications:

With the increased traffic between the Mainland and Hawaii over the past couple of years, competitive fares have been holding well below what many thought they would be. Early in 1987, we think some brand-name airlines advertising Hawaii trips on the West Coast will do their utmost to keep a few frill-less fares less than $200 each way to Honolulu, on a round-trip basis. (Add about $50 for the popular direct-to-Maui or -Kauai or -Kona flights.) Texans might estimate a barrelbottom tab of about $300 each way. From Chicago or New York the cheapest economy fare will probably run not much more than that price. (And cutthroat competition on the coast-to-coast runs may act together with the competitive California-Hawaii routes to trim those East Coast fares again, particularly if you commit yourself to a round-trip ticket.)

Some "bargain" airlines, like Total Air, may knock 20 to 30 percent off these figures. One way to be sure of getting the best fare possible, especially if you're going to Hawaii later in the year, is to buy your ticket as early as you can and take it home with you. If air fares do go up, you will have your ticket stored at home or in a safe-deposit box. Federal fare guarantee laws generally keep airlines from forcing price hikes on passengers who already have their tickets (although you may have to use them within one year after they were written).

Tip: A lot has been written about new flights from the Mainland nonstop to some Neighbor Island airports (Kauai, Maui, Kona, or Hilo). Be aware that many airlines have not found these as profitable as anticipated, and that schedules and types of aircraft are frequently changed at the last moment. For example, you may book a nonstop jumbo jet direct from San Francisco to Maui only to find yourself getting on board a DC-8 for the long trip or else to find that the aircraft will now stop at Honolulu and then double back to land on Maui an hour later. If you want to fly direct to those airports, keep an eye out for this kind of eventuality, or insist that your travel agent do so—especially if you have paid an extra premium for the convenience of skipping the hop from Honolulu.

Another tip: Even if you normally take a window seat, consider choosing one on the aisle for the 4½ to 5½ hours between the West Coast and Hawaii in Coach Class. There is not much to see outdoors, except just before landing—and if you're also going to a Neighbor Island, you'll catch your aerial views of Honolulu then. Your feet will thank you for the opportunity for an occasional stroll en route to Hawaii without disturbing anyone sitting next to you.

Incidentally, the first paying passengers to travel from San Francisco to Honolulu took off Oct. 22, 1936, traveling on a seaplane named the Hawaii Clipper. In those propeller-driven days it took 20 hours of air time to reach the Islands.

The Major North American Carriers

At this writing, there are about a dozen regularly scheduled trunk airlines on the Mainland-to-Hawaii route, and one or two more may soon be added. Some carriers can be taken from other countries, along with a few foreign airlines. Pick yours based on how well it serves your personal needs, and always choose a nonstop flight whenever you can. You may lengthen your trip by an hour each time the plane lands en route. (The list below does not include charter aircraft such as Wardair Canada or Transamerica.)

As to type of equipment (airplanes are called "equipment" in industry jargon), we vastly prefer the jumbo jets—particularly the Boeing 767 or the 747 (although the newer 767 has not yet been put on any Hawaii runs). Other aircraft classified as jumbos, or "wide bodies" (with two aisles), include the DC-10 and the Lockheed TriStar L-1011. If you're making Coach reservations on an airline flying the L-1011, ask if seats are 10-across (a 3-4-2 configuration) or a roomier 9-across (a 2-5-2 configuration). Ten-across, or "charter-style" seating, is just too cramped for many passengers.

United Airlines. United is by far the dominant carrier on the route, averaging more than 20 daily flights to Hawaii, most of them on Boeing 747s nonstop to Honolulu from Chicago, Denver, Seattle, San Francisco, and Los Angeles. Some flights originate in Toronto and New York but are not nonstops. United service now continues on from Honolulu to several Far East and South Pacific destinations. One DC-8 (single-aisle) flight (formerly a DC-10 jumbo) from Chicago via L.A. lands daily at Kailua-Kona on the Big Island. Also a few stretched DC-8 flights from San Francisco and Los Angeles travel nonstop daily to Kahului on Maui and Lihue on Kauai. The Lihue flights stop at Hilo on their return leg to Los Angeles.

Western Airlines. Traditionally second in the Mainland-Hawaii market, Western has more than 60 DC-10 flights a week to the Islands. There are nonstops to Honolulu from Anchorage, San Francisco, Los Angeles, and now San Diego. Other direct (not nonstop) flights originate in Minneapolis, New York, Las Vegas, Salt Lake City, and Washington, D.C. Last year Western also began daily direct service to Maui from Salt Lake City and Los Angeles, but recheck the type of aircraft used and the routing. At press time, Western has just been bought by Delta Airlines (see below).

Continental Airlines. This Texas-based airline offers daily flights between San Francisco or Los Angeles and Honolulu, some flights originating in Houston. Just at our press time, it announced a new four-class non-stop DC-10 flight between New York City and Honolulu, probably the only nonstop between Gotham and the Islands since TWA said it would drop the nonstop flight it tried for awhile in 1986. (Because of the jet stream, nonstop flights generally take about 10½ hours to Honolulu and 9½ hours returning to New York.) There are also new nonstops between Honolulu and Vancouver.

From Down Under, Continental flights to Honolulu and Vancouver also begin in Auckland and Sydney, some flying via Fiji, and others originate in Guam in the Western Pacific. All are on DC-10s. (*Tip:* At this writing, Continental's barrel-bottom APEX fares tend to be a little lower than those of other major airlines, although not as low as no-frills outfits like Total. For the very best deal, try to book to Honolulu on one of those more-comfortable Continental flights that also continue beyond Hawaii to the South Pacific.)

Trans World Airlines. One of the largest U.S. airlines, TWA returned to Hawaii in 1986 after an absence of almost a decade, initially flying non-stop Boeing 747 flights daily between its St. Louis headquarters and Honolulu, later adding direct service from New York. New flights from Los Angeles also were recently inaugurated by TWA in L-1011s carrying 291 passengers.

American Airlines. There are several daily DC-10 flights nonstop from Los Angeles (originating in Dallas/Ft. Worth), from San Francisco (originating in Chicago or New York), and straight from Chicago. American also has a few flights from Los Angeles and Dallas/Ft. Worth to and from Maui. No longer nonstops, however, they now go via Honolulu and then backtrack.

Hawaiian Airlines. The longtime interisland carrier now has daily nonstops to Honolulu from Los Angeles, from Las Vegas, from San Francisco, and from Seattle in its 326-passenger Lockheed L-1011s. One fare advantage is its plan which "common rates" all destinations in Hawaii—that is, it will cost you no more to fly from the West Coast to any Neighbor Island airport than it will to Honolulu. (Passengers transfer in Honolulu to Hawaiian's regular interisland flights—see below.) Hawaiian is also scheduled to roll out some new first-class seats on the Mainland runs about the time these pages roll off the press. Better recheck all of this at the last minute, perhaps through HAL's toll-free 800 number, listed in the appendix.

Delta Airlines. A relative newcomer to Hawaii, Delta now has two daily flights between Hawaii and the Mainland. Both are nonstops, one between Honolulu and Atlanta and the other between Honolulu and Dallas/Ft. Worth. Both runs are made with Delta's 241-passenger Lockheed TriStar L-1011s. Delta offers three classes to Honolulu—First (with sleeper seats), Business Class (unusual on Hawaii runs), and Coach, with sensible 2-5-2 seating (nine across) in the latter cabin. What Delta's recent purchase of Western Airlines might do to the Hawaiian service of either carrier is unclear at this writing.

Northwest Orient. Primarily oriented to the Far East, Northwest nevertheless runs daily Boeing 747 flights between Honolulu and Los Angeles, San Francisco, Seattle, and its Minneapolis headquarters, plus two daily flights between Honolulu and San Francisco.

Canadian Pacific Airlines. Formerly known as CP Air, this Canadian international airline offers four weekly nonstop DC-10 jumbo-jet flights between Honolulu and Vancouver, and about one or two nonstops a week between Honolulu and Toronto. (Coming up above from Down Under, you can fly Canadian Pacific to Honolulu from Sydney, Auckland, and Fiji.)

World Airways. World pioneered in bargain flights to Honolulu from California some years ago. Just at our deadline, it has announced that it will cease all scheduled passenger service and concentrate on charters only. (We include them in the list, just in case they have a last-minute change of heart. Check with the airline or a travel agent.)

Total Air. Total's history is just the opposite, since it is a scheduled airline which sprang up out of a former charter operation last year. Total Air has been flying TriStar L-1011s carrying 344 fully packed single-class passengers (with narrow, 10-across seating) between Los Angeles and Honolulu once a week for fairly low fares. Sorry, we know very little about them at this stage, except to point out the skinny chairs and that 101-passenger difference between Delta's and Total's TriStars. We would demand an aisle seat or nothing, and then stretch our legs often on the long, five-and-one-half-hour flight.

Regent Air. For a few years now, Regent Air, a new "all frills" airline, has been announcing plans to launch a scheduled highroller's jet service to Hawaii from Los Angeles and/or New York. The announcements have continued to keep coming all through 1986, and that's all we can say at the moment.

People Express. Just the opposite philosophy is embraced by People Express, which has expressed an interest in inaugurating a run to Hawaii, perhaps from New York and Denver. Famous for no frills, low fares, and long lines, People operates 747s with both Coach and First-Class sections. Check with the airline or a travel agent for the latest.

In the deregulated airline environment, there is good news and bad news. First, competition from the newer airlines has been credited with forcing drastic reductions in ticket prices among the big boys, especially those flying to Hawaii from California. It will be interesting to see if the fare wars continue into 1987. On the other hand, you may see some brand-new airlines come and go on the Hawaii route. An example is one we never had a chance to mention in these pages because it began flying after our 1986 edition came out and then failed long before the deadline for our 1987 edition. That one left many angry creditors, some holding special coupons they bought in advance payment for future flights.

Also last year, Pan American World Airways ceased flying to Hawaii, marking the end of service to the Islands which began during the 1930s.

Foreign Airlines. Hawaii is also served by several foreign air carriers. But if you are going from one U.S. destination to another—including Hawaii—the 1896 Jones Act prohibits you from flying merely between two American cities in a foreign airliner. (It originally covered only ships.) This means most Yankee travelers will have to skip such exotic companies as Japan Air Lines, Singapore Airlines, Philippine Airlines, Air New Zealand, or Qantas—unless they are continuing after a Honolulu stopover to some foreign destination.

Coming up from Australia, however, anyone may fly to Honolulu via Qantas, Canadian Pacific, Continental, or United. And from New Zealand your choice is probably Air New Zealand, Canadian Pacific Air, Continental, or United. These airlines generally have attractive excursion plans for residents of the two countries, worth asking Down Under travel agents about. Some of those routes include free stopovers in such places as Samoa, Tahiti, and Fiji. Also, residents of Australia and New Zealand may see Hawaii on the way to the U.S. Mainland and then return home by a different route. (See *The Maverick Guide to Australia* and *The Maverick Guide to New Zealand* for more information on these routes.)

Baggage Allowance. Currently you're allowed two large suitcases and one small (under-seat) bag free of charge. You'll pay $10 or so per extra piece. Regulations require that you affix your name to the outside of each piece of luggage. Surfboards or bicycles will cost you $20 or so to take along on the plane with you to Hawaii. But check that out with the specific airline you are considering. Different carriers have different rates for these items.

Jet Lag and Time Zones

The first time we flew direct from New York to Honolulu, we couldn't believe what was happening to our bodies. We were dead tired at 7 P.M.—maybe propped our eyes open until 8. Then the next day we were awake and up at dawn's early light, waiting impatiently for a breakfast restaurant to open. Everything was mixed up—mealtimes, digestion time, bedtime. We just could hardly cope.

The problem was not the actual distance we flew, or the physical strain of the trip, but merely the fact that we had whizzed directly across six time zones—actually seven when the Mainland has daylight saving time (Hawaii never does). In standard time, remember that when it's 7 o'clock in Honolulu, it's 8 in the Yukon and 9 in California. It's also 10 o'clock in the Rocky Mountain states, 11 o'clock in Chicago and the Midwest, and noon or midnight on the Eastern Seaboard. Add one hour to all those times for Mainland areas where daylight saving time is in effect, usually between late April and late October.

Doctors and psychiatrists believe it takes several days to recover fully from jet lag, depending on how many time zones you cross in a single day and on your own particular constitution. (A lucky few claim they are never bothered.)

We suggest a half-dozen steps to relieve (not prevent) jet lag: (1) Sleep or nap as much as you can aboard your flight. (2) Set your watch to Hawaii time when you get on the plane. (3) Take no sleeping pills and little alcohol during the flight. (4) Rest again when you arrive at your hotel (pulling the shades, if necessary). (5) Schedule no business appointments and make few decisions of any kind your first day in the Islands. (6) Stick to familiar foods and eat lightly your first day on vacation.

Interisland Transportation

For speed and comfort, most visitors to Hawaii have traditionally opted for jet trips between the islands offered by the two mainstays—**Hawaiian Airlines,** sometimes called Hawaiian Air or HAL, which flies its 85- to 170-passenger, twin-jet DC-9s between Honolulu and six Neighbor Island airports, and **Aloha Airlines,** which uses 118-seat, tri-jet Boeing 737s to most of these same destinations. Aloha flies to Kauai and Maui, and to Hilo and Kona on the Big Island. Hawaiian Air adds to that list infrequent schedules to Kapalua (Kaanapali), Lanai, and Molokai but devotes its low-altitude De Havilland DASH-7 turboprop planes to those three destinations. Holding 50 passengers, they are also used for some lower-price flights to Maui and Kauai. No alcohol is served on the DASHes, incidentally; you might get POG—a Maui punch made from a combination of passion fruit, orange, and guava juices. The planes are also pretty noisy, and we don't much like the nonreclining seats.

Hawaiian's regular Douglas fanjets are quiet, however—quieter even than Aloha's Boeings, at least in the forward areas. They have a 3-2 seat configuration, and that's another plus. In the past year, Hawaiian has been gradually replacing its larger jets with shorter, lower-capacity, faster-turnaround models of the DC-9, a badly needed operation that is beginning to improve its flight schedules. (*Tip:* For more leg room, sit in the rows by the emergency exits; they're a few inches farther from the seat in front of you.)

Aloha's plumper Boeing 737s have 6-across (3-3) seating, but the company claims they can unload baggage faster—a claim that will have less validity as Hawaiian converts to shorter planes. Aloha also has a small first-class section with wider seats set two by two in the front of the cabin, plus separate first-class check-in counters and lounges at some terminals. Hawaiian has been in the business about fifty years, and Aloha has chalked up more than thirty years of service. Both have virtually perfect safety records, with no passenger fatalities.

Although the two major lines have attempted mergers in the past, they now compete fiercely, with each other and against the smaller airlines, and each has its loyal devotees. Generally speaking it's hard to choose between Hawaiian and Aloha, although Hawaiian has lately been fighting a local reputation for late or suddenly cancelled flights, calling it a bum rap. (The new, shorter jets should help.) Both lines are hunting hard for new sources of revenue, hence Hawaiian's mainland flights described above, plus some new service to Samoa and Tonga in DC-8s. Aloha also offers weekly flights to Christmas Island, an atoll in Kiribati (the Gilbert Islands), 1,300 miles south of Hawaii. It also has plans to fly on to Tarawa eventually.

Jet flights between the Hawaiian Islands are so short—under twenty minutes from Honolulu to either Kauai or Maui, for example—that you are no more at maximum altitude than you start down again. On either of these lines, do check in at the counter no less than 45 minutes before flight departure time. Both Aloha and Hawaiian once received slaps on the wings from *Money* magazine for "bumping" passengers more than any other U.S. airlines. That may be an unfair comparison because delays are usually short. However, they do not hold reserved space for long, and during busy periods there are many hopeful standby travelers waiting to slip into any "no-show" seats. If you hold reservations and are still caught in a line at the counter 30 minutes before flight time, you might be waiting behind those checking in for a later flight. Better speak up just to make sure everything's hunky-dory.

In 1981 another company was introduced to the interisland skies, and it is still there six years later. **Mid Pacific Airlines** began flying Japanese-made Mitsubishi YS-11s—60-passenger, twin-motor, jet-propeller aircraft—between Oahu (Honolulu), Maui, Kauai, and Kona and Hilo on the Big Island. Flights are normally made at an altitude of only about 7,000 feet, which allows for better sightseeing and picture-taking than the higher-flying jets. Now, however, Mid Pacific is also flying a couple of pure jets itself, using 85-passenger, Dutch-made Fokker F-28 "UltraJets" on a few of their interisland routes. We've found them comfortable, but avoid the last row where the seats don't recline.

Mid Pacific has prided itself on offering flights at somewhat lower fares than those of Hawaiian and Aloha. And those long-haul YS-11 flights between Honolulu and Kona or Hilo, which take about an hour, include free champagne, beer, and even a light meal, unusual on interisland flights. *Tip:* The jet-prop YS-11s are noisy in the forward areas, and you might not even understand announcements on the P.A. system, so sit as far to the rear as possible for a quieter ride. For more silence on the F-28 jets, it's just the opposite; sit as far *forward* as possible.

Some of our readers have complained to us that Mid Pacific canceled their flights often, and then claimed it could not find the passengers to inform them by phone before they went out to the airport. Some regular interisland passengers on Mid Pacific or Hawaiian say they get along better by routinely calling the airline before leaving for the airport just to make sure their flight is expected to depart as scheduled.

All three of these interisland airlines now prohibit smoking while aloft, incidentally.

In the past we went into considerable detail in these pages on club memberships, special discount fares, coupon books, etc. sometimes offered by Aloha, Hawaiian, and Mid Pacific airlines, but the aerial price war is now moving too rapidly to cover them in an annual guidebook. The three lines may be expected to continue various fare dogfights in their attempts to lure tourists and locals alike, and the exact situation in the months after this edition comes off the press is impossible to predict.

Even your travel agent might not be able to keep up to the minute on this, and we suggest that if you want to get the best bargains in interisland flights it would be better to ask all the airlines about their special deals after arriving in the Islands, or else to phone their toll-free numbers (listed in our appendix) shortly before leaving home.

You might check the standby fares, too. If you can stand the uncertainty, they are usually the best deals of all, especially during the week and in off-season periods like April–May and September–October. As a general guide, normal jet fares between Honolulu and Maui or Kauai may continue to run around $50 this year—perhaps slightly more on some lines from Honolulu to destinations on the Big Island. So-called "Q" fares—available on the first and last jet flights of the day—may run around $40 to most islands. This could also be the total for the "L" fare, available on propeller aircraft flown by Hawaiian Airlines (limited capacity) and Mid Pacific Airlines (no restrictions) throughout the day. There is also a capacity-controlled "V" fare on all airlines throughout the day which may continue to run around $45 for most hops.

Important: If you *are* one of those standby passengers (whether because of full bookings or a cheaper ticket), be sure you're not waiting for a no-show seat on the very last flight of the day, unless you have all your luggage right in your hands in a container small enough to carry on the plane. Sometimes your checked bags will get on an interisland hop even if you don't. That could be a major inconvenience if you missed the last flight—but your toothbrush and clothes flew off without you. We've sweated out a few gambles like this ourselves, and one day we'll surely get stuck overnight in Kona with our pants gone to Maui. In any case, we don't recommend it to anyone.

Another tip: Regarding your luggage on any of the interisland lines, if you check in early you might find your bags waiting for you immediately, having arrived on a flight which landed before the one in which you personally rode. On the other hand, if you check in late, have to run to the plane, etc.... You can guess the rest.

Besides the three big boys, there is also a clutch of small outfits known collectively as "commuter airlines." They launch propeller-driven airplanes on regular interisland schedules. The commuter picture may change considerably in 1987 since the biggest, Royal Hawaiian Air Service, went out of business last year, and other airlines have begun rushing to pick up the slack.

Princeville Airways flies 18-passenger De Havilland Twin Otters on several interisland runs, plus a couple of Cessna 404s it picked up from the defunct Royal Hawaiian. The company began with hops from Honolulu to the short strip at Kauai's Princeville resort, which is not served by other airlines. Later it added service to Maui (Kahului and Hana), Molokai (both airports), and the Big Island, both to Waimea (Kamuela) and to a private airstrip at the Waikoloa Resort area.

Air Molokai caters to frequent local Honolulu-Molokai traffic, and they sometimes have the cheapest trip over that route. (Perhaps $15 each way between Honolulu and Molokai.) They boast a small fleet of nine-passenger Cessna 402s. Unfortunately, due to the all-pervading "insurance crisis" gripping the country, they've just had to retire their two atmospheric and dependable old DC-3s.

Reeves Air, formerly an air-taxi service only, now gives Air Molokai some scheduled competition. Reeves also flies Cessna 402s, currently Honolulu-Molokai-Maui and Honolulu-Lanai-Maui and then return flights over the same routes. And it flies to the isolated Kalaupapa Peninsula on Molokai. We haven't tried them out yet.

Surface Travel? Sadly, SeaFlite, the hydrofoil which once operated between the islands, has folded its foils and slipped away to Hong Kong. There always seem to be vague plans to bring it back for limited Honolulu-Maui service, but don't hold your breath. Meanwhile, there are a few "fun" boat trips from island to island. These are covered in section 7 of the island-chapters further along in this book.

Travel Agents

To set up a good trip to Hawaii, we heartily recommend an aggressive, enthusiastic travel agency. Avoid "assembly-line" operations (and these can be the tiny "mom and pop" agencies or the great international giants) —those who seem anxious only to book you on a prewrapped package or just to jet you off into space any old flight. A travel agency should be able and willing to take the time to tailor the ideal itinerary for you and your family. If the agent can maintain his smile while you exercise your own individuality, chances are he's the one for you.

Choosing a Travel Agent. The only reliable way to choose a travel agent is to take one other travelers you are acquainted with have used successfully. Even if you've never consulted a travel agent before and never expect to see one again, select him as you would a dentist. Don't pick one blindly from the Yellow Pages. He should be a member of ASTA (the American Society of Travel Agents), and he should be licensed by the ATC (the Air Traffic Conference). Agents who belong to ARTA—the Association of Retail Travel Agents—are also generally reliable. The most respected agents these days have the initials "CTC" after their names. That stands for Certified Travel Counselor, and it signifies an experienced agent who has completed a special two-year, graduate-level travel-management program run by the Institute of Certified Travel Agents.

Some Hawaii Experience? Well, it *might* help if your travel agent has been to Hawaii, but don't make that a requirement. Many agents have made whirlwind tours as guests of various commercial enterprises, and their recommendations may be unconsciously colored by these limited experiences. Believe me, we've gotten farther around the state and poked into more out-of-the-way corners than 100 percent of the Mainland travel agents.

Any good travel agent will try to give you what you want, so you can count on the *Maverick Guide* to help you choose your facilities and activities and then seek a good travel agent to put your plans into operation and hone the finer points of your arrangements. Take this book into the travel agency, if you want; you won't be the first to do that with excellent results.

Be Specific and Definite. Try to explain just what you want your travel agent to do for you. Make him or her have a darned good reason before talking you out of arrangements you have in mind based on your study of this guide. Also, be sure that the agent obtains letters or certificates of confirmation from hotels and rental-car outfits, giving you copies of these—including the rates agreed upon—to take with you.

Remember that travel agents seldom cost you money. Mostly they make theirs from commissions. (Airlines pay them from 7 to 11 percent; hotels and other enterprises usually give them 10 percent.) Sometimes it is proper for a travel agent to charge you a fee, but if he or she wants to do this, ask questions. If you don't like the answers, go see another agent. If the travel agent does book you on a package tour, feel free to ask him *exactly* what you are paying for. Any responsible agent will be only too happy to spell it all out.

For Lone Wolves. Many vacationers like the satisfaction of nailing down all their arrangements themselves, regardless of the availability of travel agents. That's fine, but when writing to or phoning hotels, rental cars, bus tours, etc., remember again to be absolutely specific about the type and price of what you're looking for, the days you will be arriving and leaving, etc., and then save all your confirmation letters and deposit receipts. On the phone, get the name of the person you are talking to and write it down. You probably won't need all this, but it's sound vacation practice to have the evidence of what you agreed on right along with you when you arrive. And as always, it would also be a good idea to *tell 'em we sent you.*

The Package Tour

Some people are particularly suited to taking a group tour to Hawaii. If they're lonely or gregarious, and feel for one reason or another that they can't or just don't want to make a multitude of arrangements themselves, this is an ideal alternative to more individualized travel.

Others feel that packages seal them up against the experience of personal discovery, and if they do choose such a tour it will be mainly a money-saving one that wraps up essentials like the plane, the hotel, the car, etc., and leaves out luaus, nightclubs, and other frills.

If you are considering a group tour, carefully compare the price of the deal with individual arrangements. Sometimes the savings will be significant and sometimes not. By the way, if you're a lone traveler you may pay a special "single supplement" added to the advertised price of the tour, unless you are willing to share a room with someone else.

Extras and Add-Ons. No matter how much you get as part of your package, someone will probably try to sell you more in your "orientation" meeting. Some particular sightseeing tours are good and fun, but others are just not worth it. (See section 7 in island-chapters 5 through 10.) Be aware that bus tours often list in their literature several destinations that are free and/or easily accessible anyway, and sometimes they list sights that are only pointed out briefly as you zip by in your insulated, air-conditioned coach. (And despite the "tips included" promises, you will be expected to drop some extra change here and there.)

On multi-island package tours, you and your luggage will sometimes seem to be on different itineraries. You'll have to have it battened down early so it can leave each hotel from a half-hour to two hours before you, and it may arrive in each room before or after you. Depending on the necessities (like medicine or film) packed in your Gladstones, that could be a significant inconvenience. On the other hand, you probably will never need to carry them yourself.

The Right Stuff. You're also expected to join in all the fun and develop a camaraderie with your fellow tour members, taking part in games, community sings, and other activities. Your tour conductor or escort will probably be a lively, fun-loving, and hardworking big brother (or den mother) to you all. More power to him, but he is a professional, after all. You may think you're a tolerant person, too—until you sit on bus after bus with that gum-chewing and gabby Mama from Minnehaha and good ole back-slapping Jack who sells widgets and flanges and likes to pinch bottoms.

You may hit some restaurants that give more kickbacks than good food and service, and it's not you that collects the gravy, either. And let's face it; an air-chilled bus with soundproof, tinted windows is just not the way to get out to mingle and experience the Islands.

Hawaii is certainly exotic and different, but for Americans it is *not* a foreign country. Everyone speaks your language, your money is just as good as it is at home, all the food and water are safe, and automobile driving is pretty much the same as it is back home. No one will deliberately mislead you if you choose to see the Islands at your own pace and according to your own interests. On the contrary, you'll probably find the local population the most considerate, helpful, and polite people you will meet anywhere.

So it may not be the fault of any individual tour company, and we admit we are probably wrong in some cases. But for most people, we doubt that the savings are worth joining the big on-the-bus, off-the-bus march of the packaged herds. We have never managed to sign on incognito to a full-scale, whoop-it-up package tour of Hawaii ourselves. Consequently, we particularly like to have letters from readers who have liked or disliked their own package tours. One couple who wrote us were absolutely thrilled with their Cartan Tour. We've also had good reports on Island Holidays, Trade Winds Tours, and Maupintour. Special excursions for the disabled are available through Whole Person Tours, P.O. Box 1084, Bayonne, NJ 07002-1084. And bicycle tours through the Islands are offered by Backroads, P.O. Box 1626, San Leandro, CA 94577. (As always, tell 'em we sent you.)

One more point: It may be a good idea if the tour operator is a member of the USTOA—United States Tour Operators Association—which means that he or she has subscribed to a code of ethics. The USTOA will send you a free booklet on *How to Select a Package Tour* if you send your name and address to their office at 211 East 51st St., Suite 4B, New York, NY 10022.

What if you're already on Oahu and decide to look for a combination deal to a Neighbor Island or two, possibly wrapping up the airline, a room, and a car in a single package? This is what local residents often do. Tell any Honolulu travel agency what you want, and they may be able to come up with a good deal. (Local outfits known for this kind of thing include Robert's Hawaii, Ocean Travel Service, and Rendezvous Tours.)

Also call the three major interisland airlines—Hawaiian, Aloha, and Mid Pacific—to see if they might be currently offering an air-car-and-condo special of some kind. Usually at least one of them has a deal going.

Packing and Wearing

If you've been with us all through the chapter, you now know that a "trunk carrier" is a major airline and *not* someone who will help you with your luggage. And this brings us to something you've heard a thousand times before, but for Hawaii we really mean it: Travel light!

There are two good reasons for this: (1) Hawaii honestly is warm, and life is very informal from a sartorial standpoint. Shirts are worn outside the trousers, shoes are kicked off at the slightest excuse (in fact, it is often considered impolite to wear shoes inside a private home in Hawaii), and ties and stockings are seldom wanted or needed. (2) Almost no one vacations in Hawaii without buying some clothes on the spot. Men will want to get an aloha shirt or two and perhaps a couple of those eccentric Hawaiian T-shirts. Most women can't resist a *muumuu*—long or short. You'll like the informal footwear, too. If you didn't bring sandals with you, you'll probably pick up a pair of leather ones as well as a practical pair of zoris (rubber slippers), at least for the beach.

Men's Wear. Male suit addicts should make it one lightweight model, perhaps to wear on the plane to and from the Islands. (Then if you do feel the dress-up urge you'll have that outfit along with you.) Frequent habitués of Hawaii often fly to the Islands in a blazer or sport jacket, if not simply an open-necked shirt.

If you have a couple pairs of easy-care slacks, fine. If you're young and/or plan to explore the boonies, rugged jeans would be useful. Also, white trousers for evening wear are popular (but not essential) in Hawaii, and they are often worn with white loafers (or with sandals for simpler occasions).

You may want to have one or two sport shirts with you (at least one to cover you while you sneak out to buy your aloha shirts). Tuck in lightweight underwear, pajamas, robe, etc. Laundromats are plentiful, and several of the big hotels also have their own self-service machines. Bring comfortable, soft walking shoes for general tramping around, or heavier boots for serious hiking.

If you own Bermuda shorts, by all means feel free to take them along. They're acceptable almost everywhere, although a little out of style. Island men usually prefer walking shorts or other models cut differently and shorter than Bermudas. Incidentally, local fashion is not to wear dark shoes, or shoes and socks, with shorts; instead, sandals, zoris, tennis shoes, running shoes, canvas shoes, or even bare feet are considered proper accessories for bare knees—if you don't want to look like a tourist. If you're going up in the highest mountains, it may be too chilly for shorts. Take a light sweater up with you, too, or maybe a parka or down jacket if you'll hit the Kilauea Volcano area or Haleakala Crater.

Female Fashion. Women should bring the same resort clothes they would use in southern Florida, the Caribbean, or Minneapolis in July, all preferably in loose, easy-to-care-for fabrics. As we said, keep in mind that Hawaii's vast, colorful garment industry awaits any vacancies in your wardrobe. Island fashions are different, but by shopping carefully you can take back aloha wear that can be used for at-home or hostess gowns or for informal/chic occasions. (See chapter 5, section 10, Oahu Shopping.)

Women may want to wear trousers for sightseeing, too, and Sara says a three-piece pants suit is great; the jacket goes on and off as you go in and out of air-conditioned buses, restaurants, etc. Shorts are acceptable nearly everywhere.

If you're not loading up on *Muumuus*, etc., you may want to bring something for casual evening wear, as well as regular sun or street dresses. Wear comfortable shoes; you'll be walking a lot. Sandals and zoris will be handy, whether you bring them or buy them here. You'll need heavy-soled shoes or running shoes for hiking. And since you may be in and out of the water a lot, bring a hair dryer along, too.

Men and Women. Members of both sexes will want to bring or buy a bathing suit or two. Hotels will generally provide the towels. Islanders used to short showers turn up their noses at raincoats and seldom use umbrellas, but visitors usually feel happier with either one or both, of the fold-up variety.

Women might like a head scarf to wear in the wind. Men won't need a regular Mainland felt-style hat, but they may want to buy a coconut frond or *lauhala* plantation hat. Sunbathers of either sex should be sure to have some kind of hat to wear during the day.

Toilet articles, makeup, first-aid supplies, etc., may be replenished in Hawaii, just as at home, so don't take lots of extras. All film is available, and you can even get overnight color processing and see how your pictures are coming out before you leave for home.

Besides cameras, some visitors like to bring a small battery radio (hotel rooms are short on radios even if long on TVs), plus a pair of binoculars for looking up at mountains, down into valleys, or across at bikinis. A small cassette tape record can be fun for capturing tour-guide lectures and Hawaiian music.

Don't forget sunglasses. We like the ones with polarizing lenses (Polaroid and Foster Grant are two brands that make them). Suntan lotion is important; get a kind containing PABA, a four-letter word standing for some multisyllabic monster. One of the best is PreSun, a product tested and proved in the Islands. However it will sometimes stain light-colored clothing, so apply it carefully. Other good brands are Eclipse and Sundown, both of which seem to stay on well in the water.

Sara personally recommends plenty of plastic bags of all sorts, sizes, and shapes—great for temporarily transporting wet bathing suits, washcloths, dirty clothes, old shoes, or whatever must be kept in isolation. You might even come with a roll of Baggies.

You won't need that succession of things you lug around in some foreign country, though. You can get all the familiar soaps, toothpastes, and toilet paper you want. Phrase books and money converters and the like are also superfluous. Just bring the little volume you hold in your hand right now.

When to Go to Hawaii

It might be easier to talk about when *not* to go, and we can think of two possible months. February falls into that category; not only is Honolulu packed with tourists, but it is probably the least dependable month for weather. (We seldom get several days in a row of rain, but if we do it might be in February.) Then August, the "convention month," is difficult as far as crowds, hotel bookings, etc., are concerned, especially in Honolulu. Also, if we have any month that's hot (85 degrees Fahrenheit and above), it will surely be August.

Our personal favorite months are in the fall—September to Christmas. And early January (after New Year's Day) is practical, too.

Since Hawaii's weather is much the same as a temperate zone spring the year around, the *real* spring months of April through mid-July are less in demand; too bad, because they're absolutely gorgeous. All the flowers are out, and the trade winds are never so clean and pure as on a day in May or June. And although we would never recommend suddenly zipping off to Hawaii without a hotel and car reservation, well, you might get away with it in the spring or the fall.

If you must come to Hawaii in the peak or near-peak months, that's all the more reason to visit one or more Neighbor Islands, and perhaps skip the Oahu crush entirely. If Waikiki is jammed, you'll find your tropical solitude in, perhaps, Waimea Canyon on Kauai, or the Haleakala Crater on Maui, or the Waipio Valley on the Big Island. And even in mid-August or mid-February, we'll bet you can search out that "beach without a footprint" on Kauai, Molokai, Lanai—and maybe even in some isolated areas of Maui. It's worth a try!

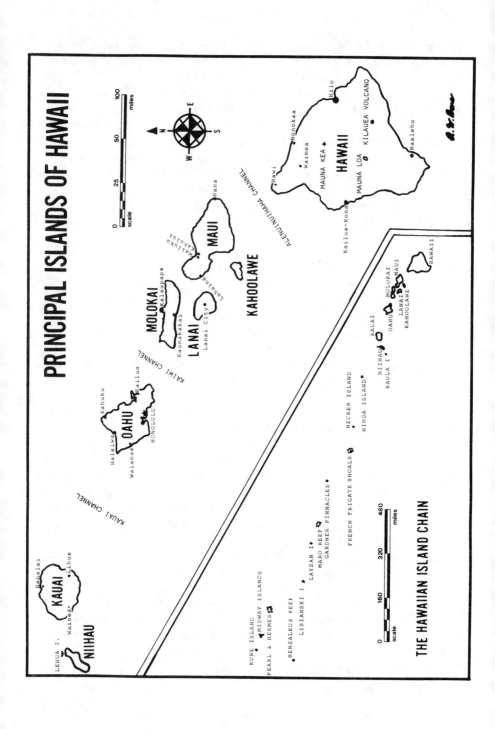

PRINCIPAL ISLANDS OF HAWAII

scale
0   25   50   100
miles

KAUAI CHANNEL

LEHUA I.
Hanalei
KAUAI
Waimea • Lihue
NIIHAU

Haleiwa
Kahuku
Waianae
OAHU
Kailua
HONOLULU

KAIWI CHANNEL

MOLOKAI
Kaunakakai
Kaluapapa

LANAI
Lanai City •

Lahaina
Kahului
Wailuku
MAUI
Hana

KAHOOLAWE

ALENUINIHAHA CHANNEL

Havi
Honokaa
Hilo
Waimea
MAUNA KEA +
HAWAII
MAUNA LOA   KILAUEA VOLCANO
Kailua-Kona •
Naalehu

KURE ISLAND
• MIDWAY ISLANDS
PEARL & HERMES

• BENSALEUX REEF
LISIANSKI I. •
LAYSAN I •
MARO REEF
GARDNER PINNACLES •

FRENCH FRIGATE SHOALS

NECKER ISLAND •
NIHOA ISLAND •

NIIHAU
KAULA I •
KAUAI
OAHU   MOLOKAI
LANAI   MAUI
KAHOOLAWE
HAWAII

scale
0   160   320   480
miles

THE HAWAIIAN ISLAND CHAIN

3

Where and What
Is Hawaii?

An Archipelago Punched from the Center of the World

Despite many intriguing theories, the original and exact meaning of
the word "Hawaii" lies, like the bones of its great warrior king, forever
hidden in a deep and mysterious past.

It is pronounced pretty much like "Ha-*why*-ee," with a catch of the
breath between the last two of those three syllables. Some people sound
the *w* like a *v*, but that's a recent affectation. Remember, though, that the
word does not in the least resemble the interrogation "How are ya?"

Today Hawaii is the official name of the fiftieth state, admitted to the
Union in 1959. That's a while back, now, so a visitor will only embarrass
himself if he announces in Honolulu that his own home is "back in the
States."

In fact, the recipe for instant popularity with your Hawaiian hosts is to
recognize their own statehood and U.S. citizenship at once by always
referring to the rest of the country as "the Mainland."

Correctly enough, some still call the archipelago "the Hawaiian Islands." And on a few British charts of the Pacific you may still see printed,
with Anglican persistence, "the Sandwich Isles." The latter label was
given the Islands by English naval captain James Cook when he came
across them in 1778, thus honoring his boss, the Earl of Sandwich and
First Lord of the Admiralty. (He was the same card-playing earl who first

placed his gambling snack between two pieces of bread, thereby winning himself a much more prominent bite in the history of the world.)

Two hundred years ago, "Hawaii" stood for only one island, the largest and southernmost in the group (and not the island where Honolulu stands). What we now call the "Big Island" still bears the formal title "The Island of Hawaii." But today Hawaii also refers collectively to all the 132 islands, islets, reefs, sandbars, and rock dots that poke up above the surface over a 1,600-mile route running from the northwest to the southeast.

As though it weren't boggling enough that Hawaii is both the name of an entire state and of one single island in that state, there are several other elusive geographic facts on which to spin your compass.

For instance, the Islands are about 2,500 miles southwest of Los Angeles, almost on the same latitude as Mexico City. Incurable romantics might refer to their location as in the "South Seas," but they are not in the South Pacific. This is the North Pacific Ocean—more than a thousand miles above the equator, but nonetheless in one of the truly tropic zones of the world.

Discounting the tinier specks, there are eight major islands in the Hawaiian chain:

• Seven of these eight main islands—all except Kahoolawe—are inhabited.

• Six of the seven inhabited islands may be easily visited. Tiny Niihau is taboo.

• Four of those six are much more popular—and populated—than the other two, and they now receive direct jet flights from the Mainland. Thus we set aside little Lanai and Molokai for the moment.

• And one rather medium-sized island—Oahu—crowds in nearly four-fifths of the state's entire population. It also serves as the traditional gateway for travel to all the islands.

From the smallest to the largest, the eight principal islands are Kahoolawe, Niihau, Lanai, Molokai, Kauai, Oahu, Maui, and Hawaii. Now let's take them one at a time.

No one other than an occasional very hardy wild goat lives on **Kahoolawe,** the smallest of the eight, although it would be large enough to set up housekeeping on if you dared. Its 45 square miles have been entirely absorbed by the U.S. Navy since 1941 and adapted primarily for use as one gigantic target range. In the past few years, the bombing of Kahoolawe has become controversial. Hawaiian activist groups have been protesting the practice, often using the issue as a rallying point to highlight their demands for social reform. The island is pronounced "kah-ho-oh-*lah-*

vay," which is not so different from the sound of the exploding ordnance as it echoes off the pockmarked ridges and valleys.

Not quite so diminutive, but also *kapu* (taboo) to most of us, is the 73-square-mile island of **Niihau** ("*knee*-ee-how"). Niihau supports about 200 people, nearly all of whom are pure-Hawaiian plantation workers and their families. One of the few places where the Hawaiian language is still in daily use, the island is private property, owned by a single family. The only island "invaded" on December 7, 1941, this Isle of Mystery has a fascinating story to tell.

The smallest island you may easily visit is the modest and unassuming dollop called **Lanai** ("lahn-*eye*"). Its 140 square miles are virtually all owned by the Dole Pineapple people, and a large portion of the island is devoted to a single giant plantation. Eventually it will be developed into a tourist resort. Meanwhile, only you, we, and its 2,000 permanent residents will know of its attractions.

The other sometimes forgotten isle is the friendly neighbor called **Molokai** ("*mole*-oak-eye"). About 6,000 are now at home on the cleared acres of its often rugged and mountainous 261 square miles. Like Lanai, one of Molokai's major selling points is its paucity of tourists; until recently, visitors were about as rare as the Hawaiian *nene* bird. On an isolated peninsula, Molokai once embraced one of the world's most compelling stories of human bondage and personal heroism. You might not be able to resist going over to experience its locale yourself.

At 553 square miles, the Island of **Kauai** is more than twice as large, and the 45,000 residents there pronounce their home "cow-*why*" or "*cow-eye*." (There's often debate about that.) It boasts the wettest spot on earth as well as a vast, dry desert canyon, and enough flowers to fill the Houston Astrodome. Its principal town, Lihue, is the seat of Kauai County, which includes the islands of Kauai and Niihau.

The next island up the size scale is 608-square-mile **Oahu** ("oh-*wah-who*"), and it is another source of demographic and geographic obfuscation. The state capital, Honolulu, is located on Oahu. And in a sense the capital *is* Oahu, because the "City and County" of Honolulu encompasses the entire island. (Actually, even more than that; for administrative purposes, nearly all the 100 or so islands in the Leeward chain—skipping over Kauai and Niihau—are part of the City and County of Honolulu.)

Oahu—or Honolulu—is populated by more than 800,000 people, or over 75 percent of the number of residents in the entire state. City and state politicians sometimes compete strenuously with each other for the affections of the electorate, due to the high proportion of voters concentrated on the one island. Oahu is also the governmental, commercial and cultural center of Hawaii. For this reason, islands other than Oahu are known as the "Neighbor Islands" or sometimes the "Outer Islands."

At 729 square miles, **Maui** (rhymes with "Howie") is significantly larger in land area than Oahu, and it is a relatively cosmopolitan Neighbor Island of 75,000. It is dominated by the vast sleeping volcano of Haleakala, today the center of the 20,000-acre Haleakala National Park. The rustic seaport of Lahaina was once capital of the entire kingdom, but sleepy Wailuku is now the seat of Maui County, which includes the nearby islands of Lanai, Molokai, and Kahoolawe.

Last, there is the king-sized **Island of Hawaii**, referred to by most who live in the state as simply "The Big Island." With its 4,038-plus square miles, it is more than twice the land area of all the rest of the Hawaiian chain wrapped up together. But for all its bulk, there are only about 105,000 people sprinkled over the vast landscape.

Honolulu folks who vacation on the Big Island are sometimes amazed to find they can drive for long periods there without seeing the sea— only the lofty and majestic mountain masses that are capped by snowfields in the winter.

It is on Hawaii that the live volcanoes of Kilauea and Mauna Loa occasionally put on a show of temper, and where the lava from deep within the earth may emerge and then flow to the sea, adding still more land area to the Big Island. From here, too, Kamehameha the Great launched his eighteenth-century war to conquer the archipelago. The small city of Hilo ("*heel*-oh") is the county seat, and it spreads out a jet airport just a coconut's toss from the city limits.

A Geologic Fluke. Calculated against the age of the earth's major natural features, the Hawaiian Islands are relative whippersnappers. It all began 25 million years ago when a rift opened up in the floor of the Pacific Ocean. A jet of red-hot volcanic liquid rock from deep within the core of the earth began pushing through the opening, seven miles below the surface of the sea. Gradually the material began spreading out to make the base of what are now Kure and Midway islands at the extreme northwest of the chain.

As each island raised itself up to a point where its own mass congealed and sealed off its birth canal, the pressure moved a little way southeastward and opened up more cracks. These built up new undersea volcanoes, some of which eventually reached the surface of the water, thereby earning the name "island."

Geologists now say the pressure didn't move along the crack, but that a "tectonic plate"—or the surface of the globe itself—moved, like some Brobdingnagian conveyor belt, over the jet of hot lava. Thus the islands were punched out more or less one by one in assembly-line fashion. And according to the same scientific theory, the islands are still drifting toward the northwest at the breakneck speed of four inches a year.

Many of the tiny islets and underwater extinct volcanoes to the northwest once stood high above the sea as respectable-sized portions of real estate. But gradually, due to the islands' own weight and the rising level of the ocean at the end of the last ice age, they began sinking again.

Coral growth sometimes delays their death, but erosion of wind and water combine to eventually wear away the oldest of the volcanic islands. Few of the northwest Leeward Islands are inhabited today, and those that are occupied have become just lonely outposts for military personnel. The rest is a 1,000-mile-long national wildlife refuge.

The eight principal islands of Hawaii also have been significantly eroded since birth. The island of Kauai is the oldest, so it has been smoothed out the most. Kauai has therefore developed a system of streams and rivers the like of which is unknown on the younger islands.

Oahu, Molokai, and Lanai are more rugged. The volcanic period that created these three islands was so long ago that virtually no trace is found of their original vast calderas. However, several smaller craters were blasted out in a later volcanic period, building such familiar landmarks as Oahu's Diamond Head, the backdrop to Waikiki, which blew up only about 150,000 years ago.

On Maui, the volcano of Haleakala is classified as dormant (not quite extinct), since it last erupted in 1790—just the day before yesterday in geologic time. The only volcanic activity in Hawaii today is on the Big Island, where lava flows and fountains from time to time around Mauna Loa and Kilauea volcanoes, the twin nuclei of Hawaii Volcanoes National Park. Kilauea and its satellite pits and vents are always bubbling and steaming, and if you should happen to catch either volcano in eruption, you'll experience one of the grandest and most awe-inspiring shows on earth.

Scenery—Unreal, but Usually True

Driving into Honolulu on the highway from the airport, you wonder at first what the difference is. Like many other American airport-to-city routes, Nimitz Highway boasts a healthy collection of car lots, hamburger stands, and gas stations. Yet there is something different, something mellowing, something that makes these commercial establishments less offensive.

Suddenly you realize it isn't what you did see, but what you didn't see. There wasn't a billboard on that entire route. In fact, there are no billboards anywhere in the state of Hawaii. There haven't been any for over fifty years, since a courageous band of women called the Outdoor Circle won a long battle to grind the oversized advertisements into the dirt. The women, many of whom were wives of Honolulu business and civic leaders, felt that the unusual and special beauty of Hawaii was being sacrificed to the two-dimensional monsters that ate up the views of mountains and valleys.

Followed by larger and larger groups of people, the ladies first boycotted and then shamed most of the outdoor advertising operations into oblivion. Finally, in 1927, there was one holdout, a small billboard firm with a few Mainland accounts. The Outdoor Circle bought the company and closed it down. Only then did the territorial legislature pass a law killing billboards completely throughout the Islands. The law continues to withstand tests up to the present.

Cynics correctly note that many of the Honolulu views once blocked by billboards have since been obstructed by a succession of Babylonian highrises. But the fact remains that many movers and shakers of Hawaii have not only cared about, but have managed to do something toward, keeping the Islands' reputation for eye-soothing tropical panoramas.

James Michener, the author of *Hawaii*, not long ago revisited the scene of his epic novel and pronounced himself "astounded" by the development since his days in residence a quarter-century ago. Nevertheless he told writer Leonard Lueras that, taking all the islands together, "It is still the most attractive single state in the country."

The Human Touch. Magnificent cliffs, waterfalls, and sunsets have no doubt been Hawaii's heritage since the days its creative fires began to cool, hundreds of thousands of years ago. But it was man's appearance on the landscape that brought to Hawaii and preserved for it the final touches to the "natural" scenery we have today.

This human concern dates back to the ancient Polynesian voyagers who discovered a naked Hawaii, almost completely devoid of trees, with only scrub bush holding tenuously to the desertlike lava fields. On return trips these early colonizers brought with them the familiar foliage of their homes in Tahiti and the Marquesas Islands, including coconut palms, breadfruit trees, bananas, and even a few flowers.

But a thousand years later, when the missionaries landed in Hawaii, there was still much gardening to be done. The New England evangelists found natural beauty in a few settlements like Lahaina, but they judged Honolulu one of the least attractive sites in the Islands, noting that it was barren and dusty, and provided neither trees nor grass.

Honolulu in the 1800s was distinguished only by its natural deepwater harbor. In fact, the word "Honolulu" is usually translated as "fair haven" or "protected bay." The commercial desirability of this anchorage led directly to the beautification of the formerly arid real estate immediately surrounding it. Travelers and immigrants brought in species after species of exotic plants, trees, and flowers, most of them with little regard to their effects on the lives of animals and other plants.

Today many of the plants considered Hawaiian can trace their family trees back to the exact date and place of germination that introduced their seed to the Islands. Some truly "native" species, brought here by winds or birds, have long ago been crowded out by the newcomers.

Three miles from arid Honolulu, Waikiki was often a dirty beach 150 years ago. It was backed by a humid, stagnant swamp that became a breeding ground for the mosquito (an insect that was inadvertently imported by man in 1827). That marsh was not drained until the 1920s, when the present Ala Wai Canal was built.

If the Islands of Hawaii were created by volcanoes, they were sculpted into aesthetic form by the actions of wind, rain, and sea—and then later by a second period of volcanic activity that further dramatized the landscape. This new round of blasting produced such prominent features as Diamond Head on Oahu and provided such new viewing platforms as the Makanalua Peninsula (Kalaupapa) on Molokai, from which the majesty of that island's north shore can be fully revered.

Dramatic Mountains. Despite the many sweeping acres of green pineapple, sugar cane, and even colorful flower fields, most of Hawaii's scenic glory is formed by its mountains. The eroded remnants of the ancient volcanoes that were the progenitors of the islands are often twisted into rugged shapes that make them seem much taller and more forbidding than the statistics bear out.

Over the centuries, the *pali* (cliffs) have been carved by wind and falling water into a series of giant buttresses, creating a pattern found nowhere else on the globe. You'll see some of the most dramatic examples of this slow-motion erosion as you travel the windward (northeastern) coast of Oahu and gaze toward the 35-mile-long Koolau range. Following a sudden rain, you can often observe these forces still at work as scores of narrow waterfalls drop for hundreds of feet along the grooved buttes.

You'll find the valleys fascinating, too. In Hawaii, valleys often slope *up* for their entire length in a gentle, narrowing incline between two roughhewn ridges. Like the famous Nuuanu Valley, behind Honolulu, they may gain gradual altitude on the leeward side of the mountains until reaching the divide, where they climax in a *pali* that plunges straight down for perhaps a thousand feet or more.

The mountains, cliffs, and valleys of Hawaii are not only rugged; they are green and rugged, an effect that may seem an incongruous combination to the outlander. There is a mountain called Olomana about a mile from our own front door, for instance. From some angles, it's almost a dead ringer for Switzerland's famous Matterhorn, except that it has been carpeted from base to tip with foliage. And again, it is much shorter than it seems. At less than 2,000 feet, it does not nearly qualify for the official term "Mount."

In a mountainous state, probably the only *true* mountains are the immense 14,000-foot volcanoes of Mauna Kea and Mauna Loa on the Big Island, and the dormant 10,000-foot volcano called Haleakala on Maui. Despite the tropic latitude, in the winter and spring these three peaks are often cloaked with snow above the tree line.

A Lack of Lakes. If you are familiar with the Pacific Northwest on the Mainland, you may notice one feature lacking in the Hawaiian environment: There are almost no natural lakes in which all the green mountains' majesty might be reflected in shimmering symmetry. Generally speaking, the porous lava base of the Islands simply won't hold much water on the surface for very long, and this also accounts for the rarity of rivers and the infrequency of streams over the islandscape.

Strangely enough, just about the highest lake in the United States is here—little Lake Waiau, 13,000 feet up near the summit of Mauna Kea. But Hawaii's only large lakes, an intermittent one of 841 acres and a permanent one of 182 acres, are on forbidden ground on the privately owned island of Niihau.

On Oahu, the only natural body of inland water, Salt Lake, was filled in by a land developer after a bitter controversy. A tiny portion of the lake serves as a callous reminder of the lost cause—it has been left as a water trap for a golf course. Today Salt Lake is only the name of another Honolulu suburb. As one might suspect, development on the populous island of Oahu has run to the point where the island's natural beauty is in danger of knuckling under to the bulldozer and the jackhammer.

Some of the beauty of the Islands has been preserved simply because many attractive sites are so hard to get to in the first place. Kauai, Maui, and Molokai contain several examples of these isolated Edens. But in heavily populated areas, environmentalists and conservationists are proving to be needed and influential voices in the community.

Although they failed in the battle of Salt Lake and some others, the good guys have gathered enough political clout to gain some impressive successes, too. Look, for instance, to the clean, green, and unspoiled hills and peaks that form the backdrop to Honolulu. They testify to the prowess of those who fully understand, like the *avant-garde* ladies of 1927, that in Hawaii there is not only an extraordinary opportunity but a definite obligation to preserve and defend our scenic heritage.

Weather, Climate, and Other Natural Phenomena

You sometimes hear a lot of fuss over the fact that the Hawaiian language includes no word for "weather." Our own judgment on this is that it indicates either an articulate deficiency in the language or a strong indifference among those who spoke it, and not much about the weather itself.

Despite what you may have heard, weather is sometimes more than a figure of speech in the Islands. And for whatever it's worth, the Hawaiians did have words for "hot," "cold," "rain," "snow," "storm," "wind," and even "fog."

Still, it is often difficult to talk about the weather in Hawaii, not because of any language barrier, but just because weather conditions are different for different people living in different parts of different islands.

From custom alone, Islanders now divide their year into four parts, including "spring" and "fall." Nevertheless, the ancient Hawaiians were right when they identified only two seasons in Hawaii—winter and summer.

Winter, which runs vaguely from mid-October through April, means approximately this:

- Daytime temperatures are in the mid-70s to low 80s.
- Nighttime temperatures run from the 60s to the low 70s. (Honolulu's lowest official temperature ever was 57 degrees.)
- The trade winds—northeasterlies, which generally bring on pleasant weather—are more erratic in winter. These "trades" are vigorous at times, but they sometimes become very weak and die completely. In fact they can be interrupted for days in this cool season, and it always seems that at least once each winter—usually in the coolest month, February—they will cease for more than two weeks straight. Strangely, the trades usually will pick up fairly well for a time in December and early January, which makes this "off-season" period a pleasant bargain for some visitors.
- *Kona* winds—westerlies and southerlies that often bring on widespread cloudiness, rain, mugginess, and even thunderstorms—are more frequent in winter. They usually rush in when the trades or other strong wind patterns die.
- Rains increase in frequency, duration, and intensity in winter, although things still might dry out before the day is through. And you can generally find someplace where it is not raining and where the sun is shining even at this time of year.
- Daylight shortens to about eleven hours in winter—still pretty long by Duluth standards.

Summer, running generally from May through mid-October, brings the following in Hawaii:

- Daytime temperatures are in the 80s. (Honolulu's record high is 94 degrees Fahrenheit, but the temperature one steaming day in 1931 reached 100 degrees at Pahala on the Big Island.)
- Nighttime temperatures run from the 70s to the low 80s.
- The trade winds are more persistent and consistent, traveling across thousands of miles of ocean from the Arctic to keep summer tempera-

tures tolerable here in the tropic zone. (Taken on a year-round basis, the trades blow for about 300 of the 365 days.)

• *Kona* winds are more infrequent in the summer. However, when the trades occasionally fail and these warm southwest winds do come in, you really know it. There is nothing worse than a sticky summer *kona* wind. If it comes on a day during August, the Islands' hottest and most crowded month, the thermometer can approach 90 degrees, and the misery factor seems much higher. On an August *kona* day, we search out targets—like the Bishop Museum, perhaps—that are air conditioned. To hang around downtown Honolulu on such a day, wandering its sweltering sidewalks, is a form of summer madness.

• Rains are more infrequent in the summer, except at high elevations, and they don't last long. Summer showers are often a matter of minutes, and you can nearly always find some place where it is not raining.

• The days lengthen to about thirteen hours. Due to Hawaii's nearness to the equator, there is little difference between the number of daylight hours in winter and summer. Such afternoon outdoor sports enthusiasts as tennis players will also note the lack of—or at least the shortness of—twilight in this latitude.

There is so much daylight in Hawaii that the state has never felt the need to "save" it by fiddling with the clocks, so it always remains on Hawaii Standard Time. That's two hours earlier than the West Coast (Pacific Standard) and five hours earlier than places like New York and Washington, D.C. When most of the rest of the country goes on daylight saving time—from the last Sunday in April through the last Sunday in October—these figures move up by one hour. (It's three hours later in San Francisco instead of two, etc.)

You may have already gotten the idea that weather is very localized in Hawaii. It's true. Somewhere on any given island the skies are clear while only a mile or two away it is just as likely to be raining at the same hour.

If you're staying in Waikiki, you may think of yourself as lucky—from the precipitation standpoint, anyway. Waikiki is one of the driest areas on Oahu. Still, if it is raining in Waikiki you might head out Makapuu way (Hanauma Bay, the Blow Hole, Sea Life Park, etc.), where it's even more likely to be dry. *Never cancel a picnic in Hawaii merely because your morning window opens on a "rainy day."* Unlike the weather on much of the Mainland, Hawaiian weather seldom remains in a day-long rut.

The driest inhabited area in the state is on the Kohala Coast of the Big Island, north of Kailua-Kona. The average rainfall is less than 7 inches a year, which means it's a big job to keep quenching the thirst of super-luxurious golf courses at the deluxe hotels there.

The wettest spot on the entire earth is probably on Kauai. It rains virtually all the time at the top of the mountain called Waialeale—nearly 500 inches a year. Luckily, there are no golf courses up there!

Hawaii's mountains have a lot to do with where it rains and how much. Moisture-laden winds pushed up the slopes are forced by the laws of physics to dump their load at certain cooling altitudes. When you plan a trip around one of the islands and you see lots of dark clouds on high, you might want to stick to the lower elevations, going *around* the mountains instead of *through* them.

Cold Weather? The tropical temperatures we have mentioned so far are operative only near sea level. Remember that the thermometer drops more than three degrees for every 1,000 feet of elevation. This is why Maui and the Big Island boast much cooler climates on their mountains. It snows at about 10,000 feet during the winter, and anyone planning to go up even 5,000 feet should bring at least a sweater to Hawaii, winter *or* summer.

Hawaii's all-time low, for those who keep track of such things, is an astoundingly frigid 11 degrees Fahrenheit. The same temperature was recorded at two places and on two different dates—on January 2, 1961, at the summit of 10,023-foot Haleakala mountain on Maui, and on February 11, 1973, at the top of 13,796-foot Mauna Kea on the Big Island. (No one skis on Haleakala, but there is some semiserious schussing on the upper slopes of Mauna Kea in winter.)

If you're like most *malihinis*, you'll wonder why we have so much artificial air conditioning. Stewart L. Udall, once the Secretary of the Interior and now the head of an environmental planning firm, called the hotel air conditioners in Waikiki an "absurd" waste of energy.

Much of the air conditioning in Hawaii is to increase the comfort of island residents, not of visitors. Studies have shown that some of us who live here have lessened our tolerance to the extremes of temperature and humidity, and are extrasensitive to small climatic changes. Personally, we have never felt the need to install air conditioning in our own home, preferring instead the natural breezes that bring to us the delicious feel and smell of Hawaii.

Some books tell you there is no fog in Hawaii, but that is not strictly correct. Clouds can descend to an altitude of only about 1,000 feet. Island roads go that high and a lot higher, and so Islanders often penetrate that cloud-fog while commuting over the mountains to work.

It's another myth that you will never see smog in Hawaii. You may, although it is fairly rare. First of all, there is the "vog," or volcanic smog, that on some isolated occasions is blown as far as Oahu by the *kona* winds when Kilauea is erupting on the Big Island. This "natural" air pollution can temporarily increase the levels of particulate matter and sulfur dioxide in the atmosphere to annoying levels, especially when combined with more pollution from Honolulu traffic. (Thankfully, there is virtually no industrial pollution in Hawaii.)

A few years ago the U.S. Environmental Protection Agency said that Honolulu is the only major city in the nation where the air is clean enough to breathe safely. Other studies have shown that the city has only 41 micrograms of particulate matter per cubic meter of air, although we guess the figure refers to the average for the entire island of Oahu, including both rural and urban areas.

Hawaii residents often speak affectionately of "liquid sunshine," the "Manoa mist," or the "Hawaiian blessing." This, of course, is rain, even if euphemized through an indulgent smile. These types of very gentle rains, however, are usually so light that their tiny drops are blown around as snowflakes are elsewhere in the world. Since the soft rains usually fall at higher elevations during daylight, they provide grist for the rainbow mills in the upland valleys, like Nuuanu and Manoa, that form the background for Honolulu. Rainbows are endemic to Hawaii, and some of them come in gorgeous double- and triple-decker models.

Natural Disasters. Violent phenomena of nature are rare in the island state. There have been a few hurricanes in the neighborhood. Two of these did serious damage on Kauai, including Hurricane Iwa in November 1982. Tornadoes can happen, but they usually become waterspouts and remain out at sea. However, one day in January 1971 a large waterspout came ashore at Kailua-Kona, destroying several buildings and injuring many persons.

Earthquakes are also not unknown in Hawaii, and, indeed, they are common on the Big Island in association with the active volcanoes there. Most of these volcanic earthquakes, up to several hundred daily, can only be perceived by sensitive scientific instruments.

Conventional earthquakes, caused by faulting, are also felt once in a while, although much less frequently than on the Mainland. A strong earthquake occurred on the Big Island on November 29, 1975. Measuring 7.2 on the Richter scale, it did millions of dollars of damage to homes and buildings in the southern portion of the island. No one was seriously injured in the quake itself, but in a freak aftereffect two persons were drowned when a portion of a beach they were camping on sank beneath the water as they slept. (Thirty-four others in their group escaped.) The shake-up was the strongest jolt felt in Hawaii since 1868.

Of greater concern are tsunamis, or seismic sea waves (and somewhat incorrectly called tidal waves). In the past, earthquakes thousands of miles away in the Aleutian Islands or in South America have generated waves that inundated Hawaii's shoreline areas.

The worst tsunami was generated by an earthquake near Alaska, and it struck Hawaii on April Fools' Day in 1946. One hundred fifty-nine persons died, 1,300 became homeless, and property damage reached $25 million. Hilo was hardest hit; several commercial buildings along the bayfront were completely destroyed. A similar wave on May 23, 1960, took 61 lives in Hilo.

Today the Islands are better protected, with an elaborate warning system involving sensors over thousands of miles of ocean and a series of sirens that cover the coastal areas of all inhabited islands. You might like to have a look at the Civil Defense Tsunami Inundation Maps and instructions in the green pages in the front of isle telephone books. You'll hear those sirens tested, usually at 11 A.M. on the first working day of each month.

Plain old sunshine—dry and not "liquid"—is the biggest natural threat to most visitors and new residents of the Islands. Wear good sunglasses (we recommend the brands with polarizing lenses), cover up between swims, and use suntan or sun-screen lotion to avoid burning, a year-round weather hazard in Hawaii.

Fish, Fowl, Flowers, and Fruit (the Natural Hawaii)

They say that if you toss a broomstick into the soil of Hawaii, it will take root and blossom before you can pull it out again. That is not quite the case, although we do recall once laying aside a branch cut from a plumeria tree and forgetting about it for a few days. We discovered bright new leaves on it before we ever got around to sticking it in the ground at all.

Not all parts of Hawaii are so fertile, of course. Some areas are genuine desert or have a surface paved with clay or even with asphalt. On the other hand, many places do live up to the image. Some sites in Hawaii are truly jungle, and it seems if you turn your head away for a moment new growth might force the works of man to crumble into the underbrush.

Even on the capital island of Oahu there are wild and rugged green mountains, treacherous to the casual hiker, that may host some exciting species of tree, flower, or bush, and maybe even a bird or two that everyone thought did not exist any more.

It is not generally known, but in the hills behind Honolulu there lives an extended family of wallabies. These kangaroo cousins are all descendants of a male and female pair that escaped from a private zoo in 1916. Heaven knows exactly what they eat as they hop from bush to knoll, but the fact remains that they do consume enough wild vegetation to keep alive and reproduce on the fringes of an expanding urban environment.

No one really lives off the land in Hawaii any more because there are

simply too many people to do so. Some folks—rugged individualists like
the late Euell Gibbons—have done it by working very hard at the project.
Personally, we are just as happy to munch on an occasional guava or
passion fruit picked up from along a country road or public park. Also,
people who have mango, orange, grapefruit, banana, avocado, or other
fruit trees in their back yards often carry a share of the soil's munificence
with them when they visit friends.

Fruits and Vegetables of Hawaii. Today almost an official symbol of the
Hawaiian Islands, **pineapple** is actually native to Latin America. This
fruit did not take much to Hawaii until James Dole began planting it
near the village of Wahiawa on Oahu in 1901. Dole inundated the Mainland market with Hawaiian pineapple, popularizing it among millions
who had never heard of it before.

Although the Hawaii hybrid continues as probably the tastiest of its
species in the world, the pineapple companies are now finding production more profitable in such places as Taiwan and the Philippines, where
labor and other costs are lower. As an Island industry, pineapple is
beginning to shrink. You may be surprised to discover, too, that pineapple in Honolulu sometimes sells for more than you would pay for the
"air-flown" fresh fruit in some cities on the Mainland.

Predating pineapple as the most important Island agricultural product is **sugar.** For years, in fact, "sugar and pine" went hand in hand to
form the main economic base of Hawaii. But sugar also has been melting
from the scene recently, even though the rich volcanic soil, the ample
sunshine, and the fluent water supply have combined to help Hawaii
produce more sugar per acre than anywhere else on earth.

Sugar cane takes about two years to mature to its maximum juice
content. Then the field is burned with controlled "cane fires" to get rid
of the leaves. The sweet stalks that remain are trucked to a mill where
huge rollers squash the stems and squeeze out the raw liquid sugar. A
small amount is refined in Hawaii, but most is sent to a cooperative
refinery in California that is jointly owned by all the Hawaiian sugar
companies. The sugar is marketed as the "C&H" brand, which stands for
California and Hawaiian.

Kids who grew up in the countryside used to hack off a length of cane
to chew on their way to school. But today many of the *keiki o ka aina*
(children of the land) no longer know how to do it.

Hawaii grows delicious **bananas,** but not nearly enough to satisfy the
demand in the local markets. Many you will see for sale are the Chiquitas
from Costa Rica or somewhere else. The tree-ripened Hawaiian varieties—
usually Bluefields or Chinese bananas—can sell for about the same price
as the imports, depending on the season.

Of course the best bananas are those you receive free. Usually they will

be given out by friends who grow more than they can use. Besides the commercial plantations, you will occasionally see fruit on the banana plants growing in the wild. But look before you leap; someone will surely claim the patch is his as soon as the fruit begins turning from green to yellow!

Almost as popular a fruit as the pineapple or the banana is the **papay** We often eat it for breakfast, in lieu of a melon, and under a squirt two of lemon juice. Its bright orange pulp has a delightful mild fla and it is low in calories (60 in a half papaya). It contains papair enzyme that helps digestion, and it is loaded with vitamins. Papaya i used in Island recipes as a meat tenderizer.

Like pineapple plants, papaya trees need lots of sunshine, wat good earth. The trees grow easily and quickly, so many homeow plant a row of them in the yard. They come in sexes, and papaya farmers must remember that the males bear no fruit. (to lots of bad jokes from tour guides about "papayas and mam can buy papaya fruit the year around, but prices will vary tr depending on the success of the current crop.

Then there are **mangoes,** which, in a good year, bust June or July. Often compared with peaches, the oblong smooth skins are oranger, juicier, and sweeter. Peel bef skin is bitter, and some folks are allergic to it. You'll se goes in the store; you'll have to pick them yourself, ha ent you with an armload, or buy them from a vendor a (Caution: Because of the occasional presence of a tin of a Hawaiian mango, it is forbidden fruit on the strong smell will lead the agricultural inspector stra before you can sneak one out of Hawaii.)

Hawaiian **coconuts** may be easily enjoyed, if yo Coconuts are often trimmed from the trees while inedible, merely so they won't fall on anyone's open a coconut until you have seen how the Samo Cultural Center. And diet watchers, please not highest in calorie count of any fruit in Hawai nut adds up to 306 calories, and a half cup of 346!

Since there are two species of **avocado** gro type ripens in winter and spring, and the ready in summer and fall—you'll find it i around. (If you're making your own, try called "Tropics Special.") Avocados are quarter of the thick-skinned West In Women who do not want to take avoc

Island beauty secret: mashed avocado makes a wonderful face cream, or so they tell us.

The ubiquitous wild **guava** can be found all year, usually clinging precariously to steep banks along the highways. In fact, guava trees are considered pests in Hawaii, and usually no one will criticize your picking all the thin-skinned, heavily seeded fruit you want, as long as your parked car is not a traffic hazard. About the size and color of lemons, guavas are pressed into nectar and used in a popular canned drink—sold on the Mainland, too—called Hawaiian Punch.

Another yellow fruit you might mistake at first for guava is **passion fruit,** more often called *lilikoi* in Hawaii. Overly seedy or too tart for most folks, it is also often squeezed and combined with other flavors—usually orange—for consumption as a fruit drink. For some unknown reason the women in our family like *lilikoi* in the raw, spooned right out of the skins, crackly seeds and all.

Fast becoming another symbol of Hawaii agriculture is the **macadamia** nut industry. Mostly grown in large orchards on the Big Island, the nuts are expensive but popular. Included in several candy combinations, macadamia nuts are also sold shelled, salted, and canned. If you visit the Big Island, you can stop in at major macadamia-nut processing plants at Honokaa and Keaau. Incidentally, in its natural state the macadamia nut is probably the most fattening nut in the world—about 25 calories per kernel.

Island agriculture also includes **Kona coffee,** which is grown there on the west (Kona) coast. It is the only coffee grown anywhere in the United States. To us, Kona coffee has never quite tasted like *real* coffee although we like its flavor in ice cream and even as a liqueur. By all means try at least one cup. It's a unique experience, and the difficulties in growing and harvesting the coffee may one year combine to close down production forever.

Maui onion, called the "Kula onion" on Maui for the area it comes from, is big, sweet, and well-loved on Island hamburgers. (Some "Maui onions" turn out to have been grown on Molokai!)

Additional edible plants and fruits of Hawaii include **lychee,** really yummy; **poha,** also known as Cape gooseberry; **mountain** apple and vaguely pear-shaped, and an ancient Hawaiian favorite; a hard-to-find prickly fruit; **Surinam cherry,** a bright red fruit makes an excellent jelly; **Kokee plum,** described in the Kauai chapter; **lilikoi,** an elongated passion fruit; **taro,** the nutritious Polynesian plant from which *poi* is pounded; **breadfruit,** tasting rather like bread, but no longer popular in the Hawaiian diet; and **Maui potatoes,** which make some of the best potato chips in the world.

Exotic *Flowers of Hawaii.* Well over 1,000 different kinds

flowers flourish in Hawaii, nearly all of which were brought to the Islands by man. Some bloom the year around. Some come out only during short seasons. One species blossoms only at night.

Several long books have been written on the flowering plants and trees of Hawaii and other tropical lands of the Pacific. You may pick up either cheap or expensive illustrated glossaries of flowers in Hawaii stores, or consult the books in Island public libraries. Meanwhile, here is a brief alphabetical list of the two dozen or so blooms everybody talks about most:

African tulip tree. One of two brilliant red flowering trees (the other is the poinciana), it blooms the year around.

Allamanda. Large, velvetlike, bright yellow blossoms you might see anywhere. Actually a periwinkle, it's a Brazilian native.

Anthurium. Once you've seen one of these naturally waxy creations, you'll never forget it. The usually red (but sometimes pink, orange, white, or green) heart-shaped collar appears to be pierced with a long, thin finger.

Bird-of-paradise. In profile, at least, the stalk looks like a bird's long neck leading to a "beak" formed by a pointed sheath. This is crowned with a gold or orange crest formed by about six petals.

Bottlebrush tree. These drooping feathery spikes look like a vermilion version of something Fuller might sell you to scrub out a test tube. (Don't confuse it with *lehua,* below.)

Bougainvillea. Not just the purple vines, but varieties of crimson, orange, pink, and even white are seen in Hawaii. Look closely; actually they are not flowers but little colored leaves. (And watch out for the thorny branches).

Gardenias. There are many kinds, including the white Tahitian with single star-shaped or pinwheel-shaped flowers.

Ginger. The heavily scented ginger comes in red, yellow, and white varieties, and two or three different shapes. One kind or another always seems to be in season.

Gold tree. One of the most magnificent of the flowering trees; the bright gold or yellow flowers usually bloom only in the spring. It's erratic, however, so you may be lucky enough to see one or two even in midwinter.

Heliconia. There are several types, but the kind we always think of is also called a "lobster claw." It's red, and it looks like several claws stacked up together.

Hibiscus. Hawaii's most "important" blossom, since it is the official state flower. There are singles and doubles, and they come at least in red, yellow, pink, orange, and white. There are no less than 5,000 hybrids, but the simple hibiscus that comes to mind is usually red and has that little thin stamen growing out of the center. A hibiscus blossom generally lasts just about twelve hours—whether you pick it or not—and then suddenly folds up forever. It is a popular flower for women to wear in their hair.

Jacaranda. "Oh, what's the blue tree?" you may hear someone exclaim. The bell-shaped lavender flowers appear most often in the spring, but you might catch them at any time of year. They are natives of Brazil.

Lehua, or *ohia lehua,* is a tuft of red stamens hanging at the end of a tight knot of grayish-green leaves. The flower can also be pink, yellow, or cream color, and it is generally found in the cool heights of Kauai or on the Big Island.

Night-blooming cereus. Between about June and October, it occasionally opens huge white buds at about 8 P.M. and closes soon after sunrise. The original was brought to the Islands from Mexico in the last century and planted on the campus of Punahou School, where it still lives.

Oleander. A tall shrub, this poisonous plant grows clusters of single and double flowers on the tips of its branches. They can come in cream, rose, pink, or red.

Orchids. Almost supplanting the hibiscus as the flower of the Islands, several varieties of orchids are now grown commercially, mainly on the Big Island. There are about 700 species, many of which grow wild. Some orchids make gorgeous *leis,* and they are popular for gifts air-shipped to the Mainland.

Passion flower. The blossom of the aforementioned passion fruit (*lilikoi*), it was named because the yellow and purple flower has oddly shaped stamens and petals that once reminded the Spanish of a style of Christian cross.

Pikake. Actually a fragrant white jasmine, it was the favorite flower of the tragic Princess Kaiulani, who was known as the Princess of the Peacocks. In her honor the blossom was named *pikake,* the Hawaiian word for "peacock."

Plumeria. Perhaps the best known and most popular lei flower, the plumeria, or frangipani, blooms white, yellow, pink, or red at the end of stubby tree branches.

Poinsettia. The "Christmas flower," the red-leafed poinsettia is brilliantly prominent in Hawaii during November and December. There are also yellow and pink varieties.

Protea. In recent years these dramatic, bulbous red, yellow or orange African and Australian blooms have been grown commercially in upcountry Maui.

Royal poinciana. Also known as *flamboyant.* Fiery red and sometimes brilliant yellow flowers cover these umbrellalike trees in June and July.

Shower trees. Delicate pink, white, coral, and "golden" varieties create feathery blossoms annually, beginning in about April and often lasting for months.

Silver sword. A dramatic native silver sunflower that grows and blooms in the dry lava near the top of Haleakala on Maui and Mauna Kea on Hawaii (the Big Island).

Ti plant. Ti, pronounced like "tea," is not really a flower, but one variety can develop very red leaves. It was considered sacred by the early Hawaiians, and it still has special meaning to some today.

Wood rose. In its best-known form, it appears to be a delicately hand-carved rose. Actually it's the dried seed pod of a type of morning glory. Popular souvenirs, wood roses are sold in flower shops. They will last for years.

Other Tropical Trees. Some trees of Hawaii that fall into neither the edible nor the floral groups include these:

The **autograph** tree is known for its thick, ovate leaves on which you can scratch a long-lasting inscription. A forest of tall, straight **bamboo** trees makes a heck of a racket in the wind. The **banyan** tree spreads out and sends down so many new roots that it's sometimes hard to tell which was the original trunk. The **baobab** tree is known in Hawaii as the "dead rat tree" because its fruit looks like small black animals hanging by their tails.

The fragrant **eucalyptus** (gum tree), an Australian native, has become a new source of timber. (Crush and smell the leaves to help clear your sinuses.) One type of eucalyptus is called the **paperbark** tree. The twisted, gnarled **hau** (pronounced "how") tree was originally grown to provide outriggers for ancient canoes. **Ironwoods,** called casuarina in Australia and elsewhere, look something like tall, fuzzy pine trees and serve as excellent windbreaks along country roads. The **kiawe** tree (also called algaroba or mesquite), with its fernish leaves and twisted trunk, appears everywhere.

Koa trees are Hawaiian natives, and their reddish wood is used for furniture and canoes. The **kukui** or candlenut tree has an oily, burnable fruit that provided a night-light for early Polynesians. The polished nuts now make popular *leis* for women or men. And providing excellent shelter from the rain, Hawaii's **monkeypod** trees are carved into bowls and trays. (Look carefully at these items before buying to see if they are made in Hawaii or in the Philippines.)

The **Norfolk pine** is a perfectly formed "Christmas tree," imported to Hawaii from its native Norfolk Island. The **octopus tree** has clusters of glossy leaves spreading out like an umbrella's ribs. The **pandanus,** also called the *hala* tree, features a fruit way up in its long pointed branches that looks from a distance something like a pineapple. It also has aerial roots that give it its other name, "the walking tree." *Hala* leaves, or *lauhala*, have been woven into baskets, hats, and even houses. (The *hala* is often falsely pointed out as the "pineapple tree.") Last, be aware that the fruit hanging from the **sausage tree** is not edible despite its name and appearance.

Animals and Insects of the Islands. A short-term visitor to Hawaii will probably see no more than one wild animal. This would be the popular little **gecko,** a tiny (two- to four-inch) lizard. The harmless creature may come inside your hotel room to eat flies, mosquitoes, and other insects. The Hawaiians considered him good luck, and you can pick him up gently in the palm of your hand. But if he becomes frightened he may run away and leave you a souvenir—his bodiless, still-wriggling tail!

There are only two mammals completely native to Hawaii. These are the **Hawaiian monk seal** and the **Hawaiian bat.** They are seldom seen by anybody, in fact, because they are the rarest seal and the rarest bat in the world. However, there is one Hawaiian monk seal in captivity, and you may find him in residence at the Waikiki Aquarium.

Driving along the road, you may catch a fleeting view of an elongated, brown furry thing skittering into the underbrush just ahead of the car. It was no doubt a **mongoose,** originally brought to the Islands in 1883 in an attempt to control the rat population. Nobody thought about the fact that rats like to run around at night whereas mongooses are daylight creatures, so the only time they meet is at the changing of shifts. Instead of eliminating the rat, the mongoose went on to contribute to the decline of the ground-nesting bird population of Hawaii. It lives on all islands except Kauai, Lanai, Kahoolawe, and Niihau.

Game hunters have special seasons in which they may shoot the following mammals: **wild cattle,** found on the Big Island only; **wild pigs,** the descendants of the European boar; **wild goats,** the progeny of Captain Cook's gifts of 1778, which are today real problems in some parts of Maui and the Big Island; **wild sheep,** generations removed from those brought by Captain George Vancouver in 1794; **Mouflon sheep,** which were imported especially for game in the 1950s; **axis deer,** particularly seen on Molokai and Lanai; the **blacktail deer,** released on Kauai in 1961; and the **pronghorn,** a type of antelope brought to Lanai in 1959.

Since **dolphins** (porpoises) and **whales** are mammals, not fish, we should mention them in this section. You might be lucky enough to see a whale if you take a boat cruise from Maui in the winter, and some dolphins frolic in a special pool at the Kahala Hilton Hotel. Most folks run across both these aquatic mammals, however, at Sea Life Park on Oahu.

You may notice a couple of lawn animals at one time or another. At night, the **bufo** (pronounced *"boof-oh"*), a type of toad, often likes to hop across the grass on a search for insects. (You might catch a few of these on the Royal Hawaiian Hotel grounds.) Then there is the large **African snail,** a pesky land animal who sometimes grows to a size of five inches. You'll usually see him following a heavy rain.

Are there any dangerous animals in Hawaii? Only one—the **wild dog.** You are unlikely to come across any unless you go in for hiking deep into the woods, and even then they are mainly found only on the Big Island. There are also **wild cats,** somewhat of a misnomer since they originated as escaped house pets. Half the 90,000 cats on Oahu alone are strays. (In the pet category, by the way, cats outnumber dogs in Hawaii by 8 to 5. Nationally it's dogs by 3 to 2.)

Believe it or not, there is one single individual **bear** some say may still be romping in the Koolau Mountains on Oahu. He escaped as a baby in 1956, but he was always very shy. If he is still alive, he is considered harmless. **Wild pigs,** of course, can be dangerous if cornered or protecting their young. There is a large benign **earthworm** (sometimes called the Hawaiian blind snake) living in the Islands, but no real **snakes,** except two of the same sex penned up at Honolulu Zoo.

There are 10,000 varieties of insects in Hawaii, and many of them exist nowhere else in the world. One of these is a clownish fellow called the **click beetle.** If he falls upside down, he snaps his body with the aid of a little spring hinge, noisily jumping up, over and over again, if necessary, until he lands on his feet.

Our most notorious insects are the voracious **termites.** There are two destructive types. With no winter to cool their appetite, they devour nearly everything and give business to about 81 pest-control companies. There are also **cockroaches.** They can get to be two inches long, and sometimes they *fly!*

Yes, Hawaii has **mosquitoes,** as well as **bees** and other things that sting. Two frightening insects include the **centipede,** which can give a painful bite, and the **scorpion,** also a nasty little stinger. Neither is considered deadly, but persons bitten by these two should call a doctor without delay. Fortunately there aren't a lot of them around. In our years of living in Hawaii we have yet to see our first scorpion, and centipedes show up about as frequently as a snake in Peoria. Californian agricultural interests are concerned about the **Oriental fruit fly**, a permanent pest in Hawaii, but which is not present in any other state.

What about the **cricket**? That "harmless" little fellow so welcome on the hearths or in the yards of temperate-zone locales is considered an unwelcome pest in Hawaii. Reason: He loves nothing more than to eat into the eyes of pineapples.

Our Fragile Bird World. Hawaii has the embarrassing distinction of having been the home of more extinct birds than any other single area in the world. At one time there were more than 70 species of native birds in the Islands. Today, 22 kinds are extinct and 26 more are on the endangered species list. That's about half the number on the list for the entire United States.

Many of the endemic birds have been crowded out by others imported and released here into the wilderness. Others simply couldn't survive the changes in the environment made by man over the past 200 years.

On the other hand, sometimes a bird thought to be extinct is discovered alive and well in some remote valley. From time to time a completely new species is found, too. And there are also programs to wipe out some of the harmful birds, such as the papaya- and banana-eating parrots that were released here carelessly in recent years.

Of the native birds, the **nene** (pronounced "*nay*-nay"), or Hawaiian goose, is the most significant. This is the official state bird, thought to be descended from a flock of migrating Canada geese blown off course several centuries ago. Its feet have evolved from webs into claws, and it lives today high on the mountain slopes and lava flows of Maui and the Big Island. No longer is it so rare as to be "endangered," but you'll still be lucky to see one outside captivity.

One of the recently rediscovered birds is the **o'o,** or more specifically the **o'o a'a** (pronounced "*oh*-oh *ah*-ah"). The ancient Hawaiians thought its cry sounded like "oh-oh." And the word *a'a* means, roughly, "dwarf." So this was apparently one of your smaller *o'o*s. The **Hawaiian stilt,** an endangered long-legged water bird, can still be found living in isolated ponds, mainly on Kauai or the Big Island.

The birds you'll most likely meet in Honolulu and other built-up areas number only three. The first is the common **mynah** bird who arrived from India in 1865, and who marches or struts on land, rather than hops. Don't confuse him with the English-speaking mynah; the Hawaiian mynahs love to engage in crowded, noisy conventions and arguments in their own raucous language. Usually these take place just above your head in some large tree or other, especially along about sunset. These birds wear basic black, but just at takeoff time they flash with white at the ends of their wings. Mynahs earn their living and the affection of the human suburban population by feeding on the grass-destroying army worms.

Also, **sparrows** are everywhere, usually noticeable picking up the crumbs in outdoor restaurants. Since there are no big grain crops in Hawaii, sparrows are tolerated and are not considered the pests they are on the Mainland. An 1871 import, the sparrow was dubbed *li'ili'i* by the Hawaiians. It means "the little bird."

The third urban bird is the **barred dove.** It has a rattling coo voice and sometimes seems to be saying "hell-of-a-lot, hell-of-a-lot." Also called "small doves," the birds are monogamous. They form couples, roost at each other's side by night, and remain forever faithful.

There are four or five birds you'll see in rural areas or in more protected gardens. The most common is the larger **lace-necked dove** or Chinese dove. (Hawaii children are taught that it often calls out, "Come to scho-o-o-l.") Both kinds of doves are fair game for hunters during the season. (See chapter 5, section 9.)

The **Brazilian cardinal** male has a bright red head and is relatively tame and friendly, if you offer him some food. The **North American cardinal** is virtually all red, or at least the daddy of the species is. This one likes to whistle a lot. Then there's the **white eye** or majiro, a greenish Japanese bird with a conspicuous white ring around the eye. All three of these were imported over less than a two-year period from 1928 to 1929. Some unusually colorful chickens reside in Hawaii. You'll probably see these **Polynesian jungle fowl** scrounging around the headquarters and restaurant area at Kokee State Park on Kauai.

One of the most interesting birds is only a winter visitor to Hawaii—the **Pacific golden plover** (that rhymes with "lover"). From May to August the plovers fly away to mate and raise their young in Alaska and Siberia. On Oahu you will likely see them between September and April, perhaps in the Punchbowl area. Anywhere there is cattle in the Islands, you'll almost surely find the **cattle egret**. It's a type of white heron which often perches on the backs of cattle, eating the insects they find there or on the ground nearby, picking off insects disturbed by the animals' movements.

Some seabirds that hover over Hawaiian waters include **tropic birds,** both the white-tailed and red-tailed varieties. They're beautiful flyers, often noticed swooping down into valleys and even volcanic craters, but terrible at takeoffs and landings, as are the **Laysan gooney birds.** Both types specialize in crash landings. The gooney (albatross) needs a runway to get airborne again, while the tropic birds beat their wings violently against the ground until they finally heave themselves into the air, seemingly by sheer will power.

The most dramatic of the seabirds is the **frigate bird,** a genuine pirate. He soars aloft, seeming to hover motionless in the sky until he spies another seabird carrying a fish. Then he harasses his victim into dropping the fish, whereupon the intruder scoops it up. The Hawaiian name for the frigate bird is *iwa,* meaning "thief."

Besides the aforementioned doves, there are a dozen birds imported for hunters to shoot in season (about November to January). These are the ring-necked pheasant, Japanese blue pheasant, California valley quail, Japanese quail, Gambel's quail, chukar partridge, Barbary partridge, mourning dove, black francolin, Erckel's francolin, gray francolin, wild turkey, and bamboo partridge.

You may notice that there are no seagulls in the Islands. Seagulls are scavengers who feed on dead fish and debris, which are only present where there is a considerable amount of shallow water. The Hawaiian Islands, being only the tip of massive underwater mountains, have grown up steeply in a very deep blue sea. The few gulls who arrive here from time to time soon leave to find places where the pickings are better.

Hawaii's Fish Story. An estimated 800 different species of fish, of both the decorative and the delicious varieties, frequent Hawaiian waters. (Selected samples of these live in luxury at the Waikiki Aquarium.)

With the rise in popularity of saltwater aquariums in American homes, so many Hawaiian fish are being sought that whole species are in danger of being eliminated. Also, certain fish that would delight aquarists elsewhere are sold as food in Hawaii markets.

Some decorative fishes—also called reef fishes because they live close to shore—are included in the following list. (Scuba divers or snorkel enthusiasts may find these at Hanauma Bay Underwater Park or other special places.)

Butterflyfishes, some 21 kinds all together; **Moorish idols,** or *kihikihi,* an old Hawaiian delicacy; **stripeys,** or convict fish; **angelfishes,** who travel in pairs; **damselfishes,** rather drab in Hawaii; **cardinalfishes,** including one type that really is all red; **aholehole,** which means "sparkling" (known also as the "silver perch"); **surgeonfishes,** or "tangs," some of which have strange single horns; the **wrasses,** of which there are more than three dozen colorful kinds; **parrotfishes,** which look like they are equipped with bills; **goatfishes,** probably called that because of their goatees; **squirrelfishes,** who are the only "squirrels" in Hawaii, incidentally; **hawkfishes,** which hunt like hawks; **scorpionfishes,** all of which are poisonous, but luckily very shy; **triggerfishes,** including the famous *humuhumunukunukuapuaa,* the official state fish; **pufferfishes,** who can blow themselves up to three times their normal size; **tubemouthed fishes,** including those long, thin vacuum cleaners called trumpetfish; and **moray eels,** who are thankfully not very aggressive despite their vicious, fanglike teeth.

There are, of course, many game and food fishes in Hawaiian waters, and you may charter boats for deep-sea fishing yourself. (See section 8, Water Sports, in the following island-chapters.) Some of these sport and eating fishes include the following:

Pacific blue marlin is the big boy, the sleek billfish everyone wants to catch. The world record is 1,805 pounds, set by Captain Cornelius Choy right out of Honolulu, but normally they run from about 300 to 400 pounds. The **striped marlin** is also a billfish, but averages about 80 pounds. There's also the **broadbill swordfish,** with a much larger bill, and the **sailfish,** with its large dorsal fin.

The favorite food fish in Hawaii is the **mahimahi**—"the fish so nice, they named it twice," goes one of the current jokes. It is occasionally known as the dorado or dolphin fish (but definitely *not* to be confused with the mammalian dolphin or porpoise, neither of which is a fish). There is also **aku** (skipjack tuna), **ahi** (yellowfin tuna), and a half dozen other types of tuna, as well as **ulua,** or jack fishes, not large but fierce fighters.

You may hear something about **tilapia,** and the most common type is also known as a "garbage fish," since it is known for swimming in less-salubrious waters. However a different type of tilapia, which lives in both salt and fresh water, has begun to be raised commercially in Hawaii as an inexpensive food fish. Image-conscious boosters have now named it the "Hawaiian sunfish."

Then there are **mullet,** which the ancient Hawaiians raised in large fishponds; the knife-toothed **barracuda,** which can reach six feet in length; and **flying fish,** seldom eaten today but appreciated for their antics on brief trips above the surface.

As in all ocean waters of the world, there are various types of sharks, including the **great white shark,** the **tiger shark,** and the weirdly shaped **hammerhead shark.** (The old Hawaiians thought sharks were gods in disguise.)

Attacks against humans by sharks in Hawaii are, fortunately—and quite honestly—very rare. In the past ninety years there have been only sixteen recorded attacks, and of these only five were fatal. Your chances of being struck by lightning anywhere in the world are greater than those of being attacked by a shark in Hawaii.

There are three interesting ray fish sometimes seen off the Hawaiian Islands. The most intriguing is the spotted and somewhat puppyfaced **eagle ray.** Also, there is the **brown stingray,** which reaches a maximum length of four feet, and the giant **manta ray,** a docile behemoth who can become as wide as twenty feet from wingtip to wingtip.

Although they are not really fish, we should mention that there are **squid** in Hawaiian waters. But when boys talk about "going squidding," they really mean they're heading out to the reef to hunt for **octopuses.** Another mollusk popular for food is the **opihi** (limpet). It is a dangerous occupation to scrape these delectables off the rocks fronting the ocean. The newspapers are always carrying stories about a sudden high wave that sweeps an opihi-picker into the sea to drown.

Also, there are **oysters** somehow still living in Pearl Harbor and bearing a few pearls. The water there is polluted, however, which means that neither the oyster nor its pearl has any value. Forget those pearl oysters in a can you see sold everywhere; they're shipped in from somewhere outside the state.

Among Hawaii's more annoying denizens of the deep are different species of jellyfish. One, the **Portuguese man-of-war,** looks something like a miniature ship under full sail. The purplish-blue animal floats into shallow, shoreline waters with the tide, usually driven by strong winds. (It even happens in Waikiki when strong *kona*—southwest—breezes come up in December or January.) If you encounter it in the water or even after it has washed up on the beach, beware; its long, dangling tentacles can cause bitter, stinging welts.

Perhaps not quite so painful is the **pololia** jellyfish, which looks like Saran Wrap floating in the water. Stings from either kind are easily treated with meat tenderizer (Adolph's is carried by some local beach goers). Lifeguards are equipped with similar substances. Well-known and usually effective folk remedies include the juice of a green papaya, or urine—although the latter may not be practical on a crowded beach.

And freshwater fish? There are a few simple shrimp and crayfish, of course. Also you will find **trout** in streams at the Kokee Public Fishing Area on Kauai, as well as **catfish** and **bass** in the Wahiawa and Nuuanu reservoirs on Oahu. These may be caught with license and permit in season.

4

Islanders—Kamaainas and Malihinis

Hawaiian History in Brief

The dramatic and often violent history of man in Hawaii has been eloquently told in volume after volume. Among the most thrilling is the semifictionalized version in *Hawaii,* by James Michener. An enjoyable account that names the real names is *Shoal of Time,* a work by Gavan Daws. And the definitive and scholarly social history is *Hawaii Pono,* by Lawrence Fuchs. A brief summary obviously can be no substitute for books of that caliber.

Much of Hawaii's thunderous and romantic past will become apparent in gentle doses in the island-chapters that follow, mostly in the Sightseeing sections. For a ready reference, however, we have included a few basics in the life story of Hawaii and its people.

Pre-Haole Hawaii—A.D. ? to 1778. Until very recently, at least, most scientists said that the Hawaiian Islands were first colonized by Marquesan Polynesians around the year 750. Some new finds indicate that date should be 300 or even earlier—perhaps even Before Christ—and archeological research on the subject is still continuing. In any case, all agree that whatever peoples there were here were joined by islanders from Tahiti and vicinity in about 1300.

These seafarers made the journey over thousands of miles in great, double-hulled canoes. The first expedition was led, according to legend, by an intrepid navigator named Hawaii Loa, who then lent his name to the Big Island. Following this initial discovery, vessels traveled back and forth for a time, bringing more family members, dogs, pigs, trees, vegetables, and flowers.

Gradually, over scores of generations, ties to the ancestral islands became less important, and eventually even the talent for making the mammoth canoes completely died out.

For a thousand years the Hawaiians lived alone, their islands composing the entire world as far as they were concerned. The verbal tales of ancient and faraway lands became indistinguishable from the religious and supernatural fairy stories that attempted to explain their environment.

There is some strong evidence that the Spanish explorer Juan Gaetano called briefly at Hawaii in 1555, and that other ships could have followed him. But the suspicious Iberians kept their Pacific secrets well, and no proof of what they may have found has survived—only a few old maps that correctly plot the general position of the Islands.

Captain Cook and the Sailor Saga—1778 to 1820. On January 20, 1778, Captain James Cook of the British Royal Navy stepped ashore on Kauai, becoming the first European known to have reached the archipelago. The Hawaiians received him as at least a great chief or a king, perhaps even a god, old stuff for Cook after his discoveries on Tahiti and the Society Islands. He paid his respects over a fortnight, reprovisioned his two ships, and then headed for the Arctic in an unsuccessful attempt to find a northern passage to the Atlantic Ocean.

Cook returned to the Islands in November, this time visiting Kealakekua Bay on the Big Island, which was one of four separate kingdoms. During this second visit some misunderstandings culminated in what might have been only a minor skirmish between Cook's men and the Hawaiians. But something went awry, and the great explorer was struck and killed on February 14, 1779. His body was later dismembered and only part of it was finally returned to his ship.

One who had been taking in all the excitement during Cook's second visit was the king's alert nephew, Kamehameha. Perhaps then and there he became impressed by the political potential of gunpowder. When his uncle died a few years later, Kamehameha set out to rule the Big Island. A decisive battle in 1791, in which he used some European cannon, won him his goal.

British Naval Captain George Vancouver struck up a friendship with Kamehameha during visits to Hawaii over the next three years, and the Hawaiian chief then revealed his plans to create one single kingdom from the entire Island chain. Kamehameha went on to award some *haoles* (whites) favored places in his inner circle, and with the use of their relatively high technology he began conquering the islands one by one, in a series of ruthless battles.

By 1795 Kamehameha ruled all the major islands except distant Kauai and Niihau. One invasion fleet was turned back by a storm, so he never succeeded in fighting for those northwestern islands. In 1810, however, he tricked their king into ceding the land to him anyway.

During this time more and more foreign ships called in Hawaii, bearing such gifts and concepts as syphilis and avarice. Kamehameha and the other blue-blooded *alii* (chiefs) developed a taste for foreign finery, but all the chief had to offer for the froufrou of the fur traders and whalers were willing young women and fresh groceries. Eventually, however, Kamehameha decided to set up some more lucrative commerce.

About 1801, the king began to sacrifice his people's entire way of life to the sandalwood trade. Shippers paid him handsomely for the stuff that the Chinese bought to burn as incense in their temples. For this, Kamehameha began breaking the backs of his subjects as they cut trees deeper and deeper in the forests and higher and higher in the mountains. These formerly hard-working people were beginning to ignore their taro patches and their festivals—even neglecting their ancient gods.

Kamehameha made a few liberal concessions, but by and large he is remembered for bloodying streams and beaches in his military victories and destroying souls wholesale in his industrial conquests. Why this Hawaiian Napoleon is so honored today remains a mystery to us.

The old monarch died in 1819, aged at least in his sixties. His body was hidden in a secret place near Kailua-Kona so that others could not obtain magical power from his bones. During his twenty-four-year reign the population of his people had plunged from an estimated 300,000 to about 135,000. Following his death, his weak eldest son, Liholiho, was named Kamehameha II.

Soon afterwards, under the influence of the dynamic Kaahumanu, his father's favorite wife, Liholiho completely abolished the ancient *kapu* (taboo) system, thereby destroying the generally oppressive gods, but at the same time throwing the population practically into religious oblivion. The immediate result as far as liberationist Kaahumanu was concerned was to allow her and other women several privileges that had been previously reserved for men.

But more changes were to come. Into this topsy-turvy atmosphere sailed, on March 30, 1820, the first company of American Calvinist missionaries.

Missionary Hawaii—1820 to 1854. At first there were only seventeen missionaries, led by two ordained ministers and bearing instructions from their Massachusetts headquarters to convert the heathen of "Owhyee" and to cover the land with fields, houses, schools, and churches.

The women in the party also took it on themselves immediately to cover the ample naked flesh of the female Hawaiians. The pullover garment they whipped up was the ancestor of today's popular *muumuu*.

After receiving the king's permission to stay, members of the company split into three teams, some remaining at Kona, others going on to Honolulu, and still more setting up a mission on Kauai. Later, another church was started at Lahaina, Maui.

The strong-willed Kaahumanu was fascinated with the new religion and the customs of the *haole* women, and, through her, the missionaries won greater favor with the king. Of course many of the king's advisors— including resident foreigners—were opposed to the missionary operations.

During this period Liholiho franchised the sale of sandalwood to his subordinate chiefs, and they, in turn, drove the people to even greater lengths to cut down and ship out this natural resource. Further epidemics of foreign diseases took their toll. At the same time, more missionaries arrived. Led by Kaahumanu and the king's mother, members of the Hawaiian royal family began to be converted to the faith, and the missionaries standardized a written form of the Hawaiian language.

In 1823 Liholiho and his queen decided to take in London. After a glorious, fun-filled visit to that city, the royal pair died there, in their hotel room, infected by measles. (Hawaiians of the period had no immunity to the disease.) The ruler's teen-age brother then became king and was named Kamehameha III.

Kamehameha III was destined for a twenty-nine-year reign, always more or less under the influence of the missionaries. Although irresponsible in his younger years, he matured to become almost a storybook wise king in later life. Senior missionary Hiram Bingham, builder of Kawaiahao Church, led the king along the path of righteousness until that minister left the Islands in 1840.

One of the later missionaries, Gerrit P. Judd, eventually left the calling to become the king's secular right-hand man. It fell to these leaders to transfer the semifeudal society into a constitutional monarchy. Under their management so many schools were established that Hawaii became one of the most literate nations in the world. Meanwhile, on the commercial front, whaling replaced the sandalwood trade as the Islands' principal means of support.

Civil liberties were born in 1839, when the king proclaimed the Declaration of Rights and Laws. This was followed quickly by a written constitution that set up a two-house legislature. For the first time representative elections were held in Hawaii.

Conflicts there were aplenty, however, often between the maritime interests and the holy word as interpreted by the missionaries. Sailors, who declared there was "no God west of the Horn," competed with the straitlaced concepts of Jesus for the affections of the loose and mellow

Hawaiians, especially the young women of the country. The missionaries continued to stamp out fornication and the hula to the tune of an occasional riot fomented from the vicinity of the waterfront.

There were also troubles with foreign policy. France, a Catholic country interested in exporting her wines and brandies, had plenty to grumble about with the strong Protestant and teetotal influence in the Islands, and she threatened to annex the tiny nation several times. But the British actually did it—sort of.

It happened in 1843 when the commander of an English frigate forced the king to submit to British rule, alleging that the property rights of Britons in Hawaii were being violated. The Union Jack flew over the Islands for only six months, however, before British Admiral Richard Thomas arrived to repudiate and apologize for the annexation. The festivities ending the occupation took place at what is now Thomas Square, named by a grateful population for the officer who renewed the Islands' independence.

Following that episode, Kamehameha III moved himself and the capital from Lahaina to Honolulu. The whaling trade reached its peak, with hundreds of ships often parked at Lahaina and Honolulu, and then began a fairly steady decline. Several Honolulu commercial establishments still in operation first opened their doors around the middle of the nineteenth century, a number of them begun by former missionaries or sons of missionaries. And agriculture, beginning with cattle ranching, began to assume a new importance in the island nation.

In 1846 the king set up the Great Mahele, which divided all real estate among the king and his chiefs, and even left a few thousand acres to the common people. Many Hawaiians did not understand what they needed to do, but most *haoles* living in the Islands lost no time in registering their claims.

Despite vigorous opposition, Catholics and Mormons had now established missions in the Islands. When Kamehameha III died in December 1854, with him went more than three decades of American Protestant missionary influence in Hawaiian politics.

The Last Days of the Monarchy—1854 to 1894. The king's nephew, Alexander Liholiho, was named the new ruler, and he assumed the title Kamehameha IV at the age of 21. Two years later he was married to Emma Rooke in a spectacular ceremony at Kawaiahao Church, and together they founded the Queen's Hospital as an institution dedicated to preventing foreign diseases among the Hawaiians.

One disease—which could not then be treated—arrived in 1860, the same year the hospital cornerstone was laid. This was leprosy, called the *Mai Pake* (Chinese malady). The board of health chose the spectacular but isolated Makanalua Peninsula (Kalaupapa) on the island of Molokai as a special refuge for its victims. The story of leprosy in Hawaii is long and sad, full of neglect and tragedy, and yet mitigated by cases of such high heroism as that of Father Damien de Veuster, the Belgian priest who worked with the lepers on Molokai until he died himself after contracting the disease.

Two personal tragedies jolted the reign of Kamehameha IV. First, he shot to death one of his own staff in a misunderstanding. Then his four-year-old son and last direct heir to the throne caught a fever and died shortly after the king had attempted to cool off a childish tantrum by holding him under running water. In a spirit of religious fervor, the king embraced the Church of England (Episcopalian) and founded St. Andrew's Cathedral in 1862.

Kamehameha IV died the following year, however, never regaining his interest in public life following the death of his son. The king was 29.

His older brother, Lot, was named Kamehameha V. By this time the population of Hawaii had declined to less than 70,000, and a very real problem was the lack of available labor to work the burgeoning sugar plantations. (Whaling had died completely as an Island industry as soon as oil was discovered in the U.S. in 1859.)

This fifth and final Kamehameha was instrumental in setting up a Bureau of Immigration to encourage the importation of contract labor. Thus began Hawaii's multiracial character as Chinese, Japanese, Portuguese, and some Europeans began to arrive, committed to work under the tropic sun.

At the end of 1872, Kamehameha V died without leaving an heir or naming a successor to the throne. William C. Lunalilo, descended from the half-brother of Kamehameha the Great, was then elected king by the legislature. King Lunalilo didn't accomplish a great deal; he died himself just over a year later.

A new legislative election brought David Kalakaua to the throne after a bitter contest between him and Queen Emma, the widow of Kamehameha IV. King Kalakaua ruled from 1874 to 1891. Now known rather inelegantly as the Merry Monarch, the king was not only into arts, music, and sciences, he was also a peripatetic ruler for the day, becoming the first king of any country to visit the United States—or to take a trip around the world, for that matter.

Kalakaua's Washington tour and visit with President Ulysses S. Grant resulted in the Reciprocity Treaty that removed the tariff barrier, a tremendous shot in the arm for the sugar industry. The king also granted Pearl Harbor to the Americans for use as a naval base. Kalakaua built the present Iolani Palace, completed in 1882, and then starred in an elaborate coronation ceremony on the palace grounds a year later.

In the 1870s and 1880s more immigrants arrived from Japan and from Portuguese islands like Madeira and the Azores to work in the sugar fields. Industrialists, foreigners, and persons under foreign influence eventually forced Kalakaua to give up much of his political power, despite a brief revolt by royalists.

King Kalakaua was a tinkerer, or perhaps a minor inventor. He was also the first in Hawaii to acquire any new gadget of the era, such as the telephone and the electric light. He became a friend of Robert Louis Stevenson, who was also interested in Hawaiian history. The king began to bring back and document the nearly forgotten culture of the ancient Hawaiians, including the formerly outlawed *hula*. Kalakaua himself wrote the words to the national anthem of the kingdom, "Hawaii Pono'i," which is still sung today as the official state song.

But political strains took their toll on the king. Kalakaua left for San Francisco for his health late in 1890. There he died January 20, 1891.

Queen Liliuokalani, Kalakaua's sister and the last monarch of Hawaii, came to the throne during an economic depression in which the sugar planters were again having trouble getting into the American market. Business interests once more put on the pressure for annexation to the United States.

When the queen attempted in 1893 to declare a new constitution strengthening the monarchy, it was either too much for an American group called the Annexation Club, or—more likely—the excuse they had been waiting for. They formed a "Committee of Public Safety," which asked the United States minister (ambassador) to land troops from a warship in the harbor.

Only one shot was fired—and that one was almost an accident—and a policeman was wounded. Queen Liliuokalani left her throne quietly to avoid bloodshed, and a provisional government was set up. The revolutionists offered the islands to the United States, but after a thorough investigation President Grover Cleveland haughtily turned down the deal. In a message to Congress, Cleveland said, "It appears that Hawaii was taken possession of by the United States forces without the consent or wish of the Government of the Islands."

The Brief Life of the Republic—1894 to 1898. Hawaii was a republic in little more than name only. Martial law was declared, loyalty oaths were required, and only men of property could vote. The Royal Hawaiian Band, among others, resigned as a body rather than swear allegiance to the revolutionaries and show disloyalty to their queen.

Nevertheless, the United States government never succeeded in restoring Liliuokalani to her throne. The new Hawaii government set about making itself into a semipermanent arrangement that would last until the climate changed completely in Washington. Sanford B. Dole, a lawyer and sugar planter—and a relative moderate among the members of the new order—was appointed president.

Shots were fired and one man died during a two-week counterrevolution in 1894. The queen did not take an active part, but she was arrested anyway and coerced into signing a document renouncing her claim to the crown and swearing allegiance to the Republic of Hawaii. Later found guilty of treason, she was sentenced to five years' hard labor. Instead, she was held prisoner in a second-floor corner of Iolani Palace for a total of nine months. During her imprisonment the queen wrote and composed music, including the Hawaiian words for the famous song "Aloha Oe." After her release she moved two blocks away to her home at Washington Place. Though she occasionally traveled in a futile appeal for her cause, Liliuokalani continued to live in the mansion as a reluctant American citizen until she died in 1916.

The election of McKinley's Republican administration certainly helped, but it was the Spanish-American War that put Hawaii's annexation cause over the top. The strategic importance of a Pacific territory was dramatized to all by Admiral Dewey's victory in the Philippines.

A formal transfer of sovereignty took place at the palace August 12, 1898. In the crowd were Americans, Portuguese, Chinese, Japanese, and Filipinos. But according to some accounts there was not a single native Hawaiian who approached the festivities closely enough to see the American flag raised.

You Had to Know the Territory—1898 to 1959. Business boomed immediately in American Hawaii. Political details took a couple of years to firm up, but by mid-1900 the Islands were handed an official governmental status. President McKinley then appointed former Hawaii president Sanford Dole as the new governor of the incorporated territory.

Meanwhile, out in the fields of central Oahu, James D. Dole, a distant cousin of the governor, was beginning to raise the first commercial pineapples. Contract agricultural laborers from the Far East continued to pour in and spread out all over the Islands.

The native Hawaiians, becoming spiritual aliens in their own land, found some solace in the election of Prince Jonah Kuhio Kalanianaole as Hawaii's nonvoting delegate to Congress. Had the monarchy survived, Prince Kuhio would have been in line for the throne. Instead he served in Washington from 1903 to 1921, and his crowning achievement was the passage of the Hawaiian Homes Commission Act. That law allows Hawaiians who qualify to lease home lots on former government lands for as little as $1 per year, and to use other, larger areas of property for agricultural production.

Upon annexation large holdings that had belonged to the crown or the Hawaiian government were set aside for military use, and Hawaii's growth as an armed camp increased, spurred even further by the activity during World War I. Cables, telephones, and airplanes began to link Hawaii more closely to the continental U.S., and tourism gradually became an important industry in the territory. The Moana Hotel was built in 1901, and the new Royal Hawaiian Hotel was completed in 1927. Both have endured to this day.

Virtually all business activities then were held in the grip of an unofficial and paternal corporate club called the "Big Five." Most of these were begun by *haole kamaaina* (longtime resident Caucasian) families who traced their lineage back to the missionaries. These companies, which still command considerable respect today, are C. Brewer & Co., Theo. H. Davies & Co., Amfac (American Factors), Castle & Cooke, and Alexander & Baldwin. Their directors ruled with iron fists over land ownership and labor activities in the first half of the twentieth century. They could—and did—decide just who would and who would not participate in business in Hawaii.

Hawaii received its worst national publicity in 1931 and 1932 during the "Massie Case," an incident that created high tension between local people and the military establishment. The wife of navy lieutenant Massie said she was raped by some local youths in the swamp now occupied by the Ala Moana shopping center. The evidence was meager against those arrested and they were found not guilty. Most civilians, at least, thought they truly were innocent.

But Massie and his wife's mother later kidnapped and murdered one of the accused. In a charged racial atmosphere, the Navy and faraway U.S. congressmen sought to have Massie released without trial. Nevertheless, he was found guilty of manslaughter. His ten-year prison sentence, however, was reduced by the U.S.–appointed governor to one single hour. The conduct of the case, therefore, left no one satisfied and everyone angry.

The Massie case led to Washington efforts to put Hawaii under a more severe form of government. Although this never came to pass, that threat of tough federal domination led others to begin pushing for the political safety offered by statehood.

Sugar, pineapple, and tourism virtually collapsed during the Great Depression, but they were given a psychological boost toward health again by the two-day visit of President Franklin D. Roosevelt in 1934.

The Islands were never the same after December 7, 1941. Although tensions had been building between the United States and Japan, the actual attack on the Pearl Harbor naval base came as a genuine shock. Thousands of servicemen and scores of civilians were killed in the raid. Martial law was declared, and many "suspicious" persons, almost all of Japanese ancestry, were rounded up and jailed.

During the war barbed wire replaced bathing suits on Waikiki Beach. The Islands became the supply and training headquarters for the entire Pacific war effort, and the population jumped by more than 400,000 active-duty military personnel. Among them was James Jones, author of *From Here to Eternity,* one of the novels depicting Hawaii during the war.

Americans of Japanese ancestry who attempted to volunteer for the service were, at first, rejected. Later in the war they were accepted in a body and formed into two units. The 442nd Regimental Combat Team and the 100th Battalion fought heroically in Italy and France. They sustained the most casualties and became the most decorated American units in World War II.

Following the war, long-overdue unionization burst upon the Island scene, in an effort to right inequities in the outmoded labor policies of the large corporations. Strikes in sugar and pineapple were bad enough, but when a crippling six-month dock strike took place in 1949, it was almost too much for the water-bound territory to bear.

The rise of McCarthyism led many to equate the union activity with Communist influence. The charges were particularly applied to the International Longshoremen's and Warehousemen's Union (ILWU) and its leaders after they organized sugar, pineapple, and dock workers, thus controlling the employees of the three most powerful industries in the territory.

The Korean War took a heavy toll on Hawaii, since the Islands contributed more men and more military casualties per capita to that action than any other state in the Union. During that war, too, a new military buildup began in Hawaii, one that has not diminished to this day. In terms of payroll, government employment now rivaled sugar, pineapple, shipping, and even tourism as the Islands' biggest "industry."

By the early 1950s labor was entrenched and beginning to influence Island political activity. The Big Five no longer held full control over the economy. Many of the *nisei* who had fought in World War II now had used their G.I. Bills to obtain new professional status. Then the largest single ethnic group in Hawaii, these Japanese-Americans became its movers and shakers. Led by 442nd veteran and future senator Daniel K. Inouye, they joined with labor elements, represented by John A. Burns (the future governor), to force a 1954 Democratic sweep of the territorial legislature. Thus they broke Republican political domination in the Islands for the first time.

Two years later Burns was elected delegate to Congress, where he began a long, hard campaign to win statehood for Hawaii. But not everyone wanted statehood. Many prognosticators of doom pointed out the "Red" influence in the labor unions and spoke direly of Japanese elements in the population "taking over." Native Hawaiians, who probably still favored a return of the monarchy, had nostalgic reasons for opposing statehood. (Tour-bus drivers were known to include their opposition to becoming a state in their patter.) Some members of the U.S. Congress also vigorously opposed statehood for various reasons, including racism and the fact of Hawaii's great physical separation from the Mainland.

Delegate Burns worked with the Alaska delegation to help pass its statehood bill in 1958. After that, Hawaii virtually rode in on the same wave. The measure passed overwhelmingly in March 1959, and President Eisenhower quickly signed it.

The Aloha State—1959 to now. The first state elections ended in a Republican-Democratic split. Republican William F. Quinn, the last appointed governor, became the first elected governor, winning in a close ballot over John Burns. (Burns captured the office from Quinn three years later.) Republican Hiram Fong won one of the U.S. Senate seats, becoming the first Oriental to join that body. (He has since retired.)

Democrat Oren E. Long, another former governor, was voted in as the other senator. The single House post at that time went to Inouye, who thus became the first Japanese-American congressman. Republicans took the wheel of the new state Senate, and the Democrats won a majority in the state House of Representatives.

Statehood and the Boeing 707 landed in Hawaii in the same year. With all the national hoopla over the fiftieth state, and a reduction of the former 9 prop hours to 4½ jet hours' time from the West Coast, tourists began funneling into Hawaii on an increasing wave.

Sadly, Hawaii again suffered disproportionate losses in the Vietnam War. In one disturbing incident, President Johnson activated a Hawaii National Guard and Reservist unit as part of a national emergency power-er play because of the 1968 "Pueblo Crisis" with North Korea. Then the men were callously kept on active duty and sent to fight in Vietnam instead. After considerable political protest, the hometown outfit was finally deactivated and sent home, but not before several of its members had died in action.

Unlike the Korean War, however, Vietnam did not hurt the tourist business. In fact, it actually increased. Thousands of servicemen were flown to Hawaii for their "R&R" time, often to see their families, who traveled from the Mainland to Hawaii to meet them.

In the 1970s, Democratic-Republican rivalries became less important than the opposing factions within Hawaii's Democratic party. Former congressional delegate John Burns had been elected governor in 1962. Reelected twice, he served through 1974.

Development-oriented, Burns was credited with improving the University of Hawaii and helping make tourism a greater industry, as well as with some progressive social legislation in public education, welfare, and labor areas. His critics complained that his growth policies worked to the detriment of pollution standards, traffic problems, the housing shortage, and overcrowding of all types.

Before he died Burns endorsed his even-tempered lieutenant governor, George R. Ariyoshi. Beginning in 1974, Ariyoshi was elected to three four-year terms, during which he continued policies similar to Burns's. He retired in 1986.

Republicans generally give only token opposition in the major races, but that has been changing a little. Honolulu mayor Frank Fasi, a longtime Democratic mayor and frequent contender for the governor's chair, was most recently elected to the top city post when he ran as a Republican. However, when three city councilmen who were elected as Democrats also tried turning Republican, they were soundly defeated in special recall elections in their districts.

The 1970s and 1980s have been marked by some renewal of ethnic pride among native Hawaiians and part-Hawaiians, who are traditionally the disadvantaged minority. That cultural renaissance was symbolized in 1976 when the large double-hulled sailing canoe *Hokule'a*, a recreation of the type used by the first settlers of the Islands, was sailed from Hawaii to Tahiti by the Polynesian Voyaging Society. The achievement was described in an article in the *National Geographic* and in a subsequent television documentary. However the triumph and celebration were marred by fights and bickering that broke out along racial lines among some members of the crew during the month-long voyage. The canoe has since made two more major Pacific voyages without incident, however.

Every now and then, Hawaii manages to impinge itself on the nation's consciousness in some way other than as the home of pineapple, ukuleles, and hula dancers. Recently, American legal history was made when the U.S. Supreme Court upheld a Hawaii land reform law which forces large property owners to sell houselots to those who live on the leased land. On a lighter note, variations on Hawaiian "aloha" fashions seemed to become the hot new look for the summer of '86 throughout the Mainland last year.

The big story of 1986, however, was the new residency of deposed Philippines President Ferdinand Marcos in Honolulu, an event with many far-reaching effects. Not the least of this has been the disruptive effect on the local Filipino community, much of which has now been divided into both pro- and anti-Marcos factions.

Today Hawaii finds herself economically dependent principally on tourism, leaving military spending—as well as traditional Island agricultural industries like sugar and pineapple—far behind. Tourists now drop a total of more than $5 *million* into the state's economy each year.

This worries many state residents, including Hawaiians (Polynesians) who see the traditional culture of the Islands being subjugated to crass outside influences. Others defend tourism by saying that visitor spending continues to support cultural activities like Hawaiian music and the hula, besides funding the continued preservation of historical sites and similar facilities.

A Rainbow of Peoples

In the volumes on Hawaii produced as school texts or as part of educational libraries over the past twenty years, there is usually a chapter entitled something like "Americans All!" The opening page might display a happy group photograph of smiling, slant-eyed, flat-nosed, olive-skinned, dark-haired, high-cheeked kids, perhaps even with a token towhead in there somewhere. All together, they are as cute a bundle of Oriental, Polynesian, and what-have-you kind of joy as you would ever want to see.

It's all true, or at least it is at that tender age. Island youngsters all learn the pledge to the flag together, and they often don't become very conscious of their different ethnic backgrounds until they near their teens. Then it's sometimes a different story.

Meanwhile the textbook goes on to explain that, yes, these children all speak English, of course, just like boys and girls on the Mainland. But the truth is something more than that; even if they do speak English, most of them would rather speak "pidgin."

The Language Is a Queer Bird. Pidgin is a conglomerate of crude English liberally spiced with several Hawaiian words plus a few from other languages. Pure Hawaiian is seldom spoken in Hawaii today, even though it *is* often sung. A few isolated communities on the Neighbor Islands do use a form of the real tongue in day-to-day life, and an older version is still spoken on the tiny island of Niihau, a privately owned strip of water-locked real estate where visitors are forbidden.

Although Hawaiian is a nearly dead language, you still need to know something about it to pick up pidgin and other flavorful aspects of Island living. The full-on Hawaiian language includes more than 25,000 words. There is a lot of vowel and throat action, and the speech is considered musical and poetic, though certainly not precise. There are supposed to be 33 synonyms for "clouds," for instance; on the other hand, it takes 8 words to express the idea "across."

The missionaries standardized an easy-to-learn spelling for Hawaiian by using only 12 letters. There are the 5 vowels—*a, e, i, o, u*—given the European pronunciation ("ah, ay, ee, oh, oo"), plus only 7 consonants, *h, k, l, m, n, p,* and *w.* To do that, the missionaries cut corners, declaring that all "T" sounds and "K" sounds henceforth would be pronounced like "K," all "R" and "L" sounds would be "L," "B" and "P" sounds would be "P," and so forth.

Thus we have the reason the Polynesian word *taboo* (forbidden or sacred) is interpreted in Hawaiian as *kapu* ("kah-*poo*"). On at least one occasion the missionaries were known to have corrected King Kamehameha II when he said his name was "Rihoriho" instead of Liholiho.

Now, in a way, there is also one additional consonant in Hawaiian. This is the "glottal stop" between two vowels, represented in print by the use of the *hamzah*. This Arabic symbol is correctly made like a backwards apostrophe or an opening inside quotation mark, as in the word 'au 'au ("ow-ow"—to take a bath). You pronounce the glottal stop by doing to your throat what the expression "oh-oh" does—a momentary stoppage of air in the back of the throat between two vowel sounds.

Some folks use a regular apostrophe for the *hamzah;* that makes things easy, though not correct (except on a typewriter). More often, the mark is left out all together and the letters joined together. It can be safely omitted where two of the same vowels are used together (*akaaka*—"ah-kah-ah-kah"—laughter)—in other words, where it's obvious the word could not be pronounced correctly without the glottal stop. (Of course, the word *Hawaii*—"Ha-*why*-ee"—which may be written Hawai'i, is another example.)

In this volume we follow the modern trend, and generally omit the *hamzah* except where there would be some definite confusion if the glottal stop were not indicated.

An example is *pau*—"pow"—finished, versus *pa'u*—"pahoo"—a long skirt, usually worn riding sidesaddle. Used in a pidgin sentence, a seamstress getting her costume ready for the Kamehameha Day Parade conceivably could say, "At last my *pa'u* is *pau!*"

As we said, you will almost never hear pure Hawaiian in Hawaii, but you will certainly hear some degrees of pidgin. The more non-English words used, together with the more unique pronunciation, lilt, and sentence structure, the heavier the pidgin that is being spoken.

Linguists say the speech of Hawaii is not a true pidgin, but a softer form of communication that strictly should be called a creole. Nevertheless, everyone *does* call it pidgin, and, hearing its spoken form, some unprepared Mainlanders have trouble knowing just what is being said.

Every visitor to Hawaii picks up some Hawaiian or pidgin words, and you'll get a head start, because the text of this guide makes use of the most common of these, just as if we were writing for a local readership.

Here is a list of several words, including some that are more often written than spoken, and help with the translation of place names. The most commonly spoken words in the following list are indicated with an asterisk. You will enjoy your visit more if you do learn their meaning and pronunciation.

aa	a rough type of lava
*akamai	*smart, wise
akua	god
ala	road, way, route (written; seldom spoken)
alii	chief, nobility
*aloha	*hello, goodbye, love, good will
auwe!	alas, ouch, wow!
blalah	heavy-set, amiable Hawaiian man
brah	friend (corruption of "brother")
bumby	after a while ("by and by" in pidgin)
*da kine	*whatchamacallit (adjective or noun)
*ewa	*generally west (toward Ewa Plantation)
hala	pandanus tree
hale	house
hana	work
hanah-buttah	nasal mucus
hanakokolele!	shame, naughty (child's word, chanted to the tune of "Johnny's got a girlfriend!")
hanau	born (not spoken—seen on gravestones)
*haole	*Caucasian, white, Mainlander
hapa	half, part
hapa-haole	part white and part Hawaiian
hapai	pregnant
heiau	ancient Hawaiian temple
hele on	"with it," "hip," or "hell-raising"
holo-holo	to visit about, make the rounds
holoku	a fitted ankle-length dress, sometimes with train
hoomalimali	nonsense talk, flattery
huhu	angry
*hula	*Polynesian dance
huli-huli	barbecued chicken
humbug	trouble, bother
humuhumunukunukuapuaa	tiny trigger fish famous for its long name
imu	underground oven
imua!	forward, onward, ¡viva!
kahili	a feathered scepter
kahuna	priest, medicine man
kai	sea, sea water (seldom spoken, except in Hawaiian)
kala	money
*kamaaina	*longtime Hawaii resident, old established family
kanaka	originally "man," but now a familiar, sometimes derogatory term for a native Hawaiian. Hawaiians use it. The rest of us had better not.
kane	men (as written on restroom doors)
kapa	tapa cloth (made from mulberry bark)
kapakahi	topsy-turvy, crooked
*kapu	*forbidden, sacred, taboo
kaukau	food

keiki	child
kokua	help
kuleana	homesite, now used like "bailiwick"
*lanai	*porch, terrace, veranda
lani	heaven, heavenly, sky (not often spoken)
lauhala	leaf of the pandanus tree (for weaving)
laulau	bundled food in leaves
*lei	*garland of flowers
lilikoi	passion fruit
lomilomi	rub, press, massage, type of raw salmon
lua	toilet (originally "two" or "twin")
*luau	*feast, party (originally a taro leaf)
luna	above, overseer, straw boss, heights
*mahalo	*thank you
mahimahi	dorado or dolphin fish (*not* a porpoise)
mahu	homosexual
*makai	*toward the sea (a direction)
make	dead (seen on gravestones)
*malihini	*newcomer, visitor, stranger
malo	man's loincloth
manini	small, cheap, stingy
*mauka	*toward the mountains, inland (a direction and opposite of *makai*)
mauna	mountain (used in names like "Mount")
*muumuu	*long, loose-fitting dress
nani	beautiful (not spoken; seen in names)
nui	big, large, huge
*okole	*bottom, rear, buttocks
okolehao	liquor distilled from ti root
ono	delicious
ono-ono	very delicious
opu	abdomen, stomach
*pali	*cliff (or cliffs)
paniolo	cowboy (Hawaiian corruption of Español)
*pau	*finished (*pau hana:* through work, retirement)
pa'u	long skirt
pahoehoe	type of lava with smooth or ropy surface (contrasted with *aa*)
pikake	jasmine flower, named after "peacock"
pilikia	trouble
*poi	*pasty food made from taro root
*puka	*hole (a *puka*-board is a peg board)
punee	couch with no back, daybed
pupule	crazy
pupus	hors d'oeuvres (literally, "shells")
shaka!	great, well-done, perfect, okay!
tita	sister, but applied to a no-nonsense, spirited, down-home country girl
*tutu	*grandmother (strictly speaking, *tutu wahine*)
*ukulele	*ukulele
*wahine	*girl, woman, wife
wai	fresh water (used in names)
wikiwiki	fast, in a hurry, quickly (also the airport shuttle bus, which often does not come *wikiwiki*)

A few pidgin postscripts: True pidgin cannot really be written down. Much of pidgin depends on the pronunciation of more or less common words, combined with some unconventional grammatical construction. But as much or more of the flavor is carried by inflection and rhythm, which perhaps could only be inscribed in musical notations, if at all.

Also, there are as many variations on pidgin as there are people who speak it. You may notice there is one general kind of pidgin used by the old folks, and a younger or more "hip" pidgin popular with the under-thirty crowd. It is combined with terms that may be in vogue with the same age group on the Mainland. (Some terms used in California's "Valspeak" actually originated as hip Hawaiian pidgin.)

Finally, remember that most of the pidgin you will hear is no longer spoken out of necessity, but in a fun sort of way in order to promote comradeship between the speakers. In other words, pidgin is often a type of private game.

Here is a jocular pidgin note we once rescued from a wastebasket. It was written by a young woman to a friend named Al to thank him for inviting her to a party.

Eh Al Brah,
Chee was one really ono luau you folks went make! All da kine kaukau stay so ono inside my opu, bumby I come fat, but ho da worth it! Ho dese kine kanakas (you and Les) good okolehao pourers you eh? You like one job in one ba? Ho, da kaukau, okolehao and da floor show you folks went make—really shaka, man.
You know da boss lady I get? She stay crack da whips on top my bod all day, so was one good time you give me. Tanks, eh? You folks went get one good lua, too. I went try em out—da flush kine.
Mahalo plenty again, and aloha.

BARBARA

Racial Groups in Hawaii. Here in the fiftieth state, everyone is a member of a racial minority group. The largest single minority in the state are the *haoles* (Caucasians), but they still make up only a little more than 26 percent of the population.

Hawaii is the only state in the Union where the whites are outnumbered by other races. Japanese add up to nearly 24 percent, Filipinos number some 11 percent, those calling themselves Hawaiian total about 19 percent. (Some believe this figure should be higher, but actually no more than 1 percent—10,000 individuals or less—are pure Polynesian Hawaiians.) And about 5 percent of the population is Chinese.

Because of this diversification, there is almost no racial friction of the bitter kind known on the Mainland. Also, love and the miracle of reproduction tend to conquer and dilute antagonistic feelings even more;

Approximate Population of Hawaii by Race

260,000	or about	26% Caucasian*
240,000	or about	24% Japanese
180,000	or about	18% Part Hawaiian
110,000	or about	11% Filipino
50,000	or about	5% Chinese
15,000	or about	1½% Korean
15,000	or about	1½% Negro
10,000	or about	1% Samoan
10,000	or about	1% Pure Hawaiian
110,000	or about	11% Mixed and miscellaneous

1,000,000   Total state population

* Includes the Portuguese, one of the traditional Hawaii minority groups, as well as Hawaii-born, Mainland-born, and foreign-born haoles.

today nearly half the state's 12,000 annual marriages—the highest marriage rate in the country—are interracial. To be sure, group hostilities do exist in Hawaii today, but they are usually shown in more subtle ways, at least among middle-aged and older adults.

Some teen-agers, on the other hand, act out prejudices and identity crises more directly, picking fights with other youngsters along racial lines. Usually these take the form of conflicts between established groups and newcomers.

Many of those exhibiting this racial antipathy are the underprivileged minority among young, native Hawaiians who harbor the belief that others have been taking away their land, their beaches, and most of the good jobs for the past century or two. There is some truth in the charge, and there are Hawaiian organizations seeking some intelligent redress of genuine grievances. Nevertheless, the active animosity of the "have-nots" for the "haves" seems to lead to police records and prison rosters that are filled with the names of young men of Polynesian blood.

One newcomer group often challenged are the Filipinos. Usually somewhat slighter in stature than the established teenagers of Hawaii, they can become the victims of racial tension. Another newish group—the Samoans—being large and pretty tough themselves, usually manage to hold their own.

The *haoles*, too, are often thought of as newcomers or outsiders, whether they are or not. Young white military enlistees can, on occasion, find themselves challenged by a squad of "locals," a term that generally covers an amalgam of backgrounds, little, if any, of which is Caucasian.

In some neighborhoods, the last day of school is known as "Kill a Haole Day." (Our own children first heard of the event at a tender age and called it "Killer Holiday.") It means no more than a day of general boisterousness and mischief-making.

Like the children at any school in the U.S.A., the offspring of Hawaii will—if they can make it past the ten thousand and two traumas of teenhood—probably come out all right.

The heterogeneous destiny of Hawaii was launched in the mid-nineteenth century, when the native Hawaiian population was at its ebb, and when the sugar planters began scouring the world for the labor needed on the plantations. They recruited peasants in Canton, Mongolia, Korea, Puerto Rico, the Madeira Islands, the Azores Islands, Portugal, Spain, Italy, Poland, Austria, Germany, Norway, Russia, Siberia, Micronesia, Polynesia, Melanesia, and the Philippines. They deliberately chose illiterates of varied and generally docile populations who could not communicate with each other in order to forestall their taking any concerted action to right the often oppressive nature of their employment.

Between 1852 and 1930, about 400,000 immigrants were transported to Hawaii to work in sugar. A few returned home at the end of their contracts, but most stayed on and began to intermarry—with each other, with the Hawaiians, and even with the *kamaaina haoles* who hired them.

All brought aspects of their culture that have remained in the Islands, and this is why we now have such "Hawaiian" institutions as the ukulele (Portuguese), steak teriyaki (Japanese), *manapua* (Chinese), and cockfights (Filipino).

In the rush to Americanize everyone after the turn of the century, Hawaii children adopted baseball and chewing gum with abandon, and they were not encouraged to learn their own individual heritages. Many young people are now understandably angry that the schools do not require Asian and Pacific studies as much as they do courses that reflect traditional American/European thinking.

Nevertheless, in the wake of the distant examples set by the black, Chicano, and Indian groups on the Mainland, a slow but encouraging resurgence of ethnic pride is developing in the Islands.

Most gratifyingly, much of this self-rediscovery is being made by one of the most interesting minority groups, the one that has had the most difficulty adjusting to the social stresses of today's world, the native Hawaiians themselves.

Government and Economics

At first glance, Hawaii's institutions are largely those of any other American state. That beautiful and dramatic capitol building, opened in 1969, houses two legislative bodies—a 25-member Senate and a 51-member

House of Representatives—plus associated governmental offices and conference rooms.

There is a popularly elected governor and a lieutenant governor. (Elections for both offices were held in late 1986, while this book was still on the press.) Hawaii's four Washington legislators include Senator Daniel K. Inouye (pronounced "in-*noy*"), who became a national figure as a member of the Senate Watergate Committee, and Senator Spark M. Matsunaga. Both are former House members. And there are two congressmen, who are also traditionally Democrats.

There are only four real counties in the state, and the largest in population is the "City and County of Honolulu," an official appellation combining what might have been two bodies into a single governmental unit. It includes the entire island of Oahu with all its smaller communities, plus, for administrative purposes, almost all of the long chain of tiny, mostly uninhabited islets northwest of Kauai called the Leeward Isles.

The other three counties are Kauai (including Kauai and Niihau islands), Maui (Maui, Molokai, Lanai, and Kahoolawe islands), and Hawaii (the Big Island). All four counties are administered under a mayor/council system.

Hawaii is the only American state with just two levels of local government. There are no separate bodies for the various towns and villages scattered over the islands, a highly touted fact that should (but doesn't) indicate that there is more streamlined government in Hawaii. The centralizing of some super-agencies, such as the State Department of Education, which controls all 217 public schools throughout the Islands, has created some monolithic monsters and inefficient bureaucratic fiefdoms.

Volatile Politics. There is a strong preoccupation with politics in Hawaii. One sociologist at the University of Hawaii has declared that the state's politics are the "politics of growth" and, at the same time, the "politics of subtle racism."

The Democratic party is firmly entrenched, and it is run mainly by Japanese-Americans, traditionally the descendants of nineteenth-century sugar plantation workers. The Republican party has an all-*haole* image and today usually provides no more than token opposition, generally leaving the most bitter fights to the factional splits within the Democratic party. (The exception to Republican tokenism is Frank F. Fasi, currently the Republican mayor of the City and County of Honolulu. However even Fasi is a lapsed Democrat who changed parties in order to give him the additional strength to successfully recapture in 1984 the office he had held during the 1970s.)

Government corruption is not unknown, and political favoritism is very much alive and well, aided by a usually apathetic electorate. If you are in real estate, construction, or allied businesses, it will help if you have friends or relatives in the city or state governments—and hurt if you don't.

Politics also thrive on a strong feeling of "localism," which some translate as racism. It is reflected in policies designed to promote cautious state development while at the same time discouraging "outsiders" from moving into the state.

Where the Money Comes From. Hawaii's main economic base has now been firmly captured by tourism, which today is a five-billion-dollar-a-year business. There is some controversy over this, with protests from a few members of the environmental community against the practice of shuttling more than 5 million vacationers a year—perhaps more than the entire United States sends annually to Europe—in and out of the state, most of them funneled through the overdeveloped peninsula called Waikiki.

However, most of Hawaii's people realize that their economic cake is iced with visitors and agree with Hawaii's Senator Dan Inouye who says that it is, with proper control, a "nonpolluting industry," and an ideal one because it draws on the traditional Hawaiian "Spirit of Aloha" —something you won't find in Miami Beach or Acapulco.

Until a few years ago the federal government provided the greatest income source for Hawaii. With Hawaii's position as the single most important Pacific outpost for the United States armed forces, the defense establishment is still an important Island "industry."

The largest industrial operation in the state, as a matter of fact, is the Pearl Harbor Naval Shipyard, not to be confused with the Pearl Harbor Naval Base next door. The shipyard repairs and overhauls more than 800 ships annually, and it has the greatest civilian payroll of any organization in Hawaii.

There are well over 120,000 military personnel and dependents in Hawaii at any one moment, almost half of them with the U.S. Navy. All service branches are represented, however, and you'll find that much of the wild outback of the Islands is still fenced off for military training and maneuvers. On Oahu, more than 25 percent of the total acreage is under direct control of the military. The unified command for the entire Pacific American forces, CINCPAC (Commander in Chief, Pacific), is at Camp H. M. Smith, in the hills overlooking Pearl Harbor.

There are more than a dozen other important military commands and installations in Hawaii, nearly all of them on Oahu. This has led to Hawaii's description in some quarters as a "sugar-coated fortress." And, sad to say, there is sometimes social antipathy between local groups and members of the military community, misunderstandings and tensions that date back to the "Massie Incident" of the 1930s.

These relationships are not helped by a system that keeps servicemen and their families generally leading separate, insular lives on military posts and generally not learning more than a superficial amount of Hawaii culture or taking part in activities of the community at large. Some military blacks, particularly singles, say they have a difficult time in Oahu, partly due to local suspicion and misunderstandings. Also there are only a few single black women around, which makes things more difficult.

Happily there are a few heart-warming exceptions to local-military tension, such as the Marines' "Toys for Tots" program, under which the leathernecks repair discarded playthings and present them to needy Island youngsters at Christmastime. The military contributes to the annual Aloha United Way campaign and also helps the community on occasion through search-and-rescue and disaster relief operations.

"Sugar and Pine." The traditional agricultural partnership of the Islands has, in the past, kept the state green in more ways than one. But sugar and pineapple have now been reduced to a long third and fourth place, respectively, in economic importance. Both were being steadily cut back until very recently, when talk of a worldwide food shortage caused some reprieves in planned plantation closings.

There are still about 15 sugar companies and several hundred independent growers in the state, employing about 5,000 persons altogether. About 200,000 acres of cane grown on Oahu, Maui, Kauai, and Hawaii compose about three-quarters of Hawaii's cultivated lands.

But compared with tourism's $5 billion plus, and the federal government's defense expenditures of nearly $2 billion, sugar's annual income of about $300 million seems very modest. Creeping water shortages are also threatening sugar in Hawaii. It takes a ton of water to produce one pound of refined sugar. Also world demand for sugar has been decreasing in recent years due to the popularity of sugar substitutes. As plantations are reduced in size it sometimes seems that the acres and acres of green sugar cane waving in Hawaii's breezes will soon be replaced by more suburban sprawls of housing developments.

Pineapple, almost the symbol of the Islands for so many years, began to face considerable problems during the 1970s because of competition from cheap-labor countries like Taiwan and Thailand. Pineapple interests in Hawaii have now reduced their domain to three companies—the main firms are Dole and Del Monte—and six plantations. It is grown on all major islands except Hawaii, employs around 2,000 fulltime workers, and garners a total income of around $90 million.

Other important agricultural products produced in Hawaii include papayas, coffee, macadamia nuts, and, of course, flowers.

Pakalolo. That's the Hawaiian word for marijuana ("crazy tobacco"), and it's true that the cultivation of illegal crops of "Maui Wowie" and "Kona Gold" now forms Hawaii's largest agricultural industry. The Hawaii state statistician has said that shipments of *pakalolo* from Hawaii County (the Big Island) alone have been estimated at 250,000 pounds per year, with annual sales from this crop running from $250 million to $750 million. Of course a certain amount of this product is regularly harvested and destroyed by the police.

Other Business. Heavy industry includes two oil refineries on Oahu, plus several factories supporting the large construction business—two cement plants, one small steel mill, an aluminum extrusion plant, a concrete pipe plant, and the like.

On a completely different scale, there are more than 100 garment manufacturers in the state, mainly producing colorful Hawaiian sportswear.

Other light industries are those that produce Kona coffee, tropical fruit drinks, jams and jellies, candies, macadamia nuts, Oriental and Hawaiian foods, dairy products, beer, sake, rum, okolehao (a ti-root "whisky"), and all kinds of soft drinks.

Labor. Employees in Hawaii's main industries have been organized at least since the early 1950s. There may be a total membership in all unions of about 150,000, but it's difficult to get honest figures. Industry-wide contracts are negotiated in plantation industries and stevedoring companies.

Two of the most influential unions are the International Longshoremen's and Warehousemen's Union (ILWU) and the Teamsters, but the largest is probably the Hawaii Government Employees Association (HGEA).

Problems in Paradise

Citizens of Hawaii are fond of calling their state "Paradise," and some members of the chamber of commerce awhile back got a lot of mileage by throwing away a preposition and turning the name of the state into an adverb: "Lucky You Live Hawaii!" the boosters wrote.

Some realists, however, characterize such catch phrases as only whistling in the sunshine. The traditional beachboy pidgin phrase "Lucky You Come Hawaii!" is more accurate. For as delightful a destination as are the Islands for an upbeat vacation, many Hawaii-philes who return year after year still feel that you *can* get too much of a good thing—that there is an enervating surfeit of surf, sun, sand, and somnolence that is fine for a vacation but not conducive to efficient and productive living on a year-round basis.

Some call the disease "Polynesian Paralysis," and others diagnose it as "Rock Fever" or "Islanditis." At any rate, it is a feeling that eventually creeps over many transplanted Mainlanders that there just isn't enough wide-open space to move around in in "Paradise," whether physically, economically, or intellectually.

(This malady is not limited to Hawaii, of course. We've come down with it ourselves after spending long stints in Puerto Rico and on Mallorca. Others have reported its effects in Jamaica, Bermuda, and the Virgin Islands.)

It is true that the Hawaiian Islands promote love and romance where the potential has existed previously. But it is equally true that many young people who meet here and later become life companions do not stay to live, work, and raise their families. They return to the Mainland to make their homes chiefly because the prohibitive cost of living in Hawaii, combined with a shortage of professional opportunities, is just too much.

For the past several years, Honolulu has headed the list of the most expensive cities for food prices in the U.S.A. (ahead of even Anchorage, Washington, and New York City), and living costs in general also make it difficult for the state to compete with Florida Gulf communities or even those in southern California in attracting the nation's retirees to some sunshine to warm up their remaining years. (The two lowest in food prices, incidentally, are Tampa and San Diego.)

There's a popular myth in Hawaii to the effect that Mainlanders are moving to the Islands in droves to escape the harsh winters, race riots, and crime waves that Islanders imagine are always gripping the Mainland. It's just not true. There is a large *turnover,* but the ratio of those who move to Hawaii and those who move out annually is not dramatically different—about 45,000 coming and 40,000 going (and about half of these are military personnel and their families).

The population of Hawaii has been increasing, to be sure. But mostly it's a natural increase (births over deaths amount to more than 12,000 annually), augmented by immigration from foreign lands (perhaps 9,000).

Now despite the higher living prices, Hawaii is generally no more expensive to *vacation in* than any other American playground—cheaper than many, as a matter of fact.

Local cynics harumph that this is because visitor expenses reflect a balance between the high cost of material goods and the lower wage scales paid to those who serve the visitor. (And they say this same combination of a low wage level and high-priced products makes life difficult for permanent residents, who are instead "paid in sunshine.")

No one can tell you for sure why things are more expensive in Hawaii. The most accused villain is the cost of shipping, but cargo costs seem to account for only a small percent of the difference. Somehow there appears to be a tradition of extra middlemen chipping away at the goods as they travel through the merchandise funnel on the way to retail shelves.

Although these are factors, it is more likely that the cost of living is tied more or less directly to the cost of real estate. Prices paid for land are astronomical, largely because there just isn't much of it available in the state.

There are a little over 4 million acres in the major islands; much of that is untenable, wild and woolly land, and a large chunk, of course, is agricultural. Be that as it may, 42 percent of all the land is owned by the state, county, and federal governments, and 47 percent is owned by a few major private owners (each one having at least 1,000 acres), who often will lease—not sell—their farm and home sites.

Less than 11 percent of all Hawaii is owned by small landowners—in "freehold" or "fee simple," to use the legal terms.

You may have heard that you can pay several times as much for a house and lot in Hawaii as you would for a comparable home in other parts of the country. That's entirely correct. Hawaii's housing units are the most expensive in the nation. The average value of owner-occupied dwellings is about $180,000, more than double that on the Mainland, and most single-family homes available cost much more than that. Many middle-class, white-collar workers have given up on the idea of owning their own homes any time soon. They rent houses or apartments instead, until such time as a relative may die and leave them enough—hopefully— for the required down payment. Even then, many forego the fee-simple house to build on a leasehold lot.

After the cost of groceries and housing, most Hawaii residents would certainly name crime as an important problem in the Islands. Crime gets a lot of attention in the media, and it's apparently causing public concern as the statistics begin to approach the crime rate common on the Mainland. Hawaii's rate of violent crimes, however, is still below those for most American states, although its property crime rate (car theft, burglary, etc.) is above average. In the 1970s and '80s, Hawaii—particularly Oahu—has suffered somewhat from some nationally publicized crimes including the kidnapping several years ago of a busload of tourists and the 1984 ambush of hikers on a trail to Sacred Falls. (In these cases and others, the perpetrators were caught and convicted and most property was returned.) Despite such stories, Hawaii's overall crime rate has been steadily dropping since 1980.

Juvenile crime, drug abuse, and vandalism exist in Hawaii as they do everywhere. A different type of lawlessness, organized crime, has accounted for a number of gangland murders, at least until recently. No, there is no branch of the Mafia. Organized crime in Hawaii has a distinctly local flavor, with the perpetrators of the violence usually called "The Syndicate," and competing factions often have been warring for power. But even that situation has improved in the past few years. Following the recent convictions of several important local hoods, the F.B.I. says it has broken the back of the local Lilliputian underworld, even if there are still a few more busts yet to come.

Honolulu's city prosecutor, a somewhat flamboyant elected official, has received considerable publicity by claiming that there is still a "godfather" of Hawaii crime around and that he has close ties to the former governor. The F.B.I. disagrees, and lately the prosecutor has received more press by tackling easier targets, conducting raids against allegedly pornographic video stores and the like.

Like its Mainland counterparts, the Hawaiian Syndicate has dabbled in gambling, prostitution, extortion, and drugs. The general public has been little concerned, though, since the victims of the occasional mayhem were virtually always fellow members of the same criminal subculture. Juvenile and amateur crime, on the other hand, has received much more public attention since they are perceived as greater threats to the average citizen.

Some violence has been attributed to an "us and them" attitude among low-income, unsophisticated youths who seek a target for their hostility among outsiders. They are most often from families of Hawaiian or mixed blood who are generally forced to live at the bottom of the economic scale. Another factor contributing to their problems is the lack of good education, both at home and in the public schools.

Critics also blame the rapid development of Hawaii, some of it by large, international corporations that have little or no sense of the social consequences of their intrusion into what was, until a short time ago, a relatively simple society.

The tensions created can erupt in fights between young locals and young military men. And unfortunately a few members of these criminal or disadvantaged groups have preyed upon visitors to the Islands who innocently wander into economically depressed areas. (Sadly, we now advise our friends not to visit the Waianae Coast on the western shore of Oahu, and not to camp overnight anywhere on that island.)

Visitors to Hawaii are invariably surprised to learn that crime is a concern here at all, since it is usually invisible over a short-term stay. But no matter how polite and friendly most Island citizens are, remember that—just as it is in any large Mainland city—it's a good idea not to leave valuable things unguarded on the beach or even in the trunk of your rental car, and not to visit dark, lonely places at night.

By the way, everyone should be aware that on Oahu, at least, policemen are *tough* and not to be argued with, even over a simple speeding ticket. Under the law, if you talk back to a Honolulu Police Department officer you can be handcuffed, arrested, and booked for "harassment." It doesn't happen often, of course, and by and large the cops are friendly, considerate, and polite, especially to visitors. But if you feel any polemics coming on, save them for the courtroom.

Virtually all HPD officers, by the way, chase around the highways in late-model, souped-up, unmarked cars that they purchase and care for themselves. A Honolulu policeman is considered to be always available for duty, whether in uniform or not, and he always carries a gun, whether it is visible or not. (And by the way, television notwithstanding, there is no "Hawaii Five-O" or any other state police force.)

Taxes take a big bite in Hawaii. Per capita, Island residents pay the third-highest state and local taxes in the nation. There is a 4 percent excise tax on absolutely everything you buy or rent.

As we mentioned in chapter 3, environmental problems come in for their share of concern in Hawaii today. Air pollution fortunately is rare, but unfortunately not completely absent in the state. A few consecutive days of stagnant or Kona winds in the winter months can combine with the effect of the thousands of infernal combustion engines and maybe some sugar-cane fires on Oahu—and sometimes with some volcanic haze drifting up from the Big Island—to create a daytime smog.

The effect has been known as "stealing the Waianaes" ever since science writer Bruce Benson observed this modern phenomenon, which occasionally eliminates the traditional view of the distant Waianae ("*Why-an-eye?*") mountain range from some parts of Honolulu. There has been talk of limiting the number of motor vehicles on Oahu, but a planned 14-mile mass transit system has stalled in the political tunnel.

A recent report from one state government bureau severely criticized overall state policies for emphasizing economic growth and development goals to the detriment of environmental protection and pollution control in Hawaii. In the past few years, pollution has often threatened island food and water supplies, largely because of agricultural pesticides. Unfortunately, pesticide control bills have been vigorously and so-far successfully fought by agricultural interests in the state.

Alternate Energy. Hawaii handled the energy crisis better than many places on the Mainland. Dr. Edward Teller, the atomic physicist, once suggested that a line of windmills might be used to harness the strong, dependable trade winds, an idea that seemed almost laughable at the time.

But there are now two serious experimental operations producing energy from the volcanic action under the ground at Pahoa on the Big

Island. Even more dramatic was the breakthrough made when the state government was the first in the nation to produce electricity through ocean thermal energy conversion. In this OTEC project, Hawaii's warm seawater is used to change ammonia from liquid to vapor within a heat exchanger. The vapor then turns an electrical generator, after which the vapor is condensed by cold water pumped from deeper in the ocean, and the cycle is repeated.

There is some interest in converting sugar cane to alcohol to make gasohol. And there is also a system to burn bagasse, the waste residue from sugar harvesting. Combined with the discarded shells from macadamia nut farms, this "biomass" energy now provides most of the electricity used by the Big Island. One firm also has an "energy tree farm" sprouting nicely.

Solar energy is also big in a state with so many hours of dependable sunshine. Hawaii has about 200,000 families, and there are 20,000 solar water heaters atop residential roofs. The main hospital on Kauai now gets most of its electricity from a field of photovoltaic cells, and for about 200 isolated homes in rural areas of the Big Island similar devices are the only regular source of power.

And what about that wind-power idea? The U.S. Department of Energy has installed some prototype windmill generators on Molokai, and a private corporation finally opened an entire "wind farm" on the Big Island in 1984. The 180 windmills can produce 3.4 megawatts, enough to serve 3,500 people. It now supplies a full 10 percent of the island's power during the evening hours.

To wrap up some of the state's other difficulties, there is vocal opposition to the storage of nuclear weapons on Oahu. One activist group claims there are 3,000 atomic bombs in the West Loch area of Pearl Harbor, but the military remains mum on the subject.

There are some union problems, made particularly difficult by the occasional threat of a dock strike, which would affect Hawaii's shipping lifeline. One of the smallest states in the nation, Hawaii suffers one of the highest alcoholism rates in the country. Incredibly, it also pays out almost as much in welfare checks as New York State.

It seems safe to say that 99 and 44/100ths percent of the visitors who came to Hawaii last year had a darn good time, but the numbers may not be so impressive for those who moved here to begin a new life. Recently Rand McNally published a *Places Rated Almanac* that rated Honolulu as the 61st best place to live in the United States out of 329. (The city ranked 15th in recreation, 22nd in climate, 36th in the arts, 40th in transportation, 92nd in health care, 142nd in crime, 197th in economic outlook, 263rd in education, and 326th in housing.)

Those of us who live in Honolulu might not agree with all those ratings. Nevertheless there are really no earthly Paradises, after all—perhaps especially for those who live their day-to-day lives where others merely come to play.

Art and Handicraft

The Hawaiians of old were adept at crafts of many types, but most of these skills were laid aside and forgotten in the face of imported talents and technology. **Tapa** is a good example, for the production of this kind of Polynesian cloth probably achieved its highest level with the Hawaiians.

In some long-lost way, they beat the bark of the mulberry tree until a material similar to felt was achieved. But today you will probably see this quality product only in the Bishop Museum. Samoans and Tongans still turn out tapa, and you'll find that sold in Honolulu today, along with a few samples of locally manufactured material using the methods developed in other Pacific islands. In the past 100 years, no one has been able to duplicate the quality of the traditional Hawaiian tapa—including the Hawaiians themselves.

In ancient Hawaii, the people were perhaps best known for their use of **feathers** in creating clothes and other ornaments. The most dramatic of the objects of feather art were the cloaks, helmets, and *kahilis* (cylinders made from feathers mounted on a pole to indicate high social status).

There were not enough birds sporting the proper colors to clothe everyone, however, so only the *alii* (nobility) wore the royal colors of red and gold produced by the tailfeathers of the *mamo* and *o'o* birds. Some feather art continues to be turned out today, but only in modest and expensive quantities. You'll occasionally see it in hatbands for the country folk and perhaps in a rare feather *lei.*

Almost the only genuine handicraft that has survived intact from the early days is the production of **leis** and **necklaces**—not usually made of feathers, but of garlands of flowers, leaves, *kukui* nuts, seashells, and even seeds. Everyone, man and woman alike, wears something around his neck in Hawaii, at least once in a while.

The art of weaving **lauhala** (the leaf of the pandanus tree) and coconut fronds has not been lost. But now, instead of fences, walls, and floors, the leaves are generally used in smaller products like hats, baskets, slippers, and table mats.

Woodcarving was an old Hawaiian art, and it's still kept alive by some modern operations in Hawaii. The traditional native woods are *koa,* monkeypod, and *ohia,* but many of these materials are now shipped in from the Orient, either as finished products or raw for working here in Hawaii.

The wooden bowl or calabash—now largely used for tossed salads—is authentically connected to the past, and it is still the traditional company retirement gift in the Islands. But you can get wood carved into any pattern imaginable, from attractive *koa* coffee tables through pregnant hula girls and up to those ridiculous giant-sized spoon and fork sets.

It surprised us to learn that some **ukuleles**—the best and most expensive ones, as a matter of fact—are made in Hawaii, although thousands of cheap (and satisfactory) ones are stamped out in Japan and then shipped to the Islands.

One of the most fascinating of Hawaiian handicrafts was begun after the missionaries showed the Hawaiians how to make bedspreads. Instead of the simple patchwork of New England, a new form of **Hawaiian quilt** utilizing island designs began to evolve. There are embroidered fruits, flowers, leaves, landmarks, and legends, usually in a single-color pattern over a solid background in white or another color. Designs are jealously guarded by the few Hawaiian quiltmakers, generally older women, who are around today.

The quilts take perhaps a month to make with the quiltmaker working full time. You will seldom find a Hawaiian quilt for sale, however. Usually they are made for a member of the family and presented to him at a special event. On the rare occasion that a price is put on a Hawaiian quilt, the tag will read about $1,000.

Another ancient art, recently revived, is **scrimshaw.** This carving on whales' bones and teeth was not a Hawaiian form, but a type of primitive etching done by *haole* sailors who spent long boring hours at sea between catches dreaming of Lahaina or New Haven while patiently scratching away at a leviathan's molar. Original scrimshaw, of course, brings antique prices. But there are several local artists turning out modern versions of the old art on whale teeth, walrus tusks, and other material.

The authentic folk arts and crafts of Hawaii are on exhibit in the Bernice Pauahi Bishop Museum in Honolulu, the repository of all artifacts of historical significance to Polynesia.

More modern handicraft or factoricraft being performed today encompasses (take a deep breath) jewelry manufacture of all types, including jewelry made from pink, black, and gold coral, olivine, and shells; several different types of porcelain, ceramic, and pottery operations; freeze-dried flowers coated with plastic; other flowers petrified in gold; collage boxes made from such Hawaiian souvenir items as macadamia nuts, shells, and ancient postcards; artificial flowers made from shells and what-have-you; various glassblowing and/or etching processes; zillions of types of scented and unscented candles; little bottles filled with layers of colored sugar; dolls of all kinds; monkeys made from coconuts;

and figurines of little hula girls and tiki gods molded from pulverized lava rock or monkeypod sawdust.

Much of the above sounds worse than it is; much of the above is even worse than it sounds. Some of it is even good, and all of it is discussed in detail in our Shopping sections, further along in the island-chapters.

Artists in Hawaii. Many artists with sketch pad and canvas have been depicting the flavor of the Islands since they were discovered by Westerners in 1778. Two talented members of Captain Cook's scientific expedition, **John Webber** and **James Clevely,** accurately documented the first visit.

Among other ships' artists was **Louis Choris,** who visited in 1816 and whose incisive, sensitive works are heavily acclaimed today. **Jacques Arago,** who drew heroic Hawaiians in 1819, and **Robert Dampier,** who sketched here during an 1825 stopover, are also important.

By the mid-nineteenth century the missionaries had begun to train a few local artists, and the Hawaiians lost the inclination to continue scratching out petroglyphs during this same period. Petroglyphs, apparently only the casual scribble of a preliterate people, have their own special charm, however, and several artists of today have incorporated petroglyphic design into their work.

In the late-nineteenth and early-twentieth centuries, many artists came to live and work in Hawaii. Today it is generally agreed that four were particularly outstanding. **Madge Tennent,** an Englishwoman who arrived from New Zealand and Samoa in 1923, is remembered especially for her bold oils of large Hawaiian women. She is often known as "Hawaii's Gauguin," and many feel her works will attain international recognition. The Tennent Art Foundation Gallery at 203 Prospect St. in Honolulu exhibits her work exclusively.

Huc M. Luquiens became famous for his landscape etchings. **John M. Kelly** was also an etcher, but one who chose the human form instead of scenery for his subject.

Jean Charlot, who came to Hawaii in 1949 already famous for his Mexican murals, remained to become the unofficial captain of Hawaii's art community until he died, aged in his nineties, in 1979. There are about three dozen other recognized artists doing significant work in Hawaii today.

The most important collection of art in Hawaii is displayed at the Honolulu Academy of Arts at 900 South Beretania St., known not only for its Western exhibits but also for its huge Oriental collections. There are several other galleries as well.

In addition to the art sold at private galleries in Hawaii, current works may be purchased at the outdoor "art marts," the best-known of which is displayed along the fence near Honolulu Zoo on Saturdays and sometimes Sundays. Similar exhibitions are held at Lahaina on Maui and at Kailua-Kona on the Big Island.

Hawaiian Music and That Ol' Hula Moon

Irving Kolodin once told us while he was music critic for the *Saturday Review* that the lure of Hawaiian music alone could account for the large number of visitors who have come here over the past several decades. "The music of the Islands has brought more people than the airplane," Kolodin said.

Certainly no other state in the Union is so musical—or at least can boast styles of music so distinctively influenced by local custom. Who can say he has listened to "Aloha Oe" or "Lovely Hula Hands" and never dreamed of experiencing the Islands in person?

Not everyone is a Hawaiian music fan, of course. Groucho Marx once grumped that all Hawaiian songs sounded the same to him, and he suspected they were all written on the same day. And Kolodin politely said that he seemed to hear the wrong kind all the time on the Mainland.

Most impressions like Groucho's are formed on hearing only a limited sample of popular tunes, usually those churned out for a Hawaiian-hungry appetite among Mainland masses during the 1930s. Hawaiian music produced today is often rich and varied, containing the traditions of the Pacific as well as the modern sounds of American jazz, rock, and country.

In ancient Hawaii, music consisted solely of chants (usually religious), for which rhythm was much more important than the few tonal changes it possessed. There was no scale at all, only a few relatively random notes. The Hawaiian nose flute, played with two hands and one nostril, dates from this early period. The conch shell, a sort of Hawaiian bugle, was also used as an ancient instrument.

When the American missionaries arrived in 1820, they made their most immediate and dramatic effect with the hymns they brought with them. Not only was the diatonic scale immediately embraced by the natives, but the whole concept of harmony almost caused a cultural revolution.

Recognizing this valuable commodity, the holy folk lost no time in organizing a singing school and in translating many Calvinist hymns into the Hawaiian language. It was music that brought the Hawaiians to church in droves—not the long, monotonous sermons that held about as much attraction for the Hawaiians as their now-discontinued chants.

The Hawaiians soon began adopting the Christian hymns and giving them new, secular lyrics in their own tongue, although they were all called *himeni*—a word still in the language for slow and dignified music. They were sung *a cappella* in four-part harmony and not accompanied by dancing, which for many years was strictly prohibited by missionary influence.

The mid-nineteenth-century *himeni* were often sad, usually reflecting a longing for some place or person far away. The reason was not only because the islands seemed very large and distances between them huge in that day; it resulted from the social legacy of King Kamehameha I who sought to "unite" the island nation by dispersing elements of the population over the entire chain.

The potential political action by the people against the king and his successors thus became a reduced threat. And a song like "The Thirsty Winds of Kohala" (a district on the Big Island) was probably composed by a sentimental and homesick Hawaiian transplanted from Kohala to Oahu or Kauai.

In the 1870s and 1880s Hawaiian music underwent several rapid changes. First there was the increased popularity of the guitar, learned by the *paniolos* (Hawaiian cowboys) on the Big Island from the Spanish-speaking *vaqueros* who had been imported to teach the local boys how to punch cattle. (The word *paniolo* is a Hawaiian corruption of *Español*.)

The *paniolos* probably had been playing the Spanish guitar in the isolated hills of Waimea for the previous twenty years, but it was only the inauguration of regular interisland shipping that brought it to the attention of the entire land. By this date the Spanish had gone back to Mexico and the Hawaiians had changed the guitar strings from the original tuning to what is now called "slack key." Basically it is a method of loosening the strings, creating a more distinctive style of plucking and strumming. (To a large extent, "slack key" guitar continued to lead an obscure life in the back country until very recently.)

Also during this period, the first of thousands of Portuguese immigrants arrived in the Islands. They, too, brought guitars and a livelier style of folk music. Further, they shipped in several other types of string instruments, among which was a relatively tiny, fourstringed affair variously called the *raga*, the *raguinho*, or the *cavalquinho*. The Hawaiians took a look at Portuguese hands strumming quickly across the *raga*'s neck and though it looked like a dog trying to scratch a persistent flea. They named the new instrument the "jumping flea," or, in Hawaiian, *uku-lele*. (It was also a play on words, since an early Hawaiian stringed instrument abolished by missionaries was named the ukele.)

In a very few years there were few thatched huts in the Islands that did not have at least one guitar or ukulele stashed in the corner, ready to serve the instant inspiration of its Hawaiian owner. And when the instrument was picked up, it was more likely to play a happy ditty than in times past. Missionary influence on the Hawaiians and their rulers decreased in the latter half of the nineteenth century, and Hawaiians began to dance again.

The newer, fast-paced numbers that accompanied the dancers became known as *hula* songs. Rhythm again became important, and the Hawaiians drew upon the old beats used prior to the missionary influence on their music. Some singers also picked up the yodeling methods put forth by the Big Island *vaqueros* and changed them into today's style of falsetto singing.

Another important development occurring at almost the same time was the 1872 arrival in the Islands of Henry Berger, the German musician hired by Kamehameha V as music teacher to the royal family and to whom was entrusted the formation of the Royal Hawaiian Band.

The Hawaiians soon found themselves led musically as well as socially by their own monarchs. King David Kalakaua wrote the words (to Berger's music) of Hawaii's national anthem, "Hawaii Pono'i," which today is the official state song. Queen Liliuokalani is credited with "Aloha Oe," which she wrote in her own hand in 1878, although nit-pickers note that the tune is much like the old hymn "The Rock Beside the Sea."

Shortly before the turn of the century, a young student at Kamehameha School for Boys, Joseph Kekuku, accidentally dropped a comb on his guitar. As it skittered across the strings he heard a new sound. One thing led to another, and soon Kekuku had changed the gut strings to wire and was turning out a steel bar in the school machine shop. He used the bar to play the world's first instrument of its type—the one the rest of the world knows now as the "Hawaiian guitar."

In Hawaii, however, it was always called the "steel guitar." No sooner had Kekuku popularized it in the Islands than he left to perform on the Mainland. There he continued to entertain and teach for twenty-seven years, until he died in New Jersey in 1932. Kekuku never returned to Hawaii, but his Hawaiian guitar was adopted by every country-and-western group in America. A few years later it was electrically amplified, and to some musical ears outside of the Nashville sphere of influence the steel guitar just plain committed suicide—killed as a serious instrument simply by overuse.

In Hawaii the steel guitar had firmly captured the melody line from the violin and flute that had led earlier Hawaiian orchestras. It generally held the lead clear into the 1960s, although today in the most modern Hawaiian arrangements the steel guitar is a much more subtle instrument or absent altogether. Nevertheless, Hawaiian musicians are nothing if not sentimental, and many are still very attached to the old twang.

In truth it is hard to imagine the likes of "Princess Pupule," "Sweet Leilani," "Little Brown Gal," and "The Cockeyed Mayor of Kaunakakai" holding up their treble clefs without a healthy dose of steel guitar. These are *hapa-haole* songs—Hawaiian music written in English or partly in English, and largely influenced by Hollywood and Broadway—which became the successors to the old *hula* songs. There are hundreds of *hapahaole* songs written over four decades, and a few are still being composed today.

During the 1960s a terrible thing seemed to be happening to Hawaiian music: It was disappearing altogether. In the bars, clubs, and showrooms of Waikiki, the ukes, the steel guitars, the melodious Hawaiian language, and the familiar themes of surf, rustling palms, and fragrant flowers all had faded from the scene in favor of hard-rock music, much of it imported from Las Vegas.

Only a few stalwarts like the perennially popular entertainer Don Ho continued to sing the traditional favorites—"Tiny Bubbles," "Pearly Shells," "Beyond the Reef"—all known widely on the Mainland but haughtily put down by hip elements of Honolulu. Ho tried to back up his own songs with some modern arrangements and a few new songs ("Suck 'em Up," "Ain't No Big Thing") with some semirock influence, but he still found himself virtually alone, patronized mainly by older-generation tourists, while the upcoming musicians of the Islands looked beyond Hawaii's shores for their professional inspiration. Loud outcries by visitors and residents alike ensued, bemoaning the imminent demise of Hawaiian music. Still, nothing they could do seemed to bring the "Hawaiian Wedding Song" or "Blue Hawaii" back onto Kalakaua Avenue.

But Hawaiian music was not really defeated. It had only made a strategic withdrawal until it was re-formed, revitalized, and ready to enter the field again. Beginning in the 1970s, some new and exciting patterns emerged, many of them traditional songs or themes clothed in some brand-new styles.

The new groups eschewed names like the Royal Hawaiian Serenaders or the Waikiki Beachboys, titles that conjured up images of happy-go-lucky brown lackeys always ready and willing to evoke whatever images you remember from Bing Crosby movies of old. Calling themselves names of the land—the Sunday Manoa, Hui Ohana, Na Keonimana—the new groups combined close harmony with hard-driving rhythms influenced by jazz, rock, and the best C&W, but above all infused with a sense of the Hawaiians' recently rediscovered cultural identity. Digging into the past, they came up again not only with the slack key guitar, but with a whole group of other instruments—strings like the tiple, the requinta, and even the mandolin, plus percussions like the *ipu* (a gourd drum), *ʻiliʻili* (stone castanets), *pahu* (a sharkskin drum), and a *ʻulili* (triple gourd rattle).

So today there are many forms of traditional and modern Hawaiian music, the latest still in transition. Those new to the medium may only be able to discern a narrow range of styles, in the same way that persons who are not accustomed to seeing faces of another race have trouble at first recognizing individual differences. But to seek out and carefully listen to Hawaiian music is to gain a special appreciation of Hawaii—perhaps the most valid experience of Hawaiian culture today.

Some musical postscripts:

• A list of Hawaiian entertainers and local musical groups, together with a brief description of each, will be found in the Oahu chapter's section 11, Nights on the Town.

• If you want to hear Hawaiian music at any hour, you may turn your radio to KCCN, the only Oahu radio station playing Hawaiian music exclusively—and indiscriminately. There at 1440 kilocycles (it's on AM only), you'll hear all the best and all the worst, side by side.

• The Royal Hawaiian Band—the same organization set up more than 100 years ago by Henry Berger—is still going strong. It's often on the dock to welcome a cruise ship to the Islands, but it's now better known for its free concerts Fridays at noon at the Coronation Bandstand on the grounds of Honolulu's Iolani Palace.

• Western classical music is not unknown in Hawaii. The Honolulu Symphony Orchestra, founded in 1900, is well regarded musically although constantly in danger of extinction due to financial problems and internal bickering of one kind or another. Recently a breakaway organization, the Hawaii Philharmonic, was set up. This eventually was reduced to a smaller ensemble, the Hawaii Chamber Orchestra. The Honolulu Symphony also sponsors the Hawaii Opera Theatre, which features guest artists and local singers during its winter season.

Some Brief Words on the Hula. Believe it or not, the first *hula* dancers were men. In prediscovery Hawaii, the *hula* was a religious ritual, and it was thought too sacred for women to perform.

The missionaries tried to suppress the *hula,* considering its gyrating motions sinful and sexually suggestive no matter who performed it. The *hula* never really died, however, although some versions of it were forgotten and others underwent several changes. By the time it reemerged into public consciousness in the late nineteenth century, most men had dropped the dance, leaving it to women who gradually adapted it into a more graceful, interpretive performance.

The grass skirt, incidentally, is a relatively recent innovation brought by Gilbert Islanders (today's Kiribati) to Hawaii. *Hula* skirts were all at least knee length 100 years ago. Usually they were longer, and there were no thighs to be seen. The ti-leaf skirt, however, is genuinely Hawaiian, although it takes fewer such leaves to make today's *hula* skirt, to be sure.

In recent decades *hula* hand motions have become almost a musical sign language, but it is not true that you can follow the story by watching these movements. And the swiveling hip motions—once downplayed in importance—have indeed been increased to a sensual display, at least in some *hapa-haole* and comic hulas.

As with Hawaiian music, there are then several different types of *hulas,* ranging from the traditional and classical to a graceful grind of good fun, vamps, and rolls. Be aware that you will see *hulas* from many other Pacific Islands performed in Hawaii. One of the favorites is the extremely fast-hipped version danced in Tahiti (remember *Mutiny on the Bounty?*) and often mistaken by newcomers for a genuine Hawaiian *hula.*

The Spirit of Aloha

John F. Kennedy once commented that Hawaii is what the rest of America is striving to be.

Like so many other public figures who have experienced Hawaii at first hand, the late president apparently admired the state's racial harmony as shown so clearly in its chop suey population. But this is merely one manifestation of a social resource dubbed in recent years the "Aloha Spirit."

In 1986, the Hawaii State Legislature passed a bill that "expresses aloha as the essence of the law in the state of Hawaii."

What is this Aloha Spirit, if there really is any such thing? This question has long perplexed many in the Islands. Some say that even if it once did exist, it is now dead. Others claim that the Aloha Spirit is around, all right, but that it often hides, leaving the pressures of the city to reside farther *mauka* (inland) and on the Neighbor Islands, where country folks more freely exude the natural, relaxed feeling of good will toward their fellow man.

A 35-member State Commission on Environmental Planning once met to find, among other things, a way to pin down and examine the supposed Aloha Spirit. At the conclusion of the session the group solemnly announced that it assumed that "there is such a thing as an aloha spirit, even though it may be hard to define, and that it is identified with empathy, tolerance, graciousness, friendliness, understanding and giving."

The same report, however, went on to issue a warning: "The aloha spirit is fragile and can be shattered by population pressures and a highly competitive society." The commission concluded, too, that the Aloha Spirit partly springs from Hawaii's natural environment as well as from the heritage of traditional Hawaiian lifestyles: "If we cannot prove that our Island geography, a benign climate, and beautiful vistas create this spirit, we nevertheless are sure that the people who live here would act very differently in a different environment."

Sociologist Harry Ball once speculated aloud that the roots of the Aloha Spirit were in the *hanai* or the "extended family" system of ancient Hawaii: "It was a totally open society. People were very open in their feelings, free of themselves, and generous," Ball said. "This openness, which I think the Aloha Spirit is all about, was really the character of Hawaiian society."

Others have noted that it was strictly *kapu* for the old Hawaiians to *helu*—to count what they did for other people in a "tit for tat" or mutual back-scratching sort of way. Favors were just done, that's all, with nothing expected in return. But as more and more members of other groups entered Hawaiian life, this system began in greater or lesser degree to break down.

Andrew W. Lind, senior professor emeritus of sociology from the University of Hawaii, wrote admiringly, though sadly, of the Aloha Spirit: "It is this universal facility of entering imaginatively and sympathetically into the experience of others, unmindful of differences of skin color, age, sex, or social position—we may call it aloha—which, if anything, 'makes the whole world kin.' Thus, however defined, aloha has a moral and emotional quality and, like love, so frequently equated with it, is fragile in nature and can easily be turned into apathy or even hatred if neglected or mistreated by those to whom it is directed."

In the book *The Frontier States* (the Time-Life Library of America), author Richard Austin Smith poetically follows a similar theme:

> The aloha spirit permeates the 50th state like a benign contagion. It can be heard in the timbre of laughter and felt in the simple friendliness of a business contact. Even a short exposure to such good will has a way of turning up the corners of mouths that hostility had clamped in a thin line....
>
> It would be a mistake to assume that all Hawaiians are responsive to the aloha spirit—they are not, human nature being what it is. Nor do those affected respond in equal measure. But there can be no doubt that what might be called a mainstream of the aloha spirit flows through Hawaiian life continuously, if variably.
>
> The result is a slow but steady tempering of self-interest, aggression, acquisitiveness, ambition. How else can it be explained that the Hawaiians are not at one another's throats like so many groups elsewhere?

Bob Krauss, the perceptive columnist for the Honolulu *Advertiser,* has taken up President Kennedy's theme, declaring Aloha to have import far beyond the shores of Hawaii and defining its spirit as a potential gift not only for the nation, but the world. Wrote Krauss: "Aloha, as a weapon of survival, may be the greatest contribution our small island state has to offer in the future of a tiny, crowded earth island as it whirls alone in space."

5

Oahu, the Capital Island

1. Around the Island—Gateway to the Fun

To millions upon millions who have coursed through the Pacific over two centuries, the island of Oahu simply *is* Hawaii. Although it was of minor importance in early history, this medium-sized landfall has, for the past 135 years, overwhelmingly dominated—politically, economically, and culturally—all the other territory in the Hawaiian chain.

Unlike the Outer Islands, Oahu does not deign to call itself by some additional identifying name or phrase. Nevertheless it is the "Capital Island" because Honolulu, once the nexus of the Hawaiian nation and now a modern high-rise city and seat of the state government, is firmly established here.

The origin of the word *oahu* is obscure, although it has been translated as "the gathering place." That is certainly an accurate description in the present day, since more than 800,000 people work and play within its 608 square miles. That number, in fact, is about four-fifths the population of the entire state.

In at least one way Honolulu and Oahu really are synonymous. The governmental body called the City and County of Honolulu encompasses the entire island, even though several smaller settlements also dot the islandscape.

The metropolitan area itself stretches several miles on the map to the

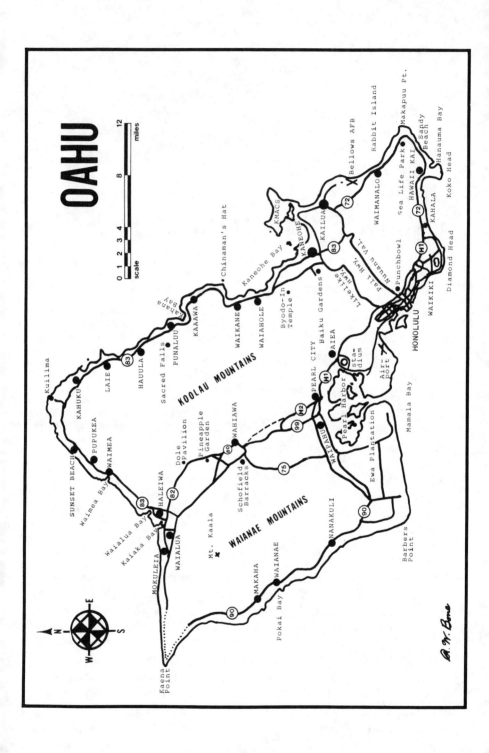

left and right of Honolulu harbor. It is one of the world's long and narrow cities, hemmed in between sea and mountains along a thin line. This two-sided squeeze causes considerable concern among job commuters and land developers.

The mountains that channel the physical growth of Honolulu are called the Koolaus (vaguely, "ko-oh-louse"), and the range runs for some 30 miles from the southeast to the northwest. They look rugged, but they're pikers by Rockies standards, the tallest peak reaching up only about 3,150 feet.

Honolulu is in the lee of the Koolaus, and there are two superhighways over these heights to take you to the area called the "windward side," dominated by the towns of Kailua and Kaneohe. A third highway has long been planned, but it has become a controversial project in this environment-conscious age, so it remains blocked—for a time or forever.

A second set of mountains, up to 1,000 feet higher but only half the length of the paralleling Koolau range, dominates the western portion of Oahu. Called the Waianaes, they are largely controlled by military installations. The only paved pass over the Waianae Mountains is not open to the public. The Armed Forces occupy fully 25 percent of the acreage on Oahu, and most of that is perpetually off limits to civilian traffic.

The gently sloping area between the Waianaes and the Koolaus traditionally has served as a wide agricultural belt, mostly composed of sugar and pineapple plantations. These green areas are still there, although there are examples of creeping urbanization now cutting into the fields.

The shape of Oahu is so irregular, and its routes of commerce so winding, that standard compass directions are seldom used. Instead, today's population has maintained the ancient Hawaiian system of direction finding. There is *mauka* for inland or toward the mountains, and *makai* for toward the sea. Otherwise, the directions are indicated by naming known landmarks that lie farther along the same general path. In Honolulu, for instance, you not only travel *mauka* or *makai*, but you can also go *ewa* ("eh-vah"—toward Ewa Plantation—generally west or northwest) or "diamondhead" (toward Diamond Head crater—east and/or south).

Oahu has been the scene of not one but two particularly violent and tragic military conflicts. The Battle of Pearl Harbor, of course, exploded the United States into World War II at 7:55 A.M., Sunday, December 7, 1941. You may visit the site of this attack and stand on the floating memorial over the rusty body of the battleship U.S.S. *Arizona*.

But a lesser known engagement that took place on the island nearly a century and a half earlier also captures the imagination of all who step up to its climactic location for the first time. This was the Battle of

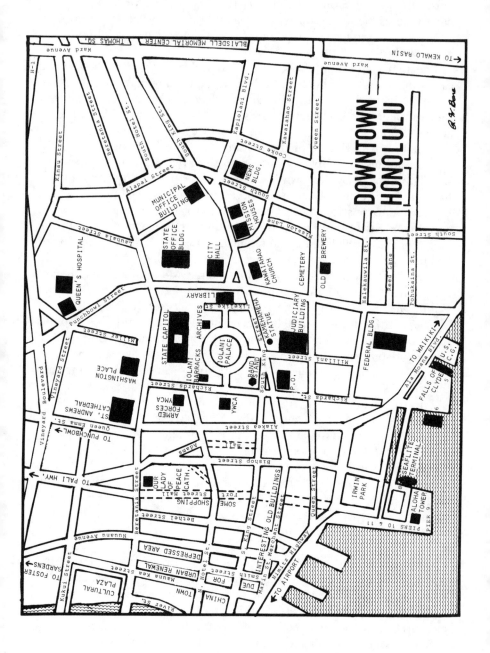

DOWNTOWN HONOLULU

R. F. Bone

Nuuanu, in which King Kamehameha I took on the forces of Oahu and drove them up the sloping and narrowing Nuuanu Valley behind Honolulu until the defending army reached the dramatic and gale-swept cliff known as the Nuuanu Pali.

According to surviving accounts of the 1795 battle, hundreds of the Oahu soldiers were driven over the sheer *pali* to plunge nearly 1,000 feet to their deaths. This was the end of the seventh and most decisive battle by which Kamehameha established his dynasty over the island chain. The spot, which provides one of the most beautiful views in the state, is made doubly dramatic by the memory of the bloody event that took place there.

In the minds of most visitors the city of Honolulu is divided into two distinct areas. First, there is "downtown," a formerly rather seedy but now mostly revitalized city center. Downtown also boasts the dramatic and modern state capitol, as well as the Victorian and quaint Iolani Palace, the royal residence of the last monarchs of Hawaii. The second area is Waikiki, the vacation suburb just three miles from downtown. Here most of the hotels vie for position on or near the gently curving and world-famous beach, backgrounded by the profile of Diamond Head, an extinct volcano.

Today, Waikiki is a seven-tenth-square-mile peninsula, bounded by the gentle surf on one side and the Ala Wai Canal on two other sides. Between the sand and the artificial waterway is a curious mixture of hotels, shops, open spaces, trees, snack bars, souvenir stands, and bikinis. A hodgepodge of architectural styles has sprung up in Waikiki, and some have justly criticized its lack of central planning.

Don't let anybody tell you, however, that Waikiki is simply "another Miami Beach." It is not, and you have only to walk it from one end to the other to verify our impression.

Begin your sandy stroll at the Hilton Hawaiian Village or Fort DeRussy and head "diamondhead" along the water at about sunset in order to keep the rays from your eyes. For the next mile or two, while the sky changes color and darkens, you will take in the smell of the sea, the sounds of Hawaiian music and laughter from the hotels, and the sight of millions of pinpoints of light that come alive in the hills beyond and the towers above, many of them reflected in the friendly moving waters lapping at your feet.

There's nothing quite like it in this world.

2. Honolulu International Airport

Honolulu International Airport is modern and well marked, but per-

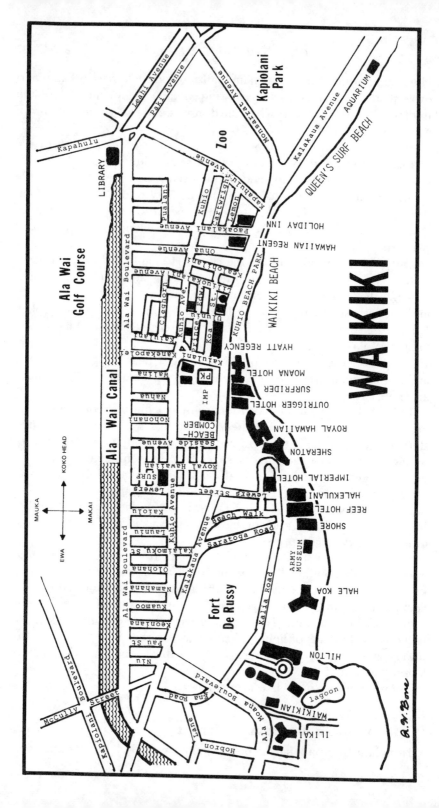

petually under construction. It's also strictly elbow-to-elbow during the peak periods of 7 to 11 A.M. and 5 to 9 P.M.

One of the busiest airports in the nation, Honolulu International is almost a small town in itself, with some 8,000 persons making a living there. Besides the usual airline accouterments, you'll find a bank, post office, restaurants, bar, barber shop, several kinds of stores, a foreign-money exchange, and a duty-free shop for foreign departures.

There is no hotel right on the campus, although two are nearby. In the main terminal building you may come across a unique facility called the Shower Tree, where at nominal fees you can shower, shave, and even nap between flights.

Be aware that like many airports on the Mainland, Honolulu International is occasionally chosen as a begging ground by members of the Hare Krishna. They may or may not be in costume.

The principal airport structure, more formally known as the John Rodgers Terminal Building, has two main floors. The ground level is set up for arriving passengers (with baggage-claim areas, taxis, rental-car booths, etc). The second level is generally for departing passengers (luggage check-in, ticket counters, and waiting lobbies).

There is a third, topmost story acting mainly as a right-of-way for the Wiki-Wiki articulated buses that shuttle to and from distant gates carrying those who don't walk.

Honolulu Airport is now equipped with small luggage carts similar to the free ones offered at airports in other countries of the world. (They're easier to steer if you pull them along rather than push.) Called Smarte Cartes, they are available only on the ground level, and they are *not* free. Use a dollar bill or four quarters to get a cart. If you bring it back to one of the cart stations, it automatically gives you a "reward" of 25 cents. (Once when we were out at the airport a cadre of small boys was cleaning up by collecting abandoned carts and either renting them out for 50 cents or returning them to the rack to claim the quarters, depending on the traffic. Some kids are even smarter than the Smarty Carties!)

Airlines that fly to and from foreign countries are generally assigned to gates at the western wing, better known as the **Ewa Concourse** (pronounce that "*eh*-vah")—Gates 26 to 31. Other jumbos, on Mainland flights, may dock there, but if they are Boeing 747s they will more likely park at the eastern wing called the **Diamond Head Concourse**—Gates 6 to 11. If your gate is near the end of this wing, you may choose to ride between the plane and the main terminal on a free Wiki-Wiki bus.

The Y-shaped **Central Concourse**—Gates 12 to 25—has facilities designed especially for DC-10s. If you have some time on your hands, wander outdoors through the yoke of the Y to see the three little interconnected gardens—one Hawaiian, one Chinese, and one Japanese.

Flocks of ducks and geese swim between them, oblivious to the screams of nearby jet engines. They must be either the most laid back or the most hard-of-hearing birds in the Pacific. Near the garden but on the upper level of the Central Concourse is the triangular main exhibit area of the new **Pacific Aerospace Museum** (Tel. 531-7747). It may be an interesting way to kill some time while waiting for your plane.

If you are being met at the airport from a Mainland flight, it is reasonable for your friends to decide not to trudge out to the arrival gate itself but instead to find you in the ground-floor **baggage-claim area** whose number is listed on the "Arrivals" TV monitor for your flight. There are three rooms: one for Areas 7 to 11, another for 12 to 14, and the third for 15 to 17.

But if you are landing on an *international* flight, everyone will have to look for you outside the **International Arrivals Center,** the sanctum sanctorum where mysterious Customs and Immigration rites are performed, and where outsiders are not allowed to enter.

Watch out, because there are *two* doors from International Arrivals. They are about fifty giant steps apart, and on crowded days they are not even quite in sight of one another. When only one door is in use, there is no problem. On other days your loved ones may be performing mad 50-yard dashes between them, hoping to catch you at the right exit. (The TV monitors there are confusing and not helpful.)

In two parts of a separate G-shaped structure at the western extreme of the main terminal complex is the traditional **Interisland Terminal.** Closest, at Gates 46 to 51, and a reasonably short walk from the main facilities, you'll find most jets operated by **Aloha Airlines** (Tel. 836-1111). First-Class passengers should note that Aloha now has a separate first class check-in counter. Aloha uses Interisland Baggage Claim Area No. 1.

Farther along, past the coffee shop and around the corner in the larger wing, Gates 52 to 56 serve **Mid Pacific Airlines** (Tel. 836-3313), whose carousel is labeled Baggage Claim Area No. 2.

And then Gates 57 to 62 are the assigned parking areas for most jets and turboprops of **Hawaiian Airlines** (Tel. 537-5100), which has Baggage Claim Area No. 3, the farthest one away from everything else. The little blue-and-white "Wiki Wiki" shuttle buses run between the main terminal (catch them outside in front of the second level) and the Interisland Terminal. The fare is 50 cents. These are less needed now with the advent of the aforementioned Smarte Carte, particularly for transferring to nearby Aloha.

Traffic is heavy in the Interisland Terminal in the early morning until 9 A.M. and from 3 to 5 in the afternoon, largely due to the number of business persons traveling between the islands. The crush has been getting steadily worse, and the airlines are carrying greater loads. A new terminal extension is finally being built further *mauka*, but unfortunately this will not be completed in 1987.

Another building, a somewhat temporary structure, has been put up at the eastern (the exact opposite) end of the entire complex—about 500 yards from the main terminal—for the small commuter airlines. At the moment, this is occupied by **Princeville Airways** (Tel. 833-3219).

Two more commuter lines are in the low-rent district on the other side of the runways, and reached by an entirely different route. First is **Air Molokai-Tropic Airlines** (Tel. 839-4040), which offers free parking at its private headquarters at 203 Lagoon Drive. The second is the more recently launched **Reeves Air** (Tel. 833-9555), almost next door at 250 Lagoon Drive.

For a description of all these local carriers—exactly who they are and where they go—please see Interisland Transportation in chapter 2.

Back at the main terminal, on the opposite side from the aircraft, you'll find the large parking lot and parking building. The building is accessible to pedestrians from the first or third floor of the terminal only, the latter reached via elevator to the overhead footbridges. (Parking has been holding at a maximum of $6 for a 24-hour day—fairly cheap as airports go.)

Near the parking lot outdoors is a line of flower lei stands where you can buy a lei for $4 that would probably cost $5 or $6 at the flower shop inside the terminal (or $3 in downtown Honolulu).

On the elevated roadway in front of the second level is the **city bus stop.** For a grand sum of 60 cents, it is the most economical way to go downtown or to Waikiki in one direction, or to Hickam A.F.B. in the other. However, the driver is not supposed to let you on board carrying anything larger than a shopping bag—not even a backpack—and this politically inspired rule supported by the island taxi industry forces us nickel-knucklers to ride something more expensive. (If you think that's mean, we suggest you call the City Office of Information and Complaint at 523-4381 and let them know your feelings.) The bus route—No. 8—takes about 45 minutes between the airport and the hotel area.

On the other hand, if you're tired it might be a better idea anyway to climb aboard the **Gray Line Airporter** (Tel. 834-1033) which waits just outside the baggage-claim area on the *ground* level. It will drop you at your Waikiki hotel in about half as much time as the bus and cost $5 per seat. If there are two or more of you, however, it may be as cheap or cheaper to share a cab, which usually runs $12 or so to Waikiki.

3. Transportation—Honolulu and All of Oahu

Not counting sightseeing buses, cruise boats, and the like, there are several ways to make your way around the Capital Island. (All those other things we cover under section 7, Guided Tours and Cruises, further along in this chapter.)

Taxicabs. You'll find most cabbies polite and friendly, the cars new and sometimes air conditioned, and the fares—set by law—fair. Current rates are $1.40 at the drop of the flag, plus 20 cents for each 1/7 mile thereafter. This means you will pay about $13 for the approximately nine-mile trip from Waikiki to the airport, or about $9 to downtown. Drivers are allowed to charge 25 cents per suitcase.

There are zillions of taxi companies, but three large ones stand out with 24-hour service, radio-dispatched cars, and island-wide service. They are **Charley's** (Tel. 531-1333), which operates a gigantic fleet of company-owned cabs, although with drivers of varying experience; **SIDA of Hawaii, Inc.** (Tel. 836-0011), a cooperative of individually owned hacks whose name comes from State Independent Drivers Association; and the **Aloha State Cab, Inc.** (Tel. 847-3566), a third biggie serving the entire island.

Limousine Service. A VIP service, complete with chauffeured Rolls Royces and Bentleys, made its Honolulu debut in 1978. The **Silver Cloud Limousine Service** (Tel. 524-7999) hires out its shiny carriages with liveried drivers for gilt-edged rates. Reserve from P.O. Box 15773, Honolulu, HI 96815. Sorry, we have had no personal experience with the firm, but it does sound elegant!

Buses—City and Others. The City and County of Honolulu is proud of its bus operation. It is known almost affectionately by the two pushed-together words painted on the sides of the white-yellow-orange-and-brown striped vehicles, **TheBus** (Tel. 531-1611 up to 10 P.M. for schedule information). Every ride now costs 60 cents, and you can travel for hours at that price, virtually circling the island, if you want, and still qualify for one free transfer to another line—if you ask for it when boarding. Students (grades 1 to 12) pay only 25 cents, and tykes under 6 travel free. *Exact change is required, in coin only.* (Paper money is not accepted. Believe it or not, even if you're paying for five people, the driver is not allowed to accept three one-dollar bills.) Senior citizens (65 or over) may apply in person for a special pass allowing them to ride free everywhere. But it does take two to three weeks for the pass to come through—an intentional and politically inspired delay.

Unfortunately the newer, more colorful bus-stop signs were apparently designed by people who don't catch buses. They are marked only on the front side—more useful in telling the drivers where to stop than the passengers where to wait. (Thus it is difficult to walk against the traffic flow while searching for a bus stop.)

Bus headquarters, where you apply in person for your senior citizens' pass, is at 725 Kapiolani Blvd., near downtown Honolulu (open until 4 P.M. weekdays).

Watch out because some buses have just been renumbered, and some printed literature and older bus guides may not be correct. If you are headquartered in Waikiki, your important bus routes will be Numbers 2, 4, 5, 8, and 19. You can always get home on those. Buses run anywhere from five minutes to one hour apart, depending on the route and time of day. Throughout this chapter we sometimes give bus routes applying to popular Oahu destinations. Unfortunately there is no official route map, although some privately published ones are sold in drugstores and other places. Probably the most detailed and accurate one is called *Honolulu and Oahu by TheBus* by Michael Brein, Ph.D.

You will see other buses (besides tour buses) occasionally making their way around town. Sometimes these are free buses that take you to commercial ventures like garment factories, boat trips, tours, etc. Another valuable bus is the commercial **Arizona Memorial Shuttle Bus** (Tel. 926-4747), which costs about $2.50 per person each way at this writing. It may save a lot of hassle on the Pearl Harbor trip.

Rental Cars. If there is a more aggressive, dog-eat-dog commercial pursuit in Hawaii than the U-drive game, we don't know what it is. You will find it hard to believe the number of auto-renting companies seeking your patronage.

During slack periods, rates will drop to amazingly low levels, and you may be stopped in the street by people who want to put you in a car with a special rate "today only." It could cut to half the rates prevailing a week ago. Yet there are times—like in August, late December, or February—when it seems you cannot find a car of any kind. In heavy periods, much of the hoopla about special deals seems to disappear down the road. Due to the wildly fluctuating situation, few firms continue to issue any literature describing the types of vehicles they offer and at what prices. Generally speaking, however, rates in the highly competitive Hawaii market are lower than in other parts of the country.

The Hawaii State Office of Consumer Protection, and yours truly, have received complaints about every rental-car agency in the state, from the largest to the smallest. Your only real protection is to be as *akamai* as you can about how they operate. Most complaints center on extra charges the customer said were not mentioned or not clear at the time of rental, so ask questions when you first make your reservations. (Don't forget the toll-free "800" numbers listed in our appendix.) Here are some things you should consider before you rent a car:

• **Mileage rates and flat rates.** An example of mileage rates is the deal that runs $20 a day and 20 cents a mile. Flat rates, with unlimited mileage, might be $25 a day. In this example, if you average more than

25 miles a day you'll save money on flat rates ($25 \times \$0.20 = \$5 + \$20 = \$25$). For either, you buy your own gas, as you do everywhere these days.

So far, we have not noticed any Hawaii rental car companies placing any "caps" on their daily mileage, as some agencies have been doing on the Mainland lately. This is a clause that may require you to pay, for example, 15 cents a mile extra if you drive over 150 miles in any one day. Such a requirement is a subtle increase in rates that might not be noticed at first.

• **Weekend and weekly rates.** These are three-day and seven-day specials that may save you more than 10 percent off the daily flat rates. (Weekend rates, however, are among the first bargains to disappear during peak periods.) If you're shopping for a car for a week or more, we suggest doing it in advance from home by using the "800" numbers in our appendix, and be sure to take into account the cost of extras such as insurance (see below).

• **Discount specials.** On a "fly-drive" deal, for example, you'll save between 15 percent and 20 percent off some rates if you fly a certain airline, either to the state or between the Islands. These may be limited to a certain number of discount days based on the number of adult tickets or adult drivers in your party. After that the rates may jump back up again. Also, the advertised special may be for one "ten-hour day" or something similar. Before going out of your way to make a fly-drive arrangement, ask some questions—like what will they do if they are out of the particular type of car the deal applies to—will they give you another at the same price? And is there any limit on the number of days you can rent the car at the special rate?

• **Mileage minimum.** This may occur in a company that advertises a very cheap daily rate. If, for example, the rent is $1 a day plus 24 cents a mile on a 100-mile-a-day *minimum,* that car is going to cost you at least $25 for any day, even if you only use it for occasional trips to the grocery store. Look these over carefully.

• **Age minimums and maximums.** Several companies won't rent cars to persons under 25 or over 70, and this is certainly a debatable practice. (Some companies will also not rent to military personnel or will do so only with outrageously high deposits, and some will not rent to Hawaii residents! We have attempted to eliminate these latter two types of companies from our list below, because we believe the feelings behind such discriminatory practices also lead to other elements of customer dissatisfaction.)

• **Deposits.** Deposits, of course, are meant to discourage folks from running away *with* a car or from running away *from* the car without paying for the rental, so don't be surprised if the company asks a lot. The only way to avoid paying a deposit is to carry a major credit card. (However, some rental agencies in Hawaii apparently no longer accept Diners Club.) By the way, if you keep the car longer than you planned, give the company a call or you may find it missing—repossessed by an agency who believes you stole it or skipped town.

- **Drop-off charges.** There are more of these around than you might think, even with the big companies. For instance, if you rent a car in Waikiki but leave it at the airport, even at the agency's own facilities, they may charge you $10 or more for that convenience.

- **"Insurance."** Auto-renting agencies are not really licensed to sell genuine insurance in Hawaii. Some companies make out like highway bandits by charging $8 to $12 extra per day for "full collision damage waivers" or some similar term, pushing hard to sell them by the use of frightening and even false statements—perhaps the only example of anti-aloha you will see in the state. Rental car clerks receive as much as 50-percent commission on the cost of these damage waivers, so now you know their motivation for threatening to take your arm, your leg and your first-born child in the event you dare to have an accident while driving their car.

If you are a licensed driver who already owns an automobile, you may already be insured to drive a rental vehicle with the same collision damage coverage you have on your own car, although any deductibles will probably apply. *Check this with your insurance agent before leaving home—or else stand the relatively small expense to phone your agent from Hawaii to find out.* If you are already satisfactorily insured, then feel free to politely but firmly decline this expensive outlay, initialing the appropriate paragraph on the contract. Despite the brass-knuckle approach you may experience, taking the extra coverage is definitely not "required," and Hawaii's "no fault" insurance law has absolutely nothing to do with it. In many cases, it is nothing less than a high-priced rip-off. (Show the clerk these words, if you need to, and then write us about it later!)

But please note this, too: If you don't already have auto insurance covering the situation, then of course do play it super-safe with the special, no-deductible coverage (especially if your rental period is only for a day or so, anyway, and the extra outlay won't make a big dent in your budget). Even if you are insured and your own insurance company takes any claims—and you are eventually determined to be at fault—an accident could increase your future premiums. (And don't turn the coverage down merely because you are a "safe driver." Damage to the car can take place in a parking lot or at other times when you are nowhere near the vehicle.)

In the event that you do have an accident without having bought the extra protection, you cannot be required to pay any more than the estimated repair costs for actual damages to the car. (I.e. they're not going to charge you $1,000 for a $100 scratch.) You'll receive documents so that you can later process a claim through your insurance company. And of course you should even get that back eventually, too, if the accident is ultimately determined to be the other guy's fault. Don't be intimidated by misstatements that your insurance company is not represented in Hawaii or that you will not be allowed to leave the island or the state without first delivering unto them a king's ransom. Understandably, a real accident certainly could delay your vacation schedule. But let's face it—Bozo's Rent-A-Car is not going to send an honest vacationer to a Hawaiian jail.

A genuine inconvenience is that the car rental agency (or the agency's insurance company) will probably not talk to your insurance company; instead, it will simply put the accident expense down on your pre-signed credit card slip. (There's not much you can do about that immediately unless it puts you way over your credit limit.) In any case it is then up to you to call your insurance company to start the bureaucratic wheels in motion so you can get back whatever you have coming to you—hopefully before your credit card bill comes in!

There are two additional types of insurance sometimes offered, although they are not the subject of a hard-sell approach. One is extra personal liability insurance with more coverage than the law requires the agency to have, which for better or worse we also routinely turn down. The other is insurance coverage on your own personal belongings being carried in the car. A relatively new option, this may be a better deal. We'll be looking into this some more this year.

A last word on the insurance subject: We would very much like to know which car companies are doing the most arm-twisting so that future Maverick readers can be warned more specifically about them. (Budget and Alamo seem to be among the pushiest lately.) We also want to hear from persons who have had an accident while driving a rented car. Please drop us a line in care of the publisher.

• **Types of cars available.** Differences in the rate you pay will depend a lot on the kind of car you want to rent. In generally descending order, they are the following: *American sedan.* This is the top-dollar car, and you probably won't get one for a flat rate of less than $40 anywhere. If you do, and you want one, grab it. *American compact.* When you can find it, you might save $5 below the flat rate for the above sedans. *Foreign compact.* The real competition is in this class. You could pay $10 below the daily flats for an American sedan, and several dollars less than American compacts.

• **Automatic and standard shift.** Where standard shift is available, it might save you another dollar or so per day off automatic transmission.

As in other parts of the U.S., car-rental rates vary widely and wildly in

Hawaii, depending on the year, the season, the weather, and perhaps the heartburn of the manager and the phases of the moon. Here is a run-down on a selection of *some* car-rental agencies in Honolulu. (Phone numbers listed here are local. You can use them while in Honolulu to reserve a car on Oahu or at Neighbor Island branches. If you're calling from the Mainland, be sure to see the WATS toll-free numbers listed in the back of this book.)

Until recently the expensive rental companies were the four who had concession booths at the airport. Three of those are still there: **Hertz** (Tel. 836-2511), **Avis** (Tel. 836-5511), and **Budget** (Tel. 922-3600). The fourth—and somewhat cheaper—airport agency is now **Dollar** (Tel. 926-4200). Other outfits will come over to pick you up at the terminal when you phone them. Now this includes the other member of the original big four, **National** (Tel. 834-7156).

One of Hawaii's own companies is **Tropical** (Tel. 836-1041). Head-quartered near the airport (550 Paiea St.), they can be over to the terminal in a jiffy. We've been recommending this outfit since it was a two-cylinder operation a decade ago, and now it's the largest car-rental operation in the state. (It no longer owns the mainland outlets by the same name, however.) There can be discouragingly large crowds standing around the offices, but that annoyance is ameliorated somewhat by the gracious Hawaiian *tutus* (grandmas) there whose only job is to be friendly to the customers. (If for some reason you don't get what you want, ask for Gerry Peters, marketing manager, or Bob Nichols, vice president for Quality Assurance.) In any case, at minimum flat rates of perhaps around $25 this year, Tropical is probably still worth waiting for.

We also like two other local choices for low prices. **Holiday Hawaii** (Tel. 836-1974) is parked where Tropical used to be at 2881 Ualena St., near the airport, and they'll also pick you up on demand. Holiday has compacts, standards, vans, and convertibles—plus a VIP lounge and *tutus,* too. On the minus side, it has been experimenting with a bother-some and rather tacky gas-tank policy. Another bargain (sometimes) is the venerable **Robert's Hawaii** (Tel. 947-3939), an efficient *kamaaina* company that will even rent to *married* 18-year-olds. Then there's **Thrifty** (Tel. 836-2388), run by about 10 members of the Kirley family, originally from Calgary, Alberta. They feature nonsmokers' cars, and they have no upper age limit for senior citizens.

Other low-priced agencies include **Alamo** (Tel. 833-4585) and **United** (Tel. 922-4605). Alamo is one where you're advised to bring back the car with an *empty* gas tank(!), which seems to us to be a sort of highway Russian roulette. Also, friends of ours booked a cheap car from Alamo recently, but when they showed up to get the vehicle, only a more expensive one was available. They had no choice but to take it—and at the higher price, too.

A few last words on car rentals:

A disturbing trend, even among the top-dollar outfits, is to provide less service at the various island airports. That is, even though you check out a car at an airport counter, the company may bus you to a separate location to pick up the car and perhaps to complete the paper work. Sometimes you may be able to rent a car and pick it up at the airport, but then you have to return it to another location, from which you will be taken back to the terminal—when they're ready, that is.

Such busing operations traditionally have been the way for the bargain outfits to provide low-cost service to those who choose them, and that's fair enough. But it is inconvenient to business people and others who are paying top dollar for their buggies and need the most efficient arrangements. If this concerns you, it would be a good idea to check the policy out in advance with any car company you're considering renting from on any island.

When returning a car, why wait in the hot sun for the lot boy to check you in on a busy day? If he doesn't arrive quickly, leave the key in the ignition, note down the mileage and the gas tank readings yourself, and then don't let anyone send you back outside again for any reason, or you'll end up having to stand in line again. They'll find a way to confirm your notes, if they need to do so. At least that's how we handle it.

Before driving away in a rented car, always make sure it is in good condition. Try the foot brakes and hand brake, the horn, the lights, the turn signals, the windshield wipers, the trunk and door locks, etc. Look for any body damage, and point it out to the agency, asking them to write it down so that you won't be charged for it (unless you took a full-collision waiver, anyway). Check the tire tread, and make sure a jack and a spare tire are in the trunk. Try to drive the car for awhile immediately after you take it; if you notice anything wrong, return it quickly.

If you're traveling with kiddies under three, be sure the agency gives or rents you a car seat. Otherwise you could be fined under Hawaii's Infant Restraint Law.

If you rent a jeep, a beach buggy, or any similar open car, there is usually no place to lock your things up if you want to take a hike away from the vehicle. And one of those fringe-topped "Fun Buggies"—usually a VW "Thing"—might be fun in the sun but a real drag in a serious downpour. Don't assume these Things and other things are genuine "off-road" vehicles, either, unless the agency tells you they are. And you'll probably need a high-wheel-base, four-wheel-drive vehicle (Jeep, Land Rover, or Land Cruiser) if you're planning on bouncing along the beach track around Kaena Point. Frankly, we'd skip it. Going camping?

We wouldn't—at least not on Oahu. If you are, though, on any island, don't tell your U-drive. Give them the name of a hotel, or they just might not let you have the car.

Hawaii on Two Wheels? We know of just one motorcycle and moped outfit that has been in business for some time. This is **Aloha Funway Rentals** (Tel. 942-9696), owned by Brad Skinner, at 1984 Kalakaua Ave., across from Fort DeRussy. (They also rent cars and Jeep-like vehicles.) Moped rates run perhaps $20 for a day, and remember that top speed on these putter-power jobbies is only about 25 mph. Motorcycles run from about $35 to $65 daily, depending on the displacement of your "hog" or "chopper."

Frankly, these two-wheeled rentals are usually rather dubious bargains compared with car-rental rates. Of course if you're a bike addict, that's something else again; you might even consider flying your own over with you.

Motor Homes? Sorry, but we don't recommend using an RV, house trailer, or similar vehicle for visiting Oahu. The Neighbor Islands are a different story, however, and we will cover these where appropriate in the following chapters.

Driving on Oahu. If you drive in your home state, you should not hesitate to get behind a wheel while visiting Oahu, or any of the Islands of Hawaii, for that matter. Laws do not vary from Mainland ordinances, any more than they do among most other states back home. Traffic is no worse than a lot of places—perhaps better than most—and other drivers are usually polite. All in all, we think driving your own route and at your own pace is the best way to experience Hawaii.

However, there are a few local quirks of the open road that should be remembered:

• One annoying traffic characteristic results from the very politeness of the drivers, and it concerns an "after you" philosophy toward left turns. An Island driver whose car faces yours at an intersection will often wait and wave you across in front of him, if he believes you would have to wait a long time to make your left. He means well, of course, but he, like you, cannot see any other car that might be coming up fast in the right lane beside him. We often refuse to make these dangerous turns.

Another aspect of the same practice is the opposite situation, where an Island driver will assume you will do him the same courtesy—giving up your right-of-way to allow him to turn across in front. (He'll also wait until the last second to signal, incidentally, if he uses the turn signal at all.) Try to remember that it's a matter of custom, be careful and patient, and you'll be all right.

• Hawaii residents have had divided highways for much less time than those living on the Mainland. Therefore there is not a well-developed tradition of staying in the right lane except when passing.

• Avoid crossing a solid white line, and never cross a double white line. This law is often mercilessly enforced in Hawaii.

• You may generally turn right, from the right lane, on a red light (after a safety stop), unless you see a sign specifically prohibiting it at the intersection. Similarly, you may make a left turn on a red light (after stopping) from the left lane of a one-way street onto another one-way street, unless prohibited.

• Horn-honking is a general no-no. It's usually not that it's specifically prohibited. It just isn't done in Hawaii, except in emergencies and the most obvious situations, and some people take considerable offense at the sound of a horn. (If you want to meet some Hawaiians badly enough to watch them all pile out of a car and march right up to your window, well, this would be one way to do it!)

• Watch your signs carefully—including arrows on the pavement—for there are a lot of exotic traffic patterns. Kalakaua Avenue in Waikiki, for instance, is one-way *except for buses and bicycles,* which are allowed to go in the opposite direction for a few blocks in a special lane! And some street signs are difficult to see—often obscured by other signs, traffic light control boxes, or whatever.

• Zoris and similar one-thonged Japanese slippers are great and popular footwear in Hawaii. But don't drive while wearing them; they have a habit of catching your control pedals in just the wrong way. We would rather drive barefoot—much safer.

• Try to avoid rush hours (7 to 9 A.M. and 4 to 6 P.M.), especially on main arteries like the H-1 Freeway or the Pali Highway.

• Like many states on the Mainland, Hawaii passed a mandatory seat belt law in 1985. If occupants of the front seat are caught unbuckled, they will each pay a $15 fine.

• About the best overall gas-station highway map of Oahu is the Shell map, but Union 76 has a better street index. For a couple of bucks, though, there's an excellent all-around map called "Travel Map, Island of Oahu" sold at bookstores in Hawaii. For very detailed maps, with every obscure street marked on them, you'll have to pick up the paperback entitled *Bryan's Sectional Maps of O'ahu,* published annually at about $5. There's also an excellent new series of full-color Oahu maps produced and published by James A. Bier, Cartographer, of Champaign, Illinois, selling in Hawaii for about $3.25. If you want to pick up some maps before leaving for the Islands, check on those sold mail order by the Forsyth Travel Library, P.O. Box 2975, Shawnee Mission, KS 66201.

• Addresses can sometimes be quite obscure, especially those on long roads and streets. If you find an address like 66-087 Kamehameha Highway (or "Kam" Highway—a road that almost circles the island), for example, you'll have to look in the front section of the Oahu telephone book to find that that's an address in Haleiwa. Also, few locals know highways by their *numbers*. If you're asking directions, it will be useless to talk about Route 83 for Kam Highway, Route 61 for the Pali Highway, etc.

• Speed limits are generally lower than on the Mainland, a factor that cuts down the auto accident rate. If you're sightseeing at a leisurely pace, however, pull over now and then to allow other traffic to pass.

• Parking meters on the streets are inoperative Sundays and holidays, but municipal parking lot meters are in effect at all times. They range from 25 to 40 cents an hour.

• Since you'll pay for your own fuel in a rental car, look for the cheapest prices. (Gasoline runs about 10 cents a gallon more than on the Mainland.) For example, you'll find discount gas at **Lex Brodie's Tire Co.,** 701 Queen St. About the only gasoline credit cards accepted in Hawaii are Union 76, Standard, and Shell, though many stations do welcome Visa and MasterCard.

• Look out for pedestrians. They have the right of way, especially on the specially marked crosswalks. (Note to pedestrians: Don't count on it!)

Pedicab Service. Shades of Saigon! Persons inspired by the popularity of two-passenger pedal vehicles in the Orient have organized a pedicab, or rickshaw, service in Waikiki. These companies have changed hands a few times, but the service will probably be in operation under some name or other. Last we looked, the fare was $5 for a point-to-point connection (for one or two people) in Waikiki or about $20 to tour the peninsula for one hour. Rates vary widely, however, since each driver is an independent operator.

Hitchhiking. State law prohibits hitchhiking, unless the counties specifically permit it. On Oahu the issue of hitchhiking has been fought back and forth for several years. As of *this writing,* and subject to change and re-change by sudden vote of the City Council, hitchhiking is permitted on Oahu from bus stops only. If you are on the roll of the Society of the Upturned Thumb, you'll have to check with your fellow members for the latest on this soon after arrival.

4. The Hotel Scene—Waikiki Havens to Rural Resorts

Unless you travel to Hawaii during peak seasons like February or August, the chances are good that you will not have any trouble with hotel rooms. Hotelkeeping is an honored and highly competitive profession in Hawaii. And now, as more and more visitors are on repeat trips, these establishments will usually knock themselves out to be helpful to their guests.

Unless you arrive in slack months, like May or October, your arrangements should be hammered down and sealed up as far in advance as possible. Many hotels will not confirm a reservation without at least one night's deposit, and this is as good a guarantee for you as it is for them. If your plane is late, delaying your arrival into the wee hours, the hotel won't have given your room to someone else, since the rent has actually been paid for that night, anyway.

In the past there have been some highly publicized overbooking scandals in Honolulu, usually in February and sometimes January. Most of these tearful incidents concerned large tour groups—few if any independent travelers with reservations were affected—and the groups squawked loudly and with justification when they were shunted to airport hotels and rural rooms far from the ocean and the action.

There are several tiresome technical reasons for this unhappy happenstance, having to do with block booking practices by tour wholesalers before they even sign up their customers. But travelers should realize that nearly all large hotels do overbook, even if they may prefer to call it "compensation for shrinkage."

Hotels will confirm up to 120 percent of their rooms, knowing that generally 30 percent of their customers just won't show up. Therefore, they end up most of the time around 90 percent full. The rub comes when more than a third of the expected no-shows do indeed arrive. The hotel is then admittedly overbooked, and no more playing with words. Although that happens to only a tiny number of Hawaii's 5 million annual visitors, the fuss can reverberate loud and long.

More than 99 percent of the visitors to Hawaii this year will not have hotel booking difficulties, but if you *are* one of the fraction of one percent who arrive holding a confirmed reservation only to discover that your hotel will not give you your room, our advice is not to budge. Do not allow the hotel merely to give you your deposit back. Do not remain satisfied to speak to the desk clerk. Deal only with the manager or the assistant manager on duty, and demand firmly and politely that he find you a room, either in his hotel or a comparable one in some other hotel.

If he will not, you point out, you will immediately describe the situation by telephone to (a) the two Honolulu daily newspapers, (b) the State Office of Consumer Protection, (c) the Visitor Satisfaction Committee of the Hawaii Visitors Bureau, (d) the Better Business Bureau of Hawaii, (e) the Chamber of Commerce of Hawaii, (f) the Hawaii Hotel Association, (g) the mayor's office, and (h) the governor's office.

A traveler and his family who stand their ground with a definite idea of the fairness and justness of their request have a good chance of ending up with a room after all—perhaps even in the presidential suite (at a lower price, of course) if no other accommodation is genuinely vacant.

Choosing a Hotel. Generally, the greatest hotel problem visitors face is simply picking one out in the first place. If you are equipped with advertisements or tourist brochures for some hotels that's fine, but look over the literature carefully. Naturally, any business wants to put its best and most attractive foot forward in a slick, full-color production.

Pamphleteers are on to lots of tricks. Like placing their cameras down low on Waikiki Beach so that a hotel that is actually far across the street looks as if it were right on the sand. Snaps of some scenes in the brochure may not have been taken on the hotel grounds at all. Other pictures of "typical rooms" may be made in the two or three luxury suites in the house. Believe me, the word pictures we have drawn in the following pages are more accurate than many of these fancy publications. Of course we can describe only some of the hotels and condominiums available (and we tend to stay away from condo operations whose apartments are not all managed by a single firm). Nevertheless, we hope that our words will help you find the room you want, even if it is not in one of the specific establishments described.

Not counting the suites, most hotels divide their rooms into three categories, traditionally called "standard," "superior," and "deluxe." There is no legal definition of these terms, however, and some hotels try to avoid "standard" as a pejorative word. Whichever are the cheapest rooms may be considered standard in the usual sense, and there may be several different price levels above that.

The three terms may or may not have anything to do with the room facilities. Often you find all the units in the hotel are exactly alike except that deluxes are high up and face the ocean, superiors might look up and down the beach from a middle altitude, and standards are often low down and/or face the mountains (fine)—or even the parking lot (not so fine). If you choose a lower-floor room, remember that you can be subjected to considerable traffic noise, particularly on Kalakaua or Kuhio avenues in Waikiki.

Seasonal Rates and Packages. Higher winter prices seem to have become established in many Hawaiian hotels in recent years. There is no good reason for seasonal room rates in Hawaii; hotels face pretty much the same level of expenses all year. It's just a question of greed—of being able to get away with it.

Hawaii hotelmen for years fought a proposed special state transient accommodations tax, the revenues from which would be used for public works that would improve the attractiveness of Hawaii to the visitor. The hotels, however, argued that even such a modest add-on would begin to send holidaymakers elsewhere—to Mexico or Europe—for their vacations. But without batting an eye, some of these same executives then arbitrarily tacked on a surcharge of 10 to 15 percent for rooms sold from mid-December through March.

Meanwhile the tax, a relatively modest 5 1/4 percent, finally did pass the Hawaii state legislature in 1986. Unfortunately the revenues from it have not been specifically earmarked for use by the tourist industry, and the rationale now is apparently that the visitor gets away without paying for various state facilities through the state income taxes that residents pay. He does, however, pay the same 4 percent sales tax as everyone else, and this means that beginning Jan. 1, 1987, taxes will total over 9 percent on hotel room rates. Unfortunately, then, this must be added to any hotel rates quoted in this book when calculating an overall vacation budget.

You can't do much about taxes, but if you don't like seasonal rates, consider patronizing those who don't lay on a big winter surcharge. It has been traditionally true that Hawaii hotel rates were significantly lower than those in most large cities and resort areas on the Mainland. In a few cases, that may still be correct, but be warned that with Hawaii's increased popularity with North American tourists over the past year, most hotel room rates have taken a giant leap upwards, particularly on Oahu and Maui. (Bargains can be found more easily on Kauai, Molokai, and the Big Island.) If you do visit Hawaii in the summer, or especially in any "soft" season like May or November, you may be able to find a better deal through a travel agent or by talking to a hotel direct. Even in high season, it never hurts to ask a hotel if there are any packages available for the dates you are interested in. Sometimes special arrangements wrap up a room together with a car rental, air fare, or both.

Dial Hawaii Direct. Many hotels in the Aloha State may be telephoned direct from the Mainland U.S. and Canada on the toll-free WATS system. These "800" numbers are a boon for individual guests or travel agents who want to make instant, accurate reservations. Our list of the latest 800 series for some Hawaii hotels and other businesses appears as an appendix in the back pages of this edition, just in front of the index. Other numbers listed in the main text of this volume are for local telephones, all in Area 808. Even if a hotel does not have a toll-free number, you may still find it worthwhile to pay the long distance bill in order to nail down the best deal you can get. (You can call the reservations people of many WATS-less hotels on Saturdays, when phone rates are very low.)

By the way, once you do have a satisfactory hotel room, remember to be burglary conscious. Valuables should be kept in the hotel safe, unless you draw a unit with the new electronic room safes. When leaving the room for the day or the evening, leave a light on and the radio or TV playing. If you're counting pennies, incidentally, be aware that local phone calls from hotel rooms are sometimes more than 75 cents each. On the other hand, a few hotels don't charge anything at all. The pay phone down in the lobby costs 25 cents, and calls from private telephones are unlimited within the monthly tariffs.

Long-distance calls from hotels can also be expensive. As much as 40 percent may be added on to the actual cost of a call to the Mainland or even to a different Hawaiian island. If this means a lot to you, ask what the markup is before you call. The only way to beat this hotel add-on is to call collect or to use a credit card.

Another way to save on hotel expenses without sacrificing quality: If you're traveling with others—two or three couples together, for instance—look into renting a suite or a condominium apartment. It could be that you'll have a lot more luxurious and commodious living accommodations—sometimes with kitchens—in a one- or two-bedroom suite that charges the same price for up to four or six persons than you would if you took the per-person tabs and applied them to the usual double hotel rooms. Large condominium management organizations in Honolulu (and throughout Hawaii) include Aston Hotels and Resorts (Tel. 922-3368), Colony Resorts (Tel. 523-0411), Great American Management (Tel. 922-3311), and Village Resorts (Tel. 521-7806). Toll-free numbers are listed in the appendix.

Whatever place you choose to call home, you will probably visit some of the other hotels described in this book. The major hotels in Honolulu are almost sightseeing attractions in themselves. You'll certainly be checking out their restaurants and nightclubs, some of which are described more thoroughly in sections 5 and 11 in this chapter.

We have divided Oahu hotels into six main categories, which we think you can use to pick your own headquarters efficiently. In Hawaii a hotel is usually not "just a place to sleep." Much of the atmosphere of your vacation and many of your memories will be affected by your surroundings. You want a hotel that answers your requests with quick, friendly service. But you may also want one with good swimming facilities, gardens, restaurants, showrooms, group activities, or whatever, and perhaps a place where you are likely to meet other people with similar interests. Hotel ambience is not something that can be precisely defined, but you'll find it an important ingredient in your Hawaiian vacation.

Because most people who come to Honolulu prefer to bed down in Waikiki—and because that's where most of the beds *are*—we lead off our discussion with those hotels, separated into four groups of six to twelve establishments each, and in each set we generally slide from our first choice to our last within the group. The categories we have set up are as follows:

- Hotels directly on Waikiki Beach;
- Waikiki hotels near the beach;
- Major Waikiki hotels off the beach;
- Waikiki budget lodgings;
- Big hideaway resorts;
- Other Honolulu hotels outside Waikiki.

As this is a volume of subjective judgment, we regularly get some brickbats on the choice of categories as well as on the entries in each classification. Nevertheless, this is the way we see it as the most helpful to you, the visitor.

And, of course, tell 'em we sent you!

HOTELS DIRECTLY ON WAIKIKI BEACH

"On the beach" means with no argument from anyone. By our definition, a hotel is not a beachside hotel if there is any intervening street or other geographic feature—despite such modern devices as the Ilikai's long footbridge or the lagoon beach behind the Waikikian. In all Waikiki there are less than a dozen choices from which you'll be able to run right out the back door into the ocean.

Of these, the undisputed champion for Waikiki sand-side luxury ever since it reopened is the new version of the old favorite called the **Halekulani** (Tel. 923-2311). The former pre–World War I cottage-style hotel has been transformed into a razzle-dazzle, stair-stepped high-rise with five interconnected wings, each capped by a stylized version of Hawaii's famous "Dickey roof." The new construction also surrounds a couple of garden patios and the spared 1931-model main building:

Friendly welcome by porters who pass your name along to Reception inside; registration accomplished in your own room; ample public areas with two oceanside restaurants, Orchids and the very expensive (and very good) La Mer, both installed in the original, historic structure; pleasant Lewers Lounge piano bar adjoining; afternoon tea served in the Living Room; 30-foot, oval-shaped swimming pool with a million (count 'em) tiles forming a giant underwater orchid; a narrow section of beach just a splash away; rebuilt House Without a Key bar/cafe still near the century-old kiawe tree and still popular for sunset cocktails; several good-quality retail stores on the premises; Hawaiiana and handicraft classes available.

A total of 456 modern, white-toned, wood-and-marble guest rooms, all unusually spacious, filled with fancy furniture and phones, and with ample *lanais;* excellent materials used everywhere; separate sitting areas in all units; deluxe amenities abounding, including hidden color televisions, refrigerators, doorbells, bathrobes, etc.; deep tub and glassed-in shower; 24-hour room service; same-day laundry and dry cleaning; some rooms designed specifically for the handicapped. Regular daily rates for 1987 have been set for (hold onto your spats!) $165 for Garden View, $195 for Courtyard View, $225 for Ocean View, $250 for Ocean Front, and $275 for Diamond Head, Ocean Front. Four categories of suites run from $325 to $650 per day. A new 15-story addition, with smaller rooms, will be under construction this year atop the garage across Kalia Road, and it is tentatively entitled the Waikiki Parc. (Reservations from the Halekulani at 2199 Kalia Rd., Honolulu, HI 96815.) The Halekulani has always mistranslated its name as the "House Befitting Heaven." The real meaning is the "House Befitting Royalty." Never mind. The dowager Halekulani, a gracious lady, is still sorely missed in Honolulu. But long live the new queen of Waikiki!

On the other side of Fort DeRussy from the touristic mainstream is the 20-acre complex of conveniences called the **Hilton Hawaiian Village** (Tel. 949-4321). In this mammoth enterprise, now the largest resort in the state, Uncle Conrad has done his name proud, although the Village actually was the dream of the late industrialist Henry J. Kaiser more than a generation ago. The hotel is a self-contained, 2,500-room resort, yet all within the boundaries of highdensity Waikiki.

We've visited this campus dozens of times, and here's the way we see it: No wider, cleaner, prettier, or safer part of Waikiki Beach than the sand bordering the Village; the only hotel with its own dock and large catamaran; decorative private lagoon (where we wouldn't swim, though); four freshwater pools (closed at 6 P.M., some readers complain); five living towers including the newest, 1,000-room, 35-floor Tapa Tower plus the traditional Rainbow, Ocean, Lower Ocean, and Diamond Head towers; beautiful grounds with ponds, putting greens, gardens, etc.; many trees and plants labeled for easy identification; free classes in Hawaiiana; a total of 9 restaurants, led by the Bali Room; several showrooms including the famous Hilton Dome and swinging Garden Bar; fantastic collection of shops, many in the unusual Rainbow Bazaar, featuring Japanese, Chinese, and South Pacific architecture; major renovations in progress in architecture and landscaping which appear dramatic on the blueprints (see the information kiosk in the Tapa Tower lobby).

Top-price, top-quality rooms this year still in the Rainbow Tower at around $195 double (nicest panoramas are on the Ewa side, but avoid the top—31st—floor with its noisy air-conditioning compressors and elevator mechanism; some readers now say the music down below is too loud on the Diamond Head side); Deluxe rooms at about $150 (high up) and Superiors at $130 or so (lower down), mostly in the new Tapa Tower in the center of the complex, just across from the convention center; Medium category rooms at $105 and Standards at about $90 in the

Ocean Tower and Diamond Head Tower. Some Standards also in the Lower Ocean Tower, with views of the grounds instead of the ocean; color TVs; some with executive refrigerators; none with kitchen facilities; new, modern telephone system; children free in their parents' rooms.

Do not confuse this establishment with the prestigious Kahala Hilton Hotel in the suburbs (see later); it's not the Kahala, but the Hilton Hawaiian Village is a fine hotel among Waikiki beach establishments. About the only criticism we might venture is that we think they should discourage swimming in the often-polluted, if visually charming, little lagoon. It is also quite a hoof for some older folks to all the rest of Waikiki. (Reservations from the hotel at 2005 Kalia Rd., Honolulu, HI 96815.) It remains an excellent bet for the world-famous shoreline.

A beach hotel in the center of the action is the twin-winged, thirty-story **Sheraton-Waikiki Hotel** (Tel. 922-4422), which has been undergoing massive refurbishment and redecoration, the first complete renovation since the hotel opened in 1971. (This work is still going on at deadline, although it should be finished by January, 1987.) It's the flagship of a fleet of five Sheraton-operated hostelries in Waikiki: Breezy entranceway, often cheerfully rattling with thousands of windchime Capiz shells; very large circular lobby now in teal blue and peach colors, with marble and oak accents; new lobby lounge sparkling here; spacious space capsule–shaped swimming pool; smaller, round pool to one side; gorgeous outdoor garden setting for the evening *luau;* a narrow section of sand; a short walk to a wider stretch at the Royal, however; several restaurants including the viewful Hanohano Room (where we've had good luck), reached by the glass-walled outdoor elevator, the very decorative second-floor Kon Tiki Room, reached by an elevating "grass shack," and the Ocean Terrace (where our own buffet was okay); Oahu Bar showroom; Sheraton guest charging privileges also in the nearby Royal, Surfrider, Moana, and "P.K." hotels.

Generally roomy rooms, all with *lanais,* color TVs, etc. (but you pay extra for the closed-circuit movies). We would opt for the oceanfront rooms, $170 for two, preferably in the Diamond Head wing. Oceanfront suites up there run from $250 up. Some high *mauka*-side rooms are considered "partial ocean view" for $150. There are also "mountain views" for $130 and "city-side views" for $115. Charges may be down $10 or so April 1 to December 20. There are no extra add-ons for children in the same room as their parents. (Reservations through any Sheraton or by mail to Sheraton Hotels, 2255 Kalakaua Ave., Honolulu, HI 96815.) The Sheraton-Waikiki is a little too architecturally overwhelming for our personal taste; nevertheless, it's a professional operation in a good position. A solid choice on the sand.

Repeaters gush over the **Royal Hawaiian Hotel** (Tel. 923-7311), also known as the "Pink Palace." Built in 1927 in a stucco Mediterranean style, the hotel is reminiscent of the days when the well-to-do came to Hawaii by ship and then moved into the Royal with their steamer trunks to stay for weeks. Now it's literally under the wing and in the shadow of the next-door Sheraton-Waikiki; both these places and several others around are owned by Japanese industrialist Kenji Osano, but are still ruled wisely and well by a local regency.

High, wide, long, and handsome corridor/lobby; crystal chandeliers downstairs; shiny, black stone floors; lots of places to sit; acres of tall mirrors; an arcade of tasteful shops; famous red-and-gold Monarch showroom usually hosting a top act; sun-blessed Surf Room for dining on the edge of the strand; outdoor Mai Tai Bar and Snack Bar nearby; the beach itself very wide and welcoming at this location; Royal Luau on Sunday nights.

There are vastly varying rooms. All have color TVs and air conditioning, but not all have been brought entirely into the current decade. Our favorites are not the $225 doubles in the architecturally Philistine tower; those might as well be in any other hotel on the beach. Instead, we like the high-ceilinged, wallpapered, old-style oceanview units in the original structure for $185, even though none have any *lanais*. There are some nice garden-view rooms, too, for $135, and some very small mother-in-law quarters ("Standard Garden") for $130. These prices could be down a little in the summer. (Reserve at the Sheraton-Waikiki's address—2255 Kalakaua Ave., Honolulu, HI 96815.) Turning 60 this February, the Royal Hawaiian valiantly maintains an elegant tradition in Waikiki.

Surrounded by the more-or-less flamboyant Sheraton entries, the **Outrigger Waikiki Hotel** (Tel. 923-0711) is the anchor on the local Kelley chain of Reefs and Outriggers. It turns out to be a pleasant, if more conventional, beachside hotel, nicer than it looks from the outside: Lower lobby admittedly a hodgepodge, more like a cheap department store; down there also—Perry's Smorgy, a cafeteria bargain, and the nautical but nice Monterey Bay Canners fish restaurant; very large pool a few steps above a good section of beach; Davy Jones Locker bar for peering under the surface; up the escalator to a very large upper lobby; friendly though busy reception folks; large showroom where the Krush and the Society of Seven have been the alternating groups for years; Malolo Kai dining room in one corner, built of bamboo, mainly; good Chuck Machado Luau outdoors once or twice a week.

We closely inspected three sample rooms: No. 701 was a nice, bright, large standard—officially a "city view," but a drop of the ocean was detectable, too—for about $90 double. No. 1521, a "moderate" (superior), had an excellent view of the sea for around $100. No. 1525, an oceanfront, was terrific with a large *lanai* for about $135. We also saw a small suite (No. 622) that would suit a team of four very well for $190. Many units are similar to these, and there were cheerful, warmtoned furnishings in all. The fifth floor has been designated for nonsmokers. Avoid the noisy first floor. All, of course, have TVs and air conditioning, and many boast refrigerators, coffee pots, etc. We haven't been in since the inauguration of the new Kuhio Club, a hotel-within-a-hotel facility at higher rates on the top two floors. (Reservations from the hotel at 2335 Kalakaua Ave., Honolulu, HI 96815. Remember that there are four or five other Outriggers in Waikiki, but this is the only beachside model.) The Outrigger is developing buoyant personality, and for the right crew she'll sail very well in her class.

The ancient, Victorian **Moana Hotel** (Tel. 922-3111), matriarch of Waikiki, at first seems to have changed little since opening day, March 12, 1901. Not unlike a big, old-fashioned, white-walled summer boarding house, the Moana has only partially succeeded in keeping up with the twentieth century, aided in recent times by the efforts of the Sheraton organization:

Excellent beach location; famous Banyan Court and its centuryold Robert Louis Stevenson tree, now rather unattractive by day, due to the setup for the nighttime show; elegance of the H-shaped building itself detectable behind the junk; Captain's Galley Restaurant in the newer wing; wide hallways, high ceilings, and double doors in the original structure, creating a romantic Old World atmosphere.

There are rooms of widely varying quality, starting at a low double price of $70. (You can be sure most un-air-conditioned models will funnel in the sound from the street or the frenetic nightly Polynesian show.) We would try hard for the $90 oceanfront rooms at the ends of the wings in the Main Building. The anachronistic appendage called the Ocean Lanai building, erected in about 1953 as the old, original Surfrider, offers the only terraces and more air conditioners. The rooms are not bad ($110, $130, and $140), but they're not the Moana, to our way of thinking. (Today's Surfrider has now moved to the Ewa side—see next entry.) Some wayfarers with an archeological bent really dig the Moana, but it helps if they groove on a lot of drums, too.

Joined to the Moana by an interior walkway is today's version of the **Surfrider Hotel** (Tel. 922-3111), and the two are often mentioned together as a single establishment (they share the same phone number): Double-deck lobby similar to the Outrigger; upper one marred by its dual purpose as a parking garage; a noisy escalator nearby; low ceilings; no pool; no guest laundry; ground-floor Beachside Cafe, doubling as a showroom at night; second-level Ship's Tavern restaurant; some dog standard rooms for $110; just so-so superiors with some decent views for $125; ocean-view deluxes, the same size and shape as others, at $140 and

$160. Frankly, we only liked the suites (about $270 by now), although renovations have helped several rooms. Despite its good beachside position, we feel the Surfrider hangs on a high-priced board for somewhat low-wave returns.

The venerable 883-room **Reef Hotel** (Tel. 923-3111, not to be confused with the very similar Moana and Surfrider number!) is fairly cheap for the beach: One of the most jumbled, overcommercial, and constantly crowded lobbies in Hawaii; reception often staffed by harassed clerks; new 40-foot marble and koa wood front desk perhaps improving their mood; wide range of beach services; good swimming pool; some rooms with maintenance and housekeeping deficiencies; recent renovation bringing the best rooms into the present day with refrigerators, personal safes, etc.; the 7th floor now for non-smokers. Some ascetic, viewless doubles may run as low as $60, but we never saw what we'd call a decent double here below about $85. (Try for something more expensive than that.) On the other hand, there's a nice large pool, the beach is good, and there's some free Sunday fun on the sand. If you must have a shoreline, mid-Waikiki hotel at a bargain price, well, this is it. Personally, if we didn't draw one of the new rooms, we might spend the night on the *offshore* reef.

Between the Reef Hotel and the Army Museum, the 100-unit kitchen condo called the **Waikiki Shores Apartments** (Tel. 926-4733) remains etched in our memory mainly as the victim of the Reef's noisy air conditioners. There is almost no lobby, no restaurant, no pool, and virtually no verve to these premises, in our opinion. There's a three-day minimum stay, and maid service is once a week. You could be lucky enough to draw one of the nicer units available at widely varying rates of between $70 and $165 or so. But on balance, we'd skip it.

For the fortunate few, there is the fairly new, 416-unit Army hotel called the **Hale Koa** (Tel. 955-0555), meaning "House of the Warrior," on the grounds of Fort DeRussy. It has some of the most inexpensive doubles on the strand, ranging between about $30 and $70. This vacation headquarters and its satellite facilities are available only to military personnel and their families, and you've got to be able to prove it or you won't even get an ice-cream cone. If you're service-connected, though, scoop it up.

WAIKIKI HOTELS NEAR THE BEACH

Generally speaking, this category covers hotels that are just across the street from Waikiki Beach, except for the Westin Ilikai and the Waikikian, which fit in here because they are just far enough away so we don't call them beach hotels but not removed enough to be "off the beach" either.

The group does not include places that are "just across the street and through another hotel to the beach." These you will find in our "off the beach" listings.

The 39-story, twin-towered **Hyatt Regency Waikiki** (Tel. 922-9292) is another link in the glittering chain that spans the country from Atlanta to Albany, from San Juan to San Francisco, and thence to Hawaii. The block-long, block-wide 1,234-room Gulliver is directly across the avenue from one of the best and most popular public sections of Waikiki Beach:

Mammoth porte cochere with acres of teak and bronze; colossal Great Hall, a 10-story landscaped atrium featuring waterfalls and band concerts; popular Harry's Bar fronting the water; Trapper's, an elegant jazz club, also at Basin Street level; grand stairway plus escalators to the second-floor lobby; separate tour-group entrance off the back street; lobby level also featuring The Colony, A Steak House, with British "Indjah" overtones; another moving stair to the third-stage promenade deck for the dinner-only Bagwells 2424 gourmet restaurant in the Ewa Tower and the Terrace Grille coffee shop in the Diamond Head Tower; tiny outdoor pool there, too, serving better as a lighted fountain at night; footbridges for crossing the Great Hall and admiring the 4,500-pound, 34-foot-high hanging metal sculpture; downstairs again to Furusato, for Japanese dining, or to Spats, an Italian *ristorante* by day and a disco after dark; about 75 different stores on all three levels; private catamaran moored at the beach; top-floor sundecks for Regency Club guests; no general public areas above the third floor, designed that way for greater guest security.

Since there are two towers in the Hyatt Regency, there are two presidential suites, each at this writing renting for $1,200 a day. Eight penthouse suites are perhaps $600, and 68 smaller suites go for around $375. Units on Hyatt's Regency Club floors sell for around $155 to $210, depending on position. Most rooms fall into doubles from $95 a night for "City View" through about $125 for "Mountain View." The "Ocean Views" go for about $145, except for the "Ocean Fronts," which are probably up to $160 by now. Some sleeping units have unusual shapes due to the octagonal architecture. Room designs are in muted tones of beige, peach, and blue. All have couches, plus the usual color TVs, terraces, and other luxury fixtures. But some penny-pinching may surprise you—like having only one reading lamp between two beds. A few rooms are for the handicapped.

Some readers have complained to us about the involved route they must take from the street entrance to get to the room elevators, although most people don't seem to be bothered. And again, because of the two towers, there are two Regency Clubs, two lounges, two concierges, etc. (Reservations from the hotel at 2424 Kalakaua Ave., Honolulu, HI 96815.) For elegant Hyatt-rise living overlooking Waikiki, it's highly recommended.

One of Honolulu's better-known establishments, even if it isn't quite in the center of the action, is the **Westin Ilikai Hotel** (Tel. 949-3811), in the old days featured often in scenes on "Hawaii Five-0." It's within striking distance of the Duke Kahanomoku section of Waikiki Beach via a long, private footbridge, and at the same time it's only a short walk in the other direction to Ala Moana Center. It also nets a reputation as the tennis center of Honolulu:

Viewful position alongside Ala Wai Yacht Harbor; three basic structures, including the Marina Tower Building for longer-term rentals; no grounds or ground floor; most facilities on a sort of main deck above the street and parking garage; programmed fountain with changing patterns and colors at night; free evening entertainment on the mall; a score of shops; four dining rooms including the up-top Champeaux's, reached by outdoor glass elevator, the Pier 7, an up-scale coffee shop, and the Maiko Japanese restaurant; several cocktail lounges; Annabelle's Nightclub; two swimming pools; extensive convention facilities; seven—count 'em—seven tennis courts in three locations.

Some low-down, viewless standards perhaps still $100 for two in the older and noisier Yacht Harbor Building; no ocean views below about $115, best units for $150 or so, with kitchens, in the Y-shaped Tower Building; some of these totaling an unusually large 650 square feet; the $290 suites surprisingly without stoves, but those above (up to $340) with full facilities; reportedly good service throughout the house. A deal to sell the Ilikai recently fell through. (Reservations from the hotel at 1777 Ala Wai, Honolulu, HI 96815.) Probably still a safe bet in any case.

Three blocks farther along Kalakaua from the Hyatt Regency is the well-respected **Hawaiian Regent Hotel** (Tel. 922-6611), also across the traffic from the same beach. The Regent has been locally known not only as a good hotel, but as the home of Honolulu's best restaurant. Now, with its 33-story Kuhio Tower, the establishment has 1,346 rooms, making it the third largest hotel around (after the previously described Hilton and Sheraton):

Excellent physical plant with intelligent landscaping; large open patio with ferns, flowers, and fountains; outdoor stairway in the older, Kalakaua Tower leading to The Third Floor (the award-winning restaurant), The Library (a cocktail piano lounge), and The Point After (a popular disco); the Summery coffee shop and the Garden Court Lounge on the ground floor; pleasant outdoor deck with good-sized pool three levels up; sunsets often visible from there; newer section boasting another pool and terrace bar; the Tiffany Steak House, the Cafe Regent, and a new Japanese-style coffee shop rounding out the restaurants; convenient hospitality suites for guests before check-in or after check-out; new 11-door shopping arcade unveiled in 1986. Ample rooms with good, colorful furnishings; sizable baths and showers, color televisions, and large lanais; handy room safes; best rooms the Oceanfront *Corners* (about $160) as opposed to regular Ocean Front (about $150) and Ocean *View* (about $125), which the corner combines. Free breakfast under some circumstances. (Ask when you reserve.) There's a $5 "winter supplement" through March 31. In the older Kalakaua Tower, avoid any lower room right on the avenue, which one reader told us was "like sleeping in a traffic jam." (Reservations from the hotel at 2552 Kalakaua Ave., Honolulu, HI 96815.) Choose your room carefully, and you'll find this a comfortable, well-run hotel.

The Regent is often confused locally with another entry a block down the street, the **Holiday Inn-Waikiki Beach** (Tel. 922-2511). At 25 stories and 636 rooms, this is the World's Innkeepers' largest in the U.S. A leap across the street from the sand, it's also only a few bounds away from the Honolulu Zoo. Perhaps in honor of its motel roots, it is one of the few inns in Waikiki to offer free guest parking:

Downstairs side-street entranceway with travel desks and the tiny Waiaha Bar; long escalator ride up and up to the brown and yellow lobby and nearly everything else; swimming pool only a splash away from the reception desk; nautical-motif Captain's Table dining room; a doctor and nurse in an office on the premises. Rates start at around $80 for no view or $90 overlooking the pool and run up to $100 and $120 for ocean views. (Like the Regent, rates are $5 more until April, 1987.) Lots of units here offer king-size beds. A child under 12 is free, but add $10 for a third adult. Try for the high floors for less noise and more views. The room furnishings are certainly adequate in this efficiency-conscious operation. (Reserve through the hotel at 2570 Kalakaua Ave., Honolulu, HI 96815, or through any H.I.) We trust that the Inn will remain a dependable Holiday headquarters.

In a jump again to the other side of the Waikiki peninsula, the modest, Polynesian-style **Waikikian Hotel** (Tel. 949-5331) huddles between the Ilikai and the Hilton. (The official name of the hotel is now the Aston Waikikian On the Beach, but no one calls it that.) It has loads of character, although we would never swim in the nearly still-water Duke Kahanamoku Lagoon that forms its "beach" (it doesn't matter, though, because you can squeeze past the end of a fence and stroll over to the sandy shore fronting the Hawaiian Village):

Entrance off busy Ala Moana into the high-peaked "Ravi Lobby"; free Tuesday Mai Tai party under the banyan tree; acres of palm trees and other tropical foliage; good, freshwater swimming pool; locally popular Tahitian Lanai Restaurant; fun and camaraderie usually available in the Papeete Bar.

We like the twenty-year-old part of the Waikikian, with rooms strung out in the four long, two-story wooden Tiki Garden buildings. Each unit there either opens onto the greenery on the ground floor or onto a private lanai on the second deck. The accommodations themselves feature lots of wood, rattan, lauhala mats, overhead fans, sliding louvres, and other South Seas accouterments. Bedrooms in these buildings generally run between about $80 and $90 in winter, and perhaps $20 less than that in summer. Also, four persons may divide up an excellent bargain in the suite (about $170). In general, we don't like the shelters in the newer air-conditioned Tiki Towers building, many of which overlook the parking lot. And in the buildings we do like there may be occasional complaints about revelers noisily departing the hotel's bar and restaurant. (Reservations from the hotel at 1811 Ala Moana, Honolulu, HI 96815.) The Waikikian may be a bit rough around the edges, but many still give it an "A" for atmosphere. Let's hope they leave very good alone.

The **Pacific Beach Hotel** (Tel. 922-1233) is an ambitious entry that falls into the category since the façade of its older section sits directly across Kalakaua from the shoreline:

No-nonsense, solid construction in one high-rise and one higher-rise; gargantuan 280,000-gallon aquarium featured in the newer, 40-story Ocean Tower; two swimming pools; three dining rooms, including the coffee-shoppish Oceanarium Restaurant, the more elegant Neptune Restaurant, and the Shogun Restaurant with Japanese fare; Atlantis discotheque. Total of 850 bedchambers, with patterned bedspreads, radio, and TV; a few kitchenettes in the older Beach Tower; double rates in four categories ranging between $87 for Standards and $135 for Ocean Fronts (a little less from mid-April to mid-December); suite prices from $220 to $425 (with four bedrooms). The hotel also offers free shuttle-bus service to Ala Moana Center and its sister Pagoda Hotel. (Reservations from the hotel at 2490 Kalakaua Ave., Honolulu, HI 96815.) Some overdue facelifting may be undertaken soon. Otherwise, it's a handsome choice along the avenue, at least in the newer section.

A low-budget entry overlooking the beach is the nearby, well-named, and unmistakable **Waikiki Circle Hotel** (Tel. 923-1571), the only cylindrical hostelry in Honolulu. About fifteen stories tall, it provides some views of the beach and mountains that would cost twice as much in other establishments. There are 100 oddly shaped, often hard-used rooms with couches that make up into beds and ample terraces. The baths and showers we saw were cramped. Rates this year will probably run between $35 and $40 double and $20 and $35 single. (Write the hotel at 2464 Kalakaua Ave., Honolulu, HI 96815.) Not bad for the low prices, maybe, and at least you won't get cornered in the rooms.

Next door, the **Waikiki Surfside** (Tel. 923-0266)—not to be confused with the Waikiki Surf—is perhaps for more ascetic voyagers. The oceanfront units at about $45 to $65 double aren't bad; they overlook a banyan tree toward the beach. There are mountain-view models for maybe $40 and some claustrophobic inside cells where the only view you'll get is a foggy one on the TV for about $35. Frankly, we think you may do better in some budget choices farther inland.

Let's hope you are not reading this book in 1988, because we will have much more information in our 1988 edition on the new 575-room **Waikiki Prince** scheduled to open that year. Developed by the Seibu Group of Tokyo, who also put up the Maui Prince Hotel, the new establishment is under construction on the site of the old Kaiser Hospital, 1697 Ala Moana, next to the Ala Wai Yacht Harbor, a block from the Westin Ilikai Hotel. The hotel will have two 28-story towers rising from a five-story base and a large swimming pool in an attempt to make up for its beachless location. Unfortunately, current plans call for it to carelessly obscure the Whaling Wall mural, which has become a Honolulu landmark and a symbol of the Save the Whales movement (see section 6). Protestors can be expected to point out that Japan is also one of the few countries in the world which still allows the open hunting of whales.

MAJOR WAIKIKI HOTELS OFF THE BEACH

There are about a dozen well-known Waikiki hotels that are neither planted right on the sand nor just across the street from it, but are all within easy strolling distance of Waikiki Beach. Some, like the "P.K." and the Beachcomber, are just across the street from other hotels that *are* on the beach. We have taken pains in this group to eliminate discussion of hotels that cater almost exclusively to large tour groups.

The generally trim and neat **Princess Kaiulani Hotel** (Tel. 922-5811) is a favorite of many annual returnees. If you want to sound local, you'll either pronounce it "Kah-ee-oh-*luh*-nee" (glottal-stopping the first two syllables) or else call it simply "the P.K." When it opened in 1956, the 29-story hotel was Waikiki's tallest building. Today it's the only hotel under the Sheraton aegis that is not on the beach, and its guests generally pad along Kaiulani Avenue, cross Kalakaua with the light, and then march through the lobby of the old auntie Moana to get to the shoreline.

Convenient location across from King's Village; L-shaped main building backed by a newer, thirty-story tower; two spacious and colorful lobbies; portrait of the princess herself (on whose former estate the house sits) opposite the front desk; large oval pool just outdoors; lots of greenery in the surrounding garden; slurpy "Beyond-the-Reef" Muzak playing incessantly, even outdoors; courtyard skyline dominated by the Moana, Surfrider, and Outrigger hotels; several restaurants including the American-style Cafe Colonnade, the Japanese-cuisine Momoyama, and the Mandarin-motif Lotus Moon; friendly Kahili Bar and poolside

Orchid Bar; several renovations in the public area continuing through-out the year.

Several different types of accommodations are available at the P.K., starting at $70 for an admittedly too-tiny inside double without view or terrace. But then even those rooms have full air conditioning, color TV, and pretty good furnishings. Others include better mountain views (and *lanais*) at $80, charming King's Village vistas at $95, and poolside pan-oramas at $100. In the tower, mountain and city views have been unified now at around $100, but insist on the fourteenth floor or above at that price. Full-on ocean views (eighth through twenty-ninth floors) sell for $120. Suites are about $160. (Reservations from the Sheraton-Waikiki address.) Heartily suggested for those to whom sleeping near the water's edge is not a must.

Not as conveniently located is the **Outrigger Prince Kuhio Hotel** (Tel. 922-0811), which is at the corner of Kuhio and Liliuokalani avenues in the part of Waikiki they used to call "the Jungle." The 626-room, L-shaped plant is well designed and generally attractive and the rooms have sever-al other features like room safes, refrigerators, and marble bathtubs. Gone are the free newspapers and some other things in effect before the cost-conscious Outriggers took over. Double rates run from about $75 to $120 for most rooms with special top-floor units in the "Kuhio Club" perhaps in the $130 range this year. (Reservations from the hotel at 2500 Kuhio Ave., Honolulu, HI 96815.) It's a little farther than most want to walk from the sands of Waikiki, but an oasis of sorts when you get there.

The **Waikiki Tower of the Reef Hotel** (Tel. 922-6424) is certainly a mouthful of words, and lately they've been calling it simply the Waikiki Tower. Despite the shared name with one hotel and shared phone num-ber with another, the WTOTRH is a self-contained establishment that does not quite qualify as a beach hotel in our book. It sprouted like Jack's beanstalk in the late, lamented garden of a battered brother, the Edgewater, which explains the strange, cutoff look of the swimming pool. But it is not a part of the Edgewater, nor the nearby Reef Towers, nor their aging grandmother on the sand, the Reef. This young sibling is the Cinderella of that otherwise lackluster family.

The rooms are small, and cost-cutting fixtures and furniture have been installed; but all we saw was neat, clean, and comfortable. Even the postage stamp–sized viewless standards have air conditioning and color TVs for two at around $55 this year. Ocean-view doubles are also good buys for about $60 and $65. (Reservations from the hotel at 200 Lewers St.) If maintenance continues high and rates continue low, the Waikiki Tower will continue to stand out as a tall bargain in the neighborhood.

The **Coral Reef Hotel** (Tel. 922-1262), not to be confused with similarly named places, has improved a little under the aegis of Aston Hotels and

Resorts. At 2299 Kuhio Ave., the establishment is now fully air conditioned, with its own rooftop pool. Rates for good-size TV- and refrigerator-equipped rooms run from $53 to $95—extra if you rent the in-room safe. (Reservations from the hotel address above at Honolulu, HI 96815 or through Aston Hotels.) The Coral Reef was almost sold last year; although the deal fell through, that places its future in doubt. We haven't been in recently, either, but it could still be a valid choice this year.

A little farther along Kaiulani Avenue than the P.K. is the second of the three or four (depending on how you count them) Outrigger hotels, the **Outrigger East** (Tel. 922-5353). Unimpressive public facilities; a second-floor lobby that looks like a shopping arcade and sometimes smells of cooking; 25 steep steps up to a prosaic pool; bedchambers, however, much better; nice views above the twelfth floor; several with refrigerators and kitchen sinks; excellent maintenance and housekeeping in rooms and corridors. Standard units at about $55 surprisingly commodious; No. 1722 and similar rooms with a great deluxe Diamond Head view for about $70; suites at $75 to $85 with full kitchens excellent buys for four sharing. (Reservations from the hotel at 150 Kaiulani Ave., Honolulu, HI 96815.) If you forget about your downstairs—and lots of people do—the Outrigger East holds up very well.

Now begins some confusion, for our next choice is another Outrigger, sometimes called the **Outrigger West** (Tel. 922-5022) and at other times referred to as the Outrigger West—Kuhio Wing. (There's also an Outrigger West—Surf Wing; see below.) This one is even farther away from the sand, around the corner on Kuhio Avenue: Tiny but attractive lobby; up the elevator to a nice pool and pool deck overlooking the street; no trees around, however; bar and snack bar next to the pool; again, some nicely kept rooms, most in this entry with complete kitchenettes (another potential money-saver), full air cooling, TV (some color), small *lanais*, etc.; double rates ranging from about $55 to $70. (Reservations from the hotel at 2330 Kuhio Ave., Honolulu, HI 96815.) If you choose your room carefully, you could get a pretty good price for the rewards.

Our last Outrigger now is the **Outrigger Surf** (Tel. 922-5777), sometimes in the past known as the Outrigger West—Surf Wing, even though it is a building or two removed from the Outrigger West—Kuhio Wing along Kuhio Avenue: Small but very neat lobby in browns and greens; poolette just outside; Rudy's Italian Restaurant extending up to the brink; generally viewless standards with B&W TVs, convertible punees, and kitchen facilities at around $55; better superiors perhaps $60 with the same amenities; very roomy deluxe models, some almost suitelike with a *shoji* screen sliding between the bed and the punee at $70. (Reservations from the hotel at 2280 Kuhio Ave.) In general, though, the rooms seemed more stale to us than the other Outriggers.

The White Sands (Tel. 923-7336), at 431 Nohonani St., is undergoing a successful metamorphosis, but primarily to attract members of its time-sharing club. Supposedly it will still take hotel guests in 1987, though, at rates from about $45 to $65, all with cooking facilities. Advance reservations may be limited, but you might snag an attractive unit with a phone call. This pleasant oasis surrounding a cool pool is justly popular and recommendable—if you can get in.

If you can't, **The Breakers** (Tel. 923-3181) has a similar feeling, but in a more frenetic neighborhood at 250 Beach Walk. Doubles around $65 to $70; garden suites much nicer at around $100; all units with kitchenettes. Swimmers like the large pool here.

The **Reef Towers** (Tel. 923-3111), farther inland on the same street, is known as the home of the Polynesian Palace, the club built especially for entertainer Don Ho, but there the fame stops. The house isn't quite as haphazard as its beachside brother, the Reef, but we thought lots of repair and cleaning operations were needed when we trudged through the sleeping areas. Double rates run between about $40 and $60. Ho doesn't play there any more, and we would prefer not to, either.

Another Reef, known as the **Edgewater Hotel** (Tel. 922-6424, same as for the Waikiki Tower), is the last member of a gang of four. On the plus side, it's the home of a good Italian restaurant, and some doubles may be worth the tab of about $40 to $60. But the Edgewater, which is not really at the edge of the water, still seems a little too soggy for us.

WAIKIKI BUDGET HOTELS

There are still decent hotels in the Waikiki peninsula where you can get a good double room for less than $40 a night—sometimes even under $30. Here are a few we explored for this volume.

One of our happiest finds is the generally well-decorated and well-managed **Waikiki Surf Hotel** (Tel. 923-7671) at the corner of Lewers and Kuhio: Convenient bus-stop location in a semiresidential part of Waikiki; small, breezy lobby with leather furniture; usually friendly but often hectic front desk (be prepared to wait); small pool and terrace off to one side; no bar or restaurant; several nice rooms in blues and greens; many with full kitchenettes and large refrigerators; bathroom/dressing rooms with flocked wallpaper.

We inspected four types of rooms and found them to be excellent bargains. Most rooms will probably rent for (depending on height above the ground) between $35 and $45 double this year (without cooking facilities). Some connect with superiors (via both the internal door and a common *lanai*), which rent for about $50 and $55 (*with* kitchenette). Deluxe corner units with all food-preparing amenities go for about $60 for two. The best bargain, however, was a four-person, two-room family suite, renting in different positions for a low of about $55 and a high of about $65. All rooms are fully air conditioned, but TV is an optional extra at additional cost. However, lower-floor units will receive traffic noise perfectly without any rabbit ears. (Reservations from the hotel at 2200 Kuhio Ave., Honolulu, HI 96815.) We didn't explore the East and West Wing extensions, and some readers have recently reported some rooms have not been maintained as well as others. Management has also just taken over responsibility for the neighboring Waikiki Malia Hotel, which we also haven't seen. All in all, we feel the Waikiki Surf is a potential budget bargain, at least in the upper stories. If you don't like your room, by all means ask to be moved to a better one—and tell 'em that's what we said to do.

A fairly short hoof from Kalakaua Avenue, the family-operated **Royal Grove Hotel** (Tel. 923-7691) is a riot of pink on its façade, but mercifully the color scheme changes once you get into the lobby. There's a nice pool out back, and a friendly-looking cardroom with a waiting piano. Bedchambers are in three different constructions. Simple units in the old *mauka* building are very small and clean, have B&W TVs, and sell for around $30 to $35, double or single. Some units there with kitchen facilities go for around $35 to $50. There's more elbow room, air conditioners, color tellies, and kitchen facilities in the newer *makai* edifice for perhaps $45 to $60. In the low, cinderblock poolside units out back are L-shaped quarters with pullman kitchens for $50, which we'd choose if we just *had* to have such a cabana. (Reservations from the Leonard Fong family, Royal Grove Hotel, 151 Uluniu Ave., Honolulu, HI 96815.) Pretty good for the category.

Over at 250 Lewers Street, the 110-room **Coral Seas Hotel** (Tel. 923-3881) is also a possibility: Wide lobby; Perry's Smorgy restaurant entrance nearby; some recent renovations; no swimming pool; some hard-used rooms; few, if any, views; rooms varying between about $25 and $50 double. So-so. One street over, a brother hotel to the Coral Seas is the **Reef Lanais** (Tel. 923-3881), which is also no beauty. Try for a high floor on the Honolulu side. If you can pick up a twin billet here for $35 or so, it may or may not be worth it.

Finally, the **Waikiki Terrace** (Tel. 923-3253) may be the cheapest hotel in town at $26 doubles, $22 singles, but we still call it overpriced for the battered and beaten rewards. Not recommended by us.

THE BIG HIDEAWAY RESORTS

There are only three—and some would say one or two—that fall into this category. These facilities generally represent self-contained vacations, which to a greater or lesser degree are enjoyed far away from the madding crowds.

The best hotel in Honolulu—and perhaps in the entire state—isn't on Waikiki Beach at all. Conveniently sited on its own reclaimed beach on the edge of a desirable residential section is the superprestigious, superdeluxe **Kahala Hilton Hotel** (Tel. 734-2211). To erase any immediate misimpression, the Kahala Hilton, operated by the Hilton International Co., is separate and distinct from the Hilton Hawaiian Village and other hotels owned by the Hilton Hotels Corp. chain. "The Kahala," as it is called locally, has been the home away from home of more kings, presidents, entertainers, etc., than all other Honolulu inns combined. It will knock itself out to give all the luxury and all the privacy that its guests may desire:

Located in the Kahala district, between the Waialae Golf Course (not affiliated) and Waialae Beach; basically two offset, ten-story rectangles with an exterior concrete trellis; balconies brimming over with bougainvillea; thousands of other flowering plants and trees on 6½ acres; specially groomed 800 feet of golden beach with two man-made islets; dolphins and other sea creatures cavorting in a tropical lagoon; 35-by-80-foot oval pool for human freshwater fun; saline waterfall, a favorite wedding backdrop.

Palatial lobby with three giant chandeliers; drinks and tea served there; interior inspired by Hawaiian monarchy-period plantation house; Thai teak parquet floors; understated, high-quality furnishings and artworks in the public areas; about 10 good shops nearby; prize-winning, orchid-filled, though windowless Maile Restaurant belowdecks; Maile Terrace (for Saturday and Sunday brunch) overlooking the lagoon; beachside Hala Terrace restaurant, also used as a supper club (perennially featuring Danny Kaleikini's show); poolside kiosk for sips and snacks; Plumeria courtyard cafe off the lobby; tiny offshore islet available for gourmet picnicking; six-court Maunalua Bay health and tennis club a short shuttle away; one-hour catamaran sails; new "reef excursion" cruise past the coastline homes of Honolulu's rich and famous.

There are 370 rooms, including 33 suites. Most are in the main structure, but 84 are in the cottage-style Lagoon Terrace near the dolphin playground. Bedchambers, about half with *lanais,* feature tasteful but muted color schemes. You'll find excellent furnishings including plenty of chairs, lamps, sofas, a desk, color television and radio, refrigerator, and the "his and her" bathrooms (he can mix drinks, shave, shower, etc., while she tubs, makes up, or does her nails in the opposite side). There are no kitchens in the units, but room service is a proud feature of the Kahala.

Daily rates are certainly high, and most depend more on position than facilities. In 1987 the $155, $175, and $195 rooms generally have mountain views. (Below $195 are without *lanais*.) Ocean or Lagoon views run from $215 (no balcony) to $310, and beachfront bedrooms are $355. The junior suites by the lagoon are $395. One-bedroom suites begin at $465. Two-bedroom suites cost $840, except in the Lagoon Terrace, where they are $1,120. The Presidential Suite is $960 with one bedroom or $1,270 with two bedrooms. (All suites are the same price for up to four persons.) Special packages are available.

The Kahala Hilton bases its reputation mainly on service, and many guests are repeaters. The house keeps records on any quirks of its residents so as to be better able to welcome them next time, and it provides unexpected homey touches like pineapples and newspapers. (Reservations from the hotel at 5000 Kahala Ave., Honolulu, HI 96816.) If you have to worry about the money, the hotel is at least an interesting tourist attraction. But to those who can well afford the outlay, there is no other place on Oahu worth considering.

The 486-room **Turtle Bay Hilton** (Tel. 293-8811), a Hilton Hotels Corp. contender, seems a little like a giant Waikiki hotel that was lifted bodily and then plunked down on a roughish piece of oceanfront land on a breezy peninsula on the North Shore, a full hour's drive from Honolulu. There's a nice piece of beach, and it is the only Oahu hotel both right on the sand and with its own golf course. Two cool pools, one large and one small; ten lighted tennis courts; three-mile jogging path; horseback riding; two restaurants; shuttle service to Honolulu; dune-buggy tours; nicest accommodations in the low-rise, fridge-equipped cottages (about $150); fares in the main three-spoke structure from around $90 to $135, depending on view and position. (Recheck these price estimates later.)

The Turtle Bay, formerly known as the Kuilima and planned as the nucleus for a whole new 800-acre resort, is owned by the Prudential Insurance Company. Prudential first assigned Hyatt to polish this outback piece of the rock. Now, under Hilton management, maybe it will become a gem, and maybe not.

The third establishment in this category, the **Sheraton Makaha Resort** (Tel. 695-9511)—way out in the boonies on the Waianae Coast, 45 miles from Waikiki—is certainly "far out" in that sense. The area is marginal, at best, and some readers have not felt welcomed by their neighbors. Golfers, of course, go for the excellent championship course surrounding the hotel, and readers who said they never left the campus during their entire stay tell us they liked it a lot. Rates holding in the $80 to $125 range this year. To us it seems an island of peaceful luxury surrounded by a sea of geographical and social uncertainty.

OTHER HONOLULU HOTELS OUTSIDE WAIKIKI

Of this final group of seven hotels, the first four are often thought of as Waikiki Beach hotels, even though they are far along the shoreline by Diamond Head. Then there are two in the Ala Moana area (within striking distance of the shopping center), and we wind up with another one in central Honolulu.

The **Colony Surf Hotel** (Tel. 923-5751), actually a condo, and its next-door companion, the **Colony East,** have been favorites with some of the "in" crowd for years: Main building in an excellent, beachside location way up by the crumbling Natatorium; a neighbor, too, to the exclusive Outrigger Canoe Club; elegant but very small marble- and mirror-walled lobby; famous and very French restaurant, Michel's at the Colony Surf, serving three meals; superhip and megafun dining in Bobby McGee's Conglomeration in the Colony East; no swimming pool, but a nice piece of beach.

Units in both buildings described as "one-room suites" with fully equipped kitchens; ample living areas (*very* large in the Colony Surf), with two queen-size beds and color TV; the Surf featuring 25 feet of windows, but no balconies or air conditioning; the Colony East rooms with a small *lanai*, plus air conditioning; all apartments well decorated, mostly in cool blues and whites. Rates depend on position and view, but we doubt that there are really any *bad* views from these two buildings. In the Colony Surf they range from $155 to $260 in 1987, and in the Colony East from $90 to $130. We didn't notice it, but the *Consumer Reports Travel Letter* said to avoid the lower two floors in the Colony East because of noisy ventilators. (Reservations to the hotel at 2895 Kalakaua Ave., Honolulu, HI 96815 or through Colony Resorts.) All together, very, very nice for the type.

Much improved in recent years is the **Diamond Head Beach Hotel** (Tel. 922-1928), at 2947 Kalakaua Ave. Gradually pyramiding, fifteen-floor pink façade; sandy yard in back; short walk on the seawall to the genuine beach; friendly reception at a window on the walkway; total of 53 units in five types, most with two double beds, a few with twin single beds, and some with one queen-size bed. All are well decorated with new furnishings and equipped with terraces, TVs, and refrigerators. Double rates will run from about $75 to $105 for most rooms, $125 to $200 for suites. Try for a high unit; the floor space may be a little smaller but the view is much better. (Reservations from Colony Resorts, Inc., 733 Bishop St., Honolulu, HI 96813.) We keep getting letters of praise for this reasonably well-polished gem, although the whole place is up for sale—$11 million was the asking price the last time we looked.

Also back up to snuff is a former favorite, the **New Otani Kaimana**

Beach Hotel (Tel. 923-1555), not far away. For years this was the head-quarters of visiting college professors and a temporary haven for returning residents, and it's becoming that again under its Japanese professional management: Cheerful, open lobby; a good section of beach outside; charmingly sited Hau Tree Lanai restaurant a breezy choice for lunch or dinner; Japanese-style Miyako Restaurant on the second floor; some popular shops, including Splash, where our daughter says she buys the best bathing suits; 156 recently redecorated but sometimes small and viewless rooms; some studios with kitchens; 18 newer luxury suites wel-come additions; wildly varying rates between about $66 and $130, or up to $180 or so for the best of the junior suites. "It has more personality than the concrete monsters in Waikiki," Janice Lawrence of Carmichael, Calif. wrote us. (Reservations from the hotel at 2863 Kalakaua Ave., Honolulu, HI 96815.) Choose your accommodation carefully, and you, too, may be pleased with the New Otani life breathed into the old Kaimana Beach.

Between Waikiki and downtown Honolulu, and next door to the shop-ping center whose name it bears, is the 36-story, 1,268-room **Ala Moana Americana Hotel** (Tel. 955-4811), not to be confused with the Moana in Waikiki. The place often advertises itself as "Nearest the Fun," and if your fun is shopping, that's certainly true. (There's even a special walk-ing ramp between the hotel and Ala Moana Center.) It's not, however, "at the entrance to Waikiki Beach," another piece of Madison Avenue hyperbole, although it is only a stroll to a city-owned beach park:

Busy location on Atkinson Drive; free shuttle bus to Waikiki; spacious lobby featuring lots of artwork and several shops of its own; dozens of meeting rooms on two floors; third-floor pool and deck; 24-hour coffee shop; Le Café for pastries and cakes; the Summit Supper Club way up on the roof; and Rumours, a popular hard-rock den. The rooms, most of which run approximately $65 to $110 for two, are ordinary but cer-tainly adequate. We recall decorations in brown and beige, quilted spreads on twin beds, radios, color TVs, nice baths, and good views from the higher floors. (Reservations from the hotel at 410 Atkinson Dr., Honolulu, HI 96814.) A perennial stalwart in the commercial area.

Two or three blocks farther *mauka* is the **Pagoda Hotel** (Tel. 941-6611), in a high-rise residential area and under the same ownership as Waikiki's Pacific Beach Hotel, and with whom it shuttles a bus. Neat lobby of bamboo, wicker, leather, straw, and a striated shag rug; tiny ovoid swim-ming pool just outside; waterfall and carp pond just beyond, surround-ing the well-known "floating" restaurant; clean but generally uninspiring bedchambers in the main building, none with balconies, but all with kitchen facilities, running between about $50 and $55 double; best bar-gains across the street in the Pagoda Terrace, maybe $45 for two, $55 for a one-bedroom family apartment holding four, or $75 for the two-bedroom units holding six. Not bad for the price.

What you might call a very basic, no-frills, but still clean and decent establishment is the **Nakamura Hotel** (Tel. 537-1951) in a nowheresville location at 1140 South King St. Nevertheless, it is on a bus route, the cinderblock building is neat, and most of the orange-and-white rooms are air conditioned. Rates? Maybe $25 for singles or doubles, and less for a longer stay. (But recheck by phone first.) Okay for the outlay.

Although we haven't had the experience ourselves, we finally know someone who recently stayed at the **Mokuleia Beach Colony** (Tel. 637-9311). It's about as far out from Honolulu as you can get on Oahu, next to the Polo Grounds on the North Shore. It consists of about 50 low-rise kitchen condo units in a dozen cottages next to a beach in an area where no one expects you to stay. This, alone, could commend it to some folks. There's a pool, tennis court, etc., amid traditional tropical foliage. One-bedroom units with all amenities run from $350 to $450 per week. (Reservations from the hotel at 69-615 Farrington Highway, Wailua, HI 96791.) Our friends enjoyed themselves there, but we didn't see them very often!

5. Dining and Restaurants on Oahu

There are few things so personal as a taste in food. Some travelers are always adventuresome—ready to try every strange new dish, no matter how exotic, haggis horrid, or squid squishy, whether the morsel is dead or alive, and regardless of how long it has been in its particular state of mortality.

Others, of course, approach their vacation fare with the grim determination that whether in Hanapepe or Dar-es-Salaam, they will root out, if it exists, the only underground ground beef and mashed potatoes joint within a hundred-mile radius.

We fall somewhere between those extremes, but have broadened our dining interests in both liberal and conservative directions for this volume. We want you to know where to look for the raw fish and where you'll find the hot dogs. Whether you regard the information at either end of the culinary spectrum as warning or invitation is up to you.

If we do lean a little toward the unusual, well, that's what this book is all about. Throughout Hawaii you will enjoy special foreign accents in the food as much as in the modes of dress and in the customs of the people. It's simply another attraction that makes a stay in the Islands more stimulating than another trip up to Moose Lake.

Local Specialties. Now there is no such thing as absolutely genuine

Hawaiian cuisine prepared today. This is true whether you are talking about the diet of the ancient Polynesian Hawaiians (who ate dog, among other "authentic delights"), or whether you mean simply a particular style of cooking that is strongly preferred today by the general Island population.

The comestibles consumed by Hawaii residents of all racial extractions during this period in history are largely American, and it's a trend that becomes more true with every generation. Some dishes do survive in ethnic purity. *Poi* is one of these. It does *not* taste like paste, by the way. There are different kinds of *poi*, too—bland, sour, thick, thin, fermented, but all made from well-pounded taro root. *Poi* is an acquired taste, like mashed potatoes, and you are not likely to fall in love with it at first smack.

Most traditional Island favorites are not so historically and culturally authentic, representing instead a polyglot of palates. Take *saimin*, for example—and you should try it at least once. A type of noodle soup flavored with chicken, beef, or shrimp and garnished with meat slices and chopped onions, it was invented in the last century by Orientals living in Hawaii. Islanders often stop briefly at a little hole-in-the-wall *saimin* stand and order a bowl or paper container for about 75 cents. It's usually served with one of those funny-looking porcelain or plastic Chinese spoons and a pair of wooden chopsticks. You're supposed to use that spoon to slurp up the broth, and the chopsticks are for the noodles. Of course there's no law against using the spoon for the noodles.

There are lots of *saimin* stands in Honolulu, but few in Waikiki, although some regular restaurants in Waikiki also have *saimin* on their menus. You can even get it at McDonald's, now, but according to *Honolulu Advertiser* writer Mark Matsunaga, who's as *saimin*-savvy as they come, the best local flavor is served up by **Washington Saimin Stand** at 1117 South King St., between Pensacola and Piikoi streets.

A second popular "Japanese" plate (and, unlike *saimin*, the basis of a full meal) is found in restaurants of many types throughout the Islands. It is steak *teriyaki*, or *teriyaki* beef. Sometimes it is known as just plain "teri." This beef is first marinated in a saucy combination of *shoyu* (soy sauce), *sake*, sugar, ginger, and garlic, and then broiled. It's delicious, and an absolute must for visitors. But again, beef *teriyaki* is almost a Hawaiian adaptation; although the *teriyaki* recipe is known and enjoyed in Japan, it is usually applied there to fish, whereas this is virtually never the case in Hawaii. There are even "teriburgers," nowadays, and they are usually darned good, too!

Teriyaki is so ubiquitous and generally well prepared all over Hawaii that we never order it at a genuine Japanese restaurant. There we would choose a more authentic imported dish instead. As a rule, delicious beef *teriyaki* may be found at any of the good American steak houses on Oahu, listed right in there alongside the prime rib and the New York sirloin.

Another important "steak house" specialty bears a Hawaiian name— *mahimahi* (pronounced "*mah*-he-*mah*-he"), and this one is a fish. A strong local favorite, when broiled or otherwise prepared properly *mahimahi* certainly deserves its popularity. Don't become confused and saddened if someone tells you the English name for *mahimahi* is "dolphin." This is *not* the charming, personable porpoise you see performing tricks at Sea Life Park. The dolphin you *eat* (that is, *mahimahi*) is a genuine fish, not an aquatic mammal. It's quite devoid of any sympathetic temperament or the smiling visage you find on the other kind of dolphin.

The lust for *mahimahi* among Islanders is so intense that the demand for it long ago outstripped the supply available in local waters. Most *mahimahi* consumed in the state today has been caught off Taiwan, Japan, or perhaps Ecuador, and then quick-frozen and shipped to Honolulu. When thawed and broiled this frozen *mahimahi* is usually still very good. Some expensive restaurants, such as Nick's Fish Market and The Third Floor, do offer the genuine island-fresh variety, and it does have a definite gustatory edge on the imported stock. But then it darn well ought to for a price tag that can run more than twice as high.

To *saimin*, beef *teriyaki*, and *mahimahi*, the three "musts" in the culinary portion of a Hawaii vacation, some would add still a fourth specialty— *kalua* pig.

This Hawaiian fresh-pork preparation is the center of the *luau*, and it is almost the only thing about that traditional Hawaiian feast that is sometimes concocted in the centuries-old manner. The entire animal, eviscerated but loaded with salt, steams for hours or all day in an underground hot-rock oven called an *imu*. It's a very salty dish, and there's where the *poi* comes in handy—to chase the pig with, and contrast favorably with that salty shredded meat.

If you don't agree that *kalua* pig is *ono-ono*, never mind. Most *luaus* serve plenty of other food, too. In a Waikiki hotel *luau*, you may find such familiar fare as baked ham or broiled steak, garnished with pineapple. (The latter, incidentally, is a recently arrived fruit that the old Hawaiians never saw.) For that reason, a hotel *luau* costs over $30 per person as compared with prices about half that for a church-sponsored *luau*, which makes almost no concessions to Mainland taste habits. (More about *luaus* later.)

Other Favorites. Our personal additions to the ethnic food list might be some Portuguese contributions to Island preferences. First, there is Portuguese sausage—mild, medium, and hot. You can eat it for breakfast, but it's also used as a base for an excellent bean soup. There is Portuguese sweet bread, which is sometimes still known as *pão dulce*. Then there's a stomach bender called *malasadas,* made of deep-fried dough that is later dunked in sugar. (Sometimes called "Portuguese doughnuts," *malasadas* are not unlike the *zeppoles* of Italy or the *bunuelos* of Spain.)

Other goodies that, like *saimin,* belong in the Japanese snack category are *sushi* (singular and plural), little vinegared rice-clump concoctions that are nearly as popular in Hawaii as they are in Tokyo. The boiled rice is tossed with Japanese vinegar, sugar, and salt, and then rolled up with tiny pieces of vegetables or fish mixed through it. Usually they are first formed into cylinders, held together by seaweed, and then sliced into sections about one inch thick. Eaten with the fingers, they are delicious and a real lunchtime bargain, too.

You may also hear a lot about another tidbit whose name, at least, is Hawaiian—*manapua.* But this is actually an adaptation of a Chinese dumpling specialty called *dim sum.* You often find *manapua* at the same shops that sell *saimin.* The original *dim sum* comes in more than a dozen different varieties. You'll find them in their purest forms at certain Chinese restaurants. Two favorites are **Yong Sing** at 1055 Alakea St., downtown, and **China House,** at the top of the ramp at 1349 Kapiolani Blvd., near Sears at Ala Moana Center.

The closest to *manapua* among these Chinese recipes is *char siu bao* (*bao* dumpling stuffed with *char siu*—sweet roast pork). Some other popular *dim sum* include steamed bread dough, coconut *bao,* curry chicken turnover, crabmeat *fun goh,* and chicken or shrimp *siu mai.* Yong Sing and China House both serve other, more familiar, Cantonese Chinese dishes too, so ask for the special *dim sum* menu when you come in.

There's a third *dim sum* restaurant in town, **Fat Siu Lau** at 100 North Beretania St., in a corner of the Cultural Plaza. There they serve *dim sum* Hong Kong–style, which makes choosing easier and faster. No menu is involved—you pick the ones you want from a circulating cart. Don't worry; they're all delicious!

While in Hawaii you'll probably hear a lot about "having *pupus*" before dinner or with cocktails. The word literally means "shells," but it is used idiomatically for hors d'oeuvres. In fact, *pupus* can mean snacks of any kind—maybe butterfly shrimp, pieces of *char siu,* some Korean meatballs, barbecued spare ribs, crisp *won ton,* or even just plain peanuts to go with your beer.

One innocent-looking little dish you may be given automatically as a *pupu* at some bars is *kim chee.* If so, watch out! It looks like nothing more than a clump of day-old tossed salad, but it's a super-hot Korean concoction that may remove the roofs of unwary mouths. This pickled *won bok* (Chinese cabbage) takes a lot of getting used to. We rather like it now—in moderation—but it took years for us to come around. Made with garlic and red-hot peppers, *kim chee* has a way of hanging around your breath for hours, and therefore it's something of a socially controversial product.

Now, what about your raw fish? That's simply a Japanese appetizer called *sashimi* (not to be confused with the previously discussed *sushi*). Usually *sashimi* are very thin slices of fresh tuna. Using chopsticks, you dip them into a mixture of *shoyu* (soy sauce) and hot mustard or in another special sauce. Strangely, *sashimi* has no "fishy" odor or taste. When made from *ahi* or *aku*, two kinds of local tuna, it feels like and has the flavor of tender beef. *Raw* beef, of course.

The specialties discussed so far cross several ethnic lines—Hawaiian, Chinese, Japanese, Portuguese, and Korean. Of course, such American snacks as popcorn and hot dogs will also be found in profusion throughout the Islands, and are beloved by everyone. In fact, you'll generally see more Orientals and Polynesians than anyone else in the neighborhood McDonald's.

The other popular dishes of Hawaii are taken up in conjunction with the different restaurants that follow. We have divided our listings into separate categories. You'll find some of Honolulu's most famous restaurants covered in the Continental/French group, of course, but remember that the capital leads the country in its choices of Pacific and Eastern specialties. It is in these that you will find the extraordinary flavors associated with living in the Islands.

Listed alphabetically, here are the categories into which we have divided our Oahu dining experiences: American/Cosmopolitan (including steak houses), Chinese (Cantonese and Mandarin), Continental/French, Greek, Hawaiian, Indian, Italian, Japanese, Mexican, Seafood Selections, and Thai. Following these, we will wrap up the major portion of our gastronomic grouping with a discussion of a few well-known coffee and snack shops and some unusual or out-of-the-way spots.

Where Are the Restaurants? You'll find places to dine out or to chow down all over the island of Oahu. Many top restaurants are, of course, in the major hotels in Waikiki and elsewhere. The Sheratons, the Hyatts, the Hiltons, etc., are guaranteed to have dining rooms which are as popular with Hawaii residents as with visitors.

There are also many restaurants in shopping centers. In Waikiki, for example, that would include several in the Royal Hawaiian Shopping Center, the Waikiki Shopping Plaza, the International Market Place, and the Kuhio Mall. In the area just out of Waikiki along the shoreline, you'll find major restaurants in Eaton Square, the Ala Moana Shopping Center, Ward Centre, and Ward Warehouse. A vast new complex of nine restaurants may be open by now at One Waterfront Plaza, under construction at this writing on Ala Moana near South Street.

Some atmospheric restaurants beckon from the old section of Downtown Honolulu. With only a few exceptions, though, these are unfortunately open only for lunch.

Outside of Honolulu and Waikiki, restaurants are spread wider apart, established sometimes in their own buildings and sometimes within other business structures. Again there are some addresses in shopping centers, but their numbers are fewer and they tend to appeal more to residents of the immediate neighborhood. On the Windward side (Kailua, Kaneohe, etc.), and on the North Shore, however, there are several atmospheric and delicious choices. So at the very end of the section, there is a brief description of some rural Oahu restaurants under our "Kitchens in the Country" heading.

Money and Prices. We think an expensive restaurant in Honolulu is one that runs $25 or $30 per person for dinner. We do not imply that such an establishment is *too* expensive. In fact, you'll usually have to pay those prices to experience the city's best culinary offerings. If the same place is also open for lunch, you probably won't get away for under $15 or so for a midday meal.

In general, we consider a moderately priced dinner as something in the $15-to-$20 neighborhood. (Of course this will vary; $15 or more for, say, a Chinese or Mexican meal—which often costs much less—would certainly be thought expensive.) A moderately priced lunch, in our view, is one that runs under $10.

Although it is less than convenient and not as much fun for many travelers, one way to eat well on a budget is to take your big meal of the day at some beautiful and delicious dining room at noon or in the early afternoon, and then just get by on a snack in the evening hours. Visitors who have rented hotel rooms with kitchen facilities can do even better by preparing something simple upstairs, and then using the resulting savings to help them take in a Hawaiian show later in the evening, or to pay for some cruise or sightseeing tour the next day.

By the way, if you are a credit-card addict it might be helpful to know that in Hawaii there seem to be many more restaurants, etc., that accept the bank-issued plastic such as Visa and MasterCard than prestigious membership accounts like American Express and Diners Club. Diners especially seems to be going out of style in Hawaii restaurants. Out-of-town checks are sometimes hard to cash in a restaurant, but traveler's checks (in U.S. dollars) are welcome nearly everywhere (although a minimum purchase may be required).

What to Wear for an Evening Out. The dress in Hawaii restaurants—even for dinner—is usually informal. Women may wear their muumuus, if they wish. Coats and ties are okay but seldom required for men. A nice aloha shirt or other neat open-neck model is fine. And wherever you go, please tell 'em we sent you. (You won't get a better price, but it will mark you as a discriminating traveler who keeps us advised of your successes and failures.)

AMERICAN/COSMOPOLITAN RESTAURANTS

Restaurants in this group cannot really be characterized by cuisine—at least not beyond the obvious specialties turned out by steak houses. Therefore our preferences in this collection often include what might be called the most "fun" dining in Honolulu. These are places that seem to operate with an overall style and flair, even if the type of cooking falls into no particular or exclusive ethnic pattern. (Unless otherwise noted, always reserve for dinner at the following addresses.)

The **Banyan Gardens** (Tel. 923-2366) has become a low-rise oasis at 2380 Kuhio Ave. in Waikiki. Here, in the middle of the concrete jungle, someone has configured a countrified, outdoorsy dining area that is tasteful and tasty at the same time:

Convenient location at the corner of Kuhio Avenue and Kanekapolei Street; waterfall in the garden and live Hawaiian music in the bar combining to mask the traffic noises; a peaceful artificial stream apparently flowing through the property; seating in two or three open-sided pavilions; tables decorated with fresh flowers and pink covers; eclectic menu that includes several spicy Chinese wok specialties; Osso Bucco and Cashew Chicken our own lucky choices; good service from beginning to end; most entrees in the $15 range. An enjoyable evening for the price.

One of our old favorites continues to be **Horatio's** (Tel. 521-5002). Just across Ala Moana Boulevard from the Kewalo Basin cruiseboat docks, the place is upstairs at the Ewa end of the Ward Warehouse shopping complex. Inspired by Admiral Horatio Nelson, the decorations are naturally nautical. On one luncheon voyage we enjoyed the Yardarm, an open-faced sandwich with chopped beef, mushrooms, tomatoes, zucchini, and Swiss cheese. Another in our crew enthused over the shellfish *sauté* and a third member of the gang gobbled up every ounce of the Admiral's Topside Broil, a thinly sliced flank steak.

Don't think of disembarking without dessert. Our favorite is the Burnt Cream, a caramel custard like we've never had before. (Ask for the recipe.) Most meals at Horatio's have been running in the (cross your fingers) $18 to $19 range, but we believe its continued popularity could force prices up to the crow's nest. At this writing it has some unusual reservations policies. Despite the mob scene often encountered at the gangplank, we still give this admiral his four stars.

Another establishment where the quality of the fare survives pretty well despite a far-out decorating scheme is closer to Waikiki—in fact, just up Kalakaua Avenue in the Colony Surf Hotel. **Bobby McGee's**

Conglomeration (Tel. 922-1282) is filled with a $300,000 inventory of hodgepodge you'd associate with a large, overfull antique and cast-off store scattered throughout five dining rooms. A couple of these, like the Indian Room or the Library, are designed in somewhat of a theme, but the others—the Victorian, the East, and the West rooms—are, well, merely a conglomeration.

Excellent service by waiters and waitresses in every costume imaginable, from a wild Wyatt Earp and a sappy Superman to flip Florence Nightingale and a hip Cleopatra; all-you-can-eat salad fixings from the bathtub; all-you-can-slurp soup of the day from atop the ancient wood stove; free potatoes (baked or French) or rice with everything. Our party enjoyed the prime ribs and the shrimp kabob, but the menu may be different this year. There are no windows and nothing to look at, save the nutty things on display in the joint itself. Although the food is good, it is not *haute cuisine*. Perhaps it's more enjoyable for a gang than a couple.

One of the lovelier and more expensive restaurants in Waikiki is **Canlis** (Tel. 923-2324), one of the few Honolulu restaurants where coat and tie are strongly encouraged. (They place you in a second-rate room if one man in your group hasn't placed his neck in a noose.) The Canlis chain was founded in Honolulu about 30 years ago, and it used to be one of the best restaurants on the island; many faithful old-timers return every time they are in town. The nicest room is the one with the chandeliers that looks like a church, and the best table is the first banquette upstairs on the left. Although the famous Canlis' salad is still good (as are some of its just desserts), the main dinner courses were a disappointment in some way to each one of our group of four. You may disagree, and we once did have a delicious lunch in the establishment.

A very Polynesian theme is carried by the torch-lit old favorite called the **Tahitian Lanai** (Tel. 946-6541), just off the beach in the back of the Waikikian Hotel. Try for a table in one of the little thatched huts along the walkway. The place is cosmopolitan with local overtones. The Hawaiian Dinner is pretty good for its type, if you want to give that a whirl. The Tahitian Style Chicken, served in a coconut, was more our own speed. There's also a good shrimp dish with garlic sauce. Some call the Tahitian Lanai a little corny, but what sarong with that?

Trader Vic's (Tel. 923-1581), in the International Market Place, is very similar in tone, except that there are fewer "American" items on the menu and more Americanized Chinese dishes. The long-gone original Trader Vic's used to be on South King Street, but they trucked over tons of the same junk and installed it here. Our meals weren't bad in the new Vic's.

Yet another of these Cosmo/Polynesian places is located in the Sheraton and is called **Kon Tiki** (Tel. 922-4422). Ride up in its "grass shack" elevator to a dramatic "outdoors-indoors" layout. We passed up the Lobster Dean Martin, but the sweet-and-sour victuals we sampled were tasty and reasonably priced. Since then, however, some readers have complained of s-l-o-w service. The place may be remodeled this year.

As good or better than the previous three entries, but far from the usual tourist haunts, is the open-air, Hawaiian-style, 40-year-old **Willows** (Tel. 946-4808). It's in a lovely inland setting under the willow trees by a spring-fed Hawaiian fishpond in an otherwise prosaic neighborhood at 901 Hausten St. This thatched-roof emporium has now expanded its menu to include several Continental classics.

Note the special Hawaiian entertainment and local foods for Thursday lunches and Sunday brunches. Also there is the "Kamaaina Suite," a separate second-level area that is a sort of a restaurant within a restaurant. It even has a separate chef, specifically Kusuma Cooray, F.C.F.A. (C.G.). All the upstairs seven-course meals are over $50 at this writing (plus tax and tip), and each table is sold only once per night, so there is never any rush. If they keep Ms. Cooray over the coming years, the top floor, at least, may remain one of the city's top dining rooms.

Another choice with a beautiful setting plus reasonable seafood and Japanese-American cuisine is the **Pagoda Floating Restaurant** (Tel. 941-6611), attached to the Pagoda Hotel at 1525 Rycroft St. Order something simple, take your time, and don't forget a stroll through the garden to admire the colorful carp. (This "floating restaurant" doesn't *really* float, by the way.)

In the "theme" category (like Bobby McGee's or Horatio's) is a Kapiolani Boulevard entry, **Victoria Station** (Tel. 955-1107), a branch line in the successful Mainland train chain. Crammed with railroad accessories and English souvenirs, Victoria Station also has portions of actual trains—strangely American, not British—tacked onto the building. Specializing in prime ribs (prices between $15 and $20, depending on the weight) and barbecue ribs (perhaps $14 for all you can eat), this wood-burner is generally a smooth express at the right fare. Once you get in, you can keep up full steam in round trips to the salad bar, etc. But then there's the hitch—"once you get in." At this writing, Victoria Station has a *no reservations policy,* and that may keep you sidetracked in the cocktail caboose for 45 minutes or more, watching your drinking budget go down the line while waiting for space in the dining cars. We try to climb aboard on a slow night.

Several dining places, some of which we like a lot, have been installed in the new Ward Centre, a chic shopping block at 1200 Ala Moana Blvd., between Ala Moana Center and the Ward Warehouse. At the top of the heap, literally and figuratively, is the noisy, bright, barnlike, crowded, and hectic **Ryan's Parkplace Bar and Grill** (Tel. 523-9132), which also doubles as one of Honolulu's better singles bars. Here's a place with no privacy at all, illuminated with institutional light globes, but with plenty of loud merriment. Somehow it all works.

It could be because of the quality of the fare. The menu proudly states that all the recipes were "personally supervised and approved by Sharon Kramis, widely known West Coast food writer, consultant and instructor." There's a lotsa pasta, scadsa salads, and about two dozen kinds of beer in addition to some innovative meat and chicken dishes. A couple dishes we remember favorably include Baked Chicken Breast Dijon and Taglietelle Bolognese. A lot of food and a lot of fun, too.

Downstairs, a modest place called the **Yum Yum Tree** (Tel. 523-9333) is a couple of notches above your average coffee shop. Ask for an outdoor umbrella table for the full tropical flavor. Some of its pies are famous. An unusual idea is a combination cafe and bookstore called **Upstart Crow & Company.** You can have salads, soups, sandwiches, etc., along with your reading material here at Ward Centre and at another branch in the Ward Warehouse.

The food is usually good also at the **Hau Tree Lanai** (Tel. 923-1555) at the New Otani Kaimana Beach Hotel, but it's the outdoorsy, beachside atmosphere underneath Waikiki's oldest hau tree that makes the place. We prefer it for a sunny breakfast or lunch, but you might like dinner if you go early enough to catch the sunset. When the sky turns into an orange sherbet, the dining can be a delicious experience. Go "diamondhead" from Waikiki to the hotel at 2863 Kalakaua Ave.

Right at the top of the twenty-five-story Ala Moana Building is **Windows of Hawaii** (Tel. 941-9138), formerly La Ronde, and the very first of the world's now-proliferating revolving restaurants. This place suffered some service problems at first, but that may be better now. In any case, with that view, it should always be worth going around at least once or twice for a drink or two.

Sorry, we know little about the **Hard Rock Café**, which is under construction at the site of the venerable Coco's, but which was torn down at the corner of Kalakaua and Kapiolani. In addition to Yankee food, it it supposed to boast Honolulu's first rock 'n' roll museum.

Steak Houses. Here's a little American/Cosmopolitan subcategory designed to answer the question "Where can we go to get a really good hunk of steak?" Besides the meat served in the places so far mentioned, we do have a few more likes and dislikes. (Don't forget, you'll probably be offered teriyaki and mahimahi along with the T-bones in these broilers.)

Hy's Steak House (Tel. 922-5555), a sparkling local link in a Canadian chain at 2440 Kuhio, has been attracting a loyal clientele to its book-lined den. (The manager bought the library from an old mansion in Philadelphia and shipped it here.) Some opt for "The Only," a 13-ounce steak broiled in Chef Arcano's special sauce for around $22. Stick with steak, and you've got a shot. A champion has always been the moderately priced **Black Angus** (Tel. 923-1919) in the Coral Reef Hotel. The Black Angus really is black inside, too, but if your eyes ever get used to firefly-power lights, you'll see some attractive Spanish appurtenances. Steaks are in the $15 range. The **Captain's Galley** in the Moana Hotel was a bummer for us, except for the sunset, which can be super.

The Colony Seafood and Steak House (Tel. 922-9292), in the Hyatt Regency Waikiki, is okay. We thought there were too many tables crowded into the room and not enough space for runs to the salad bar, although many lap up the products of its Margarita Machine. Also in Waikiki, over at 247 Lewers Street, is the below-stairs **Chuck's Cellar.** Our meat was no more than okay, and we felt rushed by their *modus operandi.* **Chuck's Steak House,** a *lower-priced* entry in the immediate neighborhood (it's in a corner of the Edgewater Hotel), is more or less dependable for the modest tariffs. However, a newer branch, up in Manoa Valley, is a much more friendly and tasty address. And in the Reef Hotel you can broil your own, now, for under $14 in the **Shore Bird Broiler.** Live music after 10 P.M.

Out of Waikiki, and back into the top-dollar steak emporia, **Byron II** (Tel. 949-8855) in the Ala Moana Center is generally dependable. The viewful **Chart House** (Tel. 941-6669) in the Ilikai Marina Apartments has successfully risen from the ashes after it was charbroiled but good in an expensive fire a few years back. Further along Ala Moana Boulevard, **Stuart Anderson's** (Tel. 523-9692) is a reliable local link in the western beef chain.

Buzz's Original Steak House (Tel. 944-9781), now at 2535 Coyne St., near the university, is okay at that address, although many prefer to drive over the Pali to the *original* "Original" in Kailua. Then, out in the Kahala Mall, some folks are faithful to the **Spindrifter** (Tel. 737-7944), which has just been brightened in a major renovation. We haven't been around recently, but *Aloha, The Magazine of Hawaii,* gives it plaudits in a review as a dependable suburban dining room. If we were in that neighborhood we might head for the **Pottery** (Tel. 735-5594), not far away at 3574 Waialae Ave. in the Kaimuki District. While waiting for a table you can watch the ceramists at work spinning out the dishes, cups, etc., which you'll use, and which you may also buy. The steaks are probably good, but you might like something different such as the Teriyaki Kabob. Happily remembered and recommended.

CHINESE COOKING IN HONOLULU

Chinese restaurants always seem more enjoyable with a group, because you can order "family style"—choosing several kinds of dishes for everyone to pass around and sample. There always seem to be some new things to try that none of the gang has ever heard of before. Probably no other style of cooking, in fact, can come up with such a large number of diverse delectable items as Chinese cuisine. In our listings below we have also tried to find places where two people can enjoy a good sampling of the bill of fare.

It is far beyond our scope to go into the intricacies of Chinese cooking. But you may want to remember that in Hawaii, at least, there are two general types. *Cantonese cooking* tends to be rather mild and sweet. Most Chinese restaurants throughout the U.S. are actually Cantonese. The other style is generally called Northern, Szechuan, or *Mandarin cooking* even though, strictly speaking, those three terms are not exactly interchangeable. The dishes tend to be on the hot and spicy side, and it's this kind of Chinese restaurant that you may not find back home. Incidentally, rice is usually *not* included "free" with a Chinese meal. Some readers report misunderstandings on the subject.

Now, a brief word about *chopsticks*. Why be intimidated? If your chopsticks are jumping and sliding over your fingers, for heaven's sake ask for a fork. This is especially true with Chinese chopsticks, which tend to be long, slippery, and hard to handle, as opposed to the shorter, wooden Japanese models. If the restaurant can provide us with disposable wood ones—the Chinese sometimes call them "picnic chopsticks"—we use 'em. Otherwise, depending on what we ordered, we might ask for western utensils, too. (Also, see our discussion on chopsticks operation under the Japanese category.)

Cantonese Restaurants. One convenient old reliable, equally practical for lunch or dinner, is the **House of Hong** (Tel. 923-0202) at 260-A Lewers St. Walk inside, past the Red Chamber Bar, and on upstairs to the Dynasty Dining Room: Ancient black-and-gold decorations (ask for the brochure explaining the artwork); high-gloss tables; low ceilings with patterned bronze characters meaning "longevity"; carved teakwood mural to one side; quiet, perhaps taciturn (but attentive) waitresses; low noontime prices; high dinner fares. We very much enjoyed our combination lunch plate (spare ribs, chicken, shrimp, pork chop suey, rice, etc.) here for around $5. Others praise the complete dinners for $13 or so. Evening reservations are advisable. Unlike many Chinese restaurants, this one has kept the same chef for years, and we keep receiving complimentary letters about it. Bending at the waist, we happily award it *Won Lo Bao*.

The reincarnated **Waikiki Lau Yee Chai** (Tel. 923-1112) is setting a high standard of Oriental opulence up in the Waikiki Shopping Plaza, near its old address at Kalakaua and Seaside. We'll try the Cashew Chicken or the Almond Duck again after the gold dust settles. Also in Waikiki is the dinner-only **Golden Dragon** (Tel. 949-4321) in the Hilton Hawaiian Village. This restaurant has had a continuously successful history for more than a decade, although it may soon move to another part of the hotel. The house specialty is the Lemon Chicken, which chef Dai Hoy Chang invented and introduced to Honolulu some years ago.

The formerly obscure **Hee Hing Chop Suey** (Tel. 735-5544) carried its loyal habitués along when it moved to new, more elegant quarters at 449 Kapahulu Ave. recently, just a chopstick's throw from the Ala Wai Canal in Waikiki. We haven't been in since the move, but it was always good and cheap and worth seeking out. The longtime champion of the chop suey sweepstakes is still **McCully Chop Sui** at McCully and King streets. Despite its traditional hold in Chinatown, the century-old **Wo Fat** (Est. 1882—Tel. 537-6260) sometimes does and sometimes doesn't keep the quality of its fare up to date. Many Wo Fat fans disagree, however, and it is certainly interesting to dine in a sort of local Cantonese museum. It's at 115 North Hotel St. in an otherwise unsavory neighborhood.

Also downtown, and in a better area, is **Fat Siu Lau** (Tel. 538-7081), "the Happy Man," in the Cultural Plaza. Although we know it for its delicious *dim sum* (served only up to 4 P.M.), it is developing a happy reputation for full meals and takeout orders, too. A similar story is the decorous **China House** (Tel. 949-6622), across the parking lot *mauka* of Sears' second floor. For cafeteria-style Chinese fun, the traditional favorite in the Ala Moana Center is **Patti's Chinese Kitchen.** It's always crowded, but the line moves pretty quickly, and to many it's worth the battered elbows to get to the Ginger Sauce Chicken and other delights.

Back in Waikiki, **The Great Wok of China** (Tel. 922-5373) is an attempt to capture some of the panache of the Japanese *teppan* table and put it in a Chinese setting. We found it enjoyable, in its convenient setting in the Royal Hawaiian Center. You might see the Butterfly Dream Beef Steak take flight before your very eyes. Lunchtime is a relative bargain; we recently noticed that the Ghengis Khan Sweet & Sour Pork was $13 at dinner and less than half that price at noon. And a Gresham, Oregon woman wrote us: "Penny pinchers may like the early dinner price... After weeks of rich restaurant food, it tastes good to eat simple stir-fry vegetables and rice."

Mandarin Restaurants. For spicy, Northern Chinese cooking, we have two favorites, neither one of which is in Waikiki. The easiest for a *malihini* to find, perhaps, is the **Mandarin** (Tel. 946-3242), at 942 McCully St., near the corner of Beretania. Back in the dark days when I thought I didn't like Chinese restaurants very well—during the Ming Dynasty, I think it was—we dined here and gobbled up everything that was brought out. They make their own noodles, which we love with beef chunks in a hot sauce. The eggplant and pork are good, as are the Shanghai-style steamed dumplings and the Mongolian beef (sauteed with green onions and red peppers). It's hard to choose between this restaurant and the following one, but strictly on consistent flavor we think the Mandarin has the edge. We annually wish the place *fu-lu-shou*—"wealth, luck, and longevity."

A better-known establishment is the **King Tsin** (Tel. 946-3273)—*not* "the King's Inn"—which has just moved near the Mandarin at Young and McCully Streets. Very neat decor; excellent service; greencovered tables often attended by owner Sylvio Wang or his family members; the hot and sour soup a must; the Crackling Chicken also a popular choice; the Szechuan beef a personal favorite; most dinners in the $14 range. The King Tsin always seems to remain very much "in." Except Tuesday, when they're out.

Also dependable, but perhaps a little harder to find for strangers in the city, is the **Maple Garden** (Tel. 941-6641) at 909 Isenberg St.—a fly ball away from the city park that used to be the old Honolulu Stadium. Home-run favorites include the very meaty Szechuan smoked duck and eggplant with hot garlic sauce. Mmm! On the other hand, we were very disappointed with the inefficient service and bland cuisine we experienced at the Honolulu branch of the attractive **House of Hunan** in Eaton Square—especially since we once stuffed ourselves happily at their parent address in Washington, D.C.

The **Mongolian Bar-B-Que** (Tel. 533-7305) has been the leader of a clutch of Oriental dining dens developing downtown in the Cultural Plaza. Besides the title dish, it also features a *Chinese* shabu-shabu, which we haven't yet dipped into. They've now opened a branch Bar-B-Que in the Kuhio Mall in Waikiki. The **Hong Kong Noodle House** (Tel. 536-5409) at 100 North Beretania sometimes has them standing in line outside— for good reason. Ditto the **Mini Garden** (Tel. 538-1273) at 50 North Hotel. But we'd skip the **Yang-Tze,** thank you.

CONTINENTAL AND FRENCH CUISINE

Some may wonder what the subtle difference might be between a "Cosmopolitan" restaurant and a "Continental" one. I don't think we can explain it, and I'm not sure we even understand it. Our personal working definition has been that Cosmopolitan restaurants are "not quite all American," and that Continental restaurants are "not quite all French."

A few things we are sure of: It takes more to make a Continental restaurant than translating an American menu into French. You also cannot merely take an island "two scoops rice" joint, expand the wine cellar, and dim the lights. Hmm. But then, if you replace the mahimahi

flawed by cumbersome serving-cart service and a young, unseasoned dining room staff, but there is a serious chef in the kitchen who cares." (Order carefully if you want to keep your final tab under $40 per diner.) Bagwells is certainly a ranking restaurant in Waikiki.

I suppose that if we'd really tried we could have kept the tab at our table for two below $135 at the oceanside **La Mer** (Tel. 923-2311). In Hawaii we're not used to having to struggle that hard to eat well and have a modest wine for a reasonable amount of cash. We cannot fault the setting and the atmosphere in this Halekulani dining room—especially at sunset—nor the service and cuisine. Indeed, I shall always remember my cooked spinach salad with truffle juice and the beef tenderloin with oranges and cream of sweet peppers. Sara's fish was also excellent. But the breezy dining room was nearly empty on our Wednesday night, and we suspect that it was the right side of the menu that frightened some others away—as it will us until there is a change of financial philosophy here. (One point: Some unordered comestibles come free—the *petits fours* that were included were enough dessert.) Men must wear jackets. If your personal or business account is fluid enough to handle the outlay, then dive into La Mer. You'll have plenty of room to sink or swim.

The downstairs dining room in the Halekulani was always known simply as the Dining Room. Now it has been renamed **Orchids** (same phone as above) and given a little extra pizzazz. A wide variety of cooking styles is offered; we saw Cajun, Italian, Thai, Hawaiian, Chinese, and French specialties. Ask about the fixed price four-course dinner, which may be the best deal. This is the Halekulani's only restaurant open for all three meals. Try to sit outdoors for the best island atmosphere.

In its own separate building at 1855 Kalakaua, **Casablanca** (Tel. 942-2151) attempts to capture the ambiance of Rick's Café Américain in 1940. Our party of four tried chicken, duck, lamb, and fish specialties, and each was almost perfectly prepared. Prices for most of the *plats de résistance* were in the $15 to $20 range. The service was quick and attentive. Live music is in the lounge after 9 until late. As time goes by, we'll be back to play it again.

Sorry, but something keeps preventing us from trying the little **Bon Appetit** (Tel. 942-3837), now firmly installed in the Discovery Bay shopping center at 1778 Ala Moana, across from the Ilikai. The owner is a former chef at Bagwells who branched out on his own. Writing in *Travel & Leisure,* Charles Monaghan said he loved the *raviolis de crevettes à la crème de morilles.* We finally did return to the **Bali Room** (Tel. 949-4321) in the Hilton Hawaiian Village to try its new French format, and we have to say we were disappointed. The setting is delicious, but the fare was only fair. Perhaps it was the chef's night out. If you go, let us know.

The Holiday Inn-Waikiki has launched the **Captain's Table** (Tel.

926-1700) in an attempt to recapture the atmosphere of "boat day" in Honolulu. Some call it a little hokey, with its recordings of shiptype sound effects, but most take it as a fun thing in this era of theme restaurants. A galley special is Steak Diane, flamed at tableside. It's not the QE-2 to be sure, but some land-lubbers lub it.

In a very different vein, the **Hanohano Room** (Tel. 922-4422), atop the Sheraton-Waikiki Hotel, is also not bad: Up the transparent lift to the end of the line; best seats by the windows or close to the orchestra/dance floor; wonderful panoramas of night-light Honolulu; usually a good orchestra for dining accompaniment and dancing; unusual terrace construction giving more inside tables a view over the city; acoustics difficult in some areas. We might stay with the beef here (the pepper steak is spectacular). If you like the Strawberry Sabayon for dessert, you may still be able to get the recipe. When you take the Hanohano Room as a whole experience (altitude, music, dancing, food), you might like it a lot. (The place is also very attractive for breakfast—particularly Sunday brunch.)

Yacht Harbor Restaurant (Tel. 946-2177) is very dignified and very pleasant—if you can find it. It's perched atop the five-story parking garage attached to the Yacht Harbor Towers apartments at 1600 Ala Moana Blvd., corner of Atkinson Drive. On foot, we had to trudge up the automobile ramp and then ask questions.

And downtown, near the top end of the Fort Street Mall, the 1940s-atmospheric **Café on the Mall** (Tel. 533-2042) deserves to succeed. This fan-cooled, palm-filled, open patio is in the rear of a former landmark hotel (the Blaisdell) and has several imaginative French menu choices for both lunch and dinner. So far we've been in for lunch but not in the evening, when live jazz is sometimes on tap from 5 to 9.

GREEK FOOD

There are two happy Hellenic choices in town these days. More convenient to visitors is **It's Greek to Me** (Tel. 922-2733), a sort of Greek "sidewalk cafe" in the Royal Hawaiian Center in Waikiki. The specialty is the Gyro (pronounced "hero") sandwich—lamb and beef on pita bread. A second, much more out-of-the-way choice, but preferred by many, is the family-run **Greek Island Taverna** (Tel. 943-0052) on the second floor at 2570 South Beretania St., near University Avenue. The dinner Gyro plate we had was excellent, and so were the dishes ordered by others in our party. A belly dancer sometimes entertains here during meals, none of which are expensive.

HAWAIIAN FOOD

Sadly, Hawaiian cooking is almost an alien in its own land. It holds onto its precarious status largely out of cultural sentiment plus the fierce devotion of a small group of fanciers who will not let it die.

In addition to *poi* (which can be fresh and bland or a few days old and nicely fermented) and *kalua* pig, both of which we mentioned previously, look for *laulau* (tender pork and beef, sometimes with butterfish, wrapped in taro and ti leaves). Also there is *lomi* salmon (a mixture of smoked salmon, tomatoes, peppers, onions, and crushed ice); if you like lox, you may like *lomi* salmon. For dessert, look for *haupia*, a coconut pudding, or *kulolo*, a pudding made from coconut and brown sugar.

Non-Hawaiian restaurants, such as the Tahitian Lanai, the Columbia Inn, or The Willows, to name three that come immediately to mind, will often offer a Hawaiian plate special of the day, and it is this that we might find ourselves ordering, rather than setting out especially to find an honest-to-*kaukau* Hawaiian restaurant.

They do exist, however. We have had occasion to lunch at one, the **Culinary Studio** (Tel. 537-4528), in the Cultural Plaza at the corner of Kukui Street and the River Street Mall. Owner Flossie Shiroma had been catering successfully for so many years previously that it was logical that her first restaurant would prove *ono-ono*. It's very simple, neat, clean, inexpensive, and worth a try. (If you're afraid of Hawaiian food, Flossie also serves a mean teriyaki sandwich.) Other favorites include **Helena's Hawaiian Foods** (Tel. 845-8044) at 1364 North King St. and **Ono Hawaiian Foods** (Tel. 737-2275), good and cheap, at 726 Kapahulu Ave., not far from Waikiki. At both you can still get a Hawaiian "plate lunch"—a paper plate-and-chopsticks takeout extravaganza that includes *kalua* pig, *laulau*, *lomi* salmon, *pipikaula*, *haupia*, and *poi* for under $5.

There are few plate lunches available in Waikiki. The exception, however, and an address where you'll see lots of locals around lunch time is **Surf Inn Snacks**, on Kalakaua next to the Park Shore Hotel. The Hawaiian Plate or Beef Stew Plate will run around $3.50.

Most Hawaiian food is experienced by visitors solely at a *luau*, a more-or-less modern version of an ancient Hawaiian feast. Since *luaus* now are usually more entertainment than authentic Hawaiian dining experiences, we will take them up in section 11, Nights on the Town.

INDIAN RESTAURANTS

Honolulu historically has had a difficult time keeping Indian restaurants. One good one that has been around for several years, now, is **India House** (Tel. 955-7552), located far from the tourist area at 2632 South King St., near University Avenue. There's no atmosphere to speak of, but the important thing is that owner/chef Ram Arora supervises everything himself. Some choose the Maharaja's Dinner, a mixture of Tandoori

Chicken, Lamb Curry, and Fish Tikka, at about $13. The curry and kabob dinner (about $12) is also popular. If you like it authentically hot, speak up. Otherwise you'll get the milder western version of everything. (Closed Mondays.)

A second entry, the **Shalimar** (Tel. 923-2693), is more convenient. It serves up both Indian and Pakistani dishes from a niche in the Waikiki Holiday Hotel, 450 Lewers St. The restaurant's kitchen with its superhot *tandoori* oven is visible through a window in the dining room. Besides the curries, you might try the Tandoori Chicken or the Shrimp Bhunna. There's also a royal Maharajah Dinner for two for around $30. Let us know what you think.

ITALIAN DINING

The usually dependable **Trattoria** (Tel. 923-8415) is in a corner of the Edgewater Hotel at Kalia Road and Beach Walk. Those experienced in the ways of Roman dining may call the place more a fine *ristorante* than a modest *trattoria* in the original sense. And the real significance of the place is that it offers some of the more subtle *al burro* dishes (cooked in butter instead of olive oil) of central and northern Italy. (They will prepare anything Italian you've ever heard of on at least one day's notice.) On our most recent visit, we thought the lasagna very good, the Correletto di Vitelo alla Parmigianna and the Pollo alla Romana even better. We have sometimes found the elbow-to-elbow seating disturbing, and although the guitarist is good we were once placed so near him that we couldn't hold a conversation among our group. Prices are generally moderate. But caution: We haven't been ourselves since Sergio, the chef, left to open his own place. (See below.)

As far as food quality and service are concerned, **Sergio's** (Tel. 926-3388) is no doubt the best Italian kitchen in the Islands: Unusual Waikiki location in the Ilima Hotel at 445 Nohonani St.; the red door somewhat of a surprise; quiet, dark, low-ceiling interior with plush upholstery; mirrors and reproductions of French Impressionists on the walls; Boston ferns also hanging around; comfortable banquettes with attractive table settings; long menu of Italian classic dishes, many of which you won't find elsewhere. We enjoyed every morsel, from the Insalata Contadina to the Piccata alla Lambarda, and experienced flawless service by a longtime professional waiter (a rare breed in Hawaii). Dinner for two with a nice Italian wine comes to around $75. Some visitors to Hawaii may find the decor's similarity to a high-class indoor New York or Cleveland address disturbing. We didn't, however, and highly recommend it to anyone who doesn't feel the need of a palm frond dipping into his soup at every meal. (Open daily for lunch and dinner.)

At the corner of Kuhio and Seaside avenues, in the relatively obscure Marine Surf-Waikiki Hotel, is **Matteo's** (Tel. 922-5551), a Hollywood-type Italian dining spot, often a haunt of local and visiting entertainers (one pepper steak is named after Frank Sinatra): Large and dark with lots of oil paintings and orange lights; relative privacy in well-padded booths; excellent house salad or antipasto; specialties in veal good and perhaps worth the price; an attentive cadre of waiters; a large selection of wines, plus an expensive (but not bad) house carafe. For the food, you'd better figure on at least $35 per person here. If that seems high for an Italian restaurant, you may be right, but plenty of people are happy to pay. (Open daily for dinner only.)

Downtown, far from the usual tourist haunts, there used to be another Matteo's. However the historic, brick-wall premises at the corner of Merchant and Nuuanu have been taken over by the **Royal Hawaiian Tavern** (Tel. 531-0422). It is said to have been a bar patronized by King Kalakaua a century ago. The address is still Italian, at least, but we have yet to try it out under the new *direzione*. The **Café Che Pasta**, at 1001 Bishop St., turns out some delicious and reasonable ravioli and other things at lunchtime, anyway. This is the one where they'll give you someting to write on the table cloth, if you want. Try the Caesar salad.

A no-nonsense spaghetti emporium is a barn of a place, the furnishing of which must have denuded the Tyrol of every antique it ever possessed. It's called **The Old Spaghetti Factory** (Tel. 531-1513, but currently taking no reservations). Amid the stained glass and bedsteads of brass are scores of happy spaghetti slurpers. Some don't like the crowds here, but large families lap up the prices. Dishes begin in the $5 neighborhood (even cheaper for kids). Light and dark draft beer or decanted *vino di tavola* is available. Hardly gourmet, but it's fun and cheap.

Another superdecorous salon is **Spats** (Tel. 922-9292) in the Hyatt Regency Waikiki. Furnished à la 1920s speakeasy—but much nicer, come to think of it—this Al Capone-ish cellar was once billed as a "family style" dining room. The menu is longer than that, although the service might be as friendly as it is at your Uncle Giovanni's. (Some booths are small, though; the tables are a more commodious bet.) Spats' Mamma Mia banks her fires about 10 P.M., although a new pasta bar keeps rolling until 2 A.M. After the family goes to bed the place turns into a disco for the *bambini*. Fun—and often very good, too.

We did try **Andrew's** (Tel. 523-8677) not long ago. It's a decent entry offering Italian food and other dishes in premises near other restaurants at Ward Centre. We thought it not expensive, but not particularly distinguished, either. Perhaps you'll disagree. Another Italian *cucina* in Ward Centre is **Il Fresco**. It's an attractive corner, to be sure, but we found this one to be little more than a fancy-dancy pizza parlor—and far from the best or the cheapest of the breed at that.

More modest Italian entries include the well-advertised **Rudy's** (Tel. 923-5949), in the Outrigger Surf Hotel, and **Bella Italia,** in Ala Moana Center. They're okay for tomato-paste lovers but far from the quality of the best Italian kitchens. We still haven't tried **Renown Milano** (Tel. 947-1933) at the Discovery Bay condo, or **Papa's** (Tel. 949-8848), a BYOW place at 1614 South King St. If you go, let us know. Angie Alongi of Auburn Heights, Mich., wrote us that she loved the **Marco Polo** (Tel. 922-7733) which she found way up the escalator in the Waikiki Shopping Plaza. **Auntie Pasto's** (Tel. 955-7891), at 1099 South Beretania St., gave us okay fare with erratic service. But the echoing noises in its high-ceilinged room were overwhelming. We first thought our waiter was dumb; as it turned out, however, he was probably deaf.

JAPANESE FARE IN HONOLULU

The Japanese are always quick to pick up on a new thing, embracing new experiences in food as they do other things of quality, so it is some-times difficult to tell what is genuine Japanese cooking. Many of the most famous Japanese dishes may have started out as Portuguese, Chinese, Korean—even American.

Such as *teppanyaki,* which has become immensely popular over the past several years. (*Teppan* means a metal plate and *yaki* means broil or fry.) It involves grilling steak, chicken, shrimp, etc., on a heavy steel top that forms the "*teppan* table" around which the diners sit. The chef cuts, slices, and sprinkles with a deft click-click, clack-clack, zip-zip, putting on a show of dexterity along with the food preparation. Then he serves the results out right there, along with bean sprouts and other vegetables.

This kind of Japanese steak house was developed in Tokyo not long ago to appeal to Americans and other foreigners, but the Japanese soon took to it themselves with equal fervor. In Honolulu some Japanese restaurants have a few *teppan* tables, some have them exclusively, and some don't have them at all. It is probably now the most popular style of Japanese cooking for Americans, although some folks don't like sharing a table—lunch counter–style—with others.

As a general rule, Japanese food is water based and cooked quickly. Fish, chicken, or beef is either broiled, boiled, fried, simmered, or steamed (never baked). There are several interesting seasonings, including *shoyu* and *sake* (rice wine). Vegetables play an important role, including such different ones as *tofu* (soybean curd), bamboo shoots, and *daikon* (white radish). Everything is served with rice—not the light, fluffy "*haole* rice," but sticky and gooey so it is easy to pick up on chopsticks! Full meals also include soup and green tea.

Another dish that is always a favorite for Mainlanders is *sukiyaki* (*suki* means "slice thin"), in which thinly sliced meat and vegetables are fried in a flat-bottomed pan. (The Japanese like it served with a raw egg, which can be whipped in at the table, but, well, frankly we always ignore or send back the egg.)

Shabu-shabu is another favorite, and works rather like a Swiss fondue. You pick up a slice of meat, cook it in the boiling broth for a moment, then dip it into some special sauce before eating. It's really very good, but a certain amount of work is involved all through the meal, of course.

Then there's *tempura,* an uncharacteristic cooking method imported to Japan by sixteenth-century Portuguese. Vegetables, fish, and, most popularly, shrimp, are cooked in a batter in very hot oil.

Japanese food is usually cut up into small pieces so it may be easily picked up with chopsticks. If you are not adept at chopsticks, let the waiter or waitress show you how to use them. In Hawaii they often come as one piece of bamboo or wood, partially slit apart. Break them the rest of the way and rub the small ends against each other to remove any tiny splinters. Chopsticks are held so that the bottom chopstick is stationary and the top one movable. The bottom stick should be in the crotch of the thumb, and the thumb forces the stick tightly against the inside tip of the ring finger. The top chopstick is held by the thumb and the first two fingers, much like a pencil, and is moved up and down by bending the fingers. If you want to try it, find a friend who knows something about chopsticks to show you exactly how, and then practice it by using two fresh, unsharpened pencils.

The best all-around Japanese restaurant is probably the very attractive **Suntory** (Tel. 922-5511) on the second floor of Building B in the Royal Hawaiian Shopping Center (very near the Sheraton). The Suntory runs the gamut in foods Japanese, although so far we've only tried the offerings in the *teppan* room, which were delicious. Everything was à la carte, and offerings are in a wide price range from $15 up. Others have praised the Shabu-Shabu dinners, the Beef Sukiyaki, or the many fish dishes. There is also an elegant version of a Tokyo *sushi* bar on the premises. Things can add up fast here. Service will probably continue to be excellent.

For *teppanyaki* exclusively, no Honolulu restaurant can beat the simple elegance of the city's own link in the ubiquitous chain called **Benihana of Tokyo** (Tel. 955-5955), on the grounds of the Hilton Hawaiian Village. We've never liked its advertising, but we do like its food: Outfitted like a very neat, old-fashioned Japanese farmhouse; a half-dozen *teppan* tables, most holding seven diners; athletic chefs with excellent memories as to who ordered what; lunchtime bargains still about $8 (for chicken) to

about $10 for a hibachi steak special; dinner prices from about $15 to
$20 for a super spread including soup, hibachi shrimp, salad, special
steak, hibachi vegetables, and ice cream. There's a local trend to look
down on Benihana for its very popularity. It does tend to be fairly expensive, and some evening diners say that after waiting too long for a table,
they feel constrained to rush through the meal. That may be true, sometimes. But it's generally delicious and fun.

The decorous little **Maiko** (Tel. 946-5151), downstairs in the Ilikai
Hotel, is a charming choice for several Japanese dishes. We cooked the
Genghis Khan Steak at our table, and enjoyed it. Then at 2057 Kalakaua
Ave., next to Fort DeRussy, is **Kyo-Ya** (Tel. 947-3911), which attracts a
considerable number of tourists from Japan. If you haven't yet tried
sukiyaki, this might be the place. The **Kobe Steak House** (Tel. 941-4444),
at 1841 Ala Moana, near the Ilikai, offers good *teppanyaki* by entertaining
chefs—once you get to the table. Despite our reservation, our large party
was kept in the bar for nearly an hour. (It's American beef—not Kobe—
by the way.) We also liked the very simple, very friendly **Regent Marushin**
(Tel. 922-6452) in the Hawaiian Regent Hotel for old-style Japanese
dining.

The traditional Japanese favorite in town is **Furusato** (Tel. 922-4991),
now in the Hyatt Regency Waikiki. It may still be the most beautifully
decorated Japanese restaurant, and it surely is the only one that announces each guest's arrival on a gong! Make special arrangements if
you don't want to sit on the floor, for there are some conventional tables
and chairs available.

If you are a party of four to six, you'll probably get your very own
small *teppan* table at **Chaco's** (Tel. 732-9333). This was the first restaurant to bring *teppanyaki* to Honolulu, several years back. Now it's a little
out of the way at 2888 Waialae Ave., at the end of Kapahulu Avenue, but
the meals are still good. At the top of the tank in the Pacific Beach Hotel,
the little **Shogun** (Tel. 922-1233) offered *teppanyaki* that was all right, but
sushi and other authentic Japanese finger foods were particularly appealing.
We were not too impressed with the **Miyako** (not to be confused with the
previously named Maiko), at the top of the New Otani Kaimana Beach
Hotel. We thought that the food was no more than okay, and that the
portions were small.

Some folks like the **Suehiro** (Tel. 949-4584), a simple establishment at
1824 South King St. We would go there again *only* if we can sit with our
own group in a *tatami* mat room. Otherwise the ambience is quite ordinary. It's inexpensive, at any rate. (Closed Tuesday.) One of the most
authentic Japanese restaurants around is **Yanagi Sushi** (Tel. 537-1525)
in a modest address at 762 Kapiolani Blvd. downtown. You can watch
them make *sushi* on the premises. Also good is the Alaska king crab, they

say, but we haven't tried it. A little more chic, perhaps, is **Chez Sushi** (Tel. 526-4007) on the ground level of Ward Centre, 1200 Ala Moana Blvd. For sushi connoisseurs, but maybe wasted on anyone else. And sorry, we still haven't visited **Tanaka of Tokyo** (Tel. 922-4702) on the fifth floor of the Waikiki Shopping Plaza. However, Monty Strauss of Lubbock, Texas, pronounced it "delicious." (Thanks, Monty!) **Musashi** (Tel. 922-9292), the new Japanese restaurant in the Hyatt Regency, is named after Japan's most famous samurai warrior. There are teppan tables, conventional dining tables, and a sushi bar. We haven't yet tried it or the **Zen Restaurant** (Tel. 923-8878) in the Waikiki Grand Hotel. But Honolulu writer Jocelyn Fujii, who really knows her Japanese cookery from A to Z, says the Zen is the Acme for classical *kaiseki* food preparation techniques. There's also an excellent sushi bar.

MEXICAN RESTAURANTS

There are always a half-dozen or so Mexican restaurants in town, but most of them are about as stable as a *serape* in a high wind—moving addresses, switching owners, or changing their names at the drop of a *sombrero*.

This year's Numero Uno is **Compadres** (Tel. 523-3914), one of the proliferating modern dining rooms in the Ward Centre, 1200 Ala Moana Blvd. Despite the central air conditioning, the establishment gives a light and airy impression with high ceilings, overhead fans, potted plants, clay urns, and tables wisely not placed too close together. Some go for the Steak Picado, or the Pollo Borracho ("drunk chicken"). Or you can probably still have a simple three-enchilada dish for around $10. We have always experienced cheerful service by a group of enthusiastic young *señoritas. Ole! (A branch of Compadres has just opened in the basement of the Outrigger Prince Kuhio Hotel.)*

A newer entry on the Mexican scene is **Popo's** (formerly Pepe's, Tel. 923-7355), sharing a *hacienda* with the South Seas Village at 2112 Kalakaua Ave. The menu is not limited to the spicy border foods, but also offers some sophisticated selections from Mexico City: Lots of stucco and wrought iron around; no air conditioning; diners in the loggia watching the passing parade; generous dinner helpings in the $10 range. We were certainly *satisfecho*. There are two newer branches: **Popo's Cantina** (Tel. 955-3326) has opened on the ground floor of Canterbury Place, a condominium apartment building at 1910 Ala Moana Blvd., on the corner of Ena Road, and not far from the Hilton Hawaiian Village. Some tables are outside. And now **Popo's Margarita Cantina** (Tel. 923-8373) has been installed in the International Market Place in Waikiki.

An attractive address in the Royal Hawaiian Center is **La Mex** (Tel. 923-2906); many have spoken well of the Shrimp Envuelto (wrapped in bacon) and other offerings. We've been twice. On one night, the billed *mariachi* entertainment was recorded, the fare was bland, and the service was almost nonexistent. The second time, things were better, but still no more than ordinary. Frankly, we prefer the much more modest **Hernando's Hideaway** (Tel. 926-3118), a well-named, hard-to-find nook down a little alley near Hamburger Mary's, off Kuhio Ave. Look for the red and green tablecloths.

For really inexpensive south-of-the-border fare, you might look into **Mama's Mexican Kitchen** (Tel. 537-3200), pretty far out in the cactus at 378 North School St. The original Mama has long ago folded her apron and moved away, but someone always seems to keep the ovens hot, for better or for worse, and for richer or for poorer. Next, far out at 1134 Koko Head Ave., is **Jose's** (Tel. 732-1833), which has been slipping and sliding in this Kaimuki neighborhood. In the same precincts, some prefer the **Azteca** (Tel. 735-2492) at 3569 Waialae Ave. **La Cocina** at Ala Moana Center is not bad, but it's cheaper at the outdoor window. (The taco you loved for $1.50 on the sidewalk becomes about twice that if you sit down inside.) There are also two branches of the ubiquitous **Taco Bell** Mexican-style takeout chain. One is on South King Street, and the other is on Kapahulu Avenue, about five blocks in from Waikiki. You can't miss it. The new **Chi-Chi's** has just opened in both the Westridge Shopping Center in Aiea and at the Kahala Mall. Sorry, we haven't been able to try either, yet. The best Mexican food on the island, however, just might be at **Bueno Nalo** in Waimanalo, far from Waikiki. A new branch has just opened in Kailua, too.

SEAFOOD SELECTIONS

As we mentioned earlier, the island's favorite fish is the *mahimahi,* which is now becoming somewhat of a rarity in Hawaiian waters. (Most *mahimahi* is frozen and imported.) Another fresh favorite now on the decline in numbers, but unfortunately not in popularity, is *opakapaka* (red snapper), and prices are consequently on the increase. Other fish favored for the table include the Hawaiian tunas—either *aku* (skipjack) or *ahi* (yellowfin)—as well as *ono* (wahoo) and *ulua* (jackfish). Of course there are several more that will be on the menu at Island restaurants along with choices air flown from just about anywhere in the world.

The most consistently excellent oceanic champion is far out of Waikiki, but convenient enough with your own wheels and a good map. That's the architecturally inspiring **John Dominis Restaurant** (Tel. 523-0955), launched by businessman/politician D. G. "Andy" Anderson, who has unsuccessfully run for mayor or governor from time to time. His restaurant, however, is a winner—both as an eye-dazzler and a tummy-tempter.

Look for it at (or take a cab to) 43 Ahui St., which is almost next to the channel entrance to Kewalo Basin (where the tour boats come in). Island fish are prepared in several different ways here. There are also delicious meat dishes in the chef's repertoire. All are expensive, to be sure, but we've never met a dissatisfied diner at Dominis.

In Waikiki many head for the modestly titled **Nick's Fish Market** (Tel. 955-6333), an underground den in the Waikiki Gateway Hotel: Very dark, stucco-walled grotto; flashlights sometimes needed to decode the menu; super-chummy waiters who just might join in your conversation (described by one local wag as "beachboys in tuxedoes"); most fish dishes excellent, especially swordfish, abalone, *mahimahi* (of course), *ualu, opakapaka,* and a superexpensive air-flown Maine lobster; accompanying vegetables sometimes bland by comparison; a superb Greek salad available, however; one of the highest-priced wine menus in town. Not everyone likes the atmosphere here, and reservation policies are erratic, but if fish is your thing—and you're willing to pay through the gills—Nick's is a good catch.

In the same general neighborhood as John Dominis is **Fisherman's Wharf** (Tel. 538-3808), which ties up next to the tuna boats and harbor cruise ships at Kewalo Basin: Decor of stuffed denizens of the deep, glass balls, flotsam and jetsam; usually friendly but sometimes overworked waitresses; checkered tablecloths; generally good local specialties; often crowded; open for lunch and dinner. Try the Shrimp Louie Salad in Abalone Shell for lunch. Admittedly more informal and more modest, and certainly less complete and less expensive than Nick's or John Dominis, the Wharf nevertheless holds up pretty well for the shallower investment.

Across the street, we don't much like the **Chowder House** at the prices asked for the small portions we were offered. But they're making quite a splash at the **Monterey Bay Canners** both at the Outrigger Hotel on the beach (Tel. 922-5761) and over at Ward Centre (Tel. 536-6197). Some diners' experiences have been more buoyant than others, but the Fish of the Day is probably fine for about $18. And a new branch of **El Crabcatcher** (Tel. 944-4911) has been installed across Hobron Lane from the Ilikai. We haven't hooked them here, yet, but we remember the restaurant as a good catch on Maui. In Waikiki, at the Royal Hawaiian Center, the **Seafood Emporium** (Tel. 922-5547) dishes out some nice choices in the $10 to $15 range under hanging lamps and to the tune of Viennese waltzes. Sara enjoyed her Sole Meuniere here. At lunch, try smoked salmon and cream cheese on a bagel.

THAI DINING

There are several Thai restaurants, now, in Honolulu. More may be open by the time our ink dries. In any case, all we have listed here we have tried and found to be dependable.

The **Mekong** (Tel. 521-2025) is the granddaddy of all the Thai restaurants in Honolulu, and in some ways it is still the best: Nowhereland location at 1295 South Beretania; Thai posters on the walls; eight tables and a bar, perhaps evocative of a waterside café in Bangkok; spicy meals served in a friendly manner; most dishes in the $11 range. Try the Thai crispy noodles, the satay beef or pork, the spring rolls, or that staple of Southeast Asia, meatball rice noodle soup. Adventurous diners conjure up the Evil Jungle Priest (sliced chicken or pork sauteed in hot spices on a bed of cabbage). Smooth the way with Ching Mai salad. For dessert, there's a dollar delight of bananas in warm coconut milk. Open daily except no lunch on Sunday. Delicious.

Much more convenient to Waikiki, and owned by the same outfit, is **Keo's** (Tel. 737-8240) at 441 Kapahulu Ave., just about 1½ blocks from the zoo. The à la carte menu offers more than 100 different dishes, and the interior is larger and fancier. And now a new branch, **Keo's at Ward Centre** (sorry, no Tel. no.) is about to open in an indoor/outdoor location at 1200 Ala Moana, neighboring such fancy dining emporia as Compadres and Ryan's. Plans call for the new address to offer a somewhat expanded menu. These, too, are enthusiastically suggested.

The newer **Thai House** (Tel. 521-1606), at 1243 South King St., lists several sea-soned specialties: steamed crab in bean sauce, fish cake with cucumber sauce, squid salad, or whole fish deep fried with chili peppers. No atmosphere, but also inexpensive—and also good. Sorry, but we lost our notes on the little **Petaya Thai** (Tel. 942-7979), at 1614 S. King St. Maybe it's because we were having such a good time. (Bring your own booze, if you want any.)

COFFEE SHOPS AND EFFICIENCY RESTAURANTS

Here are some diners that do not fall easily into the categories listed previously. Generally speaking, they offer all three meals, and some will be open around the clock.

One of the best all-around coffee shops in Honolulu for years has been the **Wailana Coffee House** (Tel. 955-1764), the main branch in the Wailana Apartment Building at 1860 Ala Moana Blvd., just across from the Hilton Dome: Open 24 hours; validated parking underneath; warm gold and yellow decor; often crowded; best booths at the window; fast, generally efficient service; choice of full dinners or snacks; the broasted chicken a best seller; steaks still at a good price; excellent dinners on holidays and special occasions; some of the waffliest waffles in town. Here are good, well-served meals in the best American tradition, yet with some flavorful local accents, too. Warmly suggested for the type.

Some like the nearby **Tops Canterbury Coffee House** (Tel. 941-5277), 1910 Ala Moana Blvd. Open 24 hours, it features booths in olde oake style, fake faded petit point, lions and unicorns etched in glass, etc. We gave it an "A" for atmosphere but a "B-minus" for bill of fare. In central Waikiki, **Trellises Garden Restaurant** (Tel. 922-0811) in the Outrigger Prince Kuhio, 2500 Kuhio Ave., is a popular site, especially for the evening buffets. The **Terrace Grille,** third floor in the Diamond Head tower of the Hyatt Regency, is a classy coffee corner.

Downtown near the state and city government buildings, the **Columbia Inn** (Tel. 531-3747) is a 24-hour favorite for many at 645 Kapiolani Blvd. It owes much of its fame to the fact that it has been the standard feeding trough and watering oasis for so many newspaper workers at the next-door *Honolulu Advertiser* and *Honolulu Star-Bulletin.* If you're an L.A. Dodgers fan, you'll feel at home in the baseball bar. The best batter is the shrimp *tempura*—at least a three-bagger and sometimes a home run.

Unpretentious, inexpensive, and down-home food, local style, is served at the **Flamingo.** One wing of the flamingo is at 574 Ala Moana, where no restaurant ought to be, and, indeed, it may fold forever this year, so recheck. The other is at 871 Kapiolani, also a rather strange address. It's hard to beat for the low prices, but another contender is the efficient **Likelike Drive In,** which is really a sitdown cafe at 735 Keeaumoku St. (And that's pronounced vaguely "leaky-leaky," like the highway of the same name.)

The **Rigger Restaurant** at 2335 Kalakaua Ave., in central Waikiki, is a good table-and-booth bazaar for burgers and the like. Decorated in slick Polynesian, it has lots of localized dishes like a Beach Boy Special, Surf Burgers, etc.

You'll find several addresses for the **Jolly Roger,** but our most recent foray was into one at the corner of Kuhio and Kaiulani avenues in Waikiki. Naugahyde and formica abound, and it was noisy with the clatter of dishes and the recorded music that tried unsuccessfully to drown out the chorus of dancing plates. The eight-foot neon hibiscus on the ceiling is considered a work of art. Our charcoal-broiled burgers and coffee tasted fine, and service was quick and good. Breakfast is fun at the 2244 Kalakaua Ave. link, especially if you draw a table by the sidewalk. We have not been quite as jolly in some of Roger's other branches, however.

Perry's Smorgy is one of those all-you-can-eat cafeterias which is perennially popular. At the moment, you can find one in the Reef, another in the Outrigger, and a third in the Coral Seas hotels. For seven or eight bucks you can fill up on spaghetti, chicken, pot roast, and several other things. Not bad for a starved trencherman on a bottom budget, but we wouldn't look for any gourmet bargains.

Another traditional penny-squeezer's pal has been the **Colonial House Cafeteria** in the International Market Place. But we thought the house was pretty battered and beaten recently, both in its dining room and in its kitchen products. In the Ilikai Hotel, the **Pier 7** is neat and popular, but we've always thought it rather pricey. There are no substitutions, either. And **Tops,** at 298 Beachwalk, was the "bottoms" as far as we were concerned. Our experience there was not good.

The meals at the Waikiki **Woolworth's** aren't bad for the low tabs. There's no longer a kosher-style "deli" on Kalakaua Avenue, but a somewhat similar establishment in the Ala Moana Center is **Lyn's Delicatessen.** It used to be a madhouse between 12 and 1, but it seems to us that they've reduced the size of their sandwiches and that the lines to get in aren't quite as hefty, either. And we now skip **Arthur's**, a downtown Bishop Street entry, entirely.

For a wide variety of Island and Mainland-style snacks, head for **Zippy's,** a diner with genuine local character. There are several sites, including one near Waikiki at 601 Kapahulu and its familiar "Saimin Lanai" at 1725 South King St. Take a minute or two to peruse the wall-mounted menu; you might like to try *saimin,* a teri beef and rice plate, *sushi,* etc. Of course it has hamburgers, chili, etc., too. Zippy's is not much more than a snack bar, but it's a good one, with a definite Hawaii accent.

Yes, there are **McDonald's** in Hawaii, as there are in Tokyo, Paris, and Melbourne. They continue to be a bargain as compared with many other places (although the Waikiki one is usually a little higher). McDonald's has made some concessions to local tastes in some outlets—adding papaya and Portuguese sausage to their breakfast menu and *saimin* at all hours of the day, but we're still waiting for them to add a McTeri burger to balance all those Mainland Macs. You'll also notice a clutch of **Kentucky Fried Chickens,** although strangely not at the moment in Waikiki. If you like it at home, you'll probably like it in Hawaii, too. Other fast-food chains represented in Honolulu include Jack-in-the-Box, Wendy's, Burger King, Church's, Taco Bell, Pizza Hut, and probably a few more we've forgotten. One local entry on the fast-food scene is the **K. C. Drive Inn,** an institution dating back to 1934, at 1029 Kapahulu Ave. Try the "Ono Ono Shake," with peanut butter on top.

SPECIAL AND UNUSUAL EATING PLACES

In an outside corner of the Honolulu Academy of Arts is one of the best and least-known culinary bargains in Hawaii, the **Garden Cafe** (Tel.

531-8865): Open only for lunch—two sittings, at 11:30 A.M. and 1 P.M. —Tuesday through Friday, about September through May; operated by volunteer ladies connected with the academy; each lunch with a different specialty soup, salad, and sandwich; no choice; all at a single price ($8 or so); sometimes dessert is an extra. *Always reserve.* (Ask for the menu of the day and the exact price by phone.) Very pleasant.

Not far away is **T.G.I. Friday** (Tel. 523-5841), at the corner of King Street and Ward Avenue, across from the Blaisdell Center Concert Hall: Outdoor section a little too close to the traffic for comfort and conversation; a cooler, quieter, and cleaner indoors loaded with antiques; large menu with unusual and clever specialty items; special champagne Sunday brunch; currently on a "no reservations" policy; bar currently a singles' meeting and mating ground. Friday's is fun any day of the week.

For ribs, try **Tony Roma's** (Tel. 942-2121) at the corner of Kalakaua Avenue and Pau Street. The barbecued baby back ribs are a bargain at lunch, more expensive at dinner. There's also a new branch under the H-1 Freeway on Waialae Avenue in Kahala. The hippest burger joint in town is called **Hamburger Mary's Organic Bar and Grill** at 2109 Kuhio Ave. Considered a "gay joint," the bamboo-walled place is popular with some of us straights, too. Most of Mary's hamburgers sell in the $6 range. Salads, sandwiches, and seafood can also be *ono-ono* (very good).

Hard to find, but worth trying, is the **Hawaiian Bagel** (Tel. 523-8638) at 753-B Halekauwila St. amid the warehouses and body and fender shops in the no-nonsense neighborhood called Kakaako. Bagels, made fresh on the premises, run from 50 cents to a buck and a half, depending on how they're served. Takeout sandwiches are in the $2 to $3 range. (Closed Sundays.)

For the past few years, the sandwich queen of Honolulu has been **Heidi's Bread Basket,** with addresses in several nooks and crannies around town, notably the Pacific Trade Center. You can get your beerwurst, headcheese, or Danish ham on about a dozen different kinds of bread. In a hard-to-find corner on the ground floor of the Davies Pacific Center (Bishop and Merchant streets,) **The Haven** builds some wonderful, healthy sandwiches. Our favorite is avocado and bacon bits on nine-grain bread. M-m-m-m-m! The branch in the Ala Moana Building doesn't seem quite as good. Instead, we would head for the new **Peppermill** on the ground-floor, mauka side of Ala Moana Center. It's a modern self-service place serving sandwiches, soups, salads, fish, vegetables, etc. Everything we tried was delicious.

The Salvation Army's half-century-old **Waioli Tea Room** (Tel. 988-2131) up in Manoa Valley suffers from TMT—too many tourists. They come in by the belching busload, often in several diesel coaches at the same time, and literally swarm through its premises. For a late lunch—after the crowds have left—it's not too bad. Try the *mahimahi,* but skip the Robert Louis Stevenson steak.

Pub Dining. The warmth and informality of the English or Irish pub is approximated in a few drinking/eating establishments in Honolulu this year. At this writing, the pub called Dickens has closed, but all the authentic Victorian froufrou and English mahogany is still in place at 1221 Kapiolani Blvd. Maybe someone will reopen it under that or another name. Stay tuned. Meanwhile, the **Rose and Crown** in King's Village concentrates on drinking and some eating. There are a few munchies like smoked sausages and "Pub Sub" sandwiches to chew with your brew. Atmosphere depends on the crowd. **Jameson's** is pretty good for Irish coffee, quiches, sandwiches, etc., at 12 Merchant St. in the revitalized downtown area. Also in the same immediate neighborhood is **O'Toole's Irish Pub** (Tel. 536-6360), 902 Nuuanu Ave., which offers a full menu and live piano music. We've yet to try their Shillelagh hamburger. Sorry, we haven't yet made it out to Aiea to investigate the **Elephant & Castle**, at Newtown Square, 98-1247 Kaahumanu St.

Turning from the Thames to the Rhine, at **Hofbrau Waikiki,** underneath the International Market Place, we liked their draft dark beer but were turned off by the dank room, which seemed to smell of Lysol on our own evening out. In any case, in 15 years of researching and patronizing Hawaii restaurants, this was the first and only one we've ever seen that added on an automatic service charge to the bill. That's just not done in the Aloha State.

Vegetarian Fare. The most charming, most delicious, most friendly, and most attractive vegetarian address is the tiny **Laulima** (Tel. 947-3844), which is somewhat out of the way at 2239 South King St. We never thought much of vegetarian food before we sat down at their shiny butcher-block tables, but the things they do with avocados, melted cheese, peanut butter, mushrooms, etc., are amazing. It opens at 11:30 A.M. daily, and if you go between 12 and 1 you probably won't squeeze in. You might have to sit on the floor here anyway, but if you're mellow about it, it's worth it. (No smoking.) Not so strictly vegetarian, but of the same general genre, is **Johnny Appleseed** at 932 Ward Ave., across from the Concert Hall. It's deservedly popular. Another choice for natural foods is **Sherrie's White Flower Inn** (Tel. 923-2664), although we haven't been in since they moved from the old house on South King to their new digs at 2117 Kuhio Ave. We'll be back sometime this year. We're also going to get to the **Guiltless Gourmet** at 1489 Kapiolani Blvd., as soon as we can get rid of some of our guilt. We hear the veggie chili dishes are pretty good. The new **Healthy's** in Ala Moana Center is not yet open at this writing.

Pancakes and Waffles. A downtown favorite is **Jake's,** at Bishop and Hotel streets, although Jake's has been expanding into other things lately. (This should not be confused with "Flakey Jake's.") Then, at the little, plain shopping center at 1414 Dillingham Blvd., there's the **Original Pancake House** (Tel. 847-1496), part of a Seattle franchise (and seemingly just about as much out of the way). A new branch has opened at 1221 Kapiolani Blvd.

Pizzas. You won't get two people to agree on this, either. We like the ones baked by the branches of **Round Table** (Tel. 946-2821 for the one at 805 Keeaumoku St.). Others swear by **Mama Mia Pizza & Deli** (Tel. 947-5233) at 1015 University Ave., or **Harpo's** in the Ward Warehouse. A decent choice that delivers in the Waikiki area is **Magoo's** (Tel. 949-5381). Its two addresses are 1980 Kalakaua Ave. and in the Kuhio Mall. **Chuck E. Cheese's Pizza Time Theatre,** on Kapiolani Boulevard, is not our cup of cheese at any time.

Submarine Sandwiches. Magoo's, above, launches them, too, but there's just one champion sub manufacturer, as far as we are concerned, and that's **Mister Sub** (Tel. 945-3511) at 1035 University Ave., next to Mama Mia's in the Puck's Alley shopping complex. M.S. makes at least 40 combinations, of which a personal favorite is the "Opu Buster" with Russian dressing. We can always dive into that one, even if we have trouble floating afterwards. Wow!

Ice Cream. Branches in the **Farrells** chain are prominent. An Edmonton visitor wrote us last year: "I've been an ice cream fan (and a fan of Farrells) ever since my university days in Albuquerque, but all four Farrells that we visited in Hawaii were marked by high prices and amateurish service. It was enough to make a guy go on a diet." Our own experience has not been that bad, although we vastly prefer **Dave's**, especially the branch at 1901 Kapiolani. Many express their preference for the hot fudge sundaes at **North Shore Fudge** at 2379 Kalakaua Ave., in the Diamond Head end of the Moana Hotel, and they *are* good. More of the same is also available at 2370 Kuhio Ave.

Shave Ice. This local dessert—compared to, but better than, a snow cone—is perhaps best sampled in Honolulu at the **Waiola Store,** a "mom and pop" grocery at 2135 Waiola St., off McCully Street. Shave ice aficionado Tom Brislin, city editor on the *Honolulu Advertiser,* likes his with vanilla and coconut syrups mixed half-and-half over a large shave ice with an ice-cream base. Mmmm! More convenient Waikiki addresses, perhaps, are those of **Island Snow** in the Royal Hawaiian Shopping Center, the Outrigger East Hotel, and the International Market Place.

KITCHENS IN THE COUNTRY

Here's a brief roundup of restaurants you may run across by design or by accident on a trip around the Island of Oahu:

PEARL CITY. The **Pearl City Tavern** (Tel. 455-1045), corner of Kam (Kamehameha) Highway and Lehua Avenue, is a first-rate restaurant specializing in Japanese food, but with several other choices including excellent lobster. Also famed for its Monkey Bar and its collection of bonsai trees. It's very busy on the weekends. To sound like a local, just call it the P.C.T.

MAKAHA. The **Sheraton** (Tel. 695-9511) on the Makaha Valley Road is expensive and certainly good. More unassuming fare will be found at the nautically decorated **Fogcutter** (Tel. 695-9404), just off Farrington Highway on Orange Street.

WAHIAWA. The most famous restaurant in this center-island community is on the shores of little Lake Wilson, across Route 99 from Schofield Barracks; it's called **Kemoo Farm** (Tel. 621-8481). Keep your eyes open or you'll miss it. It's great for a cool lunch on a hot day, overlooking the water and the eucalyptus trees. Reservations advised in the evening.

HALEIWA. Famous for baking its own pies is the **Sea View Inn.** (Try the banana or blueberry cream.) The newer **Jameson's By the Sea** (Tel. 637-4336) can be great for a sunset-over-the-ocean dinner. It's a branch of the Honolulu operation of a similar name. Getting up a lot of steam these days is **Steamer's.** Seafood is the specialty, but steaks and chops are also available. The nearby Mexican entry, **Rosie's Cantina,** does a willing, credible job with standard south-of-the-border dishes. It shares a front door with **Pizza Bob's,** which is under the same ownership. The **Tic Toc** was a waste of time, we thought. It offered little more than very cold air conditioning.

Zeke Wigglesworth, the perspicacious travel editor of the *San Jose Mercury-News,* says some of the best hamburgers on the island come from **Kua Aina,** a tiny Haleiwa shop, and we agree. Each burger seems to come in two sizes. There are five tables inside, plus three on the porch. We might also save Haleiwa as a dessert to a Wahiawa lunch by searching out the **Matsumoto Grocery** at 66-087 Kam Highway and ordering cones of shave ice (flavored crushed ice, see above). We prefer the kind with either ice cream or sweet *azuki* beans in the bottom of the paper cone.

WAIMEA. The **Proud Peacock** (Tel. 638-8513), at Waimea Falls Park, is a pleasant room in a beautiful garden setting. Our roast beef was fine.

KAHUKU. The coffee shop in the **Turtle Bay Hilton** is winning friends and influencing diners, apparently. We know less about their other restaurant; sorry.

LAIE. This is the home of the Polynesian Cultural Center, which traditionally offers great displays and entertainment but only fair fare.

Some readers have complained of long lines and cold food, but others say it was all right.

PUNALUU. There's just one restaurant, **Pat's at Punaluu** (Tel. 293-8502), and without it you might not know where Punaluu is. Although there are several who lament that it was better when the original "Pat" was alive, it's still a very pleasant beachside dining room offering seafood curry, Portuguese bean soup, and other island fare for lunch or dinner. It's now become the bottom floor in a huge beachside condo. Pat's is at its best any evening the ukulelist/guitarist duo Arna and Kimo Todd are performing. Ask before reserving, and then give them our best!

Past Punaluu Beach Park, on the *mauka* side, try the **Texas Paniolo,** if you dare. It's the only restaurant in Hawaii to offer rattlesnake meat! (Among other things, thank goodness.)

KAAAWA. Actually, the **Crouching Lion Inn** (Tel. 237-8511) is just on the *outskirts* of Kaaawa(!), nearer Kahana Bay and about two miles from Punaluu. Time was when no one would think of tripping around the island without a stop at the Inn. The lunches are sometimes so crowded that it diminishes the daytime fun. If you can get to this charming site for dinner, however, you might try the Slavonic Steak, carved at your table.

KANEOHE. For steaks, a salad bar, etc., you can do worse than the galley at **Rosey's Boat House** (Tel. 247-0039), on Kam Highway, for the evening meal. For lunch (or dinner) in a charming green setting, however, search out **Haiku Gardens** (Tel. 247-6671) at 46-336 Haiku Road, about a quarter mile *mauka* of Kahekili Highway. **Mexican Gardens** (Tel. 235-4141) is no Xochimilco, but it is reasonably good. The hard-to-find site is in prosaic surroundings near the Times Supermarket.

KAILUA. There is one very nice little French-Swiss salon in this bed-room community, open for dinner only. **L'Auberge** (Tel. 262-4835) at 117 Hekili St. is usually *très bon.* Then there's **Orson's Bourbon House** (Tel. 262-2306) at 5 Hoolai St.—a little pretentious but savory in the New Orleans style. There are two nicely decorated coffee shops, **Rob Roy's** (Tel. 262-6992), open for three decent if unspectacular squares at 26 Hoolai St., and the new **Plush Pippin** (Tel. 261-7552), next to the Foodland supermarket. The menu is uninspired, but the pies are good (and they're also sold at a takeout counter). A branch of the **Yum Yum Tree** is usually yummy. It's just off the difficult intersection at Mokapu Rd. and North Kalakeo St. Go late to avoid crying babies. There are two excellent Mexican choices in town, now. You might find us at **Cisco's Cantina**, near L'Auberge, at 123 Hekili. (Go early to avoid the crowd.) The other is the new Kailua branch of **Bueno Nalo** on Keolu Drive across from the Enchanted Lakes Shopping Center, perhaps a more difficult address to find.

If you can find the Aikahi Park Shopping Center at Mokapu Road and Kaneohe Bay Drive, near the above named Yum Yum Tree, **Harry's Cafe** and **Delicatessen** (Tel. 254-2277) is a find, too. Submarines, deli sandwiches, deluxe salads, etc., are all in the $5 range, lunch or dinner. Sit down or take out. (Closed Mondays.) For pizza, try **Alexander's,** across the parking lot from Foodland. For beef, one of our favorite feederies on the island is **Buzz's Original Steak House** (Tel. 261-4661) at 413 Kawailoa Rd., across from Kailua Beach Park. Many consider it worth driving to from Waikiki. However, **Buzz's Original Fish House,** in Kailua itself, is not nearly as good a catch.

6. Sightseeing Oahu

Face it—the Capital Island has so many targets for ogling, ooing, and ahing that it is impossible to see everything on a single vacation. And, praise be, not everything appeals to everybody. So the lists included below are designed to allow you to cut in and cut out of them as desired.

Sightwise, we've divided Oahu into five parts. The lead pair are walking tours; they are *Waikiki* first, and, second, *Downtown.*

Next we sweep nearly everything else in the metropolitan area into *Greater Honolulu.* It is arranged generally alphabetically, since no itinerary could efficiently cover all these sights in a single swing anyway.

Finally, there are two circuits more suitable for a set of wheels. The first is the relatively short *East Oahu Circle,* a good morning's or afternoon's jaunt by car. The second we call *Pearl Harbor and the Big Middle Island Round Trip.* You could almost handle that in a half-day, too, but we think it would be a mistake to do so. In both these motor excursions, as in the walking tours, we have tried to cover things in the order you may run across them.

Some sights and sites throughout the Hawaiian Islands are indicated by the "Hawaiian Warrior" markers put up by the Hawaii Visitors Bureau. Don't count on seeing them, however; many have been lost or stolen. In some areas for reasons long forgotten, they also point out public libraries. Furthermore, the symbol is not copyrighted, and restaurants, etc., have been known to erect their own Hawaiian Warrior outside, too!

A WAIKIKI WALK—THE PARK TO THE YACHT HARBOR

"Waikiki is *not* Hawaii!" someone will tell you. Unh-hunh, and we tell you, "Nonsense." Of course you could say it is no more Hawaii than, say, Kilauea Volcano *is* Hawaii, or Waimea Canyon *is* Hawaii, or Schofield Barracks *is* (or *are*) Hawaii. The point is that Waikiki is an integral and vital part of today's Hawaii, regardless of anybody's opinion as to whether it should be or not.

Travelers who have visited Waikiki in the past and then returned later almost invariably claim it was much nicer twenty years before (and when they were twenty years younger). They say it in the '80s about the '60s, just as they said it in the '60s about the '40s.

You can almost imagine the first American missionary landing on Oahu at Waikiki, looking around, and announcing to his guide, "A very nice island you have here, brother!"

"Nice?" the other man says incredulously. "Whaddaya mean, nice? You should have been here before King Kamehameha and his gang swept in and ruined everything! Twenty years ago—that's when it was really beautiful around here!"

Mark Twain came to Hawaii for a few months in 1866, when he was thirty-one years old, and then wrote and spoke admiringly of the Islands throughout the rest of his life. The Hawaii Visitors Bureau has been quoting and gloating over his words ever since. But Twain suffered from what Honolulu newsman Gerald Lopez always called the "Old Oaken Bucket Delusion," and the HVB can be thankful that the great author never returned to find that his youth was not here waiting for him. Not only would he not have composed some of that glowing prose of his later years; he would surely have angrily turned his pen to eloquently damn nearly everything in sight.

Waikiki continues to grow up, and not without a few scars inflicted and lessons learned in the school of hard knocks. To outsiders—like us—its beauty spots far outshine the marks of its mistakes. Throughout 1987, you'll see a lot of "improvement" going on in Waikiki—new and wider tiled sidewalks under construction, new benches, etc. Meanwhile, we'll bet you'll enjoy Waikiki today, and we won't be surprised if you come back again twenty years from now and say, "Oh, but you should have seen Waikiki back in the '80s!"

The dominant feature of Waikiki, and almost the symbol of Hawaii, is **Diamond Head,** a volcanic crater extinct for 150,000 years. It's only 760 feet tall, and reasonably hardy folks can climb to the top, if they want. (We made it once, anyway.) Drive via the tunnel to the little city park in the crater, then take the dusty trail. If possible, take a flashlight to help you through the dark area of the old military installation on the way and maybe a bottle of water, too, if the day is hot. The view at the top is worth the walk. Most will be content to merely gaze at the mountain the Hawaiians thought resembled a fish profile. They called it *Leahi*—forehead of the *ahi* (yellowfin tuna). Its English name came from calcite crystals discovered there by some nineteenth-century sailors who apparently thought they were diamonds.

That end—the "diamondhead boundary"—of Waikiki is more or less guarded by **Kapiolani Park,** named for the wife of King Kalakaua. On weekends, the park is almost a circus of community activities of one kind or another. Within its 140 acres are several other attractions, including the **Waikiki Aquarium** (Tel. 923-5335), a wonderful, state-owned collection of sealife, with an entrance fee currently at a reasonable $1.50, or free if you're under 16. The small aquarium, officially at 2777 Kalakaua Ave., has more than 300 species of Hawaiian and South Pacific marine life, including the giant clam, chambered nautilus, sharks, deep-water crustaceans, sea turtles, saltwater crocodiles, and harbor seals. Established in 1904, it's the third oldest aquarium in the U.S. (Open daily, 9 A.M. to 5 P.M.)

Try not to miss the free **Kodak Hula Show** (follow the crowd at 9:30 A.M. to get good seats for the 10 A.M. show Tuesday, Wednesday, and Thursday—plus Friday in the summer). The one-hour performance, which dates back to 1939, now takes place at some bleachers just off Monsarrat Avenue near the **Waikiki Shell,** another and more permanent outdoor amphitheatre. (Surprise: Film is sold there, too.)

Nearby is the **Honolulu Zoo,** which costs a buck for grownups (free for youngsters), and you'll miss an experience if you don't pop in and say hello to at least a few inhabitants. The design allows you to peek at some of the animals through the foliage, giving them a little more security and creating a natural feeling instead of putting them "on stage." A major reconstruction project has now begun at the zoo, and there is talk of raising the admission charge, too. At around 6 or 7 P.M. Wednesdays, during the summer, there's usually some kind of free show inside the zoo. (Picnic lunches welcome.) And a **Weekend Art Mart,** featuring the works of local artists, is held along the outside of the zoo fence Saturday, Sunday, and sometimes Wednesday. (See section 10, Shopping.)

Somewhat out of the way at the corner of Paki and Monsarrat avenues is the **Kapiolani Rose Garden,** with blooms taking nutrients from such exotic sources as giraffe manure from the zoo. There's no fee, but there's no picking, either. The roses are protected by some "magic *kahuna* stones." There are also picnic tables in the park, a driving range, an archery setup, tennis courts, and a special joggers' track. On the bandstand the Royal Hawaiian Band often performs weekly, usually at about 2 P.M. Sunday afternoons. It's also free.

Over by the water's edge there's the **Waikiki War Memorial Natatorium,** a crumbling 1927 structure recently saved for renovation, but fenced off in the meantime. The sections of beach along the park are known as Sans Souci and Queen's Surf. It was once a bathing area for Hawaiian royalty, but now there are showers and other facilities for us all.

The principal thoroughfare through Waikiki and the park is **Kalakaua Avenue,** named after the last king of Hawaii, King David Kalakaua ("kah-la-*cow*-wah"). Please don't let anybody tell you it is "Main Street." That's condescending, a cop-out, and decidedly unfair to the memory of a good king. Throughout 1987, several improvements are scheduled to be made to the avenue, including wider sidewalks, extensive landscaping, outdoor furniture, etc.

Just out of the park begins **Waikiki Beach,** a 2½-mile-long strand of wide, curving sand. Waikiki Beach is actually made up of several smaller beaches, and the section just at the foot of Kapahulu Avenue is called **Kuhio Beach Park.** It is particularly well protected from the heavy waves and ideal for young children and timid souls—usually. (See section 8, Water Sports.) The checkerboard tables there are also free, *if* you can find a vacant one.

At the end of the beach park, across Kalakaua from the big twin-towered Hyatt Regency Waikiki, is the **Waikiki Beach Center,** where you can rent a surfboard (look for all the racks) and take surfing lessons or maybe a surfing canoe ride. (More details in section 8.) Next to the beach center are four **Kahuna Stones,** repositories of magic healing powers perhaps for several hundred years. (A plaque explains it all.)

One of three "theme-type" Waikiki shopping emporia is officially **King's Village,** renamed that after being known as King's Alley for several years. It's a collection of nineteenth-century-style buildings that *Honolulu Star-Bulletin* writer Pierre Bowman called "Waikiki's Disneylandic confection in concrete." It's across Kaiulani Avenue from the "P.K." (the Princess Kaiulani Hotel), and there's usually free entertainment at the main entrance beginning at about 6 P.M. daily.

The other cutesy shopping arcade in the neighborhood is the quarter-century-old favorite **International Market Place,** 2330 Kalakaua Ave., which is largely sheltered by a gigantic banyan tree, complete with a treehouse. Formerly a section of an old royal estate, it's now mostly a group of rustic shopping stalls, snack bars, etc., of very varying quality, plus even a nightclub or two.

Don't miss a stroll through the old wooden **Moana Hotel,** across from the International Market Place. The Moana was built in 1901, and for a quarter-century it was the only real hotel on the beach. Today you can enjoy the banyan tree and the *makai* view as much as Robert Louis Stevenson did.

Two other landmark hotels in the immediate area include the venerable "pink palace," the **Royal Hawaiian Hotel,** still glowing cheerily in 1927 splendor (walk through its refreshing garden), plus its dramatic if gaudy young cousin, the **Sheraton-Waikiki Hotel.** On the second floor of the Sheraton is a "Waikiki Historical Room" exhibiting old photographs of the neighborhood. If the Japanese owners of the Royal have their way, it may one day exist only in old photos. There hasn't been much talk about it lately, but some $$-eyed executives still believe that the grande dame of Waikiki should be razed because it doesn't generate as much revenue per square foot as the modern highrises do.

The overlong, overbuilt **Royal Hawaiian Shopping Center,** which blocks off some traditional views between Kalakaua and the hotels, seems to have become a firm fixture in the neighborhood; it's now made somewhat more attractive by all the dripping greenery in the interior courtyards.

Kalakaua Avenue below Lewers Street (the 1900, 2000, and 2100 blocks) has become a little sleazy. Instead of going that way, turn left on Lewers. At the end of the street is the modern **Halekulani Hotel,** which also incorporates the original 1917 building, the site of the first Charlie Chan detective novel, *The House Without a Key.* Just next door is the **Reef Hotel,** where there is free amateur beachside entertainment beginning at around 8 P.M. on Sunday nights. Stroll along the beach or Kalia Road to **Fort DeRussy,** a military post maintained much like a park. (This may be the future site of a major convention center owned by the city, although the proposed project is currently embroiled in some controversy.) The **Army Museum** (Tel. 543-2639) is headquartered in the old coastal artillery battery building. If it looks something like a war ruin, that's because they once tried to batter the building down and it turned out to be too tough to raze. Admission is free, but there's an intimidating donation box at the entrance. It's open daily except Monday, 10 A.M. to 4:30 P.M., and you can reserve a guided tour by calling 543-2687.

You can't buy anything at the army's **Hale Koa Hotel** without military I.D. Of course you're welcome to swim along here; in Hawaii, all beaches are public property by state law.

Farther along the beach is the Hilton Hawaiian Village Hotel and its attractive **Rainbow Bazaar** shopping arcade. The beach ends here, but Waikiki is considered to extend just a little farther to the Ilikai Hotel and the **Ala Wai Yacht Harbor.** (This is not the harbor for the cruise boats, by the way; they leave from Kewalo Basin—see later.) The sailboats parked here are perhaps best seen by riding the glass-walled elevator that crawls up the spine of the Ilikai.

Those who walk a little farther along Ala Moana Boulevard toward Ala Moana Center may want to turn around just past the movie theater and parking lot to take a peek at what is known as the **Whaling Wall.** Undoubtedly Hawaii's largest painting, the 23,000-square-foot "Hawaiian Humpbacks" has sparked considerable controversy but survived court challenges since it was created by a young California artist in 1985. Take a look at it now. New hotel construction on the site next door will probably soon block it from view.

DOWNTOWN—HAUNTS OF MISSIONARIES AND MERCENARIES

All the tearing down and building up that goes on in Waikiki often seems to be doubled downtown, and the core area appears destined for a high state of flux over the next several years. Nevertheless, Honolulu's downtown is not a Wall Street or some other collection of impersonal blocks of stone mortared into a rectangular maze. There are happy islands of intriguing history and inviting tranquillity throughout, bordered by an active waterfront and some spicy activities in part of a decaying urban area.

You may follow the stroll we have designed below from the description, although you might like to pick up a map as well.

If you're busing from Waikiki, take the No. 2 and, after it goes along Beretania Street, get off at Alapai Street. (See the map near the beginning of this chapter.) Walk *makai*, past the tall Municipal Office Building, and at a point near City Hall cross King Street to get to the **Mission Houses Museum** (Tel. 531-0481) at 553 South King St. These are the earliest American buildings on the island. The white, wooden frame house was prefabricated in New England, shipped around "the Horn," and then, in 1821, erected as a dwelling place for the first missionaries to the Sandwich Isles. The adjoining two coral-block buildings (in one of which the visit to the museum begins) were added slightly later and also became part of the mission complex. The museum, which includes many mementos of that exciting period in Hawaiian history, is well run by members of the Hawaiian Mission Children's Society—the descendants of the missionaries themselves.

Open daily from 9 A.M. to 4 P.M., the museum costs $3.50 for adults and $1 for children. A guided tour is included in the price. A visit to the Mission Houses is essential to anyone who wants to understand some basic history of the Islands. The museum also serves as the headquarters for an excellent two-hour tour conducted by the society over the entire central historic district, including several sights listed below. (See section 7, Guided Tours, etc.)

The unusual sculpture across King Street is **Sky Gate,** a somewhat controversial work of art that is the focal point for many city-sponsored concerts and other events.

Just across the little street from the Mission Houses is **Kawaiahao Church** (Tel. 538-6267) at King and Punchbowl streets. Sometimes called the Westminster Abbey of Hawaii, the church has served as a royal chapel for the coronations, weddings, and funerals of kings and queens. But it was as a mission church for the Hawaiian people that it was consecrated. Construction began in 1837 on the 14,000-coral-block structure, which replaced four previous thatched-roof models on the same site. It was dedicated in 1842. Today services are conducted at 10:30 A.M. on Sundays in English and Hawaiian. Visitors are welcome and are often invited to tour the church afterwards.

Graves of missionaries and their families are behind the church. Those of the early congregations are on the *makai* side. In front of the church is **King Lunalilo's Tomb,** which was built in 1876. (Lunalilo did not wish to be buried at the Royal Mausoleum in Nuuanu Valley.)

Across King Street from the Kawaiahao Church you will notice **Honolulu Hale** (City Hall), built in Spanish style in 1929. But we would continue our walk along King for a block to the **Kamehameha I Statue.** This black and gold impression of the conqueror of the Islands was erected in 1883. It was the second such statue cast; the first was aboard a ship that sank on the way to Hawaii from Italy (see chapter 10). On June 11, Kamehameha Day, it is festooned with scores of long flower leis.

The statue's backdrop is **Aliiolani Hale,** now also known as the old Judiciary Building, built in 1874. Originally designed as a royal palace, it was modified for use as the House of Parliament during the monarchy. The lawmakers moved out and the courts moved in when Hawaii was declared a republic in 1893.

Across King Street and set in elaborate grounds is the highly revered Victorian structure named the **Iolani Palace.** Built by King David Kalakaua in 1882, it is now known as the only royal palace in the United States. The architecture has been called American Florentine, along with lots of other things, and it almost surely was inspired by something on King Kalakaua's world tour. One mystery is the little-known fact that it is very much like the once-famous mansion built in Athens by German archeologist Heinrich Schliemann, the discoverer of Troy.

Over the past decade the palace has been beautifully restored, and it is open for 45-minute guided tours, reservation only, from Wednesday through Saturday, 9 A.M. to 2:15 P.M. If you telephone 523-0141 a day or so in advance, you should be able to get on a tour, or you may write first to the Friends of Iolani Palace, P.O. Box 2259, Honolulu, HI 96804. Admission price has been holding at $4 for adults and $1 for children 5 through 12. (Children under 5 are prohibited.)

At this stage the palace has few furnishings, but all the architectural detail, woodwork, lighting fixtures, and other features have been brought back faithfully to 1882. The palace today is treated almost reverently. Only twelve people are allowed on a tour, incidentally, and no photographs are permitted—a silly rule, to be sure.

Out on the palace grounds you will see the **Kalakaua Coronation Bandstand,** only the dome of which remains unchanged from the 1883 ceremony during which King Kalakaua placed a crown on his own head. Today the stand is used sometimes for public events, but it primarily serves on Fridays at noon as the site for the free public concerts by the Royal Hawaiian Band.

The fortlike structure a few hundred yards *mauka* of the bandstand is **Iolani Barracks,** originally built in 1871 to quarter the Royal Household Guard. It used to stand near the present state capitol, but it was moved here stone by stone to make way for the capitol, and then was rather badly slicked up after the move.

Behind the palace is the multitrunked **Iolani Banyan,** a still-spreading tree that may be more than a century old. According to some accounts it was planted by Queen Kapiolani, wife of King Kalakaua. The modern-looking and out-of-place building next to the tree is the **State Archives,** whose tucked-away treasures are not immediately accessible, except to scholars.

Out on the grassy mall, which used to be a segment of Hotel Street, you'll see the **Queen Liliuokalani Statue,** installed there in 1982. She faces the bold and dramatic **Hawaii State Capitol,** an architectural wonder unduplicated anywhere. Completed in 1969, the capitol takes its inspiration from Hawaii's natural history. The House and Senate chambers externally resemble volcanoes rising up from a sea, represented by a reflecting pool. The columns are evocative of palm trees, and the open central court invites the gentle climate of Hawaii to enter the most important public building in the state. (The offices and chambers around the railings, however, are fully air conditioned.)

If you take an elevator to the top floor, you can appreciate the rotunda from another angle as well as walk to two opposite terraces to enjoy impressive *makai* and *mauka* views over Honolulu. The governor's office is up here, too. Look for a giant koa door that says: "E Komo Mai" (Please Come In). Sometimes there is a free booklet available inside describing the capitol and surrounding area. The state legislature is in session from January to April, and you may be lucky enough to get one of the free tours by House doorman Joe Tassill. (There is a proposal to extend the tours to other months, too.)

Outside the capitol building on the *mauka* side you will find the once-controversial bronze statue of **Father Damien,** the hero of the leprosy settlement at Kalaupapa on the island of Molokai. (See chapter 8.) It was hammered out in modern style by Marisol, the Venezuelan sculptress.

The capitol grounds are bordered on the mountain side by Beretania Street, the closest Hawaiian pronunciation and spelling could come to honoring Britannia, the ancient Latin name for Britain. Directly across this street is the new **Armed Forces Memorial,** a nonobjective sculpture with obligatory eternal flame.

A walk toward town on that side of the street will bring you to the gates of **Washington Place,** 320 South Beretania St., the official mansion of the state governor and the oldest continuously occupied house on the island. Built in 1846, it eventually was inherited by Queen Liliuokalani, who resided there until her death in 1917.

Today you can peek at it through the closed iron gate. It is not open to the public.

A few steps farther, at the corner of Queen Emma Street, is **Saint Andrew's Cathedral,** the Episcopal (Church of England) headquarters. Construction was begun in 1867, supervised by Queen Emma, the widow of Kamehameha IV, both of whom were anglophiles. The building was designed in Britain, and some of the materials were shipped from that country.

On the *makai* side of Beretania Street, and two blocks farther on, is **Our Lady of Peace Cathedral,** the modest nexus of the island's Roman Catholics. It was built between 1840 and 1843, after local opposition to Catholicism finally eased.

The cathedral fronts on the **Fort Street Mall,** which extends for seven blocks to the waterfront. The former main thoroughfare, now redesigned and relandscaped entirely for shopping and strolling pedestrians, represents a successful 1969 attempt to revitalize what was once the mercantile center of the city.

If you're running short of time, you can follow Fort Street Mall directly to the waterfront, the Aloha Tower, etc. (And if you make a one-block detour to Bishop and King streets, you'll see the new **Tamarind Park** with its 11-foot bronze statue, "Upright Motive Number Nine" by Henry Moore.) But if you're still moving at an unhurried pace, and if it's daytime, take a slight detour to experience as much of **Chinatown** as still remains since urban renewal was begun in the neighborhood.

Turn right off the mall and walk four blocks along Hotel Street, past the adult-film houses, tattoo parlors, fortune tellers, and other elements of a honky-tonk neighborhood popular with servicemen since World War II. Then turn left on **Maunakea Street** and poke around in the little Chinese groceries, herb shops, import stores, etc., on the way to King Street. (The *mauka*—inland—end of Maunakea Street is bounded by the Cultural Plaza, which is covered under Shopping, section 10. You can discover more of Chinatown, by the way, on the Tuesday-morning tours sponsored by the Chinese Chamber of Commerce, described in section 7.)

Turn left at King Street, cross King at Smith, go along Smith for a few yards, and head down tiny Marin Street past an antique gas station and several other buildings to get to **Merchant Street.** Along here several late-nineteenth- and early-twentieth-century buildings have been preserved and have been turned into shops, bars, and restaurants. The offices of *Honolulu* magazine today occupy the architecturally interesting 1910 **Yokohama Specie Bank** building, with its coppersheathed windows, at the corner of Merchant and Bishop. (The Japanese-owned bank was closed at the outset of World War II, and a Japanese-language calendar, turned to December, 1941, still hangs on one wall.) The 1871

Kamehameha V Post Office, restored across Bishop Street, may eventually become a postal museum, although recently it has been used for several courtrooms. It was the first structure in Hawaii to be built entirely of concrete. Now return to the Fort Street Mall, this time at its lower end.

Turn seaward on the mall and cross Queen Street to see what was saved from the fort, razed in 1857, that gave the mall/street its name—a single, solitary cannon. It was one of forty that once poked through the bastion built in 1817 by Kamehameha I. (A nearby plaque covers the details.)

Use the traffic lights and carefully cross Nimitz Highway, walk straight through **Irwin Park,** take the escalator to the second deck of Pier 9 (where virtually all ship passengers disembark), and follow the signs for the elevator up to the **Aloha Tower.**

Built in 1921, the state-owned Aloha Tower was for several decades the tallest structure in Honolulu. Its purpose then, as now, was to direct the ship movement in Honolulu Harbor. You can ride free to the tenth-floor observation deck for a 360-degree panorama of this part of the city any time between 8 A.M. and 9 P.M. Passenger liners sometimes tie up at Piers 9 and 10 next to the Aloha Tower. On Saturdays, these are usually the S.S. *Independence* and/or the S.S. *Constitution,* pausing in their week-long cruises around the major islands.

On the level just below the observation deck is the first stage of the new **Maritime Center,** consisting at this point mostly of a museum with photographs. Work may begin during 1987 on a massive redevelopment here that will include a hotel, shopping areas, etc., with the Aloha Tower as its focal point. What this construction will do to strolling in the vicinity in the meantime is unknown.

After leaving the tower, walk down the ramp. Below, at Pier 7, you will see other parts of the Maritime Center. First there is the restored, century-old, four-masted **Falls of Clyde,** a 266-foot-long square rigger that often called at Honolulu during the days of the tall ships. This is also the usual berth of the **Hokule'a,** the 60-foot-long replica of an ancient Polynesian voyaging canoe. Named for the star that guided Polynesians to the Hawaiian Islands, the *Hokule'a* has been sailed from Honolulu to Tahiti and the South Pacific three times since it was built in 1976. It is scheduled to return home again during 1987. Other interesting old craft will eventually be added to the area under ongoing plans. You can go on board the Falls of Clyde (Tel. 536-6373) for $3 ($1 for children) from 9:30 A.M. to 4:30 P.M. daily.

Nearby, at Pier 6, you may or may not see a flamboyant red-and-gold barge. It was a Chinese floating restaurant, towed to Honolulu from

Hong Kong in 1972. It did not win wide public acceptance, probably because of fire-safety worries, and it finally went bankrupt. (We did our part by pointing out as often as possible that floating restaurants are generally unsafe in an emergency, no matter where in the world they are located, due to inadequate exits to the shore.) At this writing there are incomplete plans to tow it back to Hong Kong, and we hope that happens before someone else tries to open it again.

If you're not driving, you can return to Waikiki from this area by catching City Bus No. 19 on nearby Nimitz Highway.

GREATER HONOLULU

As we mentioned earlier, no routing could wind through this next group in a logical order. Nor should it, since it is doubtful that any traveler will aim for every target on the list.

So now that we have wandered through Waikiki and downtown, we cover the rest of Honolulu more or less alphabetically, sometimes indicating which others in the group are in the same or nearby neighborhoods.

If your feet weren't tired from our *Waikiki Walk* above, you might have stumbled a little farther along Ala Moana Boulevard from the Ilikai Surf Hotel to **Ala Moana Center,** one of the most gigantic shopping souks in the world. (From and to Waikiki, take Bus No. 8.) There are more than 150 stores and restaurants over three levels with artwork, colorful fish and birds, children's play areas, free shows on the outdoor stage, etc. On Honolulu excursions Neighbor Islanders often stay at the adjoining Ala Moana Hotel so they can lay in supplies at this merchandising oasis. Note that some of the same articles for sale in Waikiki hotel shops may be found more reasonably priced at Ala Moana or other shopping centers. (See section 10, Shopping, for complete details.)

Across the boulevard named Ala Moana (Ocean Way) from Ala Moana Center and the Ala Moana Hotel is **Ala Moana Park,** a long strip of trees, grass, and calm-water beach popular mostly with local folk.

The man-made peninsula that juts from that park into the ocean is called Magic Island, and it was the site of an ambitious but abortive "Tivoli Gardens"–style amusement park project some years ago. Although the fun and games never got under way, the park, which forms one side of the channel to the Ala Wai Yacht Harbor, now provides an excellent view of the Waikiki coastline.

On the other side of town, the highly revered **Bishop Museum and Planetarium** (Tel. 847-1443), at 1525 Bernice St., should not be missed. Founded in 1889, it is the repository for all things Polynesian and the center for most of the scholarly archeological work throughout the Pacific. Headquartered in an old stone structure, it appears deceptively small. But winding its stairways and threading its corridors to closely examine all exhibits can easily take half a day.

Here are not only the thrones, crowns, and other relics of the elegant monarchy period of Hawaiian history, but also the feathered cloaks and carved gods of Kamehameha I and the "pre-European" ages of the Island. Next door the museum has a "living theater" structure, a sort of thatched-roof pavilion called the Atherton Halau. The arts and crafts of Hawaii are demonstrated there regularly, and classes may also be arranged. The museum's shop (in the modern Ululani Jabulka Pavilion) sells books, recordings, and artifacts you may not find for sale elsewhere.

The next-door Planetarium is also well-run. At 11 A.M. daily you can lean back, look up, and enjoy "Polynesian Skies," a lecture that might add sparkle to your late-night star gazing. Check out the old Oahu Railway train and other outdoor exhibits, too. Last time we were at the museum, admission was still running a price of $4.75 for adults, $2.50 for children 6 to 17. Open 9 to 5 every day except Christmas. To reach the museum, take City Bus No. 2—"School Street," from Waikiki (not No. 2—"Liliha," which doesn't go far enough), get off at the Kam Shopping Center, and walk *makai* for a block. With a car, take the Houghtailing Street exit from the Lunalilo Freeway, then drive to the grounds via Houghtailing and Bernice streets.

The sports arena, exhibit hall, and concert auditorium named the **Neal Blaisdell Center** is often known locally by its former name, the HIC—Honolulu International Center, or NBC, its current initials. One goes to the circular arena, at Kapiolani and Ward, for events like the circus, the fights, rock concerts, or basketball games. The nearby concert hall, at Ward and King, hosts the Honolulu Symphony Orchestra or the Hawaii Opera Theatre in season.

In the industrial area near Nimitz Highway, and also seasonal, are visits to the **Dole Pineapple Cannery** (Tel. 536-3411). They are conducted on a tour basis only at the plant, 650 Iwilei Rd. Generally the $2 rounds are made weekdays from about May through August, but hours and details vary, so phone the above number. (Take Bus No. 8/19-"Airport/ Hickam" from Waikiki.) They give you free pineapple juice, by the way. It sure tastes great—but yes, it *is* canned. Dole has explained to us that there really is no such thing as *fresh* pineapple juice.

All too often visitors miss the **Foster Botanic Gardens** (Tel. 531-1939), a large and tranquil oasis in the midst of the hustle and bustle, at 180 North Vineyard Blvd. Open from 9 A.M. to 4 P.M., this unusual city park is a living museum of virtually every type of fern, vine, tree, orchid, and other flower that can exist in the tropics—about 4,000 species.

Admission to the nearly 1½-century-old park is one dollar. (Call 538-7258 to find out about guided tours sometimes available.) Look for the gigantic trees called the earpod, the Queensland kauri, and the kapok, all planted by the originator of the garden in 1855. The orchid display is also fascinating. And wander, too, through the Prehistoric Glen, a mysterious cul-de-sac of ferns, strange palms, weird grasses, etc., that has received national recognition. Visitors are welcome to pick up anything that has fallen on the ground—seeds, flowers, leaves, etc.—but nothing off the trees or plants, of course.

You can get to the garden by a pleasant one-block walk *mauka* along the river from the Cultural Plaza. There is a parking lot for cars. Or, busing from Waikiki, take No. 4 to Nuuanu Avenue and Vineyard Boulevard. Don't forget that early closing time, but don't forget to go, either.

Across Thomas Square from the Neal Blaisdell Center concert hall is the **Honolulu Academy of Arts** (Tel. 538-1006), and entrance is free to the lovely building with its six open courtyards and thirty-seven gallery rooms. Best known for a rare collection of Oriental art, the academy also includes European and American masterpieces as well as the best work of Hawaii-based artists. (Somehow, though, the galleries are arranged so that the Eastern art is in the west and the Western works are east!) Open Tuesday through Saturday, 10 A.M. to 4:30 P.M., and Sunday 1 to 5 P.M.; 45-minute guided tours at 11 A.M. Wednesday and Friday. Closed Monday.

Besides the galleries, notice the Academy shop, which has for sale a large selection of books on art and Polynesian lore, plus some gift items. Also, the Garden Cafe there serves gourmet lunches turned out by ladies of the Academy Volunteers Council from September through May. (Reserve at 531-8865.)

To bus to the main academy building, take No. 2 from Waikiki. Your destination is 900 South Beretania St., between Victoria and Ward; onstreet metered parking is usually available in the area. If you ever visit art galleries anywhere, you should add this one to your list.

Kewalo Basin, often (incorrectly) called Fisherman's Wharf after the name of the restaurant there, is at the lower end of Ward Avenue, just across Ala Moana Boulevard. This commercial harbor, the home of most of Oahu's fishing fleet, is the place to charter deep-sea fishing boats. Also most of the dinner cruises, Pearl Harbor tours, glass-bottom boats, etc., leave from there. At the end of one pier is the Bumble Bee tuna cannery, not usually noticeable unless there is an offshore (Kona) breeze(!). Across the boulevard from the basin is Ward Warehouse, a shopping and restaurant complex. (From Waikiki take the No. 8/19 "Airport/Hickam" bus.) The area makes a nice walk on a sleepy Sunday—at least if the trades are blowing.

Up in Manoa Valley, **Paradise Park** (Tel. 988-2141) is mainly into exotic birds—teaching them to do tricks on the high wire and the like. The 15-acre park includes a rain forest and more than 100 species of tropical plants. It's certainly fun for the kids ($5.75); 13- to 17-year-olds pay $8.95 now and adults fork over a whopping $9.95 (there's a $1 discount for senior citizens). The parrots, of course, are not native to Hawaii. There's also an electronic "Dancing Waters" fountain show three times a day. The flowers and trees, at least, are authentic, and the whole park is probably a good place to take a lot of nature pictures. The tickets are steep, but visitors who are not getting out into the country or over to the Neighbor Islands may think it worth the price. The park has also inaugurated a free shuttle bus service from Waikiki. (Phone for details.)

To get there from Waikiki you can take Bus No. 5 on a long, rounda-bout route for 45 minutes to the end of the line. If you make the bus trip but decide not to hit the park, and if your hiking legs are in good shape, take the free (but often slippery) jungle trail at the end of Manoa Road behind Paradise Park and the Lyon Arboretum for one mile (about 30 minutes) to **Manoa Falls.** Freshwater swimming is permitted, and it's a wonderful place for a picnic.

Known rather simply as **Punchbowl,** the National Memorial Cemetery of the Pacific is considered the Arlington of this part of the world, a last resting place for more than 25,000 servicemen on the 112-acre floor of a long-extinct volcano. Punchbowl Crater was called Puowaina (Hill of Sacrifice) by the ancient Hawaiians, and it was indeed the site of human sacrifices in prehistory. Look for the grave of war correspondent Ernie Pyle, and near it, the grave of Ellison Onizuka, the Hawaii astronaut who died in the *Challenger* disaster in 1986.

You almost need a car or taxi to visit Punchbowl; note that there's less traffic after noon. It's at the end of Puowaina Drive, and the city buses don't go on into the cemetery. If you're truly busbound, transfer to No. 15 downtown, explain to the driver, and he'll let you off on Puowaina Drive, where your walk will be a scenic half mile or so into the cemetery. The gates are open 8 A.M. to 5 P.M. For details on the memorial and other aspects of the cemetery, see if you can pick up the Veterans Administra-tion pamphlet in the Administration Building, near the flagpole.

Queen Emma's Summer Palace (Tel. 595-3167), at 2913 Pali Highway, was once a summer retreat of the wife of Kamehameha IV. (They were the same royal couple responsible for Queen's Hospital and St. Andrew's Cathedral.) Built in 1843, the palace, whose real name is Hanaikalamalama, is now maintained as a museum by the Daughters of Hawaii. Notice the little koa-wood cradle for Emma's son, the prince, heir to the Hawaiian

throne and godson of Queen Victoria, who nevertheless was to die tragi-
cally at the age of four. The museum, open 9 A.M. to 4 P.M. Monday
through Friday and to noon Saturday, costs $4, which seems a lot for a
small place. (It's a better deal if you show up at 2 P.M. Mondays, when
you'll receive a guided tour.) Take Bus No. 4.

In the same general part of town, at 2261 Nuuanu Ave., is the 1865
Royal Mausoleum (Tel. 536-7602), which holds the remains of most
members of the Kamehameha and Kalakaua dynasties. The three-acre
grounds, the chapel, and the crypt are open daily except Sunday from 8
A.M. to 4 P.M., and from 8 until noon Saturdays. Look for a free state
parks folder inside, or you might be lucky enough to get a guided tour
by Lydia Maioho, the custodian and herself a descendant of the Kame-
hamehas. (And out of alphabetical order, here, but just around the
corner at 42 Kawananakoa Place, is the dramatically ornate **Chinese
Buddhist Temple of Honolulu.** Turn down the street. You'll know it
when you see it!)

Sand Island, the traditional dumping ground across Honolulu Channel from the Aloha Tower, has been developed into a long-overdue park—
or at least the end part of it has—that affords a nice view of downtown
Honolulu. The route to it isn't all that salubrious, however. Take Sand
Island Access Road off Nimitz Highway, but only if you're in the neighborhood anyway.

If you ask at the entrance to the U.S. Coast Guard Base at Sand Island
on the way to the park, they *may* let you go in and have a look at the two
unusual sculpted hula girls there (no guarantees). These figures, with
hair, bathing suits, and makeup in the styles of forty years ago, are all
that remain of a group of six statues that are today only a footnote to
history. They were crafted there by lonely Italian prisoners of war. For
some reason the Italians were penned in a compound on that property
in 1944.

The **Tantalus–Round Top Drive,** named after the two tall hills it crosses,
is a favorite excursion made by Honoluluans with Mainland guests, but
not an easy route for *malihinis* on their own. It sometimes provides appreciation points for Oahu's most spectacular sunsets, especially in the
winter. Part of the route goes through a tropical forest reserve, and
you'll often be able to pick up guavas or passion fruit along the winding,
two-lane road. It's cooler on Tantalus, and the few folks who live along
the way often have fireplaces to cozy up to in the wintertime. Don't miss
the little *Ualakaa Park,* and particularly its wide-angle, eagle's-eye view of
Honolulu from Koko Head to the Waianae Mountains. (The park closes
at dusk.) City bus No. 15 also makes its way along this seven-mile route.
If you're driving, check a map for Tantalus Drive or Round Top Drive;

it's hard to find the right street to start up on, but you might try it via either Makiki Street or Mott-Smith Drive.

At 203 Prospect St., on the slopes of Punchbowl, is the **Tennent Art Foundation Gallery** (Tel. 531-1987). It is devoted to displaying the works of the late Madge Tennent, probably the best-known Island artist. Open Tuesday through Saturday 10 A.M. to noon, Sunday 2 P.M. to 4 P.M.; closed Mondays. Admission is free.

The University of Hawaii and the East-West Center are on a joint 300-acre campus in Manoa Valley (take Bus No. 4). Architecturally, the institution is a disaster—a real stylistic jumble—but the grounds are botanically interesting if you're into things like that. Ask for the map and guide at the University Relations Office in Bachman Hall (Dole Street near University Avenue). Student-guided tours are sometimes offered both of the university and of the East-West Center, the unique institution set up in 1960 to promote cultural exchanges between Asian-Pacific and Western peoples. (See section 7 for more details.)

A traditional wateringhole for hundreds of tour buses through Manoa Valley is the **Waioli Tea Room** (Tel. 988-2131) at 3016 Oahu Ave. Although it is run by the good folks from the Salvation Army, and although they have installed on its grounds an old *pili* grass house that is supposed to be the one once used by Robert Louis Stevenson in Waikiki, we feel the place is generally overrated and too often overcrowded. Its bakery, however, sells delicious mango bread and other local goodies. If you stop here, go in the afternoon to avoid the morning and lunchtime hordes. They're open until 4 except on Sunday.

THE EAST OAHU CIRCLE TRIP

This trip, a good morning or afternoon tour, is designed mainly for travelers who have equipped themselves with a rental car, although two buses, No. 57 (clockwise) or No. 58 (counter-clockwise) cover basically the same route, beginning at Ala Moana Center.

Both this section and the next are circle routes. We have put it down here our way, just because that's the way we like to drive it ourselves.

Pick up a road map, of course, and if you want piped-in local atmosphere along the way, you might turn your car radio to the only Oahu radio station that plays all Hawaiian music. It's KCCN, at 1440 kilocycles, crowded in amidst two dozen island stations who vie for position on the AM dial.

Diamond Head, the extinct volcano crater that was a starting point for our Waikiki walk, also serves as a takeoff point in the opposite direction for our wheeled excursion. You can drive through a tunnel into the crater, by the way. If you stop at the park there, you'll see a trail that begins the hike to the rim. (Take Monsarrat Avenue through the zoo and then on up behind the mountain for 1.5 miles to about 18th Avenue.)

Most people prefer to save that excursion, driving instead *makai* of Diamond Head along Diamond Head Road, past the Amelia Earhart Monument and into the lush, green, and palm-shaded **Kahala District,** which holds some of Honolulu's finest homes and gardens.

If you continue on Kahala Avenue (while other traffic turns *mauka* onto Kealaolu Avenue), you'll wind up at the prestigious **Kahala Hilton Hotel,** which has hosted the likes of kings and presidents for the past decade and a half. The buildings and grounds are lovely, and you can watch the porpoises and turtles get fed at 10:30 A.M. or 12:30 and 2:30 P.M. (Ask at the front desk for a pamphlet outlining a walking tour of the grounds.)

The next-door golf course is the **Waialae Country Club,** scene of the Hawaiian Open golf tournament in January.

Return to the aforementioned Kealaolu Avenue, then drive to the Lunalilo Freeway (H-1) and take it in the *kokohead* direction (vaguely, east), being careful not to cross over the double white lines. The road becomes the famous Kalanianaole Highway. (When you can pronounce that, then you're supposed to be a *kamaaina*. And take heart, for the Honolulu Police Department usually calls it simply "Kalani Highway" when they ticket you for crossing those double lines.)

Skirting the residential neighborhoods of Aina Haina, Niu, and Kuliouou, the highway emerges alongside a sort of tropical Venice developed by the late industrialist Henry Kaiser. Called **Hawaii Kai,** the area is still growing in, around, through, and over an ancient Hawaiian fishpond. Notice that not only are there two cars in nearly every garage, but that many back doors also boast a boat dock, with a large or small craft tied up there.

Out the starboard side of your windshield, above the ocean, humps the landmark known as **Koko Head,** an extinct crater not to be confused with its steeper cousin to the left of the road which is called **Koko Crater.** (Years ago a military aerial tramway used to cut straight up the side. You can still just barely make out its route.)

If you turn into Hawaii Kai on Lunalilo Home Road at the light, the shopping center on your immediate left again is **Koko Marina.** Besides the stores installed in rustic, nautical trappings, there really is a marina. From time to time it has offered free, narrated boat rides through the surrounding waterways.

Back on the coastal highway, if you continue up the hill you can turn right to **Hanauma Bay Beach Park.** (Keep your eyes open because it's a badly marked turnoff to the right.) Park your car and go peer over the edge to view what appears to be a nearly circular bay. (Actually, it's more horseshoe-shaped, but the perspective is deceptive.) This is an extinct volcano crater, breached on one side by the sea. It now boasts a lovely beach, and also an underwater park where thousands of colorful reef fish swim among the submerged rocks, observed and enjoyed by skin and scuba divers. You can only see the creatures by using a face mask, however, and snorkeling at Hanauma Bay is one of our own favorite Island diversions.

Elvis Presley had a grass shack on Hanauma Bay in the film *Blue Hawaii,* and the beach was also used in *From Here to Eternity.* The "Beach Bus" goes there from Monsarrat Avenue in Waikiki. No. 58, the counterclockwise circle island route, also heads for Hanauma Bay.

If you continue along Kalanianaole again, you'll see HVB markers pointing out to sea identifying the islands of Molokai and Lanai, about 30 miles away. *Sometimes*—usually during the winter months—you *can* see them, and maybe even Maui as a ghostly shape beyond Molokai when the conditions are perfect.

Just a little past a small shrine, a memorial to some fishermen once swept into the sea near here, is the **Halona Blow Hole.** (The last time we were there the sign marking it needed a good cleaning.) From the lookout you can often see the waves shoot a spout of water up through an old lava tube. Lock your car or take everything with you, as thefts from "locked" vehicles are common. And watch your step while walking on the cement platform.

Sandy Beach Park, just beyond, is popular but dangerous for persons not accustomed to handling its often violent and tricky waves. It is not recommended for visitors. Even locals are regularly injured here, and a number of sharks sometimes patrol about 100 yards out, too. (See our discussion on this and other beaches in section 8, Water Sports.)

If you are into cacti, desert plants, etc., you can take nearby Kealahou Street *mauka* to the **Koko Crater Botanic Gardens,** just behind the Koko Head stables. The garden is a project of the Succulent Society of Hawaii.

The windswept shoreline beyond Sandy Beach, known as **Queen's Beach** or Wawamalu Beach, was once planned for a major resort by the Kaiser-Aetna corporation, but the state has now become interested in the area as a future park. Meanwhile, most of it is covered with huge boulders that Kaiser-Aetna dug out of its residential areas in nearby Kalama Valley.

Just past the **Hawaii Kai Championship Golf Course** the road heads through a dry, low pass, where it almost never rains, to the windward side of the island. Pull over at the lookout for a spectacular view of the windward—or northeast—coastline.

The lighthouse up on the hill marks the land's end in these parts. The most prominent islet in view is Manana, better known as **Rabbit Island.**

It is supposed to look like a rabbit with flattened ears, but then rabbits once did live there, for that matter. During the abortive 1894 counter-revolution, arms and ammunition to support it were buried on the windward side of Rabbit Island. Today it is a bird sanctuary, as is the smaller **Turtle Island** (Kaohikaipu) next to it. (The silhouette in the far distant view that *looks* like a "turtle island" is actually a peninsula on which is established Kaneohe Marine Corps Air Station.)

Perhaps the only beach more treacherous, yet more fun for body surfers, than the aforementioned Sandy Beach is the little **Makapuu Beach Park** tucked away below the lookout. It's a wonderful place for a picnic, but again, lock your car or—preferably—empty it.

Across the road from the beach is the widely hailed **Sea Life Park** (Tel. 259-7933), a highly successful commercial park operation displaying the life and antics of fish, fowl, and water animals. It costs nothing to visit the Galley Restaurant and the shops, but you'll pay about $8 (cheaper for children) to be admitted to the show portion. This includes the 300,000-gallon Hawaiian Reef Tank, where a spiral ramp leads you, in effect, three fathoms under the sea to see hundreds of creatures, including a special demonstration during which they are hand-fed by a scuba diver.

Other shows in the park include the Ocean Science Theatre, featuring a production on the training of porpoises and penguins, and the Whaler's Cove show, which includes small whales taking part in a sort of water pageant. Their tricks are complicated and good. You may also feed sea lions and seabirds, if you buy the food, and listen to minilectures at different points in the park. And you'll find a small but well-displayed collection in the whaling museum.

If you haven't seen Marineworld or Marineland in California or Florida, you should definitely go. But even for dolphin-show veterans the distinctly Hawaiian flavor at Sea Life Park makes the show worthwhile. While you're there, ask to have the "wholpin" pointed out; this cross between a whale and a dolphin was born in May, 1985, and is apparently the only one of its kind in the world. (Tip: From the restaurant portion of the park, which you may enter without an admission charge, you can see the museum and the sea lion pools. Use the lower level entrance past the restrooms, etc.) The park is open from 9:30 A.M., and the last show goes on about 4:30 P.M. The setting is also gorgeous, and if price is no object, then don't miss it.

(Remember that you can also reach Sea Life Park by public bus. Climb aboard any Route 57 or 58, although from its beginning at Ala Moana Center it may be a slightly shorter trip if you use the 58, the clockwise route—via Kailua, Waimanalo, etc.—rather than the opposite system we've been following here.)

Throughout this whole Makapuu area—especially on a Sunday—you may cast your eyes skyward to see Hawaii's most daring sport. The up-drafts along the nearby cliffs are particularly suited to hang-glider flying, and as many as a dozen gliders at a time wheel and turn as they jockey for air space in the neighborhood. (In 1986, hang-glider pilot Jim Will stayed aloft here for 34 hours, breaking Lindbergh's solo endurance record.) Unfortunately, over the past few years there have been some fatalities registered in this popular activity here.

Continuing via the highway, you'll see at the end of a long pier the **Makai Undersea Test Range,** a commercial marine research station (visitors not permitted).

Waimanalo Beach Park, farther along, is attractive, but we do not consider it safe to camp there overnight. As a matter of fact, it leads the list—along with Makaha and Nanikuli parks on the western coast—of sites that have been the scenes of crimes and unpleasantness. If you see a rough crowd here, better let them have the place all to themselves.

Under a long row of ironwood trees behind a white fence *mauka* of the road, you may catch sight of several portable stands selling everything from pickled mangoes to puka shell necklaces. These vendors and craftsmen, who used to create a colorful if hazardous collection directly alongside the traffic, have banded together into a *hui* (cooperative) called Pine Grove Village. It's still somewhat experimental, and you may have to search out the parking area. But some visitors have been picking up good handicraft bargains under the trees, especially on weekends.

The entrance to **Bellows Air Force Base,** today only a recreation installation, is along here on the right. Its park areas are open to civilians for camping and general frolicking on weekends and holidays. The beach is lovely, clean, uncrowded, full of beautiful waves, and generally safe and fun for ocean sports like swimming and body surfing.

The village of **Waimanalo,** formerly the nucleus of a large sugar plantation, is now somewhat of a poverty pocket. The rich soil in the area is used today for flower and fruit production. Most of Oahu's banana, papaya, and anthurium supplies come from Waimanalo. It is not, however, considered much of a visitor attraction.

The sharp, double-spiked mountain you can see in the distance past Waimanalo is **Olomana Peak.** Hikers often like to tackle that one, but sometimes they become stranded on its slopes and must be picked off by rescue helicopters.

If you're not running late, take the main junction with Kailua Road (Route 63) to the right (*makai*) to visit **Kailua,** a small beachside community within easy commuting distance of Honolulu. Ask directions to **Kailua Beach Park,** basically at the corner of Kailua Road and Kalaheo Avenue, for a popular beach. (Many think it's the best all-round beach on the island, as a matter of fact.)

Returning up Kailua Road again toward Honolulu, a short way out of the village and behind the YMCA is the hard-to-find **Ulu Po Heiau.** To the nonscholar it looks like a mere pile of rocks on the edge of **Kawainui Swamp.** If you're going to search out the Puu-o-Mahuka Heiau on the North Shore (see the next section), you can certainly skip this one.

Beyond the intersection at which you turned toward Kailua, the Kailua Road becomes for all intents and purposes the four-lane Pali Highway (Route 61). It winds its way up into the Koolau Mountains to dive through the twin Pali Tunnels into the upper reaches of the **Nuuanu Valley.**

Now please don't strain your neck or let your car run off the road, but if weather conditions are right, you may see far up in the right-hand rim of the valley "Waipuhia" or **Upside Down Falls.** Strong winds and heavy rain runoff often combine here to blow the waters *up* once they reach the edge of a small cliff. (However some claim you can see it better from the other direction.)

A half-mile farther is the turnoff to take you back up the old road through the rain forest to the point above the tunnels called the **Nuuanu Pali Lookout,** the most dramatic elevated view on Oahu and ranking among the two or three best in the state. Your viewpoint is a lower area eroded in the Koolau Mountains, through which the trade winds usually rush with such force that you can virtually lean against them. But watch anything you're carrying. It just might be blown right out of your hands. Glasses-wearers may have to hold onto their specs, too.

Here is the dramatic, 1,000-foot cliff over which Kamehameha I drove the forces of the king of Oahu in 1795. Somewhere between 400 and 10,000 warriors (casualty lists were casual) jumped or were pushed over the *pali,* and for a hundred years afterward their bones were taken by souvenir hunters from the ledges below the cliff.

Try to ignore the terribly overbuilt concrete observation platform, and enjoy the aspect from the little railing below it. But watch your step everywhere. When the old, two-lane highway ran over here, it was at this lower point that you stopped to enjoy the panorama of mountain, sea, and shore, which—thankfully—has not appreciably changed over the centuries.

The view is most dependable and the light is considered best in mid-morning, but in those hours you may have to share it with the occupants of scores of large tour buses. We like to hit it between noon and about 4 or 5 P.M. The overlook is also open at night, but it is deserted and unguarded, and we don't think the views of the lights of Kailua and Kaneohe are worth the potential risk. It is fun and safe during daylight, but again, be sure to take your valuables with you when you park the car.

(If you do not follow the route we have been describing here, you may come up the Pali Highway directly from the Honolulu side, turning onto a different, well-marked spur just before the tunnels. After your ooing and ahing, you can either come back to the highway there and continue through the tunnels into Kailua, or you can return to Honolulu via the old road just described. Unfortunately there is absolutely no way to travel to the Pali Lookout by public bus.)

However you get there, the site is Oahu's crowning glory. You cannot go home without experiencing it firsthand. When the weather's good, we absolutely defy you to shrug your shoulders and walk away!

From the Lookout, return to the Pali Highway, which will take you into downtown Honolulu again. For simplicity's sake we suggest you check the map and then use Bishop Street, Ala Moana Boulevard, and Kalakaua Avenue to return to Waikiki.

PEARL HARBOR AND THE BIG MIDDLE ISLAND ROUND TRIP

Like the East Oahu Circle route, you really need a car for the excursion as we've outlined it here, although several of the targets may also be hit by public bus (most of them with Routes No. 52 or 55, which go in a four-hour circle). Allow all day for this trip, and be aware that although we have included Pearl Harbor and the Polynesian Cultural Center here, you may prefer to make those trips on separate days to give each of them the time it deserves.

By car, there are two different ways to reach the Arizona Memorial and associated facilities at Pearl Harbor. The seaward or *makai* route is basically via the partially elevated Kam (Kamehameha) Highway past Honolulu Airport, past Hickam Air Force Base, and past the main (Nimitz) gate to Pearl Harbor, continuing north on Route 90. Then keep watching your signs carefully for "Halawa Gate" or "Arizona Memorial." You'll eventually make a left turn to your destination.

Some prefer to take the more inland road, which passes a couple points of interest en route. This *mauka* method means the Lunalilo Freeway through the city, traveling west or north. At about Exit 19 merge onto the Moanalua Freeway (Route 78).

If you're picnicking, a good stop about halfway along is at **Moanalua Gardens,** a private, 26-acre park open to all. The monkeypod trees are magnificent, and the cottage on the grounds was built more than a century ago for bachelor King Kamehameha V and his card-playing cronies.

Back on the highway, keep a lookout for the 50,000-seat **Aloha Stadium,** a history-making construction that moves into baseball or football configurations virtually at the touch of a button. (Across from the stadium is **Castle Park,** a home-grown dizzy-land appealing more to residents than transients.) Near the stadium, bear right at the sign to "Aiea" first, and then left to merge into Kam Highway (Route 90) *south* to go to Pearl Harbor. Soon after, you make a right turn through the Halawa Gate to get to the shuttle boat landing for the **U.S.S. Arizona Memorial** (Tel. 422-0561).

The shoreline waiting arrangements for the memorial have been vastly improved in recent years. No longer are there long lines to stand in regardless of the weather. The modern Visitor Center includes boat docks and an attractive building with a museum, a movie theater, a bookstore, and a snack bar.

After arriving at the Center (any time between 8 A.M. and 3 P.M.), you'll be issued a free ticket and a group number by the National Park Service. You can walk around, take pictures, muse through the museum, or browse through the bookstore until your group is called to view the film. It is a 20-minute documentary on the Battle of Pearl Harbor and subsequent events. Then you all file out of the theater and onto a U.S. Navy launch to go to the memorial.

The boat lands you directly *on the memorial,* a 184-footlong floating bridge of white concrete that was dedicated in 1962. It spans the width of the sunken U.S.S. *Arizona,* which stands upright on the bottom in 38 feet of water. (The flag is mounted on one of the few parts of the ship's superstructure that is still above the surface.)

The memorial is magnificent and a fitting tribute marking the grave of 1,177 men. Their bodies are still aboard the battleship whose hull you can discern in ghostly outline just below. You may notice a slight oil slick coming from the depths; it is said that after four and one-half decades, the ship itself is still bleeding.

Be sure to enter the shrine room, at one end of the memorial, where the names of all who were killed on the ship December 7, 1941, have been engraved on a wall of white marble.

The Navy has several rules and regulations, of course, some of which prohibit children under 45 inches tall and anyone wearing a bathing suit or persons not wearing something on their feet. Also the Center is closed and boat trips are suspended on all national holidays *except* Memorial Day, Independence Day, and Veterans Day. The trips may be suspended, too, for any period when it is raining hard or when there are high winds.

The Arizona Memorial is the state's most popular tourist attraction, and more than 1.5 million will go through it again this year. As it stands, now, boat trips to the memorial are *suspended on Mondays* (although the center itself is usually open). This makes Tuesday the heaviest day for tourist traffic, gradually reducing to lighter crowds later in the week. The morning is usually your best bet, too. Some Tuesday-afternoon waits are over two hours long, and if you wait until too late, tickets may not be available.

For the latest official information on the hours, tours, etc., take pencil in hand, and then telephone the recording at the phone number above. You can also take City Bus No. 20 westbound from Waikiki. It's a faster trip on the special shuttle bus (Tel. 926-4747), which costs $2.50.

Remember that if you take the $8 to $16 three-hour *commercial* cruises from Kewalo Basin to Pearl Harbor, they're not allowed to let you off on the memorial.

Within walking distance of the Visitor Center, on the other side of the Ford Island ferry landing, you may now visit the U.S.S. **Bowfin,** a World War II submarine. It has been installed there through the auspices of the Pacific Fleet Submarine Memorial Association, which restored the old vessel, and you will be asked for a donation to walk through it. The *Bowfin* went on nine Pacific combat patrols and is credited with sinking 38 Japanese ships. Some readers have told us that the sub was the most interesting part of their visit to the area. (Closed Monday.)

A little-known military sight at another part of Pearl Harbor is the **Pacific Submarine Museum** (open Wednesday through Sunday, 9:30 A.M. to 5 P.M.). To get there, however, you'll have to ask directions to Nimitz Gate (the Main Gate), or take Bus No. 3. Tell the Marine at the gate where you want to go, and he'll issue you a special pass and point you in the right direction. Again, it's better to have a car; otherwise it's a 20-minute walk after you get off the bus and pass the Marine guard. For military buffs, however, the museum is essential. It includes portions of actual submarines (both American and captured foreign models), and you can twiddle the dials to your heart's content.

Also, on the first Saturday of every month you may visit a designated Navy surface ship by seeing that same Marine at Nimitz Gate. (Phone the Navy at 471-0281 for further information.) In any case, visiting the sub museum or the monthly surface ship may be the only way you can get onto the main base at Pearl.

Now, to continue the circular trip, head back north (*ewa*) on Kam Highway, continuing either on that or (better) the H-1 Freeway through the towns of Aiea ("I-*A*-ah") and Pearl City.

We do not recommend driving out to Nanakuli, Waianae, or Makaha unless you have a specific reason for doing so. Parts of that coastline are poverty-stricken, high-crime areas where rebellious youths have been known to take out their frustration on strangers in the area.

Check your map and take Kam Highway (when it is numbered 99) or Highway H-2 inland through the sugar cane and pineapple fields to the former plantation town of **Wahiawa,** which now borders the home of "Hawaii's Own" 25th Infantry Division, **Schofield Barracks.** If you drive onto the post, and find the barracks look familiar, maybe it's because you remember Burt Lancaster on the roof shooting down attacking airplanes in *From Here to Eternity*.)

Also in Wahiawa, at 1396 California Ave., a mile off Kam Highway, is the free **Wahiawa Botanical Gardens** (open daily, 9 to 4). We might give it a short stroll if it's not raining. Pick up a free pamphlet to find out just what you're looking at, and be sure to crush and sniff a leaf of the allspice tree. The rest of Wahiawa, a former plantation town, has now become a soldier's town, with all that that implies. Drive on by the roadside vendors selling ghetto blasters and tapestries of dogs playing poker.

Kam Highway out of Wahiawa (Route 80) goes over a bridge and then on the left passes a dirt road that leads about 300 yards to Kukaniloko—the **Hawaiian Birth Stones.** It was to this sacred site that Hawaiian *alii* preferred to come for ceremonial births, and you can sit on the same stones as they did for the royal blessed events. The area has been slated for restoration, and the access road eventually may be moved to the west—but they've been saying that for a long time.

Continuing on Kam Highway, you'll pass Del Monte's **Pineapple Variety Garden** (illustrating the evolution of the pineapple from primitive to modern varieties) on your left, and then almost immediately on the right you'll come to the **Dole Pineapple Pavilion** (open 9 to 5). There you may purchase hunks of fresh pineapple for a dollar or so and then chomp on it while wandering over to the edge of the fields to see how they grow. (Grab plenty of napkins, first.) We've noticed that when pineapples are plentiful you can often buy whole pineapples at this pavilion at prices cheaper than in the stores. When the fruit is in short supply, however, the Dole pavilion doesn't seem to raise prices; they just stop selling whole fruit entirely, offering only the little packages of spears and chunks, and cups of juice. The juice, as we've mentioned, is canned.

Again continuing along the highway, glance to your left to the **Waianae Mountains.** Yes, there is a road over them, but you can't take it because of military restrictions. The Army at Schofield Barracks will sometimes let you go up their side, but if you don't have military identification the Navy won't let you go down theirs. (In many ways, the Armed Services still seem to think of Hawaii as a foreign country, and they have placed much of Oahu permanently "off limits" to the taxpayers. The image of the Islands as a "sugar-coated fortress" is thus perpetuated.)

The tallest peak in the Waianaes—the tallest on the island, in fact—is **Mt. Kaala,** 4,046 feet.

We have directed you away from Kaukonalua Highway (Route 803), which you may notice on the map. It's one of the most dangerous roads on the island, due to some deceptive illusions and other effects along its curves.

At the Weed Traffic Circle, you might head west to **Mokuleia** ("mo-cool-lay-*ee*-yah"), where the polo matches are held on Sunday afternoons in the spring and summer, or on a little farther to the **Dillingham Airstrip** where you may watch the gliders any day of the week, or even take a ride in a three-seat sailplane yourself with members of the Hawaii Soaring Club. Never having quite made it aloft ourselves, and being a little unsure of our insurance policies, we can't vouch for it one way or another, but it sounds like fine fun for the daring.

Retracing the route somewhat brings you to **Waialua** ("whya-*loo*-wah"), another old sugar plantation town. There are several ways to wend through it until you cross the stream into **Haleiwa** ("Holly Eva"). At the turn of the century the village was a fashionable beach resort at the end of a railroad line. Today the tracks are gone and the grand hotels are closed, but it's sometimes fun for just poking around in, admiring the little boat harbor, etc. At the country stores, you can buy cones of shave ice. (See section 5, under Kitchens in the Country.)

Continuing east along the north-shore Route 83, you will pass several beaches and beach parks, not nearly as populated as any near Honolulu. During the week they can be completely deserted. Seven miles from Haleiwa, just at a lovely little bay, is the turnoff for **Waimea Falls Park,** a privately owned nature reserve (Tel. 638-8511). Open 10 A.M. till 5:30 P.M., admission about $8—less for children.

The park is usually a much more pleasant stop for the money than other expensive commercial gardens. You can take the mile-long ride in a free electric road tram to the 55-foot falls, and then swim if you want in the pool at the base. (*Careful:* The water is not always clear, and diving is dangerous in any case unless you know *exactly* where the rocks are.) There are plenty of beautiful trails in the area, some of them recommended for hiking shoes only. You can walk around most of the central area easily, occasionally meeting up with helpful young guides, or else take the guided tours at no extra charge. Also featured are cliff-diving demonstrations, hula shows, and ancient Hawaiian games.

At one time the entire Waimea Valley was the home of thousands of Hawaiians, and Captain Cook's ships stopped there to take on fresh water in 1779, after his death, on their way home. Today it's a lovely place for a picnic, and you can either bring in your own basket or buy the fixins at the park's "Country Store." Waimea Falls Park also includes an arboretum and a few exotic birds—some caged and some free. Our only caveat is that the park is sometimes just too darn crowded. We now avoid it on weekends, particularly in the afternoon. (Like most of these sites, it's on Bus Routes No. 52/55.)

Back on the main drag, **Waimea Beach Park** is across the road. This coast is a famous winter surfing area where waves often break up to 35 feet high (see section 8). Just around the bend—if the weather is dry—

take the Pupukea Road (next to the supermarket) up the hill for about 7/10 mile, then look for an HVB marker and a red dirt road that leads, after another 7/10 mile, to the **Puu-o-Mahuka Heiau.** The ruins of this ancient Hawaiian *heiau,* or temple, are now a registered National Historic Landmark. Human sacrifices took place within this rectangular pile of rocks, including those in 1794 of three of Vancouver's crewmen who ran afoul of the local population.

In 1780, a famous *kahuna* headquartered at this *heiau* predicted that Oahu would eventually be conquered by *haoles.* In case you doubt that all the old pagan beliefs are now dead, have a look around you at all the sacred *ti* leaves held down by rocks, or tied around them, given as recent offerings. The view from the bay side of the *heiau* is beautiful, and not so different than it was when the structure was built several centuries ago.

Just up the road, **Sunset Beach** is near the infamous Banzai Pipeline, a curl of fast-breaking waves over rough coral rock and a supreme challenge for super surfers. This whole shoreline is often the site of winter surfing championships and the center of a whole youthful subculture in Hawaii.

Somewhere midway up a cliff *mauka* of Sunset Beach you're supposed to see the **George Washington Stone,** a natural formation that tour-bus drivers say looks like a bust of the first president. The old Hawaiians noticed it, too, and called him Kahiki-lani—a surfing prince who was turned to stone for being unfaithful. We generally don't think much of this kind of thing, since it usually takes a powerful amount of imagination, plus knowing just exactly where to look. Near the stone, by the way, is the COMSAT (Communications Satellite) station, which is much easier to see. It's the one with the big white dish.

Almost at Oahu's windy and most northerly point is the **Turtle Bay Hilton Hotel,** representing an attempt to plunk a luxury resort down into the sticks. Eventually it will be the center of a large resort community in the immediate area. Incidentally, if you think you hear cannon fire in this neighborhood, you may be right. The U.S. Army has a major field training area in the hills beyond. There are also some ponds raising commercial prawns in this vicinity. You occasionally see them on island menus.

A very unusual sugar-sweet museum is—or was—the **Kahuku Sugar Mill.** The mill closed in 1971 after ninety years of processing sugar cane, when it became an unprofitable operation. Five years later it reopened, its machinery turning slowly in a color-coded demonstration of how such mills operated. The irony is that as a tourist attraction the mill is again closed at this writing, although we suspect that it will come to life again eventually. Somewhere along here, though, look to the hills to see some more modern mills. The Hawaiian Electric Company is installing an entire wind farm in this area, and 15 of these turbines may be whirling away there by now.

The town of **Laie** (pronounced "*lie*-yay") is headquarters for the Mormon Church in Hawaii. (The Church of Jesus Christ of the Latter Day Saints is the formal title.) Here it operates Brigham Young University–Hawaii Campus, and the nearby 1919 **Mormon Temple** is considered a point of interest.

The big presentation at Laie is the church-run, 24-year-old **Polynesian Cultural Center** (Tel. 293-3333, 923-1861). Open daily except Sunday, the center consists of replicas of seven different Polynesian villages, where there are demonstrations of art, craft, music, dance, and costumes given by natives of the islands they represent. Most employees are students at BYU-Hawaii working to earn their academic tuition. In some ways it's almost like a trip through the cultures of ancient Hawaii, Samoa, Fiji, Tonga, Tahiti, the Marquesas, and New Zealand (the Maoris).

The PCC has been experimenting with different schedules, but in any case the entire experience now takes a full seven hours from beginning to end. (Gates may open at 11 A.M. to 12:30 P.M., but recheck by phone.) *Unlike in previous years you now have to pay for everything, whether you decide to take it all in or not.* The required package includes a meal, activities and demonstrations at the villages, a brass band concert, the water-bourne "Pageant of the Long Canoes" (a sort of river review), and the big "This Is Polynesia" show. While not totally authentic, the 90-minute performance is probably the most entertaining Polynesian music-dance-and-costume show in Hawaii. If you have a choice between daytime or nighttime performances, it is much more effective at night.

At this writing, the total tab adds up to a whopping $36 per person, except that children from 5-11 get away for $27—amounts which some readers have lambasted as simply greedy. There's no longer any way to experience the PCC without shelling out for all the shows plus a dinner which is not exactly *haute cuisine*. (And remember that this is Mormon country: No alcohol, tobacco, coffee, or tea is available, and smoking is prohibited in many areas.)

Add it all up carefully in advance, for it could cost a family of four from $126 to $144 for the whole enchilada. If you can okay the outlay of time and money, the PCC earns a high entertainment/cultural recommendation. If you can't, don't feel badly; it isn't exactly Mecca, and one doesn't have to visit the PCC to become whole. We suspect that management is still under pressure to reduce the "all or nothing at all" requirement; it's worth asking to see if that has happened yet. (Again, a reminder—it's open *never on Sunday*.)

Just on the other side of **Hauula** ("how-*oo*-la") are a couple of nice beach parks. A little farther, about four miles from Laie, those with a hiking itch might like to keep an eye out for a sign on the right indicating the way to **Sacred Falls,** now a state park. You may take a sometimes rough trail mostly through dense vegetation along the stream for about an hour—two miles—and then swim in the clear pool at the base of an 80-foot waterfall.

The falls are lovely when you get there, but you should definitely avoid the trek in wet weather. The trail is particularly treacherous when muddy, and there is some danger of flash floods if it's raining in the hills beyond. (If you're going to Hilo, Hawaii, or Hana, Maui, you may see nicer waterfalls for less effort.)

Back on the highway, continue through the village of Punaluu. (Unless you're stopping at Pat's for lunch.) Just past Kahana Bay Beach Park you might notice the ruins of **Huilua Fishpond,** one of several such mullet-raising pens created when the ancient Hawaiians built stone walls out into the sea. This one was in use until the 1920s.

Beyond the inn and restaurant by the same name is a mountain ridge profile called the **Crouching Lion.** You've got to get in just the right position to see this leonine illusion, of course, and it took us several trips here to find it. In Hawaiian lore it goes as usual: Somebody—a demigod, not a lion—was turned to stone for some kind of religious transgression.

You'll pass the ruins of an **Old Sugar Mill** along here. It's just about the first one on the island, dating back to 1863 and operated only until 1871. Out to sea, you'll recognize the little conical island known as **Chinaman's Hat.** Its Hawaiian name is Mokoli'i, which means "little dragon," and it's supposed to be the visible part of the li'l fella's tail. The rest of him is apparently stuck somehow underwater. The **Molii Fishpond** you may be able to make out along here is actually still in commercial fish-raising operation. It was built before recorded history in the Islands, probably as long ago as 700 years. You can see it better if you enter the nearby **Kualoa Regional Park.**

Farther along the road the lush areas full of papaya, taro, bananas, etc., and often dotted by very modest Hawaiian dwellings are known as **Waikane** and **Waiahole.** Together they are currently becoming a symbol of modern-day struggles in the Islands as the agricultural leaseholders, most of whom are native Hawaiians, are being forced off the property by landowners who want to develop new housing in the area.

We do not believe the several souvenir shops along here will provide any better bargains than you can find in Honolulu, although some may be attractively arranged. Others are tourist traps that survive because of the under-the-bus payments made to tour drivers who choose to stop there. Fruits and vegetables sold along the road, however, can sometimes be genuine bargains, especially if you're staying in a condo with a kitchen.

Just beyond Waiahole, near a local landmark incredibly called the

Hygienic Store, you'll have to choose routes at a fork in the road. Route 83 (Kahekili Highway) goes to the right (inland) and leads to the charming **Haiku Gardens** at 46-316 Haiku Rd., a former private estate now crowned by a restaurant. The highway also goes to the **Byodo-In Temple,** a beautiful replica of a famous Japanese structure in Kyoto, for which you'll have to go through the Valley of the Temples (a cemetery) and pay $1 a head. (The Byodo-In is lovely, but we liked it more when it was free.)

If you're a clever map reader, you can backtrack later to either or both of those last two targets. You would instead take the left-hand fork at the Hygienic Store (Kamehameha Highway, Route 836) along the shoreline to the **Heeia** area ("hay-ay-*ee*-yah"). At the end of the pier there used to be a glass-bottom boat in occasional operation, but the last time we checked it was nowhere to be seen.

In **Kaneohe** ("connie-*o*-he") you can turn right on the Likelike ("leaky-leaky") Highway (Route 63) to return to Honolulu via the Wilson Tunnel. Or you may take Kam Highway (Route 83) farther on to the Pali Highway (Route 61) described at the end of our East Oahu Circle Route and return via the Pali Tunnels. Either route will bring you to the Lunalilo Freeway, which you take diamondhead (eastish) toward Waikiki. Drive carefully!

7. Guided Tours and Cruises

A-lo-o-o-o-*ha!* Hawaii's equivalent of the school cheer is the word *aloha,* but not spoken straight and simple. When the tour guide gives you his *aloha,* he intones it slowly, ending with a special oomph, and then cocks his ear so that his faithful dozens of charges can shoot it back to him in a resounding echo—ah-lo-o-o-o-o-*HA!*

There is no definite record of who first started giving this *banzai!* Geronimo treatment to such a kind and gentle sentiment as *aloha.* It is certainly not authentically Hawaiian and surely did not exist before the tourist industry developed in Waikiki.

According to humorist H. Allen Smith, the long, drawn-out *aloha,* although spoken more softly, originated with a little man named Freddie who used to operate the elevators at the Moana and the old Surfrider Hotel in the 1940s and '50s. But those elevators are self-service now, and if there really was a Freddie, he has long ago alo-o-ha-ed himself into obscurity, officially unrecognized for his contribution to Hawaiian culture.

The tours in this section are not the umpteen-day, "all-inclusive" type (these "packages" are discussed in chapter 2). The kind of guided tour we're talking about here usually goes in a bus, limousine, or taxi, for anywhere between three hours and all day. It may or may not be part of one of your large package tours. But whether yours was all-inclusive or not, your bus driver's last and most dramatic trick will be his demonstration of the fastest hand in the Islands—palming with a "secret handshake" any tip you may offer him.

He generally hopes for at least a buck a head. However, we have quite successfully slipped him less and even stiffed him completely on occasion. No driver ever said a word—just smiled in anticipation of shaking the hand of those directly behind us. Therefore, if we were going to give any advice on this, we might say that if you're *not* going to tip, it might be wise not to be the last off the bus!

There is no official standard to which guides must measure up. Since they do have to pass a government test to be drivers, chances are they will be better at manhandling a bus than they will be at accurately pointing out the interesting things about their islands.

You might like to know, too, that some of the stops made by a bus driver have more to do with the kickbacks he receives from nearby commercial interests than with any determination that the point of interest will be of particular interest to you.

Nevertheless, many a driver/guide is fun and smart and genuinely likes showing off the things he is proud of about his island. It is difficult to ask him a question he hasn't heard and answered a hundred times before, usually with just as big a smile and as much patience the hundredth time as the first.

How to get a good tour. There are three or four things to remember that may help: **(1)** The smaller the vehicle, the more rapport and responsiveness there will be between the driver/guide and passengers, and a better time will be had by all. Of course taxis are the most expensive tour vehicles. Limousines or "stretch-outs" (carrying 11 passengers) or else small vans are less expensive and a good compromise. The big motor coaches (carrying 40 passengers or more) may be the least costly. But you have a somewhat higher chance of drawing a dud for a guide, and it will be harder to get to know him, in any case.

(2) Try to find out if your guide is a graduate of the voluntary Hawaiiana class taught by the State Department of Education. If he is, you're probably in good hands. Unfortunately, the tour companies generally don't send their drivers to this class. Those who go do so on their own time, although the best companies might reimburse their drivers for the tuition—providing they finish the course.

(3) In general, remember that long tours tend to be better than short tours, since there is more chance for passengers and guide to get to know one another. The worst tour, for instance, would be a short trip on a big bus. We are reminded of the "City-Punchbowl" trip we suffered through one morning. Unfortunately, that particular tour—by whatever company—is often the "free" tour included in the price of a package. The other tours—those you have to pay extra for—are likely to be better.

(4) It is a strange and interesting fact that if you are a member of a group, all of whom know each other from back home, you will probably have a better time on a guided tour. You may end up by voting your driver an honorary member of the club!

Most standard bus and limousine tours cost exactly the same prices regardless of the company. The tariffs for each are approved by the State Public Utilities Commission, and the firms must justify any applications for increases.

There are only a few major tour-bus companies (and scores of small ones) on Oahu. Without going into exhaustive detail, here are some larger ones, more or less listed in our personal order of preference. As we mentioned, you might draw a dumb driver in the best of them, or a really snappy, entertaining, and informed expert in the worst. (We would be very happy to hear of your experiences with these outfits—good, bad, or indifferent.) All have sedans, stretch-out limos, and full-size buses available.

Charley's Scenic Tours & Transportation, Inc. (Tel. 9553381), 1682 Kalakaua Ave., Honolulu, HI 96826. Charley's caters also to local business, and seems responsive to the potential of repeat trade. **Gray Line Hawaii, Ltd.** (Tel. 834-1033), P.O. Box 30046, Honolulu, HI 96820. We like its "no kickbacks" policy and the fact that it sometimes sends out undercover company personnel posing as passengers to check out the drivers. **Robert's Hawaii Tours, Inc.** (Tel. 947-3939), 444 Hobron Lane, Honolulu, HI 96815. It also prohibits its drivers from accepting commissions from roadside businesses. **Trans Hawaiian Services** (Tel. 735-6467), 2440 Kuhio Ave., Honolulu, HI 96815. A new company, it seems to offer a wide variety of tours, including some unusual ones like a hike to the top of Diamond Head. And **Aloha State Tour & Transportation** (Tel. 841-8031), P.O. Box 22612, Honolulu, HI 96822.

The following are a few sample tours offered by these and some other companies on the island of Oahu. Generally speaking, half-day tours run around $20, full-day tours around $35 or $40 (but please don't hold us to those estimates).

City-Punchbowl (Honolulu Tour). Morning. Three hours. University of Hawaii, Waioli Tea Room (a stop), Manoa Valley, Punchbowl Cemetery (a stop), downtown Honolulu, and Iolani Palace. (This is often the only tour included in a package from the Mainland. Because of all the passengers on large buses that take this tour, Punchbowl is mistakenly said to be the most popular tourist attraction in the state.)

Pearl Harbor and Punchbowl. Half day. Includes the Navy cruise to

Pearl Harbor, central Oahu pineapple fields, the Nuuanu Pali Lookout, Punchbowl Cemetery, and downtown Honolulu.

Little Circle Island. Half day. Diamond Head, Koko Head, suburban Honolulu residential neighborhoods, Hanauma Bay, the Blow Hole, Makapuu Point, and Windward Oahu, returning to Waikiki via the Nuuanu Pali Lookout (a stop).

Circle Island. Seven hours. Nuuanu Valley, Pali Lookout (a stop), Kaneohe, Mormon Temple (a stop), Sunset Beach, Waimea Bay, Haleiwa, Wahiawa, Pearl Harbor. (Or reverse.) A lunch stop is made—probably at the Hilton Turtle Bay Hotel.

Sea Life Park. Afternoon. Four hours. Diamond Head, Koko Head, Hawaii Kai, Hanauma Bay (a stop), the Blow Hole (a stop), Sea Life Park (admission not included), Waimanalo, Wilson Tunnel.

Polynesian Cultural Center. Afternoon and evening. Includes center admission, buffet dinner, and evening show. About $60.

Small-group tours, specializing in (but not limited to) waterfall and nature itineraries, are offered by the minibus-equipped **E Noa Tours** (Tel. 941-6608), 1110 University Ave., Honolulu, HI 96826. The excursions can vary somewhat depending on the interests of the passengers and the predilection of the driver. Prices vary from around $15 for a brief City Highlights Tour to about $70 for an all-day, eight-hour, round-the-island excursion, stopping at Pearl Harbor and at the Polynesian Cultural Center. E Noa also runs the 90-minute, 34-passenger "trackless trolley" tours of Waikiki.

E Noa pioneered in the van tours, but several more are now being cranked up. **Polynesian Adventure Tours** (Tel. 922-0888) has recently received accolades in letters from our readers. **Akamai Tours** (Tel. 922-6485) may also be a smart bet. Others include **Hauoli Tours** (Tel. 836-3656) and **Kiwi Tours** (Tel. 942-2343).

All four have slightly different itineraries but comparable fares. The only danger with these tours is that they may grow large. At groups of a dozen or so with a driver/guide, they form an ideal way to get a good feeling for Hawaii. Another point is that big buses tend to be resented by the local population. (They block traffic, create fumes and noise, and interrupt TV reception in rural areas.) Smaller vehicles, and by extension all who sail in them, receive a better blessing throughout Hawaii.

History buffs should not miss the **Historic Downtown Walking Tour,** a two-hour stroll offered by the volunteers from the Mission Houses Museum (Tel. 531-0481). For $8 or so, the ladies will meet you about 9:30 A.M. weekdays. After a tour through the museum (see section 6), the ladies or gentlemen conducting the tour will lead you downtown through the historic government center. *Reservations are essential.* We recommend it particularly for a Friday. Then you can finish the morning off with the noontime band concert on the lawn of Iolani Palace.

The **Walking Tour of Chinatown** (Tel. 533-3181) is also pretty good. Sponsored by the Chinese Chamber of Commerce, the tour goes every Tuesday at 9:30 A.M., rain or shine, from the CCC at 42 North King St. Last time we checked, it was still $3.00 for the tour itself plus $4 if you want the optional Chinese lunch following the three-hour excursion.

The free **University of Hawaii Tour** and the **East-West Center Tour** take place one right after the other Monday through Friday. Meet at the entrance to Bachman Hall, at the corner of University Avenue and Dole Street, at 1:30 P.M. After about an hour viewing what *Honolulu Star-Bulletin* writer Murry Engle calls "a phantasmagoria of architecture set in an impressive collection of plant life," your student guide will leave you at Jefferson Hall, the headquarters of the East-West Center. Another guide will pick you up there a few minutes later and explain the purposes of the East-West Center, etc. Interesting for those with a definite academic or botanical bent—a bore for others.

AIR TOURS

For years we did not recommend any one-day flying tours of all the Islands. One such company has an unenviable safety record, and another has an unenviable public relations image. The problem usually comes—as it does with so many tourist activities—during busy periods when somebody gets greedy and wants to pick up all the fares he can. In this kind of business, it's a temptation to scrounge extra planes and extra pilots besides the regular ones when necessary. The substitute personnel and/or equipment just might not be satisfactory.

Many readers have written to disagree with this assessment because their own experience has been good—or lucky. Still, we decided over 10 years ago that as long as there was any possible problem, we wouldn't recommend or even list these outfits.

Now, however, the picture has changed for the better with the entry of **Hawaiian Airlines** (Tel. 537-5100) into the air-tour business with its "Islands in the Sky" program. One of the long-established scheduled interisland airlines (with an impeccable safety record), Hawaiian Air flies neither its big jets nor the tiny puddle-jumpers of other tours, taking off instead in its 50-seat British-made De Havilland DASH-7 turboprops.

The peripatetic trips cover eight islands in eight hours, viewing Oahu, Molokai, Lanai, Kahoolawe, the Big Island, and Niihau from the air, and making stops at Kauai and Maui. The program is divided into totals of about 3½ hours of flying time and 4½ hours on the ground. The fare of about $200 per person includes breakfast on board, lunch on the ground, a boat ride to the Fern Grotto on Kauai, and a van tour on Maui. One reader, unused to small planes, wrote us that the ride was sometimes bumpy. Some passengers will certainly be exhausted after the long day, but others are sure to love it. And again, this is the only such trip we would consider taking.

One-day tours are also being cranked up by **Mid Pacific Airlines** (Tel. 836-3313) to either Maui, Kauai, or the Big Island at a price of around $100 per trip, which includes air fare, breakfast, and ground transportation and guide. We know less about this project, but the plans look good for the price, and the airline is also dependable.

Helicopter Operations. You may or may not find some whirlybird sightseeing trips of Oahu available. Chopper firms have a way of cranking up and shutting down so fast that many in existence today will have flown into a cloud tomorrow.

One outfit that has become fairly well established is **Hawaii Pacific Helicopters** (Tel. 836-1566), headquartered at the Ala Wai Heliport behind the Ilikai Hotel. (Viewers of TV's "Magnum P.I." will recognize the site, but this is decidedly *not* "T.C.'s" operation.) Hawaii Pacific has been offering seven "Cloud 9" tours ranging from a short $25-per-person six-minute skip along Waikiki Beach to a $200 excursion to the end of the Koolau Mountains in four- and six-passenger Bell Jet Rangers. It has now opened up a branch operation at the Hilton Turtle Bay Hotel on the North Shore (Tel. 293-2155).

Two others that may be offering tours this year are **Kenai Helicopters** (Tel. 836-2071), which has four- and six-passenger Bell Jet Rangers, and **Royal Helicopters** (Tel. 941-4683), which flies Hughes equipment.

We have yet to climb on any commercial helicopter trips on Oahu and can offer little advice, except to be sure to confirm how long each trip lasts for the amount you're paying. Better check by phone with any of these, as a matter of fact, just to be sure you'll find them out at the pad. Happy landings!

CRUISES ON OAHU

There are several interesting trips on the briny from the Capital Island, at all price ranges. And, in fact, we think it would be a dogfish shame if any voyager to Hawaii did not manage to get out on the water at least once. The sea is an important part of Hawaii's heritage, and it should be experienced, even if only in the most minor or cornball way.

The most informal of these are the barefoot beachside sails that push off from time to time from the sands of Waikiki. One of these is the 42-foot **Leahi Catamaran** (Tel. 922-5665), the green-sailed craft that pulls up by the Sheraton-Waikiki. A 1½-hour sunset cruise, with beer, wine, or mai tais included, will probably cost about $20—less for non-drinkers.

SUNSET AND TWILIGHT DINNER CRUISES

Affectionately called "boogie boats" by their crews, a half-dozen or more craft swing out at 5:15 or 5:30 P.M. daily, usually from Kewalo Basin ("Fisherman's Wharf") for a two-hour cruise toward Diamond Head and back. Most run pretty smoothly, although we generally prefer the sailboats to the mechanical-power operations. There's a lap dinner (usually barbecued chicken), free drinks, live music, an emcee, and dancing. Fares are running around $35 to $40 this year.

One company offering the sunset/twilight cruises is **Aikane Catamarans** (Tel. 538-3680), whose newer boats are the *Aikane I* and the *Aikane VI*, both of which resemble ancient Polynesian canoes. Also its 28-year-old humpbacked cat, *Ale Ale Kai V,* made famous by Henry Kaiser in the 1950s, has been refurbished. All offer tables-and-chairs seating. And all three are docked at Kewalo Basin.

Another well-established outfit is **Windjammer Cruises** (Tel. 521-0036). Windjammer has owned several boats, but it's currently most proud of its massive, refurbished *Rella Mae,* a sort-of replica of a clipper ship, which was a New York–based Hudson River excursion boat before they added on the sticks and sailed it to Hawaii. This 284-foot, three-deck, four-masted, 40-year-old leviathan almost seems to feature everything an ocean liner does, and it can carry 1,500 passengers. It takes about 20 minutes to hoist the 20 sails. The *Rella Mae* is based at Pier 7, near the *Falls of Clyde* museum ship.

A dinner operation is conducted, too, by **Rainbow Cruises** (Tel. 955-3348). Their catamaran with the distinctive striped sails leaves from its own dock off the beach at the Hilton Hawaiian Village in Waikiki. Two that cast off from the Aloha Tower area are **Ali'i Kai and Hula Kai Catamarans** (Tel. 524-1800). The newer, 167-foot *Ali'i Kai,* billed as the world's largest catamaran, indeed carries 1,000 passengers. It is patterned after the double-hulled canoes of ancient Polynesia. The *Hula Kai* catamaran, 65 feet long, is now saved for other cruises (see below). Also leaving from the Aloha Tower area currently is **Hokunani Cruises** (Tel. 523-6155), which has been parking its 95-foot Polynesian-style craft at Pier 8 (on the Waikiki side of the tower).

Also under way now is **Merry Monarch Cruises** (Tel. 949-8472), which has been piloting a magnificent 160-foot, all-aluminum vessel called the *Royal Prince.* (Formerly the *Avalon,* it used to carry passengers between San Diego and Ensenada, Mexico.) The launch, which originally cost a reported $3 million, seats 500 persons.

Then **Hawaiian Cruises** (Tel. 923-2061), which formerly offered only a Pearl Harbor trip, has jumped on the sunset dinner wagon with their double-decked *Adventure V.*

MOONLIGHT AND STARLIGHT TRIPS

This is the same two-hour dinner cruise as above but repeated later in the evening, usually at 8:30 or 9 P.M. Aikane Catamarans, Windjammer Cruises, and the *Ali'i Kai* catamaran (see above) all offer it. Rainbow Cruises didn't, at last report. Aikane also operates a two-hour "Rock-n-Roll Booze Cruise" leaving Kewalo Basin at 9 P.M. three days a week for around $18, and the *Hula Kai* catamaran also has a "Booze Cruise" for around the same price. Both feature live bands on board. (Check with Aikane about a "No-Booze Cruise" for under 18s, at a lower price.)

PICNIC CRUISES

Picnics are seldom definitely scheduled. It depends more on the demand than anything else. The most dependably offered *pikiniki* this year will probably be by the *Hula Kai* catamaran (see above) for 2½ hours. Usually there's a cold lunch, complimentary mai tais or soft drinks, an offshore swim, and dancing to live music. It should be priced around $30 or so.

PEARL HARBOR BOAT RIDES

Most commercial Pearl Harbor cruises—not to be confused with the free Navy tours—last 2½ to 3 hours and depart Kewalo Basin twice daily, at 9:30 A.M. and 1:30 P.M. The fare now varies between about $8 and $16. Passengers view, *but do not get off at,* the U.S.S. *Arizona* and U.S.S. *Utah* memorials. The trip will be narrated, and hard and soft drinks and snacks are for sale on board. Color slides and various souvenir books will also be hawked, to be sure.

This year, we expect the sailing cruises to the harbor to cost more than the power operations. Aikane Catamarans will probably get $15 for the trip, the *Ali'i Kai* will cost around $12, and Rainbow Cruises may charge $16. (See above for phone numbers.)

The power boats include **Hawaiian Cruises** (Tel. 923-2061), with their 110-foot vessel *Adventure V,* and **First Pearl Harbor Cruise** (Tel. 536-3641) in either the 128-foot *Pearl Kai* or the 110-foot *Pearl Kai II.*

GLASS-BOTTOM BOATS

The only glass-bottom company is **Glass Bottom Boats Hawaii** (Tel.

923-2061), a subsidiary of the above Hawaiian Cruises. It has been operating the 74-foot, 149-passenger *Ani Ani* in a one-hour cruise off Waikiki
for more than a decade. (The *Ani Ani,* which has glass viewing ports,
used to be the old *Captain Cook VI* from the Kona Coast on the Big
Island.) We'll make an educated guess that the fare for bottom viewing
and skyline viewing will run about $8.50 this year.

CRUISING INTERISLAND

The traditional regular sailings from Honolulu to the Neighbor Islands are the week-long luxury trips offered by **American Hawaii Cruises**
(Tel. 521-0384) aboard two historic 800-passenger sister ships originally
built in 1951. Grace Kelly and her wedding party sailed to Monaco on
the S.S. *Constitution;* it was also used for filming *An Affair to Remember* with
Cary Grant and Deborah Kerr. And President Harry Truman traveled
aboard the S.S. *Independence,* when both ships were owned by the old
American President Lines. Amazingly they still have much of their original furniture and decorations.

Sometimes both vessels are in operation, but on slightly different itineraries. At other times only one ship may be making the island rounds
while the other is used for a Trans-Pacific cruise (between Honolulu
and San Francisco or Los Angeles), routine maintenance, or other
activities.

Both itineraries call for the ship to leave the Aloha Tower in downtown
Honolulu on Saturday night and do a full day of cruising on Sunday on
the way to different areas of the Big Island. Then the ship will make four
port calls, three lasting one day and one lasting two days. The ships call
at both Hilo and Kailua-Kona on opposite sides of the Big Island, at
Kahului, Maui, and at Nawiliwili, Kauai. Either Maui or Kauai is the
two-day stopover. We have no strong preference between the two itineraries as they now stand. One problem the line has always had is that the
islands are so close together that it has had to use up extra time to travel
between them. One idiosyncrasy, for example, is that one ship will sail
from the Big Island on Tuesday night all the way to the other end of the
island chain to Kauai, and then backtrack past Oahu as far as Maui on
the next leg of the voyage. Then it dog-legs it back to Honolulu.

Of the two ships, we believe the *Constitution* is the more attractive.
Other differences: The *Independence* has a gymnasium, a video games
room, a Teen Room, and a larger dining room. The *Constitution* sports
two separate dining rooms, plus the attractive Starlight piano bar open
into the wee hours on the top deck (where the gym is located on the
other vessel). Both ships have three other bars and each has two swim-

ming pools, four elevators, a shopping arcade, and a children's playroom. Interiors are done up in a sort of '50s revival of the '30s art deco style.

American Hawaii, headquartered in San Francisco, is fully versed in the traditional cruise activities, keeping you busy almost around the clock or allowing you to laze every day in a deck chair if you'd rather. All nightclub acts, music, movies, games, and other entertainment is included, as, of course, are food, accommodations, and your built-in transportation. (Drinks on board and shore excursions—available at Hilo, Kailua-Kona, Maui, and Kauai—are extra, payable with cash or credit card, but not with personal checks.)

Letters from Maverick readers who have traveled on either ship have been generally favorable. We enjoyed our own inaugural cruise on the *Constitution* awhile back, except perhaps for the feeling of isolation from the world at large and even from today's Hawaii. (Newspapers are seldom available, no magazines are sold on board, it is difficult to get radio news, and there is no TV for passenger use.) Understandably, many will find all that a big plus. Sensitive to past criticism that the operation felt somewhat more "Mainland" than Hawaiian, the line said it has now increased the amount of Hawaiian entertainment and other local influence on board both vessels. It has also pepped up the shore excursions, offering more active alternatives than before.

We thought the meals were generally good, although within a limited range of cuisine due to central menu planning in San Francisco. But there was plenty of food, especially when you count afternoon tea, the midnight buffet, pizza parties, etc. Open seating for breakfast and lunch means that you may have to stand in line a lot. The generally young crew (more than 300 in number) were almost universally pleasant to everyone. (Count on a minimum of $35 per passenger in tips, by the way.) You'll save time on returning to port if you can carry your own luggage off. Disembarkation can be hectic.

Fares for 1987 will probably run from about $1,300 to $2,800 per person in a dozen different categories. (There are special low fares for children under 18.) Choose your accommodations carefully, consulting a deck plan and a good travel agent. (You might save $150 or more apiece if a porthole doesn't mean that much to you—maybe more if you forego the "prestige" of residence on an upper deck. Or you might get more elbow room lower in the ship for the same amount of money.) All cabins have private toilets and showers. Many have separate lower berths. Several have double or king-size beds (but watch out for kings in cabins that are really not large enough for them). A few have upper bunks.

For full details, write American Hawaii Cruises, 550 Kearny St., San Francisco, CA 94108, or call the toll-free number in the appendix. (Either way, tell 'em we said to ask for the 68-page brochure.) All in all, we judged it a trip to remember.

Special bargain tip: American Hawaii also sometimes sells shorter cruises of three and four days. These *kamaaina* cruises are intended to attract local residents. They are being marketed in Hawaii only, so you would have to chance making arrangements after arriving in the Islands. Fares currently range upwards from about $400 for the three-day trip and from about $600 for the four-day version.

Probably launched by the time you read these words is an unusual interisland cruise by the Seattle-based **Exploration Cruise Lines** (Tel. 206/625-9600) aboard its new, 104-foot, four-decked catamaran, *Executive Explorer.* It carries a maximum of 49 passengers in 23 outside staterooms, all equipped with TVs and VCRs. Rates per highrolling explorer run from a low of around $1,600 to a high of around $2,600 for a week-long voyage touching all six major Hawaiian Islands, sometimes landing at out-of-the-way places. The company is also looking for convention and other group business to charter the entire vessel. The brochures and literature for the Hawaii program seem interesting if a little unfocused at this early stage, apparently a result of long-distance planning. Nevertheless, the line has had a good track record exploring other areas of the world over the past decade or so. We'll report more thoroughly on this operation in our 1988 edition.

We know less about another new interisland cruise operation being planned by **Aloha Pacific Cruises**, based in Alexandria, Va. Aloha Pacific plans to bring back to Hawaii the 35-year-old S.S. *Monterey*, once one of the four famous Matson vessels which sailed between the Mainland and the Islands. The ship, which carried 365 passengers, is being renovated to accommodate 639 passengers on its cruises between Oahu and the Neighbor Islands. No date has been announced for the launching of these trips.

8. Water Sports on Oahu

Oahu's beaches are generally gorgeous, and of the island's 50 miles of sand, 2 miles of the safest and the most fun line right up against the vacation precincts of Waikiki.

Many of the things you want to do in the water you can do very well at Waikiki Beach. You can swim, you can surf (better for boards than for bellies), you can paddle, you can skin dive (snorkel), and even scuba dive in calm and clear waters, including the famous "100-foot hole" beyond the reef. And with no talent at all you can also shoot the waves in an outrigger canoe, or even catch wind and wave together on sail boards or the small-size catamarans that run up onto the sand. Or you can sun yourself (not too much, too soon!), and maybe learn to play the ukulele.

WAIKIKI BEACH

After years of careful grooming, Waikiki Beach today runs uninterrupted for the entire length of the peninsula. It is considered to begin at Kapahulu Avenue and end in front of the Hilton Hawaiian Village. (To the left or "diamondhead" of Kapahulu Avenue is a narrow half-mile strand not strictly part of Waikiki. Called Queen Surf Beach, it runs generally along Kapiolani Park and is a popular place for Island families to picnic and play.)

For most, Waikiki Beach begins just past Kapahulu at a small and protected portion of shoreline called "Kuhio Beach." With the long breakwater cutting the rough waves down to kiddie size, it's a good place to take young children. Curiously, Kuhio Beach is also popular for strolling, wading, and sometimes swimming tourists from Japan. If you don't swim, watch out for deep holes here.

Just along from Kuhio Beach is the **Waikiki Beach Center,** repository of several scores of red surfboards. It is just one of a half-dozen similar concessions along the beach. You may take surfing lessons for about $10 an hour, including board and instructor.

If you're already into surfing, you can rent the board alone for maybe $5 an hour (be sure it has wax on it). And if all that seems a little too tricky, you might approximate the thrill very well on an outrigger canoe ride. Usually the beachboys will take you and others out and let the boat catch three waves—which takes about 20 or 30 minutes—for about $4 per person.

Similar beach concession outfits along the shore include the **Aloha Beach Service** (which serves the Sheraton hotels and has extensions on their phones) with desks in front of the Moana/Surfrider, the Royal Hawaiian, and the Sheraton.

The **Outrigger Beach Services** are operated by the Outrigger Hotel, and we like the way this group cleans up the cigarette butts from the sand along here. The **Halekulani Hotel** also has its own beach stand. Two more beach concessions are operated by a single firm at the Reef Hotel and at Fort DeRussy Beach. Like the Outrigger and the Halekulani, the **Hilton Hawaiian Village** runs its own beach operations.

Each section of the beach has its own particular characteristics, and the surfing areas in the water in front of them are nearly all named. The aforementioned Kuhio Beach, tame close in, has fast, crowded waves called "Queens" out in front of its seawall.

The wide Moana/Surfrider beach section has a lovely outdoor bar, and that's a good place to sit and watch surfers and outriggers taking the "Canoes," a group of waves that break close enough so you can get good views and photographs of the action. The Outrigger's beach is also wide, but usually jammed anyway. The Royal Hawaiian is less crowded, partly due to the ropes set up above the high-water line to give its guests a little more elbow room. The "Malihinis," gentle waves in front of the Royal, are close in and a good spot for beginner's surfing lessons.

The beach narrows at the Sheraton, then widens a bit at the Halekulani. The "Populars" offshore are often populated with surfers. The Reef beach might have a festive atmosphere, perhaps with impromptu ukulele music and lessons on Sunday evening. The long Fort DeRussy Beach you'll find primarily used by military men and their families. Finally, the Hilton Hawaiian Village Beach has an affluent air about it. You'll see lots of Sunday volleyball here on the wide, tree-studded sand.

At several points along Waikiki Beach there are catamarans pulled up onto the shore. Usually they offer one-hour rides for around $7, perhaps half that for the *keikis*.

Before leaving Waikiki Beach, a few words about the famous—or notorious—beachboys. James Michener wrote about the fabled Kelly Kanakoa, a bronze Adonis who was no smoother on a surfboard than he was at satisfying the fantasies of hundreds of lonely *haole wahines* who felt far away from home and reality on a prejet Waikiki Beach. This extra-curricular image may be slipping a little in the 1980s, but the fact is that the beachboys' *official* talents, at least, are not. All beachboys must be licensed by the Hawaii State Department of Transportation. They not only have to know how to teach surfing, but they must also be regularly qualified in lifesaving tests. The requirements are even stiffer for surfing canoe captains, and catamaran skippers must also be licensed by the U.S. Coast Guard.

Still, beachboys will be beachboys, and they shouldn't be confused with life guards, of course. The younger instructors still are good at good-natured hustling—lessons and rides by day, and maybe a few free drinks, a meal, and impromptu friendships after dark. They give the appearance—like one of their traditional songs—of "Livin' On Easy." Nevertheless, they know their job.

OTHER BEACHES ON OAHU

If you don't remember anything else about Oahu beaches, note that although most are beautiful, several are downright dangerous. Lifeguarding isn't all that it should be, and some Mainland beachgoers may be shocked to learn that beaches are always open, whether a life guard is on duty or not. Even if you're an Olympic swimmer, it's a good idea at *any* beach to see if there's a guard tower nearby, and, more important, to see whether or not that tower is occupied.

Safety Rules. Here are several precautions specifically for *malihinis* in Hawaiian waters.

• *Never* swim alone. The powerful waves of Hawaii can tire a swimmer almost before he knows it. Have someone around to call to.

• Don't swim where the waves are large, along a rocky coast, or at a steep beach.

• If you're caught in a riptide (undertow), don't fight against the current. Swim parallel or diagonally in relation to the beach toward the white water until you're out of the current, then turn back toward shore.

• If you're in the water but not surfing, stay clear of surfers. Runaway boards are dangerous.

• Obey warning signs, red flags, etc., at the beaches.

• Avoid all freshwater swimming unless you know exactly what you're getting into. There are sharp rocks at the bottom of mountain pools. Also some clear natural pools—especially those near residential areas— are nonetheless polluted.

Progressing from Waikiki in order along vaguely the south, east, and north shore of Oahu, here are several beaches or beach parks you may run across. Most parks will also have picnic facilities—barbecue grills, etc. (We do not recommend stopping at any beach along the western shore—the Waianae Coast. A large number of burglaries occur from rented cars—even from locked trunks—in that area while the drivers and passengers are on the beach or in the water. And sometimes visitors and military men have been victims in more violent incidents with residents of this high-crime area.)

Diamond Head Beach Park, on Diamond Head Beach Road below the lighthouse. Poor and dangerous swimming, but a nice place for a walk and observing life in the tidal pools.

Waialae Beach Park, 4925 Kahala Ave., and others along a five-mile shoreline including **Wailupe, Kuliouou,** and **Maunalua Beach parks.** Poor swimming in all due mainly to shallow underwater coral. Scuba divers know, however, that off Waialae lies the famous Fantasy Reef, accessible only by boat.

Hanauma Bay Beach Park, 7455 Kalanianaole Highway. Yes, there is good swimming in this beautiful, semisubmerged volcanic crater, but its *raison d'être* is the easy yet dramatic snorkeling and—in the deep water beyond the rocks—gentle but still lovely beginners' scuba-diving waters.

The bay is a Hawaii underwater park, so no fishing is allowed. The fish seem to know this, now, and if you look under the surface with mask and snorkel, even in shallow wading areas, you can see hundreds of different kinds and colors of reef fish. Bring a crust of bread into the water, and we'll guarantee it! Hanauma Bay is one of our favorite excursions. (If you take snorkel or scuba lessons, the chances are they'll bring you out here. There's no better place of the type on Oahu.)

Farther along the highway is **Sandy Beach,** also known as **Koko Head Beach Park.** *Do not even think of entering the water here!* This is the most notorious and dangerous body-surfing beach in Hawaii. There are hazardous, crunching shorebreaks and submerged rocks causing broken necks among many but the most expert body surfers who have grown up with these waters. Strong currents and riptides are common. Regardless of how many people you see here, skip it!

Around on the windward side, now, you'll note below the scenic lookout **Makapuu Beach Park,** a famous body-surfing beach. But to all but the expert it is virtually as dangerous as the previously named Sandy Beach. Swells over four feet will bring in hazardous currents (riptides) on top of everything else.

Waimanalo Beach Park, at 41-741 Kalanianaole Highway, has good swimming, but you occasionally see a rough crowd hanging around. We skip it and go on a couple miles to Bellows (below).

Bellows Field Beach Park is administered by the U.S. Air Force and is only open to the civilian public from Friday noon to Sunday midnight and on federal holidays. There is excellent swimming and good, safe body surfing, plus lots of excellent picnicking facilities.

Follow your map carefully to find **Kailua Beach Park,** 450 Kawailoa Rd., at the edge of the windward bedroom community of Kailua. There is excellent swimming, but the little "Flat Island" you'll see is farther away than it looks! Body surfing is sometimes fun when the "surf's up." Sailing and boating are also excellent.

Kaneohe Beach Park, as well as others like **Laenani and Waiahole Beach parks,** border polluted Kaneohe Bay. These parks are fine for picnics and sunning, but don't go near the water.

Kaaawa Beach Park, 51-392 Kam Highway, near Kaaawa, has good swimming and snorkeling. But skip **Swanzy Beach Park,** about a mile along, where swimming is difficult due to a coral shelf.

Kahana Bay Beach Park, at 52-222 Kam Highway, is a real sleeper. Here is a beautiful location with good swimming, fishing, and boating. There's a nice beginners' body and board surf close in to the beach, too.

Punaluu Beach Park, 53-309 Kam Highway, also has good swimming, but **Hauula Beach Park,** three or four miles farther, has poor swimming due to a rocky bottom.

Ehukai Beach Park is the site of the experts-only "Banzai Pipeline" and other high winter surf. In the summer, when the ocean is flat, this is a pretty good swimming and snorkeling area. **Sunset Beach,** nearby, has body and board surfing, but for experts only. Both of these are killers in the winter. They're not even safe for strolling.

Waimea Beach Park, 61-031 Kam Highway, often features dangerous swimming and very strong currents. In the winter, as a matter of fact, there's a danger that beach strollers may be picked right up off the beach by high waves and then washed out to sea. In the fall and winter avoid the water here as well as at nearby **Pupukea Beach Park** like pariahs. Snorkeling is fun in calm surf during the summer. Remember, in the winter the entire shoreline between Kahuku and Haleiwa, including the preceding four entries, is often *exceedingly dangerous.* If you can't find a life guard to tell you the latest information, *don't even walk at the water's edge!*

Haleiwa Beach Park, 62-449 Kam Highway, features good swimming and snorkeling in the spring and summer. Surfing for experts only (dangerous reef and current farther out). **Waialua Beach Park,** 66-167 Haleiwa Rd., now renamed Haleiwa *Alii* Beach Park, also has good swimming in spring and summer. And **Mokuleia Beach Park,** 68-919 Kaena Point Rd., a popular camping spot, has poor swimming.

SCUBA DIVING AND SNORKELING

During the winter, at least, the best scuba diving sites are found on the southern and western shores. There are sunken vessels to explore, plus lots of interesting rocks and caverns plus, of course, colorful tropical fish, sea turtles, etc. The aforementioned Hanauma Bay is almost legendary. During the summer, when the surf is down, several good spots are also safe on the North Shore, too.

Serious divers will want to touch base with **Destination Hawaii** (Tel. 922-0975), a non-profit association of more than two dozen dive operations throughout the Islands. The association has also published a 24-page Dive and Snorkel Guide highlighting many popular sites on all islands. It's available for $3 from the group's executive director, Barbara Brundage, P. O. Box 90295, Honolulu, HI 96835. (Tell her we said to write.)

Several "dive shops" offer lessons in how to get along underwater, but stick to the big ones who have been in business for at least five years—especially for scuba, which has some dangerous aspects. A half day of classes and diving will run about $45 or so. (Snorkel lessons will total maybe $20.) Prices usually include transportation from and to the hotels and all necessary paraphernalia. (Of course, if you are already a certified scuba diver, you can rent equipment from most of these shops, too. You'll have to have your "C" card to prove it, however.)

There are three "old reliables" on the scuba scene: **Dan's Dive Shop** (Tel. 536-6181), at 660 Ala Moana Blvd., offers a catamaran scuba tour for around $55, a five-day scuba course for about $300, and a half-day snorkel tour for $25 or so. **South Seas Aquatics** (Tel. 5383854), in the Ward Warehouse shopping center, has half-day beginning scuba lessons for about $65, two-tank boat dives for around the same price, and half-day snorkel tours for around $20. And the **Aloha Dive Shop** (Tel. 395-5922), in Koko Marina out at Hawaii Kai, has one-tank dives for about $45, two tanks about $55. A newer outfit, **Steve's Diving Adventures** (Tel. 947-8900), has beginner's and advanced dives, plus a Hanauma Bay snorkeling expedition.

For snorkeling lessons only, the best deal is to latch onto the inexpensive classes given by the City and County of Honolulu Department of Parks and Recreation. They usually take place March through June and cost $5 or $6. For information, call the department at 524-1257. Other possibilities are newer outfits that offer snorkel tours to Hanauma Bay. These include **Hanauma Bay Snorkeling Excursions** (Tel. 944-8828), with half-day tours for $12.50, **Waikiki Diving** (Tel. 922-7188), with half-day tours for $9, and **Steve's Diving Adventures** (Tel. 947-8900), with half-day tours for only $6, at this writing. (Some of these also offer scuba instruction, but personally we would rather depend on the previously mentioned old standbys.) One reader complained recently that **Blue Water** only gave her snorkeling equipment and transportation to and from Hanauma Bay—no instruction.

SAILING LESSONS AND RENTALS

Figure $75 or so per day for sailing lessons. One outfit is **Yacht Charters Hawaii** (Tel. 521-6305), formerly Hawaiiana Yacht Charters, and now moved to 902 Maunakea St. They also offer interisland courses as well as sailboat rentals (both crewed and uncrewed).

By the way, if you're already qualified on a Hobie Cat, that 12- to 15-foot beach-based catamaran, you can rent one from the beach services desk at the Hilton Hawaiian Village. Please do not attempt to handle these tricky craft without experience!

For beginning or advanced windsurfing experiences, the top firm to see is currently **Windsurfing Hawaii** (Tel. 261-3539) at 156-C Hamakua Drive in Kailua. A beginner's lesson runs around $30. You can rent a board and sail for around $20 a day.

DEEP-SEA FISHING

Hawaii has some of the best sport fishing in the world, and on Oahu you may charter boats from 40 feet to a luxurious 63 feet in which to try your luck. Of course marlin and other billfish are the most famous and dramatic catches, but even when they aren't running you can fish for skipjack tuna (*aku*), *mahimahi,* jack crevalle (*ulua*), wahoo, yellow fin (Allison) tuna (called *ahi* locally), bonefish, or even barracuda.

Most bookings are made from the **Kewalo Marine Basin** in Honolulu (Ala Moana Boulevard, foot of Ward Avenue, next to Fisherman's Wharf restaurant). If you make your inquiries and your Honolulu bookings through the addresses listed below, you'll most likely get a good boat and a fine captain and mate. All these boats must maintain high standards and they generally keep the latest equipment aboard. By and large, it's not worth saving a few pennies by trying to find some independent operator, who may have trouble staying...well...shipshape.

The newer and better sport-fishing boats have at least a flying bridge above the deck house so the skipper can get an elevated view of the telltale seabird action and even see the distant fish breaking the surface while feeding. The very latest boats might even have a "tuna tower," a tall framework that extends even higher over the flying bridge.

If you're new at the game, say so. Hawaii charter skippers won't take you for a ride you don't want. And if you want to fish for Pacific blue marlin, and the marlin aren't running, they'll probably suggest you'll have more fun after putting out lures for something else, like wahoo or maybe *mahimahi.*

The best season for blue marlin, incidentally, is summer. And the tuna run around Oahu begins about the second week in June and continues until the end of September. Winter is fairly quiet, with few big fish, except for periodic battles with a type of young, striped marlin (up to about 130 pounds). These marlin appear shortly after Christmas and may continue running through Hawaiian waters to the end of February.

Charter rates will run from $325 to $450—but mostly hold at about $375—for a full day (about 7 A.M. to 3:30 P.M.) for up to six persons. Half-day trips cost from around $275. Tackle, lures, etc., are included, but not lunches. If there are only one or two of you, call the booking offices anyway. They may be able to fit you in on a boat short of its full complement of anglers. (On a share-boat basis, per-person rates will run between $70 and $75 for a full day, $55 to $65 for a half day.)

The largest association of Kewalo Basin skippers is **Sport Fishing Hawaii** (Tel. 536-6577), guided by Captain Bill Shelton. Queen of that fleet is Shelton's 63-foot *Catherine S.,* which is certified for up to 18 persons. (She has several staterooms, too, and is often chartered by the more well-heeled for interisland cruises.) Shelton's association books more than a dozen different boats.

Nearly as hefty an outfit is **Island Charters** (Tel. 536-1555), which represents some of the same boats as Sport Fishing Hawaii, plus a handsome, twin-diesel-powered sampan fisher called the *Aukai,* a popular boat owned and operated by Captain Freddie Knight.

There are other small groups of boats that are "self-booked." They include **Coreene-C's Charters** (Tel. 536-7472), which charters out the *Coreene-C II* and the larger (60-foot) *Coreene-C III*. Although the legendary Captain Cornelius Choy, famous as the skipper who caught the world's largest marlin, has died, his family continues to operate the charter business.

There are some other outfits which charge more, for perhaps less return. We firmly recommend you make your arrangements with one of the three listed above.

It's customary to tip following a fishing charter. If everything has gone really swimmingly (the captain and the mate have worked hard, etc., and especially if they've gotten you some fish), someone in your party should hand the skipper at least a $20 bill—maybe a higher minimum if you're going to have the fish mounted rather than give it to him. Normally the captain does expect to keep the fish.

If you do tip the captain, he'll take care of the mate for you. Some folks prefer to tip the mate only, and if he's worked hard—fish or no—it's nice to slip him a ten-spot. Of course if you didn't like your boat or your crew, don't tip at all. (And then please write us and tell us why you were dissatisfied.)

Is sport fishing a thrill? You bet it is, and if you're visiting Hawaii in the summer, at least, it seems a shame to pass it up. If, of course, you can swing the price.

9. Other Sports and Games on Oahu

Blessed with a year-round mild climate, Hawaii seems ideally suited for any sport, except those few that actually call for cold weather. Islanders, in fact, have always been sports crazy, apparently because of their natural heritage as an outdoor people.

The ancient Hawaiians had a wide variety of athletic events, all of which were effectively shut out by the missionaries. Due to this Calvinist upset, the old games are no longer popular, nor indeed are they really remembered, although there are occasional efforts to revive such activities as *ulu maika*, a kind of bowling, and a few other obscure pastimes. The Hawaiians also had a large number of warlike games involving spear throwing, wrestling, boxing, etc.

But today the popular sports in Hawaii are much like those of most areas of the Mainland. High-school football is followed avidly. Now a member of the Western Athletic Conference, the University of Hawaii plays against first-rate Mainland competition in football and basketball, and it enjoys popular local support in both. Professional golf and bowling make annual stops, and professional boxing does better here than in

most Mainland cities. Amateur and professional baseball also have wide
followings.

SPECTATOR SPORTS

One of the earliest American sports in the Islands was *baseball.* This
was undoubtedly because the father of modern baseball, Alexander J.
Cartwright, moved to Honolulu from New York City not long after
designing the baseball diamond and setting up the first clubs and written
rules in 1845. He was just as active in promoting his sport here in the
Islands as he had been in New York.

Today the state is proud of its professional baseball team, the Islanders
of the Pacific Coast League.

The Islanders play in the new 50,000-seat **Aloha Stadium** near Pearl
Harbor. This gigantic contraption can be shaped for football or baseball
by sliding its massive grandstands on a thin cushion of air, a trick that
received world attention when it was first performed in 1975.

In the *football* configuration, the stadium accommodates several high-
school and University of Hawaii football games. It also is the home to
three post-season contests that are telecast live to the Mainland, including the traditional Hula Bowl in January, which brings the country's
leading college senior players to Honolulu for an all-star game. Then
there's the Aloha Bowl, which pits two top collegiate gridiron teams in a
Christmas-week game.

Finally, Honolulu now hosts the Pro Bowl, the last football game of the
season, usually played the first weekend in February. This is the National
Football League's all-star game, putting the American Conference up
against the National Conference.

On game nights there are usually express buses to and from the stadium. They usually leave from the suburban bus stop on Kona Street, next
to Ala Moana Center, and sometimes also from Monsarrat Avenue near
Kapiolani Park. (Telephone 531-1611 for details on times and fares.)

The island is nuts over *basketball,* too, particularly University of Ha-
waii basketball. The U.H. Rainbow Warriors play in the 7,852-seat **Neal
Blaisdell Center** arena at the corner of Kapiolani Boulevard and Ward
Avenue. The same arena is host to the annual Rainbow Classic Basketball
Tournament during Christmas week, which brings some of the nation's
leading college teams to town.

You'll find that same arena also used for professional *boxing* events
from time to time, as well as for Japanese *Sumo wrestling* and various
other forms of martial arts.

Out in the countryside next to the obscure village of Mokuleia, a
popular spectator sport every Sunday, beginning at 2:30 P.M., is *polo.*

The season opens in early March and continues into September. Admission price this year is uncertain, perhaps around $3 for adults.

There is no pari-mutuel horse racing in Oahu, but there are several other kinds of races. *Outrigger canoe races* are sponsored by two different associations on Saturdays and Sundays between June and August off several different beach parks around Oahu. Statewide, there are more than 50 clubs, some of which trace their history back to the nineteenth century. There are numerous regattas all summer long, and there is even a high-school league.

Members of the Hawaii Power Boat Association hold *motorboat races,* usually the third Sunday of every month at Keehi Lagoon from around 0:30 A.M. to 2 P.M. Just take the road to Sand Island, turn right, and follow the noise. It can be an exciting free show.

And *automobile races* at **Hawaii Raceway Park** are often held on Friday and Saturday nights. To get there, take the H-1 Freeway past Makakilo and turn *makai* on Kalaeloa Boulevard. Recommended only for car nuts.

Something quiet, more genteel, perhaps? Head for Kapiolani Park at noon, and somewhere, right about in the middle of that large green space, you might run across a rousing match held between teams formed by the Honolulu *Cricket* Club. You may not be surprised to learn that because of Honolulu's ideal weather—as opposed to that of Merrie England—some authenticity must of necessity be lost: In this climate, there simply is no such thing as a "sticky wicket."

PARTICIPATION SPORTS

Perhaps inspired by the annually televised Hawaiian Open at the end of January and beginning of February, many newcomers head directly for one of Oahu's twenty-six *golf* courses, at least fifteen or sixteen of which welcome visiting drive, slice, and putt artists. The eight military clubs are off limits to civilians, and that's too bad, because the Navy/ Marine club at Leilehua and the Air Force course at Hickam, for instance, are beautiful. (Incidentally, we suggest that you do not bring your own clubs to Hawaii, especially if you'll be golfing on more than one island. That way you won't have to worry about how the airlines take care of them. Rental clubs come complete all over the state.)

The Waialae Country Club, used for that Hawaiian Open, and the prestigious old Oahu Country Club in Nuuanu Valley limit play strictly to members and their personal guests.

The **Ala Wai Golf Course** (Tel. 732-7741), just across the canal from Waikiki, looks tempting and convenient, but you'd better skip it. There's just too long a wait to get a starting time. The 6,350-yard **Hawaii Kai**

Championship Course and the 2,545-yard **Hawaii Kai Executive Course** (Tel. 395-2358 for both) are in a beautiful setting, fanned by trade winds, although way out by Sandy Beach. Green fees average around $30 on the Championship Course, including required cart. The Executive Course will total around $20.

The best deal going may be at **Olomana Golf Links** (Tel. 259-7926). It's a lovely location, and a challenging but not sadistic course. Green fees may still be $16 weekdays, $21 weekends and holidays. The **Pali Golf Course** (Tel. 261-9784), the one you see from the Pali Lookout, is also soothing and stimulating. Green fees including required carts at last report were still holding at $23 weekend, $19 weekdays.

Of those less convenient to Honolulu, the big one is the **Sheraton Makaha Country Club** (Tel. 695-9544). The West Course, at 7,091 yards, is the longest on the island. Another important club is the **Turtle Bay Hilton & Country Club** (Tel. 293-8811), a 7,036-yard course supposedly laid out with the wind in mind. *Golf* magazine said the course "is reputed to have some of the finest conditioned greens in Hawaii."

Other golf links include the par-three **Bay View Golf Center** (Tel. 247-0451) at Kaneohe; the **Hawaii Country Club** (Tel. 621-5654) on Kunia Road, *makai* of Wahiawa; the **Kahuku Golf Course** (Tel. 293-5842), nine holes at the northern tip of Oahu; the **Mililani Golf Club** (Tel. 623-2254), six miles past Pearl City on Kam Highway; the **Moanalua Golf Club** (Tel. 839-2411), a nine-holer near Tripler Hospital; the **Pearl Country Club of Hawaii** (Tel. 487-3802), which overlooks Pearl Harbor; and the **Ted Makalena Golf Course** (Tel. 671-6488), located on Waipio Peninsula.

In recent years *tennis* has become popular—so popular, in fact, as to nearly overrun the courts available on Oahu. There are free county courts at 26 different locations, only 4 of which are even remotely in the area of Waikiki.

Visitors who want to get on a court with less waiting should play weekdays, and even then only before 4 P.M. (You are allowed 45 minutes per turn. And foursomes take preference over twosomes.)

There are ten lighted courts at **Ala Moana Park,** 201 Ala Moana Blvd., but that does *not* mean no waiting. Still, it may be a smash compared with **Diamond Head Tennis Center** (Tel. 923-7927), 3908 Paki Ave., which has seven courts—and for which there can be as much as a two-hour delay (you'll see players reading books to pass the time).

You'll probably do better at **Kapiolani Tennis Courts,** 2748 Kalakaua Ave. Its four courts are some of the best public ones in town, and a good place to find friendly competition. They're lighted at night, too, and you'll sometimes find spirited matches going at 4 A.M. The courts just mentioned are closest to Waikiki, but visitors sometimes drive the short distance to the six-court **Koko Head District Park,** 423 Kaumakani St. in Hawaii Kai.

Private courts available for public use include six courts at the **Iolani Tennis School** (Tel. 941-9555), 563 Kamoku St., and the **Punahou Tennis Club** (Tel. 946-2951) on the campus of Punahou School, 1601 Punahou St.

You may reserve a specific time at the **Westin Ilikai Hotel** (Tel. 949-3811), which has seven courts—including two stadiums—scattered around its various rooftops. They're open 7 A.M. to 5 P.M. There's also a single court at the **Hawaiian Regent Hotel** (Tel. 922-6611). Out of Waikiki, a better bet might be the **King Street Courts** (Tel. 947-2625), 2220 South King St. Its four lighted courts rent for about $8 per person per hour.

There are lighted tennis facilities at the Turtle Bay Hilton & Country Club on the North Shore and at the Sheraton Makaha Inn on the Waianae Coast. There is no fee, but they are normally reserved for hotel guests only.

Surprising to many, *hunting* is very big throughout Hawaii. But of all the islands, Oahu is the worst target for that activity. There is a year-round season for feral goats and wild pigs on the island, and bird-hunting season runs from approximately November through January. Game birds include several types of pheasant, quail, partridge, dove, francolin, and wild turkey.

There are twelve hunting areas on Oahu, but we advise skirting the often muddy and dangerous grounds near Kaena Point. Nonresident hunting licenses run $15. For more information, see the Division of Fish and Game, State of Hawaii Department of Land and Natural Resources (Tel. 548-4002). You'll find it in the new State Office Building on Punchbowl Street across from the capitol (Honolulu, HI 96813).

If you want to go *horseback riding,* we know of three outfits that may be saddling up trail rides this year. One is **Koko Crater Stables** (Tel. 395-2628), which offers guided rides into Koko Head Crater. **Kualoa Ranch** (Tel. 237-8202) has rides in that windward area out near Chinaman's Hat. And a newer operation is **Gunstock Ranch** (Tel. 293-1183), offering trail and beach rides for $10 or so per hour.

Running has been making great strides in Hawaii, as it has everywhere, and Honolulu has been called the runningest city in the nation. If you want to join the sessions of the Marathon Clinic, show up at the Kapiolani Park Bandstand at 7:30 A.M. Sundays (March to November). The Honolulu Marathon itself is run by thousands on a Sunday in early December.

If you're into *hiking and backpacking,* we strongly urge you to contact one of three organizations before trekking out into the wilderness. The most all-encompassing is the **Hawaii Geographic Society** (Tel. 538-3952), which runs a small bookstore upstairs at 217 South King St. (Their mailing address is P.O. Box 1698, Honolulu, HI 96806.) If you send a check for $5 and mention our name, they'll send you a veritable care package of information. (They might even do it if you don't say you read it here!) Then drop in and see them after you come to Honolulu.

The **Hawaiian Trail and Mountain Club** meets at the *mauka* side of Iolani Palace, usually at 8 A.M. Sundays (or sometimes at 1 P.M.) for a weekly hike, and they welcome newcomers. The club frequently gets special permission to hike on private lands normally unavailable to the public. If you write them in advance and send a stamped, self-addressed business envelope, the club will respond with schedules of their upcoming hikes. The address is Box 2238, Honolulu, HI 96804. The other outfit is the Hawaii chapter of the **Sierra Club** (Tel. 946-8494), which has hikes about once a month. Its address is Box 11070, Honolulu, HI 96828. Tell 'em all that we sent you.

Hikers who just want to poke around on their own may pick up a free trail map from the Division of Forestry, State Department of Land and Natural Resources, on the third floor of the State Office Building on Punchbowl Street. Also the city has a free, safety-conscious booklet on hiking trails. Pick one up at City Hall or at any fire station. Due to unusual geological and climatic conditions, there are special hazards to hiking in Hawaii. Talk to local hikers before going out, and *never* hike in Hawaii alone!

If you're going *camping*—whether by backpack or by wheels—you'll need a free permit from the City and County to bed down in the various public beach parks. Obtain that document between 8 A.M. and 4 P.M. on Monday to Friday at the ground-floor office of the Parks and Recreation Department (Tel. 523-4525) in the Honolulu Municipal Building. That's the tall, fortresslike structure at the corner of King and Alapai streets. Then see our general remarks on some of these beaches in our Water Sports section. Frankly, we don't recommend camping on Oahu unless you can get in at the new and well-patrolled park named **Ho'omaluhia** (Tel. 235-6636), a city-owned botanical reserve near Kaneohe. Chances are everything will be okay in the beach parks, too, but be warned that there have been occasional middle-of-the-night incidents between campers and young toughs out on a toot. It is always better to camp in groups of four or more—and only where you see other campers, too.

Visitors who refuse to have an ordinary land-locked or waterlogged vacation might get their trip really off the ground by *gliding* or *soaring*. The more "conventional" version of such things is to go out to Dillingham Airfield near Mokuleia and buy a ride in one of the all-aluminum gliders stationed there. (Tel. 623-6711 for information.)

Believe it or not, the ancient Hawaiians reportedly had a similar game to that, too. According to some old accounts, they practiced gliding on air currents near the Nuuanu Pali, using a kind of feathered contraption. This, too, apparently became a lost art. But among the more far-out activities in Hawaii over the past several years has been something very like it—*hang gliding.*

For this, the more daring set sail on little more than wings of song and Dacron off the Makapuu cliffs. Despite several fatal accidents, some say the location off the ridge provides the finest hang-gliding site in the world.

Hang-glider pilots may want to write the **Hawaii Hanggliding Association, Ltd.,** Box 22232, Honolulu, HI 96813. If you're not an old hand and want to give it a whirl, lessons are available from **Tradewinds Hang Gliding** (Tel. 396-8557). You start by leaping off gentle dunes, then work your way up to the 1,000-foot cliffs. Beginners pay $40 for three hours. Or, for $75, you can be an instant copilot on a professionally flown glider right off the highest precipice.

You might enjoy this sport more by watching it from below the cliffs near Sea Life Park. Actually taking off from those heights is not for the fainthearted ... and that includes *us* chickens!

10. Shopping and Browsing on Oahu

There are at least fifteen definable areas in which to shop in Honolulu, and we will discuss below some that are relatively good and convenient.

But first, what should you buy? That depends on your own taste as well as the preferences of the folks for whom you are buying. With just a little attention paid to our own prejudices, here is a list of things for sale that have interested other visitors to Hawaii, together with some particular kinds of shops.

Three points to remember: One is that Hawaii has a refund law that states that stores can refuse to give you your money back if they conspicuously post a notice of their no-refund policy. A second caveat is that you will seldom receive a bargain by taking a special free bus to shop at a "factory" or some other remote location. We think such shopping tours are a waste of time and money. The third tip is generally to avoid buying products that are supposed to be shipped, at least from small stores. The Better Business Bureau is sometimes flooded with complaints about packages that didn't arrive. And don't have something shipped to friends as a gift. You may never know if they received it or not, and you'll be too embarrassed to ask!

ITEMS SOLD AND TYPES OF STORES

Aloha wear—Bright and light-hearted patterned shirts for men and gaily designed *muumuus* or *holokus* (long, loosefitting Hawaiian dresses) for women are called aloha wear. The cheaper and gaudier models from the "Garment Factory to You," etc., will probably hold up long enough to use while your vacation lasts, and may look out of place back home anyway. More expensive, tasteful, and better-made aloha styles from prestige stores like Liberty House will last much longer and will probably serve on festive occasions back home, too. (In Hawaii, everyone wears aloha clothes at one time or another, but it is not the local fashion for couples to don *matching* aloha outfits.)

Antiques—You may find some that are related to Hawaii here and there. Try Anchor House at 471 Kapahulu Ave., near the library. **Artworks**—Honolulu has about four score commercial galleries, often featuring paintings of people and places in Hawaii. Avoid galleries pushing the so-called "investment art," unless you know *exactly* what you are doing. Art salesmen are often perversely persuasive. Good Oriental art is featured at Robyn Buntin at Eaton Square near the Westin Ilikai. **Artificial flowers**—Some good ones, and some bad ones, are made of shells. The best of the shell group may be those crafted by Sue Lange, and they are sold in several stores.

Bamboo and rattan—Bamboo is made into lots of things, from flutes to furniture. **Books on Hawaii**—You'll find hundreds in bookshops, department stores, and the five and dime, along with special cookbooks with Pacific accents. Many good ones are published in Hawaii and never make it to Mainland stores. **Calendars**—Some have nice Hawaiian pictures, but the ones with the months and days written in the Hawaiian language may drive you nuts after the novelty wears off. **Candles**—You see different designs in candles all over the place. Some supposedly give off the scents of Hawaiian flowers. **Candy**—There are candies shaped like Hawaiian flowers, but macadamia-nut candy is perhaps a better bet to take back home. **Caricatures of yourself**—The ones drawn by the artist in the International Market Place are usually pretty good. **Ceramics**—Lots of pot-throwers come to Hawaii, and you'll see their work everywhere. **Chinese goods**—Several stores carry Chinese objects along with other things. These may be from Taiwan, Hong Kong, or even the People's Republic of China. (For the latter, look into the China Friendship Store on the third floor of the Royal Hawaiian Shopping Center.) **Chinese preserved seeds**—Sometimes called "crack seed." Islanders love 'em and chew them up like candy; most Mainlanders do not.

Clothing stores, men's—Besides the department stores, some of the big names are Ross Sutherland, Andrade's, Reyn's, Kramer's, Palm Beach, and Sato. **Clothing stores, women's**—Well-known shops, not counting department stores, include Carol & Mary, Andrade's Women's Store, Alfred Shaheen, Chocolates for Breakfast, Fumi's, Villa Roma, and Ethel's.

Clothing, large sizes—The traditional place is the Trunk, in Kilohana Square, but there is also one shop that has had at least a couple of name changes near the top of King's Village. **Coconuts**—If you can find, or buy, the kind with a smooth husk, you can paint on an address, paste on the stamps, and post them home just like that. **Coffee cups and mugs**— You can get them with your name in Hawaiian baked right on. Most we've seen were overpriced.

Coral jewelry—There are polished necklaces, rings, pins, etc. fashioned out of three types of Hawaiian coral—black, pink, and gold. Some of the best is produced by Maui Divers, but you should see and price it in several locations before choosing; price tags can vary by more than 50 percent for similar pieces. (Be aware that the very deep red coral, which you'll also see, is Mediterranean, not Hawaiian.) **Craft shops**—There are several, but you may want to drive directly to Lanakila Rehabilitation Center, somewhat inconveniently sited at 1809 Bachelot St. in the Nuuanu area, where everything is made on the premises by handicapped workers. In Waikiki, look into the Little Hawaiian Craft Shop in the Royal Hawaiian Shopping Center.

Department stores—The big ones are Liberty House, Sears, and Penney's, all in Ala Moana Center and other locations. **Discount department stores**— These include Holiday Mart, Gem, and Gibson's. **Dolls**—There are dolls in Hawaiian clothing at several stores, including a Hawaiian Barbie. **Drugstores**—Kuhio Pharmacy and the Outrigger Pharmacy are the main ones in Waikiki. *Discount* drugstores include Long's and Thrifty, both outside Waikiki. **Duty-free shops**—Designed largely for Japanese tourists, they have few genuine savings for Americans.

Fabrics—Many stores sell colorful printed Hawaiian yardage for persons who want to sew their own. **Flowers**—You'll find orchids or dozens of other Hawaiian flowers you may wear as leis or mail or take to the Mainland. Remember that there are quarantine restrictions: Most fresh flowers are okay, except those of mauna loa, gardenia, rose, and jade vine. Plants in soil are also forbidden. **Fruits**—Like flowers, many are prohibited for shipping to the Mainland. All pineapples and coconuts are okay. Avocado, banana, litchi, and papaya must be treated first. *All other fresh fruits are banned.* (For information on flowers or fruit, telephone the USDA at 836-1491.) **Glassware**—Some of it is made with etchings of Hawaiian flowers. (We like those turned out by Arts Hawaii.) **Gold-plated items**—Shells, flowers, etc. that have been dipped in gold are sold all over the place. Check the item to see if it has retained fine detail. (There are even gold-plated Hawaiian *cockroaches*!) **Grass skirts**—Generally only souvenirs for children. They should, of course, be marked "flame resistant," or something similar.

Hats—Coconut hats, webbed out of palm leaves before your eyes, are the tourist traditional (about $5). Some kind of hat is advisable for the hot Hawaiian sun in any case. Men sometimes like a straw-style "planter's hat," a wide-brimmed legacy from plantation days. **Jade**—Due to the popularity of jade among the Chinese, you'll generally find a greater variety available and more technical knowledge among Hawaii dealers than in many places on the Mainland. **Jams and jellies**—Several are made from tropical fruits like guava, passion fruit, mango, papaya, poha, etc., and are packed for gifts or mailing. **Japanese stores**—Some of the best-known include Shirokiya (a Japanese department store), Hotei-Ya, Iida, Dai'ei, Hakubundo, and Musashiya. You might like to check these for good deals in kimonos, hapi coats, and other Oriental items.

Kona coffee—Make sure you really *like* Kona coffee first. We like Honolulu's own Lion brand coffee and sometimes drive to 831 Queen St. to grind our own. **Kukui nut leis**—A traditional necklace for women and men, these are finely polished nuts from the official state tree. Buy them only from reputable stores, and save your receipt. If they weren't prepared properly, they may burst or rot. **Kukui nut oil**—We'd skip it. All of it is high priced and we can find no useful purpose for it. It's no good as a suntan lotion, by the way.

Lauhala products—Lauhala is about the only genuine traditional Hawaiian handicraft left in the Islands. You can get it in floor mats, table mats, hats, slippers, purses, and other things. These are made from the leaf *(lau)* of the pandanus tree *(hala)*, and you can often watch the actual process under the banyan tree in the International Market Place. **Lava products**—We don't think there is much artistic merit in most stuff made from lava. The little statuettes—most of which are not historically accurate designs—are not carved lava, but powdered lava mixed with resin and poured into molds. They're solidly made and hold up pretty well, however. If you want this kind of thing, the best is made by Coco Joe. (The outfit also makes some figures out of "Hapa-wood." It's the same process, but using local sawdust instead of pulverized lava.) **Lava flower pots**—They're porous, so supposedly they allow the plant roots to "breathe." By the same token they also leak. **Lava-lava**—This wraparound cotton skirt for men is not worn in Hawaii (except sometimes by Samoans), but it is sold here.

Leis—In addition to the familiar flower ones, there are those made of kukui nuts, various kinds of seeds, and even from feathers (rare and often beautiful). **Liquor and liqueurs**—In the old days, Hawaiians drank a kind of ti-root "whiskey" called *okolehao* ("iron bottom"). Virtually nobody partakes of it nowadays, but you can still buy it, along with lots of alcoholic "cordials" made from pineapple, passion fruit, etc. The best of these liqueurs is Kona coffee, which some people compare with Kahlua. There is also a Honolulu-made *sake* (Japanese rice wine); and rum, beer, and wine coolers are produced on Maui. Primo brand beer, however, is now brewed on the Mainland and shipped to Hawaii.)

Macadamia nuts—Grown principally on the Big Island, there are two main brands. We generally like Mauna Loa (the blue can) best, but Hawaiian Holiday has a larger choice of types—flavored with hickory smoke, Maui onions, etc. The two are competitively priced, but relatively expensive everywhere. (Nobody likes to talk about it, but some macadamia nuts sold in Hawaii actually come from Kenya, Costa Rica, Brazil, or other foreign sources and then are secretly mixed in with the Hawaiian nuts, a dishonest practice that has not yet been prohibited.) **Music and recordings**—Hawaiian music, of course, is distinctive. The best prices in records are at the department and discount stores (and you *won't* find them when you get back home). For sheet music and books, check the House of Music in Ala Moana Center, although their record prices are usually higher than some other places. **Olivine**—Unless you really go for this green gem, we think you should pass it up in Hawaii. Virtually all olivine for sale is brought into the state, generally from Arizona or Mexico. It is *not* mined here, and it only occurs in "sand sizes" on the famous Green Sand Beach and a few other shorelines.

Palaka shirts—A historic Hawaiian plaid derived from "factory woven" 100 percent cotton cloth introduced from New England in the 1800s. **Patterns**—You can buy patterns for making Hawaiian dresses, etc. (look for the ones called "Patterns Pacifica"). Some places they come together with the suggested material already precut to the right length. **Perfumes**—Royal Hawaiian has the big local factory, but there is also Paradise Fragrances, Perfumes of Hawaii, and Perfumes Polynesia. Supposedly they capture the essence of Hawaiian flowers. The better perfume displays have tester bottles, so you can sniff each one on a piece of your own skin. (There is even a perfume scent called "Hibiscus," which is a flower without a smell!) **Photographs of old Hawaii**—For something different, pore through the albums at the Archives of Hawaii downtown and order some prints specially made. They usually cost about $3 each. **Pineapples**—If you're taking them home, get them packed in a carrying box with a handle, etc. The better prices are usually at the supermarkets or perhaps at the Dole Pavilion out near Wahiawa. Pineapple Hawaii (Tel. 922-5077) or Tropical Fruits Distributors (Tel. 847-3234) cost a little more but will conveniently have everything you order ready for you at the airport. **Posters**—Several stores sell surfing posters or others with Hawaiian photographs or scenery.

Shells—Some of the most beautiful individual shells in the world are gathered from Hawaiian waters. Check what's for sale at Shell World Hawaii, 2381 Kalakaua Ave. We thought their personnel a little snippy, but their selection is snazzy. (Prices start at two for $1—no, not one for 50

cents!—on up.) Some of the most sought-after shells are the eensy ones
from Niihau. **Straw mats**—Islanders lay them out on the sand instead of
using beach towels. You see them at variety stores for a dollar or two.
Sugar—We think some of the most doubtful things for sale are those
little jars of colored sugar—the ones poured into layers to create a sort of
swirly, rainbow effect. The price is about $5 for five ounces. If you're
going to use it at a party soon, so be it. Otherwise, be aware that the
colors might fade within a few months after you put it on display.

Supermarkets—There are four big food chains here, listed in our
personal order of preference: Times, Safeway, Foodland, and Star. In
those you'll save as much as 50 percent over some stores on Kalakaua
Avenue. *The only supermarket in Waikiki is the Food Pantry, 2370 Kuhio Ave.,*
and it is not very cheap. **Surfboards**—More than a dozen shops make
and/or sell surfboards. If you get into the surf scene in Hawaii, you'll
pick up better and later recommendations than we can give you here.
That goes for related products like boogie boards and skim boards, too.

T-shirts—There are lots with distinctive Hawaiian designs. Some of
the best are made by Crazy Shirts, which has several outlets. Count on
paying as much as $25 for the best ones. At Woolworth's you'll get them
for a few dollars less. **Tapa cloth**—Tapa designs are usually good and the
beaten bark material is texturally interesting. It all comes from Samoa,
Tonga, or Fiji, however; tapa-making is a lost art in Hawaii. **Ti logs**—The
kind you take home, water, and grow are okay. They come in red or
green varieties. **Tiki torches**—These are a popular way to light up a
garden party. Just buy the heads and put them on your own poles.
Tunafish—See if you agree that the Coral brand, available only in Hawaii, beats anything else in a can. (Hawaiian tuna are caught by the pole
method, too; there's no chance of any porpoises getting pulled in with
the nets, as in waters near the Mainland.)

Ukuleles—Lots of ukes sell for $10 or $15 (OK, but mostly made in
Taiwan or Japan). No really good ones go for under $50 or so. Kamaka is
the best local brand. **Wood products**—Monkeypod and koa are the two
popular—and expensive—woods of Hawaii. Much of what is for sale is
cheaper and imported from Taiwan or the Philippines, even though it
may be nicely finished off in Hawaii. Salad bowls are often a good buy,
but look at lots of samples. Something different is sandalwood jewelry.
Videotapes—We haven't been able to review them all, but "Hawaii—
Adventure Thru Paradise," produced by Don Mapes, is probably one of
the better travelogues. **Wood roses**—A seed pod that looks like a flower
makes a practical gift that will last indefinitely. If you've never seen a
wood rose before, it might look like some kind of delicate carving.

Zoris—Sometimes called go-aheads, thongs, or jandals, they are a type
of one-thong Japanese slipper. The cheap thin-rubber varieties may cost

$1.99. But there are also thick-soled kinds called Kamabokos and a personal favorite made out of mats called goza slippers. All zoris are practical for this brand of indoor-outdoor living, particularly since it's polite to slip off your footwear before entering a private home in Hawaii.

ALA MOANA CENTER

The gigantic, well-architected emporium called Ala Moana Center is a five-minute bus ride (via No. 8) west of Waikiki. (On the map the 50-acre lot is bounded by Ala Moana Boulevard, Piikoi Street, Kapiolani Boulevard, and Atkinson Boulevard.) It's open seven days a week—until 9 P.M. weekdays, with most stores closing at 5:30 P.M. Saturday and 4 P.M. Sunday.

If you're staying in Waikiki, your first serious shopping should be done at Ala Moana, in the same stores where much of the permanent population of Honolulu shops. Then, if you want, hit every other place in town.

Guarded on opposite ends by Sears and by Liberty House, the shopping center is lined up along two basic levels and includes more than 150 shops and stores. With notable exceptions, you'll generally find food and restaurants on the street level and more concentrated shopping activity up on the mall level. (Parking is easier up there, too, although hotter in the open sun.) Ala Moana is currently going through major reconstruction which has still not been completed by our deadline.

With its sunlit wide spaces, trees, and fishponds, the mall area is more casual, open-air, and fun for strolling. The street level seems a little darker, and during heavy traffic periods like the Christmas season, it traps a large amount of automobile exhaust fumes. Progressing on that level, now, from one end to the other with some sample establishments:

Sears, Roebuck & Co. (Tel. 947-0247) turns out everything you'd expect in a Mainland Sears, *plus* a wide, wide selection of local goods, including pretty dependable souvenir items and lots of generally good aloha wear. For years it's been the largest single store in the state. Moving down the mall, **Long's Drugs** (Tel. 941-4433) is crowded but inexpensive. Next door, several new boutiques are scheduled to open soon in a large area.

Across the mall, **Security Diamond** (Tel. 949-6432) is one of the big-name jewelers. Their Hawaiian Heirloom rings, bracelets, etc., nice as they are, are *inspired* by the monarchical period, and are not a re-creation of particular antiques. **Watumulls,** nearby, is a link in a local chain, and sometimes has a few interesting aloha items. **Sato Clothiers** (Tel. 949-4191) is one of several good men's stores. Mod clothes for the teens and twenties are in the **San Francisco Rag Shop** (Tel. 946-2808). **Reyn's** (Tel. 949-5929), nearby, offers some nice traditional clothing on the expensive side. (They also produce their own line, called No Ka Oi). **Ethel's** (Tel. 946-5047) has a fairly wide, middle-of-the-road selection of dresses.

Across on the *mauka* side again, we're not fond of the duds at **Hartfield's** or at **Aloha Fashions.** Between them, **Chocolates for Breakfast** has the very late-late-latest in expensive young-women's apparel. We don't know much about **Guava Lane**, which has just opened in the large premises once occupied by McInerny's.

Again on the *makai* side, the Hawaiian gift shop thereabouts is representative of several small souvenir stores in the neighborhood that generally leave us cold. But **Andrade's Women's Store** (Tel. 949-3951), which appeals to a mature clientele, is pleasant and well stocked.

Across Fashion Square and the central court, now, and on the mountain side of the street again, **Carol & Mary** (Tel. 946-5075) has chic women's and children's clothing styled for the carriage trade. There are many designer items and European modes—including furs, believe it or not. The **Ritz** store we think crowded (with merchandise) and unappealing.

Two large stores take up most of the remainder of the block on that side. **Penney's** (Tel. 946-8068) is a branch in the Mainland Penney tree, but with a definite Hawaiian bent. You'll find some good aloha fashions there, some Hawaiian-type jewelry, and a souvenir section running the gamut from el schlocko on up. Then there's the intriguing Japanese department store **Shirokiya** (Tel. 941-9111), and it really is Japanese. A wonderful place to browse and discover some unusual gadgets. (Also, check the upstairs food section.)

Across from Carol & Mary is **Ross Sutherland** (Tel. 946-2888), appealing to the older, well-heeled man. The next-door **Center Art Gallery** we think unexciting, but if you really know what you like and can afford to pay for it, go for it. **Waltah Clarke's,** an old timah, has a wide selection of Polynesian dresses generally well displayed. **Villa Roma** is another fashion outlet for young ladies, but perhaps not as expensive as the above-named Chocolates.

Along here are two more men's stores. **Kramer's,** with nice, if limited, selections, also has a separate **Big and Tall** shop right alongside. **Andrade's Men's Store** (Tel. 949-3951) sets out lots of quality wear for older men. An Andrade man might find his daughter next door in **Otaheite** (Tel. 941-5470), a sort of far-out Polynesian boutique. The **Pocketbook Man** has a nice selection of luggage and traveling accessories. And right next door the snazzier, snobbier **Louis Vuitton** displays some superclassy *mallettes* that M. Baedeker might have carried across the Alps.

At the end of the mall is **Liberty House** (Tel. 941-2345), Honolulu's best all-around department store. It's the most up-to-date in Island styles and trends in all merchandise, all attractively displayed on three big floors. We've always thought the clerks the most polite and most helpful of any department store in Hawaii. (Some California readers have complained to us that their Mainland Liberty House cards aren't accepted. We've found, however, that LH cardholders may quickly make arrangements for a "courtesy account" at the store's credit office.)

Down on the *street level*, now, some Ala Moana shops chosen at random include the following: **Foodland** stocks the usual groceries on the inside but some interesting prepared foods around the outer edges of the store. **Honolulu Book Shops** (Tel. 941-2274) stacks up the island's widest and most complete selection of reading material. A Japanese store—**S. M. Iida** (pronounced "E-*e*-dah," Tel. 946-0888)—has paper lanterns, simple toys, nice teacups, wooden trays, etc. **The Prides of New Zealand** spreads out some cuddly sheepskin rugs and seatcovers at prices that are pretty good unless you're going Down Under yourself. **Tahiti Imports** (Tel. 941-4539) hangs up some nice aloha wear. **Hale Kukui Makai** (Tel. 949-6500) has a large variety of candles, some made on the premises. **The Jeans Machine** (Tel. 955-0649) displays young, casual fashions. **Crazy Shirts** (Tel. 949-6900) turns out the widest selection of Hawaiian T-shirts.

Right beside the Peppermill restaurant, the **ABC Store** posts some of the lowest prices for tourist junque in town, and also does pretty well with macadamia nuts, liquor, etc. It's often crowded—with good reason. Next door to that, at **Fromex One-Hour Photo System,** you can watch your color pictures coming right off the production line. (You'll probably find lower film prices at ABC, Longs, or Sears, however.) Back near the bookstore, **Morrow's Nut House** is attractive but expensive. How expensive? Well, you have to go inside to find out. After you're hooked, *then* they'll tell you. Absolutely no prices are posted, and that's one reason we never go in.

There are some lovely imported fabrics at the **China Silk House,** and we like the little gifties we find in the midget-size **Summer's Place.** Nearby, **Paniolo Trading** seems to be an urban tack stall cashing in on the rhinestone cowboy concept. At the **Crack Seed Center** you can try that gooey stuff that island kids are so in love with, if you want. And **Mrs. Fields' Chocolate Chippery** sells the most delicious cookies in town (about 50 cents each).

This may be more appropriate to our restaurant section, but about the time this volume comes off the press, the bazaar-like **Makai Market Food Court,** with 20 different tenants, will open on the ground floor of the center. (We can't wait to try them out!) And here's a valuable tip: The U. S. Post Office at Ala Moana is the only one in town that stays open until 4:30 P.M. on Saturdays. This is an efficient branch, too. Even when the line snakes out to the sidewalk, you'll be surprised how fast they get you up to a window.

INTERNATIONAL MARKET PLACE AND KUHIO MALL

Back in Waikiki, the second most popular visitor shopping bazaar is the outdoorsy International Market Place at 2330 Kalakaua Ave., across from the Moana Hotel. This quarter-century-old casbah crowds in dozens of stalls and stores, all gathered under, around, and near a gigantic banyan tree, and it's probably the only place in town where you might find someone to paint a tiny palm tree on your finger nail. There's a lot of trash for sale, but a few places worth wandering into, including the **Gem Tree,** just at the entrance, for coral and similar goods (there are even some you can string yourself or have mounted at home). Some well-designed women's clothes (aloha and other) are at **Harriet's,** way in the back. A souvenir shop a cut above the others is **Diamond Palace**, behind Farrells. Up on the second floor, you'll find a branch of **High Performance Kites**, with prices ranging from sea level to sky high.

To the rear, across Kuhio Avenue, is the new **Kuhio Mall.** It's a three-story Polynesian/Oriental complex designed around a central courtyard with fountains, tropical plants, and the like. Shops and carts sell craftwork from Southeast Asian countries.

At either location (or anywhere else, for that matter) watch out for the pearl/oyster scam. It only costs a little to buy an oyster, have it opened, and see if there's a pearl inside. There usually is, but it costs a lot more to have it mounted. So look out; unless you stop them quick, some of these fast-talking Speedy Gonzales types will have your pearl mounted and then present you with a larger bill so quickly it'll make your head swim! (And then we recently had a letter from a woman whose pearl fell out of the mounting and rolled into oblivion as soon as she got it home.)

KING'S VILLAGE (NEE ALLEY)

After a decade of calling it King's Alley, a pretty good name, by and large, the owners of this cobblestone souk across from the P.K. Hotel decided to promote it to a "village." It's a sort of gossamer version of Hawaii's sentimental monarchy period (the 1880s), all gussied up into a winding street of shops. At night it affects an especially festive air. Evenings at about 6:15, a costumed drill team "changes the guard" with a free precision rifle and marching show. You'll probably find that many local people still refer to the place as King's Alley.

The best part of the alley/village is the little "Open Market" square right at the top. The storelets there change hands often, of course. You'll also find in the alley small branches of some well-known quality stores like Liberty House and Alfred Shaheen.

WAIKIKI SHOPPING PLAZA

At Kalakaua and Seaside avenues, the Waikiki Shopping Plaza is making a big splash. Its principal feature is a 75-foot-tall "water sculpture," best enjoyed while traveling the escalators flanking the fountain. Lately there have also been free hula shows at 6:30 and 8 P.M.

The bottom floor is devoted to fast foods—pizza, sushi, tacos, and burgers. Then there are four floors of stores. **Chocolates for Breakfast** and **Villa Roma** are branches of the chic Ala Moana boutiques of the same names. The **Center Art Gallery** has works by Red Skelton and seems to feature clowns with big red noses. We much prefer the **Artists' Gallery,** a showcase for about 70 local artists. **Waldenbooks,** a link in a well-known chain, has a good selection of best sellers and Hawaiiana. The two highest levels in the plaza are devoted to individual restaurants, some of which seem to be having a hard time drawing folks to the top of the fountain.

KALAKAUA AVENUE IN WAIKIKI

It's not a shopping center *per se,* but there are nevertheless several interesting stores right on Kalakaua Avenue, Waikiki's "Main Street." If aloha wear at the cheapest possible price is what you want, head for those multibranched stores at several Waikiki addresses called **Island Fashions— Garment Factory to You.** There's no "factory" in Waikiki, of course. The stuff is stamped out in long-used patterns, but at $10 or so for aloha shirts and perhaps $20 or $25 for muumuus, it's a way to get into Hawaii at less than half the price of some other stores. They have same-day or overnight alterations.

However, it might be a good idea first to see what the best and most current Hawaiian fashions look like and add up to. You can do this at **Liberty House,** whose Waikiki store is at 2314 Kalakaua Ave. It has some of the most tasteful goods in town. A small shop nearby on the avenue with nice aloha and Hawaiian wear is **Casa D. Bella II** at 2352 Kalakaua.

Next door to the above, **Le Cadeaux** has the most modern and antique dolls together in one spot this side of Barbie-town. An interesting display.

Several good shops have been installed in the Hyatt Regency Waikiki on Kalakaua—not the ground-floor shops, which generally seem to have the same froufrou as everywhere else, but the quality establishments on the Hyatt's second-floor mezzanine. Among them are **Chapman's,** a good men's shop, and **Alfred Shaheen,** a somewhat conservative but very nice women's-wear store. There's also a branch of **Crazy Shirts**, an old standby for fancy T-shirts and the like.

At the little stands and pushcarts in **Duke's Lane,** an alley beside the

Waikiki Beachcomber Hotel, you can sometimes haggle your way into a bargain.

The only dry-goods store left in Waikiki is the **Cherry Blossom** (Tel. 923-6844) at 2184 Kalakaua. Hawaiian tapa and pareu prints in cotton and cotton blends are sold in this family-owned store that's been on the same spot for 35 years. An unusual store featuring a 40-foot-long wall of military patches, **The Military Shop of Hawaii** also spreads out other "militaria" at 1921 Kalakaua.

THE ROYAL HAWAIIAN SHOPPING CENTER

The massive Royal Hawaiian Shopping Center, a three-block-long emporium walling off the Royal Hawaiian and Sheraton hotels, features more than 150 shops. It's anchored by **McInerny's** (pronounced "Mac & Ernie's"), a branch of a long-time Honolulu department store. There are three levels, but most of the best browsing areas seem to be on the ground floor.

Andrade's is also considered a dependable department store for both men and women. **Winners**, next door, features casual, summery wear for teens and young women. Look into **Jungle Jason** for safari-type clothing—a poor man's Banana Republic? For modern and authentic "surf clothing," try **Surfsports Hawaii** or, at the other end of the complex, **Paradise Express.**

If you think you know what's available at **That's My Bag**, you might be wrong. We saw only hats, hats, and more hats, priced from about $4 to $40. Try **Raku Leather** for some quality materials with a western look. We doubt you'll find a leather jacket there for under $200, though. Gifts and souvenirs are displayed nicely in the **Hawaii Country Store**, just in from the Lewers Street side. Some nice leis, for not too much *kala*, may be found at **Auntie Bella's Lei Stand.** Authentic Japanese clothing is at the **Pagoda Kimono.** Kimonos run from around $30 to $60. Hapi coats, slippers, and dolls are also available.

Affordable art reproductions are sold at **Sea Art Hawaii** in perhaps the $15 to $25 range. **Left is Right, Too** is a specialty shop for tools and other things designed for left-handed people. And all types of casual footwear is sold at the **Slipper House.**

THE RAINBOW BAZAAR

Like the International Market Place and King's Village, the Rainbow Bazaar, at the Hilton Hawaiian Village, is a "theme" shopping center. It is divided into three sections—Imperial Japan, Hong Kong Alley, and South Pacific. The settings are very well done, and it generally features quality merchandise at premium prices. Some of the Oriental furniture at **China Treasures,** for example, is as good a rosewood or teak as you'll find anywhere west of the East.

FORT STREET MALL AND DOWNTOWN

In downtown Honolulu, the former Fort Street has been almost entirely converted into a walking and sitting street in a noble experiment somewhat more successful here than in some other cities—at least for resident weekday shopping. The best time to visit is around noon Friday when you will see office workers shopping or lunching in attractive aloha clothing. (Use Bus No. 2.)

The big stores downtown are now **Woolworth's,** not quite as interesting as the ones in Waikiki and Ala Moana, and **Liberty House,** the department store that has moved to fancy quarters at King and Bethel streets. **T & H Leather Wear** (Tel. 538-1214), at 1120 Fort St. Mall, is the only place in town that will still custom make leather sandals. They're priced from about $40.

THE CULTURAL PLAZA AND CHINATOWN

An idea a little ahead of its time is the struggling but still charming Cultural Plaza, on the fringe of Chinatown in the block bounded by Kukui, Maunakea, and Beretania streets and the Nuuanu Stream. It's an easy stroll from Foster Gardens. (Bus No. 2.) When more urban-renewal projects are completed in adjacent neighborhoods, this project—designed to exhibit the multicultural makeup of Hawaii—might really bloom. Meanwhile, there are several interesting restaurants and stores in this ethnic center, most of which are Chinese.

If you're going to seek out what's left of shopping in Chinatown proper, it's somewhat of a hoof from the Cultural Plaza through a sometimes unattractive area. Most interesting stores are in a one-block stretch on the east side of Maunakea Street running between Hotel and King streets. There are Chinese jewelry shops, ceramic shops, spice shops, herb shops, grocery stores, and acupuncture supplies. If you want to chew on lotus-root candy, you'll almost have to buy it along here. By the way, there are several lei shops on Maunakea Street, where the flowers are usually much cheaper than anyplace else in town. The best lei shop of all, though, is **Sweetheart's Lei Shop,** around the corner at 65 N. Beretania St., still run by the Lau family after more than 50 years.

Note: Some people understandably consider Chinatown a marginal district, and it's true that around Hotel Street Chinatown does cross with Porno Town. It's a safe and sane area in the daytime, at least, but, de-

pending on your predilections, you may feel better staying away from
that part of Hotel Street at night. It is, however, heavily patrolled by
police after dark, and it usually features more barkers than biters.

THE WARD WAREHOUSE AND WARD CENTRE

Across Ala Moana Boulevard from Kewalo Basin is The Ward Warehouse, 1050 Ala Moana, and a block or so further along is Ward Centre
at 1200 Ala Moana. The Ward Warehouse is a contemporary shopping
center with a natural wood-beam feeling that mixes retail and light industrial establishments.

Some folks wander over to the Warehouse after coming off one of the
daytime cruises. Check the beautiful hand-blown art glass at **Rare Discovery** (Tel. 524-4811), the lovely artificial flowers at the **Miyuki Art Flower
Studio** (Tel. 521-5512) on the ground floor, and the products of local artists
at **The Artist Guild** (Tel. 531-2933). **Kinnari** is a ladies' apparel emporium
featuring appliqué patchwork designs by its owner. **Erida's Music Boxes**
has hundreds of pleasant tinkling sounds from all over the world. A combination bookstore and European-style cafe is **Upstart Crow & Company.**

There's also an Upstart Crow (*sans* coffee) at Ward *Centre,* a newer wood-
and-brass specialty shopping center. A popular stop for local folk
is the **R. Field Wine Company,** with lots of wines, cheeses, and other
goodies to take home. Restaurants seem to dominate Ward Centre, but
you'll also find some burgeoning boutiques and fashions for both women
(e.g., **Susan Marie**) and men (e.g., **Polo/Ralph Lauren**). An interesting
classic toy store is **Allison's Wonderland.** Shop ownerships seem to turn
over very quickly, however, so don't hold us to these examples. Take Bus
No. 8 to both Ward Centre and Ward Warehouse.

PEARLRIDGE CENTER

The top suburban shopping center now is Pearlridge—out of the way
for most visitors, but convenient to many military personnel and their
families—way out at Pearl City, near the intersection of Kamehameha
Highway and the Waimano Home Road. (Suburban buses from Ala
Moana Center—Nos. 53, 51, 50, or 50A.) Hawaii's first and only mono-
rail is here, connecting the two parts of the center, which are 1,000 feet
apart. There are 90 stores, one of the most interesting of which is **Dai'ei**
("*die*-yay"), a Japanese department store.

KAHALA MALL AND KOKO MARINA

In the high-priced residential district of Waialae/Kahala near the H-1

Freeway is Kahala Mall. (Bus No. 14.) It was Hawaii's first fully enclosed, air-conditioned shopping mall. You might check into a husband/wife import store called **Fabulous Things** (Tel. 732-7070).

The island's only shopping complex at the water's edge is the 15-acre Koko Marina, sometimes called the Waterfront Village, which borders the lagoon harbor much farther out at Hawaii Kai. (Bus No. 1.) The 16-acre, nautically inspired center unfortunately has often had economic troubles, and individual stores have opened and closed unpredictably. It is now owned by the Prudential Insurance Co., which seems to be breathing new life into the place. We always liked to stop at Koko Marina for hot pretzels, but what with the corporate twists and turns, we can't guarantee the dough will still be around this year.

11. Nights on the Town

Only one oasis in the United States is a bigger entertainment town than Honolulu. That's Las Vegas, which draws crowds to the desert bright lights with the aid of games of chance. In Hawaii gambling is strictly illegal, but night life goes on, perpetuated by a strong local tradition of music, song, laughter, and booze, with thanks to the millions of tourists who help finance all this nighttime revelry. (Speaking of booze, a new state law says you have to be at least 21 to drink in Hawaii.)

In Waikiki you will find big, professional headliner shows, largely designed to appeal to visitors to these shores. But you may also attend performances by accomplished entertainers who are stars only to those who avidly follow the latest trends in contemporary Hawaiian music and entertainment.

Outlanders are often bemused by this local audience/entertainer rapport, not being blessed with the necessary Island background to appreciate it. There might be lots of in-jokes in pidgin—sometimes at the expense of the *haoles*—that have special meaning to a resident crowd only.

Nevertheless, most accomplished Hawaiian entertainers succeed in spanning the distance between both cultures, sizing up their audiences and gearing their acts to the people responding to them.

Dinner Show Vs. Cocktail Show. Many well-advertised, high-priced performances will be offered at both a mid-evening dinner show and then later at a cocktail show. Usually the sit-down or buffet dinner will begin at 6 or 7 P.M., with show time set for 8 or 9. We usually feel that to pay for the dinner merely because it is connected with a certain show is a waste of money. We'd rather pick a restaurant on its own merits and then go on to attend a show we think will be good entertainment, even if it is under a different roof—and even if we have to pick a different show than the one we chose first. Often so many are crowded side-by-side at these tables that you may feel you're on an airplane again, trying to eat with your elbows tight at your sides.

In fact, the only reason for going to a dinner/show combination as far as we can see is that you're a little more likely to get a good position to see and hear the performance. This we will do on some occasions, if we don't have to pay in advance. If we don't like the position we are taken to, we can always leave immediately without owing a thing.

Showroom reservations people who tell you that the *only* way you can go to a certain show is to take the dinner too are often being less than truthful. We have frequently skipped the dinner/show combination (perhaps at $30 or $35) and showed up later at showtime to pay only about $15 or $20 to catch the act without having absorbed the "required" $15 plate of chicken or roast beef. Incidentally, you might save by making dinner/show reservations yourself directly with the hotel. As part of a tour operator's "package," it could be 20 percent higher.

If you arrive to see the show *only*, there will likely be a cover charge and/or a two-drink minimum (sometimes both combined in a show charge), whether you see the early show (maybe 8 or 9 P.M.) or the cocktail show (starting somewhere between 10 and 11 P.M.). At that second show you will almost surely pay both cover charge and minimum (or a hefty show charge), especially if it is a Friday or Saturday night.

Standard cover charges vary between about $5 and $8 per person. The drinks might be $3 or $4 each.

Some acts have a very late or post-midnight show, perhaps on a Friday or Saturday only. These are almost always presented without a cover charge, although sometimes they keep the drink minimum.

If you can take the hours, they usually are a good deal. You might find that other Waikiki entertainers whose shows finish earlier have walked in to catch the act. Often they are enticed onstage.

All of these factors—starting times, cover charges, drink minimums, etc.—change regularly everywhere, so we always try to reserve shows by calling ahead, asking all the questions right there on the phone. If any showroom doesn't take the time to spell out everything we want to know, we say bye-bye and look for another production.

Most entertainment events are listed in the half-dozen or so "throwaway" tourist publications in Waikiki. The free papers or thick magazines are usually the most complete, probably because they are well established and are bountifully favored by advertisers.

Remember, however, that these and any other free visitor publications generally don't list anything commercial that has not bought advertising space. Your best bet may therefore be in the local newspapers. Look for

"TGIF—The Great Index to Fun" in Friday's *Advertiser* or "Weekend Pass" in the *Star-Bulletin.*

Watch out for the slump season on the club show circuit. Any time between November and late December—after Aloha Week and before the holidays—the big names of Honolulu entertainment may be found on vacation or in Vegas. In some big rooms there are substitutes—some on the way up and some rusting old stars perhaps beginning to dip below the popularity horizon.

Drinking in the Tropics. We always ask for standard drinks by their brand names in the clubs ("Dewars," "Jack Daniels," etc.). By asking for "scotch and soda" or "bourbon and water" you might open yourself up for an injection of Olde Rotgutte, which is probably no less expensive than the Chateau Real McCoy, anyway.

However, *"exotic" drinks*—Mai Tais, Blue Hawaiis, Chi Chis, Wipeouts, Catamarans, Zombies, or whatever—may be ordered by those names without fear. Most of them are rum concoctions and are filled up with sugar plus pineapple and other fruits of the tropical loom. They will cost considerably more than call drinks, however.

The two-drink requirement in many clubs usually works for any kind of drink, incidentally—even beer, although you may have to pay $3 for a bottle of Primo. By the way, this formerly Hawaiian brew is no longer made in the Islands. It is "imported" from California!

If you want to change your poison in mid-show, you'll have a hard time catching your waitress on the fly. She might be so busy that the next time you see her will be when she swoops in on automatic pilot with the second round of exactly the same stuff that you originally ordered.

One advantage of whooping it up in Waikiki, of course, is that you usually don't have to drive anywhere afterwards. If you *do*, however, limit your drinks severely—to one or none. Honolulu police have special tough DUI ("driving under the influence") teams who come down hard on drinking drivers. They set up frequent unannounced road blocks, and if you don't pass breathalyzer or other sobriety tests, you could find yourself spending the rest of your vacation in the slammer—or worse!

WAIKIKI SHOW BIZ—WHO'S WHO AND WHAT'S WHAT

Most Waikiki entertainers and some big productions move around from clubroom to clubroom too frequently for us to pin down their particular shows and admission prices in an annual publication. But here are some of the big names—people and show titles—currently on the night scene. Only a few will be performing at any one time, and some may only appear in guest spots.

The Aliis—A six-man Hawaiian vocal group that successfully blends music and yuk-it-up humor. Plenty of variety in a big, well-paced show. **Baltazar, Gabe**—Known today as Hawaii's premier jazz musician. **Beamer, Kapono**—Son of a famous Hawaiian musical family who is now performing on his own. **"Blue Kangaroo"**—A somewhat far-out comedy act. **Borges, Jimmy**—Popular and informal Island singer, even more at home in jazz than on Hawaiian numbers. (Perhaps still at the Captain's Gallery in the Moana Hotel.) **Bumatai, Andy**—Hawaii's most popular and most talented stand-up comedian, who returns home occasionally from California, where he is now working.

   Cabang, Mel—A wild-eyed comedian with a flashlight and a heavy local flavor. (He may be at the Plaza Lounge in the Waikiki Shopping Plaza.) **Cazimero, Roland and Robert**—Now billed as the "Brothers Cazimero," this duo offers one of the most popular entertainment experiences, appreciated by both locals and visitors. (Now in their fifth year at the Monarch Room of the Royal Hawaiian Hotel.) **Chillingsworth, Sonny**—One of Hawaii's best slack-key guitar artists. **Conjugacion, Brother Noland**—He has successfully fused rock-pop music with Island themes. **Conjugacion, Tony**—Don't let the last name fool you. Noland's younger brother is part-Hawaiian, with a great falsetto voice, who sings traditional and contemporary Hawaiian music. **Courtney, Del, and His Orchestra**—Big band dancing at twilight on Monday at the Royal Hawaiian Hotel's Monarch Room. **Cypriano, Nohelani**—Island singer with a Mainland wallop. (She recently moved into Trappers, the jazz club at the Hyatt Regency Hotel.)

   Davis, Charles K. L.—A Hawaiian operatic tenor and the first son of Hawaii to sing at the Met. He also has a vast repertoire of old Hawaiian songs, and seems to have become a fixture in recent years as Sunday brunchtime entertainment at Keemoo Farms. **DeLima, Frank**—He mixes music and mirth successfully along with a comic pair called Na Kolohe. Wild, local-style humor. (He's probably still at the Noodle Shop in the Waikiki Sand Villa Hotel.) **Denny, Martin**—Pianist/composer/orchestra leader trying to outlive his bird calls and jungle-sound fame of bygone years. **Garner, Loyal**—Once the biggest thing to hit Waikiki in years, and she's still pretty big. A radiant personality with voice and piano ability to match. Sometimes schmaltzy, but always fun. **Harrington, Al**—Another leading Waikiki professional who formerly played a regular part on "Hawaii Five-0." An appealing personality, but not a strong singer.

   Ho, Don—Mister "Tiny Bubbles" himself, the king of Hawaiian entertainers, and the handsome prince for the thousands of grandmas he's kissed on stage over the decades. It is unfortunate that Ho is almost the only Hawaiian entertainer known on the Mainland, but he's usually good on your first trip to Hawaii. (Young people are less enthusiastic in the letters we receive, however.) In any case, the Ho show is just about the most expensive in town—as a guess, close to $50 with drinks and dinner this year, or maybe $30 or so for the cocktail show. He's probably still at the Hilton Hawaiian Village Dome.

Jensen, Dick—Another powerful, first-line Hawaiian showman, Jensen stands 6-foot-2, and they call him "Giant." Lots of excitement, dancing, etc., in his show, and he's known for a slip, glide, and slide routine as well as a group of humorous sound effects.

Kaaihue, Henry "Kapono"—A former member of a duet, now going it alone. He appeals to a younger audience. **Ka'eo**—A popular Hawaiian music group. **"Kailua Madrigals"**—A delightful chorus of high-school students. **"Kalo's South Seas Revue"**—The Polynesian show probably still thump-thumping it up in the Hawaiian Hut, a nicely designed showroom in the Ala Moana Americana Hotel. We would rank it about third in Waikiki shows of the type.

Kaleikini, Danny—Almost as well known as Don Ho, he has been the star at the Kahala Hilton for two decades. *Honolulu Advertiser* critic Wayne Harada says he offers "Hawaiiana with simple elegance." In a brisk show, he demonstrates several talents including his famous nose flute performance. Kaleikini's good voice can retreat to the back of his throat, and then the orchestra might overpower it. We had one of the bad tables in the Hala Terrace, certainly not the best of showrooms. **Kamahele, Sonny**—A well-known Island steel guitarist, perhaps still at the Halekulani. **Kamae, Eddie, and the Sons of Hawaii**—An all-Hawaiian string and song group led by ukulele virtuoso Kamae.

Keale, Moe—A gifted ukulele player with a pure Hawaiian voice. **Keawe, Genoa**—She's a genuine, old-time Hawaiian entertainer, a great-grandma specializing in falsetto voice. **Keawehawai'i, Karen**—A popular singer and comedienne. **Kimura, Andy**—A singer/musician who plays guitar and performs his own compositions. **Krush, The**—Energetic eight-member modern musical group.

Larrin, Jay—A lounge performer whose own piano and voice compositions are appreciated by locals and visitors alike. **Leed, Melveen**—Hawaii's hottest female down-home-style singer, known as the "Tita" (pidgin for "sister") from Molokai. Specializes in "Hawaiian country" music, and was the first Hawaiian singer to appear at the Grand Ole Opry in Nashville. **Lincoln, Bill**—A solid, old-style Hawaiian falsetto singer and guitarist. **Lupenui, Darrell** (and his Men of Waimapuna)—An expansive figure leading a prize-winning hula group, noted for its earthy Hawaiian songs and dances.

McCall, Azure—A jazz trouper with a powerful voice. **Makaha Sons of Niihau**—An excellent down-home Hawaiian group. **Mendes, Sonya**—A 5-foot-2 bundle of energy, she's considered Hawaii's "new rock" music queen. A vocalist who can double on keyboard and guitar. She and her group, "Revolucion," are often at the Wave Waikiki. **Morris, Freddy**— Young Island singer/ventriloquist, performing with his blockhead companion, "Moku Kahana." **Moon, Peter**—A talented guitarist and composer specializing in modern Island songs, he heads his own "Peter Moon Band." **Namakelua, "Auntie Alice"**—Now in her eighties, she is still among the foremost slack-key guitar players and composers in the Islands. She seldom performs in public, however.

Nievera, Roberto—A former member of the "Society of Seven," now on his own. Once known as the "Johnny Mathis of the Philippines," he has now gone far beyond that. **Ohta, Herb**—Known also as "Ohta-san," he's probably the Islands' foremost and most accomplished ukulele artist. **Paulo, Rene**—Quick, nimble, and precise, he ranks as the dean of the keyboarders in Hawaii. His wife, Akemi, often sings with him.

Sai, Marlene—Powerful singer with a regal style. Hawaii's only gold-record female vocalist. **Santos, Jerry**—Singer and guitarist who writes and performs folk-pop Hawaiian music popular among Island youth. The **"Society of Seven"**—Also known as S.O.S., they're a long-run, Vegas-style favorite at the Outrigger Hotel's Main Showroom, often alternating weeks with the Krush.

"Tavana's Polynesian Spectacular"—Sometimes called simply "Tavana," the show has perhaps remained the best Polynesian review in Waikiki, surpassed only by the teetotaling show out at the Polynesian Cultural Center in Laie. Tavana has changed venues several times. He *may* still be in the Long House at the Hilton Hawaiian Village. Of the same ilk, the **Moana Polynesian Review** in the Banyan Court behind the Moana Hotel is also pretty good. **"Tihati's South Seas Spectacular"**—Another all-Polynesian review, probably still performing in the Bora Bora Room of the Waikiki Beachcomber. It's also fine, even if we still prefer Tavana's. **Tiki, Varoa**—An up-and-coming entertainer successfully combining shticks and songs.

Vaughan, Palani—Singer and Hawaiiana scholar, specializing in songs of the King Kalakaua era. **Veary, Emma**—Affectionately dubbed "Ol' Golden Throat," Emma brings a cultured, classical voice to her Hawaiian songs and a special misty-eyed reverence for the monarchy period of Island history. (Lately performing with the Brothers Cazimero at the Royal Hawaiian Hotel.)

"Zoulou" (who used to spell his name "Zulu")—Always pointed out as that fat guy who played in the first three or four seasons of "Hawaii Five-0." That's unfortunate, for Zoulou deserves his own good reputation as a first-rate, versatile showman; he's a singer, dancer, and comedian, and a top-grade performer on the uke, too.

THE LUAU SCENE

Stop thinking of a luau as a "feast." It is not, especially as set up in Waikiki at present. It is true that you will sample some Hawaiian food, and that may be a valuable cultural experience. Nevertheless, less than one percent of the visitors to Hawaii actually like Hawaiian food, and as far as we are concerned luaus are better in direct proportion to the amount of nonauthentic comestibles one is offered in addition to the traditional fare.

Most folks are most interested in the entertainment, and there's where a luau can be fun. Depending on the emcee, the other entertainers who take part, and the camaraderie in your own group, the luau should be a whoop-it-up, happy-go-lucky Hawaiian experience.

Remember that a luau should be *outdoors* to capture the full flavor of the event, and we recommend skipping any that are not. Don't expect to sit on the ground in this day and age, however. They do this in other islands of the Pacific, but not in Hawaii.

Here's a list of four good bets in Oahu luaus for 1986. All may run in the neighborhood of $30 to $40 for adults, $25 or so for children. Reserve in advance, either by phone after arrival or (in some cases) using the toll-free numbers in the back of this book.

Chuck Machado Luau (Tel. 836-0249)—A long-established, well-regarded local firm presenting luaus outside the Outrigger Hotel, and perhaps less expensive than most.

Royal Luau (Tel. 923-7311)—The regular Sunday luau presented by the Royal Hawaiian Hotel at 6 P.M. on their Ocean Terrace.

Sheraton-Waikiki Luau (Tel. 922-4422)—A good show *if* it's held out on the lawn. (We were once packed into an indoor version here, which was not much fun.) Tuesdays.

Paradise Cove Luau (Tel. 945-3539)—Guests are bused from Waikiki a long way out to the old beachfront estate of the late Kamokila Campbell near Ewa. In general, we would rather not consider any luau that involves a bus trip out of town, but this *might* be an exception. (Germaine's, however, is now off our list.)

DISCOTHEQUES, CLUBS, AND CABARETS

Nearly all establishments serving liquor must by law close their doors at 2 A.M. The exceptions are those with "cabaret" licenses, generally singles' rock music and dance spots, which the city allows to jump until 4 A.M. They're not truly "discotheques," by the way. One requirement for the cabaret license is that there must be live music—no records.

The most popular such spots featuring the best musical groups are usually easy to find—there's a capacity limit, so they're the ones with the longest lines outside. And it may not be fair, but some of these admit card-carrying "members" before a newcomer to the scene.

The best honest-to-groove discos and rock clubs are restaurants that have banked their fires and heated up the hi-fi along about 10 P.M. Beginning generally with the best, those the local discomaniacs dig the most include **Spats** at the Hyatt Regency, **Scruples** in the Waikiki Market Place, 2310 Kuhio Ave., **Nick's Fish Market** in the Waikiki Gateway Hotel, 2070 Kalakaua, and **Bobby McGee's Conglomeration** far out at the Colony East Hotel, 2885 Kalakaua Ave.

Annabelle's, under the aegis of the prestigious Juliana's of London, is on the top floor of the Ilikai Hotel. Newer discos include **Cilly's,** in the basement under 1909 Ala Wai Blvd., **Masquerade,** in its own building at 224 McCully St., near Kalakaua, and **The Pink Cadillac**, parked not far away at 478 Ena Rd., just off Kalakaua.

The big rock-band clubs, most with a 4 A.M. weekend closing time, are—in approximate order of descending desirability—**Wave Waikiki** at 1877 Kalakaua Ave., the **Point After** on the second floor of the Hawaiian Regent Hotel, and **Rumours** in the Ala Moana Americana Hotel. All are 110-decibel dating-and-mating grounds for singles. You'll find a cover charge (for men) and a two-drink minimum on live band nights. There are plenty of other hot spots opening and closing their doors and changing their names almost monthly. The scene will surely be shifted by the time this perishable research hits the strobe lights.

By the way, the drinks in most clubs will be at least $2.50—even for a Coke. Big outfits like the Point After will levy cover charges, too, but generally not the places that are restaurants earlier in the evenings.

Mellower music and dancing? One of the traditional favorites is the sophisticated lounge called **Trapper's** in the Hyatt Regency Waikiki. For a few days each month, it has been featuring one of the world's jazz greats. Les McCann, Stan Getz, Wynton Marsalis, Freddie Hubbard, etc., have let loose here at one time or another. Then they might walk across the street to the **Captain's Gallery** at the Moana Hotel to finish up. Then a brand new club attracting dancing devotees is **Casablanca** at 1855 Kalakaua Ave. Something more mellow and traditional are the piano, bass, guitar, and drums you may find encouraging after-dinner dancing at the **Hanohano Room** atop the Sheraton-Waikiki.

Forty minutes beyond Waikiki, in Pearl City, there are jazz jam sessions at **Reni's**, 98-713 Kuahao Place. Reni's was opened recently by "Magnum P.I." co-star Roger E. ("T.C.") Mosley. And speaking of jazz, Dixieland performances have long been a Sunday-afternoon tradition at the **Gar-**

den Bar in the Hilton Hawaiian Village. The downbeat usually sounds at around 2 P.M.

HONOLULU ON THE SLIGHTLY SEAMY SIDE

There is no real Sin City in Hawaii, but there is plenty of racy action for anybody with the curiosity, the inclination, and, of course, the money. Traditionally much of this has been centered around the porno palaces, kook-book shops, and X-Y-Z-rated film houses in the low numbers on North and South Hotel streets downtown. Some cheap sleaze has also invaded Waikiki, from the 1900 to the 2100 block of Kalakaua. (If you can read Japanese, you might be appalled at the content of some of those signs.)

Honolulu's long-standing strip-tease and burlesque joint is downtown— the **Club Hubba-Hubba** (Tel. 536-7698), at 25 North Hotel St. The action is continuous and exhausting from about 4 to 4—that's P.M. to A.M., of course. No cover, and no cover.

You'll also find nude go-go dancing at places like the **Lolli-Pop,** 2131 Kalakaua Ave., and now in many of the hostess bars. Probably due to the Oriental influence in Hawaii, the B-girl enjoys just a little more *geisha*-like respect in Honolulu than in Mainland cities. Also, the places in which she works are a little less likely to be ripoffs. They are known in Honolulu generally as "Korean bars," although the young women who will sit on a customer's lap for as long as he buys the drinks are today often Vietnamese. In any case, they seldom admit to knowing much more English than a breathy "yes-s-s." And if there are ten tables in the joint, you'll probably find there are ten hostesses there, too.

Her drinks may cost $15 or more, whether they're real drinks or not, and of course it's all on your tab. Perhaps that's harmless enough, but look out when she gives you her only other English word—"Champagne." Then your wallet has begun to get serious. Of course if you can afford $80 for an $8 bottle of Barney's Backyard Bubbly, great.

The free *pupus* in the better Korean bars are usually delicious, and you *can* turn down the professional companionship if you just want to sit and talk business with your buddy. (Of course a regular date would feel pretty uncomfortable in there.)

Among the more popular and "respectable" Korean bars are **Crystal Palace** at 735 Sheridan St., **Misty II** at 1661C Kapiolani Blvd., **Butterfly Lounge** at 903 Keeaumoku St., and **Sir John's** at 1210 Queen St. There are about 50 more, however, usually recognizable by a woman's name following the word "Club" or preceding the word "Lounge," as in "Club Penelope" or "Geraldine's Lounge." (To our knowledge, at least, neither of these examples exists at the moment.)

Most are all right as long as you accept their basic premises. And don't expect the girl to topple over on the stuff *she's* putting away.

There may be a Korean bar around someplace that will try to make you pay for something you didn't order. We'd talk loudly about notifying the Honolulu Liquor Commission—*if* we were sure of our ground.

A tough bar in a tough neighborhood? Not for everyone is a sociologist's dream and a yuppy's nightmare called **The Pantheon**, also billed as "the oldest bar in Honolulu." Established in 1883, the Pantheon now hosts what *Honolulu Advertiser* writer Will Hoover described as "floozies, philanderers and flesh peddlers...hucksters, live wires, grape mongers, dipsomaniacs, misfits and elbow benders of every human persuasion." King Kalakaua drank there, according to owner/bartender Pete Peterson. Will concluded that Toulouse-Lautrec, anyway, would have loved the place. Look up the address in the phone book, if you want. You're not likely to run across the Pantheon by accident, and we're not going to be responsible for telling you how to get there!

GAY BARS

The gay scene changes quickly, but at this writing there is no bar or club devoted exclusively to the fraternity. Gays do frequent the aforementioned Club Hubba-Hubba, but then so do lots of others. In Waikiki, and billing itself as a "megasexual discotheque," is **Hula's Bar and Lei Stand,** 2103 Kuhio Ave., at Kalaimoku Street. The scene also flows over next door to **Hamburger Mary's Organic Grill.**

DRINKING AND CHATTING

There are several nice lounges, but one of our favorites is a quiet piano bar called **The Library,** next to The Third Floor in the Hawaiian Regent Hotel. The pubs mentioned near the end of our dining suggestions (section 5) are also good and popular, as is the aforementioned **Trapper's.** After dining hours, restaurants catering to a casual clientele include **Canlis**, at 2100 Kalakaua Ave., and **Andrew's**, a few minutes outside of Waikiki at Ward Centre, 1200 Ala Moana Blvd.

AND AFTER 4 A.M.?

Night owls who get hungry following their evening hoot often float back to earth at the **Wailana Coffee Shop,** 860 Ala Moana Blvd., or perhaps sit down for awhile with **Eggs 'n Things,** nearby at 436 Ena Rd. Happy landings!

12. The Oahu Address List

Art supplies— Pacific Gallery and Art Supplies, 1253 South Beretania St. Tel. 533-1197.

Bakery— Leonard's Bakery, 933 Kapahulu Ave. Tel. 737-5591.

Barber— Percy's, 2255 Kalakaua Ave. (Sheraton-Waikiki). Tel. 922-1591.

Beauty salon— Paul Brown's Cutters, 1347 Kapiolani Blvd. Tel. 947-3971.

Bus information— Tel. 531-1611.

Camper rentals— Beach Boy Campers, 1720 Ala Moana Blvd. Tel. 955-6381.

Camping equipment rental— Hawaiian Rent-All, 1946 South Beretania St. Tel. 949-3961.

Chamber of Commerce of Hawaii— 735 Bishop St. Tel. 531-4111.

City Office of Information and Complaint— 530 South King St., Room 301. Tel. 523-4381.

Dry cleaners— Al Phillips, Waikiki Market Place, 2310 Kuhio Ave. Tel. 923-1971.

Fire department— Dial 911 for all emergencies.

Fishing supplies— Charley's, 745 Keeaumoku St. Tel. 949-7373.

Florist— Polynesian Exotics, 410 Nahua St. Tel. 926-3556.

Hawaii Visitors Bureau— 2270 Kalakaua Ave., Suite 804. Tel. 923-1811.

Health-food store— Aloha Health Foods, Ward Warehouse. Tel. 531-7703.

Hospital— Dial 911 for all emergencies.

Laundromat— Outrigger Hotel Arcade, 2335 Kalakaua Ave. Tel. 923-0711.

Medical clinic— Ala Moana Family & Emergency Medicine (open 24 hours), 1860 Ala Moana. Tel. 943-1111.

Pharmacy— Outrigger Pharmacy, 2335 Kalakaua Ave. Tel. 923-2529.

Police— Dial 911 for all emergencies. Headquarters is at 1455 South Beretania St. (near the end of Kalakaua Avenue). Tel. 943-3111.

Post office— Waikiki Branch Post Office, 330 Saratoga Rd. Tel. 941-1062.

Public library— Waikiki-Kapahulu Library, 400 Kapahulu Ave., at the Ala Wai. Tel. 732-2777.

Supermarket—Safeway, 1121 South Beretania St. Tel. 538-7315.

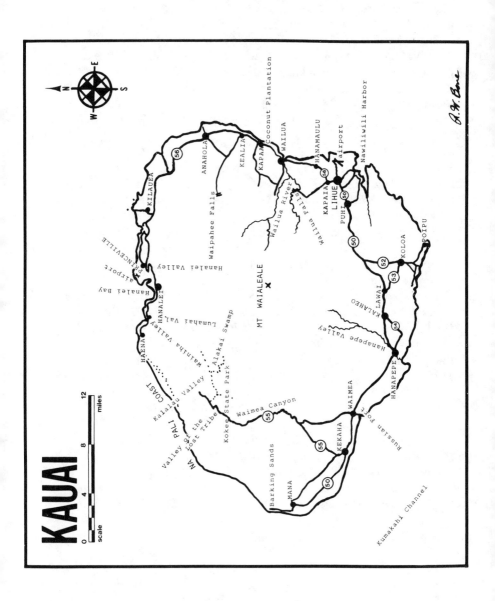

6

Kauai,
the Garden Island

1. Around the Island—A Verdant Outpost

Is there really no such thing as a sleepy tropical paradise any more?
Are such ingredients as rustling palms, fragrant *mokihana* vines, pure
untouched sands, azure seas, wheeling frigate birds, and an unhurried
pace of life all mixed together solely in someone's imagination—a scenic
recipe only affirmed in the films of Hollywood?

Maybe. But then where do the moviemakers go to capture these images of Elysium?

They go to the Island of Kauai. Perhaps the director must cart along
an improbable collection of characters, but there is virtually no need for
anyone called a set designer.

Honoluluans often save Kauai for their honeymoons. The 100-mile
distance from the capital serves as a psychological barrier to state residents. They may visit all the other islands in the chain before they fall in
love and set out for Kauai.

Together with its satellite isle of Niihau, Kauai is the only major piece
of real estate in the archipelago that cannot be seen from any of the
other Hawaiian Islands.

Maps produced by airlines and other commercial operations often
draw Kauai artificially closer—to the point where it is nearly touching
Oahu. This is a usurpation of artistic license, for the island's distance and

more northward latitude help us to understand its bucolic isolation and somewhat cooler mien.

Kauai is not on the way to anyplace else, unless you count the uninhabited atolls, islets, and shoals that form tiny, wave-swept stepping stones dotting the direction to Japan. In the eighteenth and nineteenth centuries, this separation from the islands to the southeast saved Kauai residents considerable bloodshed. Here is one island that was *not* conquered by Kamehameha the Great. It was finally given to him, though a little less than amicably, by Kaumualii, the king of Kauai, in 1810.

To statisticians, the Garden Isle consists of 553 square miles, making it the fourth largest of the islands. It is also the oldest, since it thrust itself above the sea about 8 million years ago. It has had considerably more centuries to be eroded and otherwise molded by wind, rain, and tide. Perhaps partly for this reason, it could also be called the Island of Rivers, features that are generally missing from the younger islands in the state.

Kauai was built by one massive volcano. Today's tallest peak, Mt. Waialeale ("why-ollie-ollie") is all that remains of that volcano's eastern rim. The 5,243-foot mountain, whose name can be translated as "overflowing water," is said to be the wettest spot on earth. A geologic fluke has created a funnel that collects masses of moisture-laden trade winds and forces them up to an altitude where they must cool and condense. The rainfall atop the cloud-shrouded *massif* averages more than 460 inches annually, and one pluvial year it measured 624 inches.

Most of Kauai's 45,000 residents live around the rim of the island, leaving the sprawling and often rugged interior to sugar cane, wild goats, and feral pigs. Two natural features dominate the outback—the deep gash called Waimea Canyon, and the virtually impenetrable sloping valleys and green sea cliffs on the northwest shore called the Na Pali Coast. Because of this rugged obstruction, no road will ever completely circle the island. There are gorges in Na Pali that have not felt a human foot for centuries, and there are others that have never been explored at all.

The first Polynesians came to Kauai in about 800 A.D., but there are tales of mysterious groups of people having preceded them. Hawaiian legends speak particularly of the *Menehunes* ("many-*hoon*-ies"), a race of "white dwarfs" who were adept at stonemasonry but who were physically subjugated by the more powerful Polynesians.

Did the Menehunes really exist? You will see examples of very sophisticated fitted stone on Kauai that are found nowhere else in the Islands. And even the journals of Captain James Cook tell of a servant class on Kauai—men and women he saw who were shorter and lightskinned.

For more than 150 years, the Hawaiians have been telling us that the Menehunes simply went away one day. According to legends, they pulled up stakes and disappeared into one of the hidden valleys along the Na Pali Coast. Some say they could be living there still.

2. Airports—Lihue and Princeville

Most travelers to Kauai enter through **Lihue Airport** after a 17-minute jet trip from Honolulu via either of the two scheduled jet air carriers, Aloha Airlines (Tel. 245-3691) or Hawaiian Airlines (Tel. 245-3671), or the prop-jets flown by Mid Pacific Airlines (Tel. 245-7775). A few take the 50-minute propeller flights between Honolulu and Princeville via Princeville Airways (Tel. 826-3770). See chapter 2 on interisland flying. Now a significant number of visitors jet direct to Kauai via nonstop flights from Los Angeles on the DC-8 aircraft of United Airlines (Tel. 245-9533). Jumbo jets may come along in a year or two, after the runway is lengthened.

Lihue Airport has been getting several badly needed technical improvements. Recently it inaugurated its long-overdue and much safer ocean-approach runway, which does not require a sharp bank in order to miss a range of hills. Nevertheless, the old runway is also still in operation, used mainly by smaller aircraft. Because of this, we take the advice of pilot friends and never fly into or out of Lihue in obviously bad weather or at night.

The new Lihue Airport terminal may be open or partially open by the time you read these words, although construction is slated to continue through 1995. On the surface, it appears to be shaping up as something similar to Hilo's barn-like facility. It can handle six airlines (only four needed at the moment), and twin baggage carousels are located at either end of the long main structure. The air-conditioned building with its fancy big-city weatherproof jetways will certainly be comfortable. However many lament that it lacks the charm of the outpost airfield that island residents were accustomed to for so many years. We'll go into greater detail on the airport layout and facilities in our 1988 edition.

Kauai's second and much smaller landing strip is **Princeville Airport,** alongside the road a couple of miles or so east of the resort community of Princeville. It's one of the most beautiful green sites for an airport in the country, backdropped by the distant Hanalei Mountains. The only scheduled commercial service is provided by Princeville Airways in their Twin Otters, direct from Honolulu.

3. Transportation on Kauai

To travel from the airport to your hotel, your choices are simple: Take a shuttle bus, hire a taxi, rent a car, or—if that's your duffle bag—hike.

Hotel transfers (shuttle service) from the terminals now have standardized prices on all bus companies. It will cost you somewhere between $5 and $20, depending on the distance, to be carted off with your luggage to most lodgings via these buses or limousines. They currently are run by three outfits: Robert's Hawaii Tours, Gray Line Kauai, and Kauai Island Tours (see Section 7).

There is only one taxi company stationed at the airport: **Garden Island Taxis** (Tel. 245-3523), an old stalwart. Sample and very approximate rates to some destinations run as follows: Lihue—$8; Poipu Beach hotels—$25; Coco Palms Resort Hotel (Wailua)—$15; Coconut Plantation hotels—$18; and Princeville or Hanalei—$45. Drivers are allowed to charge 25 cents extra per large suitcase. There are several other taxi ownerships on the island at this writing, each generally associated with separate communities. Check with your hotel for specific taxi information.

Most travelers not on conducted tours will prefer to rent a car. In Kauai, too, this is a highly volatile and very competitive business. As of yesterday afternoon, there were no less than 20 competing companies there. Impossible? You bet, and there are bound to be many changes by the time you're ready to slide into the driver's seat. (Please see our long discussion on rental-car agencies in chapter 5, section 3.) Here are some Kauai rental-car agencies, and an observation or two about them. For all except Watase's, you may make advance reservations by calling their Honolulu offices. (Check the Oahu telephone directory for those numbers.)

Avis (Tel. 245-3512) is a dependable perennial. **Budget** (Tel. 245-4021) once laid the damage-waiver pressure on us hard here. But we resisted and found the car itself satisfactory. **Dollar** (Tel. 245-4708) may still have a good deal on renting camping equipment to go with the car. **Hertz** (Tel. 245-3356) is generally the top-dollar car here as in many other places. **National** (Tel. 245-3502) presumably still gives Green Stamps. **Robert's Hawaii** (Tel. 245-4008) may also have jeeps and vans. **Thrifty** (Tel. 245-7388) is now open both in Lihue and Hanalei, offering some "no-smoking" cars. **Tropical** (Tel. 245-6988) is a longtime personal favorite for low flat rates and usually good service (there's no airport office; call and they'll come pick you up). **Watase's** (Tel. 245-3251) is a good local outfit that has mileage rates only. **Westside** (Tel. 332-8644) serves the Poipu area with cars and jeeps. Used cars can be taken out from **Rent-A-Wreck** (Tel. 2454755). But if you're heading into the boonies up in Kokee or elsewhere, look into **Rent a Jeep** (Tel. 245-9622).

Until recently, driving on Kauai was a pretty casual thing. But not long ago the very first stop lights came to the island, and now there are nearly a dozen. Traffic is one of Kauai's most nagging problems, particularly on the east side between Lihue and Kapaa, and it is probably part of the reason for the increased popularity of resorts on the north (Hanalei/

Princeville) and south (Poipu) shores. Except for Sunday, try to schedule your arrival on Kauai for around noon—never around 4 or 4:30 P.M., which is *pau hana* (quitting time), or you could spend two hours inching along Kuhio Highway getting to your "nearby" hotel.

Kauai drivers tend to be informal in their traffic habits. The *Honolulu Advertiser*'s barefoot Kauai correspondent with the untenable name, Jan TenBruggencate, points out that there are still three things any *malihini* driver is just going to have to grin at and bear up with: following in the wake of a tour bus, getting stuck behind a giant sugar cane truck loaded with stalks (don't try to pass one in an open convertible), and nosing the exhaust pipe of a little old retired plantation worker who chugs along at 35 miles per hour no matter where he is.

Bicycles, Motorized and Not. There are usually two or three outfits renting mopeds and bikes. Try **South Shore Activities** (Tel. 742-6873) next to the Sheraton Kauai at Poipu. Whatever the moped rates are, we'd advise comparing them carefully with what you would pay for a rental car. Chances are, if there are at least two of you, you'll be further ahead in something with four wheels.

4. The Hotel Scene

You'll probably base your choice of a Kauai vacation headquarters as much on location—whether you prefer to be the village mouse or the country mouse, or to be a club-jumper or a beachnik—as you will on the particular amenities offered by hotel managements. And if you're a budget-squeezer, remember that even the most modest twenty-dollar Kauai double is planted in lush, springlike surroundings that money simply can't buy in the most prestigious establishments in Chicago, Cleveland, or Milwaukee.

Kauai hotels and condos generally fall into three major geographical sectors. First is *Lihue-Kapaa*, which is about as close as you can get to "downtown Kauai." Second is *Poipu*, a haven for beach lovers which is somewhat isolated from the mainstream and other strands, about 20 minutes' drive southeast of Lihue. And third, we looked into some fairly expensive havens in *Princeville-Hanalei*, which may be about as far removed from reality as you can get, way up on the north shore.

Hotels we have listed in the *Expensive* category rent out most of their double rooms from about $100 per day on up. In our *Medium* group, two persons can pay from about $50 to $100 for 24 hours. And *Budget* hotels will happily put up a pair for something between $25 and $50, all calculated before taxes. Prices may change, of course, so those mentioned on these pages should be thought of only as a general guide.

EXPENSIVE HOTELS

Now pay close attention, because the grand-hotel picture is changing rapidly in Kauai. A big splash in 1987 will certainly be made by the new Westin Kauai when it opens at Nawiliwili, a suburb of Lihue, late in the year. (See end of this category.) This may be enough to pull the center of vacation luxury back into East Kauai.

Meanwhile there is only one contender for the crown of opulence, comfort, and tropical luxury on the Garden Isle. That is the visually dramatic 11,000-acre resort community of Princeville, and in particular its long-awaited world-class hotel, the 300-room **Sheraton Princeville** (Tel. 826-9644) —not to be confused with two other Sheratons on the island. The Sheraton Princeville forms the "hub" to the previously isolated golfing community near Hanalei. What's left of that isolation is the feeling of bedding down somewhere special, far away from the cares of the outside world. Even the annoying traffic patterns of East Kauai can be avoided now by flying Princeville Airways non-stop from Honolulu to the resort:

Unsurpassed site at Pu'upoa Point, with a perfect postcard vista of the mountain-and-shore panorama of Hanalei popularly if incorrectly called "Bali Ha'i"; unusual architecture with three main structures descending the steep hill in a sort of triple-terrace arrangement; 11 stories, with the entrance level on number 9; brick-paved lobby with separate check-in areas for groups and FITs; public rooms in classic Island designs, marked in some cases with the breadfruit patterns often seen on traditional Hawaiian quilts; several bars and restaurants down on the eighth floor; viewless Victorian-style Noble's, the signature dining room, in British colonial motif; open-air Hale Kapa serving three meals overlooking the bay; brick-lined Hale Kapa, the "country kitchen" style restaurant; plant-filled Ukiyo entertainment lounge/sushi bar with Oriental/theatrical accents; Lime Tree bar in the lobby; a long hike and two elevator rides for some to reach the pool, pool terrace, and beach; 24 tennis courts available; nearby 27-hole golf course already famous as one of the country's best; lots of activities available on and off the property.

In this, Sheraton's first genuinely up-market hotel in Hawaii, there are no rooms under $160 for two, and those overlook the golf course instead of the ocean; most will be from $200 to $260. Special features include, for example, a television disguised as a nineteenth-century "pie safe." Each room comes equipped with a Teddy Bear (for sale, if you want it). The 10th level has been designated a "no smoking" floor. (Reservations through the Sheraton organization or through the hotel at P.O. Box 3069, Princeville, HI 96722.) About the only detrimental thing we can say is that it normally rains more on this side of the island, generally in

January or February; that's what keeps it all so green. Rains are often short, however, and when things are dry, this hotel may be Hanalei Heaven.

We'll return to the Princeville/Hanalei area in a moment. If we couldn't get in at the Sheraton Princeville in 1987, we might skip over Lihue and its busy environs and head for some of the best, brightest, and biggest beaches on the island at Poipu on the southern shore. Our top selection there is the elegant **Waiohai Hotel** (Tel. 742-9511), a 460-room Gargantua right on Poipu Beach. Previously the plushest hotel on the island, the Waiohai occupies the site of a modest and fondly remembered lodge of the same name that was about one-tenth the size; today it tries to recapture the slower pace of an earlier day with its plantation-theme decorations:

Four-level, W-shaped plant on 11 well-landscaped acres; marble-floored, open-air lobby with four-story windows; teak and brass accents abounding; the largest, most artistic lobby wind chime you ever did see; two garden areas between arms of the W—the Ginger Courtyard with fragrant white flowers, and the Rainbow Courtyard with multicolored blossoms; each court with a pool, but one surrounding a semisunken bar (neither deeper than five feet, so no diving, please); six tennis courts; three high-priced restaurants, including the Waiohai Terrace (on the viewful site of the old hotel's restaurant), the haute-cuisine Tamarind (see section 5), and the cellar-sited Wine Room; Jackstraws, an atmospheric bar; the Tamarind Lounge a good piano bar; expensive but worth-it champagne brunch on Sunday; a large physical-fitness center with all the appropriate accouterments to help you compensate for that food.

Rooms (nearly all ocean view) with hidden color televisions; prestocked refrigerators; wet minibars; mirrored doors; patterned walls, upholstery, and bedspreads; small couches with tiny coffee tables; some rooms without desks or sit-down tables; very fancy bathrooms; small *lanais* with difficult outdoor furniture. Due to design deficiencies, some rooms do not admit enough sunlight during the day, especially the one we drew in the armpit of the W. At least one guest has complained that the fluorescent bed lamps are unflattering. Room rates for '87 are set at $125-$135 for Standards, $160-$170 for Superiors, and $190-$200 for Deluxes. Suites may begin at about $350 this year. (These are all FIT rates, and no, that doesn't really stand for what you'll have when you get the bill. Groups, etc., can probably wangle some lesser amounts.)

The Waiohai was controversial among local residents who fought its construction and did succeed (thankfully) in limiting it to four stories. (Reservations from Amfac Hotels, P.O. Box 8519, Honolulu, HI 96815.) Although we, too, miss the old Waiohai, the newer model is still recommended for Kauai capers—at least if price is no object.

Some say, and with good reason, that the title for South Shore elegance should go to the lively **Sheraton Kauai** (Tel. 742-1661), one of the three Sheratons on the island. Much of the Sheraton Kauai was destroyed three years ago by Hurricane Iwa, but now the hotel has been rebuilt very well. Its gardens are much more attractive than they were, and the establishment also seems to have developed an *esprit de corps* that matches its improved facilities:

Ideal location on a perfect section of sand; several four-story buildings scattered around lovely grounds on two sides of a small public street; many structures connected by elevated walkways; some garden sections forming an architectural impression of a small Japanese village; high-peaked, open lobby with tile floors and baskets of greenery; downstairs still guarded by grouchy old Waha, the parrot (he barks, too, but his bite is worse!); two large swimming pools, one by The Trellis, a pool bar, the other across the street near the beach; popular Pareo Pub for happy hours and sunsets; Lawai Terrace Steak House restaurant (where the catch of the day sometimes has been caught by fisherman/chef Bert Matsuoka himself); the Outrigger Dining Room for three meals in the Ocean Wing, sometimes featuring a Polynesian Show at night; the ocean-view Drum Lounge beating merrily next door.

Six Garden Wing buildings with accommodations oriented either to pool or ponds; Garden Wing rooms at $110, $120 and $130, depending on the views; fourth-floor units featuring high "cathedral" ceilings; ground-floor models convenient to pool or gardens via the *lanai* doors; beds all double-doubles or king-size; good furnishings throughout; TVs and *TV Guides;* paintings by Honolulu artist Pegge Hopper in nearly every room; 114 rebuilt Ocean Wing units *makai* of the road; deluxe rates over there mostly above $175; rates down about $10 during the summer and fall; some accommodations in all categories equipped for the handicapped. Two new buildings of about 120 rooms will be under construction during most of 1987. (Reservations from Sheraton Hotels in Hawaii, P.O. Box 8559, Honolulu, HI 96815.) Like the song goes, the Sheraton has mended its broken wings and learned to fly again—perhaps higher and better than ever before.

Also on Poipu Beach, the **Kiahuna Plantation** (Tel. 742-6411) is a resort condominium haven: About 300 apartments in some 40 cottage-style cedar and redwood buildings rambling over 35 acres; some units right on the sand; others set back a long, long way; famous, charming Plantation Gardens restaurant on the property (see section 5); ten tennis courts (free to guests); swimming pool a long hike from the beach; 18-hole golf course (the only one in the neighborhood); Hawaiian cultural lessons and demonstrations; special children's program available; accommodations decorated in bright colors; ceiling fans instead of air conditioners. The operation has finally broken its original vow of TV abstinence and put color sets in all the units. Some excellent rates for families or friends: One-bedroom models as a guess about $90 to $225 for up to four people as 1987 begins; two-bedroom units for up to six persons from $160 to $300, perhaps. (Reservations from Village Resorts, Inc., Suite 1000, 841 Bishop St., Honolulu, HI 96813.) Kiahuna Plantation tries to swing less like a condo and more like a resort. For golf or tennis buffs especially, it could be a winner. (But see below.)

Confusing the picture in a manner typical of so many condo operations—and one reason we cover so few of them in this book—is that there are now *two* Kiahunas. A half dozen duplicate buildings within the same boundaries are managed by a different outfit, now called **Kiahuna Beachside** (Tel. 742-7262), and guest registration is in a separate building far removed from the previous one. These well-landscaped buildings are all near the beach and have similar amenities to the other Kiahuna. However maid service is every *other* day, and during some periods there is a three- or five-night minimum stay. Rates at the K—Beachside are similar to and maybe a little less than those at the K—Plantation. We had a letter from one reader who was happy with his unit at the little Kiahuna, but said he could not obtain sand chairs, towels, snorkel equipment, etc., from the nearby Beach Hut since that facility turned out to be part of the big Kiahuna. And would you believe there are some smaller rental pools that represent a few units in *both* Kiahunas? Gadzooks! (Reservations and information from Hawaiiana Resorts, 1100 Ward Ave., Honolulu, HI 96814, or call their 800 number for the latest.) Also recommended, as long as you can keep everything straight.

There are several other condo operations in the Poipu area, ebbing and flowing with the tide, and we just can't keep up with them all. When reading their literature, watch out for terms like "ocean front condominiums," which are probably on a rocky shore and not as desirable as "beach front" units right on the sand. (And even in a "beach front" condo, that doesn't mean that your particular unit is going to be on the beach.) In addition to receiving information on maid service and minimum stays, ask about fans or air conditioning; "ocean breezes" are often not enough to keep you cool. One interesting condo we saw is **Poipu Crater** (Tel. 742-7260), whose buildings really do line the inside circumference of an extinct volcanic crater. There are no ocean views, but the units are apparently quiet and cool. **Poipu Shores** (Tel. 742-6522) is another reliable old-timer, on an ocean (not beach) front. The **Poipu Kai** (Tel. 742-6464) won praise from a reader recently, and it has one-bedroom units going from around $110 up and two-bedroom units for around $200. With its five pools, restaurant, bar, and other facilities, it feels more like a hotel, and it's also within reasonable walking distance of

Brennecke's Beach Park. Eight different outfits rent out apartments in the Poipu Kai, notably Colony Resorts, which has the management contract.

Switching now to eastern Kauai, specifically to Wailua, our traditional favorite there has always been the venerable **Coco Palms Resort Hotel** (Tel. 822-4921):

High-peaked, churchlike lobby with mammoth chandeliers and stained-glass windows; new main entrance, marble floors, and lighter tones coming this year; lovely grounds with three outdoor swimming pools; tiny zoo out back; nine tennis courts, including three new clay-surfaced models; thatched Chapel in the Palms, built for "Sadie Thompson" (weddings easily arranged); interesting private museum on the grounds; three restaurants—the Lagoon Dining Room, the menuless Flame Room, and the new ocean view coffee shop, still under construction; Sea Shell restaurant across the road also under the C.P. aegis; nightly entertainment; miles of pathways wandering through hundreds of palms; trees and lagoon remaining from a royal retreat of a century ago; famous torch-lighting ceremony nightly around the lagoon (the honors Elvis Presley performed in "Blue Hawaii"); the public Wailua Beach (no beach services) across the busy highway from the resort; a new pedestrian bridge to the sand hopefully coming this year.

Only a very few of the Coco Palms' 392 rooms are Standard doubles at $90. We prefer the Superiors for $110 in the refurbished Sea Shell wing with their blue-and-white decor, famous genuine giant clamshell washbasins, refrigerators, and several other extras. Try for Shell rooms overlooking the lagoon. Deluxe rooms in the Alii Kai ("Chief of the Sea") section are now $125. We saw Room 444 with its custom tiles, wrought iron, and white rattan furnishings. (All rates will be down about $5 from April 1 until Christmas.)

The Kings' Cottages and Queens' Cottages, running in the $165 range this year, often popular with honeymooners; decor in red and green and stone and wood; some with small, hidden yardlet with a unique outdoor lava-rock bathtub for private soaping in the sun. (Make sure you don't get the cottage right next to the dining room and its late-night, early-morning kitchen noise.) The newer Prince of Hawaii cottage ($225) is larger, although one guest who had it complained to us that the outdoor bath was plagued by mosquitoes. The Coco Palms has just been taken over by the Park Lane hotel people, a Hong Kong firm, and lots of refurbishing is on the drawing boards for this year. (Reservations from the hotel at P.O. Box 631, Lihue, HI 96766.) The Coco Palms has always been a sort of crazy, grew-like-Topsy sort of place, but it has always had genuine individual character, too. We still like it, and we're keeping our fingers crossed.

The brand-new 350-room, deluxe **Kauai Hilton** (Tel. 2451955) opened last year four miles from the Lihue Airport, and it is becoming known among travel agents for its swimming pools and among Kauaians for its discotheque:

Breezy, beachside site down a long entrance road off Kuhio Highway; 25 acres of well-landscaped grounds; several black, white, and black-and-white swans aswimming in the free-form lagoons; three meandering pools (counting a shallow kiddie pool) surrounded by artificial caves and cascades; a dangerous section of beach—for viewing, not for swimming or surfing; four lighted tennis courts; Wailua Golf Course a short drive away (by free shuttle); new luau building under construction; main four-story hotel edifice in a horseshoe shape with red-tile roofs; pleasant, sprawling lobby in pink and cream, with potted palms and a low ceiling; scored terrazzo tiles causing loud rumbles from the luggage carts; several lounges and bars, including Gilligan's—now the island's most popular disco; two respectable restaurants, the Jacaranda Terrace, an indoor/outdoor cafe with tables and wallpapered booths, and the green-marbled Midori, featuring Continental cuisine in an Oriental decor in two smallish rooms.

Sound-proofed, air-conditioned hotel rooms, with small triangular lanais, refrigerators, direct-dial phones, and cable televisions; a decor described by Hilton as "mulberry ice, deep raspberry and seafoam"; king size beds or double-doubles; seating areas in the king rooms only; well-designed baths; 1987 rates not decided by our deadline, but probably running around $100 or so for the few mountain/garden views, much more for the ocean vistas; 150 much older but refurbished Beach Villas rental condo units, with large lanais, self-cleaning ovens, etc., now managed by Hilton and perhaps running $100 to $175—maybe a better deal than some of the regular hotel rooms. The Hilton is pegged heavily to group and convention business, which may make some FITs (independents) feel a little lonely in the crowd. (Reservations for all through the Hilton Hotels Corporation). If a good swimming beach is your thing, the Hilton is not. But if you confine your water activities to the pools, the jacuzzi, or gazing into the duck pond, it just might be.

The 311-room oceanside **Sheraton Coconut Beach** (Tel. 822-3455), not to be confused with the Sheraton Kauai or the Sheraton Princeville, is at the far end of the Coconut Plantation complex, a five-minute stroll from the shops, along the beach or along the road:

Attractive, rambling, four-story structure with a modernistic, 40-foot waterfall in the lobby; koa wood planters and lots of stained glass and tapestry on the ground floor; Voyage Room restaurant, partly outdoors, and Cook's Landing, a comfortable, underutilized indoor/outdoor bar near the pool, with live cocktail music; a silent elevator that sneaks up on you; special *hale* under the palms for the Sheraton *luau;* several sports activities including tennis (three courts), volleyball, shuffleboard, and a putting green; narrow beach plagued with tiny, rough "cones" from the ironwood trees that may prickle sensitive feet; waves often too heavy for ocean sports in this area.

Rooms with color TVs, 80 percent with ocean views, but nearly all with tiny, triangular *lanais;* doors that do little to coax soothing trade winds indoors; air conditioners a welcome salvation in the warmest weather. For bigger balconies, and more air, choose the oceanfront Deluxes at $155 for two. Other rates go down to $100, but don't accept the unit we once had across from the Coke machine and noisy laundry room. We have been happy at other locations in the building, however. Prices are $10 lower April to mid-December. Sheraton recently sold the hotel to Pleasant Hawaiian Holidays, the largest wholesaler of package tours to Hawaii, but Sheraton continues to manage the property. (Reservations from Sheraton Hotels in Hawaii, P.O. Box 8559, Honolulu, HI 96815.) Wear your zoris to the beach, confine your swimming to the pool, cool your room by machine, and you may love it.

We haven't been through the 140-room **Poipu Beach Hotel** (Tel. 742-6681) lately, but it pales considerably in the shadow of the next-door Waiohai, under the same Amfac management. Rates range from around $80 to about $105 this year. At one time there was a plan to make this a *part* of the Waiohai, and we hope that idea never surfaces again. Actually, the place has been redecorated since our last go-around, and all units now have kitchen facilities. The beach, of course, is terrific, and we'll try to get around to doing a new site inspection again during 1987.

Back on the North Shore, now, besides the Sheraton Princeville Hotel, there are also some rentable condominium clusters administered by the Princeville Management Corp., notably the **Makai Club Cottages** (Tel. 826-6561). None, incidentally, is right on a beach, but the sands are not too far away.

The "front desk" for some cottages is in a building fronting the shops at Princeville Center, just off Kuhio Highway. We've seen beautiful interior furnishings at these condos in big-sky country, and they are certainly convenient for drive, slice, and putt addicts. Tennis courts and a swimming pool are also available, and there are a number of pleasant restaurants in the vicinity.

Daily rates run from about $100 for one-bedroom apartments to about $120 for three-bedroom apartments (up to six people), all with daily maid service. (Reservations from Princeville at P.O. Box 121, Hanalei, HI 96714.) We've never heard a discouraging word about Princeville from its guests, and dedicated golfers surely rate it much better than par.

Another condominium operation, **Hanalei Bay Resort** (Tel. 826-6522), is also in the Princeville complex: Well-known Bali Ha'i Restaurant in the central building; popular Happy Talk lounge; 11 tennis courts; two swimming pools; generally attractive one-, two-, and three-bedroom units in buildings named after fruits—or was it after trees (we checked out the "Guava Building"); lots of space and fine facilities, including washer/dryer and good kitchen equipment with garbage disposals; no air conditioning; overhead fans instead. Rates begin at about $75 for two in a "Mountain View" or maybe $80 for an "Ocean View" (but both of those are without kitchens). Fully equipped units begin at $100 or so and go up to about $300 for a three-bedroom apartment sleeping seven. (Reservations from Village Resorts, Inc., Suite 1000, 841 Bishop St., Honolulu, HI 96813.) Expensive, certainly, but certainly nice, too.

Two other large condo outfits at Princeville with which we're less familiar are the **Cliffs at Princeville** (Tel. 826-6219), with 200 small and large units beginning around $80 (they have an unusual plan that will prestock your fridge), and **Pali Ke Kua** (Tel. 826-9833), with 100 units beginning at around $100. The several Princeville condo operations can be confusing, to say the least, with some sets of cottages split between a half dozen or more different management agencies, each with its own scale of prices. Generally speaking, however, the accommodations are pleasant, even if some might be considered overpriced.

At this writing, the new $190 million, 837-room **Westin Kauai** (sorry, they couldn't tell us the telephone number yet) is still under construction on Kalapaki Beach at Nawiliwili, scheduled to open in late 1987. There will be 553 expanded rooms in the shell of the original 10-story Kauai Surf Hotel plus 284 rooms in an entirely new building, all planned and executed by multi-millionaire Honolulu developer Chris Hemmeter.

Many details of the resort are not out, but extravagant plans call for horse-drawn carriages to travel over 200 acres of lawns and gardens within the property, 40 acres of lakes and lagoons (with ferry boats) within a 36-hole golf course, an 11-court tennis complex (counting one stadium court seating 1,000), three shopping centers, a cliff-side Japanese inn, and other dramatic facilities on property that reaches from Kalapaki Bay to Lihue Airport. There will also be a 31,000-square-foot swimming pool and fountain surrounding an artificial island and capped by a glass pavilion with hot springs, a special wedding chapel by the sea, and seven to 10 restaurants—including the Tempura House, in a Japanese garden, and Prince Bill's, with views of the ocean and sunset. The beach, one of the best public strands on the island, will be bordered by a crushed marble and mosaic tile promenade. In the only high-rise buildings allowed on the island, all rooms will have a mini-bar and refrigerator, and rates are expected to begin at about $180 a day.

Although we can never recommend a hotel we've not seen in operation, we're certainly following the Westin developments with bated breath.

Last, we should mention that a brand-new luxury hotel, perhaps a Hyatt or something similar, will be built on Shipwreck Beach, a really great stretch of historic sand beyond Poipu, and it is expected to be open during 1988. If you are reading these words in 1988, maybe half of this volume will be out of date by then! Get ahold of a copy of the 1988 edition of this book, and we'll fill you in with the latest on that new hotel, a review of the new Westin, and everything else that has happened in Hawaii tourism during the previous 12 months.

MEDIUM-PRICE HOTELS

Although their snazzier rooms may run higher, here is a group of hotels and condos where you can usually come up with a decent double for less than $90 or so per night.

Besides those establishments listed below, sometimes private homes can be rented for short terms at comparable rates. If you're already on Kauai when you read these words, you might want to drop in to some local real estate agencies that handle vacation rentals.

The top medium-budget place is occupied by the 243-room **Kauai BeachBoy** (Tel. 822-3441), two strokes and a kick from the Sheraton Coconut Beach along the same shoreline in the Coconut Plantation complex: Friendly reception in a somewhat cluttered lobby; dining in the high-ceilinged Hale Kai restaurant (where the food has been pretty good); Hale Kai Boogie Palace Bar (outrigger canoes "fly" from the roof); parquet dance floor; downstairs beauty parlor; several shops; angular pool in well-kept lawn; Menehune Snack Shop beside the kiddie pool; myriad extracurricular activities including tennis, volleyball, ping pong, etc.

Some units directly on the beach; neat bedrooms; all air conditioned; washbasin separated from sleeping chamber only by a room divider; shower and john, however, with a genuine door; some teaklike furnishings; sliding door to the *lanai;* light-patterned wallpaper (unusual in Hawaii); clock radio (also a rare blessing); no room service. Doubles beginning at $65; then $78 for the best sand-side locations this year. (Reservations from Amfac Hotels, P.O. Box 8519, Honolulu, HI 96815.) The Kauai BeachBoy is tanned, healthy, and usually a handsome choice for the price.

We've always found the **Kauai Sands** (Tel. 822-4951) hard to rank. Adrift on a hard-to-snag road just before you get to Coconut Plantation, its facilities seemed undistinguished, except for an erratic decorating scheme. Not so its bubbly staff, however, who couldn't have been more friendly, warm, and helpful on our visit. These kinds of attitudes make up for a lot of kitschy furniture. Calling theirs "the only Hawaiian-owned and -operated hotels in the world," Hukilau Resort Hotels, the owners, also have one hostelry on Maui and three on the Big Island. On Kauai, neat doubles went for about $52 to $66 when we looked in, and that "higher" price included a kitchenette! (Reservations from Hukilau Resort Hotels, Suite 1201, 2222 Kalakaua Ave., Honolulu, HI 96815.) Our verdict? Somewhat of a plain Jane, but perhaps with a great personality.

Another hostelry about which you may disagree is the **Kauai Resort Hotel** (Tel. 245-3931), which we thought lacking in atmosphere on our own stay: Pleasant location alongside winsome Lydgate Park; gigantic high-roofed lobby that can fill up with 200 milling tourists at the crack of a bus door; overdone rock garden outdoors; tiny, perfectly round swimming pool, and access to park beach; very-decorated restaurant. Our standard double in the big building seemed sterile; it sells for about $65 now. We have had several complaints about mediocre service, substandard food, peeling paint, and bugs. Sorry, it's not for us this year.

It's been so long since we've seen the **Hanalei Colony Resort** (Tel. 826-6522) that we weren't going to mention it. But our sagacious friends, Dan and Gale Myers, have just returned to Honolulu from a week on the premises, and they enjoyed it a lot. Just about as far out toward the end of the northern road as you can go, this Haena condo has a dozen buildings, each with four ample apartments with all facilities. There's a swimming pool outside and Charo's restaurant is also on the property. Rates currently run $70 to $115. There are no televisions or telephones, and the adjoining beach is too rough for winter swimming. (Reservations from the resort at P.O. Box 206, Hanalei, HI 96714). A good layout for the modest outlay.

Two possibilities out at Poipu include the four modest cottages at **Koloa Landing** (Tel. 742-1470) on Honani Road. It rents studios for around $45 and two-bedroom units for $65-$75. The other is the nearby **Garden Isle Cottages** (Tel. 742-6717) with nine units and wide-ranging prices between $40 and $140 a day. We intended to see these two this year, but somehow didn't make it.

BUDGET HOTELS

The best in this price range probably is the 26-room **Coral Reef** (Tel. 822-4481) at 1516 Kuhio Ave. (the main highway), now under new ownership in Kapaa: Attractive palm-fringed setting for two buildings; office in the older wooden structure fragrant with many blooms; open-air loungette with Japanese garden; narrow beach outside, not great for swimming; a short walk to the town pool, at least. Some rooms with small refrigerator; nicest nests in the newer building about $40 for two; private lanai in the upstairs units; downstairs units put the Pacific right out your back door; doubles in the old building maybe $30 now; no discount for singles. There are also two spacious, two-bedroom family rooms, perhaps $40 for a couple and two *keikis*. Some readers reported difficulties making reservations by mail, but that was under the previous administration. (Write to the hotel at 1516 Kuhio Highway, Kapaa, Kauai, HI 96746, or use their new toll-free number in the Appendix.) It's not the Ritz, but then who needs the Ritz? In any case, we doubt you can beat it on Kauai for those prices.

A brief, incognito stay in Spike Kanja's **Ocean View Motel** (Tel. 245-6345) in Nawiliwili kept alive our appreciation for the place: TV lounge downstairs; absolutely no frills like pictures or phones in the rooms; popular with a young, budget-conscious crowd; some older folks reporting they feel out of place; not quite Spartan but usually spotless doubles for around $20 or so; singles beginning at about $18. And is there an ocean view at the Ocean View? You bet! It's way in the distance across the road, but you can walk there as well as to the terrific Kalapaki Beach where you may play footsies with those who will be paying several times your O.V. rate at the superluxurious Westin Kauai once it opens. Write Spike at 3445 Wilcox Rd., Nawiliwili, HI 96766.) It's priced right for the right crowd.

An unusual bargain, if the location is okay, is at the stateowned **Kokee Lodge** (Tel. 335-6061). This is not a hotel or condo, but a collection of a dozen cabins about 4,000 feet up in the cool forest at Kokee State Park, on the edge of the Alakai Swamp, a l-o-o-o-n-g way from the action. Surrounded by miles of hiking and hunting trails and several troutfishing streams, the apparently rustic accommodations are nevertheless furnished with refrigerators, stoves, showers, dishes, utensils, sheets, towels, pillows, and blankets. (But "no soap," said one reader.) A small restaurant/bar is nearby. Rates are still only $25 per cabin for either the small units (sleeping up to three) or the large ones (sleeping up to seven). Understandably this relatively nontropical, high-altitude haven is popular with Hawaii residents in the summer; but with last-minute cancellations, you may be lucky with a phone reservation. The *maximum* length of stay is five days. (Reservations from Kokee Lodge, P.O. Box 819, Waimea, Kauai, HI 96795, and a $25 deposit is required.) The revitalized operation is now run by Olson and Johnson, personal friends of ours, along with another couple, all of whom are serious about doing a good job.

If you want to establish yourself in the center of "Metropolitan Lihue," try the **Tip Top Motel** (Tel. 245-2333), whose bakery is justly famous for Portuguese sweet bread (*pão dulce*) and macadamia-nut cookies. There's a cafe, of sorts, and clean *air-conditioned* bedrooms still ran about $25 single and $30 double the last time we looked in. Better recheck those rates later, though. (Reservations direct from the Tip Top, 3173 Akahi St., Lihue, Kauai, HI 96766.) Actually, it's not really tip-top, but then neither are the prices.

Three other tiny places we didn't get to see include the **Hale Lihue** (Tel. 245-3151), 2931 Kalena St., Lihue, HI 96766; the **Ahana Motel Apartments** (Tel. 245-2206), 3115 Akahi St., Lihue, HI 96766; and the **Motel Lani** (Tel. 245-2965), P.O. Box 535, Lihue, HI 96766. All have some double rooms for $30 or less. Singles run around $25.

5. Kauai Restaurants and Dining

Of the four relatively populous islands in the state, Kauai is probably the least known for culinary excellence. But all things are relative, and happily there are some delicious exceptions to the general bill of fare.

LIHUE-NAWILIWILI DINING

In Lihue, the traditional favorite for steak-lobster-*mahimahi* and the like is **J. J.'s Broiler** (Tel. 245-3841), 2971 Haleko St., which some say put the "cow" in "cow-why." It's in the refurbished quarters in the third of four nineteenth-century German plantation foremen's houses. It's always great for lunch. Unfortunately, flying bugs can be an annoyance in the evening, depending on the weather and the season.

Lihue now boasts four Chinese restaurants. One of the best bargains is **Ho's Garden Restaurant** (Tel. 245-5255) at 3016 Umi St., in a tiny building near the Hawaii Visitors Bureau office in the center of town. Then there is the **Lihue Cafe and Chop Sui** (Tel. 245-6471) at 2978 Umi St., not far from Ho's. We haven't been in, but we heard from a couple couples, all of whom enjoyed it. Closed Mondays. The third is **Kauai Chop Suey** (Tel. 245-8790), in the Harbor Village across from the Westin Kauai construction site. It's a little more expensive, but some think the pleasant establishment is worth every penny. Try the Shrimp Canton. Last, and perhaps least from the strictly culinary point of view, is the revered old **Club Jetty** down at Nawiliwili Harbor. The people are friendly, and the combination "down-home" and nautical atmosphere is fascinating. Nobody really goes there for the food, but it's certainly okay if a little pricey. The place is much more lively late at night (see section 11).

Moving into the Japanese column, now, the best low-price bargain has to be the recently enlarged **Restaurant Kiibo** (Tel. 245-2650) at 2991 Umi St., across Rice Street from the County Building. (It's in the phone book under "R.") Try the shrimp tempura, and wash it down with *sake* or Japanese beer. Much better known, more expensive, and perhaps a little more tasty overall, too, is **Kintaro** (Tel. 822-3341). Also with Nipponese specialties is the little stucco **Barbecue Inn** at 2982 Kress St. Sorry, we haven't been in, but we've heard a good word or two from those who have.

The only Italian address in Lihue now is the **Casa Italiana** (Tel. 245-9586), which is winning friends for its long menu as well as its *northern* Italian goodies. It's at 2989 Haleko Rd., near J. J.'s, in a little *casa* said to be haunted by the German plantation manager who built it 100 years ago. He may stamp around upstairs from time to time in his jackboots. If the spirit is willing, perhaps the Italians and Germans will remain in peaceful coexistence when you and your doppelganger float by.

There are usually a couple Mexican entries in Lihue. The old La Luna has gone into eclipse, but something else will probably come over the horizon. In the same neighborhood, we still recommend **Rosita's** (Tel. 245-8561) in the Kukui Grove Center. It's decorated in almost a Mexican musical-comedy motif, with many high-backed, very *grande* booths. The food was innovative and generally *muy bien, gracias.* Try the unusual crab enchiladas or stuffed steak Tapacania.

Other popular choices in the same shopping center include the **Kukui Nut Tree** (Tel. 245-7005), where the food is uncomplicated but good, the service is quick, and the place is spotless. **Woolworth's** also has a convenient dining room in the same area.

Across the highway from the center, and about a mile further on, look for the former plantation estate called Kilohana. Its atmospheric courtyard dining room is called **Gaylord's Restaurant & Wine Bar** (Tel. 245-9593), and at the moment, it's open only at lunch for sandwiches and salads. Dinner plans may be in effect by the time of your visit, however. But out back, in the former area occupied by the servants and plantation workers, is the unusual **Original Plantation Cookout** (Tel. 245-9595), an outdoor experience featuring grilled fish, chicken, and steaks and all-you-can-eat salad and dessert bars. This is modeled after some successful operations in Alaska, by several Alaskans, and some Alaskan specialties like salmon and halibut are also on the menu. Most plates are priced between $11 and $16. Dining is on checkered tablecloths in an open-sided pavilion. We enjoyed it a lot, including the music by Daddy Cool, an Alaskan who plays jazz from the '30s and '40s.

There's plenty of genuine, penny-pinching local atmosphere at the **Tip Top Cafe,** which is a bit of a misnomer, at 3173 Akahi St., near the Lihue Shopping Center. Another local choice is **Ma's Family, Inc.** (Tel. 245-3142), formerly Ma's Place, at 4277 Halenani St. just in back of the Kress store, particularly for fresh malasadas. Catch these unusual operating hours: Open Monday to Friday from 5 A.M. to 1:30 P.M. and on Saturday and Sunday from 12:30 A.M. to 10 A.M. Kauaians disagree with my own Ma, who used to say nothing good ever happened after midnight, and point to their Ma's as the proof. And now Ma's nephew has opened **Dani's** (Tel. 245-4991) at 4201 Rice St., next to the fire station. Another "local kine" coffee shop, Dani's also has some strange hours: Monday to Saturday 5 A.M. to 2 P.M., Sunday 5 A.M. to 11 P.M. (Don't ask me, ask Ma's nephew!)

Before we leave the Lihue area, let's assure all timid souls that yes, the county seat does have a **Kentucky Fried Chicken,** where the public waits while the colonel cooks, and a **McDonald's,** which is like any one anywhere else, except maybe pricier. There's also a **Wendy's,** for hot and sloppy addicts (come the revolution, we're going to outlaw square burgers on a round bun), a **Burger King** for whopper–lovers, a **Pizza Hut** with the familiar red roof, and a **Dairy Queen** or two, where we would keep strictly to the one product that made it famous and skip everything else.

Those places draw a late-snack crowd, of course. But for something with more fun and local flair, try the **Hamura Saimin Stand** at 2956 Kress St. The saimin and barbecue sticks are cheap and really *ono-ono*. It doesn't close its doors until 2 A.M.—sometimes an hour or two later.

DINING FROM WAILUA TO KAPAA

Despite that awful name, **The Bull Shed** (Tel. 822-3791) continues to round up beef lovers over in the Waipouli/Coconut Plantation area. Some tables have terrific views over the ocean, so try not to get seated in the hallway. (Don't confuse this with its viewless branch shed at Nawiliwili.) Also excellent for lunch and dinner is the new **Plantation Buffet House** (Tel. 822-7714) under the theaters in the Coconut Plantation. The catch of the day is usually pretty good, says our Kauai spy. If you don't mind cooking your own, try **Create a Steak** (Tel. 822-1869), also in the Coconut Plantation.

What used to be just a lunch wagon in Hanalei has now been parked in a more or less permanent pink-stucco address in the Kapaa Shopping Center. That is **Tropical Taco** (Tel. 822-3622), and it has been known for several years, now, as the home of Hawaii's best tacos, all containing tons of refried beans, large amounts of ground beef, plenty of lettuce and tomato, heaps of shredded cheese, hot sauce, and a whopping lump of sour cream on top. You need a spoon, a fork, and maybe a half-hour to do justice to it. The original Tropical Taco itself is now up to $4.50—and worth it. We have also enjoyed their burritos, enchiladas, etc. The table service can be a bit *mañana*-like, but maybe that's part of the atmosphere.

Also in Kapaa, a friendly reader said he found Hawaii's finest breakfast at the **Kountry Kitchen.** We followed up and substantially agree— although things can get greasy at times. A good bet is the Polynesian omelette. Another excellent choice for down-home cooking is the **Ono**

Family Restaurant, 4-1292 Kuhio Highway, at the southern entrance to Kapaa, especially for eggs. We enjoyed our $8 Gourmet Burger last trip, and the pleasant family who runs the place. (No alcohol.) But the best choice for miles for a more serious lunch or a night out to dinner might be the **Kapaa Fish and Chowder House** (Tel. 822-7488) at 4-1639 Kuhio Highway, open daily at the north end of Kapaa. It's one of those old plantation-era stores, now painted white and battleship gray and filled with nautical gear from the rooftop lobster pots to the ship's wheel at the bar. Seafood is the thing here, and there's plenty of it, although you'll find some beef and chicken plates in the $14-$15 range.

And a good deal for a trencherman with a multicultural outlook may be the new International Buffet, which serves up an all-you-can-eat special from a different country every night of the week. It's in the Hale Kai Dining Room at the **Kauai BeachBoy Hotel** (Tel. 822-3441) in the Coconut Plantation. All-inclusive prices range from around $10 to $15.

KOLOA-POIPU DINING

The finest restaurant on this end of the island today has to be the **Tamarind Room** (Tel. 742-9511) in the Waiohai Hotel, and some would logically rate this classical Continental and Asian establishment the best on Kauai. No atmospheric vistas, here; the Tamarind must rely on an elegant brass, pink, and blue decorating scheme within its dark, windowless cavern. (We always carry a penlight for places like this just to illuminate the menu.) One anachronistic pretension is handing women a menu without prices listed; Sara immediately demanded—and got—the real thing. We experienced very attentive, professional service. Our party of four enjoyed the Hong Kong Steak, steamed fish, Hot and Spicy Chicken, and the house wine and got away for something reasonably reasonable. Incidentally, out of a hundred or more different restaurants we've patronized in Hawaii, this was the very first ever to hand us silver chopsticks!

The traditional fine-dining restaurant in Poipu is the **Plantation Gardens** (Tel. 742-1695), a former sugar plantation manager's nineteenth-century home, planted in the center of seven acres of exquisite tropical foliage which is now part of the Kiahuna Plantation resort. While waiting for a table, examine the museum/lounge with its *poi* pounders, tapa beaters, game stones, feather gourds, and calabashes preserved from Old Hawaii. Be careful with your drink if you wait at a "cocktail table" that was once a hollowed-out *poi*-pounding board. (I spilled my Bloody Mary into history.)

After all that, we must say that over the past few years the chefs have rolled in and out of here like waves off Poipu Beach, so the cuisine has simply been inconsistent. Our advice is to go while it's still light, sit at a table on the *lanai* by the window, and order something dependable like the catch of the day and maybe a Caesar salad. After dinner, finish off with a cognac or liqueur in the outdoor bar. The Plantation Gardens has it all over almost anyplace else on the South Shore for atmosphere.

At the moment, **Brennecke's Seaside Bar & Grill** (Tel. 742-7588) is still the neighborhood rage. Across Hoona Road from the Poipu Beach Park, it's a two-tier address serving snacks on the ground level and kiawe-wood broiler specialties in the open-air topside. The menu broils down to steak, lobster, a little pasta, and some excellent fresh seafood specialties. There's a terrific wine selection, and you can order many of these by the glass. To many, the ocean view at sunset is the most delicious offering on or off the menu. Sometimes a long wait—but usually worth it.

In a very different vein, we have remained fans of a do-the-work-yourself place in Koloa called the **Koloa Broiler** (Tel. 742-9122), for lunch or dinner. Inside a rickety old green-and-white building right on the strip you can still enjoy a burger, beans, and salad bar for around $4 at lunch (or $6 at dinner), top sirloin for perhaps $9.50, and several things priced in between. While you're salting and turning your meat, you can read the nearby sign: "Known worldwide for our famous chefs!" (You might like the outdoor *lanai* at lunch.) Then, if you insist on sitting down and having a good fish selection, the **Koloa Fish and Chowder House** (Tel. 742-7377) has opened in Old Koloa Town, sponsored by the same folks that fired up the aforementioned Kapaa operation. The atmosphere is noisy, but the fish is well prepared.

Sadly, the old Beach House Restaurant was carried out to sea by Hurricane Iwa. But happily, a new **Beach House Restaurant** (Tel. 742-7575) reopened in Poipu on Lawai Road near the Kuhio Shores condo. Sadly, we still haven't made it since the post-storm reincarnation, although it's popular with a faithful local cadre. Go before dusk to watch the waves break while the sun sinks. At the other end of the Poipu area, Kauaians who can find it like to dive into the **Aquarium** (Tel. 742-9505), specializing in Italian food. It's at 2301 Nalo Road, but you'd better get directions when you make your reservation. Then in the Kiahuna Shopping Village, **Keoki's Paradise** (Tel. 742-7534) is overstating it a bit in the name, judging by the snippy service we received. Next time, we're going only for drinks, pupus, and the sunset, and we hope things are sunnier.

HANALEI-PRINCEVILLE RESTAURANTS

The restaurants at the new Sheraton Princeville are doing a good business, although apparently drawing more of their clientele from in the house than outside. The signature restaurant is the Victorian-decorated but viewless **Noble's,** which boasts a Dutch chef. Sorry; it's a major oversight of ours this year not to have tried this place out yet. We'll try to correct that by the next edition, of course. If you like sushi, **Ukiyo's** in the Sheraton is the only true sushi bar on this side of the island. Some stare at the Oriental cut-glass artwork on the walls for awhile before its true meaning becomes clear.

There are several other dining salons open in the Princeville resort and golfing complex. The **Beamreach** (Tel. 826-9131), a neat, second-story entry overlooking the greens near the Pale Ke Kua condos, features hand-carved sandwiches at lunch and steak/seafood at dinner. It's a de-serving favorite. Also smacking a lot of happy Kauai lips is **Chuck's Steak House** (Tel. 826-6211) in the shopping center.

A popular address in Hanalei itself is **The Dolphin** (Tel. 826-6113), in a rustic cabin on the side of the Hanalei Trader general store: Lacquered tables in tapa designs; glass-ball and paper lamps; captain's chairs; screens over the windows; Bombay fans; lots of wooden fixtures; lighted aquarium by the bar. We had a pleasant breakfast there, but it is well loved for dinner, too. *Honolulu Star-Bulletin* columnist Dave Donnelly praised the ratatouille appetizer. There are several steak, lobster, chicken, and fish entrees, adding up to seven to eleven clams, and a surprisingly complete wine list. The Dolphin knows some good tricks. And sorry, we haven't been into **Charo's** (Tel. 826-6422) since it was named that after being bought by the Latin American singer/dancer who was Xavier Cugat's wife. It's the only place in Haena, however, and if you go, let us know.

Also in Hanalei, a nightclub that used to serve a few meals on Fridays has now heated up the fires on a daily basis. **Tahiti Nui** (Tel. 826-6277), indeed owned by a woman hailing from Big Tahiti, dishes out breakfast, lunch, and dinner. The Friday-night *luau* just might be the best of its type on the island. The Chinese restaurant in the Ching Young Village, **Foong Wong** (Tel. 826-6996), has been packin' 'em in lately, too. And the new **Hanalei Shell House** (Tel. 826-9301) specializes in such variations as Italian fare, clam chowder, and large burgers. There's usually at least one gourmet choice for dinner.

THE ROUTE TO KOKEE

Turning now to the southern route, there are four or five stops highly recommended by Kauai *cognoscenti*. The new **Lawai Restaurant** (Tel. 332-9550), featuring Chinese/American fare, has just opened in the old post office at Lawai. Chop suey is sucked up by the gallon at lunchtime. Kalaheo's claim to fame among some travelers on this road is **Brick Oven Pizza**. There are several different sizes and types, and all are local favorites.

In Hanapepe (or actually between Eleele and Hanapepe), about 17 miles from Lihue, is the **Green Garden Restaurant** (Tel. 335-5422), serving all three meals in an open green garden. The food is generally good, but the daytime crowds are sometimes discouraging. (If you're around in the evening, however, the "family style" dinners just might be great.) Try the famous *lilikoi* (Hawaiian passion fruit) chiffon pie. A short way past that, on the same highway, something has happened to the former Conrad's and Wong's restaurant. At last report, it was only **Wong's** (Tel. 335-5066) and operating as a Chinese take-out only. Mr. Wong told me he may reopen this year. In Waimea, you might mosey over to **Wrangler** (Tel. 338-1218) in the historic Ako Building, which dates back to 1907. Our resident Kauai *paniolo* publisher Peter Wolf likes the cowboy atmosphere and its giant menu featuring everything from Mexican to seafood.

Near the end of Route 55, way up in the heavily forested Kokee (that rhymes with "okay") State Park, is the recently refurbished, revitalized, and remanaged **Kokee Lodge Restaurant** (Tel. 335-6061). Now serving all three meals, the Kokee dining room and its connecting bar have taken a giant step up from "okay" to *ole!*

6. Sightseeing Kauai

With just a little advance attention, semi-circumnavigating the island could hardly be more fun or more easily planned. The good two-lane road runs about three-fourths of the way around, and the starting point must be more or less in the middle of that highway. Unless you're staying up at Princeville or Hanalei, Kauai almost automatically divides itself into two one-day round trips for the casual wanderer.

On the other hand, dedicated explorers determined to exhaust the possibilities could poke around for two weeks, or even two months, for that matter, and still leave some important stones unturned.

Here is our own highly personalized list of sightseeing targets. We've eliminated some (the library, the state building, etc.) from the standard itinerary whenever we felt they might take some time and attention from others we felt were more worthwhile.

They are listed in the order you'll come across them using the two-route system. In either case, plan on following the road to the very end (46 miles each way from Lihue on the southern branch and 40 miles on the northern one). Each has its own pot of gold waiting there to be enjoyed.

Leave early in the morning to avoid driving behind tour buses, and you may want to tuck a picnic lunch into the car. (Some hotels will make these up for you on request.) If you're going to Kokee in the winter, toss a sweater or a jacket for each of you in the back seat. You may need them when you reach cooler altitudes.

LIHUE TO KOKEE, AND THE KALALAU VALLEY

From the airport, it's 2 miles (via Route 57) to **Lihue** ("Lee-*hooey*"), the county seat. The twin stacks of the **Lihue Sugar Mill** (no visitors) will tell you you're there. Rice Street (Route 51) is the main drag.

About two blocks down Rice Street on the left is the double-structured **Kauai Museum** (Tel. 245-6931). Admission is $3 for 18 and over; open 9:30 A.M. to 4:30 P.M., Monday through Friday. Permanent "Story of Kauai" exhibit in the Rice Building; art shows and changing exhibits including cultural heritage displays in the Wilcox Building; authentic materials and Hawaiiana books for sale in the gift shop. The professionally managed little museum is known especially for its Hawaiian quilt and calabash collections. (If you're making an early start on a driving trip, though, you'd better save it for the trip back or even a separate day.)

Continue on Route 51 to see **Kalapaki Beach** fronting the island's only tall buildings, the luxurious eleven-story Westin Kauai. The area is called Nawiliwili, and its harbor is used by ocean-going and interisland vessels, including the interisland cruise ships *Independence* and *Constitution*.

At the point where Route 51 ceases to be Route 51, a spur called Niumalu Road—then Hulemalu Road—continues on to the **Alekoko Fishpond,** a mysterious mullet-raising lagoon said to have been built by Menehunes, the "little people" who may have been the island's first residents. Whoever did it constructed an ingenious wall more than 900 feet long in order to cut off a bend in the Huleia Stream. Legend says the Menehunes engineered the entire project overnight for a princess and her brother but under the stipulation that no one would watch them at work. Unable to restrain their curiosity, the royal *keikis* crept up to have a peek, were seen by the elves, and were turned into twin pillars of stone for their transgression. They still stand on the side of the mountain above the pond.

If you want, you may continue on the gradually worsening road to eventually hit Route 50 at Puhi. However, we recommend retracing your route back to the junction with 580 and turning left on it. On your right are the **Menehune Gardens** (Tel. 245-2660), although they may not be too well marked. Admission perhaps around $2.50 for adults, 50 cents for children under 12, and it's open 10 A.M. to 4 P.M. daily. You'll probably be guided through the garden by owner Melvin Kailikea, who often wears his WW II air-raid warden's helmet while describing the flowers, plants, and trees you rub noses with along the long, meandering pathway. The garden's guardian is the gigantic, undisciplined Chinese Weeping Banyan tree, planted in 1896 and still growing. (Mrs. K. told us she had measured some of the aerial roots lengthening at a rate of five feet in eight months!) Although a piece of the banyan was taken out by Hurricane Iwa in 1982, this may still be Hawaii's largest tree, occupying nearly an acre of land. The enthusiasm of the Kailikeas makes the hike worth the price of admission.

Not far away is the **Grove Farm Museum** (Tel. 245-3202), a private, 80-acre historic site recalling plantation days on Kauai. The buildings comprise the former home of the Wilcox family, who ran the Grove Farm Plantation for more than a century. Things are almost exactly as they were when it was lived in, including furniture and household items dating from several different periods, ending in 1978 when the last resident Wilcox died. Admission may still be $3 for adults, $1 for children, on a 1½-hour guided tour in small groups. Tours begin promptly at 10 A.M. and 1:15 P.M. Monday, Wednesday, and Thursday only, and *advance reservations are required.* (Call the above number, a day or more beforehand if possible. They'll give you exact directions to the homestead.) We thoroughly enjoyed it; tell 'em we sent you!

When you reach Route 50 (Kaumualii Highway), take it to the left. Less than a mile past the shopping center called Kukui Grove, you'll see on the right a sign indicating **Kilohana** (Tel. 245-7818). Follow the entrance road toward the large Hawaiian flag and the 1935 building which was the home of another Wilcox, while he was plantation manager. The mansion and grounds have become a sort of museum-like shopping complex, and occasionally there are rides on old carriages drawn by Clydesdale horses. Admission is free, but the operators of the property hope you will patronize their restaurants, shops, and art galleries that have been installed in the various bedrooms and outbuildings. Not as academically pure as the Grove Farm Museum, of course, it's been done very well nevertheless, and certainly worth a stop.

Continue on the highway through the village of **Puhi.** In another mile or so you'll come across one of those HVB warrior markers labeled **Queen Victoria's Profile** and pointing with undue assurance to a mountain ridge a few miles away. We passed that area and strained our eyes dozens of times before we finally were able to trace out Queen Victoria's stubby form. The secret is to know not only that her hair is tied in a bun, not only that she is lying on her back in a most unroyal manner, but also that she has an admonishing finger raised toward Nawiliwili Harbor. She is supposed to be scolding, "Now, Willy Willy!" (Nawiliwili). The legend dates back about 70 years, the "Willy Willy" being Victoria's cousin, Kaiser Wilhelm of Germany. Good luck and God save the queen if you want to search for this kind of thing, but just be careful not to drive off the road. In September and October we are much more interested in gathering the *lilikoi* (yellow passion fruit) off the road and trees in the immediate neighborhood. Delicious!

We suggest another side loop to the south onto Route 52, or Maluhia ("Serenity") Road. Drive through its wonderful tunnel of towering eucalyptus trees to the traditionally somnolent town of **Koloa.** A glance at that main street with its weatherbeaten false fronts always took us back 150 years or more. We always liked Koloa with its rusty tin roofs, sagging porches, bulging walls, and cockeyed windows, but now the new "Old Koloa Town" commercial restoration and shopping project with its slick landscaping has prettied up the genuine, rickety atmosphere in the central area. At night it really looks hokey, with lines of lights outlining the roofs, etc. (Some of the longtime merchants couldn't afford the new high rents and moved out.) Kauai's first sugar mill (1835) stands in ruins across the street from the business block.

To reach the most beautiful beach in southern Kauai, take the Poipu Road down to Poipu Beach. Some nice hotels and condos are located here, although there is public access to the same sands at **Poipu Beach Park.** This is a fine location for swimming and snorkeling.

Before returning toward Koloa, you can first take the side spur to **Spouting Horn,** which is one of those shoreline lava tubes through which the waves sometimes shoot very dramatically (often on a day other than the one you happen to come down to see it). It's very much like the Blow Hole on Oahu, but when this one is working well, it emits a strange, low moan or "deep breath" between the eruptions.

Some may object to the line of craft and trinket salesmen in the park next to Spouting Horn. Nevertheless these people have been there for years, so the small bazaar now has taken on the respectability of "tradition." (And occasionally you can pick up a bargain in hand-made jewelry or metalwork.)

Kauaians, incidentally, agree that the Spouting Horn has changed to only a little squirt in recent decades. One story told is that in pre-tourism times it used to shoot hundreds of feet into the air—until the owners of nearby sugar fields determined that the windblown saltwater spray was ruining their crops. Their solution was to dynamite the rock, making the hole larger and the fountain much less tall. Could be, but we'd certainly rather believe the opening has just become naturally eroded over the years!

At Koloa again, take Route 53 (also called 530) west. If you're lucky, and it's a Tuesday or Thursday, you can turn left on hard-to-see Hailima Road for about two miles and then find the 186-acre **Pacific Tropical Botanical Garden** (Tel. 332-8131). Not widely known, this private tropical plant research center gives two-hour morning tours for $10 on some days. We finally took the tour last year ourselves and learned a lot of botany from our guide. Be sure to crush and sniff an allspice leaf, and you might try a berry that will set every taste bud in your mouth on "sweet" for 45 minutes. Despite the apparently high fare, some Maverick readers who have gone through this garden have praised it as the highlight of their trips. (Better phone first for information and reservations, and have a pencil ready to take down exact directions. Also the tours are cancelled in rainy weather.) Tell 'em we sent you.

Rejoining Highway 50 at Kalaheo, you might keep an eye out for the much smaller **Olu Pua Gardens** (Tel. 332-8182), a former plantation manager's estate now opened as a botanical attraction. The gardens are attractive and interesting, but seemed a little pricey to us at $6 a ticket. (Maybe you can get a two-for-one discount coupon in your rental-car *Kauai Drive Guide* magazine, as we did.) Incidentally, former President Richard Nixon was a houseguest here in 1979.

Make a brief stop at the **Hanapepe Valley Lookout,** indicated by an HVB warrior marker. Years ago the view was capped by a dramatic windswept 326-foot-high waterfall. But in recent decades its headwaters have apparently been tapped for sugar field irrigation—perhaps by the same folks who played around with Spouting Horn. Still, the valley forms an impressive vista.

A mile past **Eleele** ("elly-elly") is the village of **Hanapepe** ("hah-nah-*pay*-pay"), which boasts that it is the "Biggest Little Town on Kauai." It's a happy place today and bears no mark of its 1924 tragedy, when at least 20 people were killed here in an all-out battle between police and striking Filipino sugar-cane workers. (We once saw a hillside covered with hundreds of multicolored flowers at one of the two entrances to this town.)

If you find you've been clipping right along, you might take the one-mile detour on Highway 543 to the ancient **Salt Ponds** (look for Lokokai Road, then Kaalani Road) and the nearby mild beach. Here the Hui Hana Paakai O Hanapepe (Syndicate of Hanapepe Salt Makers) has kept alive the ancient Hawaiian art of salt-making, during the spring and summer months. The salt-drying beds date back at least to the seventeenth century and perhaps to several hundred years before that. Captain James Cook's crew observed and wrote about the Hanapepe salt ponds in a description that is still accurate today. The salt is still popular with modern Hawaiians for seasoning, and some family recipes call only for red Hanapepe salt. Supercautious health regulations now prohibit its sale, and we suspect that it's the "impurities" that provide the special flavor. The salt is highly prized for gifts, however, and you may be able to talk somebody out of a pinch or two.

In and around the village of **Waimea,** the former Polynesian capital of the island, there are three "musts," at least two of which don't impress us a lot. (If you're running late, we suggest saving them all as possibilities for the return trip, pushing on first toward Kekaha and Kokee.)

The first of the three is the old **Russian Fort,** a pile of lava stones on your left, about 5½ miles from the junction of Highway 543. It was built in 1817 in the shape of a six-pointed star by a German doctor named Georg Anton Scheffer, who was also a former Moscow policeman and international adventurer. Although built ostensibly for Kaumualii, the King of Kauai, it flew the Russian flag over its 30-foot-thick walls. Scheffer also built a Russian fort in Honolulu, where the Aloha Tower now stands, leaving the capital only with the name "Fort Street" today as a reminder. And there were two more Russian forts built by Scheffer near the Waioli River on Kauai's north shore, but those have virtually eroded away.

At any rate the czar never backed up his ambitious Hessian, being more interested in Russia's well-established colonies in Alaska. Scheffer and his soldiers eventually left. For some unknown reason, King Kaumualii continued to fly the Russian flag over the structure for a number of years. So the tumble-down fort remains symbolic of what might have been. (Statistically it's one of the most visited sites on Kauai, but that's because of the convenient rest rooms there and the fact that almost every tour bus stops at the site for that reason.)

Just past the bridge over the Waimea River, you may turn left toward Lucy Wright Park to see **Captain Cook's Landing,** a spot on the beach now denoted by an unimpressive marker. Captain James Cook was credited with discovering the Sandwich Islands just about here, stepping on the sand just at the river's mouth at about 3:30 in the afternoon, January 20, 1778.

If you stop at the public library, you may be able to pick up a pamphlet produced by the West Kauai Main Street Project. It outlines a fairly extensive self-guided walking tour of Waimea. Some of the points of interest may fascinate scholars more than casual visitors.

Off the highway, on Menehune Road opposite the suspension bridge, about 1½ miles in, is a low, mysterious structure, most of which has long ago been buried in the thoughtless construction of the road. The **Menehune Ditch** is said to be the work of this strange, small race, built either prior to the arrival of the Polynesians or, according to one account, at the bidding of the Hawaiians when the Menehunes lived on Kauai as a low-caste people.

That legend says a Hawaiian king named Pe, who sought to improve lowland irrigation, hired the Menehunes to build the aqueduct. As usual in such stories, the Menehunes completed the job during one night, and they received a *luau* of shrimp as a reward. With great joy, they returned to the mountains back of Puukapele, and their shouts are still recalled in an old Hawaiian chant: "The hum of the voices of the Menehune at Puukapele, Kauai, startled the birds at the pond of Kawainui at Koolaupoku, Oahu."

We happen to live not far from the pond of Kawainui on Oahu and we can state with some assurance that there would have to be lots of Menehunes for their hum to carry more than 130 miles! At any rate, they were marvelous stonemasons, and archaeologists agree that the Hawaiians were not capable of building such sophisticated cut and keyed masonry. It is also doubtful that the work could have been performed with stone tools, which gives rise to even greater mysteries. Look carefully for the low stone wall; many still drive up here and miss the whole point of the place.

We'd recommend going on Route 50 as far as **Kekaha** before turning on Route 55 toward Kokee. (Better not take the road *up* from Waimea because of cane truck traffic.) Check your gas gauge; by the time you return to the coast, you'll have traveled about 40 more miles, no mile of which passes a working pump. Picnickers should note that this is the last neighborhood with a full grocery store before they head up into the mountains.

We always recommended not taking Route 50 on to **Barking Sands,** because travelers have been very disappointed when the military folks wouldn't let them in—something we have criticized in these pages every year since 1977. Now the situation has improved since the Pacific Missile Range has opened the area to small groups for free two-hour tours at 9:30 A.M. on the first and third Wednesday of each month. Reservations are required; they can be made by telephoning 335-4393 in advance, preferably at least the day before. We haven't yet taken this new excursion, but we expect to do so eventually if we can ever get out there on just the right Wednesday. Some friends who have done it, however, say it's worth the time spent, especially since the people you meet are not smooth-talking professional tour guides, but are happy to describe their jobs.

At other times determined hikers can invade along the beach for a ways, however, since the shoreline is state of Hawaii land up to the high-water mark. To lend credence to the name of the area, you're supposed to slide down a certain sand dune to hear the "woof-woof" of a German shepherd. And they say that you can also pick up some of the sand, clap it together, and produce something like the "yap-yap" of a Chihuahua. The sand includes ground-up coral and lava, and that's the secret of its "bark." But on top of every other difficulty, it's supposed to sound off only on a very dry day.

On the way up, up, up Route 55, you will eventually catch a good view of isolated **Niihau,** about 17 miles out into the ocean. Called the "Forbidden Island," it is the last example of old—really old—Hawaii. Fewer than 250 people live there, virtually all of whom are pure-blooded Hawaiians. They still speak Hawaiian in day-to-day conversation, although their English has improved since the invention of the transistor radio. There is no electricity—nor telephone, television, guns, doctors, liquor, or jails—on Niihau. All these are forbidden.

Visitors are absolutely *not* welcome, but this time it's not the military that declares the *kapu.* Nor is it the Hawaiian *paniolos* you'll see waving in friendly fashion if you fly over Niihau by helicopter. Since 1864, the entire 72-square-mile island has been owned by one *haole* family, and all the Hawaiians work on their ranch. Contrary to legend, the residents of this twentieth-century semiserfdom *may* move back and forth, although some who did leave reportedly had difficulties competing in modern life and returned to the island permanently to tend the cattle and sheep or gather wild honey.

Sights there must be on the Forbidden Island. A unique white coral *heiau* (ancient temple) is rumored to survive in good condition there. And the island contains Hawaii's only large (841 acres) natural lake. But few non-Hawaiians have visited Niihau—including us.

Eleven miles up from Kekaha at a fork in the road, an HVB warrior sign indicates the main lookout for **Waimea Canyon.** Park the car and take the steps to experience a startling sight for such a small tropical island. Mark Twain supposedly called the chasm the "Grand Canyon of the Pacific." That's an exaggeration, and Twain never visited Kauai in any case. Nevertheless its size and depth are still amazing for its location.

The opposite side of the canyon is broken into three enormous tributary canyons, giving some added depth to this panorama. There are many colors at midday with pinks, greens, and browns predominating. Later in the day, purples, blues, and lavenders usually take over the scene.

To your left you may see the distant Waipoo Falls tumbling 800 feet over a cliff, its narrow flow disappearing behind a hill before it hits bottom. There is seldom any wind, and if there are few people at the lookout you'll be impressed with the overwhelming quiet of it all. You can sometimes see the ribbonlike Waimea Stream about 3,000 feet below, but everything is so far away that there is neither sound nor movement. The only motion you can perceive will be the flight of the long-tailed, white *koai* birds as they scout out the crevices and pillars.

Waimea Canyon alone is worth the 38-mile trip from Lihue, but we think the very best vista is a little farther along the same road. First, push on another 8 miles into the cool, 4,345-acre **Kokee State Park** (Tel. 335-5871). There in the forest you will find a restaurant, rental cabins (see section 4), a natural history museum, and 45 miles of hiking trails. These range from the one-tenth-mile Nature Trail through a *koa*-wood forest to a picnic site, to the Canyon Trail, a 1.7-mile trek that skirts a hidden swimming hole and then climbs to a lookout point. A couple of trails also traverse the 30-square-mile **Alakai Swamp.**

From mid-June until early August, you may pick up to the limit of ten pounds of the delicious Kokee plums that grow in the state park. Some folks come all the way from Honolulu to do just that. Near the restaurant, notice the colorful wild chickens. These are Polynesian Jungle Fowl, protected by law, and descended from those introduced to Hawaii from Tahiti before white men discovered the Islands.

But then head for Kokee's crowning glory, the **Kalalau Valley Lookout,** and pray that no clouds will drift along to obscure the view. At an elevation of 4,000 feet, it is a magnificently impressive panorama over a vast valley that slopes steeply down to the shore far—very far—in the distance. To try to describe the hogback cliffs, the lush vegetation, the distant narrow waterfalls, the feeling of endless space, seems useless.

We had read Jack London's description of the valley and have since looked at many photographs taken from this point, but no writer or photographer has ever managed to capture completely the feeling we experienced standing right there for the first time.

The Kalalau Valley below you today is completely unpopulated, although the natural vegetables, fruits, and other foodstuffs that once supported hundreds of families are still growing there. No highway could ever reach it, and plain old loneliness drew nearly everybody out about a hundred years ago. Please be warned that despite what you may have heard, there is no trail from here down to the beach. Hikers regularly get into trouble in the area, and not long ago one man was killed while trying to make it down.

Only experienced mountaineers can enter the valley from Kokee. But almost anyone in good physical condition can make the 11-mile hike to the Kalalau beach from Haena on the north shore. (See later.) And from May through September, when the seas are calm, it's fairly easy to land on the beach in a canoe.

Kalalau Valley, by the way, is the setting for the Jack London short story "Koolau, the Leper." In the tale, one man defends his right to live and die with his family alone in the valley, killing off one by one the authorities who would ship him away to live alone in the leprosy colony on Molokai. It's based on tragic events that did take place here around the turn of the century.

On the way back down the mountain, look carefully for the Canyon Rim Road on the left about two-thirds of the way along. (On our last trip it was poorly marked.) It's a twisting and turning route, but the road is paved, and it provides several other views of Waimea Canyon. Drive carefully and you'll end up in the village of Waimea (not Kekaha), so you can see its sights—the Menehune Ditch, Cook's Landing, and the Russian Fort—if you missed them before.

THE NORTH SHORE AND HANALEI—HOME OF BALI HA'I

You definitely will not need your sweater for *this* trip, but you may want to dredge up an ancient Hawaiian curse if you should forget your bathing suit. There's also a rough but famous hiking trail at the end of the road, so you might throw a pair of "sensible" shoes in the car, if not a good set of boots. (Two miles along that trail, incidentally, you may feel more in style streaking into the water *without* any bathing suit.)

The highway runs about 40 miles. Stretches of the route that go along the beaches are in the Wailua and Kapaa areas and on part of the road past Hanalei to Haena. There are beautiful views of ocean and mountains, bays and valleys, and many unmarked beaches that may be reached by well-worn paths. The more intrepid sand-seekers will use this route to find their goal—the beach without a footprint.

About a mile north of town there's a wide spot in the road called **Kapaia.** Turn onto the dusty pavement of Route 583 (Maalo Road) to your left and wind through the sugar cane fields for a long, dull four miles on a narrow road to reach **Wailua Falls.**

Wailua means "twin waters," and if you look over the side of the road you'll see a double torrent of water throwing itself over an 80-foot cliff. It's particularly dramatic after a heavy rain. The pool at the bottom is ringed with *hala* trees and tropical flowers. It's somewhat disappointing that you can only get a single angle on this sight. No head-on view is possible, except from a helicopter. If the falls look familiar, maybe it's because you've seen them from a chopper in the opening scene of the TV show "Fantasy Island."

Back on the main highway, go past the golf course and turn right on hard-to-see Leho Road (by the electrical substation) and follow it around behind the Kauai Resort Hotel to the end at **Lydgate State Park**, the site of an ancient temple of refuge. The ruin is still there, under the palms next to the Wailua River and the sea. It was to this place that a Hawaiian of any rank could run after he had broken a sacred *kapu.* No one could touch him in the temple of refuge, no matter how serious his crime. (You can walk to this point easily from the hotel.)

Nearby, when the tides remove the sand, there are a group of black rocks bearing mysterious primitive carvings called **petroglyphs.** Some believe they had fairly sophisticated meanings. Other experts say that they are little more than centuries-old doodles. Snorkeling is sometimes excellent in this area.

Back across the main highway, just before the Wailua River bridge, is the **Wailua Marina,** where two competing boat tour outfits conduct cruises up the river to the **Fern Grotto.** (See section 7 in this chapter.) Unless you know someone with his own canoe, the only way to reach the grotto is along with a score of others, all in the same boat, and usually along with more folks in other boats. (Try for the first one so you won't be bothered by diesel fumes from the vessel ahead.) Rather cloying music and entertainment are provided along the route. Be aware that not everyone likes this trip, but the river is pleasant, and so is the grotto, where ferns grow upside down and hang from the top of the cave. By the way, there are few ferns when water is short, and now they're talking about piping in water to spray the grotto during dry weather conditions.

"We endured mediocre entertainment from a disinterested trio and the world's sourest-looking hula dancer," an Edmonton man wrote us recently. "The grotto itself was so disappointing that I didn't even take a picture." We hope that won't be your experience.

The broad Wailua River is known as the only navigable river in the Islands. It was deeper and swifter in times gone by before it was tapped upstream for irrigation. Sailing vessels used to beat their way up the river, and during the American Civil War a northern ship made it over the sandbar to hide on the river while dodging the Confederate ship *Shenandoah,* then thought to be prowling Hawaiian waters.

Almost next door to the Wailua Marina is one of those commercial garden parks which was called Kauai's Paradise Pacifica until they went bankrupt. Now, at least temporarily, the name is **Smith's Tropical Paradise.** It's a 31-acre botanical collection where you used to be able to take a guided open tram tour or walk around by yourself if you wanted. We remember a couple of strange elements, like a fake Easter Island statue that looks rather like former president Nixon and a puce-colored "Filipino Village." The flowers and trees are beautiful and interesting, but we never were too fond of the place under the previous administration, and it remains to be seen what the new owners will do. We've heard the new luau show ($35 with dinner, $11 without) is pretty good. General admission to the garden is now $3, which is at least a little better than the former $5 gouge. If you go, let us know.

Just across the Wailua River bridge on Route 56 and to the left is the **King's Highway,** so called because his majesty, upon beaching the royal canoe, would be carried to his house while still seated in the craft rather than take the risk that his royal feet might be soiled by common ground. Today the King's Highway is called Number 580 (or Kuamoo Road), and it will lead you first to the **Holo-Holo-Ku Heiau** (although another sign there identifies it perhaps incorrectly as the **Ka Lae O Ka Manu Heiau**). It's perhaps the oldest *heiau* on Kauai and one of the few such temples in Hawaii where human sacrifices were taken. Look for a huge rock on the *mauka* corner of the ruins. The blood has washed away, but that was the sacrificial stone.

A few yards away is the **Pohaku-Ho-o Hanau,** a collection of sacred stones where royal mothers came to give birth to royal babies. The sanded platform in front is thought to be the floor of the shelter built for the expectant *alii wahine.*

Further along the same road, an HVB warrior marker will tell you where to get a distant view of **Opaekaa Falls.** Park and walk along the barricade. The falls might be nicer if you could get closer, but you can't. Across the road is the entrance to the Fernandez family's **Kamokila Hawaiian Village** (Tel. 822-1192). It's a sort of spruced-up replica of an ancient Hawaiian village where you might learn how to pound *poi*, weave mats, and experience other aspects of prediscovery life. The admission price is $5. If you drive down the road, try not to be intimidated by the naively forbidding signs along the way and hope that Mrs. Fernandez will be there to greet you and guide you around the property. Take a picnic lunch; there's a lovely place to eat it beside the river, but you still have to pay your five bucks. As the sign says: "No excuses!"

Back on Route 580, it looks like the road might eventually lead you to a good mountain viewpoint, but we've made that mistake for you. Instead, return toward the sea again. Just after leaving the falls (or the village), there are three unmarked overlooks to the Wailua River on the right. The first features a steep and dangerous path, so skip it; the second (perhaps indicated only by a "one way" sign) is better. Then the third pull-off, at this writing only marked by a "falling rock" sign, leads after 20 yards or so to a pair of interesting and very large old rocks. Supposedly these are **bell stones**, which ring if you hit them in just the right position with another stone. We felt like fools pounding away recently and never did find its secret ring spot. One stone sports a petroglyph, however. And an overgrown path leads to a river overlook which may have been an important site in ancient times—perhaps the Poliahu Heiau— or maybe the Ka Lae O Ka Manu Heiau.

Returning to the main highway, on your left is the Coco Palms Resort Hotel (see section 4), set down in a once-sacred coconut grove formerly owned by the last queen of Kauai. Later it served nicely as a copra plantation. The charming little lagoon, around which the resort now holds its evening torch-lighting ceremony, was in ancient times a pond to sweeten and fatten saltwater fish.

A mile north of Wailua and Coco Palms is Waipouli, now the home of the **Coconut Plantation** complex. It includes an attractive shopping center called the Market Place (see section 10, Shopping). Two hotels are there, the Sheraton Coconut Beach and the Kauai BeachBoy, plus a couple of condos and three or four restaurants.

Photographers used to love the village of **Kapaa** farther up the road for its weatherbeaten, false-front main streets. Would that it would never change, but gradually it's doing so.

Because everybody talks about it, and because there's an HVB marker pointing it out, be aware of a mountaintop configuration visible from Kapaa that's supposed to look like a **Sleeping Giant.** Just like Queen

Victoria's Profile on the southern route, this doesn't wake us up, either. So if you can't make out the Sleeping Giant, have a look later at the somewhat enhanced photograph on the luncheon menu at Coco Palms. There you can see something of what you're supposed to grasp on the mountain. (And the "legend" printed on that menu is as good as any other for justifying the Kauai Gulliver.)

Look closely in this area to see if you can spot any Kauai "beefalo," a cross between a cow and a buffalo, sometimes seen on ranches in western and northern Kauai. (No, we're not kidding.) The hump over the shoulders gives it away.

Returning to Route 56, the road through the townlet of **Anahola** used to cut through acres and acres of green pineapple fields. But nearly all Kauai pineapples have now *pau*-ed out. More's the pity, because Kauai pineapple has always seemed to us to be about the sweetest grown in the state. It will be some consolation, though, if the land is given over to the raising of the famous Anahola watermelons. Some of the island's best papayas are also grown around here. (Not mentioned in our restaurant section, because it is not in the specific areas covered, is Duane's Ono Burger, a roadside stand at Anahola that makes some of the best burgers on the island.)

At **Kilauea,** either on the way out or on the way back, take the two-mile-long road to the 1913 **Kilauea Lighthouse,** operated by the U.S. Coast Guard. The grounds are open to all between noon and 4 P.M. Sunday through Friday. (Closed Saturday.) Perched on a high bluff above a restless sea, this unusual clamshell lens beacon is the world's largest of its type. Nevertheless, the lighthouse has outlived its usefulness, and it blinked out in 1976 for good. A smaller, electronic beacon nearby now does the job. In spring and summer the comical red-footed booby birds make their somersault landings near here to nest and raise their young. The Laysan albatross, wedge-tailed shearwater, and other marine birds are also seen in profusion, and no bird watcher should miss it.

Sadly, the **Slippery Slide** in this area has been closed. But if you run across the Jacques Bakery in Kilauea, you should know that it produces some of the best French pastry in the state. Farther along is the **Kalihiwai Valley Lookout,** then **Anini Beach.** (Two miles from the highway, this could be your "beach without a footprint" on a weekday.) Swimming is excellent.

Nearby is **Princeville,** a 1,000-acre recreation community, known especially for its two championship golf courses. The two hubs are the Princeville Shopping Center and the Sheraton Princeville Hotel.

The next stopping point is a scenic vista indicated on the left. If you miss it on your way out, don't speed by coming back. The **Hanalei Valley Lookout** is one of the famous views in the Islands. The broad panorama

includes taro patches, vegetable crops, sugar cane, and a few rice pad-
dies, all bisected by the gleaming Hanalei River and backdropped by
three majestic mountains.

The main road descends a hill, and you'll find yourself crossing the
rickety 1912 bridge you probably saw from the Hanalei Valley Lookout.
Bless this bridge, for because of its load limit, you'll find no large tour
buses from this point on. Along the river, you might notice a herd of
contented cattle. On wet days, the distant mountains can spring forth
with dozens of waterfalls, some of which drop a thousand feet or more.

In **Hanalei,** headquarters for members of the counterculture and wealthy
escapists, there are two general stores, two restaurants, and one interesting bar (Tahiti Nui). In the Ching Young Village is the new **Native
Hawaiian Museum,** run by the Hanalei Hawaiian Civic Club. Admission
is free. Nearby, the club has also taken over the privately owned **Hanalei
Museum** (adults $1, children free, irregular hours) with its small collec-
tion of artifacts gathered from an earlier day.

The **Waioli Mission House,** one of those nineteenth-century New
England prefab jobs, was put up here in 1836. It's completely outfitted
with period furniture, including a bed warmer brought around the Horn
by a missionary wife who just didn't know what to expect of the climate
so far from home. Admission is free, although donations are welcome;
the house is open and guided tours are available from 9 to 3, Tuesday,
Thursday, and Saturday. (Large group tours and special tour days may
sometimes be arranged by phoning 245-3202.) Follow the double-track
cement driveway through the white picket fence to locate this charming
building.

You can swim at the majestic beach on **Hanalei Bay,** but only if you stay
near the old pier where waters are calmer. As with any of Hawaii's
beaches, it's safer to enter deep water only where you see others doing
so. (See section 8.)

From here on, the road will wind over tiny one-lane bridges and along
scores of beautiful beaches. One shoreline you won't want to miss is
Lumahai Beach, on which Mitzi Gaynor vowed to "Wash That Man
Right Out of My Hair" in *South Pacific.* You'll see it first from on high
(sometimes an HVB sign is posted there). There's a steep trail down
through the pandanus trees to the sand itself if you want to comb the
beach for the little green grains of olivine that often wash up there. But
swimming is safe on that beach *only in the summer* when the water is
calmer and even then only for the expert. There is an undertow and the
ocean currents are very tricky at this point.

Pass **Haena Beach Park** *(absolutely no swimming),* and you'll see three
sets of caves. The first is **Maniniholo Dry Cave,** named after the head

fisherman of the Menehunes. It's the end of a lava tube running for several hundred yards under the cliff.

About a mile farther are the **Waikapalae and Waikanaloa Wet Caves.** The Hawaiians claim they were dug by Pele, the fire and volcano goddess, when she first sought a home in the Islands. Twice she hit fresh water instead of the fire in the center of the earth, so she moved on. The usual clear water in Waikanaloa mysteriously turns milky from time to time, and no one knows why. We'd skip the cave up the steep, difficult side road.

The road ends at **Haena Point,** directly in front of Ke'e Beach, where there is usually good, reef-protected swimming close to shore and excellent skin diving. Archeologists have excavated some ancient Hawaiian home sites in this area.

At Haena Point begins the 11-mile trail to Kalalau Valley Beach along the famous and rugged **Na Pali Coast.** Lots of young folks (and that once included us oldsters) hike along the trail at least 2 miles to the mellow-minded beach called Hanakapiai ("hah-nah-*cop*-pee-eye"), where they sometimes find more people without clothes than with them. Don't go swimming in the dangerous ocean currents here, however.

Don't even make the short trip late in the afternoon, however. The trail is treacherous in lengthening shadows and impossible after dark. It is also very difficult when wet. (For more information on hiking on Kauai, see section 9, Other Sports.)

7. Guided Tours and Cruises on Kauai

There are five tour bus companies on the island, including three old big-bus standbys with offices at Lihue Airport, and two more laid-back outfits that specialize in small van tours. All prices are sample estimates based on last-year's fares, and with a pickup from east Kauai hotels. They will cost less or more from Poipu or Princeville addresses, depending on the distances involved.

Taking the latter two first, the former Holo Holo Kauai has been bought out by **Chandler's Kauai Tours** (Tel. 245-9134), specializing in personalized 14-passenger van tours. Some of its tours at this writing: Hanalei and Haena with breakfast and barbecue lunch, $45; Waimea Canyon, Polihale Beach, breakfast and lunch, $50; Waimea Canyon/ Wailua River, $35; Hanalei/Waimea Canyon, $40; Waimea Canyon/Wailua River/Hanalei, $60; half-day Waimea Canyon, $25; half-day Hanalei, $20.

Trans Hawaiian Kauai (Tel. 245-5108) uses 12-passenger vans: Waimea Canyon, $25; Hanalei/Haena, $20; Waimea Canyon/Wailua River, $40;

Waimea Canyon/Hanalei/Haena, $40; Wailua River/Hanalei/Haena (including boat trip), $40.

The three more traditional companies include **Robert's Hawaii, Inc.** (Tel. 245-3344), now a statewide company for which Kauai was the ancestral stamping ground. Robert's has big motorcoaches as well as 5- to 11-passenger vehicles. **Gray Line Hawaii** (Tel. 245-3344) also has large and small buses. **Kauai Island Tours** (Tel. 245-4777) specializes in big bus tours. As an example, all three charge about $15 for the Waimea Canyon trip or maybe $25 for a Hanalei trip.

The trend toward more "adventurous" tours has come to Kauai, and we recently enjoyed our trip through the outback regions of Kokee State Park with **Kauai Mountain Tours** (Tel. 245-7224), the only commercial excursion with permission to explore the back roads and trails of the large park. In special eight-passenger, four-wheel drive vehicles, Kauai Mountain fords streams and plows through dirt and mud to discover and describe deserted areas of forests and flowers that can't be seen from the standard bus and car routes. Don't forget your binoculars and a jacket. Our only regret was that we decided on the relatively rushed half-day tour (about $55) instead of the more leisurely full-day excursion (about $75, including lunch). Maybe we'll go again.

A newer outfit we haven't yet traveled with personally is called **Local Boy Tours** (Tel. 822-7919), a one-man hiking operation through trails at Waimea Canyon and Kokee by naturalist Lloyd Pratt. Lloyd grew up on Kauai and knows a lot about the identification of local plants and how they were used by the ancient Hawaiians. He also specializes in teaching traditional arts and crafts and other aspects of the Hawaiian culture. (He begins every hike with the Lord's Prayer, recited in Hawaiian.) Currently rates run $40 for a four-hour hike, $50 for a six-hour hike and $60 for an all-day excursion. Overnight camping trips are sometimes available. (For details, call the number above or write Lloyd at P.O. Box 3324, Lihue, HI 96766.)

BOAT CRUISES

Two companies compete on the three-mile river run to Fern Grotto. **Smith's Motor Boat Service** (Tel. 822-4111) has been in business much longer, and it offers scheduled trips every half-hour daily from 9 A.M. to 4 P.M. Each lasts an hour or a little more and costs $7 for adults and $4 for children under 12. They also cast off on a Hawaiian Night Luau Cruise Tuesday and Thursday at 6:15 P.M. for 2½ hours. Adults are $20 and children $10 for that. For a ticket without a dinner, the prices are $14 and $7 respectively. Fares may be up a little in '87. The other company is **Waialeale Boat Tours** (Tel. 822-4908). Prices are similar, but some individual travelers have said they prefer this company to avoid the battalions often booked on the Smith armada during the day.

Several interesting "cruises" are now being offered by Gary and Bob Crane through their **Island Adventures, Inc.** (Tel. 245-9662). We enjoyed Gary's company on their kayak trip up Huleia Stream. The two-hour tour, one to a boat, includes a box lunch for $25 or so. (These boats are special models, called "Royaks," and are much less likely to tip than the traditional Eskimo variety.) Trips depart from the Small Boat Harbor adjacent to the main Nawiliwili Harbor. (Information from P.O. Box 3370, Lihue, HI 96766.) Island Adventures also has a half-day "Beach Party" which provides snorkeling, sailing, and windsurfing instruction for about $40.

Unusual excursions are also offered by **Na Pali Zodiac** (Tel. 826-9371), sometimes called "Captain Zodiac," which has been taking 10 or 15 passengers in rubber boats to virtually inaccessible beaches and coves along the rugged Na Pali Coast for over a decade. Four trips and probable prices include the Morning or Afternoon Excursion for $50; Camper Drop-off at Kalalau Valley for $50 one way, $95 round trip; the popular 5-hour Day Expedition for $85, including lunch and a 2-hour beach landing; and the Sunset Cruise for $35. (Children's fares are about 25 percent less.) We have yet to make one of these trips ourselves, but we will. Meanwhile, all our reports are favorable. (You can write them at P.O. Box 456, Hanalei, HI 96714.) Be aware that these trips are often cancelled under difficult winter wave conditions. Also there are two or three other Zodiac trips along the same coast, but the Captain is the original. Tell him we sent you.

A large 20-passenger rubber boat trip on the *south* shore has been launched by **Fantasy Island Boat Tours** (Tel. 742-6636). They depart from Kukuiula Harbor at Poipu Beach and explore cliffs and caves along the nearby shoreline. Four-hour cruises with lunch are running about $50.

Lady Ann Cruises (Tel. 245-8538), a husband-wife operation, is offering several types of cruises (depending on the season of the year) from offices at Nawiliwili Harbor. There are two vessels, a 32-foot, 23-passenger cruiser and a 36-foot, 42-passenger double-deck cruiser. At last report, Ann and Don's summertime 2½-hour Na Pali Coast Cruise was running about $35 per person, and the five-hour snorkel cruise to remote bays and beaches was about $75 per person, including lunch. December-to-April whale-watching cruises run about $35. Readers have been pleased with these trips.

BIRD'S-EYE VIEWS

The popularity of Kauai helicopter flights over the past several years has resulted in a proliferation of competing companies offering tours in and out of some of the most spectacular scenery in the Pacific. At last report, there were no less than 18 whirlybirds on the island, and more have plans to migrate to the Garden Isle in the future. (Some local residents have been fighting these flights and the most responsible pilots are also calling for some sort of regulation.)

The companies buzzing around at this writing all fly four- or six-passenger Bell Jet Rangers, headquartered at different airports and heli-ports around the island. You can either charter the entire aircraft, for $450 or so per hour, or you can buy tours on a per-seat basis. Fares will vary from around $50 for a 15-minute flight to around $100 for a 45- to 60-minute flight.

Corporate and personnel changes may be made so rapidly in helicop-ter companies that it's sometimes difficult to recommend any one over the others. However, we will say that the granddaddy of the chopper firms is **Jack Harter Helicopters** (Tel. 245-3774). Harter's wife is a pro-fessional photographer, and he's used to covering all the good angles. Harter has a perfect safety record to date, and advance reservations are a must. If we couldn't get Harter, we might try for **Will Squyres Heli-copter Service** (Tel. 245-7541), another owner-operated firm. Then **Kenai Helicopters** (Tel. 245-8591), a statewide firm, is also popular and usually good. **Island Helicopters Kauai** (Tel. 245-8588), a one-man operation, was set up after its owner split with Kenai. **Rainbow Helicopters** (Tel. 245-4661), **South Sea Helicopters** (Tel. 245-7781), and **Menehune Heli-copters** (Tel. 245-7705) are three newer firms we know less about. You may run across three or four even newer ones. We will not fly with **Papillon Helicopters,** which does not have as good a safety record as we would like.

Remember that unlike boat operations, no commercial helicopter is allowed to actually land you in remote areas of the island. Helicopters can be nice any place in Hawaii, but somehow Kauai retains the reputa-tion as the most fun in a chopper—*if*, of course, you can stand the financial altitude.

There are also a couple of fixed-wing sightseeing planes in opera-tion. **Aero Service Kauai** (Tel. 245-6035) advertises a three-passenger Cessna with fares per person varying from $30 through $75. Another operation is **Garden Island Aviation** (Tel. 245-1844), with flights be-ginning at $30 for 30 minutes. We know absolutely nothing about either firm, except that both have been been going for several years, now.

Last, and also technically under "bird's-eye views," we guess, is the new **Balloons Above Kauai** (Tel. 822-5059), which plans to start taking you and everyone else aloft in a tethered hot-air balloon from Coconut Plantation. We don't want to put it down, so we'll just say sorry, it's not our bag.

8. Water Sports on Kauai

There are at least 23 major beaches and bays on the island, but not all of them are safe beyond the shoreline. Generally, the north shore is best for winter surfing and summer swimming. The south shore is the opposite—fine for a summer surf and for milder winter swimming. Obviously there are several exceptions, and the east side is good off and on for both water activities the year around. Here are some of the beaches:

Anahola Beach Park. Excellent swimming and wading; good skin diving; good surfing a long way out; fishing and shelling okay; barbecue pits and picnic tables; tent camping only.

Anini Beach. Excellent swimming and wading; well protected; excellent skin diving; winter surf for experts only; excellent windsurfing; reportedly great torch fishing; shelling; barbecue pit and picnic tables; tent camping only.

Haena Beach Park. Swimming positively unsafe! (But there is good swimming and good skin diving at Ke'e, a little farther at the end of the highway.) Fishing; shelling; picnic tables; barbecue pits; tent and mobile camping permitted.

Hanalei Beach Park. Swimming safe at the old landing only; excellent surfing early morning and late afternoon; tables, barbecue pits, and pavilion; tent camping only.

Hanamaulu Beach Park. Former water pollution problems said to be corrected; poor skin diving; shelling okay; tables, pits, and pavilion; playground; tent and mobile camping permitted.

Kapaa Beach Park. Good swimming; fishing; tables, barbecue pits, and pavilions; tent and mobile camping permitted.

Kekaha Beach Park. Rough surf; strong ocean currents; tables, pits, pavilion, and playground; tent camping only.

Lydgate State Park. Good swimming; picnic tables; barbecue pits; no tent camping due to problems with local bullies.

Lumahai Beach. Not recommended for swimming. Beachcombers look for small, green olivine crystals in the sand here.

Na Pali Coast. Dangerous swimming everywhere, especially in winter.

Nawiliwili Park. Excellent swimming at Kalapaki Bay; good for beginning surfers; fishing; picnic tables and barbecue pits.

Poipu Beach Park. Good swimming and fair skin diving; good body surfing; fishing; shelling.

Polihale State Park. Good swimming in mid-summer; hazardous in winter, spring and fall; fishing; shelling; tables and barbecue pits; tent camping only.

Salt Pond. Good swimming; occasional summer surfing; shelling; fishing; tables, barbecue pits, and pavilions; tent camping only.

Wailua Beach. Good swimming; good beginners' surf when waves are small; dangerous when surf is big due to strong currents.

SCUBA, SNORKELING, AND WINDSURFING

Some of the best snorkeling and skin-diving waters in Hawaii can be found in Kauai, and now there are four diving firms to help you enjoy them.

We were very impressed with the efficient yet fun-loving operation run by Terry O'Halloran and Barbara Brundage at **Fathom Five Divers** (Tel. 742-6991) from modest headquarters next to the Chevron station in Koloa. Snorkeling lessons and tours start at around $25, and introductory scuba runs may be $60 or so for a half-day trip. (Tell 'em we said hello.) Other dependable outfits include the three headquartered in or near Kapaa: **Sea Sage Diving Center** (Tel. 822-3841) at 4-1378 Kuhio Highway, **Aquatics Kauai** (Tel. 822-9213) at 733 Kuhio Highway, across from the Sheraton Coconut Beach, and **Ocean Odyssey** (Tel. 822-9680) in the Market Place at Coconut Plantation.

Windsurfing rentals and instruction are now available from several firms. These include **Sailboards Kauai** (Tel. 245-5955) and **Kauai Windsurfing & Hobie Co.** (Tel. 245-9290), both in Lihue, and **Hanalei Joy** (Tel. 826-6647) and **Garden Island Windsurfing** (Tel. 826-9005), both in Hanalei. We have had no experience with any of these firms; sorry. Please let us know if you do.

9. Other Sports

The most famous and beautiful *golf* course on Kauai is the 27-hole **Princeville Makai Golf and Country Club** (Tel. 826-6891), site of the 26th World Cup Golf championship tournament in 1978 and 1979 and currently the headquarters for the LPGA Women's Kemper Open. The **Kiahuna Golf Club** (Tel. 742-9595), now an 18-holer, has cheaper rates if you live in the area. The county-supported **Wailua Municipal Golf Course** (Tel. 245-2163), which you probably won't book through a travel agent, is a sleeper. Golfing writer Grady Timmons has reported that the back nine may be the best nine holes in the state. For us duffers, there's the nine-hole **Kukuiolono Park Golf Course** (Tel. 332-9151), which charges reasonable green fees; a cart is optional.

Tennis. Several hotels have courts that are available (usually free) only to their guests. The Hanalei Bay Resort has 11 courts, and the Kiahuna Plantation has 10. Free public courts are open in the villages of Lihue, Kalaheo, Kapaa, Hanapepe, Koloa, and Waimea.

Hotels that have courts available to nonguests, too, include Coco Palms (Tel. 822-3831), Kiahuna Plantation (Tel. 742-6411), the Princeville Tennis Garden (Tel. 826-9823), and the Hanalei Bay Resort (Tel. 826-6522, Ext. 1024).

Kauai has two *riding* stables: the **Highgates Ranch** at Wailua Homestead (Tel. 822-3182), where a reader suggests asking for "Rose," and **Po'oku Stables** (Tel. 826-6777) at Princeville. Both charge about $15 for an hour ride or $50 for an all-day Water Fall Picnic Ride.

Hiking enthusiasts should write the Kauai Forest Reserve Trails, Department of Land and Natural Resources, Division of Forestry, P.O. Box 1671, Lihue, Kauai, HI 96766 (or visit them in the State Building at Eiwa and Hardy Streets), to ask for lists and maps of trails on Kauai. Permits are not needed for hiking, but you must have them for camping. They're free for state parks, however, and available from the above office in the State Building, corner of Hardy and Elua streets in Lihue. Camping permits for county parks cost $3 per person per night and are issued at the Kauai War Memorial Convention Hall, 4191 Hardy St., Monday to Friday, or by the police department after hours. Kauai Kops, incidentally, are notoriously merciless if you have no permit.

Nonresident *hunting* licenses are available for $15 from the same state department and address as the above, except it's the Fish and Game Division you go to see. They'll bring you up to date on the latest regulations, bag limits, and seasons for wild goats, wild boar, blacktail deer, pheasant, quail, doves, and partridge. (There is no commercial hunting guide service on Kauai.)

10. Garden Island Shopping

There is not a lot for sale on Kauai that you won't also find—usually cheaper—in Honolulu. There are now about 10 shopping complexes worth noting, including the following: The **Lihue Shopping Center** in the center of town, now of little interest except for the Foodland supermarket; the **Rice Shopping Center,** a group of 16 shops congregated at 4303 Rice St.; the large and snazzy **Kukui Grove Center,** just out of Lihue off Route 50 (lots of souvenirs available in Woolworth's); the **Harbor Village,** formerly the Menehune Village, at Nawiliwili just across from the Westin Kauai; the **Market Place at Coconut Plantation,** now more than 60 shops among the three hotels and several restaurants at Waipouli (free hula shows at 4 P.M. the last two or three days in the week); the **Princeville Shopping Center,** an 1800s-style, wood-frame center up near Hanalei; the **Ching Young Village** in Hanalei itself near the old Ching Young general store; the new super-cute **Old Koloa Town** (free open-air jitney service to and from Poipu hotels and condos); and the new **Kiahuna Shopping Center** right in Poipu.

Many hotels have shops on the premises, but remember that in Kauai, as elsewhere, hotel shops usually must recover more from their customers in order to pay for higher real estate costs.

Arts and Handicraft. Some of the best and most expensive of both can be found in the dozen or so galleries and shops in **Kilohana**, the restored old plantation homestead off Route 50, about a mile past Kukui Grove Center just out of Lihue. **The Kauai Museum Gift Shop** (Tel. 245-6931), 4220 Rice St. in Lihue, offers imported Polynesian and local handicraft, jewelry, shell leis, and Hawaiiana books and prints. You need not pay the entrance fee to the museum to visit its shop. Just north of Lihue, in Kapaia, **Kapaia Stitchery** (Tel. 245-2281) has many locally made clothing items for men and women.

Rehabilitation Unlimited Kauai (Tel. 822-4975), across Highway 580 from the Coco Palms Resort Hotel, invites visitors into its workshops where the handicapped manufacture coconut, *lauhala,* and shell products. Prices run from about a dollar to $35. Open Monday through Friday, 8 A.M. to 4:30 P.M. Closed Saturday and Sunday.

John Engstrom, travel editor of the *Seattle Post-Intelligencer,* said he found some Hawaiian gold and enamel jewelry at the **Goldsmith's Gallery** (Tel. 822-4653) in Waipouli Plaza. Eelskin products have been featured lately at **Hannah Bananas** in the Hee Fat Marketplace in Kapaa. You'll see "Hannah" standing outside the old green-and-white store.

The **Kong Lung Store** (Tel. 828-1731) up in Kilauea, sometimes known as the "Gumps of the Pacific," usually has a wide choice of specialty items. Some beautiful Niihau leis go for several hundred dollars—not unusual for these rare strands of tiny, tiny shells. (Open daily until 6 P.M.)

Hawaiian Wear. The **Happy Kauaian** now seems to have branches scattered everywhere over the island. Some better-quality aloha wear seems to be at **Pomare** in the Kiahuna Shopping Center. You might also look into **Tropical T's** in the same center. In Kukui Grove Centre, we thought **Deja Vu** a rather strange name for a clothing store until we realized that indeed we had seen most of their fashions before.

Bookstores. Competing on opposite sides of the mall at Kukui Grove Center are **Waldenbooks** (Tel. 245-7162) and **Rainbow Books,** which shares digs with a coffee shop and art gallery. They are obviously run by sage business people, since we saw copies of the Maverick series at both of them! (Tell 'em we sent you.)

Incidentally, for anyone planning an extended stay on Kauai, we highly recommend a self-published volume with the space to go into tremendous detail on restaurants, beaches, and enjoying Kauai with small children. That is the *Underground Guide to Kauai* by Lenore W. Horowitz. We have no connection with the book nor have we even met the lady. And though we don't always agree with her, of course, we do admire her work. It costs about $6 in bookstores in Hawaii.

Department Stores. The island's only homegrown department store, Kauai Stores, has bit the dust. Opposite ends of the Kukui Grove Center are anchored by **Liberty House,** a branch of the Honolulu firm, and **Sears, Roebuck and Co.,** of Chicago and points north, south, east, west, *mauka,* and *makai.* **Penney's** has also opened at Kukui Grove.

Antiques. An amazing collection of memorabilia from the past, several with special Hawaiian accents, is displayed at Paul Wroblewski's **The Only Show In Town** (Tel. 822-1442). The 1927-model green-and-white building at 1495 Kuhio Highway is about two doors from the Kountry Kitchen restaurant and almost across from the Coral Reef Hotel in Kapaa: Glass ball fishing floats from $4 up; old Hawaii license plates $6 up to hundreds; antique bottles from $5; old "silkie" aloha shirts, maybe $45 to $65. Paul says he's open 10 to 7 every day—"unless I'm fishing." If you go in just to browse, well, at least buy one of Paul's ice cream cones. (Tell him we said hello.)

11. Nights on the Town on Kauai

Few come to Kauai to "make the scene," and if they do, they must have gotten it mixed up with somewhere else. Most folks say that Kauai after dark is just that—dark. There are a few up-beat and bright exceptions, however, mostly in the hotels.

At the Kauai Hilton, the disco currently taking the island by storm is **Gilligan's.** Chic decorations are capped by a large-screen video. It's open 'til 4 A.M. Thursday-Saturday, 2 A.M. on other nights. It's hopeless on Friday or Saturday night when the line waiting to get in stretches out to the street. Incidentally, the place was named after the lead character in "Gilligan's Island," a fellow who would have never passed the strict dress code to get in.

Another discothèque in favor with Kauai yuppies is **Park Place** down at Harbor Village, across from the Westin. No one under 21 is admitted. If you're looking for the once-popular dance club called the Vanishing Point, well, you guessed it. It's completely disappeared.

At Poipu, you might find some action, live bands, etc., in the new **Poipu Beach Club,** which has replaced the old Mahina Lounge in the Poipu Beach Hotel. It now bills itself as "the South Shore's only night spot." Over at the Waiohai, more casual entertainment is by Kimo Garner at the keyboard in the Tamarind Lounge. He'll play just about any request from classical to rock 'n' roll. Nice bars include **Cook's Landing** anchored in the Sheraton Coconut Beach—especially during happy hour when "Happy" Oyama is fingering the guitar strings, and at the **Drum Lounge** in the Kauai Sheraton, the beat goes on until at least midnight—a good spot for tippling and terpsichore.

The **Club Jetty,** right on the pier at Nawiliwili, is a local institution. It's the oldest nightclub on Kauai, it looks it, and it's better for it. There's a Polynesian show about 9:30 P.M., and dancing after that (the owner, Auntie Betty, becomes the deejay). Sometimes it imports modern musical groups from Taiwan, Japan, Hong Kong, the Philippines, etc. Note the sign declaring: "Barefoot Dancing Prohibited." The fact that they have to put up such a sign in the first place tells you a lot about the Jetty in the second place. Open until about 4 A.M. Closed Tuesday. We like it for its special atmosphere.

You may find good Polynesian dinner shows (luaus) at four or five hotels: The Kauai Hilton (the "Flames of Fantasy" production); the Coco Palms Resort; the Kauai Resort Hotel; in the open longhouse pavilion at the Sheraton Coconut Beach; or in the Outrigger Room at the Sheraton Kauai. However this scene can change quickly.

The piano bar in the **Jolly Roger** restaurant at the Coconut Plantation is popular with the twenties and thirties crowd. Nearby, the **Boogie Palace Bar** in the Kauai BeachBoy Hotel usually starts throwing hard rock into the night after 9:30. Sometimes live shows are brought in, too.

The shining nighttime star in Hanalei is generally the **Tahiti Nui,** which serves up local entertainment on a spontaneous basis. Songs are mainly Hawaiian, but its female owner is an expert in Tahitian melodies, too. At this writing, it also fields a Polynesian show on Wednesday night and an Oldtime Hawaiian show on Fridays. This is a favorite bar with a hip, local crowd, and when it's hot, it's hot.

12. The Kauai Address List

Art supplies— The Art Shop, 3196 Akahi St. Tel. 245-3810.

Barber— Benny's Barber Shop, 3204C Kuhio Highway, across from Datsun. Tel. 245-6062.

Beauty salon— Shimazu's Hair Design (women and men), 2891 Kalena St. Tel. 245-4544.

Camping supplies— Hanalei Camping & Backpacking, Ching Young Village, Hanalei. Tel. 826-6664.

Chamber of Commerce— 2970 Kele St. Tel. 245-7363.

Dry cleaners— Up-To-Date, 3088 Akahi St. Tel. 245-6621.

Fire department— 4223 Rice St. Tel. 245-2222. (Emergency number: 911.)

Fishing supplies— Lihue Fishing Supply, 2985 Kalena. Tel. 245-4930.

Florist— Flowers Forever, 4444 Rice St. Tel. 245-4717.
Hawaii Visitors Bureau— 3016 Umi St. Tel. 245-3971.
Hospital— Wilcox Hospital, 3420 Kuhio Highway. Tel. 245-1100.
Laundromat— Lihue Washerette, lower level, Lihue Shopping Center.
Pharmacy— Longs Drug Store, Kukui Grove Center. Tel. 245-7771.
Police headquarters— 3060 Umi St. Tel. 245-9711. (Emergency number: 911.)
Post office— 4441 Rice St. Tel. 245-4994.
Public library— Main branch, 4344 Hardy St. Tel. 245-3617.

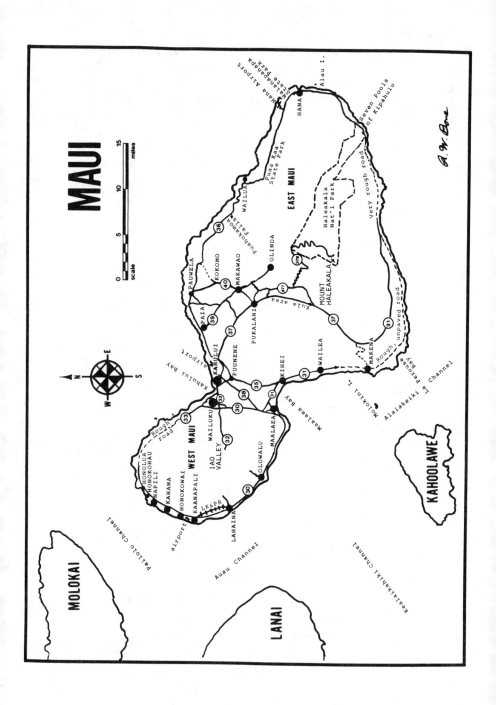

7

Maui,
the Valley Island

1. Around the Island—the Beauty of Success

Local pride flatly sums up Maui in an often-seen declaration: *Maui no ka oi!* In older and more warlike times the phrase was translated as "Maui over all!" Today it simply means "Maui is the best!"

Maui is certainly a three-way favorite. First, it attracts more visitors than any other Neighbor Island. Second, it is the fastest-growing island in the state; its population stands at 75,000, having taken a giant jump over the last decade, and is expected to reach 140,000 by 2005.

Third, its economic future looks particularly bright. Although the other islands are phasing out their traditional sugar and pineapple plantations in greater or lesser degrees, Maui continues to produce these products in relative abundance. Maui is also particularly suited to raising several other kinds of agricultural products.

Some worry about Maui's rapid growth, predicting mistakes that would create a hodgepodge of uncontrolled development. But blessed with some cool heads, the county and the builders have so far managed to make generally high-quality plans for both vacationers and residents.

Maui is the second largest of the Islands in land area. It measures nearly 729 square miles, 120 square miles more than Oahu, where Honolulu is located. Yet Maui numbers less than one-tenth the population of Oahu. All things considered, Maui is lucky that the king moved the capital from Lahaina, Maui, to Honolulu back in 1843.

As every Island has its sobriquet, Maui is known as the "Valley Island." In recent years it has been explained that because Maui was created by two massive volcanoes, an isthmus appeared between them and that this is the "valley" of the Valley Island. But this effect occurs on Oahu and the Big Island, too.

Author Stanley Porteus was more likely correct fifty years ago when he said the old Mauians nicknamed their island for the Iao Valley, the dramatic green slash that cuts nearly to the heart of the ancient West Maui volcano and that figured so prominently in the island's history. There thousands died when Kamehameha the Great, with the help of his *haole* technical advisers and their cannon, finally decimated the defending army of Maui after trapping it in that exitless gorge.

Topographically, the island displays three great natural characteristics: the incredibly rugged, often impassable, and largely unexplored mountains of West Maui; the low ground in its center on which are planted the towns of Wailuku and Kahului and thousands of acres of sugar cane; and the massive, sleeping volcano of Haleakala (pronounced "holly-ah-kah-*lah*"), whose cool and rarefied summit looks down 10,023 feet to the warm ocean below.

It's been said that residents of Maui may choose their climate. They can live in Lahaina, whose name means "merciless sun." Lahaina is warmer much of the year because steep, brooding mountains block it from the cool trade winds. These refreshing breezes do reach Kaanapali just three miles away, however. And they ventilate Napili, a few miles farther on, even more.

The trades also sweep the central isthmus most of the year. And the farther you drive up Haleakala, the cooler it gets, winter or summer. On the fertile slopes grow Mainland fruits, vegetables, and flowers that would never survive at tropical sea level. Here are the delicious Maui onions, russet potatoes, rows of rosebushes, and fields of African protea blossoms.

Some years, perhaps in February or March, it really does snow atop Haleakala, transforming that already beautiful but desolate landscape into a white, nonobjective sculpture unduplicated anywhere else in nature.

Last, those who seek the lushness of a rain forest, or perhaps a tropical version of a green Irish countryside, may settle at Hana. The village and its surrounding area receive an annual rainfall of more than 70 inches, almost all of which blessedly falls during the night.

The island is named after the demigod Maui, whose exploits are celebrated in the legends of all Polynesian peoples. In Hawaii, his fame was assured after he ascended Haleakala (literally, "House of the Sun") one night, determined to set a lower speed limit for the sun's trip across the sky. As the sun arose from its house, Maui took careful aim and lassoed the hot beast by its genitals, not releasing it until it promised to proceed more slowly in the future. This fantastic feat was accomplished mainly so Maui's mother would have more time to dry her tapa cloth in the sun's rays.

The sun told its captor it would take it easy henceforth, and it may now be safe to say that the whole world benefited from Maui's imposed daylight saving time. Today you may ascend the House of the Sun, wait for the dawn, and watch the sun lift himself from his bed at the end of the sky. It's one of the most beautiful, moving events on earth.

2. The Maui Airports

The Valley Isle has three airports, including the state-run fields at Kahului (for jet traffic) and Hana (prop planes only) and the new airstriplet near the luxury resort area of Kapalua. Like Hana's, it operates only by day. All these handle scheduled interisland flights.

The island's main terminal, which is most often hopelessly overcrowded, is at **Kahului Airport** in the flatland between Maui's two mountainous areas. Look out for a blast of wind on disembarking, and follow the bare footprints to the terminal. Distances will be important on Maui, so remember that these runways are 2 road miles from the Kahului business district, 5 miles from Wailuku, 9 miles from Kihei, 15 miles from Wailea, 25 miles from Lahaina, 29 miles from Kaanapali, and 35 miles from Kapalua.

Kahului is the only Maui airport that operates at night. But unless you know you're going to your hotel by taxi or bus, plan your landing in full daylight, leaving enough time to rent a car and find your way home before dusk. The first time we set foot on Maui, we had one dickens of a time finding Kaanapali after a long drive in the dark and in the rain.

Kahului Airport now accepts several direct flights from the Mainland (although not yet on jumbo jets due to the shorter runways), and the terminal building has begun a long-overdue massive expansion program. As of the day before yesterday, anyway, here was its layout:

It is basically one large room, completely open on the side away from the runways, like an outsize Hawaiian *lanai*. (Unfortunately the wonderful old banyan tree and its colony of chirping birds that dominated the inside of the building has finally been removed to make more room for the human population.) The check-in counters for Aloha Airlines, Hawaiian Airlines, Western Airlines, and American Airlines are on the east wall. On the south wall, the runway side, are the check-ins for Mid-Pacific Airlines and United Airlines.

The Hawaii State Agriculture Department inspection area for Mainland-bound passengers is in the center of the building. The airport restaurant is up the stairs on the east side, just above the Hawaiian Airlines departure lounge. Some small shops are on the west side. The Aloha/Mid-Pacific departure lounge wing extends outward from the south side.

Through the nearby west door—on the outside of the building—you'll find the temporary baggage claim areas for all airlines, a visitors' information kiosk, and a lighted board offering free telephone service to some hotels and rental car agencies, as well as other counters serving a taxi company, etc. Across a narrow roadway are a line of rental car booths. Headquarters for the small commuter airlines such as Princeville Airways, Air Molokai, and Reeves Air are a short walk away in a tiny wooden building just past the control tower.

Fifty twisting road miles and more than two hours of hard driving from Kahului Airport is the **Hana Airport** (Tel. 248-8208). By light plane, the two strips are less than 15 minutes apart. There's not much at the Hana terminal but a check-in counter for Princeville Airways, a drinking fountain, two rest rooms, and benches (choice of outdoor or indoor).

If the Hotel Hana-Maui or the Hana Kai Resort is expecting you, there will be a hotel minibus to pick you up from the airport. Or you can order a rental car from either of these two hotels to meet you at the terminal. Otherwise you're on your own, four miles from the village. (Special note to backpackers, however: It's only a short hike from Hana Airport to Waianapanapa State Park, where camping is permitted and where cabins are for rent if there's a vacancy.)

Maui's third airstrip, scheduled to open about the time the ink dries on these pages, is the new facility carved out of a sugar cane field and tentatively named the **Kapalua-West Maui Airport,** about midway between the Kaanapali and Kapalua resort areas on the new highway. The 3000-foot runway and two-story terminal were built by Hawaiian Airlines, and at the moment, at least, it is set to receive and launch only flights on Hawaiian's propeller-driven DASH-7 aircraft.

3. Transportation on Maui

By taxi, it may cost you more than $25 for the long run between Kahului Airport and your Lahaina or Kaanapali hotel. If four persons take the cab and share it equally, the rate is better—about the same or less per person as **Grayline** (Tel. 877-5730) will charge you for a seat on the bus.

But for that $25 you can probably rent a car and drive it yourself for 24 hours. Automobile rental turns out to be the best transportation bargain on Maui, since the distance between the airport and the most popular hotels is so great.

First of all, be sure to read our general tips on this subject in the Oahu chapter. Car rental on Maui is such a fiercely competitive and volatile industry that the rates and companies seem to change daily. At last count there were at least forty (right, we said 40!) different rental-car companies on the island. Honestly, we have never seen fewer than thirty such companies there at a time.

This competition serves more to confuse the picture than to clarify it. But if you are searching for the lowest rates, the principle remains the same: Pick a company that has an address far from the airport high-rent district. (The heck of it is that even if you do choose a company from among the rental-car booths on the property, you will probably have to be vanned to the company's parking lot a mile or two away from the terminal, anyway.) And if you're planning to bring your car back late, be sure to find out if the rental agency closes before your flight out.

Here's a piece of advice from Dave Donnelly, the well-driven columnist for the Honolulu *Star-Bulletin:* Don't rent a standard-shift car if you're planning to twist and turn over the 50-mile route to Hana. "So I saved a buck, but 2½ hours later I was a basket case!"

Speaking of Hana, it is virtually impossible to rent a car there unless you are a guest at one of the two main hotel operations.

During peak periods—June through August and December through March—it's pretty risky to arrive on Maui without advance reservations for cars. Following is a list of some of the better-known companies. As we said, there are a lot more, but these have all been around for a few years. All these except Tropical, Kamaaina, El Cheap-O, Sunshine, and Rent-A-Wreck have offices at Kahului Airport. All but Rent-A-Wreck, Sunshine, and El Cheap-O have Honolulu offices with numbers listed in the Oahu directory, so you can make reservations before leaving the capital. The Maui numbers, however, are given here:

American International (Tel. 877-7604); **Avis** (Tel. 871-7575); **Budget** (Tel. 871-8811); **El Cheap-O** (Tel. 877-5851); **Hertz** (Tel. 877-5167); **Kamaaina** (Tel. 877-5460), a Maui outfit that sometimes has good summer rates; **National** (Tel. 877-5347), which still gives Green Stamps; **Rent-A-Wreck** (Tel. 877-5600), which offers used cars for rent; **Robert's Hawaii** (Tel. 871-6226); **Sunshine** (Tel. 871-6222), which offers convertibles and jeeps; and **Tropical** (Tel. 877-0002), an old standby in Hawaii.

Motorcycles and Bicycles. Motorized bicycles (no license required) have invaded Maui. **Go-Go Bikes Hawaii** (Tel. 661-3063) are racked up at each of the four big hotels in Kaanapali. They putt out for perhaps $20 a day. Some of the Go-Go stands also rent conventional pedal bikes for $10 a day. In Lahaina, try the **South Seas Moped Rental** (Tel. 661-8655).

There are some special bike paths on Maui, by the way. One well-used trail has now been paved all the way from Lahaina to the Kaanapali resort area. Nevertheless, Maui motorcyclist Ron Youngblood, an avid hog and chopper addict, points out that in other areas—like the central valley and places such as Olowalu and Pukalani—any kind of two-wheeler will have to fight winds that habitually gust at speeds up to 40 miles per hour.

Driving on Maui. You'll feel safer with a four-wheel-drive vehicle—a Jeep, a Bronco, or a Land Cruiser (a sort of Japanese Jeep)—if you're planning to drive the rough northern route on West Maui or the rougher portions of the southern route on East Maui, either one a piece of potentially axle-busting terrain. These dirt roads, incidentally, are prohibited to you under normal rental-car contracts, so if you break down on them, you'll have to bear all the expenses.

Except for the teeth-rattlers just mentioned, the main roads on Maui are as well maintained or better than those on Oahu. There are usually two lanes only, however, and you'll find no real divided highways on the island. Local drivers are generally considerate; many other drivers seem confused, since there are so many cars driven by visitors to the Valley Isle.

The road to Hana (Highway 36) is feared by some for its 617 twists and turns, and the possibility that a landslide might block the road in rainy weather. Any one of its miles of splendiferous views also may distract a driver from his steering wheel.

And when going up Haleakala, remember that you will end up at 10,000 feet, which is high enough to make some folks feel a little woozy from the rarefied atmosphere. We never take that trip without another driver in the car.

Driving to Kaanapali, be aware that the resort has three entrances off the Honoapiilani Highway, three miles past Lahaina. Take the third entrance for the the Maui Kaanapali condominium. Take the second for the Royal Lahaina Hotel. Take the first for everything else.

Other Forms of Transportation. There is no genuine public transportation on Maui, and there are no buses between Kahului Airport and the major resort areas. A private outfit called **Shoreline Transportation** (Tel. 661-3827) runs its blue-and-white buses from Kapalua about every half-hour through Kaanapali, Lahaina, Maalaea, and Kihei to Wailea and back. Fares depend on how far you go—probably from about $1.50 up to $5 or so. Another shuttle, called **The Shuttle** (Tel. 667-7170) runs between the Wharf shopping center (658 Front St.) in Lahaina and the Kaanapali hotels for fares of about $1.50 one way. Then there's the **Kaanapali Resort Jitney,** a green, double-streetcar-like vehicle that runs on rubber tires. It tours the Kaanapali area only, chugging between the hotels, the Whalers Village, and the Kaanapali station of the LK&PR railroad line. The fare may be $2 or so for an all-day ticket this year, and $1.50 for a single ride.

And the train? Yes, there really is one, but it's mostly for the thrill of the ride and seems rather costly when considered as straight transportation. See the details in section 6, Sightseeing.

4. The Hotel Scene—Luxury in Lilliput

For most Maui visitors, there is one area for a Maui vacation headquarters that far outdistances all others on the yardstick of desirability. This is the short stretch of shore that runs from **Lahaina to Kaanapali.**

Lahaina, the once-bawdy old capital of the Sandwich Islands, is today a living museum. It hosts no luxury hotels, and has no beach to speak of. However Kaanapali, just three miles farther along the road, was once *only* an area of beautiful beaches. The only thing that extended higher in the air than a grass shack was a 100-foot-tall volcanic promontory called Black Rock. Today the grass shacks are all gone, and Black Rock is the foundation of the Sheraton Maui Hotel.

And the Sheraton is only one of a group of a dozen hostelries that have sprung up along the breakers over the last two decades. These hotels, now part of the 500-acre Kaanapali Beach Resort, are all tied together by the bright green strip created by the 36-hole Royal Kaanapali Golf Course.

Farther along the same coastline are the villages of **Honokowai** and **Napili,** which reach just about the limit of remoteness for staking your claim in the sands. Then the superdeluxe Kapalua resort is virtually at the end of the line.

A more recently developed shoreline runs from **Kihei** ("*key*-hay") through **Wailea** ("why-*lay*-ah") and out the other side. These lie along some lovely and sparsely populated beaches down the southern neck of the low area separating West and East Maui.

The smaller Wailea neighborhood now rivals Kaanapali in attractiveness, and sun-seekers searching for a more peaceful, somewhat less peripatetic vacation than they might find at Kaanapali are settling in nicely at Wailea. Unlike Wailea, nearby Kihei has been built up by many different condominium developers, and that area appears somewhat hodgepodgy, architecturally speaking. However some see it as more mellow and "laid-back" today than it was in previous years. Both Wailea and Kihei have at least taken the pressure off the West Maui areas.

There are also a few hotels in the twin communities of **Wailuku** and **Kahului,** two little workaday towns that serve as the county seat and airport gateway respectively.

Certainly in a class all by itself is the little bay, village, and state of mind called **Hana.** A tropical and sociological wonder, "Heavenly Hana" stays that way mainly because of its isolation from the rest of Maui and from the rest of the world. There are only two hostelries in Hana with more than five or six rooms, and one of them is one of the most costly hotels in the Islands.

Maui Condomania. If you drive along the coast from Kaanapali to Napili, you may see some modern apartment buildings, a few of which may hang out signs: "Beautiful double room, $45 nightly." These are not hotels, but the simplest version of an innkeeping concept called "condominium hotels" or "resort condos." Hawaii has the largest number of hotel condo units in the nation, and Maui has more than any other Hawaiian island, except Oahu.

Resort condominiums are not set up by a person or a corporation, but by a limited partnership, a venture that may include as many as 200 people—investors or second-home owners—who usually have proprietary rights over at least one of the units. Owners share in the maintenance costs, and all common areas are held jointly. The number of units available for rental varies, depending on how many are occupied by owners or long-term lessees.

The smaller places offer rooms or apartments—period. There may be no restaurant, no beach services, infrequent maid service, and no professional management. The amenities in your flat will depend largely on how often the owner of the unit stays there himself. If he visits frequently, there may be a large color TV, fine furniture, and a set of good china. If he doesn't, there may be nothing in the unit except the basic equipment all the partners have agreed to provide for the rental pool.

The larger condominium operations, however, have been coming into their own in the past few years, especially on Maui, offering more hotel-like facilities. Many of these are now excellent bargains that can compete with hotels offering the same luxury amenities. And beyond the usual hotel arrangements, most include full kitchens for no more money than you might pay for a comparable room without such conveniences in a conventional hotel. Rates are often (but not always) based on the size of the unit itself—seldom on the number of people who will be occupying it. And this sometimes makes for an excellent bargain for two families renting together. If you're reserving a condo, be sure to ask questions about maid service, whether there is a minimum length of stay, what equipment is provided, what public facilities are there, how old the unit is, and—especially if you won't have a car—how near it is to shopping and recreation areas. (Few will be within walking distance of both.)

If you're interested in a condo on Maui, it might make good sense to talk to a central reservations agency that handles several different kinds of accommodations. One which has been in business for several years is **Maui 800** (Tel. 877-2749), and it represents scores of condos, not only on Maui but on other islands, too. A newer outfit, making a big splash in the past year, is **The Maui Connection** (Tel. 979-6343), which also has several addresses and price levels in its book. (These are local phone numbers, but both outfits have toll-free numbers, listed in our appendix.) These companies talk mainly to travel agencies, but you should have no trouble dealing with them direct. Be sure to ask if they have any combination car-condo specials. (And as always, tell 'em we sent you.)

We have divided up our selection of sample accommodations below (mostly hotels, but including a few proven condos) into Expensive, Medium, and Budget categories, and we have listed them generally in the order of our personal choice within those groupings. (The exception is the Hana hotels—there are only a few possibilities—which are listed at the end of each price classification.) Rates we have mentioned should only be taken as a general guide, although we believe they are correct at press time.

EXPENSIVE HOTELS

At this writing, Maui folks are waiting for the new Westin to open (see later). In the meantime, the 815-room, triple-towered, $80-million **Hyatt Regency Maui** (Tel. 667-7474), which debuted in late 1980 on Kaanapali Beach, set out unabashedly to outdazzle anything else on the island. In many ways it still succeeds admirably:

Mammoth entranceway flanked by massive, million-dollar Chinese vases; valuable Oriental artworks scattered over the 20-acre campus; two dozen elegant shops in the ground-level promenades; scads of tropical gardens with scads of tropical birds; dramatic, free-form, one-acre swimming pool (divided into two areas by a swimmable waterfall hiding the Grotto Bar, and also featuring a 130-foot slide).

Long list of guest facilities and activities including saunas, massage room, exercise room, jacuzzi, library, pool table, electronic game room, scuba and snorkeling lessons and excursions, volleyball, shuffleboard, tetherball, boating, etc.; five tennis courts, with a teaching pro; Kaanapali golf links next door; special children's programs; four expensive restaurants, including the mirror-lined Swan Court, the chocoholic-bar-equipped Lahaina Provision Company (above the waterfall), the Italian-flavored Spats II, doubling as a popular basement disco, and the poolside Pavilion Restaurant, the priciest "coffee shop" you ever did see; several bars; entertainment in the Sunset Terrace or the plastic-roofed, tree-full Grand Ballroom; unfortunately inconvenient parking in the back lot behind the hotel.

Guest bedrooms in three wings—the rectangular Napili Tower to the west and Lahaina Tower to the east, and the atrium-hollow Kaanapali Tower in the middle; all units with at least a peek at the ocean; all with luxury facilities, except strangely with narrow *lanais;* decor running to brown and beige; most rooms divided by a credenza into sleeping and sitting areas. Rates for 1987 (single or double) are expected to be as follows: Garden View, $175; Mountain View, $205; Ocean Front, $245 to $275; Regency Club, $290; and Regency Club/Ocean View, $320. Suites run from $375 to $1,500. An extra person in the room costs $25. These are much higher tabs than even the Hyatt on Waikiki Beach. Our reader reports have been somewhat mixed on service standards (one person complained to us that he had to get down to the pool by 8 A.M. every day to get a lounge chair; another thought the bathrooms were small on the Regency Club floor), but all praise the dramatic layout. (Reservations through the Hyatt chain or the Hotel Hyatt Regency Maui, 200 Noheo Kai Dr., Lahaina, HI 96761.) In any case, as 1987 begins, the Hyatt wins our highest destination recommendation on Maui.

Far beyond Kaanapali, a double-deluxe resort on West Maui's most beautiful beach is the **Kapalua Bay Hotel and Villas** (Tel. 669-5656), created by Laurance S. Rockefeller, picked up for awhile by Regent International, but eventually bought by a group formed largely of its own guests (although one of the new co-owners is Mark Rolfing, who worked his way up to operations director after starting out at the hotel a decade before, gassing up and washing down the golf carts). It is the only hotel in the Kapalua resort, and it is at last more accessible since the opening of the new West Maui Airport:

Developed alongside two championship, 18-hole golf courses designed by Arnold Palmer; sloping site made even more gentle by design of the hotel on four levels in six buildings joined in a "modified C" plan; three-story-tall lobby with views to trees, grass, pool, the ocean, and the islands beyond; Bay Lounge in the lobby with evening entertainment; two-tiered The Garden dining room for lighter meals and a spectacular brunch one level below, bisected by a moving waterway; separate and well-regarded Bay Club Dining Room a beach length away; the Grill & Bar, a casual local favorite up by the Golf and Tennis Garden; Crown Bar (with evening entertainment) next to the Dining Room; usually excellent Plantation Veranda, an enclosed, U-shaped, Hawaiian-look room serving dinner only; nightly movies on the property; 10 all-weather tennis courts; large, 12-corner swimming pool with bar/snack bar; many organized athletic activities.

Rooms are divided into 108 Ocean Views, 83 Garden Views, and 3 suites. The "E" Wing is most convenient to the sand. Modified American Plan (two meals daily) is available at about $50 per person per day extra. Room rates for 1987 will run from $175 for some Garden View rooms up to $325 for some of the Ocean Front units. Suites run from $400 to $950. (There are no longer any rate reductions during the summer.)

Most regular hotel units are large and also near duplicates of one another, with rate classification based on their position relative to the ocean; all decorated in either blue or rust tones; air conditioning, but also Bombay fans; original art in each unit; hidden fridgelette under the tiled dry bar; color TVs; his-and-hers bath with separate double sinks, separate double closet, and separate tub and shower; lots of spacious condo "Villas" now under the same management, running from $125 through $550 daily.

This hotel has dropped its original elitist plans and turned partly to groups to keep the room night count up, a policy that drew criticism in one letter we received from a guest. We also received a complaint last year that with no notice the hotel decided to turn off its air conditioning at night. August visitors may be interested in the annual classical music festival held on the property. (Reservations from the hotel at One Bay Drive, Kapalua, HI 96761.) It's a far-out beauty, to be sure, but perhaps no longer too far away.

Way over in Wailea, the 1,450-acre luxury resort community built by *kamaaina* sugar firm Alexander & Baldwin, Inc. is anchored by the 600-room **Maui Inter-Continental Wailea** (Tel. 879-1922). Its far-out location on the bosom of East Maui affords some spectacular views of Kahoolawe, Molokini, and West Maui: Greens beckoning from the nearby Wailea Golf Course; 14-court Wailea Tennis Club also a short serve away; windsurfing and hobie-cat clinics. White stucco and dark wood architecture throughout; towering, eight-story Lahaina Building suitable for tour groups; one Main Building for central services; long, open-air lobby with its Lobby Bar; a dozen tasteful shops; string of eight low-rise structures generally housing non-group travelers; lava-rocky coastline between lovely Wailea Beach and Ulua Beach; three pools (at least one always sheltered from the wind); one of Maui's most attractive outdoor luaus; miles of meandering pathways with benches; full beach services; sports, crafts, and many extra activities for guests; always a full calendar of special events; handy "guest relations desk" with concierge-type services; five restaurants, including the fancy seafood dining salon named La Perouse; an excellent Sunday brunch; good entertainment in the Inu-Inu Bar.

There are neatly appointed bedrooms in browns, yellows, and oranges. Several have king-size beds; some have twin doubles. All have good baths, individual *lanais*, TV/radios, and air conditioning. Figure $155 to $195 daily for two in normal rooms, or $125 to $165 from mid-April to mid-December, depending on your view. But we saw no bad views—just some that gazed toward Haleakala instead of the waves. Suites, with several special extras, run from about $200 to $700. Children under 18 free in their parents' room at any price level. Special golf, tennis, or family plans sometimes available. (Reservations from the hotel at P.O. Box 799, Kihei, HI 96753.) The Inter-Continental is now completing a multi-million-dollar refurbishing program. A handsome choice in a beautiful location.

Next door to the Inter-Continental is the newer and smaller **Stouffer's Wailea Beach Resort** (Tel. 879-4900), a bright alternative that some logically place higher on the list: Colorful, cheery lobby; same Wailea Resort golf (36 holes) and tennis (14 courts) as the neighboring Inter-Continental; large pool amid attractive and innovative landscaping (also fine for wheelchairs); waterfall and meandering lagoon; lovely crescent of beach beyond; Hawaiian language and history classes; special honeymoon packages; a summer children's program; three restaurants, including the award-winning Raffles, the Palm Court, and the friendly Maui Onion down by the pool; drinking on the Sunset Terrace or at Lost Horizon, almost a Shangri-la for the disco set; large game room.

A total of 350 well-furnished, nicely decorated, not-too-large units with full luxury amenities (including refrigerators); two rooms especially equipped for the handicapped; four sleeping wings with the Mokapu Beach Club, the separate "hotel within a hotel" down near the beach, the most desirable and most expensive; the Makai wing our second favorite; some readers warning against the few rooms near the noisy service entrance. Daily double rates for 1987 probably on the following scale: $215 Mountain Side, $235 Ocean Side, and $350 Makapu Beach Club. Suites begin at $450. This has always been one of our favorite hotels on Maui, with some of the highest service standards around, although the rates have climbed astronomically. (Reservations through the Stouffer organization or direct from 3550 Waialae Alanui Dr., Wailea, HI 96753-9597.) Stouffer's may mean more to you as a TV dinner, but this could be a delicious selection.

Meanwhile, back at Kaanapali, the **Sheraton Maui** (Tel. 661-0031) has two "ground" floors, one with the lobby, the other eight stories up on top of Black Rock, the extinct volcano crater from which the ancient Hawaiians said warriors leaped off to join the spirit world. Today leaps are being held nightly. As the climax of the evening torch-lighting ceremony, a *malo*-clad employee dives into the sea from a rocky ledge. We've stayed at the Sheraton from time to time, and here are our impressions of this unique establishment:

Large, moon-shaped swimming pool; wide, wide, wide beach a few steps away; smaller pool by the cottages; three tennis courts; golf privileges on the nearby courses; pathways for explorers winding around Black Rock; elevator making a faster and easier route up the Cliff Tower; viewful and entertaining Discovery Room restaurant at the top; Barkentine Bar next door; informal Black Rock Terrace restaurant serving three meals by the main pool; Aloha Luau several nights a week on the grounds.

At the moment there are 510 bedrooms in three areas, ranging from Standard doubles at $150 in the Garden Tower through Deluxe units around $200 in the Ocean Lanai buildings on the face of the rock, to the Ocean Front Cottages at $225. (Make sure you get a good location; a few of those cottages may have a better view of the luau pit than the ocean). Recheck these advance-announced rates later. (Reservations through the Sheraton chain or from Sheraton Hotels, 2255 Kalakaua Ave., Honolulu, HI 96815.) After a quarter century, there is evidence of hard knocks on the premises, and the Sheraton is now undergoing an overdue major renovation. Later—perhaps next year—it is also scheduled to add 373 new rooms. You'll find parking problems here on luau nights. Meanwhile, as an architectural achievement and a convenient base for Kaanapaliing, we still declare this choice almost as solid as the rock on which it sits.

Also at Kaanapali, the twin-winged, 720-room **Maui Marriott Resort** (Tel. 667-1200) is Marriott's 100th link in the chain, and the first to be forged in Hawaii: Breezy, 15-acre, oceanfront site near the Hyatt; recently improved landscaping; open-air lobby surrounding pools and fountains; conveniently separate group and independent check-in; pleasant folks on duty there; long, open courtyard acting like a walk-in Venturi tube; many outdoor activities; two grown-up pools and one kiddy pool; sometimes dangerous section of beach (walk a few minutes one way or the other before entering the water); five tennis courts; often difficult parking; four restaurants, including the Kaukau Grill, a poolside snack bar, the reasonably priced Moana Terrace (open to the ocean when weather permits), the equally well-liked Nikko Steak House (featuring Japanese teppanyaki), and the fine-dining Lokelani Room; several bars, including the swinging Banana Moon "entertainment lounge" for the younger generation.

Accommodations in two nine-story towers, the Lanai Wing and the Molokai Wing; generally large rooms with king-size or twin-double beds; convertible couches sleeping two more; luxury accouterments including color TVs, *lanais,* room safes, etc.; 1987 rates from about $150 with a golf-course or mountain view through several stages to $250 for increasingly greater vistas of the ocean; suites beginning at around $450.

We thought the hotel not too well designed for the site on which it sits. One of its most scenic spots, on the ground floor by the beach, is used for that Japanese steak house, which is air conditioned and only open after dark. (Reservations through the Marriott chain or from the hotel at 2341-A Kaanapali Parkway, Lahaina, HI 96761.) Our own stay was okay, and letters from readers have been generally favorable too, especially toward a friendly staff.

A well-maintained resort that offers a lot for your money is the **Napili Kai Beach Club** (Tel. 669-6271), almost as far away as Kapalua on the long road west. However the resort will be easier to reach now, with the new West Maui Airport in operation, even if it is still a long stretch out to explore some of the rest of the areas of Maui by car. (It is about 35 miles from Kahului.) But if semi-isolation is no problem, here is a total outdoor activity center in one hotel-condo complex:

Large, well-landscaped grounds snuggling up to two beautiful beaches; tremendous selection of *alfresco* sports including tennis courts, croquet, shuffleboard, putting, snorkeling, you-name-it; no extra charge for most sports equipment; some organized activities like Mai Tai parties; new outdoor *huli-huli* barbecue now sizzling; new luaus being planned around it; dependable Sea House Restaurant (formerly "Teahouse of the Maui Moon"); entertainment nightly; four swimming pools; new jacuzzi; eight buildings including a tiny "Hideaway Cottage."

The rooms we saw were lovely, in neo-Japanese decor, and all overlook the ocean. To be right next to the sand, however, ask for Standard rooms in the Lahaina Wing at around $125. Studio prices for two run about $160 in the more luxurious units. Suites in the Honolua Wing go for around $200, and the price is about $325 for four to six persons in that Hideaway Cottage. *Credit cards are not accepted.* (Reservations from Napili Kai Beach Club, Napili Bay, HI 96761.) A devoted clutch of annual returnees wouldn't consider anyplace else.

When we recently inspected the new 300-room, Japanese-owned **Maui Prince Hotel** (Tel. 874-1111), out past the Wailea Resort in the new Makena Resort, it was not quite open to the general public. One thing that tends to recommend it in our book, however, is the fact that it is out to capture FITs—free and independent travelers—and is not looking for the large group trade:

One single, V-shaped, five-story building aimed toward the nearby white-sand beach; the company's own 18-hole Makena Golf Course a nine-iron shot away; guests offered a cool, damp towel on arrival; large open lobby with colorful carpet and giant teak shutters; a 30,000-square-foot courtyard with two running artificial streams; free entertainment alternating between classical and Hawaiian; a mirror pond specially designed to reflect the sunset; two too-small, too-shallow circular swimming pools (which we predict will eventually be augmented or replaced); three restaurants, including the large, open-sided Cafe Kiowai coffee shop on the ground floor, the fancy Prince Court, and the well-decorated Hakone, an authentic dinner-only Japanese restaurant on the second floor; 24-hour room service announced at the outset anyway.

Free newspapers for every room; the third floor reserved as a special no-smoking zone; all units with an ocean panorama; nice views of Molokini and Kahoolawe; clever cross-ventilation design for the doors; remote control Sony TVs (at least until somebody walks away with the remote control); fridges in every room; somewhat smaller living areas on the higher floors, due to architectural limitations; extension phones in the johns; beach towels conveniently available in the rooms. Double rates beginning at about $200 a day, so they say. (Reservations from the hotel at 5400 Makena Alanui, Kihei, HI 96753.) There are lots of pluses and minuses, so a lot will depend on the quality of service seen throughout 1987.

A veteran contender still loved by many is the **Royal Lahaina Hotel** (Tel. 661-3611), a neighbor of the Sheraton. The hotel is now owned by Pleasant Hawaiian Holidays, a large tour wholesaler in California, and this means more group traffic, but the management continues to be by Amfac Hotels, certainly a plus. Today the formerly large campus has been reduced mainly to one 11-story building with rooms overlooking the cobalt blue ocean or the electric green Kaanapali Fairway Number 8, with a few smaller buildings and 31 very nice, recently redecorated cottages:

Check-in facilities in the monkeypod-paneled lobby; Franciscan-tiled floor; a bellhop for your bags only if you ask for one; three swimming pools besides that most beautiful pool of all called the Pacific; great views (Lanai on the left, Molokai on the right); eleven tennis courts; two putting greens; several restaurants, including the Royal Ocean Terrace, the Alii Dining Room and its nightly Polynesian show, and Chopsticks, an unusual Oriental-theme dining room.

Bedrooms in cool greens and blues; generally excellent appointments with imported rattan; double rates ranging from $105 to $190, depending on position; magnificent sea-view corner suites about $400. But the cottages—*no ka oi!* There are four units per building, but somehow each seems private. Bedrooms open to the breeze on two sides; muted salmon and teal blue colors with peach accents; good rattan furnishings; second-floor units with private *lanai;* bottom units with back door opening right to the beach; all equipped with refrigerator, TV, and several extras; cottage rates about $145 to $210. (Reservations from Amfac Hotels, P.O. Box 8519, Honolulu, HI 96815.) Still a professional operation.

Today there are a few nice hotel/condo operations in Kihei, an area we wouldn't have considered a few years ago. One of these is **Kamaole Sands** (Tel. 879-0666), across the street from the county's Kamaole Beach Park No. 3. A total of 440 apartments in a half-dozen buildings are arranged in a deep U shape around a recreation area, grassy slope, and artificial meandering stream. There's a swimming pool, wading pool, and a couple of jacuzzis. Farther down the slope you can make use of one of two barbecue areas. Four tennis courts are free to guests. Some 134 units are in the rental plan; we would choose one of the cool, double-storied top-floor units if possible. Apartments have all appliances, including washer/dryers, etc. Current rates run from around $100 to $175 or so, depending on size and position. You'll probably need a car for most of your stay, though; there's not much within walking distance except the beach. (Reservations through Colony Resorts, 733 Bishop St., Honolulu, HI 96813.) We enjoyed a brief stay here once ourselves.

The 364-unit condominium operation called the **Papakea Beach Resort** (Tel. 669-4848), a little north of Kaanapali, has been winning friends and influencing visitors for a few years, now. There's a narrow strip of beach, at least at low tide, a couple of inviting pools, tennis courts, nicely landscaped gardens, and several guest activities. Well-furnished living units on four floors offer color TVs, washer/dryers, good kitchenettes, and overhead fans, but no air conditioning. Like some other condos, this one has maid service only *every other* day.

Exact rates for 1987 are unavailable at this writing, but based on past schedules will probably run from around $100 to $110 for studios through $125 to $135 or so for one-bedroom models sleeping four, to about $175 for two-bedroom apartments. Substantial discounts, however, have been in effect from April 1 to December 19. (Reservations from the resort at Kaanapali, HI 96761.) Perhaps a happy find.

Sand-side accommodations in Lahaina itself are possible in the seven-story **Lahaina Shores Hotel** (Tel. 661-4835), a condominium-apartment operation, often flying the biggest American flag you ever saw in your life: On the water at the east end of town; a narrow beach of sorts, a rarity in Lahaina; old-style facade with colonnades and balustrades; large lobby; swimming pool and jacuzzi out on the AstroTurf; no restaurant or bar, but plenty of those near enough anyway. Units with full kitchen, air cooling, and color television; black-out draperies; lots of lemon-yellow and lime-green decorations; a panorama outside that just can't miss. Mountain-view studios for around $75; similar rooms on the ocean for $85; deluxe separate-bedroom units for about $110 facing *mauka* or $120 on the water-and-sunset side of things; some deluxe penthouses in the $125-to-$140 range; ground-floor units with access from inside or outside, a convenience for beachniks. (Reservations from the hotel at 475 Front St., Lahaina, HI 96761.) It may be showing a few scars. Nevertheless it's a good choice if you want that convenient location.

More condo possibilities include the popular **Kaanapali Shores** (Tel. 667-2211) with all hotel amenities near Papakea, and the **Whaler** (Tel. 661-4861), right on Kaanapali Beach. Both are in the $100-to-$150 per couple range. We have not yet been on a full inspection of these two, although we have had good reports on both.

Last on our basic list of relatively high-priced choices for West Maui is the **Kaanapali Beach Hotel** (Tel. 661-0011), on the beach for which it is named, and not to be confused with any similarly named establishments. The rooms are okay (try for the ground-floor units for easy access to the beach and the cartoon whale–shaped pool). But we think the general layout is less than inspiring. It seems heavily used by groups, making some independent visitors feel alone in the crowd. One reader complained that there was no longer any room service here, another that the balconies of the next-door Whaler condo gave them no privacy, and another that the staff at the beach activity center were "flip, high-handed, pushy and arrogant." On the other hand, the housekeeping staff are reportedly friendly and responsive, and the hotel has also undergone a major refurbishment since our last visit. Standard doubles for $105, Superiors for $125, and Deluxes for $145. (Reservations through Amfac Hotels.) It's never been our favorite, but perhaps things are looking up.

Opening sometime in the middle of 1987 will be the $155 million, 762-room **Westin Maui** (sorry, no phone number at this stage) on Kaanapali Beach, at the site of the old Maui Surf, and incorporating that building in the plans. Rumored to be Maui's most flamboyant hotel, the Westin is supposed to have more than $2 million in fine art and a swimming pool which is the largest in the state. (Actually there are five pools on the drawing board, together with slides and waterfalls.) Also planned are nine restaurants and bars, including the Island Bar in the center of the swimming pool area and the Villa Restaurant, with a view of the Pacific and the pool playground. Like other Kaanapali resorts (the Hyatt, Marriott, Sheraton, etc.), it has access to one of the largest and best beaches in the state as well as to the Royal Kaanapali Golf Course. A health club is also under construction. Room rates for this superman resort are expected to begin at $180 and move up, up and away. (Reservations through the Westin organization.) If you check in in '87, please let us know your gut reaction.

An even later opening, in December '87 or January '88, will take place for the **Embassy Suites Maui**, an "all-suite" hotel now under construction at Kaanapali. About 415 suites, each with a separate bedroom, will be included in the plans.

Now, how about Hana? To a large extent, the attraction of the **Hotel Hana-Maui** (Tel. 248-8211) is simply the lush, unspoiled environment of Hana itself. Located smack in the modest little village, it's a collection of several low-roofed buildings, around which wind its own private gardens and small pitch-and-putt golf course:

Open patio-style lobby with a fountain of flowers; several public areas indoors including sitting room, cardroom, etc., off the restaurant and open-air cocktail lounge; many outdoor facilities and activities including heated swimming pool, two tennis courts, shuffleboard, croquet, table tennis, golf, weekly cookouts, *luaus,* and so on.

Swimming is on Hamoa Beach with private access a few minutes away by hotel shuttle. The staff will handle all arrangements for car rentals, horseback riding, hula and ukulele lessons, bicycling, and nearly anything else you can think of except a Broadway show. There are many different types of accommodations, all single-story, running from about $250 per day for two (including all meals) on up to the Alii Executive Home for over $700 per day. There are no TVs or air conditioners available or needed. Better book a year in advance for a Christmas vacation. The hotel and surrounding ranch are now owned by the Rosewood Hotels people from Dallas, who have been conducting a massive renovation program without closing the hotel, and promising not to ruin it in the process. Sorry, but we have been unable to see the results at this writing. (Reservations from the hotel direct at Hana, HI 96713.) It's expensive, but to many its unique style may continue to be worth every blue chip.

MEDIUM-PRICE HOTELS

First, here are some lodgings on which Sara and I do not agree. I happen to like very much carrying my own bags up the creaky wooden stairs of the octogenarian original building of the **Pioneer Inn** (Tel. 661-3636) on the waterfront in Lahaina. There in a lopsided old room with a fan circling overhead and whose shivering timbers are only held together by multitudinous layers of white paint, I can lie down and hear the rinky-tink piano coming from below in the Old Whaler's Grog Shop. That's a genuine antique bar like none other in Hawaii. Then I can wander out on the ancient veranda and scan Lahaina Harbor, the scene of drama, history, and the passing Hawaiian parade for two centuries. There is a pool, of sorts, but no room service. Doubles in the original building are about $50 with bath or perhaps five dollars less with down-the-hall facilities. Creatures of comfort who choose the new wing in the rear (we must admit, it *is* nice) will pay about $70 for two. (But the Spencer Tracy–Katharine Hepburn Suite is in the old section up front.)

Now, why do I like it? Listen to some of these house rules posted on opening day in 1901: "Women is not allow in you room. If you wet or burn you bed you going out. You are not allow in the down stears in the seating room or in the dinering room or in the kitchen when you are drunk. You must use a shirt when you come to the seating room." (Reservations from the hotel at 658 Wharf St., Lahaina, HI 96761.) Sara says it's like sleeping in an old museum, and I say yup, that's just why I like it!

The 49-unit **Noelani** (Tel. 669-8374), out past Kaanapali at Honokowai, is one of the nicer small condo buys around: No lobby or central meeting place; two palm-lined pools, however, both near the ocean; pleasant grounds; postage-stamp beach a short stroll away; nicely furnished units in three buildings; full kitchen facilities, dishes, etc.; all with cable TV; some with washer/dryer; all with ocean views; maid service once a week.

Studio units only in the older two structures and larger studio units in the new building in either blue or orange motif, all for about $60 for two; one-bedroom apartments for about $80 double; two-bedroom units sleeping four for around $100 to $110; monthly discounts available. (For the latest scoop, write the Noelani at 4095 Honoapiilani Highway, Lahaina, HI 96761 or use the toll-free number in the appendix.) A happy find.

Much further out the same highway, the 41-unit condo, **Coconut Inn** (Tel. 669-5712), has been highly recommended by at least a couple of readers and a parrot for its friendly, helpful attitude as well as good facilities. It's a little hard to find at the end of the dirt Hui Road in the Napili area, and a 10-minute walk from the beach. As indicated, we haven't seen the place personally, but our information places it in a price range of $60 to $70 for studios and apartments, including color TV and a continental breakfast at the pool. (Write Box 10517, Lahaina, HI 96761 or call the toll-free number in the appendix.) And tell 'em we'll be out to take a look around in '87, too.

Good ole **Maui Lu** (Tel. 879-5881), the pioneer in the Kihei area, is especially popular with Western Canadians. It's across the road from the beach where Captain George Vancouver is thought to have landed in 1792, now marked by a Canadian totem pole. You'll find a swimming pool shaped like a large map of Maui, two tennis courts, Jesse's Restaurant (perhaps renamed now that Jesse has left), the Hale Kope coffee shop, and the Maui Lu-au, packing them in three nights a week.

The rambling collection of buildings makes for widely varying rates and types of accommodations, but all have refrigerator, coffeemaker, TV, and air conditioner. Some feature cooking facilities. Doubles run from around $60 on up to $80 or so. (Reservations from the hotel, 575 South Kihei Rd., Kihei, Maui, HI 96753, or through Aston Resorts.) Stay with the lower rates for the best deals.

Back in Lahaina, the **Lahaina Roads** (Tel. 661-3166) is somewhat removed from the main drag at 1403 Front St. The "beach" is better for snorkeling than for wading, but there's also a pool. Parking is underneath the building: Total of 42 condo apartments; private *lanais;* wall-to-wall carpeting; all with TV, washer/dryer; all kitchen facilities; no maid service; no restaurant. One-bedroom apartments for about $65 to $70; two bedrooms for $70 to $75; penthouse (sleeping four) for perhaps $130; long-term rates available. (Write to the above address at Lahaina, HI 96761.) The Roads is no superhighway, but it's passable.

In Kahului, the **Maui Beach Hotel** (Tel. 877-0051) and its Siamese twin, the **Maui Palms Hotel** (Tel. 877-0071) are not recommended by us until further notice. (The Maui Hukilau is cheaper and better; see below.)

Now, out at Hana again, the traditional "other" place to stay in town is at the **Hana Kai Resort Apartments** (Tel. 248-8435), a 20-unit condominium with daily maid service. Two buildings in a lovely setting right on the water; nearby swimming pool; no restaurant (bring your own fixin's or eat dinner at the expensive Hotel Hana-Maui); free pickup from the Hana airstrip. The hotel will arrange rental cars, horseback rides, and other activities. Studio apartments with all equipment for about $65 double; one-bedroom apartments for $75, extra people for $6 each. Naval Commander (retired) Joe and Sina Fornier are your hosts, and they keep everything on an even keel. (Reservations from P.O. Box 38, Hana, HI 96713.) A shipshape choice.

We have not yet managed to look at any of the **Hana Bay Vacation Rentals** (Tel. 248-7727). This is a group of small houses featuring one, two, or three bedrooms in various locations in the village of Hana itself. All feature fully equipped kitchens, appliances, etc., and daily rates range from around $50 to $95. Details are available from P.O. Box 318, Hana, HI 96713. Last, we almost hate to mention the **Heavenly Hana Inn** (Tel. 248-8442), only because it's so small that if you count on it you may well be disappointed. There are only four rooms in this attractive little beach house, and they rent for between $55 and $85 for a double. You can reserve, however. (Write Alfreda Worst at P.O. Box 146, Hana, HI 96713.) Maybe you'll be lucky.

BUDGET HOTELS

No doubt about it, the best bargain in low-priced hotels on Maui today is still the little **Lahainaluna Hotel** (Tel. 661-0577), especially if you land one of its better units: Upstairs in one of those reconstructed buildings in the Lahaina historic district; 99 percent air conditioned; B&W TV in all units; good, glass-door showers; clean floors. Best bargains are the units on the front, with honest-to-whale waterfront views; cheaper cells in the back seem more claustrophobic but still neat; at last report even the most expensive units were still holding at under $30. Single rates the same as doubles; $6 per extra person after two; no checks (except for deposits), but credit cards okay; absolutely no confirmation without a deposit; maid service three times per week; two days' minimum stay. (Reservations from the hotel, 127 Lahainaluna Rd., Lahaina, HI 96761.) We've tried it and—for the Bare Bones category, at least—we like it.

Over on the windward side, the best deal is the **Maui Hukilau** (Tel. 877-3311). Although physical facilities are pretty good for the price, the dullsville location plus the number of groups that pour into Kahului hotels combine to rank them lower on our scale than they might otherwise be. If you arrive on Maui without reservations, you might snag a decent leftover double for $45 or $50, plus the price of a phone call. Speaking of phone calls, absolutely no long-distance or interisland calls can be made from the rooms. (Boo!) On the other hand, local phone calls are free. (Yay!)

And now, Hana for the budgeteer? Since we wound up each of the previous two categories with accommodations in Hana, we'll try to do it again here. The dedicated low-cost traveler might be put up there in the rustic cabins at **Waianapanapa** ("why-a-noppa-noppa") **State Park.** There are furnished units sleeping four to six at rates from $10 to $30 a day. All are completely equipped with kitchen, etc. (For the most up-to-date report, write to the Division of State Parks, P.O. Box 1049, Wailuku, HI 96793. On Maui, telephone the Parks Division at 244-4354.) Why-a-not?

5. Maui Restaurants and Dining—Supper by Sunset

Does Maui have restaurants? Does it ever! They roll in and roll out, sometimes appearing and disappearing with the rapidity of the waves off Kaanapali. Occasionally a famous name will stick around for a while, but even then there may be a swinging door back in the kitchen to accommodate the incoming and outgoing chefs. It is not uncommon at all for a cook to prove his giblets on Maui, only to be shanghaied and hauled off to a juicier kitchen in Waikiki.

Some bargain tips: Many Maui dining rooms offer "early bird" specials, meaning if you don't mind having dinner between about 5 and 7 P.M., you might save a significant amount of bread (the green kind, that is). Special reservations are sometimes required. Then if it's Sunday, look for the special champagne Sunday brunches, an extravaganza laid out for an all-you-can-eat price by several of the major hotels.

Dining with a show, to boot? There are several places like that. See section 11 for a few old standbys.

LAHAINA AND VICINITY

Longhi's (Tel. 667-2288), hard by the traffic in the quaint, white building at 888 Front St. (corner of Papalaua), has now expanded to the upper story. There are no reservations and no menus, and the first surprise comes when your waiter pushes aside a Boston fern and sits down at your table. Oozing sincerity, he leans forward and in respectful tones recites the "verbal menu." Notwithstanding some of these "hipper than thou" attitudes, the classic Continental and Italian food is always

good, usually excellent, and occasionally superb. Better get there early—
maybe around 6 for a minimum waiting period. Looking back, our only
grouse was the background of street noises penetrating the open-air,
curbside structure. Some readers thought the tables a little small and
some say they have trouble remembering the menu. It's also open for
lunch.

Just off the sidewalk in the Lahaina Market Place, **Gerard's** (Tel. 661-8939)
is the latest Gallic champion in Lahaina. Monsieur Gerard Riversade
tends everything himself in the kitchen. We found pleasant but unpretentious surroundings, with two dozen or so white-clothed tables set on a
brick floor. The menu varies daily, depending on the availability of ingredients, but many classic veal, duck, fish, and chicken specialties are
served, all with a variety of French sauces. Order carefully to keep your
bill at a respectable level.

The traditional longtime French kitchen on the island is all by itself
nearly six miles east of Lahaina at **Chez Paul** (Tel. 661-3843). It's en-
sconced at the end of a wood-frame general store and almost hidden in a
clump of trees off the highway at Olowalu. (Don't try to find it at night if
you didn't see it during the day.) Only about fifteen tables in one modest
room; reservations a must; seatings only at 6:30 and 8:30; single diners
not taken; candles on white tablecloths; no view; no fancy decor; just
excellent *cuisine française* and good service at prices that are *not* cheap.
We had Filet of Sole Meuniere and Veal Valdotin, a casserole dish with
veal, two sauces, and ham and cheese. Others swear by the creamed
soups. Former owner/chef Paul Kirk has died, but the new owners seem
to be carrying on in the same tradition.

La Bretagne (Tel. 661-8966) is an oasis of elegance in a desert of
commercialism, according to some diners. Although the address is officially 562 Front St., it's actually an old house some ways off the street and
across from the softball field at Malu Lulu O Lele Park. Sink back in
comfortable old chairs with antique clocks and other furnishings and
order from a menu of frequently changing French classics, from onion
soup to *noix*. Try the veal, the roast duckling or the catch of the day.
Madge Walls, the savor-savvy dining critic of Maui, says Chef Claude
Gaty is an absolute master of home-made desserts. Count on dropping at
least $25 a person, plus drinks, but the wine prices are actually a little less
than in some other Maui dining rooms.

Back in town center, the 1901 Pioneer Inn Hotel (Tel. 661-3636) hosts
two restaurants. The **Harpooner's Lanai** is open for breakfast and lunch,
but we recommend it heartily *only* for breakfast. You'll see and hear a
marvelous selection of town characters along with your pancakes. At
lunchtime, however, we have been gassed in our chairs by the battalions
of tour buses that leave their diesel motors idling nearby. On the other

side of the same historic building is the dinner-only **Harbor Room** featuring steaks and seafood. We haven't been in recently enough to comment, but prices are probably still moderate.

Under the same management is the **Lahaina Broiler** (Tel. 661-3111) at about 885 Front St. At night the Broiler is lit up literally like a Christmas tree. Whaling-ship decor with kegs, floats, glass balls, and wooden pilings; open-air view from the rail of the islands of Kahoolawe, Lanai, and Molokai; pounding waves seemingly threatening the underpinnings. We've had some delightful breakfasts here for reasonable prices and enjoyed playing footsies with the little crabs who sometimes search for crumbs along the rail. Watch out for your valuables. A slip and a splash, and they belong to King Neptune. Service is unprofessional but friendly. One reader praised the French toast. We have had some complaints about evening dinners; certainly good for the forenoon, anyway.

On the *makai* side of the street, but not nearly so far along, is the well-named **Oceanhouse** (Tel. 661-3472) at 831 Front St. It's a double-decked nautical emporium with both the downstairs dining room and the overhead Carthaginian Bar gazing down on floodlit waves. You can take the salad bar alone at a good price, if you want. Meals run from sauteed filet of *mahimahi* for about $13 to lobster tail for $20 or so. Some readers praise the scampi and pasta. A few creole specialties, too. Not a fancy place, to be sure, but over the years we have experienced fast, friendly service at both lunch and dinner.

Down an alley called Wahie Lane behind 834 Front St. is an Italian hole-in-the-wall called **Alex's Hole In The Wall** (Tel. 661-3197). Pasta dishes are in the $9 range, with lasagna at $14 or Veal Scallopini for perhaps $17. Now you reserve, a change from its earlier policy. Closed Sundays. Small, to be sure, but still deservedly popular. Across the street at No. 839, **Greenthums Over The Ocean** almost places you *in* the ocean on heavy sea days. We had a hearty salad and a fancy sandwich for lunch, but watch those waves!

Across Front Street from the town park and the banyan tree is the **Banyan Inn** (Tel. 661-4489), an old cement-floor, no-nonsense place that has now been renovated. It's fish and steaks, mostly, at around $13 dinner, $7 lunch. Top it off with *lilikoi* (passion fruit) or some other fresh-fruit pie. Some good local entertainment is served with the fixin's on some nights.

The **Whale's Tale** (Tel. 661-3676), next door to The Wharf, deserves its own long-taled reputation. The high-beamed ceilings, stained-glass lanterns, and open-air balcony are typical of Lahaina reconstruction decor, restaurant division. We enjoyed drinks in its Whale Watchers Saloon, but somehow never got back for dinner. It serves until 11 P.M. (sinfully late for Lahaina dining). Try the Korean baby backribs or the chicken in artichoke. Still a reliable choice. Next door in the shopping center, the attractive **Harbor Front Restaurant** (Tel. 667-7822) on the Widow's Walk level specializes in seafood for lunch and dinner. Perhaps a good place to try broiled *mahimahi*.

A favorite Lahaina bakery is **The Bakery,** strictly a carryout, but one of the best, at 991 Limahana Place on the other side of the highway near the train station. Pastries are excellent and the croissant sandwiches are the greatest. It's a terrific place to pick up a box lunch for a picnic or a cruise. Next door is the **Cafe Allegro** (Tel. 667-6743), a well-run Italian dining room.

We do not suggest setting your course for the **Chart House** at the north end of town (although not all nighttime navigators agree). The expensive submarines at **Togo's Eatery** might just blast your wallet out of the water. Nevertheless, they make for a hearty meal. Keep a lookout for these subs in the Lahaina Shores Village at 505 Front St. **Chris' Smokehouse** (Tel. 667-2111) has been serving up some delicious ribs, chicken, and barbecue specialties lately in the Lahaina Square. Nearby, **Fujiyama**, in the Lahaina Shopping Center, is a pretty good choice for Japanese food, but it adds up to a lot of yen. The perennial **Golden Palace** is just about the only sit-down Chinese restaurant right in Lahaina. It's okay, but no more than that in our book.

KAANAPALI

Generally speaking, Kaanapali dining means hotel dining, and some of these inns are not always consistent in the quality of their meals, perhaps because some of the chefs are as transient as their customers.

One of these exceptions is the proudly strutting dining room called **The Peacock** (Tel. 667-6847), a Continental/Polynesian entry firmly installed in the former golf clubhouse at 2650 Kekaa Drive (near the Maui Eldorado condo): Shining ceiling of LED indicators inside plastic tubes; long, low room with wicker tables (the bases can get in the way of long legs); open to island breezes (no air conditioning). Our party enjoyed some excellent dishes including turtle soup (you add the sherry yourself), Veal Oscar, Tournedos Forestiere, and fresh island *opakapaka* (red snapper), all attractively prepared and deftly served. Wide-ranging prices from $20 to $35 for dinners. Better bargains at lunch. One reader told us her family ate there every night for four nights! It's perhaps the most dependable Kaanapali address for lunch and dinner.

Also sailing smoothly on the pond of *haute cuisine* is **Swan Court** (Tel. 667-7474) in the Hyatt Regency Hotel. It's an elegant outdoor tropical setting for classic continental choices like roast duckling or rack of lamb. Several excellent seafood choices are also on the *carte*. Fresh Island Fish

Eichenholz is an unusual favorite. Many fork over an arm and a leg—and say it's worth the price.

A little less imposing than the previous two is a seafood room on the shoreline next to the Whalers Village complex called **El Crab Catcher** (Tel. 661-4423). You can choose the full dinners for around $18 or some "light suppers" (crab custard quiche or crab Louie salad, etc.) for less money. This one is also drawing discriminating local traffic from Lahaina and points east. (Incidentally, parking at the Whalers Village is sometimes impossible after 6 p.m. Consider having an early dinner or perhaps a cocktail hour first for any restaurant in the complex.) Now open at the entrance to Kaanapali is **La Familia** (Tel. 667-7902), the Mexican favorite that closed its antique doors in Wailuku. Not everyone loves it here in its new home (where we haven't tried it yet) as we all did in Wailuku and do now in Kihei. The Mexican entry in the Whalers Village is **Chico's Cantina** (Tel. 667-2777) with complete meals or selections from the Taco Bar. For Italian, we wouldn't consider any other place in Kaanapali than **Spats** in the Hyatt Regency.

A fairly new contender is **Leilani's on the Beach** (Tel. 661-4495), also in the Whalers Village, and it has been winning good reviews, especially for Sunday brunch. Downstairs, their bar with umbrella tables opens right onto the sunny sands of Kaanapali. Upstairs, it's a grand lanai offering a wide variety of steaks, chicken, and seafood selections in the $10 to $15 range, with some specialties especially smoked in koa wood ovens. A good place for Portuguese bean soup, too. It serves until 10:30 P.M.

If hotels were to seek a plethora-of-restaurants prize, it would probably be won by the several kitchens on the grounds of the Royal Lahaina (Tel. 661-3611). **Moby Dick's** is one of the better ones for seafare-ing. The new place on the Kaanapali campus, though, is **Chopsticks,** which is designed for "grazing"—serving a large variety of foods from several Oriental countries in appetizer portions. It's an interesting concept, but brand new and we haven't even been to see it yet. If you go, let us know.

The **Rusty Harpoon** (Tel. 661-3123) in the Whalers Village, which traditionally offered broil-your-own lunches and dinners for a young, hip crowd, has changed its character somewhat. But it still is for pretty casual dining. You might get a "Burger & Beer" special here before 5 p.m. for, maybe, $5.50. Later dining runs to pizzas, pastas, and prime rib (cuts at $13.95 and $16.95). **Ricco's** in the same area may be the place for pizza, made from Ricco's mother's own recipe. One reader complained that the female staff wore torn, disheveled clothing when she was there. The **Ming Court** (Tel. 667-7781), a Whalers Village sister operation to Kahului's famous Ming Yuen, is certainly the best Chinese restaurant in the neighborhood, for both Cantonese and Szechuan cooking. Look for it up on the balcony. Try the duck smoked in tea leaves for around $8.50 or the spicy Chengdu Chicken for $7.50 or so. Some dishes may seem expensive, but this is a top-of-the-line sleeper that may wake up any second.

Over at the Sheraton Maui Hotel (Tel. 661-0031), the somewhat barnlike **Discovery Room** may be found atop Black Rock, providing unequaled views over the nearby land-, sand-, and seascape. It may be worth dropping into when Rodney Arias and other slick entertainers are on stage, but there are several bad tables and service can be a bit iffy. When the show is on, it's almost too dark to see your plate, too. (One reader objected, naturally enough, to receiving three checks—separate ones for food, wine, and cocktails.) The teppanyaki at the **Nikko** Japanese steak house in the Maui Marriott is expensive, fun, and usually good, too. The pleasant **Lokelani Room** in the same hotel is getting along swimmingly with a different lobster specialty every night. And the **Moana Terrace,** also in the Marriott, has been receiving rave reviews from our readers for good quality and low prices. (Tel. 667-1200 for all three dining rooms.)

NAPILI

The dining rooms associated with the Kapalua Bay Hotel (Tel. 669-5656) are expensive, but usually excellent. **The Garden** now offers a "Mayfair Luncheon Buffet," similar to other hotel Sunday-brunch extravaganzas except that this one is served seven days a week. Jackets are strongly suggested for men at dinner in the Bay Club, which is down the beach a bit and not attached to the hotel. There's no view at the **Plantation Veranda,** an elegant inside room. Expensive but delicious specialties include Noisettes of Lamb. (Jackets are a must for men in the evening here.) A local favorite between the tennis garden and the golf club is the informal **Grill & Bar,** especially for lunch.

The restaurant in the Napili Shores Resort has been changed from French to Szechuan Chinese and Thai cuisine and renamed the **Orient Express** (Tel. 669-8077). The "Orient Express" dish itself is a hot beef and seafood combination. Jeffrey Geddes from Carol Stream, Ill. especially recommends the drinks the nights when "Karen" is tending the bar.

The nearby **Sea House** (Tel. 669-6271), in the Napili Kai Beach Club, has changed its name several times, but its quality is consistent. It generally features Continental cuisine with island accents. There is entertainment nightly except Sunday, the Friday-night show featuring offspring of the hotel staff. Dependable and enjoyable.

Not far away is the dinner-only **Pineapple Hill,** a former plantation manager's home in a lovely hilltop setting. Prices are usually low enough, but the bill of fare seemed only fair. We'd be interested in your reaction.

KIHEI

A French restaurant called **Robaire's** (Tel. 879-2707)—and it *is* spelled that way—is shepherded by Robert (pronounced "Robaire") Goueytes, who used to be at home on the ranges at New York's Le Pavillon, Le Jockey Club in Madrid, and the Cafe de Paris at Biarritz. The secret to his success here may be his personal supervision over each dish. You'll find the place at 61 South Kihei Rd., next to the Suda Store.

Also in Kihei today is **La Familia** (Tel. 879-8824), a branch of the Mexican Familia from Kaanapali (and formerly Wailuku). Probably as good or better a bet here at 2511 South Kihei Rd. as there, although one reader reported to us that he finally had to chase down the waitress to get his change. The **Island Fish House** (Tel. 879-7771) is deservedly popular for finny fare. It's tied up to 1945 South Kihei Rd. A fellow Maverick wrote that he enjoyed his steak with sunset on the *lanai* of the **Outrigger Maui** (Tel. 879-1581) at 2980 South Kihei Rd.

WAILEA

The restaurants at the Maui Inter-Continental (Tel. 879-1922) are gaining recognition now from both local and traveling folk. The seafood-oriented **La Pérouse,** decorated in a wide variety of Oriental silks, African antiques, etc., seems to specialize in French cuisine prepared with a distinctive Hawaiian accent. The Callaloo Crabmeat Soup (about $6), made with coconut milk and taro leaves, has become famous. Ditto the Lobster Tail Americaine (about $30). We enjoyed the pepper steak. Jackets or *long sleeved* aloha shirts are considered the proper attire for men, but we saw some wearing short sleeves. If you don't get to La Pérouse, try the Champagne Sunday Brunch in the Makani Room—honestly worth $18.95. The viewful **Lanai Terrace** is now the main coffee shop, serving all three meals.

Next door, in the Stouffer's Wailea Beach Resort, the award-winning restaurant called **Raffles** (Tel. 879-4900) has been making a name for itself. The restaurant editor of *Travel/Holiday* magazine, Robert Lawrence Balzer, once invaded the kitchen, donned an apron, and created some new dishes, which were then added to the menu. The atmosphere seeks to re-create that of the Singapore Raffles Hotel, with polished teak floors, Oriental rugs, bronze chandeliers, and the like (but not those chairs on wheels!). One reader told us she thought the portions seemed small for the prices asked, and we thought the bread a little ordinary. But wait 'til you see that five-tier dessert cart! We very much enjoyed the three meals we've had there, but we must say we have always been in with a special group, not dining incognito. In the same hotel, the **Palm Court** has been offering a good daily champagne brunch. But our favorite spot for lunch at Stouffer's is the **Maui Onion** under the flowering trellis down by the pool.

Near the golf course, the **Wailea Steak House** was for sale the last time we drove through. Its score will have to remain a question mark for the moment. **The Set Point,** dressed in yellow and white at the Wailea Tennis Club, offers second-floor fans a chance to munch some sandwiches while keeping tabs on the action on the courts below. This may be the only dining room on Maui that keeps your jaw moving from side to side as much as up and down!

WAILUKU-KAHULUI

Maui is not particularly known for Oriental fare, but **Ming Yuen** (Tel. 871-7787) no doubt still serves the best Chinese food on the island. It's off the main track (Route 380) at 162 Alamaha St. in the Kahului Industrial Area. Then the all-you-can-eat Imperial Teppanyaki Buffet Dinner, a seven-days-a-week Japanese extravaganza in the **Maui Palms Hotel** (Tel. 877-0071), is *ichi ban*. Also on the Japanese file, try **Tokyo Tei** (Tel. 242-9630) at 1063 Lower Main St. for the shrimp tempura (and other goodies) or **Archie's** (Tel. 244-9401), on the same street at No. 1440 (lots of soups). Both are in Wailuku, and both are often jammed at lunch.

The nicest place for a businessman's lunch these days is the **Island Fish House** (Tel. 871-7555) at 33 Lono Ave. in the Alexander & Baldwin Building in Kahului. This one was launched by the parent Island Fish House in Kihei. Midday reservations are a must. Things are much quieter at dinner. In the Wailuku Business Plaza (2065 Main), try **Pino's** (Tel. 242-9650) for Italian pastas and other goodies. The *mahimahi* with ginger comes highly recommended. Open for lunch Monday to Friday and dinner only on Friday and Saturday.

A good local place for breakfast—and a modest lunch—is **Ma-Chan's** (Tel. 877-7818) in the Kaahumanu Shopping Center in Kahului. No fancy surroundings, but a popular place with permanent residents of the neighborhood.

KULA

On the way up—or down—Haleakala there is now only the **Kula Lodge** (Tel. 878-1535) in Kula. It serves up breakfast and heaps of mountain atmosphere along Highway 377, although it's not for people in a hurry.

For fast snacks, Ron Danzig, a Maverick from Marietta, recommends the **Sunrise Country Market** near the beginning of the Crater Road (Route 378). On the other hand Jeff and Laura Kaplan from Milwaukee had good words for the breakfast at **Doreen's** in nearby Pukalani.

MAKAWAO

The **Makawao Steak House** (Tel. 572-8711) has a good salad bar and offers intimate dining in this Up-country neighborhood. It's very popular with island residents. Jerry Hulse of the *Los Angeles Times* discovered **Kau Kau Korner,** a tiny, inexpensive restaurant operated by 77-year-old Takeshi Kitada for some 40 years on Baldwin Avenue. Local specialties include delicious *saimin,* beef hekka, and pork tofu. Also, check out **Kimoda's Bakery,** which bakes some of the most popular pastry on the island. It opens about 6 A.M., usually to a line waiting outside. Then in nearby Pukalani, right on Highway 37, the cafe called **Bullock's of Hawaii** has been serving up "moonburgers" and guava milk shakes to satisfied customers for years.

PAIA

In this tiny town, a jumping-off place for the Hana trip, there are two traditional choices for semiserious dining. **Dillon's** (Tel. 579-9113) is right in town, and a good choice for steaks, chops, and fish. And there's the more-famous **Mama's Fish House** (Tel. 579-9672), which is actually about a mile out of town at Kuau Cove. It still serves up a good seafood dinner—including Mama's papaya-seed salad. (It opens at 5 P.M.) Local fans admit Mama's is now expensive and hectic, but think she's still worth every sweaty penny of it. (Not everyone agrees.) Sheila Sackawitch, who works for CBS Sports in New York, reported she scored a winner at another new place in Paia called **Picnics:** "We picked up box lunches with huge sandwiches, soda, Maui potato chips (the best potato chips I ever had) and fruit!"

HANA

In Hana itself, there is literally one single address for dinner, and that's the expensive spread at the **Hotel Hana-Maui** (Tel. 248-8211). We've enjoyed the buffet lunch there, too. You can also eat a meal from about 11 A.M. to 4 P.M. for $7 or so at the **Hana Ranch Restaurant** (Tel. 248-8255), whose precise address we've misplaced (just ask anyone). Down at Hana Beach Park, **Tutu's Snack Bar** keeps turning out *saimin,* hot dogs, hamburgers, etc., until about 5 o'clock. One reader wrote us that

Tutu served him the best hamburger he had had in Hawaii, but we haven't reconfirmed that opinion.

A last word on Maui restaurants: For the *real* last word, you might want to pick up a modestly priced volume entitled *Eating Out on Maui,* by Madge Tennent Walls. A decidedly honest appraisal of the local scene, it's apparently the only publication devoted to Maui restaurants that accepts no advertising.

6. Sightseeing Maui

Points of interest on the island of Maui divide themselves naturally into four general areas, and many visitors schedule their Valley Isle stay for a total of four days.

This is not to say you can't have a good time on only a two-day trip. And you could easily spend more than a month on Maui, devoting a week to exploring thoroughly each of the different Island neighborhoods, with an occasional day of rest on some deserted beach. There are also miles and miles of trails, virtually impassable without four-wheel drive, not to mention even more obscure paths through the wilderness, elusive to all but dedicated hikers.

As described in this chapter, the four areas include the following:

West Maui, beginning at Kaanapali, concentrating on Lahaina, and continuing down the coastline as far as the village of Maalaea.

Central Maui, which takes in Kihei, Wailea, and everything in the "neck" of the island. It also includes the airport village of Kahului, the county seat of Wailuku, and Iao Valley—its parks and its "needle."

Haleakala, for which the trip first runs along some 30 miles of mountain greenery in "Up-country Maui" and then winds on up to the crater rim itself at 10,023 feet.

Hana, the unique and unspoiled village and its lush countryside. It is reached by a route so long and winding that many visitors save it for a separate trip on another visit—and that's just what keeps Hana the virginal tropical wilderness that it is.

WEST MAUI—KAANAPALI, LAHAINA, OLOWALU, MAALAEA

If you're staying in the neighborhood, one of the first things you'll notice about **Kaanapali Beach** is how really gorgeous four long miles of gently curving, wide, wide sand can be. Twenty years ago this was about 1,000 wild acres, used largely as a dumping ground for bagasse, the waste product of the Pioneer Sugar Mill. Today, two golf courses provide a neat, green carpet along the strand, studded here and there by a hotel or resort building.

Across the water you will see the outlines of Molokai and Lanai, giving you the feeling as nowhere else in Hawaii that you are indeed living among a community of islands.

The beach is divided in two halves by a large volcanic cone called Kekaa, or **Black Rock.** A sacred cliff in ancient times, the rock today is used as the base for the Sheraton Maui Hotel. Even the most severe critics of modern building in conflict with natural wonders must give the Sheraton its due. The effect is magnificent, and a walk over its grounds is certainly recommended.

Nearby, still in Kaanapali, is the answer to a common husband-wife dilemma, the genuinely unique **Whalers Village.** This handsomely designed museum and shopping bazaar occupies us elders easily for an hour or two. There's plenty of room for the kids to run, too, plus a whaleboat to "sail," old bells to ring, and the like.

The 100 exhibits show the effects of whaling on Maui's past. There's an entire skeleton of a 40-foot-long sperm whale hanging around, plus scores of shops, three or four restaurants, and a movie theater in the same complex. (See also section 10, Shopping.) It's a marvelous browsing place.

Kaanapali also provides the western terminus for the little **Lahaina, Kaanapali & Pacific Railroad** (Tel. 661-0089), a reconstructed 1890 sugar-cane train (with passenger cars) operating between Kaanapali and Lahaina. The six-mile, half-hour run is made about five times daily in each direction. Strictly on a per-mile basis, the fare is a little steep—about $4.50 one way and $7.50 round trip for everyone aged 13 and older; half price for preteens. You can walk to the two Kaanapali depots, one just across the highway from the airstrip and the other across from the Maui Eldorado condo, or take the green articulated Kaanapali Resort Jitney to the station (about $2). The railroad provides a free bus on the other end of the line to get its passengers from the Lahaina depot to the center of town. Getting there is all the fun, and you may find the LK&PR worth the tab.

Lahaina, the scene of so much adventure in James Michener's novel *Hawaii,* was the capital of the Islands from the time Kamehameha the Great rested there after conquering Oahu in 1795 until 1843, when his son, Kamehameha III, moved himself and the seat of the kingdom to Honolulu.

Lahaina's turbulent period ran from the early 1820s—when the whaling ships and the missionaries first arrived, bringing all at once the concepts of both sin and salvation—until late in the century when the rise of the petroleum industry reduced the demand for whale oil. The missionaries, whose homes and missions had even been shot at by waterborne cannon, apparently won by default. The whalers stopped coming, and the principal "sights" of Lahaina today are the real beneficiaries of all this—the whales themselves.

If you visit Maui between late November and early May, you will probably see whales rolling, jumping, and skylarking offshore. Often they are within the nine-mile span of water between Lahaina and the island of Lanai, cavorting on the very spot where as many as 400 whaling vessels once tied up deck to deck, almost forming a floating bridge across the Auau channel.

You can walk to most of the interesting spots in Lahaina. We'd begin with the East Indian **Banyan Tree,** the oldest and perhaps the largest in all the Islands. It was planted in the center of the square on April 24, 1873, to celebrate the fiftieth anniversary of Protestant missionary work. In 1973, more than 500 persons gathered in its 2/3-acre shade to mark its first century.

Fronting the mammoth tree is the **Lahaina Courthouse,** built in 1859 from stones cannibalized from Kamehameha III's old decaying palace several blocks away. Today it serves as Lahaina's police station, but the jail cells below it have been cleverly converted into galleries for the Lahaina Art Society.

The crumbled walls you see nearby represent the corner of the old **Waterfront Fort,** put up in 1831 as a show of force to the whalers. They had been picking fights with the missionaries who disagreed with the sailors over visitation rights for native girls to their ships, and some cannonballs had even whistled into the church compound. The fort was demolished in 1854. In recent times, when Lahaina began honoring its lusty past, there wasn't much that could be done about rebuilding the fort without the unthinkable act of removing the banyan tree. So they rounded up some coral blocks and rebuilt just a corner of the structure— as a sort of "ruin" that never existed in the first place!

In front of the courthouse is the **Lahaina Small Boat Harbor,** filled with a colorful mixture of private and commercial craft. Most of the local cruise boats, fishing charters, and glass-bottom vessels are tied up there.

The original building of the **Pioneer Inn,** across the street, was put up in 1901, when economic activity in Lahaina was at a low point. It was mainly built as a convenience for passengers on the interisland ferry that used to dock nearby. Incredibly, the landmark has remained virtually untouched. There's a wonderful old bar there on the other side of a pair of swinging batwing doors that appears to be right out of Somerset Maugham. It's a favorite watering hole for yr. obt. svt. at least once in every voyage to the old capital.

Tied up to the wharf out front is the museum ship now dubbed **The Brig Carthaginian** (Tel. 661-3262). There once rested here a lovely old square-rigger called the *Carthaginian,* used during the filming of *Hawaii.*

But someone ran it up on the reef in 1972, hopelessly foundering it, and the community was heartbroken. The steelhulled vessel now parked at the same pier was obtained at great effort from Denmark by the Lahaina Restoration Foundation, sailed 12,000 miles to Lahaina, and determinedly renamed *Carthaginian II*. It has gradually been converted into an accurate replica of a square-rigged vessel of the 1800s (though the ship actually dates only to 1920). The exhibits and video below deck are interesting. (Open 9:30 to 4:30 daily; admission $2.) Although we all miss the original, this newer incarnation of the *Carthaginian* is certainly worth a visit.

Just inland from that ship is a set of low ruins partly under plexiglass, the remains of the **Brick Palace.** Almost certainly the first western structure in the Islands, the palace was somewhat amateurishly built around 1801 by two ex-convicts from Australia expressly for the first King Kamehameha.

A short walk along the waterline from the above is the **Hauola Stone,** believed to have been a sacred healing place for the early Hawaiians. You'll have to look over the edge of the seawall to find it. It is shaped like a chair.

Catercorner across Front Street from the back of the Pioneer Inn you'll see the **Baldwin House Museum** (Tel. 661-3262), the proud showpiece of the Lahaina Restoration Foundation. Built in 1834, it housed the medical missionary Dr. Dwight Baldwin and his family from 1838 until 1871. He saved the people of Maui, Molokai, and Lanai from the smallpox epidemic of 1853. The admission price includes a house tour by one of the gracious Lahaina ladies of the foundation. (Open daily 9:30 A.M. to 5 P.M., admission about $2 for adults, free for children.) We also recommend the little booklet "Story of Lahaina," which they sell there for about $1. (Ask also for the free pamphlet outlining a walking tour of cultural points in the area—more sites than we can outline here.) Next door is the **Master's Reading Room,** a two-story coral building built by missionaries for the use of ships' officers. Today it serves as headquarters for the Restoration Foundation.

The foundation has also opened the **Wo Hing Temple** (Tel. 661-5553) much farther along at about 860 Front Street. It depicts the contribution of the Chinese to Lahaina and costs $1 to enter.

A 10-minute walk from the Baldwin House down Front Street and up Prison Road will take you to the place all the coral stones from the demolished waterfront fort went to. The **Hale Paahao,** translatable as the "stuck-in-irons house," is a prison built by convict labor at a leisurely pace from 1852 to 1854. (The walls are original, but the wooden cellblocks inside have been rebuilt.) It housed drunken sailors and Hawaiians alike.

If you have time, you can walk along Wainee Street to Shaw Street and look behind the recently rebuilt Wainee Church for the **Wainee Church-yard.** Perhaps a third of the stones mark the graves of children—missionary babies who just couldn't make it because of hardship and disease. Many famous citizens of old Lahaina are also buried there.

You'll have to drive or ride toward Lahainaluna to see the **Pioneer Sugar Mill,** which has been in continuous operation since 1860. Even farther *mauka* along the Lahainaluna Road is the **Lahainaluna High School,** built by its own first students in 1831 as a mission seminary school. It's not open to the public, but on its grounds is the **Hale Pa'i** ("House of Printing"), which is open daily except Sunday. That 1834 printing house, recently restored, is the site of the first newspaper printed in the Islands—or west of the Rocky Mountains, for that matter. The volunteer curator there may print a page from an old school book for you while you wait. (Admission free.)

Six miles east of Lahaina along Route 30 is the easily overlooked village of **Olowalu,** which is the entry point for the equally obscure dirt road to the **Olowalu Petroglyphs.** The way is no longer marked by a Hawaii Visitors Bureau "warrior" sign. There are about three dirt roads leading *mauka,* but the right one runs by a water tower maybe 100 yards west of the Olowalu general store, almost hidden itself in a clump of trees.

About a mile in, you may see the remains of a wooden stairway that used to help everyone up to inspect the 200- to 300-year-old rock carvings. Today, most of that has been removed to discourage vandalism, and you will have to make like a mountain goat to scramble up the side of the cliff. If you're not that agile, and/or if you're going to the Big Island—where the petroglyphs are somewhat more accessible in the Puako area—these just might not be worth the effort necessary to see them.

Continuing on Highway 30, you might look up the hill from time to time to catch a glimpse of the winding old road, especially above the outcropping which you burrow through in a tunnel. That's the route people like Herman Melville and Mark Twain used to travel on horseback between Lahaina and Wailuku. Maui seemed a much bigger and more adventurous island in the last century, we'll wager.

Stop at **McGregor Point,** which is now only labeled "Scenic Point," to obtain a good view of East Maui (and Haleakala); Kahoolawe, the island the U.S. Navy uses as a great big bomb and shell target range; and Molokini, the little islet that pokes up above the water about halfway between Maui and Kahoolawe. From the air, it's obvious that Molokini is a little volcano crater, breached on one side by the sea, giving it a half-moon shape. A fish sanctuary, it's ideal for snorkeling and scuba diving. (See section 7 for tour information.)

A few miles farther along the road, on the shores of Maalaea Bay, is

Maalaea, today sloppily pronounced "mah-*lie*-ya" by local folks. The tiny village has a small market, a gas pump, a Coast Guard station, a small boat harbor, and Buzz's Restaurant.

CENTRAL MAUI—KIHEI, WAILEA, AND IAO VALLEY

First of all, an interesting target that is a little outside of the route we describe here is the **Maui Tropical Plantation** (Tel. 244-7643) at Waikapu, about halfway between Maalaea and Wailuku on Route 30. The 120-acre Plantation is designed as a living exhibit of Hawaii's tropical agricultural products, including sugar, pineapple, macadamia nuts, coconuts, guavas, bananas, passion fruit, Maui onions, Kona coffee, and other fruits, flowers and vegetables. There's no admission charge to the main facility itself, which of course sells a lot of stuff either to carry away or to ship home direct. But a 20-minute narrated tram tour of all the growing things costs $5. Two or three nights a week, there's also a hayride, square dancing, a paniolo (cowboy) barbecue, and live entertainment. (See section 11.) All this is in a lovely setting, and in a little over two years it's become one of the most popular visitor attractions on the island.

The coastline from Maalaea to Kihei has formed the traditional war-canoe invasion beach for centuries. The U.S. Armed Forces in the 1940s were aware of this; along Route 31 you may still catch sight of one or two structures overgrown by weeds or sugar cane. These were the World War II Block Houses, hastily constructed to prevent the Japanese invasion that never came. You may also still see some tank traps—cement boulders with spikes of railroad rails bristling from them.

Several little beaches along the highway may be reached by short access roads. On some you will find no one else in sight, probably because of the steady and often bothersome wind that comes up at noon and continues until dusk. (The windmill you may see is an experiment by Maui Electric Co. It generates enough electricity to power about 150 homes.) On many of these beaches, members of the 4th Marine Division who were stationed on Maui in 1944 and 1945 trained for the assault on Japanese-held islands in the South Pacific during World War II.

Opposite the Maui Lu Resort is the **Vancouver Monument,** thought to mark the point where Captain George Vancouver landed in the early 1800s. The marker is a totem pole, recalling Vancouver's association with western Canada. The Maui Lu Resort across the road is run by and caters to western Canadians, and somehow all this ties in together.

The little village, area, or whatnot of **Kihei** ("*key*-hay") is not especially attractive, and many tasteless condos sprouted up in the area in the 1970s. A few better ones have come along in the 1980s. In any case it may help that the new *mauka* highway now manages to bypass all of the jumble.

If you continue driving on either road you will enter the **Wailea Resort,** the well-planned vacation community executed by Alexander & Baldwin, a *kamaaina* company that once devoted its attention entirely to sugar. Instead of cutting the public off from the five beautiful beaches next to its land, A&B built a minipark at each with parking lots, paved access, and some rest rooms for everybody, and then turned these facilities over to the county government.

There are two beautiful 18-hole golf courses, plus an 11-court tennis club. The luxurious Hotel Inter-Continental Maui is between **Ulua Beach** and the larger **Wailea Beach,** and the handsome Stouffer's Wailea Beach Hotel is on nearby **Mokapu Beach.** The Wailea Shopping Village, a smallish complex, is also on the property near the highway.

The paved route (Wailea Alanui) ends a short way past **Polo Beach** at the brand new Maui Prince Hotel and the Makena Golf Club. The dirt road beyond it is passable at least to **Makena Beach,** one of the most popular public swimming and surfing shores on the island. (*Warning:* Leave nothing valuable in your car, and watch your belongings in general, if you go swimming in the area.)

Unless you have a rugged vehicle, you should turn back at this point. We *do not* recommend the temptingly short but very rough winding road up the mountain between Makena and Ulupalakua, even if someone tells you the route is okay. (It may be reasonably passable one day, but perhaps not for the next 10 days.) Improvements will come here some day, and when this route is finally smoothed out, we will be among the first to try it as an attractive alternate course to "Up-country Maui" and access to Haleakala. Sometimes the road is officially closed to all traffic of any kind, anyway.

Retracing your route past Kihei, you can turn off onto Highway 35 for a quick march to **Kahului,** Maui's deepwater port and site of the island's jet airport. **Baldwin Beach Park,** near Paia, is about the only good beach on the windward side of the island. Personally, we don't like the atmosphere there all that much.

The rest of Kahului is composed mainly of shopping centers, gas stations, and housing developments. You can continue along Highway 32 (Kaahumanu Avenue) into its twin city, **Wailuku,** the older county seat. The earliest section of Wailuku is in the foothills of the West Maui Mountains. Of the things that are generally pointed out to visitors, we like the little 1832 **Kaahumanu Congregational Church,** the oldest extant church on Maui. It's across from the county government buildings on Route 30, just off Main Street.

The only "don't miss" in Wailuku with which we strongly agree is on the left and just a little farther along Highway 32, the same road that leads to Iao ("ee-*yow*") Valley. This is the **Hale Hoikeike,** the Maui Historical Society museum (Tel. 244-3326). The first part of the stone structure was put up in 1842, and it became the home of local schoolmaster and artist Edward Bailey. Several of his works are exhibited there. There are also many artifacts from both Stone-Age Hawaii and post-Cook periods on display, including items brought to the Islands by the missionaries. (Open 9 A.M. to 3:30 P.M., Monday to Saturday; about $3 adults, $1 children.)

Farther up the road you'll see **Kepaniwai Park,** whose charming, peaceful grounds belie its violent past. Kepaniwai, which takes its name from the stream running through it, means "damming of the waters" and refers to the 1790 slaughter by Kamehameha of the Maui army. The bodies filled the brook, causing *kepaniwai.* (And the water ran red down the valley, too, causing another name change in the village at the bottom: *Wailuku* means, loosely, "Bloody River.") Kamehameha won the battle, incidentally, by introducing cannon into local power politics for the first time. The cannon, named Lopaka ("Robert"), was manned by the king's *haole* advisors John Young and Isaac Davis. Some of the first and still highly revered whites in the Islands were not exactly men of peace and good will. Anyway, Kepaniwai Park was built in recent years as a cultural tribute to the ethnic groups that settled on Maui. There are separate pavilions for Japanese, Filipino, Chinese, Hawaiian, early American, and Portuguese groups.

A little farther up the valley, and on the right, is a strange natural formation known as the **John F. Kennedy Profile.** At one time it was thought that the natural rock formation closely resembled the late president. But as memories of the Kennedy era begin to dim, it does not appear nearly as effective an illusion as it seemed during the 1960s. It seems incredible that the face apparently was not noticed until after the president died.

The end of the road is in **Iao Valley State Park,** the spot that Mark Twain in typical hyperbole called the "Yosemite of the Pacific." The park is at the eroded center of the ancient volcano that created West Maui. The valley floor is already 2,250 feet above sea level, but the most startling feature is a spire of gray and moss-green rock called **Iao Needle.** It doesn't look very tall because there's nothing on top of it to provide a comparison, but this natural basaltic form rises another 1,200 feet above your head.

The green-carpeted cliffs in the valley inspired another writer, Robert Louis Stevenson, to coin a word to describe it—*viridescent.* The moss and small ferns do seem almost to glow when the sun catches them at just the right angle. The cliffs rise about twice as high as the needle, incidentally.

When there has been a heavy rain in the neighborhood, a spectacular waterfall is often seen nearby.

There is a 1½-mile-long trail in the valley, but in the winter you should remember that the sun goes down quickly, leaving you in a very cool shadow as early as 3:30 P.M. The Hawaiian word *iao* is often translated as "facing the dawn," and the steep valley that bears the name has no sunsets.

THE HALEAKALA TRIP—KULA AND POINTS UP, UP, AND UP

Measured from the airport, the trip to the summit of Haleakala, the "House of the Sun," is only 36 miles. It will take you about 2 hours in each direction, however. With the stops you'll want to make in Kula and at the observatory points, it would be a darn good idea to start early. The crater will probably be cloudy at midday and clear in midmorning or late afternoon. Dial the National Weather Service recording, 877-5124, for a weather report on viewing conditions. There is also a national park recording, updated less frequently, at 572-7749. (It is probably updated at about 4 P.M. and 8 A.M.) If you want to check with the park rangers live, try 572-9306 between 8 and 4.

No matter how warm it is at sea level, take a wrap to put on at the summit. (Going up to see the sunrise, especially, many borrow blankets from their hotel rooms.) It will be downright chilly at 10,023 feet at any time of year. A second caveat: If you suffer from high blood pressure or have any other trouble with rare air at high altitudes, let someone else drive the car. Pull over to the side if you begin to feel lightheaded at any point during the trip.

If you've got plenty of gas in the tank, water in the radiator, and perhaps a picnic lunch and a thermos of hot coffee in the back seat, start off along Highway 37 out of Kahului.

Your first sign of civilization over the rolling hills of "Up-country" will be **Pukalani.** There are a couple of gas stations operating there, in case you really *did* forget to fill up down below. Bullock's of Hawaii, a snack and gift shop, is not bad for a "moonburger." (See section 5.) Some on the way up to the sunrise, however, may detour to **Makawao** and search out Komoda's Bakery, 3674 Baldwin Ave. (Route 390, just off Makawao Ave.), which opens at 6:30 A.M., for their delicious cream puffs and long johns. (Or hit it on the way back down if the sunrise is too early.)

Turn onto Route 377 when you reach the junction. It's also known as the Upper Kula Road, and it will lead you over some particularly pleasant pastureland and along stands of eucalyptus and pine trees to **Kula,** the center of the vegetable and flower-growing industries on Maui. The air is nearly always more bracing up here, giving rise to the local slogan

"It's cooler in Kula." In late spring and early summer, you may see many flowering trees in the vicinity. Around the turn of the century the then-thriving Chinese community in Kula was the frequent refuge of Dr. Sun Yat-sen, the leader of the 1912 revolution in China. But Kula is considered a Portuguese community, and if you're driving around this area later you may come across St. Joseph's, the lovely octagonal church, whose altar was brought here from Portugal.

You'll soon come across a modest chalet-hotel at the 3,300-foot level. The Kula Lodge (Tel. 878-1535) has a dining room, cozy lounge, and a fireplace. Persons who plan to spend hours hiking or riding in Haleakala might want to consider their rooms. Doubles run around $50-$60.

A little farther along is the junction with Highway 378, the route that will eventually take you to the top. Almost immediately it begins its twists and turns, and along about here you'll be glad you brought your sweater or jacket.

If it's still morning, you may be able to see all the way down to the ocean while you continue to climb. If it's later in the day, you may be driving through mist and rain. If it seems foggy, don't give up. It could still be a beautiful day where you're going, in the land beyond the clouds.

At about 7,000 feet above the ocean there's a side road off to the left to **Hosmer Grove Campground** about one quarter mile in. If you brought a picnic and you're hungry now, this glen full of exotic shrubs and trees is the traditional place to eat it. There are rest rooms, a couple of picnic tables, a barbecue pit, and perhaps no one else to talk to.

Just ahead is the entrance to **Haleakala National Park** and soon after, the park headquarters. Incidentally, this was the first building we ever saw in Hawaii that was centrally heated, radiators being about as common as snowmen in the state. Load up here on information, literature, etc.; this is also the place you secure your camping and hiking permits, if needed.

In the front yard of the building are planted several examples of the rare silversword, that strange, delicate plant that grows only on Haleakala and high up on the Big Island, and nowhere else in the world. It blooms just once, and dies shortly afterwards. (By the way, the silversword, like everything else alive in the park, is of course strictly protected by law. Recently some idiot pulled up a silversword intending to grow it at his home in Baldwinsville, N.Y. He was quickly caught, arrested, and fined; the fragile specimen was replanted immediately but soon died.)

And in case you don't see them in the wild, there are a couple of specimens of *nene*, the Hawaiian native goose, penned up in the back yard at park headquarters. The *nene* has a black patch over his eye, but more significant is the lack of webbing between the toes. Over the centuries, this feature has evolved for living among the rough lava flows, whereas webbing, of course, is more suited for paddling around in a lake.

From headquarters it's 11 more miles to the summit. There are two overlooks to the crater on the way, Leleiwi and Kalahaku, but save them for the trip back. Push on to the Visitor Center at 9,745 feet, where the park rangers give occasional talks. (It used to open at dawn to welcome the sunrise crowd, but because of recent federal economy moves, the hours have been restricted to 8 A.M. to 3 P.M.) A little farther, the unattended observatory at the summit (open 24 hours) is the traditional place to watch the sunrise.

The beautiful scene of desolation spread out in front of you has been compared to the mountains of the moon. It's an awesome crater—seven miles long, two miles wide, 8,000 feet deep—supposedly enough to hold the entire island of Manhattan, Bronx to Battery, East Side to West Side, subways to skyscrapers. Throughout this huge crater are smaller craters, a miniature mountain range of cinder cones. Everywhere there are muted colors—rust, gray, purple, brown, black, yellow, and an occasional pink.

The way to really experience the Haleakala Crater is to hike or take horseback trips into it. There are 30 miles of well-marked trails, and excursions are occasionally conducted by park rangers. Three cabins are within the crater, none closer than 7½ miles to the rim observatory. Fees are cheap, but the cabins are booked months in advance, and the bookings are made by National Park Service lottery since requests far outnumber the bunks available.

Full information on hiking, riding, and camping may be obtained in advance by writing the Superintendent, Haleakala National Park, Box 537, Makawao, Maui, HI 96768. On Maui itself, you may telephone the park headquarters at 572-9306.

Also near the summit of Haleakala are several scientific and military technical installations, once called Science City. One ground station here keeps constant surveillance on satellites and all objects in deep space. In 1985, a low-power laser beam from here was bounced off one of the space shuttles in one of the first tests of the proposed "Star Wars" missile defense technology.

If you didn't enter the crater and missed seeing examples of the silversword there or at park headquarters, you will have another chance near the **Kalahaku Overlook** on the way back down.

At the bottom of the crater road—Route 378—you may want to turn left (south) on 377, Kekaulike Avenue, and search out a commercial protea flower farm. One we like very much is the **Maui Sunburst** (Tel. 878-1218), on the somewhat hard-to-find Copp Road, which is about a mile and a half from the end of 378. Say "Hi" for us to Carver or

Skelly, the two friends who run the operation. (Closed Saturday.) Unfortunately, Copp Road is marked better at its junction with the lower road, Route 37.

Even farther south, another 10 miles or so along the narrow and twisting portion of Route 37, you will eventually arrive at Ulupalakua Ranch and the tasting room of the **Tedeschi Winery** (Tel. 878-6058), in a century-old jailhouse (open 10 A.M. to 5 P.M.). Beginning in 1972, the winery had only pineapple wine to offer—Maui Blanc and the sparkling Maui Brut. But in 1983, Emil Tedeschi finally unveiled some real stuff—a champagne made from Carnelian grapes grown on the side of Haleakala. Production of this Blanc de Noirs has been low, and it's hard to find outside of Maui itself. It retails for around $17 a bottle at the winery. A new fruity young red, Maui Nouveau, debuted in 1985, and another, more full-bodied red, Maui Blush, was released in 1986.

HANA—THE SPIRIT OF OLD HAWAII

"Heavenly Hana," they call it. And maybe it is that way because it's almost as hard to get to. Officially it's just under 53 miles from Kahului Airport on Route 36, but that's a trip that will take nearly three hours each way when the weather is good. When it's not, well, you just don't go. If there's a washout on the road, you could be trapped for hours.

We've been to Hana both by land and by air, and you might want to consider taking the plane, too. Princeville Airways flies there, and so do some charter or tour operations out of Kahului like Paragon Air. When we flew in once, we rented a car to explore the immediate area. But you can't "deadhead" a rented car into or out of Hana. You either have to fly both ways or drive both ways.

Check your gas and your tummy in the village of **Paia,** a last-chance stop on the way. (You may want to look into the Paia General Store or the Maui Crafts Guild store there.) Paia seems a sleepy place today with no sign of the activity of World War II, when it was the closest real town to Camp Maui, headquarters of the Fourth Marine Division. (Camp Maui now has been completely demolished, but there's a commemorative plaque on the Kokomo Road.) Ten miles after Paia the road gets rough and your Hana safari has begun.

Now right about here is where we should say that travelers vary widely in their reaction to the Hana road. We get letters annually from some readers who ask how we could have the nerve to put them on such a terrible, difficult, and winding road with narrow, one-lane bridges. Others write to tell us that they don't know what we were making such a fuss about. The route was fine, they say, with the rewards well worth the extra effort. Perhaps it has to do with what one's driving experience has been in other areas. In any case, you'll have to make up your own mind, but don't say we didn't warn you. We suggest, however, that if you have a choice you'd be better off not traveling the route on Saturday or Sunday when there is more local traffic around. If you notice a line of cars following just behind you, pull over when you can and let everyone pass.

You'll find plenty of tempting places to stop, but don't lose track of your time. There are some occasional freshwater swimming holes. A favorite of ours is at **Puohokamoa Falls** almost halfway to Hana, 25 miles from Kahului (just before you get to Kaumahina State Wayside Park). The falls are just out of sight, but only a few yards along a pathway beyond a low stone wall. Then, many like to drive down the steep hill onto the **Keanae Peninsula**, once the site of a large Hawaiian community, now populated by a few houses and horses. Back on the road, a little further along, is the short turnoff for **Wailua**. (One of these days we're going to stop there to see the "shell lady" who makes shell jewelry in her home across from the Coral Miracle Church in Wailua. Let us know if you meet her first.)

Other wonderful picnic spots include **Puaa Kaa State Park,** about four miles further along, where two waterfalls and a pair of natural pools occur right beside the highway. In fact, if you didn't stop back at Puohokamoa, be sure to do so now, at least for a minute or two, at this photogenic spot.

You'll see fascinating vegetation along most of the road to Hana, like the giant *ape-ape* ("*ah*-pay, *ah*-pay") leaves, African tulip trees, and breadfruit trees. If you like guavas, sometimes you can pick up hundreds along the road to **Hana Airport,** for example.

About a half mile farther from the airport road is **Waianapanapa State Park** ("why a *nah*-pah *nah*-pah"), which offers camping or rustic accommodations in a dozen cabins (if you've made advance reservations). Also in the park are trails through the *hala* or pandanus trees to hard-to-find **Waianapanapa Caves,** where you can swim underground in some water-filled lava tubes.

Here's another trick we haven't tried, but some readers have managed to make it under these instructions: At low tide, there's a second chamber in the cave which you can locate only by floating something ahead of you like a surfboard with a light on it. If you do, you will find a natural rock throne where a Hawaiian princess once tried to hide from her jealous husband. But he saw in the water the reflection of her feather *kahili* (the symbol of royalty), entered the secret chamber, and killed her there along with her servant. Today the water is supposed to turn red one day every spring in supernatural testimony to that tragedy.

A mile before Hana is the privately owned **Helani Gardens** (admission $2). Trees and plants are labeled not only with genus and species but by various literary quotations and aphorisms that its septuagenarian owner has found interesting enough to pass on.

As you enter Hana, there's a fork in the road. Either route will take you into the village, but the rougher road on the right follows the high ground and provides the first distant view of the lovely **Hana Bay.** The beach park down below is a beautiful picnic site, but the swimming is not all that great. In ancient times this gentle and peaceful inlet witnessed countless invasions from the Big Island, only 30 miles away. The **Hotel Hana-Maui,** the town's principal means of support, is the only place in town open for dinner. (See sections 4 and 5.)

Across the street from the hotel is the charming little **Wananalua Church,** built in 1838, appropriately enough on the site of a *heiau,* thus physically supplanting the old religion with the new. As much of a sight as any in Hana is the funky commercial establishment made famous in the now seldom-sung song, the **Hasegawa General Store.** Here's where you get the bumper stickers with Hana's solution to gasoline and pollution problems—"Get a Horse," it advises. (And it looks like Hasegawa's just might sell you one, too, right off the counter.)

The paved but now increasingly rough and rutty road (Route 36) continues through the lush and unhurried countryside for ten miles or so beyond the village of Hana. On quiet weekdays, you may have trouble skirting the sleeping dogs in the road in order to drive through. But dogs aren't the only hazards.

On one trip, we saw a sign that declared in no uncertain terms: "Beware of Goat!" Suddenly we saw the Big Gruff Billy himself, trying to stare us down from the shoulder of the road. And another notice farther on slowed us even more. "Caution for Little Pigs Crossing Road," it said, alongside a silhouette of three little porkers. These we didn't see in the flesh, but it wasn't for lack of looking!

A few miles out of town a sign indicates **Hamoa Beach,** on a separate loop off the main road. Not as beautiful as it's sometimes cracked up to be, the sand is reached over land owned by the Hotel Hana-Maui, which maintains the beach as part of its private facilities. (Some Mavericks have reported that they have successfully invaded this beach despite all the intimidating signs.)

Continuing along the main road, you may be able to catch sight of the Big Island across the Alenuihaha Channel. In the winter, look for the snowcapped peaks of Mauna Kea and more-distant Mauna Loa.

The large cross you will soon see at the side of the road is dedicated to Helio Kawaloa, an early Catholic Hawaiian who converted 4,000 more to his faith. He is buried down the hill in the ruins of the deserted Wailua village. A little ways farther is **Wailua Falls,** a dramatic cascade that thunders down beside the road. You may get a better look at it on the way back if you have time then.

Just when you think there is no such thing, you round your last curve to find the **Seven Pools of Kipahulu,** sometimes (incorrectly) referred to as the Seven Sacred Pools, 10 miles from Hana. Since the Kipahulu Valley down to the ocean is now part of Haleakala National Park, you will probably find a ranger there to answer your questions about the area. (Sometimes he conducts special field trips. Telephone 248-8260 for information.)

The road crosses the stream between pool number four and pool number five. Park your car in the parking area beyond the bridge and walk back to it and then down along the lower pools to the ocean. Swimming, picnicking, and camping (with permit for the latter) are certainly allowed, but bring your own drinking water. The area has become so popular that it can be unpleasantly crowded on weekends. And some readers have complained of hordes of mosquitoes during wet weather.

If you want, you may continue for a little over two miles farther along the road to visit **Charles Lindbergh's Grave.** The great aviator picked out and cleared the site himself more than a year before his death. He chose the churchyard of the 1850 Kipahulu Hawaiian Church, a couple of hundred yards off the road. (Not to be confused with St. Paul's Church nearby.) The grave, now marked with a simple marble stone, is *makai* of the church near a natal plum tree. Lindbergh died August 26, 1974, and was buried the same day, in accordance with his instructions.

Unless you have a Jeep or something similar, you're now supposed to return the same way you came. The unpaved road from this point west for the next 10 miles miles or so is rough, and to travel it is a violation of a rental car contract, invalidating the insurance, etc. (Depending on the weather and other transient factors, the road is indeed often impassable.) Those who continue on successfully eventually find themselves on the Kula Highway at Ulupalakua Ranch, the Tedeschi Winery, etc.

7. Guided Tours and Cruises on Maui

Robert's Hawaii, Inc. (Tel. 871-6226) and **Akamai Tours,** both all-Island companies, **Maui Island Tours** (Tel. 8716226), a Maui agency, and probably **Trans Hawaiian Maui** (Tel. 8777308) begin their tours in Kahului. Two other companies—**Grayline Maui** (Tel. 877-5507) and **Holo Holo Maui** (Tel. 661-4858)—offer theirs originating at Kaanapali. Arrangements can be made with any of these for pickup in the Wailea area. All but Holo Holo Maui and Akamai Tours use big buses, limousines, and vans. Holo Holo and Akamai pride themselves on offering tours in minibuses only. A newer outfit recently recommended by a reader is **Ekahi Tours** (Tel. 572-9775).

Some typical bus tours include the following:

Iao Valley–Haleakala Crater. 10 hours. From your Kaanapali or Wailea hotel, via Wailuku, to see the Iao Needle and then way up to the crater. This is a long trip, and in winter it will be dark before you get back to your hotel.

Kaanapali–Iao Valley–Kula Drive. 8 hours. Similar to the above, but instead of continuing up to see Haleakala Crater, you turn around in Kula, the village on the slopes.

Lahaina. 3 hours. From your Kaanapali hotel, the tour takes you to old Lahaina town, stops at the old prison and the fort, and brings you back again.

Small van or minibus tours are much more numerous, flexible, and changeable. As of this writing, Holo Holo Maui, for example, has the following set of tours in 12-passenger vehicles (don't hold us to these estimated prices): Heavenly Hana, $65; Haleakala Sunrise, $55; Haleakala and Central Maui, $55; Iao Valley and Lahaina, $70; Haleakala Sunset, $65; and the Circle Island Tour, $65. (Reservations at P.O. Box 1591, Lahaina, HI 96761.) We've taken one tour with the laid-back Holo Holo operation, and we like them very much.

Another small van tour for those who make it into Hana on their own, whether by air or by any other means, is the unique and personalized **Tiny's Hana Tours** (Tel. 248-8685). Tiny's is one van and one man, named Viewed "Tiny" Malaikini, a 300-pound-plus musical Hawaiian born in Hana who's been around the world and come back home again. A large part of the attraction is Tiny's jovial but respectful personality, and he'll tailor his tour to the wants of his passengers. At the moment, Tiny's tours are selling for $25 per person for three hours and $50 for six hours. (You can reserve in advance by phone or by writing him at P.O. Box 41, Hana, HI 96713. Bookings are also made through Paragon Air—see "Air Tours" later.) Tiny's is the only game in town—and it's a good one, too. We've enjoyed Tiny's tour ourselves, so say hello to him from us!

MAUI BY HORSEBACK

We used to file these under section 9 (Sports), but we've changed it now since in theory, at least, the horses get more of a workout than you do. In any case, there are a few good riding tours on the island. (We'd particularly like to have your reaction to any of the outfits listed below.)

One of the best is run by Jerry and Margaret Thompson at **Thompson's Ranch and Riding Stables** (Tel. 878-1910) up in Kula. The Thompsons offer one- and two-hour escorted trail rides around their Up-country ranch, which is certainly scenic enough, for about $15 per person per hour. But the best deal is probably the all-day trip into Haleakala Crater for perhaps $125. (*Honolulu* magazine writer Brett Uprichard put it well when he said that Jerry offers "tame rides with wild views.") To get to the ranch take Route 37 past the main part of Kula, turn left at the sign to the Kula Sanatorium and Hospital, then take an almost immediate right onto Thompson Road, which, after a mile and a half, leads to the ranch. Jerry says many of his riders have never been on a horse before, so he has some gentle mounts available. Wear long trousers and long-sleeved shirts, and say "howdy" for us, too.

Pony Express Tours (Tel. 667-2202) features a similar all-day crater ride at a similar price. But P.E. also has a half-day, abbreviated crater tour for around $80, provided at least four riders can be assembled. Everybody meets at the crater rim, but call the above number for details. Or write in advance to P.O. Box 507, Makawao, Maui, HI 96768.

In West Maui, you might try **Kaanapali Kau Lio** (Tel. 667-7896), which offers two-hour guided rides a half-hour away from Lahaina on the sloping meadows above Kaanapali for about $40 per person. You can't drive there, though. Call the phone number and they'll pick you up. Then there's **Adventures on Horseback** (Tel. 242-7445), where Frank Levinson limits his riders to only four per excursion, and you should have at least some riding experience. His most popular excursion is the day-long "Waterfall Ride" for around $100. A newer operation is at **Rainbow Ranch** (Tel. 669-4991), 11 miles north of Lahaina near the end of the new highway near Napili. There are rides designed for both amateurs and experienced horsemen. Sorry, we haven't been personally, and don't know anyone who has.

BOAT CRUISES FROM MAUI

The situation on the docks is bound to be at least a little different by the time of your arrival. In this buoyant and buffeted business, cruise boats come and go with the tide. Maui is probably the best island from which to go sailing, however, and here is how we see it for 1987. (Be sure to tell 'em we sent you.)

Heading into the waves directly from Kaanapali Beach is **Sea Sails** (Tel. 661-0927), headquartered at the Sheraton. Their catamaran *Seahorse* offers a three-hour luncheon cruise with a snorkeling expedition for perhaps $55, and a sunset cocktail sail with open bar for about $45.

There are several vessels to choose from at the boat harbor in front of the old courthouse in Lahaina. Those designed primarily for fishing or scuba charters will be found under our section 8, Water Sports. Here are those offering regular cruises:

Three boats are now under the command of Captain Jon S. Dilloway, probably all tied up at about Pier 1, even if they do have three different phone numbers: The 65-foot glass-bottom powerboat, named (with no apologies for the spelling) the **Coral See** (Tel. 661-8600), cruises clearer waters than those on Oahu. Half-day picnic/snorkel tours to Molokini, with equipment, instruction, and lunch, now run $55 or so. Then the souped-up, 52-foot Chinese junk called the **Lin Wa II** (Tel. 661-3392) offers 1½-hour glass bottoming for around $12 about five times a day. If you bring a bathing suit, you can help feed the fish. And the **Spirit of Windjammer** (Tel. 667-6834), a 65-foot schooner, makes all-day trips to Lanai for around $80 and dinner cruises off Lahaina for $40 or so. From December through May, whale-watching excursions are usually scheduled on all three boats for around $25. Children's fares are about half price on all trips. Just at deadline, the Coral See operation has just announced a new excursion to Molokai and back aboard the 50-foot yacht *Leilani*. Round-trip tickets are around $60—proportionately more depending on whether your want a tour or rental car for the day on Molokai. (Reserve for any of these from Captain Jon at P.O. Box 596, Lahaina, HI 96761.)

Scotch Mist Charters (Tel. 661-0386) launches several sails aboard the 36-foot sloop *Scotch Mist* or the 50-foot yacht *Scotch Mist II*. Look for them at Piers 10 and 11. Afternoon Snorkel Sails run perhaps $55 (or all-day for around $90), including equipment, refreshments, etc. A two-hour Champagne Sunset Sail goes for around $35, at this writing. Call Skipper Paul Schatzkin or his wife Georja (who quit the Hollywood TV rat race so they could have this kind of life) or write them at P.O. Box 845, Lahaina, HI 96761 to make advance reservations.

The 50-foot trimaran *Trilogy*, built by the late E. J. Coon, is still operated by his family as **Trilogy Excursions** (Tel. 661-4743). Day-long sails to Lanai go Monday through Friday for about $110, including breakfast, a car tour of Lanai, snorkeling, and lunch. This is a popular trip, and parties are kept small. (If necessary a second, 40-foot trimaran, the *Kailana*, is also put in service.) We've had several letters praising the Coons' operation, although we've never gone ourselves. Phone or write Jim Coon or his family at P.O. Box 1121, Lahaina, HI 96761.

All-day cruises to Lanai are launched from Pier 2 by **Seabird Cruises** (Tel. 661-3643) in the two-masted ketch *Viajero*. With breakfast, lunch, snorkeling, and Lanai bus tour, the whole excursion may run around $100 this year (half-price for junior sea scouts). There may also be a five-hour Picnic Snorkel Sail for around $45, a Sunset Mai Tai Sail (two hours) for around $30, and a Cocktail Dinner Cruise (roast beef, open bar, entertainment) for around $50. We once took a rough trip to Molokai aboard their catamaran, the *Olo Mana* (formerly the *Aikane II*), although one reader told us he enjoyed it a lot when combined with the optional bus tour by "Uncle Ben" on Molokai.

We may have erred in passing on a critical comment by a reader about **Alihilani Yacht Charters** (Tel. 661-3047). Understandably annoyed, Alihilani sent us pages of compliments Xeroxed from their guest book that can't be denied. The company lists several trips from a two-hour sail for around $30 to all-day trips to Lanai for $120 or so. We haven't been aboard ourselves, and we'd like to hear from some more who have. (Reservations from P.O. Box 1286, Lahaina, HI 96761.)

Newly in operation in Maui now is **Captain Zodiac Raft Expeditions** (Tel. 667-5351), an outgrowth of the successful parent firm on Kauai. The rubber-boat operation charges around $75 for a six-hour snorkeling cruise to Lanai and back.

Pat Morgan of Milwaukee has written to us of a "great" time with the new **Kamehameha Catamaran Sails** (Tel. 661-4522) aboard a 40-foot catamaran that limits its passengers to only 15 per trip: "We saw several whales and porpoises on the two-hour trip which cost $20." Kamehameha also has snorkel tours and sunset sails.

Turning from Lahaina, now, two very well-run snorkel cruises sail out of the Maalaea Harbor every morning at 7:30 A.M. One is aboard the *Wailea Kai*, run by the **Ocean Activities Center** (Tel. 879-4485). The 65-foot catamaran heads for the tiny, half-moon-shaped islet of Molokini, which cradles a marine conservation area. On the way the crew instructs you in safe and fun snorkeling activities, then turns you loose under their watchful eyes to observe the hundreds of kinds of multicolored fish under the surface. With breakfast and lunch, the price will be around $55 in 1987.

The other is an all-day snorkeling and land tour to Lanai aboard the 56-foot "power cat" *Maka Kai*. The price is about $90, including lunch at the little Hotel Lanai. Since Maalaea Harbor is a long way from Lanai (as compared to Lahaina Harbor), the trip between the two islands takes at least two hours, however. We've been on both Ocean Activities excursions and were impressed by the friendly and knowledgeable crew. In season, the same company also operates two-hour whale-watching cruises in Maalaea Harbor for around $25. And there's a Sunset Champagne Sail, with dinner and drinks, for around $45. (Reservations from the phone number above, at either of the two Wailea hotels, or from the Ocean Activities Center at 3750 Wailea Alanui D-2, Wailea, HI 96753.) Tell 'em we sent you!

We have had a letter from an Alabama couple praising **Sail Hawaii** (Tel. 879-2201), which takes a maximum of six people direct from the beach at Kihei. Price is around $55 per person for a two-hour trip, including lunch. Sail Hawaii's mailing address is P.O. Box 573, Kihei, HI 96753.

Maui's newest, fastest, and largest cruise vessel is the 250-passenger *Prince Kuhio*, a power craft custom-built for **Maui-Molokai Sea Cruises** (Tel. 242-8777). It specializes in full-day excursions from Maalaea Harbor to Lanai or Molokai (with lunch and a bus tour) and back for about $125 per adult passsenger (half fares for small fry). The 92-foot *Prince* boasts such royal amenities as air conditioning, sit-down tables, etc., and may be more comfortable for the less active. Still, there's an open-air upper deck, it also runs some snorkel cruises to Molokini or La Perouse Bay for around $60, and it even has a freshwater shower so you can get the salt off without waiting until you return to your hotel.

Besides the above cruises, there will surely be others riding the waves this year. Three booking services try to stay afloat on a changing sea of information. Besides the aforementioned Ocean Activities Center, you might check with the **Aloha Activity Center** (Tel. 667-9564) in the Whalers Village and at The Wharf in Lahaina, or the **Maui Visitor Information & Activity Center** (Tel. 661-8340) on Halawai Drive in Lahaina. These agencies draw a commission from the boats themselves, so it should not cost you any more to make your bookings through them.

AIR TOURS ON MAUI

The flight patterns change rapidly, but the current big whirlybird for sightseeing seems to be **Maui Helicopters** (Tel. 879-1601), with two four-passenger Hughes 500D jet helicopters stationed at the Hotel Inter-Continental Maui. Three tours include "Remote Excursion" (40 minutes)—the central valley, rain forests, waterfalls, and Hana town, for around $110 per passenger; "Panoramic Journey" (55 minutes)—Hana, Seven Pools, and Haleakala Crater, about $140; and "Maui Unlimited" (80 minutes)—the entire island for $200 or so. We've been with this outfit and would probably fly them again—something we would not say about all companies.

Three other chopper firms are on Maui. **Kenai Air Hawaii** (Tel. 661-4426), an extension of the Honolulu company, has three Maui tours with departures from Kaanapali and Kapalua. They are the "Maui Deluxe," including Haleakala Crater and Hana, with a touchdown in an otherwise inaccessible area for about $200 per person; "West Maui and North Shore of Molokai," including Kalaupapa and a stop at an otherwise inaccessible beach, $165; and "Maui's West Coast and Mountains and Iao Valley," about $120.

South Sea Helicopters (Tel. 667-7765), a newer company, also offers several tours, including a 1½-hour flight called "Pacific Fantasy" covering the entire island. With a beach stop and a meal, it may run over $150 this year. We will not fly on **Papillon Helicopters,** which does not have as good a safety record as we would like (although most of their problems have been on Kauai, not Maui).

Touring helicopters get most of the publicity, but good bargains can sometimes be found on fixed-wing aerial tours in Hawaii. The best one-man operation we found is **Paragon Air** (Tel. 244-3356). Pilot Peter Wolford and his wife have organized several aerial programs, including a one-hour tour of East Maui for $100 or so, and an hour-and-45-minute tour that adds to that Lanai and Molokai for around $150. Combination air-ground tours have been set up, too, including one that connects with the above-mentioned Tiny's Hana Tours. We've flown with Peter in his sleek, high-winged Italian Partenavia, and enjoyed every thrilling second of it. If you go, give him our warmest happy landings!

SPECIAL TOURS

One of Maui's most unusual tours is provided by **Cruiser Bob's Haleakala Downhill** (Tel. 667-7717), headquartered at the Lahaina TraveLodge. For $85 or so, C. B. will take you to the top of 10,000-foot Haleakala, give you breakfast, then put you in a specially equipped bicycle, and lead you and others in a coasting tour down the mountain for 38 miles. Some have called it "an experience of a lifetime." The newer, competing operation is **Maui Downhill** (Tel. 871-2155), which at this writing charges slightly less than Bob's for a similar trip. Reports are that this one is pretty good, too.

Hiking? We have some general notes on hiking in section 9, but we should mention that guided hiking tours are offered daily by **Hike Maui** (Tel. 879-5270). At this writing, this is a one-man operation run by experienced naturalist Ken Schmitt, who has favorite spots in the outback you're not likely to see otherwise. We haven't met Ken yet, however. Call his number or write him at P.O. Box 10506, Lahaina, HI for further information.

8. Water Sports on Maui

Of Maui's 150 miles of coastline, some 32½ miles are lined with beaches. Many are not even named, which does not dim their popularity with beachcombers, surfers, swimmers, snorkelers, or fishermen.

We stick stubbornly to the southerly shores. Local pride notwithstanding, there is virtually no good swimming along the entire windward coast of Maui—or if there is, please tell *us* about it. We couldn't find a decent beach over there except for **Baldwin Park,** near Paia on the road to Hana. It's often populated by youthful beer drinkers, and some say that the sharks are all on the shore at Baldwin. The offshore current is also strong. Just a little further along, however, is **Hookipa Beach,** famous as one of the first and best areas in the country for wind surfing.

Kahului Beach behind the Kahului hotels is almost a joke. Supposedly, however, it's good for hunting "Maui diamonds," which are actually little white quartz stones. We never saw any, but then we didn't look very hard.

All the most desirable beaches are leeward, or on the southern shores. Here are some selected targets for beachniks there, progressing generally from west to east:

D. T. Fleming Beach Park, formerly known as Honokohau Beach, near the end of the paved portion of Highway 30. Good swimming, surfing, fishing, and shelling. **Pokakupele Beach,** sometimes called Windmill Beach, is better for fishing and shelling than for swimming.

Honolua Beach has good swimming, surfing, skin diving, and scuba diving. One of the finest habitats for live coral and reef fish in the state, it has now been named a State Marine Life Conservation District.

Makuleia Beach has good swimming and fishing. **Honokahua Beach** has good swimming, snorkeling, and skin diving.

Kapalua Beach, once known as Fleming Beach, is one of the finest beaches on Maui for swimming, snorkeling, skin diving, and scuba. The Kapalua Bay Hotel opened right on this beach, but there is public access from an obscure road.

Napili Beach fronts the Napili Kai and other hotels on Napili Bay. There's good swimming, snorkeling, surfing, skin diving, and scuba diving there. **Honokowai Beach Park,** at Honokowai, offers fair swimming and snorkeling off narrow sands.

Kaanapali Beach. Three miles of beautiful sandy beach fronting more than a half-dozen luxury hotels and condos. Good swimming except when the surf is high (look for the red flags put out by the hotels). Good body surfing fronting the Sheraton.

Lahaina shoreline. Little beach—except a bit of sand at the Lahaina Shores Hotel—but there are excellent spots dotted along the entire Lahaina coastline for swimming, surfing, shelling, fishing, snorkeling, and skin diving in shallow water.

Launiupoko State Park, a wayside picnic park you'll notice between Lahaina and Olowalu. Nobody likes to talk about it much, but the surfers call this area "Shark Pit." It is indeed a breeding ground for small sharks during May, June, and July. It's not a good swimming area, anyway, although it's okay for fishing and hunting shells.

Olowalu Shore, near Hekili Point. Not only are there good swimming, surfing, fishing, skin diving, and scuba diving, but this is the best place for hunting those "Maui diamonds," described above at Kahului Beach.

Kihei Memorial Park. No swimming. Picnic only. **Kalama Beach Park.** Heavy coral here makes for poor swimming. **Kamaole Beach Parks I, II, and III** all have excellent swimming and good snorkeling and fishing.

Keawakapu, Mokapu, Ulua, Wailea, and Polo beaches. These five beaches, which were developed by the Wailea Resort, are excellent for swimming. There's also good fishing and snorkeling around the rocks. When the waves come in during the summer months, they are excellent for body surfing.

Makena Beach. Popular until recently with an exclusive surfing coterie, but now gaining in general use. The winter surf is big, but when waters are tame it's also a good swimming, fishing, and shelling area. (*Caution:* There are often thefts from cars in this area.) **Little Makena Beach,** just the other side of the rock promontory at Makena's north end, is Maui's most famous nude beach.

The Nuu Shore. Running from the Makena beaches to La Perouse Bay, this rugged area of dirt trails and steep cliffs does offer good shelling and fishing. Surfing is for experts only at La Perouse Bay due to the steep cliffs and razor-sharp lava fingers in the area.

Hana Beach Park. This picturesque beach at the village of Hana does offer good swimming and fishing. **Hamoa Beach.** Near Hana, all land access to this beach is controlled by the Hotel Hana-Maui, making it almost a private beach for the hotel's guests only. Swimming and snorkeling are excellent, but the grey sand is certainly not as lovely as many other beaches on West Maui.

Freshwater Swimming. There are several natural pools along Highway 36 to Hana and beyond, nearly all at the bottom of waterfalls. Some of these include Waikamoi Stream, Puohokamoa Falls, Haipuaena Falls, Koolau Park, Puaa Kaa State Park, Hanawi Falls, and the famous Seven Pools of Kipahulu.

SCUBA DIVING AND SNORKELING

Some of the best diving grounds in Hawaii are found in the channel running from Olowalu to Kaanapali. The coastline from Kihei to Makena is also good, as are Napili Bay and Fleming Beach. But divers should check with local experts to be fully aware of hazards in these waters.

Snorkelers will also find beautiful viewing in the same areas, but generally close in to shore. (An exception is at Molokini Island; see section 7.)

Instructions and equipment rental are available at several dive shops in Lahaina. These include **Central Pacific Divers** (Tel. 661-8718), the granddaddy of most of them, at 780 Front St.; **Lahaina Divers** (Tel. 667-7496) at 710 Front St.; **Hawaiian Reef Divers** (Tel. 667-7647) at 129 Lahainaluna Road; and **Captain Nemo's Ocean Emporium** (Tel. 661-5555) at Front and Dickenson streets.

One dive shop now has a Kihei address: **Maui Dive Shop** (Tel. 879-3388) in the Azeka Place Shopping Center. At any of these, figure $50 or so for a half-day of scuba instruction, if the shop arranges everything.

Accomplished divers may experience some fascinating underwater adventures on Maui. Central Pacific and other dive shops like to take their clients to the huge underwater caves called the Lanai Cathedrals, 60 feet down.

SPORT FISHING

No license is required for deep-sea fishing. Catches include marlin, *mahimahi, aku* (skipjack), barracuda, *kawakawa* (bonito), *ulua* (jack crevalle), *ahi* (yellowfin tuna), wahoo, and bonefish.

There are several well-known charter outfits, many of which sail from the small boat harbor at Lahaina and some from the marina at Maalaea. All officially charge about $300 for a half day (four hours) and $500 for a full, eight-hour day for the entire boat (up to six persons). Some will stick to these official rates, but you might try to make your contacts in person to see how good a deal you can snag when the captain doesn't have to pay an agent's commission. Many will also set up trips on a "share-boat" basis.

The number of skippers who have skipped on and off the Maui charter scene over the past few years has been too much for us to keep up with, so we can no longer list individual boats and crews. If you're interested in deep-sea fishing, either (a) go down to the docks in Lahaina or Maalaea and strike up a conversation with a captain or his mate; (b) seek advice from your hotel activities desk; or (c) call any of the three Maui activities centers, who are all up on the latest boats and rates available. The Aloha Activity Center (Tel. 667-9564), the Ocean Activities Center (Tel. 879-4485), and the Maui Visitor Information & Activity Center (Tel. 661-8340) should have all the dope on charter fishing, and, of course, lots of other activities.

MORE WATER SPORTS

If you dislike booking a cruise but still want to get out on the water, you can be your own captain. "Bareboat charters," as they're called, are available to experienced sailors at **Seabern Yachts** (Tel. 661-8110). Boats range from 27 to 36 feet and are available from half days at about $45 on up to a week's cruise, varying between $700 and $2,000. We have no personal experience with this firm. You may want to write them first at P.O. Box 1022, Lahaina, HI 96761.

There is now water-skiing at Kaanapali Beach, something that was missing on the local scene for some time. **Ski Hawaiian** (Tel. 244-9451) offers excursions for up to four people ranging from $40 for a half hour to $120 for two hours the last time we looked. Better call for details. A similar pleasure—for some—are those motorized monsters you can rent at **Jammin' Jet Skis** across from Suda's store on Kihei Beach. The rate for jammin' up and down the beach at last report was $35 per half hour or $50 per hour, and two people are allowed to spell each other as needed. You might want earplugs.

9. Other Sports on Maui

On Maui, *hunting* is becoming almost as popular a sport as fishing. Year-round game mammals include wild boar in the West Maui mountains and goats on the northern and western slopes of Haleakala. Bag limit is two each per day. Game birds include pheasants, doves, quail, wild turkey, francolin, and chukar partridge in the Kula-Kahikinui Game Management Area.

Licenses for nonresidents are $15. All hunting is under State of Hawaii jurisdiction, so up-to-date information on Maui hunting should be obtained from the Division of Fish and Game, Hawaii Department of Land and Natural Resources, State Building, Wailuku, HI 96793. The telephone number is 244-4352.

There are at least eight *golf* courses open to the public on the island, and naturally they are used all year round. Fees can be expensive, however, and you might want to shop around for the best deal. The most famous course is the **Royal Kaanapali** (Tel. 661-3691), North and South Courses, which wind regally through the Kaanapali resort area.

The **Wailea Golf Club** (Tel. 879-2966) is split into a Blue Course and an Orange Course. The **Kapalua Golf Course** (Tel. 669-8044), designed by Arnold Palmer, is the nucleus of the Kapalua Bay Resort. Each of these resorts has 36 holes. Green fees are $35 for guests in the two Wailea hotels, a whopping $50 for others.

Other courses include the **Maui Country Club** (Tel. 877-0616) at Sprecklesville, the **Waiehu Municipal Golf Course** (Tel. 244-5433) at Waiehu, the **Makena Golf Course** (Tel. 879-3344), past Wailea, and the **Pukalani Country Club** (Tel. 572-1314) at Pukalani.

There are three obvious *tennis* centers serving Maui. First is the 14-court **Wailea Tennis Club** (Tel. 879-1958) in the Wailea Resort near the Hotel Inter-Continental Maui. Three courts are lighted; another three are grass. Court fees are around $15. Play in the morning or early afternoon to avoid the wind.

The **Royal Lahaina Tennis Ranch** (Tel. 661-3611) has 11 courts, at least 6 of which are lighted. Spectator tennis is often centered at the hotel in the stadium court. The **Kapalua Tennis Garden** (Tel. 669-5677) is now open at the Kapalua Resort.

Community courts are set up at Wailuku, Lahaina, Kihei, and Hana, all administered by the Maui County Department of Parks and Recreation (no charges). In addition, a few courts are set up at some other hotels (one or two courts each), which are primarily available to guests in those hotels.

Horse racing? Sometimes. Usually every other Sunday during the summer at the County Fairgrounds in Kahului, at the annual fete itself in October, and on other varying occasions throughout the year. But caution: Betting on any horse race is strictly forbidden by state law!

Hiking and Camping. Write or visit the Division of State Parks, Hawaii Department of Land and Natural Resources, State Building, Wailuku, Maui, HI 96793 (Tel. 244-4354) for the most up-to-date regulations on hiking and camping in state parks. Camping permits are required, but the state ones are free.

The three state parks with camping permitted are **Kaumahina** (tent only) on the road to Hana, **Waianapanapa** near Hana Airport, and **Polipoli** on Route 37 near Kula.

County camping information is available from the Maui Department of Parks and Recreation, War Memorial Gymnasium, Kaahumanu Avenue, Wailuku, Maui, HI 96793 (Tel. 244-5514). Permits are $1 per day. County campsites include **Baldwin Park** in Paia, **Hookipa Beach** off the Hana Highway, and **Rainbow Park,** also near Paia.

There are 30 miles of hiking trails meandering inside Haleakala Crater, and the National Park Service offers conducted tours in the summer. There are also several campgrounds within park boundaries. For detailed, up-to-date information, write the Superintendent, Haleakala National Park, Box 537, Makawao, Maui, HI 96768 (or Tel. 572-9306).

Dedicated hikers may also want to touch base with the **Mauna Ala Hiking Club** (Tel. 572-8338), P.O. Box 497, Makawao, Maui, HI 96768. The club conducts Saturday and Sunday hikes, and visitors are welcome to join in. Also, see the commercial hiking tour we mentioned above at the end of section 7.

10. Valley Isle Shopping

You will find a surprising number of unusual gift items on Maui—Polynesian fabrics, clothes, wood, lauhala, and shell products; jewelry made from such locally harvested material as pink, black, and gold coral; and "Maui diamonds." Local handicrafts in wood, clothing, leather, shell, etc., are sold as well as modern scrimshaw—delicate carving on whale teeth, walrus ivory, or similar material. Outside the more expensive hotel shops, prices often rival those in Honolulu. And there are genuine bargains to be found in some Maui establishments by dedicated shoppers.

In **KAANAPALI** you'll find the local equivalent to clever bazaars like Honolulu's International Market Place or King's Village. This is the **Whalers Village,** a combination shopping center and museum containing about 50 stores and rambling over 10 acres adjacent to the ocean near the Kaanapali Beach Hotel. The village is open seven days a week, 9:30 A.M. to at least 5:30 P.M., but until 9 P.M. on Thursday and Friday. Here are a few shops that interest us there:

Ka Honu (or the Wood Shop) is owned by local name sculptor Sam Kaai, but he no longer sits down there to carve. He imports crafts from the South Pacific, many of them of museum quality. Interesting antique maps, engravings, reproductions, etc., are sold at **Lahaina Printsellers**. Also, **Lahaina Galleries**, an elegant establishment next to the whale boat, sells works by about a dozen artists with Hawaii connections including Guy Buffet, Robert Nelson and David Lee. At **Liberty House** (Tel. 661-4451), the West Maui branch of the famous Honolulu department store, look for good-quality resort wear, Polynesian clothing, lingerie, gourmet foods, and many other items. There's also a branch of **Crazy Shirts**, popular with young folks.

In **LAHAINA,** the most interesting establishments are still generally along Front Street, the town's main thoroughfare which fronts the ocean. This is not some centrally engineered set of shops, but a collection of ramshackle buildings, many of them left over from Lahaina's days of gore and glory. There are a few newer structures, but they are strictly converted according to a conscientious code so they will retain the nineteenth-century motif of the town.

We recommend you start your ramble in the Hotel Street arcade of the Pioneer Inn and then move into Front Street for a five-block shopping serendipity, perhaps ending with a snack at any of the little restaurants or sandwich stands along the way:

Jack Ackerman's Maui Divers, the first place you come across, disappoints us. The black coral is okay, if you like it. But the "Maui diamonds" we saw there are actually quartz cut, shaped, and polished so they look like real diamonds. They are *not* real diamonds, of course, and they are not even from Maui. **Super Whale,** also in the Pioneer Inn Arcade, specializes in children's wear. And the nearby **Wardrobe** seems to have generally good prices.

Across Front Street from the square is the relatively new complex called The Wharf, a high-density, thick-wood, heavy-handed shopping center that is out of key with Lahaina's more delicate architectural pattern. The shops there are nicely air conditioned, however, a plus in this sunny and warm neighborhood. One we especially like is **Upstart Crow and Company**, which manages to marry a delicious coffeehouse with a well-stocked bookstore. The **Maui Mad Hatter**, which we always thought was fun in Wailea, has now moved in here. Lending credence to the name these days is the prominent and somewhat testy notice prohibiting several activities in the mad hatter's establishment, including photography!

Moving along Front Street, now, we don't know much about **Apparels of Pauline** (Est. 1958), but remembering the movie *Perils,* we've always enjoyed the name. **High as a Kite** nearby has kites running from a modest mylar model at $7.95 on up to $200 for a hand-made "sun kite." At 709 Front, the **Vagabond** should be called the "Bagabond." Just about every kind of Gladstone and duffle is sold there, along with lots of other stuff.

The Gallery, at 716 Front across the way, features a veritable museum of art and antiques from the Orient. Exquisite pieces of jade, porcelain, etc., are for sale to collectors.

The former Whaling Port Curio and Shell Shop, at 724 Front St., has been sold by the malacologists and turned into another ABC Discount Store. And the former Hop Wo Store, an atmospheric plantation-era hold-out at No. 728 Front for many years, has now been converted into the glitzy **Lahaina Galleries**. The old department store at No. 744 is more interesting on the outside these days than for the one-more muu-muu shop that now occupies the premises. We also skip any "investment art" stores that spring up along here from time to time.

The brick-paved **Lahaina Market Place,** which contains several shops at the corner of Front and Lahainaluna, is worth entering for a short stroll. Watch the glass blower and check out the peddler-type carts parked here. A few steps down Lahainaluna Road is the **Nagamine Poster and Photo Gallery.** It has some nice things, although they weren't all that friendly to us when it looked like we weren't going to buy.

David's of Hawaii, now moved to No. 815, carries some unusual vintage "silkie" aloha shirts from $75 to $250, besides the modern variety. They also have several good T-shirts.

Set back from the street, behind a yard full of greenery in a 75-year-old green house, is the **Old Poi Factory**, where we saw some good, modern designs in women's wear. If there are any earring nuts in the crowd, they should stop in at the **Moonbow Boutique** at 835 Front St. There Ms. Ronnie Steinfeld will show you lots of baubles, bangles, and beads. We also like the attractive display at the **Lahaina Scrimshaw Factory** at 845 Front St., next to Kimo's. Next door, the **South Seas Trading Post** offers generally expensive—but good—handicraft from several South Seas islands. These folks seem to know their stuff.

Sea Breeze, 855 Front St., is a pretty well-equipped souvenir shop where you can lean right in the window over the display cases. We almost bought one of those cheerful wind chimes for $12, but settled for a $2.50 poster. Like some other readers, you may enjoy meeting **Claire—the Ring Lady** in the arcade at 858 Front St. **Crazy Shirts**, across the street at 865, has Hawaii design T-shirts for $10 and up. Go in (and look up) to see the figurehead from the old *Carthaginian*, the photographs of her 1972 sinking, etc.

An attractive address for scrimshaw and other nautical items is **The Whaler** at 866 Front St. The owner is Chuck Sutherland, one of Maui's senior scrimshanders, and he and his staff tell some interesting—and authentic—stories.

Off Papalaua Street, just *mauka* of Front Street, is the **Lahaina Shopping Center,** with groceries, drugstores, hardware shops, and other places suited to more prosaic needs. Two establishments worth noting are the **Nagasako Variety Market** (Tel. 661-4108), which carries condo sizes in soap powders, etc., and its sister organization, **Nagasako Super Market** (Tel. 661-0985), which we like better than Foodland. Nagasako's market may be the best place in the neighborhood to stock up on staples.

A short drive or long walk further along Front Street is a fascinating collection of generally expensive engravings and maps for sale at the **Lahaina Printsellers** (667-7843). It's headquartered in the historic old Seaman's Hospital, dating from a century ago, at 1024 Front St. Still further along, a new shopping center, the **Lahaina Cannery,** was still under construction on our recent research rounds. It may open in early 1987.

Out at **WAILEA** is a small complex called the **Wailea Shopping Village,** not far from the Hotel Inter-Continental. You'll find a branch of **Chapman's,** an expensive Honolulu shop for resort wear. High fashion for women is sold at **Michele's.** Try **Susu's** for upscale, generally good quality Hawaiian attire, too. **Isle Style** has handicraft, paintings, etc.

KIHEI now boasts a couple of modest modern shopping centers. There's the Rainbow Mall, which opened on the mountain side between Kamaole Beach Parks I and II. Check there for a nice card shop we've somehow lost the name of. Also the **Maui Fudge Kitchen** turns out some terrific cookies. The other center is Azeka Place, 1280 S. Kihei Rd., four miles from Wailea, which has a branch of **Liberty House** and **Crazy Shirts,** both Honolulu-headquartered stalwarts, plus **Lobster & Roses,** a good-quality women's boutique.

One of our favorite stores is the nearby indoor-outdoor hodgepodge at neither center, called the **Paradise Fruit Stand**. It's open 24 hours at

1913 South Kihei Rd., next to Kihei Town Center. If you want an apple or a pre-wrapped sandwich after midnight, join the locals who flock in here.

In the old town of **WAILUKU** you might like to peek into the **Maui Rehabilitation Center** (Tel. 244-5502) at Cameron Center, 95 Mahalani St., which has authentic Hawaiian handicrafts made by the handicapped on the premises. Also in Wailuku, many search out the famous Japanese cookies with the sweet bean filling called *manju* at the **Home Maid Bakery** (Tel. 244-7015), at 1005 East Lower Main St., or at **Shishido's** (Tel. 244-5222) at 758 Lower Main St. Some prefer those turned out by **Sam Sato's** (Tel. 244-7124) in his restaurant at 318 No. Market St., and one day we will have to try all three recipes side-by-side. Sato's apple turnovers are also a local specialty.

In **KAHULUI.** Progressing from east to west along Kaahumanu Avenue, there are three non-connected shopping centers—the Maui Mall, the Kahului Shopping Center, and the main mall of all, Kaahumanu Center. At the Maui Mall, **Star Super Market** is about the cheapest choice for groceries on the island, although some prefer **Ooka's Super Market** (Tel. 244-3931) at 1870 Main St. Also in the Maui Mall, now, is an excellent branch of **Waldenbooks** (Tel. 877-0181) and a smellorific store called **Sir Wilfred's Coffee, Tea and Tobacco Shop** (Tel. 877-3711). Look for the antique Indian outside. Almost next door is the famous **Tasaka Guri Guri Shop,** which makes the best *guri guri* ("goody goody") Japanese ice cream in Hawaii. Actually it's a kind of sherbet, and locals like it on top of sweet *azuki* beans. The Petroglyph Garden in the mall is a *recreation*—well done, but not authentic petroglyphs.

We usually drive right by the Kahului Shopping Center these days. (If you find something interesting there, let us know.) The prestige complex in Kahului is Kaahumanu Center. In some ways it's an architectural echo of Honolulu's Ala Moana, studded by **Sears** on one end and by **Liberty House** on the other, with lots of Honolulu-headquartered emporia in between. We like to browse through the **Book Cache.** You'll find island fashions at **Otaheite,** a boutique. **Camellia Imports Seed Shop** has those dried Chinese seeds Island youngsters like to chew on. At **Karen's Fruit and Floral Boutique** you may see samples of protea blossoms, if you missed them up at Kula. In the center of the center is the **Center for Performing Plants,** also known as the Nani Pacifica, a green boutique run by Judith Cohen. (It also has some hand-made Christmas ornaments.)

Across the parking lot and the busy avenue from the same center, shophounds like to sniff around the recently refurbished Old Kahului Building. There you'll find the **Artful Dodger Feed 'N' Read,** a used bookstore/restaurant combo, the **Tiger Lily,** an exquisite dress shop, the

Bamboo Breeze, with furniture and *objets de* tropical art, and another interesting store or three.

PRODUCTS OF MAUI. Foremost among miscellaneous Maui specialties is pineapple, of course. All the pineapple grown on Maui is, in theory, reserved for canning. Actually you can buy some Maui pine fresh from the fields if you find the **King of Hawaii** brand. The sweetest, tastiest Maui onions are those from **M. Uradomo Farms.** And the best pastries (aside from the previously named *manju*) are those turned out by the **Komoda Bakery** in Makawao. We've already discussed wine under Sightseeing, but be aware that just at our deadline, the first bottles of **Maui Lager** are coming off the production line on the Valley Island. You may have a chance to try the new local brew before we do. So far they can't make enough of it to ship it to any other island. The same people are also getting ready to turn out a new Hawaiian wine cooler, this one manufactured on the mainland but supposedly using traditional Hawaiian fruits.

Finally, a word about potato chips. Ever since articles on Maui's potato chips appeared in the *Wall Street Journal* and some other Mainland publications, there has been a run on virtually all potato chips on the island. However there is more than one potato chip factory on Maui, so it is distinctly possible that you may crunch into Brands X, Y, or Z. To be sure to buy the right product, search out the "Kitch'n Cook'd" label. If you can't find them in the stores, you could go direct to the **Maui Potato Chip Factory** (Tel. 877-3652), at 295 Lalo Place in Kahului.

11. Maui Nights on the Town

The Valley Island swings like a tree-full of mynahs in a high wind. In fact, Maui's *hele on* stance after dark is precisely what makes it difficult to publish an up-to-date report. You may find a night-life scene with a volatile collection of bars and clubs opening and closing about as frenetically as a family of octopuses swimming through a revolving door.

If there is any consistency on the night scene, it will be found in the cocktail lounges and clubrooms of the major Kaanapali and Wailea hotels. THE disco on the Kaanapali Kampus this season is still **Spats** in the Hyatt Regency Maui. It's recorded rock, but the beat goes on 'til nearly dawn. Rocker-readers have reported that it's hopelessly crowded on Friday and Saturday, though. A similar attraction, but for a younger set, is the **Banana Moon** lounge in the nearby Marriott. It's also often mobbed on Friday and Saturday.

Polynesian and other shows are offered at several hotels, and with meals they run about $40, maybe half that for children. The best luau/entertainment combinations now are probably the **Aloha Luau** at the

Sheraton Maui in Kaanapali (Tel. 677-9564) and **Maui's Merriest Luau** at the Hotel Inter-Continental (Tel. 879-1822) over in Wailea. The **Luau at the Maui Lu** in the Maui Lu Resort (Tel. 879-5858) in Kihei also has its loyal fans. (They've finally stopped calling it the "Maui Lu-Au!") The **"Drums of the Pacific"** show at the Hyatt Regency (Tel. 667-7474) may be okay, too. And **Jesse's Luau** (Tel. 879-7227) features Jesse Nakooka, who was a fixture at the Maui Lu for many years. Jesse and his gang now whoop it up at the Mana Kai Maui Hotel, a condo at 2960 So. Kihei Road in Kihei.

The best long-running and consistent stage show on Maui has to be **"Here is Hawaii"** in Kaanapali. It recently moved to the Kaanapali Beach Hotel, but it could be somewhere else by the time you read these words. In any case, it's worth searching out because unlike the usual poly-Polynesian shows, this one is *all* Hawaiian (no Tahitian or Samoan hulas, etc.). It stars Audrey Meyers and Keola Beamer, two well-known names on the local entertainment scene. You'll find a lot of good history and good fun here. The dinner/show package will come to $38 or so in 1987, and it begins at 6 P.M.. It may be worth trying to buy the 8 P.M. show only if you don't want the dinner, but during busy periods it may be booked out by those who took the entire package.

Outside the Kaanapali hotels, but still in the resort area in the Whalers Village, the **Rusty Harpoon** (Tel. 661-3123) sometimes hooks some up-and-coming groups for its lounge acts. It's a smooth place for a sunset, but also mellow for midnighting. Its resident mixologists, by the way, specialize in about a dozen different daiquiris. (Cash only. No credit cards or traveler's checks accepted the last time we were there.)

In **LAHAINA,** our all-time favorite Maui bar is the **Old Whaler's Grog Shop,** the lopsided landmark tavern in the corner of the old Pioneer Inn. Good drinking and a spirit of camaraderie are generally available at any hour, but the seasoned old floorboards really jump when someone sits down at the rinky-tink piano late in the evening. It's very popular with the young singles crowd, but some of us in our Fabulous Fifties like the place, too.

The top-deck Carthaginian Bar above the downstairs dining room in the **Oceanhouse,** at 831 Front St., is inviting. Sit next to the windows for a floodlit view of the breakers below. Perhaps ideal for a quiet *tête-à-tête,* not for a foot-stomping hoedown. Open until 1 or 2 A.M.

Another top-floor entry, particularly pleasant for early-evening tippling, is the bar at the **Whale's Tale Inn** at 666 Front St., behind the Pioneer Inn. Sit on the *lanai,* near the corner, to overlook the famous Banyan Tree, the courthouse, the ocean, and, perchance, the whales in the channel.

Not far away, on Friday and Saturday nights, you'll find an appreciative local crowd taking in the Hawaiian music at the **Banyan Inn,** the open-sided restaurant at 640 Front St., opposite the big banyan tree. Jazz fans lately have been gathering about three days a week to hear musicians at **Blackie's Boat Yard** (Tel. 667-7979), also known as Blackie's Bar, on Route 30, just out of Lahaina toward Kaanapali. (We haven't tried the Mexican food, though.) And a good bar for getting to know locals and nonlocals might still be at **Moose McGillycuddy's** (Tel. 667-7758), featuring rock videos at 844 Front St. in Lahaina. (Earlier it is a relatively undistinguished restaurant.)

Way out in **NAPILI,** the Napili Kai Beach Club is proud of its **Sea House Restaurant** (formerly "Teahouse of the Maui Moon"), which offers the usual Polynesian show on most nights. But on Fridays there's a welcome change: All the acts are performed by about 40 offspring of the hotel staff. Telephone 669-6271 for show time. It's a real refresher.

AT **WAIKAPU,** we recently enjoyed the Plantation Barbecue at **Maui Tropical Plantation** (Tel. 244-7643), which currently hoes down at least two nights a week. The festivities include a sunset hayride, an all-you-can-eat buffet dinner, and a *paniolo* (Hawaiian cowboy) show led by long-time Maui showman Buddy Fo and his country band. We expect the fare for the fun will run around $40 in 1986, maybe $30 for kids. We were not here incognito this time, but it didn't matter. Every one we saw seemed to have a good meal and a good time—including Buddy and his talented musicians and dancers. (Tell him we sent you!)

In **KIHEI,** "Maui's largest dance floor" is supposed to be at the **Maui Lu Resort** (Tel. 879-5881), which offers live music nightly.

A good living-room bar in **KAHULUI** may still be **Apple Annie's** (Tel. 877-3107) in Kaahumanu Center, next to Liberty House. (But better recheck that by phone; we haven't been there in a while.) In the neighboring township of **WAILUKU,** an often-colorful tavern at 2080 Vineyard St. is the **Hale Kukui Lounge.** There's frequently a live band, at least on weekends. This one can get rough, though, so give the crowd the onceover before sitting down. If you see any Kukui nuts, pick another Hale.

Not exactly night life, but certainly grand entertainment, is the annual Na Mele O Maui, "the Songs of Maui," a three-day festival held in Lahaina and Kaanapali one weekend every November.

12. The Maui Address List

Barber— Agena Barber Shop, 782-B Panaewa St., Lahaina. Tel. 661-3187.
Beauty salon— Hair Horizon, Lahaina Shopping Center. Tel. 661-3466.
Chamber of Commerce— 26 North Puunene Ave., Kahului. Tel. 877-0452.

Doctors— Maui Medical Group, 130 Prison St., Lahaina. Tel. 661-0051.

Dry cleaners— Maui Dry Cleaners, Lahaina Shopping Center. Tel. 667-2659.

Fire department—Dial 911 for all emergencies.

Florist— Lahaina Florist, Lahaina Shopping Center. Tel. 661-0509.

Gas station (open 24 hours)— Kahului Shell Service, 137 Kaahumanu Ave., Kahului. Tel. 877-3023.

Hospital— Maui Memorial, 221 Mahalani St., Kahului. Tel. 244-9056.

Laundromat— There's one at the Lahaina Shopping Center.

Liquor— Party Pantry, 1217 Front St., Lahaina. Tel. 661-3577.

Pharmacy— Craft's Drugs, Lahaina Shopping Center. Tel. 661-3119.

Police headquarters— Old Lahaina Courthouse, Town Square. Tel. 661-4441 (but dial 911 for all emergencies).

Post office— In Lahaina Shopping Center. Tel. 667-6611.

Public library— Lahaina branch next to Pioneer Inn. Tel. 661-0566.

Supermarket— Nagasako, Lahaina Shopping Center. Tel. 661-0985.

Tourist information— Hawaii Visitors Bureau, 172 Alamaha, Kahului. Tel. 871-8691.

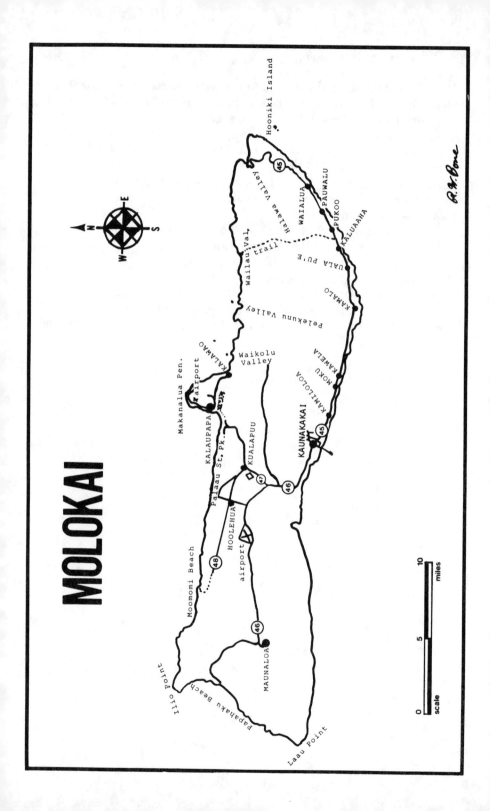

8

Molokai,
the Friendly Island

1. Around the Island—A Land in Limbo

Like the populace of a small town in the Midwest, Molokaians are traditionally interested in people—talking because it's fun to talk, and being helpful just because it feels good to be helpful. For this reason, Molokai over the past fifty years or so has earned the subtitle "The Friendly Island."

In old Hawaii, Molokai supported a native population of at least 10,000. During the 1800s, however, opportunity beckoned elsewhere, and the number dropped severely. The population reached a low of 1,000 in 1910. During this black period, Molokai was known as "The Lonely Island" or "The Forgotten Island."

The establishment of pineapple was the island's salvation. In the 1920s and 1930s, there was a rush to return home to unspoiled Molokai and work in the booming industry. Everyone's mood improved, and eventually 7,000 happy people were being supported directly or indirectly by pineapple paychecks.

Then again, fortune turned for Molokai. In the 1970s the island was the only one in the state that was losing population, dropping down to around 5,000. With cheaper pineapple production available in foreign lands like Taiwan and the Philippines, Dole closed its Molokai plantations. Del Monte announced that it would do the same, but at this writing it continues to run a small pineapple operation on the island.

Today Molokai spirits have been raised again, sparked by the construction of the Sheraton Molokai Hotel and other projects. Population is again on the rise, now standing at over 6,000. Unemployment remains at about 20 percent, however, with welfare payments accounting for over 40 percent of the residents' income. And at least some Molokai residents believe that rich "outsiders" are controlling the island's destiny.

Molokai is being dragged into the late 1980s, and visitors should realize that there is still some controversy on the island on the ultimate social value of tourism. Thousands of acres of land have been bought by a large Mainland firm with big plans for recreational facilities and other modern development. If some skepticism toward this and other things results in slow, intelligent growth, then it will prove a healthy influence in the coming years.

Meanwhile, treat Molokai with respect, and you'll come across some of the most genuine and ingenuous Hawaiian charm to be found anywhere.

2. The Airports—Hoolehua and Kalaupapa

Flying over to Molokai from a vacation headquarters on either Oahu or Maui is one of the least expensive interisland hops. At this writing, some two-way trips still total under $30. It is not unusual for folks to make the round trip in a single day—e.g., to fly over to Molokai or Kalaupapa from Honolulu for the day or for residents or visitors staying on Molokai to hop over to Honolulu or Maui for a day of shopping or sightseeing.

The terminal buildings at either airport are uncomplicated. The one down at Kalaupapa is not much more than a one-room shack. The airport at Hoolehua is eight miles west of Kaunakakai, and it is this one that is usually referred to simply as "Molokai Airport."

Hawaiian Airlines (Tel. 567-6510) serves Molokai Airport, about a 20-minute flight from Honolulu, in its DASH-7 turboprops. It has counter space inside the airport building. **Air Molokai** (Tel. 567-6881) and **Princeville Airways** (Tel. 567-6115), two of three interisland commuter airlines, also have indoor terminal space. The third, **Reeves Air** (Tel. 553-3655), which also maintains scheduled flights, occupies counter space outdoors on the opposite side of the structure from the runway, along with the booths for the island's three rental-car outfits. There is also a tiny bar and snack shop in the building.

Molokai's two airports form the gateways to two very distinct and different places. *There is no ground transportation between them* (unless you count pack mules—see later). The simple landing strip at Kalaupapa serves the leprosy settlement there near sea level on the little Makanalua

Peninsula. Molokai Airport, on the other hand, is "topside"—meaning more than 1,000 feet up the cliff—and it accepts passengers destined for all other parts of Molokai.

If you are going to Kalaupapa, therefore, the most practical way is to *fly down* to it from topside. Air Molokai and Reeves Air (mentioned above) plus **Polynesian Airways** (Tel. 567-6647), inside the terminal, have been making these short hops once or twice a day, but recheck by phone before going out to the airport. Air Molokai and Princeville Airways sometimes fly direct to Kalaupapa and back from Oahu or Maui. (Hawaiian Air does not fly to Kalaupapa, and Aloha Airlines does not fly to the island at all.) Most flight schedules are set up so passengers can meet up with Kalaupapa tours (see section 7).

3. Transportation on Molokai

There are no buses or other means of public transportation on Molokai. The hotels sometimes provide complimentary service for their guests to and from the airport, but don't count on that. It will cost you a hefty $25 or so each way to take the special bus to the Sheraton, so you almost certainly will be better off renting a car. There are no taxis to be had at all.

Currently, there are three rental-car competitors on the island, all with offices at Molokai Airport. They include **Molokai Island U-Drive** (Tel. 567-6156), a long-time local outfit now affiliated with Dollar Rent-A-Car, **Tropical Rent-A-Car** (Tel. 567-6118), which has generally been a favorite, and **Avis Rent A Car** (Tel. 553-3866), all headquartered at the airport in outdoor booths facing the parking lot. (You may find another company or two has set up shop there in 1987.) There are no car rentals available at Kalaupapa.

Driving on Molokai is pretty easy. There are still no traffic lights on the island, the main roads are well paved, and there are several sightseeing targets to which a passenger car will easily take you. You'll should have a jeep or another four-wheel drive vehicle if you want to prowl the back lanes, however. (They're sometimes hard to find, though; hunters sometimes choose to rent out the old World War II military ammunition truck owned by Molokai Fish & Dive, Tel. 553-5926.)

Local residents think the traffic gets heavy on Molokai. Most of the time, however, you might judge it only slightly busier than in the Mohave Desert on a Sunday afternoon.

4. The Hotel Scene

You don't have to stay overnight to have fun on Molokai, but if you want to explore more thoroughly, there are three full-fledged hotels to put you up, plus a few other possibilities. Only one hotel qualifies as a luxury establishment, but comfortable rooms may be found in all. The hotels also offer pretty good Polynesian entertainment on busy evenings.

The **Sheraton Molokai** (Tel. 552-2555) has rooms strung out in several *ohia*-wood and redwood two-story buildings, many of them a fair hike from the dining room and lobby. It's the sole Molokai hostelry right on an attractive beach, although it's generally too dangerous for swimming there. There's no air conditioning, and indeed none is needed with the dependable breezes (and sometimes gales) that sweep across the 6,800-acre Kaluakoi Resort on the west end of the island, 20 minutes' drive from the airport. By day, the faint outlines of Oahu may be seen about 25 miles away, making the Sheraton the only Neighbor Island hotel with the coveted view of Diamond Head. For nighttime strollers, Honolulu glows against the distant sky.

You can't fault the facilities: four lighted tennis courts, all surrounded by a high windbreak; the 18-hole championship Kaluakoi Golf Course; a small shopping arcade; one nice pool next to an attractive bar and dining room; a snack shop; classes in Hawaiian crafts; willing, hard-working, and friendly service; live music most nights until 11 P.M. Doubles under the twirling fans running $90 to $125 (ask for a room near the center of things); regular suites for perhaps $145; the best facilities by far in the beachside Ocean Cottage Suites at around $175 for two.

The success of Sheraton's Molokai venture now seems assured, although we wouldn't swim in the often-treacherous surf in any case. (Reservations from Sheraton Hotels in Hawaii, P.O. Box 8559, Honolulu, HI 96815.) All in all, it's an admirable attempt at carving an oasis from a Hawaiian desert.

The recently renovated **Hotel Molokai** (Tel. 553-5347) is a collection of low, swaybacked buildings in a palm grove on a narrow, gray-sand beach about two miles east of Kaunakakai: Rustic, open-air lobby; Polynesian-wear shop and florist; well-kept lawns; oceanside and poolside dining room with carved totem posts; newly redesigned horse-shoe bar to one side; entertainment two or three nights a week; blimp-shaped but not blimp-sized swimming pool; 57 heavy-timbered accommodations; some with lofts or loft-like effects and 17-foot ceilings; natural wood or shingled walls; some lanais with swings; no room telephone service; new shuttle bus to the Pau Hana Inn (see below). The most expensive upper-floor, ocean-view units still cost $72 for two as 1987 begins. There are better bargains in the ground-floor building bordering the parking lot at $45 or so, while mid-range and cooler rooms next to the garden can be had for $52 to $62. (Reservations from the hotel at P.O. Box 546, Kaunakakai,

Molokai, HI 96748, or telephone the hotel toll-free from Honolulu at 531-4004.) Still a solid choice.

The traditional runner-up in hotels on Molokai is the venerable **Pau Hana Inn** (Tel. 553-5342), and many think this is the only Molokai place with real, down-home, local-kine atmosphere: Conveniently located on the fringe of Kaunakakai; modest entrance with palm growing through the roof; dining room with lava-rock walls and overhead fans (one outside wall to be removed soon); outdoor bar near a century-old, Bengalese banyan tree; terrace a popular gathering place for a local crowd; ample swimming pool; weekend entertainment sometimes on tap. The doubles near the pool (about $75) are newer and pleasanter, and some have air conditioning. The lowest-priced accommodations (about $40 for twin pillows) are quite basic but adequate for the most dedicated pinchpennies. (Reservations by mail to P.O. Box 860, Kaunakakai, HI 96748; in Honolulu, telephone direct at 536-7545.) At press time, the Pau Hana Inn has just been bought by Molokai Beach, Ltd., the same *hui* that owns the Hotel Molokai. The new owners plan some upgrades that, if successful, could make this one a real sleeper. If you go, let us know.

There are four decent choices for condominium-apartment living on Molokai, all of which have TVs and swimming pools and none of which have restaurants. The nicest is probably still the 102-unit **Molokai Shores** (Tel. 553-5954), which is a little past Kaunakakai on the southern shore, near an ancient Hawaiian fish pond. We saw overhead fans, wall-to-wall carpets, white furniture, and well-equipped kitchens. Ground-floor units have direct back-door access to a narrow sandy beach and good-sized pool. There are lanais and tall beamed ceilings on the upper stories. One-bedroom apartments were renting for $68 and the two-bedroom jobs were hovering at around $90, the last information we had. Minimum stay is two nights. (Reservations through Hawaiian Island Resorts or the hotel at P.O. Box 1037, Kaunakakai, HI 96748.) We liked it.

Then there are two choices near the Sheraton and the golf course on the Kaluakoi Resort lands. First is the 77-unit **Paniolo Hale** (Tel. 552-2731). Daily apartment rentals in the well-designed, plantation-style buildings begin at about $65 for studios and continue to about $100 or so for some two-bedroom combinations, with grand verandahs and some with hot tubs. There is a pool and paddle tennis. The way to two attractive beaches is across a major golf course fairway. (Fore!) One is called *Make* ("mah-kay"—dead) Horse Beach, and we won't speculate on how it got that name. (The resort people are trying to beat the Dead Horse moniker by popularizing it as "Eleventh Hole Beach" instead.) The second condo is the **Ke Nani Kai** (Tel. 552-2761), not far away. The latter's more hilly site provides generally excellent ocean views throughout all the apartments, but it is not close to a beach. There are also tennis courts and an excellent pool and barbecue area. Last we knew, fully equipped units were renting there for around $65 to $100.

In the other direction, about 25 miles from the airport on Molokai's eastern shore, is the out-of-the-way **Wavecrest** (Tel. 558-8238) at Ualapue. You'll find two lighted tennis courts and a grocery store. We thought the units were not too inspired, but at about $70 for two bedrooms, they could certainly be bargains for groups of four. (One-bedroom units for two vary between about $50 and $60 this year.) There are full kitchen facilities, and maid service is every third day. The whole thing is on the water's edge, although we didn't think much of the beach.

There are three tiny bed-and-breakfast family operations on Molokai. Interested persons can write Mrs. Marian Mueh, Star Route, Box 128, Kaunakakai, HI 96748 for more information.

5. Restaurants and Dining, Molokai Style

The salons where you can load up on serious viands are all at the hotels. The Ohia Lodge in the **Sheraton Molokai** (Tel. 552-2555) captures a lot of attention, now, especially with its Sunday-night dinner buffet. There are open beamed ceilings, rattan furniture, and ocean views, too. The hotel also has its Paniolo Broiler, featuring steaks and chops over *kiawe* charcoal and a salad bar.

At the **Hotel Molokai** (Tel. 553-5347), we have enjoyed a casual open-air lunch in the attractive oceanside restaurant, the Holo Holo Kai, on a number of occasions. For breakfast, try the French toast with Molokai bread. Entertainment is often on tap with dinner, which has a generally good local reputation. The dining room in the **Pau Hana Inn** (Tel. 553-5342) has been somewhat of a roller-coaster operation in recent years. But all bets are off, anyway, since the place has just been bought by the owners of the Hotel Molokai. One wall will be knocked out, to give the place a more open-air feeling, and we would presume some changes in the cuisine would be a high priority.

Let's see. Outside of those, there's a tiny Chinese restaurant called the **Hop Inn** (Tel. 553-5465), where we once had an excellent evening meal with local residents Travis and Marlene Werner, who dragged us in there and then almost had to drag us out. There's a modest place with a few booths and tables called the **Mid-Nite Inn** (Tel. 553-5302) on Ala Malama Street, the main drag of Kaunakakai. It serves all three meals. The Mid-Nite Inn, incidentally, closes at 9:30 P.M. Sorry, we haven't tried **Oviedo's** (nicely kept) or **Rabang's** (more rustic), both of which specialize in Filipino cuisine.

Breakfast? Try those wonderful fresh doughnuts, sweet rolls, and special Molokai bread at the **Kanemitsu Bakery.** They have a counter and booths behind the shop, but don't expect things to always move swiftly and efficiently. (Closed Tuesdays.)

6. Sightseeing Molokai—Delightfully Lonely Exercise

With a rented car, most people find they can see what they want in a day or two. With a jeep, you'll need at least two days to cover it all, since more sights that are relatively inaccessible to low-slung sedans will be open to you.

We divide our "topside" trips into west and east below. Following that is a separate discussion on visiting the leprosy colony at Kalaupapa. (Add a "0" to all route numbers on our map, which was drawn before the change was made.)

THE ROAD WEST

The principal village, **Kaunakakai,** is pronounced "cow-na-cock-*eye*," and is the reason a songwriter composed "The Cockeyed Mayor of Kaunakakai" during the 1930s. Incidentally, there is no official mayor of Kaunakakai because Molokai is merely a part of Maui County—which does have a mayor in the county seat of Wailuku on the Island of Maui.

Kaunakakai, population 500 or so, is known principally for its main thoroughfare, Ala Malama Street, with its wide, empty pavement flanked by a collection of wooden, false-front commercial buildings. It is somewhat reminiscent of Tombstone, Arizona, in the 1860s. With new prosperity, however, the paintbrushes have come out, reducing some of the old and weatherbeaten look which carried the town into the early 1980s. Nevertheless, there are still no stop lights, no elevators, and no chain stores in Kaunakakai—or on the whole island, for that matter.

Kaunakakaians are proud of their **wharf,** on which you may drive nearly a half-mile out over the ocean. Until recently, huge barges were berthed here to load tons upon tons of pineapple grown on Molokai and destined for the cannery in Honolulu. Pineapple production has been virtually phased out, and in the past few years the island has been busy trying to ship out export quantities of other agricultural products like sweet potatoes, onions, green beans, watermelons, alfalfa, and bell peppers. Meanwhile, it is still fun to go down to the pier on Monday and Wednesday mornings to watch the unloading of the barges.

Near the canoe shack just west of the approach to the landing is the foundation of **Kamehameha V's Summer Home.** That monarch, who reigned from 1863 to 1872, is a sort of unofficial patron of the past to Molokai. He had a ranch on the island, and several things are named for him, including Route 460.

A couple miles west along the Kamehameha V Highway is the **Kapuaiwa**

Grove, which still contains hundreds of coconut palms, the remnants of the 1,000 planted by the king in the 1860s. The spring that still bubbles there marked the center of a town square. You may explore what's left of the grove, but be warned that there is always a danger of falling coconuts.

Directly across the road from the coconut grove is **church row.** There are about ten houses of worship there now. Any church with at least a few Hawaiians in its congregation may build there on lands granted by the Hawaiian Homes Commission. Molokai's only rush hour occurs here— at noon on Sundays when they all let out at once.

If you're not pressed for time, continue on Route 460 to the left after the junction with Route 470. (If you are in a hurry, skip the next three paragraphs.)

At **Puu Nana** ("Viewing Hill"), elevation 1,381 feet, you may be able to see 30 miles over the ocean to the Island of Oahu on a clear day. At the end of the paved road is the former Dole plantation village of **Maunaloa,** built in 1923. (Dole has now closed down its Molokai pineapple operations.) Look for a post office (Zip 96720), and a branch of Kaunakakai's Friendly Market. The main street has been converted into shops selling crafts, etc. (See section 10.) The fancier residences up on the hill were the managers' houses.

Through the scrub growth in this area there is now a network of newly paved streets, many of which were built in anticipation of development which has not kept pace with the road program. If you follow the signs carefully, one of these (Kaluakoi Road) will eventually take you to the Sheraton Molokai Hotel at **Kepuhi Beach.** Another leads to several other white strands, including the attractive **Papohaku Beach Park.** Also in this area is a wildlife park that has been stocked with such exotica as giraffes and antelope, but you may only visit them on guided tours. (See section 7.)

Returning along this spur of Highway 460, you may want to take the little road that circles behind Molokai Airport. If we had not been traveling with the Imamura family of Kaunakakai, we never would have known it, but those little hills or mounds along the road are actually overgrown hangars and bunkers left behind by the Army Air Corps after World War II. Carolyn Imamura told us she explored the ruins as a child, but now they are largely caved in and dangerous.

At the junction, take Highway 470 north. You will pass the **Kualapuu Reservoir,** a water source of some local pride. Holding 1.4 billion gallons, it is the world's largest rubber-lined body of water and the home for a few families of mallards. Is it worth a stop? Well, we are more impressed when we see it from an airplane.

Above **Kualapuu,** formerly a Del Monte company town, the countryside becomes greener and more hilly. The yellow fruit you may see in the bushes lining the road are guavas, and they're delicious raw or made into jams and jellies. If you see what looks like a whole field of tiny A-frame houses, these are the homes for Molokai's highly pampered "feathered gladiators." Cockfights may be illegal, but it is not illegal to raise fighting cocks.

Continue on the road into **Palaau State Park** and to the parking lot at the end of the highway. Two short trails lead from there. The footpath to the north will lead you in about three minutes to the **Kalaupapa Overlook.** From a 1,600-foot cliff you look through space down to the Makanalua Peninsula holding the last few remaining residents of the leprosy colony. The colony was established in 1866 originally as a place of quarantine. Today, of course, leprosy has been contained by sulfone drugs. About 100 residents remain—partly because the location is beautiful, but mainly because it is home. The view from this point, from which you also catch a glimpse of the inaccessible north shore and its 3,000-foot cliffs (the highest sea cliffs in the world, according to the *Guinness Book of World Records*), is one of the most famous and dramatic in the state. Don't miss it.

The other trail runs through about 150 yards of forest, a 10-minute walk accompanied by the whistling wind in the eucalyptus trees, to the famous **Phallic Rock,** also called Kauleonanahoa. A Brobdingnagian natural feature, the stone organ has naturally given rise to certain legends, and one is explained on a nearby plaque. In ancient times, barren women made a pilgrimage to this sacred rock so that they might be able to conceive.

Just outside the park, at the sign marking its entrance, is a route to the **original Kalaupapa Overlook.** The road is muddy in wet weather, but some believe this angle provides a more dramatic view of the peninsula than the one we previously described. You cannot see the north shore cliffs from here, but in the foreground you will catch sight of the beginning of the century-old **Kalaupapa Trail,** a 1,600-foot switchback route down to the leprosy settlement below.

At one time it was known as the Jack London Trail, after the author wrote about it in one of his stories. You may follow in his footsteps for a short way or, with proper permission, you may hike or take a mule to the bottom. The trail is still the only land route to and from the isolated peninsula.

Some hereabouts may favor re-naming the trail after Chuck Yeager. Not long ago the famous test pilot, who is used to traveling at somewhat higher speeds, dutifully rode his mount on the way down. But coming back up he decided to hike, beating the mule train to the top by a considerable length of time.

On the return trip, you might turn right onto Route 480 and go through the village of Hoolehua. At the end of Route 480, a dirt road continues through private property to **Moomomi Beach.** If you want to go, you may have to open a gate or two on the way. Just remember to close them behind you. Moomomi and nearby, but hard-to-reach, Keonelele Beach, boast what is practically the only collection of sand dunes in the state. There are also several endangered plant species found nowhere else in the world.

Back on Highway 460, just about a half-mile south of the junction with 470, a dirt and gravel Forest Reserve jeep road leads toward the east. *If the weather is neither too wet nor too dry, this can be a dramatic and lovely excursion, although be aware that it is generally a violation of your rental-car contract to travel on it.* (In dry weather, a gate is sometimes closed at the road's beginning because of the danger of forest fires. If so, the key to enter may be obtained from the Division of Forestry in the State Building at Kaunakakai. The man to see there is Jim Lindsey.)

About nine miles in is the famous **Sandalwood Measuring Pit,** a depression in the ground the size and shape of a sailing ship's hull. In the early 1800s, the Hawaiian chiefs had their workers measure the cut sandalwood here before it was sent to the white traders. Use of the measuring pit was discontinued about a century ago when all the sandalwood trees were finally stripped from the island.

Another mile or two brings you to the **Waikolu Valley Lookout,** a dramatic viewpoint over a 3,000-foot-deep gorge. About three miles away in the sea you may catch sight of Okala Islet, the same feature you may see from quite a different angle if you journey to Kalawao Park, across the Makanalua Peninsula from Kalaupapa. The view of the valley is usually clear in the morning—but don't count on it. Just past the lookout is the gate to the **Kamakou Preserve**, a 2,774-acre forest and bird conservation area established in 1982 by the Nature Conservancy. Entrance is permitted to hikers or four-wheel-drive vehicles only. Anyone entering the preserve should get advice and a pamphlet outlining all the rules first. Sometimes special tours are run by the Conservancy. Telephone 567-6680 on Molokai or the headquarters at 537-4508 in Honolulu for information.

THE LONG ROAD EAST

To Halawa Valley and back (60 miles) is at least a half-day trip, and we prefer to make it in the morning so that we are less likely to be worried about rain clouds along the steep dirt road into and out of the valley. There is no place to get gas en route, so don't forget to check your gauge.

Another step in preparation: If you are planning to make the short hike to visit the Iliiliopae Heiau, you should have permission and perhaps a gate key from Mrs. Pearl Petro (Tel. 558-8113).

Some travelers prefer to drive directly to Halawa Valley and then hit the other sites on the return trip. To avoid confusion, however, we will describe each point in its order along the route. Don't count on being directed solely by those Hawaii Visitors Bureau warrior signs, incidentally. Many of them have disappeared or been placed at the wrong sites.

Route 450 is the portion of Kamehameha V Highway that goes east (as opposed to Route 460, which is also Kamehameha V Highway, but westbound).

Almost immediately you will see the first of 58 original **Hawaiian fishponds** built along this coast from the fifteenth to the eighteenth centuries. Some have been wrecked by tides or silt, but many others remain and a few are even operated commercially. The walls, constructed of coral and basalt, formed enclosures used to raise and fatten saltwater fish.

Next, you will come across a village with ancient roots called **Kawela,** six miles from Kaunakakai. Kawela was named by a Maui chief, according to research gathered by Cadette Girl Scout Troop No. 311 of Molokai. The chief landed at the nearby **Pakuhiwa Battleground** and saw that the first wave of soldiers were already engaged in a bloody slingshot war. "Kawela!" he shouted, meaning "The heat (of the battle)!" The area has been called Kawela ever since. (And according to our good friend "Molokai Mar," the place also lives up to its name by being one of the hottest areas on the island.) The battle itself, incidentally, was one of the decisive ones by which Kamehameha the Great conquered the Islands. They say his war canoes lined the now peaceful beach for four miles and that sling stones are occasionally found there even today.

St. Joseph Church, about 11 miles from Kaunakakai, was built by Father Damien de Veuster in 1876. Father Damien, famous for his work with leprosy victims in Kalawao and Kalaupapa, also used to hike to East Molokai to tend to this and other parishes.

A little farther along, a small monument marks the **Smith and Bronte Landing.** In 1927, aviators Ernest Smith and Emory Bronte came down here somewhat inelegantly in a clump of *kiawe* trees, thus completing the first civilian trans-Pacific flight. There's not much to see, however. Also forget the "bell stone" you may see an HVB marker for along the highway. It's hard to get to, and it doesn't ring any more when you do get to it.

Past Kaluaaha, less than a mile off the road, is the aforementioned thirteenth-century **Iliiliopae Heiau.** This temple, 268 feet long, is said by many to be the most magnificent in all Hawaii. If you have the previously mentioned permission (and the gate key, if needed), you may pass through the green gate on the *mauka* side of the road and follow the short trail and cross the stream to see this structure, the scene of ancient human sacrifices. Almost as long as a football field, it deceptively looks much smaller than that.

Almost beside the heiau is the start of the **Wailau Trail,** a difficult all-day trek to Wailau Valley on the north shore. The valley once held a large community, but it is now virtually deserted except for a few fishermen and *pakalolo* growers who hike to the lonely chasm. Don't set off on that particular trip without boots and other good equipment.

Back on the highway, you will run across a sign indicating the **Maupulehu Mango Patch,** a family-run operation at the end of a dirt road beside the ocean. There you can try and buy perhaps 35 different types of mangoes, plus mango milkshakes—if mangoes are in season, that is. (That's about April-July.) At other times, you might try fresh fruit smoothies and the like. Continuing on the main road, at Pukoo you will soon run across a church-run Neighborhood Store, which sells a lot of refreshment—but nothing made of red meat. (The hot dogs are turkey dogs. It's the only game for miles around, and your last chance for a soft drink, a chicken burger, or whatever.) On the drive you will begin seeing the island of Maui across the Pailolo Channel. In this area are several coves with deserted sandy beaches and good swimming. When the water is calm, it is also clear and ideal for skin diving.

As the road begins winding up to a higher altitude, you'll catch sight of the **Isle of Mokuhooniki,** a turtle-shaped offshore rock used as a bombing target during World War II. Today's pilots say it resembles a different animal from the air. They call it "Elephant Rock."

At the top of the bluff is the **Puu-O-Hoku Lodge and Ranch,** which once raised the largest herd of Charolais cattle in the world. Puu-O-Hoku means "Hill of Stars," and there must be a zillion visible on a moonless night from this isolated place.

A few more turns and you will catch your first breathtaking view of the magnificent **Halawa Valley.** Far, far below is a curving beach, then a broad, grassy plain headed by a thick jungle three or four miles inland. There you will see at least one of a pair of large waterfalls which plunge down the side of the cliff. To know that hundreds once lived in that deep gorge adds to its overwhelming beauty and loneliness.

The very rugged three-mile descent into the valley has now been paved, but that doesn't help a whole heck of a lot. The road is still narrow and dangerous, and frequent honking at blind curves is certainly advisable.

Halawa Valley is popular with campers, picnickers, and beachcombers. Only a few families live there on a permanent basis today, and they must make do without electricity or telephones. Several houses are just plain deserted, although services are held there every Sunday in the little church.

There are two waterfalls at the head of the valley, and since our last edition, we hiked back, generally following the stream and an old PVC pipe to the base of the 500-foot **Hipuapua Falls** while on assignment for *Off the Beaten Path*, published by Readers Digest Books. The last part was a rough climb. Others have crossed that stream and followed another one to reach the perhaps more easily attainable, 250-foot-high **Moaula Falls**. According to ancient Hawaiian legend, you may swim in the "bottomless" pool under the falls if the giant lizard woman who lives below the surface is happy. To test her mood, throw a ti leaf on the water. If it floats, she won't bother you. If it sinks, the creature is testy, and is stirring up the currents below. So you should save your swim for another day. (For either hike, allow an hour in each direction, and don't go if it looks like rain.)

THE TRIP TO KALAUPAPA

The Makanalua Peninsula, usually called the Kalaupapa Peninsula these days, was the scene of tragedy and heartbreak in the latter half of the nineteenth century. Today it is being turned into Kalaupapa National Historical Park, and it may be visited easily and safely. About 100 leprosy patients, whose age averages 65, still live there because of their sentimental attachment to the place. For years, there has no longer been any medical need for the natural barrier cliffs to keep these victims of Hansen's Disease isolated from the rest of Molokai and all the world. And there is also no longer any need to use a euphemism for leprosy, since it is not, after all, a crime or an immoral act. But for the same reason it is terribly cruel to label a person as "a leper."

There are only three ways to reach the settlement on the spit of land so far below the northern *pali*. You can fly from Molokai Airport (or from Oahu or Maui) to the airport at Kalaupapa. (See section 2 for airline information.) Or you can either hike or ride a mule down the 3.2-mile switchback trail that descends the 1,600-foot precipice. (Figure from an hour to 1½ hours each way.)

You are not permitted to tour the peninsula entirely on your own hook. You may fly down—or hike down—and arrange to be met at the airport or the bottom of the trail by Father Damien Tours, run by Mr. and Mrs. Richard Marks, who live in Kalaupapa and are themselves patients. (See section 7, Guided Tours and Cruises.)

On the tour, you will see **Kalaupapa,** the sleepy town that is the site of today's hospital and settlement on the western side of the peninsula. The town is noted for its large number of pet dogs, which are loved by the patients in lieu of the children they were not allowed to have. Young children, who are still considered susceptible to leprosy, remain strictly forbidden in the area. In the old days, newborns would be sent away to live somewhere else. (There are now no residents of childbearing age.)

More beautiful than Kalaupapa is the setting for the original village of **Kalawao,** now in ruins, on the other side of the peninsula. There still is the little St. Philomena's Roman Catholic Church, built by Father Damien de Veuster. Known today as the Martyr of Molokai, the Belgian priest came ashore in 1873 to help the leprosy victims who were banished there without shelter or provisions. Father Damien himself caught the disease and died in 1889, soon after the church was finished. He has been nominated for sainthood.

Notwithstanding the magnificent scenery at Kalawao, the colony eventually moved across the peninsula to Kalaupapa, where it was warmer and less windy. But Kalawao is the place to have your picnic. Sara and I sat down there with Mrs. Marks one sun-filled day and thoroughly enjoyed the incomparable view of the rugged north coast. We watched turtles play in the surf and gave silent thanks that this place of beauty will never again be marred by the tragedies of long ago.

7. Guided Tours and Cruises on Molokai

The just-mentioned **Father Damien Tours** (Tel. 567-6171), Box No. 1, Kalaupapa, HI 96742, offers probably the best standard 4-hour tour of the Makanalua Peninsula (Kalaupapa) for about $13 per person daily except Sunday. An equally well-established competing operation is **Ike's Scenic Tours** (Tel. 567-6437), which has set up some air/ground packages from topside with Polynesian Airways.

The most interesting way down to Kalaupapa is via the **Molokai Mule Ride** (Tel. 567-6088), also known as Rare Adventures, Ltd. For about $60 per person, you will descend the trail and sway along the 26-switchback route, down, down, down to the point where you are met and given a guided minibus tour of the peninsula. The rate includes the trail guide, the mule, a box lunch, and the tour, but not transportation between your hotel and the corral. The entire enchilada takes about six hours.

If you don't want to trust your lives to an animal, you may now arrange a hike down the rocky trail through the same outfit. The price is currently about $25, including lunch and the same tour at the bottom of the trail. Oh yes, the hikers do leave about a half-hour *in front of* the mule train. Whew! Rare Adventures will also set up a combination air/ground tour of the area for around $50, or you can arrange to hike in and fly out, if you want.

Another strange excursion is the **Molokai Ranch Wildlife Safari** (Tel.

553-5115), a one-hour photographic hunting trip through the Molokai Ranch Wildlife Park, for about $15. It departs from the Sheraton. Passengers in open-windowed vans may view and photograph several types of African and Asian animals being raised to supply other animal parks in the world. These include giraffe, aoudad, Indian black buck, eland, oryx, impala, and the greater kudu. (Incidentally, some of these game animals now end up as gourmet dishes in selected restaurants on the other islands.) Sorry, but the tour is not as good as it was in the days when the animals were allowed to be fed by the driver/guides; the beasties are catching on, now, and they seldom come over close enough to be thoroughly enjoyed and photographed.

For conventional bus and car tours, check with **Robert's Hawaii, Inc.** (Tel. 552-2751) or **Grayline of Molokai** (Tel. 567-6177). Just what will be offered on half- and full-day tours in 1987 isn't clear at press time.

We recently enjoyed an exciting powerboat trip launched by **Hokupaʻa Ocean Adventures** (Tel. 558-8195). The cruise is captained by Glenn Davis, who lives in Halawa Valley, and he takes you almost from his front door along the dramatic 3,000-foot sea cliffs and isolated valleys of the island's north shore clear to the edge of Kalaupapa. The cost for the four-hour cruise is $50 at this writing, and reservations are required. There is also another firm advertising kayak adventures along the north shore. We can't speak from experience, but we know we would *not* like to have been in such a vessel in the kind of waves that we've seen in that area. Maybe this kind of trip is for very special people, but as for us, we would rather go again with Glenn while sitting high above his dependable twin motors!

Whale-watching, sightseeing, and snorkeling cruises are available aboard the **Rodonis** (Tel. 553-3311), a handsome 50-foot cutter at the Kaunakakai wharf. Three-hour cruises go out for around $50; shorter sunset cruises run around $35; full-day cruises to Lanai are offered for around $100. We haven't been. Similar cruises may be offered aboard the **Noio** (Tel. 558-8910), which normally specializes in sport fishing. (See below.)

Aerial tours are now offered on Molokai by **Royal Helicopters** (Tel. 567-6733), part of a Honolulu outfit. At this writing a 15-minute Kalaupapa Tour costs about $40, a 30-minute tour of the North Shore goes for around $80, and a one-hour tour of the entire island costs about $160. We've never had a report from a disinterested passenger, and we've not been personally. If you go, let us know.

8. Water Sports—Privacy on the Sands

There are no good beaches at Kaunakakai. The very best sandy shoreline is on the extreme west coast of Molokai, at 2½-mile-long **Papohaku**

Beach, which is one of the longest and widest in the entire state. Nearby, Kepuhi Beach is next to the Sheraton Molokai. However the currents at both are often dangerous, so we recommend against going into the water.

Local folk like to swim on the north shore at **Moomomi Beach.** To reach it, follow Highway 480 to the end—and then keep going on dirt roads and hope.

The easiest beaches to drive to are those on Highway 450 to the east. They begin about 10 miles from Kaunakakai, but our favorite is **Waialua,** about 20 miles down the road. Swimming and skin diving are usually excellent at this unmarked strand. Along there the shore fishing becomes good, too, particularly at **Morris Point.** (Your luck may also be running at the end of that half-mile-long pier back at Kaunakakai.)

The beach in picturesque **Halawa Valley** is popular for skin diving. Nearby is one of the few good surfing spots on Molokai, and fishing is fine in the bay from August to November. You can swim in the bay and sometimes in the fresh pool at the foot of **Moaula Falls,** about an hour's hike inland from the beach.

Some of the best deep-sea fishing in the Islands is found at Penguin Bank, a submerged peninsula off the southwest coast of Molokai. Although this wide, shallow area is mostly plied by charter outfits out of Honolulu or Lahaina, there are two or three Molokai operations who also know the waters. Check with **Alele II** (Tel. 558-8266), a 35-foot inboard, the **Noio** (Tel. 552-2622), a 48-foot cruiser, or the **Molokai Fish & Dive Corp.** (Tel. 553-5926), which may be running various snorkel and scuba excursions besides fishing trips.

9. Other Sports on Molokai

The championship 18-hole **Kaluakoi Golf Course** (Tel. 552-2739), 6,705 yards, is available at the Sheraton, and the **Ironwood Hills Golf Course** (Tel. 567-6121) offers a hilly nine-holer at Kualapuu. Also, the Del Monte people have another nine holes at Maunaloa.

Mountain and valley horseback rides may be available this year at **Ekahanui Stables** (Tel. 558-8981) at Kamalo, Molokai, HI 96748. Last we heard, you mounted up for $12.50 per hour, with guided rides running $25 and overnight camping trips for $150. (No checks.) We know less about **Halawa Valley Horse Rides** (Tel. 553-3214), a three- or four-horse operation down in Halawa Valley, which offers trail rides to Moaula Falls from the owner's home in the valley.

Then for experienced *English saddle* riders only, look into **Hawaiian Horsemanship Unlimited** (Tel. 567-6635), recently set up by Sarah Selnick and her photographer husband, Howard. They have been given free rein over some of the most beautiful horse country on the island. Rates and hours have not been firmed up at this writing. (The couple is affiliated with FITS Equestrian, which arranges riding tours in several parts of the world.) Reservations are essential at any of these outfits. We haven't tried them, but we have met the Selnicks, at least, and were impressed with their enthusiasm and ability.

For hunters, there are several thousand acres of public game. As on Lanai, you may hunt axis deer and wild goats in season, as well as several kinds of game birds. Full information on the latest season dates, bag limits, etc., is available from the Department of Land and Natural Resources, Division of Fish and Game, 465 South King St., Honolulu, HI 96813.

The Sheraton offers tennis, horseshoes, volleyball, and other activities to its guests. Similar facilities are available at Hotel Molokai and at the Wavecrest condominium at Ualapue.

10. Shopping—Just Looking?

Kaunakakai has all the shops and stores needed to provide most day-to-day needs of a community of 6,000. Most of these are located on Ala Malama, the main street of the village. Check into the **Molokai Fish & Dive** shop for local designer T-shirts and caps and an eclectic collection of other things for sale—plus interesting items on display like live parrots and dead boars which are not. Then some unusual food products may be found down Mango Lane, around the corner from the Fish & Dive, at **Molokai Buyers' Inc.**, a cooperative specializing in local produce. (It's the only place in the state where we ever saw "female" papayas for sale.)

There's a tiny branch of Honolulu's **Liberty House** at the Sheraton. And at the Hotel Molokai, drop in at the **Jo's of Molokai Gift Shop** (Tel. 553-3444), operated by Jo and Bob Johnson, retired TV folk. (Bob is the recorded voice on "Mission Impossible" who promises to self-destruct in five seconds!)

We haven't yet looked into **Purdy's Nuts**, a macadamia nut grove, store, and museum operated daily by Harry Purdy on Hawaiian Homestead land at Hoolehua. It's on Lihipali Avenue, behind the high school. Maybe we'll meet there this year.

An unusual establishment in the old plantation community of Maunaloa is the **Big Wind Kite Factory** (Tel. 552-2364), where Jonathan Socher sells kites from all over the world. In the same village, you might also check out **Red Dirt Shirt** (Tel. 552-247), which has some unusual T-shirts and various graphic designs. Some other craft stores are also in the vicinity.

Browsers also enjoy reading the two bulletin boards set up in Kaunakakai. There's a wealth of fascinating information about bazaars, garage sales, festivals, and anything else that is *au courant* in Molokai. A couple of nice souvenir books available locally include *Molokai, the Friendly Isle,* by Molokai resident Marlene Freedman and *Molokai* by Philip Spalding III, a local photographer and historian.

11. Nights on the Town

The last time we looked, there were three places to make the night scene: the **Sheraton Molokai,** the **Hotel Molokai,** and the **Pau Hana Inn,** all three of the hotels. At the latter you'll probably find a more local crowd gathered out back underneath the beautiful old banyan. Live music and dancing are also available at all three, but sometimes only on the weekends.

12. The Molokai Address List

Molokai folk don't hold much with the names of streets and numbers. There aren't even many of them; the island takes up less than eight pages in the Maui phone book. Just ask anyone for what you want. They'll be happy to tell you and sometimes go out of their way to take you there.

One address you might want to make a note of, however, is the Destination Molokai Association (Tel. 553-3877), P.O. Box 200, Kualapuu, Molokai, HI 96757. The Honolulu phone number is 537-1845 and they also have toll-free numbers from the U.S. mainland and Canada (see appendix). If you're planning a trip to Molokai, they'll give you a hand. (Tell 'em we said to call.)

9

Lanai,
the Pineapple Island

1. Around the Island—A Green and Rugged Experience

Somehow a myth is perpetuated in Honolulu to the effect that the Island of Lanai consists of nothing but pineapples. It's true that there is an abundance of the big, fat, golden, and delicious fruit there. The 16,000 acres planted on Lanai make up the largest single pineapple plantation in the world, and it is the island's only industry.

But Lanai doesn't consist of a mere 16,000 acres. It totals about 90,400 acres—nearly 140 square miles—so less than one-fifth of that island is planted in pineapple. The rest? Well, much of it is ripe for your exploration.

"But it has only 20 miles of roads!" the mythmakers exclaim. Wrong again. Lanai has only 20 miles of *paved* roads. We put well over 100 miles on a jeep on Lanai one time and had a darn good time doing it, too.

True, Lanai is not for everyone. If you aren't prepared to bounce around in a jeep over dusty and rocky routes, don't go. But if you're young or in good health, want to blaze some trails and find historic sights with few signs to guide you, and maybe meet only two or three fellow visitors, then you'll enjoy Lanai as much as we do.

The Dole Company bought the entire island in 1922 for $1.1 million. That firm is now owned by Castle & Cooke, Inc., which eventually bowed to union pressure and sold nearly 2,000 acres of company housing to employees at very cheap rates. Today about 65 percent of the families

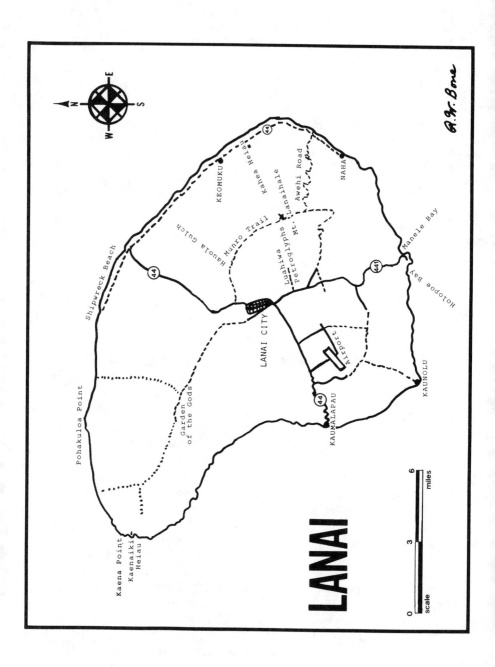

who live there proudly take care of their own tiny houses and gardens. Nevertheless, the company still owns nearly 98 percent of the island, and some residents and others in Hawaii are worried about plans to develop Lanai for tourism in the coming years. Castle & Cooke and its subsidiaries (Dole, the Lanai Company, and the Koele Company) are now controlled by mainlanders with a strong "bottom line" orientation.

Meanwhile, if you stay overnight at the Hotel Lanai, you might wake to hear the whistle blow at 4:30 A.M., in the middle of the dark, cool night. That means the weather's dry and there's work today.

If you were one of the 2,000 Filipino workers who live in Lanai City, you would eat your breakfast swiftly and then get dressed as quickly as you could in an incredibly thick outfit to protect you from the hot sun and the sharp crowns of the pineapple. If you got to the trucks in an hour and a half, you'd be in the fields in time to earn a full day's pay.

2. Lanai's Airport and Flights

As you descend closer and closer to the prickly pineapple fields, it's hard to believe that there's really a smooth runway down there. Hawaiian Airlines used to land their DC-9 Fanjets there, as a matter of fact, but today they serve the island only in their funny-looking, 50-passenger DASH-7 jet props.

Aloha Airlines doesn't fly to Lanai, so your choice of craft is either Hawaiian Air or the smaller commuter planes flown by Princeville Airways, Air Molokai, or Reeves Air.

About the only point to remember about the Lanai terminal building itself is that it is only open when flights are due. Otherwise its doors—including its lavatories—are securely locked. This becomes important after a day of jeep riding on dusty, red-dirt roads if you thought you could clean up quickly in the rest room before catching the plane out. For other types of emergencies, talk to the airport firemen in the corrugated metal shack next door.

The airport is five minutes' drive from Lanai City.

3. Transportation on Lanai

The scheduled planes into Lanai are often met by the island's only taxi, driven by "Molokai" Oshiro, Mrs. Oshiro, or their son, Glenn. If they are not there, you can use the pay phone on the outside of the terminal to call them at **Oshiro Enterprises** (Tel. 565-6952). If you are going to arrive on Sunday, be sure to make advance arrangements.

The Oshiros also own one of Lanai City's two gas stations, and one of only two rental-car agencies. We signed out a jeep from them once, and with the occasional use of the compound low gear (four-wheel drive), we were able to reach any point on the island where any other vehicle had ever preceded us. Expect to pay at least $70 a day for a jeep (or similar) or $30 for a conventional car.

The other gas station, **Lanai City Service** (Tel. 565-6780), is also in the U-drive business, but with compact cars only. Current rates are about $30 per day plus gas and tax.

There is little reason for renting a normal passenger car unless you are in Lanai on business and have no reason to sightsee. Nearly anything of interest can only be reached with a more rugged vehicle. Not every road will require switching into four-wheel drive, but the high undercarriage will serve to carry you safely over rocks and other objects hazardous to low-slung passenger automobiles.

The unpaved roads, particularly those through pineapple fields, are very, very dusty—and, on occasion, very, very muddy. Although it may be fun to take the top off and put the windshield down on trips through the mountains or along the beaches, we'd advise against it in the red-dirt plantation areas.

Traffic is no problem on the few miles of asphalt. On the one-lane dirt jeep trails, get in the habit of honking your horn on blind curves. However unlikely, another vehicle could come along. There are no traffic lights, but there are stop signs within the city limits plus about six policemen who do, they tell us, hand out tickets to tourists. Parking is free everywhere, and we never saw a "No Parking" sign on Lanai.

There is no public transportation on the island. Young folks generally have good luck with hitchhiking, except that local residents are seldom heading as far as such sites as petroglyphs, ancient *heiaus*, ghost towns, or the Garden of the Gods. If you have a pack on your back for serious exploring, however, and just need a lift to where the trail begins, chances are somebody will take you closer to it.

There are no bicycles, motorcycles, or horses currently for rent on Lanai. Hawaiian Airlines will fly your own bicycle to the island for around $5, however.

4. The Hotel Scene—Your Choice of One

Castle & Cooke has plans to build a luxury hotel on the island in 1988, so there's not much time left to stay in the little old **Hotel Lanai** (Tel. 565-6605). Built around 1927 by the Dole Corporation for its official visitors, today the white wood frame building is open to all comers.

It's set atop a grassy knoll in a cool forest of stately Norfolk pine trees, 1,600 feet above sea level. There's a charming, knotty-pine dining room with a fireplace at one end, and a new outdoor barbecue area. The hotel's spacious, creaky veranda now serves as the town's only bar.

There are 10 rooms, all with a john and shower. A few have private entrances so you won't have to track all that red dirt through the house after a day of sightseeing. At this writing, all accommodations rent for around $60 for two, $55 for one. (Reserve at the Hotel Lanai, Lanai, HI 96763, and include one night's deposit.) We haven't been over to stay since the hotel was bought by the new operators, the Ocean Activities Center of Maui, but initial reports are good.

For more intrepid wanderers, there are six approved campsites on the island, administered by the property owners. Costs are $5 for registration and then $4.50 per night per camper. Make arrangements with the Koele Company (Tel. 565-6661).

5. Dining and Restaurants

The best restaurant in Lanai City has always been the dining room in the **Hotel Lanai** just mentioned. At breakfast, lunch, or dinner, you'll probably find yourself exchanging sightseeing information with other guests.

For lunch only, there's a sort of all-around goody shop called **S. & T. Properties** on Seventh Street. It has a soda fountain inside, and it used to be named the Lanai Fountain. Lots of folks hereabouts still refer to it as "The Fountain." Anyway, it serves pretty good hamburgers. Next door, **Dahang's Pastry Shop** is now serving a local-style breakfast and lunch. Prices have always been low.

Or you can buy food fixings at Richard's Shopping Center, 434 Eighth St., or the Pine Isle Market, just up the street at No. 356. Both are general stores.

For our own lunch, we had the hotel make up some sandwiches and other accessories that we consumed on the road, high, high up at Lanaihale, and far, far from the maddening mob. You never knew a crunch into ham and cheese could taste so good—and sound so loud!

6. Sightseeing Lanai—Fun, but Rugged

Lanai has its fair share of sightseeing points, but they're about the hardest targets to hit of any in the Islands. Frankly, there's some serious local sentiment for maintaining the obscurity of many of the historical locations, under the theory that those who really want to find them badly enough will manage it somehow, and that casual wanderers can be dangerous. And it is true that such valuable relics as petroglyphs, ghost towns, and archeological sites have been defaced and damaged. Unfortunately, there are no facilities for guarding these important sites.

Once upon a time there were as many as twenty Hawaii Visitors Bureau warrior markers on Lanai, but all except two or three of these seem to have disappeared. Even some road signs in the hinterlands have been uprooted or at least not replaced when knocked asunder by wind, rain, or the wrath of the *akuas*.

Another problem in traversing Lanai is simply that there are *too many roads*. Every time a pineapple field is replanted or redesigned, the bulldozers are brought in to cut some new roads along the rows of fruit. Even some old routes indicated on maps are impossible to tell from just another pineapple road as it makes its way through the plantation.

One of the helpful techniques we have found for locating old roads is simply to drive along the periphery of the pineapple plantings, e.g., on Kaupili Road, keeping the fruit on one side of the jeep and the undeveloped scrub growth on the other. Then, when you see one of the "pineapple roads" cross your path and head off into the bushes, it could be the track you're looking for.

Use our directions here as general guides, but the way to improve your chances of finding the right road is to ask first at the Hotel Lanai. There's probably still a map on the wall that marks several sites you may not find listed elsewhere. (If you're reading these words before leaving for Lanai, hie yourself down to Honolulu Bookshops or another place that sells the University Press of Hawaii's map of Molokai and Lanai. It's a good investment even if it, too, isn't entirely accurate.)

The courses to follow generally divide themselves into five. Each one of four routes heads off more or less in a different direction. And a fifth road makes its way up along the ridgeline to the top of the mountain and down again. All radiate more or less from Lanai City, a patchwork of little houses in the pines positioned in the approximate center of the island.

THE NORTHWEST ROUTE

A well-traveled dirt road variously entitled the Kanepuu Highway or the Awalua Highway begins its trek to the far corner of the island by running through pineapple fields, but eventually emerges into the open, dry country that has probably not changed much for hundreds of years.

After about seven miles, the road comes to the **Garden of the Gods.** Most dramatic at sunrise or sunset, the bizarre landscape is dominated by a canyon of buttes, pinnacles, and weird lava formations, all cut into the red dirt and bordered by green grass.

Farther along, the road gets rougher, but you may be able to follow it when the weather's good to **Kaena Iki**, the site of the largest *heiau* on Lanai. There used to be a spur from there to **Kaena Point**, which served as an exile colony for adulterous Hawaiian women for a brief period in 1837. Lately the road has been closed, however.

THE NORTHEAST ROUTE

Here's one that's paved, or at least it is for the first eight miles down the slope as far as the windward shore. That's where it begins to be interesting, and it divides into two sections.

Just before the end of the macadamized section, take the Poaiwa Road to the left. This winding, dirt-and-sand track dives through tunnels of *kiawe* trees (plenty of ducking necessary if you're in an open jeep) and eventually leads to **Shipwreck Beach.** You may pass some squatters' shacks built out of the timbers of foundered vessels. At the very end of the road, you'll see at least one modern-looking ship aground, deserted and just waiting for the waves to pound her into submission against the offshore reef. The craft is an old "liberty ship," still holding out since its beaching there during World War II.

With the trade winds funneling through the Pailolo Channel between Molokai and Maui (both islands visible in the distance), hundreds of large and small craft have been scuttled on this shore, either by accident or design, during the past 150 years. There have been fewer shipwrecked in this century since whaling vessels no longer congregate in the Lahaina Roadstead across the nine-mile channel between Lanai and Maui.

Leave your jeep at the end of the road and head on foot for a cement structure that looks like it might have been a World War II gun platform. Near there, the rocks on the ground have been marked with white paint and an occasional arrow by Lanai Boy Scouts. Follow these for a few hundred yards to see a good collection of **Hawaiian petroglyphs.** The gateway boulder to this ancient grotto of pictorial graffiti is marked in commanding strokes, "Do Not Deface!"

If you return to the end of the paved portion of Highway 44, you can continue south on the dirt along the waterline to the ghost town of **Keomuku.** The village was abandoned in 1901 when the nearby Maunalei Sugar Company failed. Nestled in a lovely coconut grove, most of the old houses were razed only in 1973. The rickety wooden church remains, however. The nearby century-old boat landing has just been restored, supposedly opening up the area as a low-density tourist attraction for cruises from Lanai, but we haven't been by since that took place.

Just down the road you'll see why the Hawaiians say the plantation closed down. There is the **Kahea Heiau,** some of whose sacred stones were taken by the *haoles* to build the sugar railroad. Not long after the shrine was disturbed, the mill's sweet water turned salty for no earthly reason. (We also saw some interesting petroglyphs on the large stones near the *heiau*.)

If you follow this windward dirt road for the full 15 miles, you'll eventually come to the site of the old Hawaiian village called **Naha.** There is some "paved" road here—paved in stones by the old Hawaiians centuries ago. But cobbled or not, here your jeep road ends. Unless there's been a new cut made by the bulldozers since we were there, you'll have to turn around.

THE SOUTHWEST ROUTE

A really good stretch of two-lane highway, this end of Route 44 goes past the airport road and winds down the bluff to **Kaumalapau Harbor,** and it is a busy thoroughfare during the picking season. The harbor was built to transfer millions of tons of pineapples annually from the enormous trucks to the enormous barges which then speed them off to the enormous Dole cannery in Honolulu. In the summer, you may watch this operation in progress.

Just past the airport road, long before you get to that harbor, however, there is another paved road that turns off the Kaumalapau Highway to the left. (It may or may not be called Kaupili Road.) If you have a jeep, a rugged constitution, a determined nature, plenty of time, and a deep interest in seeing the vast remains of a once-populous village frequented by Kamehameha the Great, you can turn here to begin the trek to **Kaunolu Village.** A rough shoreline community, now completely deserted, it was Kamehameha's favorite fishing ground.

The pavement peters out into a dusty red pineapple road at a point nearly opposite the end of the airport runway (the elevated area to your left). Now scan the horizon to your right on a search for the only man-made structure in view, a tubular building that is the covered antenna for an aircraft electronic navigation station. From this distance, it looks something like a rocket ship or a lighthouse. Head out across any pineapple road over the rolling plantation until you reach that building, located right on the border between the pineapples and the uncultivated countryside.

Next, continue to drive generally south along the edge of the plantation, always keeping the pineapples (or plowed pineapple fields) to your left and the rugged grassland to your right, for about 2 miles. There, the Kaunolu Road heads into the bush to your right. If you're lucky, there *may* be a wooden sign there to reassure you.

The incredibly rough road bumps down, down, down for two miles (it may seem more like ten) before you reach the rocky ruins of the village. But then, wow!

Park your jeep, and climb around the "city," being very careful not to stumble and fall into any ravines or over any *pali.* There are the ruins of **Halulu Heiau,** and you can soon begin to imagine the place full of activity as it must have looked with a hundred or more grass houses scattered over the terraces, where only piles of rocks and remnants of hillside trails now remain. (The rocks, incidentally, are believed by some to contain the spirits of the former residents. Those who want to stay on good terms with these Hawaiian ghosts will demonstrate it—as we did— by piling at least one rock on top of another, larger rock, thus restoring a fallen warrior to his former dignity.)

You may find yourself standing on the brink of the eastern bluff, just above the gulch. This, they say, was the site of the king's house. From here, you can see **Kahekili's Jump,** a 62-foot-high cliff from which the king's bravest soldiers would, on his command, leap into the sea. Those who were strong and pure of heart would have no trouble clearing the 15-foot ledge that protrudes below. Others, who could not, would instead enter the spirit world, leaving their broken bodies with the rocks at the water's edge.

THE SOUTHEAST ROUTE

This, too, is a main paved road to the shore with almost a Mission Impossible side trip that is nevertheless of unusual value. The conventional route is to follow Manele Road (State Highway 441) to **Hulopoe Bay**—a lovely beach park with picnic tables, barbecue pits, and excellent swimming. (The new hotel will be built near here.) A nearby fork in the road leads to **Manele Bay,** the site of a rather plain, small boat harbor where you might land if you're one of the few visitors to Lanai to arrive by sea. (Several cruise boats from Lahaina, Maui, offer excursions to Lanai, and this could be an unusual way to effect an interisland trip. See the Maui chapter, section 7.)

But the side trip off Highway 441 to see the **Luahiwa petroglyphs** is the most tantalizing—and the most frustrating—project for many visitors. Among the best preserved in all the Islands, this large collection of boulders engraved with hundreds of Hawaiian figures would be easy to reach if the roads were marked, but they are not.

About a mile south of Lanai City on Route 441, look east toward the foothills until you see a silvery water tower, an easy landmark to find. Below this tank, almost down to the level of the pineapple fields, is a more obscure little yellow building (or at least it was yellow the last time we were there) that houses a humming electric transformer. The petroglyphs are approximately 50 feet up the hill above this high-voltage shack, and just a little south of it.

After parking our jeep at the little building and making an agonizing climb up a near-vertical cliff through the underbrush, we finally came to—another road! (Later we found the same road on wheels, but it is hopeless to describe the maze of rust-colored trails we blundered through in order to do so.)

The scattering of inscribed boulders in the grove of trees and sisal plants on the nearby hillside was magnificent. There were petroglyphs we hadn't seen represented in any books, and we marveled at such images as the magnificent large war canoes, complete with sails and outriggers. Also there were men on horseback, so these were apparently drawn after the *haoles* came to Lanai with their strange snorting beasts. We thought then that it was an historical pity that the Hawaiians did not bring the newcomers to such stones to describe what significance was attached to their scratches, if not to read aloud the stories inscribed there.

The boulders appeared to march up and up the hill, one by one, in a zigzag pattern. Each rock seemed to call us to climb again and see just one more group of pictures, farther and farther up the bluff in a continuing quest to pry some meaning from it all. It seemed each rock had a different story to tell—about families, dogs, pigs, birds, and little concentric circles that could mean trips around the island, or, perhaps, rainbows. There were petroglyphs on top of petroglyphs, so surely they have not yet all been studied exhaustively. Who would perceive the solution to their mystery?

THE MUNRO TRAIL

Sometime after the turn of the century, a New Zealand naturalist named George C. Munro came to Lanai with seeds, plants, and flowers from his native land that he decided would flourish up along the ridgeline of Lanaihale, the 3,370-foot-high mountain that today watches over Lanai City and the pineapple plants below.

So Munro proceeded to sow a little New Zealand way up high, and not the least of these botanical wonders were hundreds of Norfolk Island pine trees. These proved to be so efficient at gathering moisture from the air that they were also successfully seeded in and around Lanai City to alleviate the desert atmosphere.

Our jeep trip through the upland rain forest along the Munro Trail was a particular delight for Sara, herself a displaced New Zealander. She recognized such familiar home-grown specialties as *manuka* and other wildflowers and tree ferns that descended from her countryman's munificence long ago.

The Munro Trail is often—and rightly—the first excursion taken by a visitor to Lanai. Pack some sandwiches and take Route 44 past the golf course about a half-mile; then turn right onto the dirt road at Koele. Always follow the more well-traveled track, even when it appears to go down instead of up, not far from the beginning of the route. Or, better yet, get some up-to-date advice from the Hotel Lanai. (The cemetery road is now supposed to be a better beginning to the trail.) Keep a sharp eye out, and you may see an axis deer, as we did on our own gambol over the trail.

You'll pass the **Hookio Ridge,** the fortified notches in the landscape where Lanai warriors unsuccessfully defended their home from an invasion launched from the Island of Hawaii in 1778.

Nearby is the 2,000-foot-deep **Hauola Gulch,** seen best from a foot trail that leads to an overlook. But where we shut off the motor, were deafened by the silence, and settled down to picnic was at the **Lanaihale Overlook.** There you can see the islands of Maui, Molokini, Kahoolawe, and, on a clear day, Oahu, Molokai, and Hawaii.

From Lanaihale you must continue around the remainder of the seven-mile circular route until it joins Highway 441 via Hoike Road.

The Munro Trail is Lanai's zenith—a "must," we think, for all comers.

7. Guided Tours and Cruises

Jimmie Nishimura, now in his seventies, has sold the gas station and tour operation he ran for most of his life. However, Jimmie is still there at **Lanai City Service** (Tel. 565-6780), although semiretired. If you could talk him into giving you a tour, it would probably be first-rate.

Lanai Sea Charters (Tel. 565-6958) will tailor its trips to suit you, the sailor. Several different arrangements are available. Bob Moon, captain and instructor, will meet you at Lanai Airport or even send out his boat to bring you over to Lanai from Maui, if you prefer. Better write him in advance at P.O. Box 401, Lanai City, HI 96763 to find out the latest information.

Some other sailing trips may be organized from Lanai in 1987. Chances are all the latest nautical scuttlebutt will be available from the Hotel Lanai.

8. Water Sports on Lanai

There is good swimming, some snorkeling, so-so surfing, and several excellent spots for shore fishing.

Hulopoe Beach is one of the best beaches in the state, usually safe for swimming except during rough seas. Sometimes there is good body surfing. Camping is possible with a permit from the Koele Company.

Manele Beach, next door, is more suited for docking of small boats than swimming, although there is some sand leading up to the calm waters. Most people swim at Hulopoe, however. There are picnic tables and grills at both.

Shipwreck Beach is fine for wading, shore fishing, and certainly beachcombing.

Kaunolu, which was Kamehameha's favorite fishing grounds, still is good fertile territory for shore casting, they say. We wouldn't swim in these crashing waves and near those rocks, however, on a *kahuna*'s double dare!

Kaumalapau Harbor is also popular for shore fishing, once the pineapple truck and barge activity has ended for the day.

There are no charter boats for *sport fishing* stationed at Lanai, but some will come over from Maui on request. Waters around Lanai are known for catches of *ahi, aku, kawakawa, mahimahi,* and *ulua.*

9. Other Sports on Lanai

There is the nine-hole **Cavendish Golf Course** ($5 a day for out-of-towners; no carts, and bring your own clubs) and four free tennis courts at the school (bring your own rackets and balls). You can also use the archery club's range free (again, only if you've tucked your bow and arrows into your bags).

If a Honoluluan knows anything more about Lanai other than that "it's paved with pineapple," he knows it's an island of good *hunting*. In the latter fact, he is correct. The island has been stocked with several kinds of game especially for hunters.

Axis deer, Mouflon sheep, and pronghorn antelope are the larger animals in season, although the recently imported antelope have not been surviving very well on the island.

Many game birds are hunted, some of which will make a quick bag limit. These include the ubiquitous Chukar partridge, bamboo partridge, ring-necked pheasant, barred dove, black francolin, grey francolin, lace-necked dove, Gambel's quail, and the Rio Grande turkey.

Seasons, limits, and hunting licenses are set up, both by the Koele Company (which controls hunting on and near pineapple land) and the state (which sets the rules everywhere else). For information on hunting on private property write to the Chief Ranger, Koele Company, Lanai City, HI 96763, or call 565-6661 on Lanai or 531-4454, a direct line from Honolulu.

Basic charge for hunting on Koele (Castle & Cooke) land is perhaps still $180 per hunter per day. If you've never hunted there before, a guide is required, and they cost around $150 to $200. The guide will take care of just about everything except firing the shot, including picking you up at the airport, providing a light breakfast, finding the deer, gutting it later, packing the meat and the trophy, etc. If you don't stay at the Hotel Lanai, the Koele Company can sometimes provide basic one-bedroom hunter's cottages, sleeping two, for $50 or so a night. If you forget your gun, the Koele Company will rent you that, too.

If you're interested in hunting on state land, on Lanai or elsewhere in Hawaii, write to the Department of Land and Natural Resources, Division of Fish and Game, 465 South King St., Honolulu, HI 96813.

One other sport, which is not regulated—except that it is completely illegal—is *cockfighting,* which is very much part of the tradition and culture of the Filipino plantation workers. By asking around, they say, you can attend a cockfight any Sunday. (We haven't.)

10. & 11. Shopping and Nights on the Town

The first isn't recommended for the visitor. And the second just isn't. Have a short one on the *lanai* of the Hotel Lanai and then go to bed early like everyone else. (The bar usually closes at 9:30 P.M. anyway.)

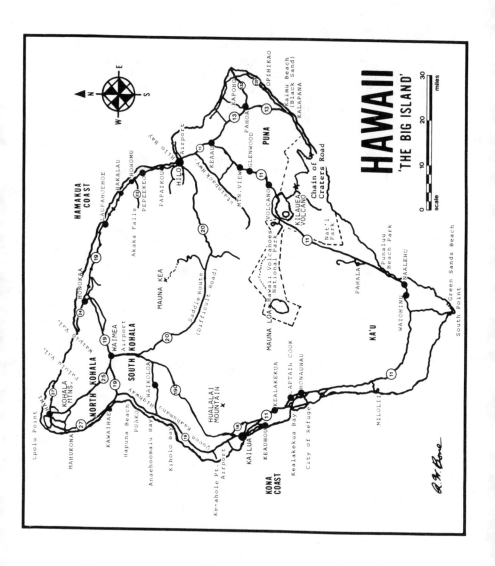

10

The Island of Hawaii
—the "Big Island"

1. Around the Island—A Sizable Hunk of History

The Big Island is what Hawaii is all about.

Just under its surface, the liquid fire of creation still lives, its vaporous breath always visible and smellable, even in the most quiescent periods. Sometimes it emerges in a spectacular display to remind us that human life is only a very recent and relatively insignificant feature on this or any other island.

New lava may pour forth, either from one of the great calderas in the Volcanoes National Park or squeezed through massive fissures that open far away in the earth, perhaps near villages and farms and nowhere in the vicinity we think of as the volcano area.

The hot material, at once destructive and constructive, then moves over the land, decimating the works of man until it reaches the sea, there building up a new shoreline and still more real estate on the Island of Hawaii. It is the only such island in the chain that is physically still growing in size.

According to Hawaiian legend, the island is the dwelling place of Pele, the goddess of the volcano. Her house is said to be in whichever crater is currently the hottest and most frequently active. The ancient Hawaiians were justly afraid of Pele, for her wrath claimed a number of their souls. It is interesting, though perhaps not significant, that lives have virtually ceased to be lost to Pele in modern times, and her antics have become relatively predictable. During a volcano eruption, the National Park Service does its best to find safe places for everyone to watch the show and to direct the public to these areas.

Three mountains dominate the Big Island landscape. Hualalai, the shortest, and Mauna Kea, the tallest, are considered dormant (but not extinct) volcanoes. Mauna Loa, nearly as lofty as the 13,800-foot Mauna Kea, is officially an active volcano, although its eruptions are relatively infrequent. Mauna Loa was quiet for twenty-five years, in fact, before it let loose with a dramatic one-day eruption in 1975. Then in 1984 it burst forth again in a spectacular eruption for 22 days, sending toward Hilo a lengthening, potentially destructive finger of lava that stopped growing just outside the outskirts of the city.

Hawaii's most active volcano, and considered the most active volcano in the world, is Kilauea, which does not seem to be a mountain at all. Its major crater (or caldera) is a gigantic, two-mile-wide ever-steaming circular pit on a plain at about the 4,000-foot level on the gentle slope of Mauna Loa. Between 1959 and 1975, Kilauea erupted two or three times a year, either from the crater area or farther down the "rift zone" in the Puna District. After that the action slowed for a time, with an eruption about every other year. In 1982 there were two short outbreaks of lava directly inside Kilauea crater, and these drew thousands of spectators to the rim day and night to watch the sound-and-light show below.

Then, in 1983, Kilauea began to erupt spectacularly off and on in a more frequent series of eruptions that has continued for four years, so far, although almost always away from the crater in out-of-the-way forests on the rift zone. On two occasions, however, lava flowed slowly down the flank into an isolated country residential area, and eventually it claimed about 10 houses. As always, no one was hurt.

The Big Island has hosted many key events in human history, not the least of which was the visit of the great British navigator Captain James Cook, at first honored and then killed by the Hawaiians at Kealakekua Bay in 1779. It was on Hawaii, too, that Kamehameha the Great first plotted and fought his way to power before going on to extend his empire over the entire string of islands. Christianity gained an important step here in 1824 when the converted Chieftess Kapiolani publicly and successfully defied Pele in a ceremony at Kilauea crater in front of scores of trembling witnesses.

Today, of course, the Big Island is not all volcano. Its county seat is Hilo, a mixture of modern and rustic structures at the mouth of the Wailuku River, and a center for the colorful orchid and anthurium industry. North of Hilo is the dramatically rugged Hamakua Coast, ending in the deep green slash of Waipio Valley. And near that is the vast, rolling cattle and cowboy country of Waimea.

Still farther north is the former sugar land and economically depressed peninsula of Kohala. The western coast is called Kona, a sunny and dry neighborhood that includes the former stamping ground of Captain Cook, King Kamehameha, Captain George Vancouver, and the first missionaries to the Islands. Today the Kona Coast boasts the only commercial coffee crops in the U.S. and perhaps the best deep-sea fishing area in the world.

The southern land mass is Ka'u, which received the first Polynesian settlers to the Islands and is now sparsely populated. It is the home of the "southernmost" everything in the United States.

Then there is prosperous Puna, which has, at the same time, some of the most desolate parts of the island in its volcanic areas and some of the most tropical and lush acreage where the soil has escaped the flows of lava.

Strangely, the Big Island has few tourists for its size, due at least partly to the confusion caused by its own name. (Local boosters complain that even travel agents have been known to get off the plane in Hilo and ask the way to Waikiki Beach—and worse, to ask in Honolulu to be taken up to the volcano!) This is a shame, for in many ways this island offers unique sights and experiences that cannot be duplicated in the state—or in any other state, for that matter. For its special features, it just might be the best bargain for visitors who want to choose a single destination with lots to see and do but without the hustle-bustle of Honolulu or Maui.

So islanders virtually never call the island Hawaii, unless they can use the term "*on* Hawaii" to contrast with the phrase "*in* Hawaii." There have been attempts to nickname the Island of Hawaii "The Orchid Island" or "The Volcano Island," but those terms usually fall on inattentive ears at home. The island's dominant characteristic will always be its size—more than twice the land area of all the other islands combined—and its name will always remain simply "The Big Island."

2. The Airports on Hawaii

Five civilian airports are scattered over the Big Island, but three have been fast fading from the scene. The **Kona Village Airport,** serving an exclusive resort community, no longer has scheduled flights. Except for an occasional helicopter, it now serves only as an emergency strip. The tiny **Upolu Airport** on the windswept land's end at the northernmost tip of the island is also all but closed down. And the attractive **Waimea-Kohala Airport** at Waimea, like the Upolu and Kona Village strips, has been doomed by the Kaahumanu Highway. The center of the ranch and cattle country, Waimea may be occasionally served by a charter flight only.

Over on the windward side of the island, the half-mile-long terminal at Hilo's **General Lyman Field** serves all interisland flights as well as those from Kona on United Airlines, which gas up and pick up more passengers in Hilo before leaving for the Mainland.

Passengers from all jets enter the terminal on the second floor through one of seven loading bridges attached directly to aircraft doors. Baggage-claim carousels are down the escalator on the ground floor. In one end of the building there is a state VIP (Visitor Information Program) booth, three *lei* stands, and a gift shop. The cafeteria-style restaurant is just across the hall and a package food store (macadamia nuts and all that) is nearby.

Some rental-car agencies are outside opposite the center of the complex. As in Kona, there is no public transportation from the airport. But since the airport is practically inside the city and near many hotels, taxis are not so bad—about $5. (Backpackers may prefer to hoof the three miles into town.)

The terminal is attractively landscaped and even features some small waterfalls using water collected from the building's roof. (And in Hilo, that should certainly be a dependable source!)

On the leeward side of the island, Kona's breezy, outdoorsy **Ke-ahole Airport,** about 15 minutes' drive north of Kailua-Kona, is also a full-size gateway to the Big Island. It has several flights a day from all other islands via the jets of Aloha Airlines, and the jets or jet props of Hawaiian Airlines and Mid Pacific Airlines, as well as the propeller-driven DeHavillands of Princeville Airways. It also receives some DC-8 flights to or from some Mainland cities via United Airlines.

Set up in a string of about ten little Polynesian-style, open-sided buildings, the terminal is divided into two general areas. Hawaiian Airlines occupies the southern or Kailua extremity, while Aloha Airlines has the opposite end, with facilities arranged in a near-mirror image to Hawaiian's. Consequently, there are two of nearly everything at the airport—two snack bars, two sets of rest rooms, two state information counters, et cetera. (So watch out if you're going to meet somebody for a hot dog.) Under construction in the center of the complex is the pavilion and museum honoring Ellison Onizuka, the Hawaii astronaut from Kona who died in the *Challenger* disaster.

Over a footbridge in the very center is a small building devoted to a line of automobile rental counters, with their vehicles either parked in the lot just behind them or a five-minute shuttle ride away. You'll find about a dozen firms represented at the airport. Two or three other companies are in Kailua and will arrange an airport pickup for customers. (See section 3.)

There is no municipal transportation available at the airport. It will cost you about $9 for a seat on the Gray Line limousine for the nine miles to Kailua or perhaps $11 via one of the three or four taxi companies available—up to $16 to hotels in Keauhou. Some hotels on the Kohala coast send their own transportation to pick up hotel guests at the airport, usually by prior arrangement.

3. Big Island Transportation

The most practical transportation for visitors on the Big Island is a rental car—or even a jeep, if you are heading to more rugged and wilder areas. At any given time, there are at least a dozen very competitive car-rental firms on the island. Those with offices at the two major airports are more convenient, of course, and usually more expensive, too.

Since distances are so great compared with other islands in the state, many will prefer to rent a car on flat rates—with no mileage charges. Be aware, however, that this is difficult to do during the busiest seasons of the year when there are many customers and fewer cars available. Flat rates for most companies go into hiding in February and don't come out again until about April. They might disappear again in July and August.

Here is a list of some Big Island car-rental companies as they exist at the moment. Unless otherwise indicated, all have offices at the airports in both Kona and Hilo, and the phone numbers listed here are for those terminal locations. (If you are in Honolulu planning a Big Island trip, you can look up and call the Honolulu phone numbers for some of these outfits, questioning them on their rates and then making reservations for cars.)

Be aware that if you rent a car in Hilo and turn it in in Kona—or vice versa—you'll probably pay a hefty drop-off charge, so compare this with your air fares. To drive from Kona all the way around to Kona again and then fly back to Honolulu may only cost you about $3 or so more than turning in your car in Hilo and flying to Honolulu from there.

National chains:
Hertz (Kona 329-3566, Hilo 935-2896), which specializes in Ford products; **Avis** (Kona 329-1745, Hilo 935-1290), which generally has GM or Japanese cars; **National** (Kona 329-1674, Hilo 935-0891), which usually features GM products; **Budget** (Kona 329-8511, Hilo 935-6878); **Dollar** (Kona 329-2744, Hilo 961-6059); **American International** (Kona 329-2926, Hilo 935-1108); and **Alamo** (Kona 329-8896, Hilo 961-3343) which has an annoying empty-gas-tank policy.

Statewide chains:
Robert's Hawaii (Kona 329-1688, Hilo 935-2858), which is well established and well known in the Islands; **Holiday** (Kona 329-1752, Hilo 935-6861); and **Tropical** (Kona, 329-2347, Hilo, 935-3385).

Local Big Island companies:

Phillips (Kona 329-1730, Hilo 935-1936) and **United** (Kona 329-3411, Hilo 935-2115).

Used cars are rented in Kailua-Kona by **Ugly Duckling** (Tel. 329-2113) at 74-5491 Kaiwi St. and by **Honolulu** (Tel. 329-7328) at 74-5588 Pawai Place. We have had no experience with either firm.

Keep in mind that the rental situation sometimes changes daily in regard to rates, ownership, types of deals, etc. Before renting a car anywhere in the Islands, please see our discussion on the subject in chapter 5, section 3.

A scooter, bike, and moped rental outfit, **Continental Rental** (Tel. 329-3250), has opened in Kona at 74-5622 Alapa St. We have had no experience with them.

Camper Rentals. For those intrepids who want to guide their own hotel rooms over Big Island byways, there are now two firms to consider. The long-established recreational vehicle renter is **Travel/Camp** (Tel. 935-7406), where you can rent three sizes, from a compact cabover sleeping two for about $55 a day on up to a 24-foot motor home, sleeping six, with full bathroom and generator for around $100 a day. Write for details to P.O. Box 11, Hilo, HI 96720.

Beach Boy Campers (Tel. 967-8144) may still have a Datsun "mini-cabover," sleeping four, from about $50 to $90. (We've tried neither of these outfits personally, and strangely we haven't heard from any readers who have.)

Driving on the Big Island. In general, the roads are good and well marked, with a couple of notable exceptions. Some maps you may pick up list the old route numbers in the Waimea-to-Kona neighborhood, which has changed around somewhat. (Part of Route 19 has become 190, Route 26 has become part of 19, etc.)

• In Hilo, watch your stop signs carefully. There are a few streets that look like they ought to be through ones for you but aren't. And by all means be sure your windshield wipers are working all right.

• The Saddle Road (54 miles on Route 20 between Hilo and Waimea) is not for every driver. In addition to its being narrow with several rough spots and some very tight turns, the road is often wet and foggy and sometimes used in massive military maneuvers. There are no gas stations or emergency services of any kind, and in case of any mishap, help could be a long time coming—and expensive. If you do try it, do so in the morning and when the weather is clear. The Saddle Road may look on the map like a faster way to Kona than the northern route, but it decidedly is not. Also, driving on the Saddle Road is a violation of most rental-car contracts. We do not cater to the U-drives, of course, but we want to point out that this means you may have insurance difficulties if you do have an accident there.

● Make a practice of keeping your gas tank full all over the Big Island. Stations have a way of closing early when you don't expect it, and there are such frightening stretches as that 50 miles between the villages of Captain Cook and Naalehu with not a gas pump to be seen! (It's even worse than that when Naalehu and Captain Cook roll up their respective sidewalks.)

County Buses. An island-wide operation, the 11-year-old **County of Hawaii Mass Transit Agency** (Tel. 935-8241), is fine as long as the buses are going where you want to go. Taking a cue apparently from Honolulu, they made the new vehicles colorful, painting most of them lavender and white, and labeled them with the pidgin slogan *Hele-on.* (That may be loosely translated as "go-go.")

The Hilo bus terminal is between Kamehameha Avenue and the Bayfront Highway, about opposite the foot of Mamo Street. You pay on the basis of how far you *hele* (small change for some short trips, but it's $5.25 from Hilo to Kailua-Kona), and schedules are usually designed to be of more service to workers than to island visitors.

4. The Hotel Scene—Kona, Hilo, and Inns Between

Lodgings on the Big Island traditionally fall into two general areas. There are the hotels and condos in the popular resort area of *Kona,* often in the neighborhing villages of Kailua (sometimes called Kailua-Kona) and Keauhou ("kay-ow-*ho*"), which are seven miles away from each other. And second, 100 road miles across the island, some other hotels in the county seat, the citilet of *Hilo* (either in the shoreline Banyan Drive area or downtown).

In addition to these, there have always been a half-dozen or so modest country hotels scattered about the island. Recently these have been augmented by some magnificent exceptions such as the deluxe Sheraton Waikoloa and the superluxurious Mauna Lani Bay.

Last, but certainly farthest from least, there are a couple of exclusive hostelries that qualify not just as hotels but as entire centralized vacations themselves—the Mauna Kea Beach Hotel and the Kona Village Resort. These luxurious retreats were designed for the most affluent travelers to Hawaii, and have very special features that place them in a category of their own. They bring up the end of this section.

HOTELS IN KONA

Many consider the resort area of Kona to be bounded by the village of

Kailua on the north and Keauhou Bay seven miles south, so the principal hotels and condos appear in those two areas. (Kona Coast hotels outside those boundaries will be discussed later.) As it happened, on our research rounds the Kona accommodations we saw fell into three price categories, which we have labeled "expensive," "medium," and "budget." Expensive hotels will be found in both Keauhou and Kailua, but all the medium and budget entries are in Kailua only.

EXPENSIVE KEAUHOU/KAILUA-KONA HOTELS

The unusual architecture and landscaping in the 535-room **Kona Surf Resort** (Tel. 322-3411) in Keauhou makes it a favorite: Huge, rambling structure in five irregularly shaped wings (ask for a hotel map, and watch the color-coded elevator banks); walking distance to Keauhou Bay, with a little beach and cruises available; large open-air lobby with intaglio mural (ask at the reception desk for the beach guide folder); several lush gardens; lots of sports activities including golf on the nearby Keauhou Resort course, three tennis courts, volleyball, driving range, putting green, two swimming pools (one huge saltwater model with a slide); sauna bath; massage salon; many shops; Pacific and Asian art and sculpture collection spread throughout the structure; occasionally visiting manta rays in the floodlights after dark.

The hotel boasts several attractive restaurants and bars, including the cavelike Puka Bar (7:30 to 12); Poi Pounder show bar and discotheque; Pele's Court coffee shop; open-air Nalu Terrace sometimes serving buffet breakfast; Nalu Bar, next to the salty pool; the S.S. James Makee Dining Room, named for an early interisland steamship.

The bedrooms are in five wings named after five islands; the Maui Wing our preference; some rooms with king-size beds; others with double-doubles; eye-soothing views over rocks and seas; large *lanais;* tapestries in Hawaiian quilt designs; carpeted baths; generally colorful decor throughout; a few lower-floor standard doubles at about $90 a day, unchanged from last year; superiors and deluxes $110 to $125. Best nonsuite room in the house for $140. (Reservations direct from the hotel at Keauhou-Kona, HI 96740.) The hotel has been bought and sold several times recently. That's a shame, for maintenance has become a little spotty as a result, at least temporarily. But we think the basic plant is good and the staff is ready and willing. We hope and believe the Kona Surf will again be the area leader in 1987.

At one end of the village of Kailua, the unusually contoured **Kona Hilton** (Tel. 329-3111) sails the southern skyline: Walking distance to village sights along the shoreline; dramatic exterior with lots of hanging plants, bougainvillea, and other flowers; three large main structures;

massive Grecian pillars in the public areas; airy, breezy lobby reached via a bridge over a lagoon (drop a piece of bread and watch the carp crowd around); small beach nearby; large pool; four Laykold tennis courts; several shops; Windjammer lounge; elegant Hele Mai dining room (high prices); Lanai Coffee Shop a better bargain.

Total of 452 well-decorated rooms with views over ocean, mountains, or village; several with original paintings on the walls; all with TV, coffee-makers, refrigerators, etc.; widely varying prices running from around $75 to $125 for twins all year. Forty-eight hours advance notice is required for cancellations, a policy that upset a reader last year when his flight was delayed until the following day. (Reservations through Hilton Hotels, or P. O. Box 1179, Kailua-Kona, HI 96745.) The Hilton is now owned by Pleasant Hawaiian Holidays, a wholesale tour operator, so that may mean more groups and fewer independent guests these days. Nevertheless, it's still convenient and generally recommended.

Some may logically prefer the **Hotel King Kamehameha** (Tel. 329-2911), which has ruled the north end of Kailua town since the venerated old King Kam was dynamited off the beach. The grounds, with their historical displays, are beautiful and interesting, the nighttime torch-lit atmosphere around the pool and the ocean is delightful, and the location is convenient, with a regal shopping center built right into the twin-hulled complex. There are four tennis courts off to the side and a tiny bathing strand along a calm cove. We have remained generally disappointed with the food service, but it doesn't matter since all of Kailua is at your feet.

Upstairs, the suites are fit for a king all right, but many other rooms are simply too pawn-sized for a luxury-class Hawaii hotel. Five classes of accommodations will run from around $70 to about $120 this year. The friendly, helpful staff here makes up for a lot. (Reservations from Amfac Hotels, P.O. Box 8519, Honolulu, HI 96815.) The Kam is not a bad King, to be sure, and he seems to be improving.

Last on our luxury scale is back in Keauhou again at the 454-room **Kona Lagoon Hotel** (Tel. 322-2727), an architectural curiosity next door to the Keauhou Beach Hotel: Three bodies of water—the ocean, a kidney-shaped pool, and the artificial lagoon helping to justify the name; large reception area decorated with pictures of last night's luau; electronic games for lobby loungers; two tennis courts; Tonga bar and dining room with tapa designs; high-peaked Polynesian Long House dinner/show room across from the huge porte cochere; Club CJ's disco on weekends. Rooms are rather small, and nearly all (except suites) are priced from around $65 to $75. (Reservations from the hotel at 78-6780 Alii Dr., Kailua-Kona, HI 96740.) We don't really object to this hotel, but all things considered—little beach, group-heavy, distance from the action, room size, etc.—we do prefer all the previously listed Kona addresses this year.

A probably good condo operation we haven't inspected yet is the **Royal Sea Cliff** (Tel. 329-8021) at 76-6040 Alii Drive, just south of Kailua-Kona. Administered by Aston Hotels and Resorts, there's a shoreline swimming pool and tennis court plus air-conditioned studio, one-bedroom and two-bedroom apartments renting from around $70 to $125. If you go, let us know.

MEDIUM-PRICED KAILUA HOTELS

A moderately priced Kona sleeper is the 123-room **Kona Bay Hotel** (Tel. 329-1393), administered by members of the younger generation in the family of Uncle Billy Kimi, proprietor of the Hilo Bay Hotel. There's a pool and four restaurants on the premises.

The air-conditioned units, virtually all alike, come in standards (B&W TV) for perhaps $40 double, superiors (color TV) for $45, and deluxes (color TV and small refrigerator) for about $50. (Add $7 for an extra person, or $8 for a unit with kitchenette.) We were happy with our own short stay awhile back, although one reader wrote us several more recent complaints. (Write the hotel at 75-5739 Alii Drive, or phone the toll-free number in the appendix.) Perhaps a good bet at those rates—and perhaps not.

A more whoop-it-up favorite with many is the **Kona Seaside** (Tel. 329-2455), owned by the Hukilau chain, which seems to cater to a lively singles crowd. Midtown location at the corner of Kuakini and Palani, a *maika* stone's throw from the King Kam; set back behind the bougainvillea and the old outriggers; darkish, low-ceilinged lobby with large tiles; wood paneling; windows on high; ample swimming pool; deluxe rooms on the fourth floor for about $70 with ocean view; superiors on the street corner maybe $64 (where some staff members say you can watch the cars crack up at the intersection below!); some first-floor standards in the $60 range for two; same prices for singles in each category. All rates down about $5 mid-April to mid-December. (Reservations from Hukilau Resorts, 2222 Kalakaua Ave., Honolulu, HI 96815.) Plainer than some Hukilaus, but perhaps a good place for a crash.

BUDGET KAILUA HOTELS

There are still a couple of addresses where you might get double accommodations for $60 or less. One standby is the **Kona Hukilau** (Tel. 329-2455), which is connected with (and almost connected *to*) the above-mentioned Seaside: Convenient address, in the center of everything;

rustic lobby right on Alii Drive; popular, low-priced tapa-walled restaurant and aquarium-studded bar; unusual hillside design placing the pool and "ground" floor upstairs. A common *lanai* with chairs in front of several rooms at once means you'll run into your neighbors—or at least their feet! There are 104 simple, neat, clean rooms at around $50-$60, double or single. Walk-in room rates may be cheaper than the published sheet. (Reservations from Hukilau Resorts, 2222 Kalakaua Ave., Honolulu, HI 96815.) You won't find a lot of frills, but we actually prefer this one to its slightly more expensive Seaside sister.

Then there's the **Kona Tiki** (Tel. 329-1425), a small, three-story structure about a mile south of Kailua: Just 15 modest but clean units, all with *lanais;* everything directly on the ocean; no beach, but a nice pool next to the salt spray; free Kona coffee and donuts every morning on the terrace; outdoor barbecue for guest use; ceiling fans in all the rooms. Twins at around $40 have cooking facilities; those for around $30 do not. There's a three-day minimum stay. (Write the hotel at Box 1567, Kailua-Kona, HI 96740.) A car would help, for it's a little way from the action, but not at all bad for the price.

The general manager of the **Kona White Sands** (Tel. 329-3210) has written us, asking to be mentioned in this book. While we can't specifically recommend a place until we've had a chance to inspect it, we rather like the sound of this condo for the price. We have had a reader letter praising the view and the housekeeping, although mildly criticizing the furnishings. There are just ten apartments in an office building across the road from White Sands (Disappearing) Beach, 3½ miles south of Kailua. With full kitchens and an ocean view, rents run from about $40 to $45 a day for two, a potential bargain. (More details from the hotel at P.O. Box 594, Kailua-Kona, HI 96740.) We'll sift through the White Sands in more detail one of these days, we promise.

HOTELS IN THE CITY OF HILO

Hotels in Hilo are traditionally in a cluster along Banyan Drive, an attractive waterfront avenue not far from the airport, or else nearer the center of Hilo itself, where they are somewhat separated from one another. We prefer the location on Banyan Drive for general atmosphere and the opportunities for casual strolling in pleasant, not-too-commercial surroundings. (Remember that there are no—none—absolutely zero—Hilo hotels located on a sandy beach.)

The hotels we have considered in Hilo certainly are not expensive, by international standards. We have divided them into two price ranges, calling them "higher-priced" and "moderate."

HIGHER-PRICED HILO HOTELS

There is one outstanding choice. That is the somewhat beleaguered **Naniloa** (Tel. 935-0831), formerly the Naniloa Surf: A rambling internal structure based around two 10- and 12-story wings; location set back just enough from Banyan Drive; airy lobby opening onto a viewsome *lanai;* wonderful vistas of Hilo Bay and—when the clouds lift—faraway Mauna Kea; two main floors, the lower on the sea side; spacious and green grounds featuring an unusual barringtonia ("fish poison") tree; two tennis courts; meandering walkways along the lava-studded shore; bayside kidney pool with more sun space than water content; poolside Samurai Bar (for afternoon pupus and music); dependable dining at the adjoining Hutu Terrace dining room; cozy Hoomalimali Bar for later dancing and tippling; sometimes some local or Waikiki acts in the Crown Room, the city's premier nightclub.

There are 386 generally well-appointed bedrooms, and the ones we saw sported TV, radio, air conditioning, and a few extras. Unfortunately, windows don't open in 503, 504, and a few other cheaper chambers, so watch out for those. Generally good housekeeping and maintenance; twin bedrooms from about $55 for standards through $65 and $75 levels to $85 for the Surf Deluxes—large rooms with direct ocean views. The hotel was recently sold and is no longer part of a local chain. (Reservations from the hotel at 93 Banyan Drive, Hilo, HI or use the 800 number in the Appendix.) The Naniloa remains the best on Banyan Drive.

Nearby, the **Hilo Hawaiian Hotel** (Tel. 935-9361) captures a solid second, and almost anyone would be happy there: Not too inspiring green-and-white architectural design; massive porte cochere offering plenty precipitation protection; best location on the drive, right next to Liliuokalani Gardens; large lobby/*lanai* featuring Coconut Island in the back yard, Mauna Kea in the background; less outdoor real estate of its own than the nearby Naniloa; a larger swimming pool, however; four resort shops in four pagodas out front; Menehune Land cocktail lounge with leprechaunish murals; cool blue Queen's Court dining room with a pleasant view.

Total of 290 rooms; individually controlled air conditioning; color TVs; striped bedspreads; some units needing more pictures on the walls; modest twin standards facing town for around $60, oceanfront superiors a little more; deluxe and roomier accommodations for perhaps $70, $80, and $90. Full suites in the $150 to $190 range. (Reservations from Hawaiian Pacific Resorts, 1150 South King St., Honolulu, HI 96814.) We call it a little cool, but comfortable and fairly priced.

MODERATELY PRICED HILO HOTELS

Unless you want to drive up to the Volcano House for the night (see later), nothing is unusual or outstanding. In Hilo itself, the best bet for the price is still the rustic **Hilo Bay Hotel** (Tel. 935-0861): Surprisingly homey lobby with lots of light rattan and thatching, even including the chandeliers; tapa cloth everywhere the grass won't go; smells a bit like a haymow (but not objectionable); attractive, bucolic bar; informal restaurant attached; shopping arcade; Hawaiian garden out back between two residential wings; pond full of colorful carp; lots of bamboo and *hala* trees; attractive bay views at the end by the ample pool.

Generally spacious rooms, with some ground-floor models opening right onto the garden (as well as the hall); TVs and air conditioners in all rooms; several with fridge and kitchen sink (costing $5 extra); housekeeping sometimes a little spotty; room prices perhaps holding between $45 and $60 for doubles, $40 to $55 for singles, depending on location. This is a Hawaiian family operation under the avuncular wing of "Uncle Billy" Kimi, who also owns the adjoining Uncle Billy's Restaurant. (Write him at the hotel, 87 Banyan Drive, Hilo, HI 96720.) We haven't been back recently, and you may want to check out your room before checking in. But most still rate it relatively high on the APC Scale—for atmosphere, personality, and character.

Better in some ways for some folks is the 139-room **Hilo Hukilau** (Tel. 935-0821), which sits almost at the end of the airport runway, a little bit off Banyan Drive, and not next to the ocean: Open, lauhala-and-tapa-cloth lobby overlooking pleasant pond and greenery; two internal patios, one with lava rock garden, the other with tables and pool; locally popular restaurant and bar off the lobby; some slippery corridors. Widely varying rooms (one we stayed in once had a TV but was short on windows); the nicest units with *lanai* overlooking the lagoon; double or single prices perhaps $55 to $60. (Reservations from Hukilau Resorts, 2222 Kalakaua Ave., Honolulu, HI 96815.) A friendly place, and peaceful, too—between landings and takeoffs, anyway.

We once got to stay at the engaging little **Dolphin Bay Hotel** (Tel. 935-1466), which has only 18 units far away from the ocean in a Hilo-green residential area called Puueo. There is no pool, and no air conditioners, but plenty of space cooled by oscillating desk fans. All units have kitchenettes, and their managers manage to keep it all as deliciously clean as the inside of a fresh coconut. (They might even give you a fresh coconut to compare with!) Doubles may run from around $30 to $55 this year, with $7 per extra person. Singles start at around $25. A car is a must, and you should reserve far in advance for peak periods. (Write to

John Alexander, the helpful manager, at 333 Iliahi St., Hilo, HI 96720, and tell him we sent you.) A real tropical charmer.

The **Hilo Hotel** (Tel. 961-3733) is cheaper, and that's as it should be: Midtown location near the corner of Kinoole and Kalakaua; rocking chairs on the front porch; tiny lobby in beige and black; well-regarded Restaurant Fuji with Japanese menu; swimming pool out back; TV for all in the rec room. Total of 57 well-used billets; singles all running around $30 per key. (Don't write; drop in and have a look first.) Affectionately regarded locally—just like the Old Gray Mare.

HOTELS IN THE COUNTRY

There are lodgings of differing quality in Hawaii Volcanoes National Park, Honokaa, Waimea/Kamuela, Hawi, Puako, the Kohala Coast, Holualoa, Captain Cook, Naalehu, and the Waipio Valley.

THE NATIONAL PARK

You won't find anything anywhere that compares with the unique **Volcano House** (Tel. 967-7321), now run by Sheraton, and parked smack-dab on the edge of Kilauea crater: Wonderful, commodious sitting alcove off the lobby; large, cheery *ohia* wood fire on chilly evenings; leather chairs and nine-foot suede sofa; glassed terrace for volcano-watching or reading; same view from Uncle George's Cocktail Lounge and the Ka Ohelo Dining Room; sometimes overcrowded lunch buffets (see section 5); usually a good choice for dinner, however; natural volcanic steam sauna (*tip:* ask them to heat it up considerably before you go in); golf course almost across the road.

Just 37 well-furnished, well-maintained, and heated (when the heating works) sleeping quarters; most strung out in a line and overlooking the crater; a few at the same price facing the opposite direction. (Unless you're an early riser, try not to get rooms next to the maids' service closet, where you won't avoid the 8 A.M. clatter and chatter.) All double rooms still renting for under $55 this year (although some are better than others); no charge for youngsters in the same room, but extra adults are $10; roughing-it camper cabins three miles away for about $10 a day without baths, etc. (Write Sheraton, P.O. Box 8559, Honolulu, HI 96815 for reservations.) The Volcano House has a long and fascinating history dating back to at least 1864. Even if it's only for a single overnight, the volcano—and its House—should not be missed.

HONOKAA

Just off Route 19, some 40 miles north of Hilo in the hamlet of Honokaa, is the old and well-weathered **Hotel Honokaa Club** (Tel. 775-0678). There is a sort of restaurant and bar, and in an emergency you can try for Room #16, an $18 double with a view of a couple of back yards and the ocean farther away. All the second-floor units are worth the asking price, as a matter of fact. The first-floor units are cheaper, but offer much less, too. Many accommodations have been taken by more-or-less permanent residents, who may know something more about the place than we.

WAIMEA (KAMUELA)

The venerable **Kamuela Inn** (Tel. 885-4243) has painted cinderblocks and always reminded us of an old motel in northern Georgia. On our own cool overnight, we found the sheets clean, the water hot, and an electric heater a pleasant accessory. Doubles run perhaps $35 to $50. Possibly nicer is **The Lodge** (Tel. 885-4100), run by the Parker Ranch. Incredibly, we ran up against an un-*akamai* desk person who wouldn't let us peek at a room. According to lodge literature each unit has a kitchenette and a gas heater. We saw a color TV in the common cardroom. Rates at this writing are about $50 for two. Sorry, but we can't recommend what we can't see. Many folks now push on to Kailua-Kona (under an hour) on the new highway.

HAWI

The 23-unit **Old Hawaii Lodging Co.** (Tel. 889-5577), formerly Luke's Hotel, across from the old sugar mill smokestack in Hawi, is an old, old institution in an old, old town. With the only bar and restaurant around, it is probably still the social activities center at *pau hana* time. Some dwelling units are grouped around a scraggly garden courtyard featuring a thoroughly undisciplined flowering cactus. Doubles run around $23, singles around $20. (Their mailing address is Box 521, Kapaau, HI 96755.) We haven't been in since the new management took over and gave it that glorified name, but we wish them all the luck they'll need.

PUAKO

A modern condominium rental establishment, the **Puako Beach Condominium** (Tel. 882-7711) welcomes visitors in this outback community. All 38 units are well-appointed apartments with full kitchen and/or wet bar plus laundry facilities, as well as a *lanai* overlooking the small beach. One-, two-, and three-bedroom apartments will probably rent for about $50 to $95 this year. (Reservations from the condo at 3 Puako Beach Dr., Kamuela, HI 96743). If you like Puako, a sleepy place we think of only for its large collection of petroglyphs, it might be an attractive alternative.

KOHALA COAST

A few miles south of the Mauna Kea Beach Hotel (see later), the dramatic new **Mauna Lani Bay Hotel** (Tel. 885-6622) was opened by Tokyo-based Emerald Hotels in 1983 with its sights set on capturing clientele from its more prestigious neighbor to the north:

A beautiful site bordering one of the best golf courses in the nation, part of the same 3,200-acre resort; 10-court tennis garden; architecturally fascinating six-story, arrow-shaped structure aimed toward the sea; several resort shops; pristine white beach on a protected cove just a coconut's toss away (love those canopied cabanas!); several ocean activities available; two open atria with gardens, streams, and waterfall; glass-walled elevators for viewing the greenery; spacious, breezy, blue-tiled public areas with Oriental accents; ample, free-form swimming pool; separate cloverleaf-design jacuzzi; historic fishponds with leaping mullet; cottage museum on the grounds; several areas of archeological interest; three restaurants, including the excellent Third Floor (inspired by Honolulu's famous restaurant of that name), the partly open-air Bay Terrace (where we enjoyed our breakfasts), and the new "fresh-ingredient" Gallery (where substitutions are encouraged); all but the Gallery requiring jackets for men in the evening (not the kind of laid-back Kona we remember!); several lounges and bars; summertime program for youngsters.

A total of 351 rooms, more than 90 percent with ocean views; a few gazing toward Mauna Kea (the mountain, not the competition); some of the most commodious accommodations in the 50th state; all in maroon, beige, teak, cane, and marble; some with king-size beds, some with double-doubles; all with fridges, bars, tiny coffee tables, and discreetly hidden color televisions; no radios; good lighting; air conditioning and ceiling fans; large, well-designed triangular *lanais;* luxurious bathrooms. Announced rates for '87: $195 for Mountain or Garden View, $240 for Ocean View, and $270 for Ocean Front. Those are all European Plan—no meals included. Modified American Plan (two meals daily) is available at around $50 per person per day extra. For all its flamboyance, the best things the Mauna Lani has going for it are its gorgeous site and its friendly, energetic, unpretentious staff. (Reservations from the hotel at P.O. Box 4000, Kawaihae, HI 96743.) It has set its sights high, and in time, it could become the dominant resort on the Kohala or the Kona Coast.

About five miles south of the Mauna Lani, in the developing residential/ recreational area of Waikoloa, the 543-room **Sheraton Royal Waikoloa** (Tel. 885-6789) opened in late 1981 next to the magnificent, half-mile-long palm-studded beach at Anaehoomalu Bay, 20 miles north of Keahole Airport. Also beside an ancient Hawaiian fishpond, the twin-wing building rises six stories above the palms, sands, and old lava flows in North Kona on what they now call the Kohala Coast:

Public areas garnished with *koa*, the strong wood once favored by the Hawaiians for their spears and war canoes; green-and-white raffia furnishings in the breezy, open reception area; free-form pool next to the luau garden; field of petroglyphs a short stroll away over the black lava desert; nearby 18-hole golf course; six tennis courts; unusual brassaia tree gracing the sunken Garden Room restaurant; two other dining areas, including the Royal Terrace, a dinner showroom, and the Tiare, a pleasant crystal-and-china room open in the evenings; an outdoor/indoor luau every Sunday.

Until May 15, the bedrooms, all with *lanais*, run from $160 for Garden View through $200 Mountain View, and from $225 to $250 for lesser or greater views of the ocean. There are also the Lagoon Cabanas for perhaps $275. These are normal rates these days for the amenities offered. *But from May 15 to September 15*, these amounts may be cut in half. This makes the Sheraton Waikoloa a good summer bargain for those who seek a champagne hotel on a beer budget.

As time goes on, and as this resort area develops more, the establishment may overcome the faraway feeling some guests experience there. (Reservations through the Sheraton organization.) The hotel itself is fine and the site is, again, simply terrific.

You may have also heard of the fantabulous $360 million, 1,260-room **Hyatt Regency Waikoloa,** designed to knock the socks off anything else on the island. However, the 60-acre resort extravaganza, Venetian gondolas et al, will continue under construction all through 1987 and then some. We'll have a full report on this spread in our next—1988—edition.

HOLUALOA

An old country inn in somnolent Holualoa, a little rain-forest town about five miles *mauka* of Kailua, is called the **Kona Hotel** (Tel. 324-1155), and it should not be confused with any other hotel of a similar name. This wooden structure was put up by owner Goro Inaba's parents in 1926, and it has hardly changed a whisker since. There are even views over Kailua, when the weather is clear. None of the 11 units have private plumbing. Rates are now around $12 per person per night. (Address: P.O. Box 342, Holualoa, HI 96725.) At those low tabs some folks find themselves in a state of euphoria. Others might pick a different state.

CAPTAIN COOK

Another antique hostelry, but one that has kept up a little better with the times, is the 1917-model storefront **Manago Hotel** (Tel. 323-2642) in the village of Captain Cook near Kealakekua Bay. When we stayed there, our son, six at the time, called it "very creepy." Actually, Mr. and Mrs. Harold Manago have done a pretty good job, especially with their new addition out back. The 22 "community bath" rooms in the old ("creepy") section run around $15 single, $20 double. The 42 rooms with ocean view and their very own baths were from around $20 to $25 single and $25 to $30 double, the last we checked. Ask to see the very special "Japanese Room," dedicated by Harold and Nancy to his parents. There guests sleep Oriental style on *tatami* mats, etc., for around $35 or so for two, and that's the only one with a TV. (You can write the Manago at P.O. Box 145, Captain Cook, HI 96704.) Again, recommended only to genuine seekers of authentic atmosphere.

NAALEHU

The southernmost place to stay in the southernmost town in the U.S.A. is the **Shirakawa Motel** (Tel. 929-7462) at Naalehu. Well, actually it's in Waiohinu, about halfway between Kona and Hilo on the southern road (Route 11), about one minute from the monkeypod tree planted by Mark Twain. Lee and Takumi Shirakawa, coffee and banana farmers, run these modest units on the side in the midst of lush, flower-filled surroundings. Rates run around $20-$25 for two, and if you're stuck in this area, this is it. Mark Twain might have loved it, but he came by just a little too soon.

WAIPIO VALLEY

Somewhat mischievously, we list here for the first time the **no-name hotel** (Tel. 775-0368), although we've known about it for years. Tom Araki's modest place, 2,000 feet down in barely accessible Waipio Valley (you need a four-wheel drive to get there) is the ultimate in rusticity. Each of his five rooms is provided a kerosene lamp because there is no electricity. John and shower are "down the hall." Propane stoves are available in the common kitchen. Rates? Ten dollars per person, double or single. If you can't reach Tom at the above phone number, call his

Hilo line, 935-7466. (Reservations by phone or at 25 Malama Place, Hilo, and make out your check to Tom personally since his hotel really has no name.) To be sure, this place is not for everyone, but we liked Tom a lot and think he does a good job. (And ask to try the sweet and delicious green fruit from his unusual Japanese *sapote* tree on the hotel property; eat it skin and all.)

LUXURY VACATION RESORTS

There are two more-or-less self-contained destination resorts on the Big Island, and they are so different in conception that they cannot be compared with each other. The larger is the 310-room, 22-year-old **Westin Mauna Kea**(Tel. 882-7222), which has just changed its name from the Mauna Kea Beach Hotel.

The Mauna Kea and its own surrounding 18-hole championship golf course sit alone on a desert, alongside one of the few beautiful beaches on the island. It almost never rains at Mauna Kea, and its 500 acres of greenery are kept alive via a network of midnight-activated hidden sprinklers. If the Mauna Kea has no one distinctive characteristic, it must take justifiable pride in the fact that whatever one liked somewhere else, one might like it better here. It is a formula that has worked on presidents, kings, emperors, and rulers of the silver screen. Here is the way we saw it:

Semi-isolated location 32 miles from Kailua-Kona; driveway to the hotel winding through the beautiful links designed by Robert Trent Jones Sr.; two wings, 208 rooms in the original structure and 102 in the just refurbished Beach Front building; long, low, terraced façades not obtrusive despite size; everything nestled neatly into the side of a hill; trees, plants, and waterfalls extending from outdoors to inside the hotel edifice; two large gardens, one north and one south (ask for the booklet, the "Gardens of Mauna Kea"); spacious lobby overlooking a flower-filled interior court; one flight down to "Promenade Level" and tasteful collection of shops (any vase we picked up in The Gallery was priced at at least $100); four award-winning restaurants, The Terrace, for the luncheon buffet and lighter, more informal (jacketless) evening dining, the spicy Batik Room and bar in Ceylonese *houda* motif, three-tiered Pavilion (formerly Dining Pavilion) with live music nightly, and the newer Garden (formerly Garden Pavilion), now featuring local specialties; the Hau Tree snack shop in the beach area; sauna and massage nearby; large, circular, palm-shaded, blue-bottomed pool back from the beach; widely acclaimed 13-court tennis park; lots of other lawn and sea games; 58-foot catamaran *Mauna Kea Kai* for cruising, scuba, snorkeling, etc.; hunting and horseback riding available; special children's programs offered.

A museumful of Oriental art scattered throughout the buildings (more than 1,600 *objets*—ask for that booklet or take the special art tour); some good Hawaii artists also represented; mirror-bright, brass-walled elevators with parquet floors; elegant bedchambers, some with separate entrance foyers and dressing rooms; plain, white walls; excellent local artwork; framed seashell collections; bright, solid colors; thick throw rugs on smooth hex-tiled floors; wicker and cane furnishings; custom-carved Thai lamps; no TVs in the rooms (by design, of course); sliding louvered doors to the large *lanais;* bathrooms with mirrored wall; Italian marble basins; hidden teak-doored refrigerators in all units.

Most expensive ocean-view doubles ($378) and the least costly mountain-view rooms ($298) in the original structure; beachfront units in the newer wing (running $368) closer to beach, pool, and golf shop; suites perhaps twice these amounts. All these fares include breakfast and dinner—Modified American Plan. *But in a major change in policy the hotel no longer requres MAP from Easter to December 15, so deduct $100 from those rates for the optional summer European Plan.* (Reservations through the Westin Hotels organization or the hotel itself at P.O. Box 218, Kamuela, HI 96743.) The nearby Mauna Lani may have siphoned off some of the clientele, but the Mauna Kea still seems to be where the "old money" goes. You'll find there a self-contained vacation in almost a Mediterranean style (you still dress up for dinner, etc.), but today with some stronger Hawaiian accents, too. Within this framework, the hotel and its *modus operandi* are superb accomplishments.

The other destination resort is the very private, very posh, and still very Polynesian **Kona Village Resort** (Tel. 325-5555). It is designed for those who want a vacation that is a full escape from reality, free from care about almost anything, and perhaps even some sort of transferral to a separate, very personal world.

There is a perfect, sand-lined cove, rimmed with palm trees and no large buildings. It has little guest cottages scattered here and there along the shoreline and a neighboring pond. These amazing thatched-roof huts, called *hales* ("*hah*-lays"), are constructed in the architecture of several South Seas islands—Hawaii, Samoa, Fiji, Tahiti, and others. They are interesting as much for what they do not contain as for what they do.

There are no televisions, no radios, no air conditioners, and no keys for the doors. There are excellent decorations, lovely baths, and impeccable maintenance standards. All this is carefully installed on the site of an ancient Hawaiian fishing village.

Entrance to Kona Village is through a private gatehouse on Route 19, where the guard lets absolutely no one in who is not known or expected. After this, a narrow roadway for about two miles over the lava fields to the verdant *kipuka* (an "island" untouched by the molten flow); lobby/office a separate building at the end of the road; the only phone in there;

flower leis and special rum punch for all arriving guests; famous Hale Samoa, the former main restaurant; Hale Moana dining room in Vanuatu motif; large, circular, lava-lined swimming pool; nearby Shipwreck Bar made from an honest-to-schooner, genuine shipwreck; Island Copra general store. Beach with every facility imaginable; three tennis courts; petroglyphs and other archeological tours; all at no extra charge.

All together, 100 thatched *hales* built with "plush primitive" amenities and representing seven different Pacific Island groups; ventilated by trade winds and overhead fans; no room service (but no one seems to miss it); most units with king-size beds; 24 family units; everything closed for redecoration two weeks at the beginning of December. Current 1987 prices are Full American Plan daily double rates of $425 for the oceanfront deluxe, $395 for oceanfront superior deluxe, $385 for the superior ocean view or superior garden suite, $350 for the moderate garden *hale,* and $295 for standard garden *hales.* (A third person is $150.) All rates include all meals, and there are no extra charges for games, equipment, etc. Special wedding and honeymoon packages can be arranged. (Write the Kona Village at P.O. Box 1299, Kailua-Kona, HI 96745.) For the special kind of rustic/elegant isolation it offers, it can't be beat. We've been twice, and we hope to return again and again.

5. Big Island Restaurants and Dining

Since there are two main headquarters on Hawaii, we divide our dining section into choices in Kona (generally, the Kailua to Keauhou area), and then in Hilo. After that, there is a brief wrap-up of several country tables.

DINING FROM KAILUA- TO KEAUHOU-KONA

Unfortunately, we are not sure there is any absolutely dependable *haute-cuisine* restaurant in the Kona mainstream at the moment, although we wish someone would prove us wrong. There *were* two, and they're still around, however. You've got a shot at **Dorian's** (Tel. 329-3195) in the small Magic Sands apartment building next to White Sands ("Disappearing") Beach. But disappearing, too, seems to be the consistency of Dorian's, which once served us an excellent meal and then a couple of mediocre ones. Similar reports combine now to give this salon a yo-yo rating in our book. It's still a lovely location, especially since a terrace was tacked on to take advantage of the delicious sunsets. Other than that, we are reminded of the "little girl who had a little curl..."

Some still assert the finest galley in the neighborhood is installed in the **S.S. James Makee Room** (Tel. 322-3411), in the elegant Kona Surf Resort at Keauhou. Also known for Continental cooking, the room was named after a famous old interisland steamship of long ago: Naturally nautical decor; orange lanterns everywhere; locally caught fish on the *table d'hote*. Steak Au Poivre about $18.95. Sadly, service standards sometimes seem to slip astern. To sum up, the SSJMR may not always be a shipshape choice; but depending on your crew, she may get you where you're going.

For lighter dining, also at the Kona Surf, there is **Pele's Court** (Tel. 322-3411), an open-sided terrace on the ground floor with waterfalls and greenery abounding. There's only a patch of sky, but plenty of sunlight is reflected from the hotel superstructure. The oceanside lunch served at the hotel's **Nalu Terrace** is pleasant.

Reports are now almost all good on **La Bourgogne** (Tel. 329-6711), a French Provençale entry at Kuakini Plaza South, about five minutes' drive on Highway 11 from Kailua. The tables may be a little too close together, but the food and ambience are generally superb. Now one of the best bets this end of the island.

A consistently good choice for prime rib of beef fans is back in Kailua at the Kona Hilton. The **Hele Mai** (Tel. 329-3111) at the hotel also features seafood. Prime rib and *mahimahi* are now also the stars at the **Sunset Rib Lanai** (Tel. 322-3441) at the Keauhou Beach Hotel.

The **Kona Ranch House** (Tel. 329-7061), an attractive building near the Shell station at the corner of Kuakini Highway and Palani Road, is another very professional operation, especially for breakfast, brunch, or lunch.

Longtime Kona returnees have been happy to learn that the **Kona Inn** (Tel. 329-4455) is alive and well—as a restaurant, not a hotel. The old inn that ruled Alii Drive from 1928 to 1978 mostly has been converted to a shopping center. But one part that wasn't was the 8,000-square-foot dining room and bar, and, in fact, new life has been breathed into the seaside site by a California firm called Wind and Sea. Ask for a table next to the stone wall. Choose from an assortment of steaks and chops, or maybe the Chicken Cordon Bleu, the Hawaiian Chicken, or vegetable casserole. Fish of the Day, no doubt unloaded that afternoon onto Kailua Wharf, is the most dependable. Lunch or the champagne Sunday brunch is also atmospheric and fun. Note those overhead fans, still driven by rubber bands after more than half a century. Today the Kona Inn is spinning along better than ever!

Hurricane Annie's (Tel. 329-4345) is the latest to open in the Kona Inn Shopping Center, and it should not be confused with the previously described Kona Inn. With a cabin full of ship's antiques, Annie's churns out steaks, fish, barbecues, and Italian specialties. Some folks especially like the 25-item fruit and salad bar. The nearby **Don Drysdale's** serves food, but it's the collection of local characters hanging out in the bar that makes this an interesting place.

We remain unimpressed with the restaurant operations in the Hotel King Kamehameha in Kailua, by the way. The **Marlin Room** and especially the **Veranda Room** are off our list. Across the street, **Quinn's** (Tel. 329-3822) is a moderate-price entry catering more to local residents, perhaps. There's a very "laid-back" garden patio in the rear where they have some good sandwiches and salads. Here's one for night owls, too: Dinners are served until 12:30 A.M.

Just across Palani Street from the King Kam, on an upper deck, you'll find the justly popular **Kona Galley** (Tel. 329-3777): Overlooking Kailua Pier, an ideal setting at sunset; tastefully decorated in a lantern-lit, seafaring motif; awnings rolled down when trade and the trades are both brisk; steak and "today's catch" fish dishes in the $14 range; chicken somewhat of a "?"; popular with a knowledgeable local crowd; open 11 A.M. to 10 P.M. Usually a winner.

Strict nickel-knucklers might like to sit in at the **Ocean View Inn** (Tel. 329-9998) on Alii Drive right in the center of things. The ocean view is there, all right, seen through a fine-mesh screen. Decor is, well, somewhere between unfancy and none at all. There's a large menu, and a faithful neighborhood crowd choosing and chewing some of about 75 to 100 different dishes in Chinese, American, and Hawaiian styles. It's okay for the budget-conscious; incredibly, some major plates may still be around $5 or $6. (Closed Mondays—and maybe Septembers.)

Huggo's (Tel. 329-1493), next to the water near the Hilton, has been a favorite hangout for years. There's always a beautiful view and a friendly atmosphere, and it's a dependable choice for sizable sandwiches, steaks, and uncomplicated dinners.

Probably a little more expensive, but also with a terrific view, is the **Spindrifter** (Tel. 329-1344). One reader says it's great for breakfast, and we agree. At lunch, try the seafood pastas. The newer **Eclipse** (Tel. 329-4686) supposedly has the longest bar on the island, but we doubt that claim. The Eclipse seems to be almost totally eclipsed until around 10 P.M.; it's apparently trying to build a reputation more as a disco than as a restaurant.

Steak Houses. The leader in the group has been **The Pottery** (Tel. 329-2277). It no longer makes pottery in the restaurant, although they do sell some. Some reports indicate something may be slipping here, however. **Marty's** (Tel. 329-1571), occupying an attractive, second-story, torch-lit Alii Drive location, has good steaks and fish—and sunsets. (A better selection for an early dinner.) And **Cousin Kimo's** in the Kona Bay Hotel also combines excellent beef with some chicken and fish dishes the locals call *shaka!*

Mexican/Italian Food. On the Latin spice file, there is a terrific south-of-the-border spot (headquartered in Southern California) called the **Old Kailua Cantina** (no reservations) above the Jug 'n' Jigger at 75-5669

Alii Drive, and opposite the Kailua Wharf. The delicious view is only surpassed by the food. Try the Chimichangas at maybe $8.95. The pineapple margaritas are also good, but one reader complained to us about generally poor service. Then there's old reliable **Jose's** (Tel. 329-6391), about 10 minutes' drive south of Kailua along Route 11. Full meals about $10, and *muy popular,* too. A more modest address than either is **Paniolo Pizza,** which features several Mexican and Italian specialties in the Kona Coast Shopping Center. Their giant-size pizza is called "The Big Island." Spaghettis are also on tap. For some unknown reason, Italian food (except for pizzas) is something of a rarity in Kona.

DINING IN HILO

Hilo is not exactly headquarters for the gourmet army of Hawaii, either, and we have found it difficult to keep up with the openings and closings and other maneuvers of dining rooms in the county seat. Just when we think we've got a dependable winner, something changes—the chef, the manager, or even the owner of the place.

Dining in the hotels is considered dependable, if seldom spectacular. When Hiloans go out on the town, they often head for a steak house, and there is always one currently in vogue. Of course it may or may not continue to sizzle the imagination next year.

One long-standing beef emporium with an excellent local reputation is **Rosey's Boat House** (Tel. 935-2112), slightly out of the way across from the tennis stadium at the corner of Piilani and Laukapu streets in a lava-rock and shingle building. We stuck with steak and salad bar here and were happy enough. Other Maverick readers have liked the fish and the crab, too. There's some live music every night in the bar.

In the Naniloa Surf Hotel, the **Hutu Terrace,** formerly a modest, though attractive, coffee shop, has now been made the main restaurant, offering a large variety of food styles. There's entertainment nightly in the adjoining Samurai Bar.

Outside the hotel complex proper is **The Banyan Broiler** (Tel. 961-5802), which has been building a good dinner reputation. Fellow Mavericks report that some of the best steak, prime rib, and especially oysters and *opakapaka* (snapper) now hang out here, along with a good salad bar. Prices are reasonable, and there's a live band after 9 P.M. daily except Sunday. Across the street near the golf course is **Club CJ's** (Tel. 935-7700), which seems to be building its reputation more as teen-and-twenties disco and meeting ground than on kitchen products. **Harrington's** (Tel. 961-4966) continues to be popular, however, serving steak and seafood from its watery address at 135 Kalanianaole Ave., right on Reed's Bay. And Cajun cooking is supposed to be the thing in the new **Roussel's**

(Tel. 935-5111) at 60 Keawe St. It's on our "to try" list, but that's the most we can say up to this moment.

If it's raining, but you still want to feel outdoorsy for breakfast or lunch, head for the **Queen's Court** (Tel. 935-9361), a pleasant coffee shop behind huge plate-glass windows in the Hilo Hawaiian Hotel. When the weather's nice, the views over the bay are delightful from either the window seats or the cleverly conceived raised booths farther inside. Our Geisha Sandwich was hokey in concept, but tasted quite nice. (It was a cheese, egg, and bacon concoction where the only thing "geisha" was a paper parasol.) The Sunday brunch is probably a better deal these days.

Much more fun for dinner, though, is **Uncle Billy's** (Tel. 935-0861), stuck on the side of the Hilo Bay Hotel: Lots of tables crowded together; Hawaiian entertainment (perhaps a 2-girl hula show); Polynesian decor; a friendly, supercasual atmosphere. The food was in the moderate range for dinner, and not really fancy, but the whole family scooted in here one night awhile back and enjoyed almost every minute of it. Go early. One diner did complain to us recently that they were out of salad by 8 o'clock! Strictly a shoes-off place, remember.

We always seem to eat a good breakfast at **Ken's Pancake House** (Tel. 935-8711), Kamehameha Avenue and Route 11, perhaps still the *only 24-hour restaurant* in Hilo. Strictly a coffee shop in mood and manner, but they're quick, friendly, and the pancakes and waffles are usually delicious. Try their omelets, too. Right alongside Ken's, now, is the Waiakea Kai Shopping Center with several fast-food stands.

We did check out **Roy's Gourmet,** which seems to get a lot of attention from barrel-bottom-budget visitors. The name is a gross miscarriage of definition, in our opinion. We didn't like our meal or the half-dozen others we smelled simultaneously. For substantial fare at reasonable tabs, check into **Dick's Coffee House** (Tel. 935-2769) in the Hilo Shopping Center. It's also an excellent place for bargain breakfasting.

Another good economy choice is the little **Hukilau Restaurant** (Tel. 935-4222), in the hotel of the same name and within walking distance of Banyan Drive hotels. Sort of a green, white, and yellow decor; Polynesian overtones with overhanging canoe; lots of growing greenery; best positions in the window booths; lines on the glass marking height limits of the 1957 and 1960 tsunamis; substantial meals (steak, fish, chicken) at down-to-earth prices. This place was understaffed on our Sunday-night visit, but it's popular with an understanding, local crowd. The food was certainly okay for the outlay.

Chinese Restaurants. There are several in Hilo, of consistently varying quality. Often praised for its Cantonese cuisine is the **Sun Sun Lau Chop Sui House** (Tel. 935-2808), a family operation in barnlike surroundings at 1055 Kinoole St. (Closed Wednesdays.) **Leung's Chop Suey House**

(Tel. 935-4066), at 530 East Lanikaula St., receives high praise from Shirley and Sig Rich of Los Altos, California. And Ferd Borsch, Honolulu's top baseball writer, who also scores hits in his dining-room contests, recommends **Mun Cheong Lau** (Tel. 935-3040), at the corner of Keawe and Kalakaua streets. (Local cats sometimes call it the Munch & Meow, or Munchin' Meow.) As for Ferd, he managed to gulp down a gallon of bird's nest soup and then made a steamed pork of himself. This wide-awake place is open until 2 A.M.—except on Friday and Saturday when folks keep munchin' until 4! (A good stop after a night on the town, says Stephanie Salazar, news editor for Hilo's KBIG.)

Japanese Dining. There are three or four we should mention in Hilo. The traditional favorite is the **K. K. Tei** (Tel. 961-3791), for which we lost our notes, dammit! We remember it as a long, low building with diners seated in two areas, one very informal, one a little spiffier, next to a well-designed rock garden. Some call its menu a little *haole*fied, but there were gentlemen gourmets from Japan in there with us, too. Prices are apparently very reasonable.

In the venerable old Hilo Hotel downtown is the **Restaurant Fuji** (Tel. 961-3733), at 142 Kinoole St. Here the dishes run a little more toward the traditional—less *teriyaki* and more *sushi*—than you might find elsewhere. The *shabu-shabu* still might be the best in town. (Some report that the service shuffle-shuffle is the slowest in town, too.) Also dependable, if a little pricey, is **Nihon** (Tel. 9691133), a Japanese restaurant and *sushi* bar installed in an art gallery at 123 Lihiwai St. There's a nice view of Hilo Bay from some tables. Maybe a good choice for lunch.

Food Chains. Yes, the two old reliables are now in Hilo. **Kentucky Fried Chicken** whomps it up downtown at 348 Kinoole St. and at 670 Piilani St. until 8 or 9 P.M. daily, and **McDonald's** is at 177 Ululani St. and 88 Kanoelehua St.

Hot dogs and ice cream? Try the weiners served on a sweet bun by **Mr. K's Hawaiian Ice Cream**, which opens at 5 A.M. (!) at 89 Lihiwai St., right next to the famous Suisan Fish Market (see section 6). They make their own ice cream, too.

KITCHENS IN THE COUNTRY

After a dining discussion of the volcano area, we begin a culinary swoop around the island, starting north of Hilo and heading counter-clockwise using Routes 19 and 11. Restaurants worth mentioning are at Honokaa, Waimea, Kawaihae, Captain Cook, Naalehu, and Kalapana.

NATIONAL PARK AND VOLCANO AREAS

Nothing in the immediate neighborhood compares with the **Volcano House Restaurant** (Tel. 967-7321): Located in the famous old hotel, right on the rim of the crater; day views always good; night views superb only when there's some fiery action down in the hole; Early American decor; patterned wallpaper; glass-ball chandeliers. Many changes have been taking place in the restaurant, and things frequently seem to be as unsettled at the Volcano House as they are at the volcano.

At noontime, the hordes of tour groups that are bused in by the gross for the buffet lunch make the Volcano House impractical and unpleasant for a midday meal. There is also an expensive snack bar nearby. If you're stuck up there without a car, you'll have to put up with it or gnaw on your boots.

With a car, your choices open up slightly. There's a little-known alternate place to grab a bite about a mile and a half away from the Volcano House at the **Volcano Golf Course Clubhouse** (Tel. 967-7331). It can be quite nice, and they sometimes bake their own sourdough bread. The hamburgers are usually good, too. (Take a right immediately after the military camp, then cross Route 11. It may now be closed on Mondays.)

But if you find you are on your way along that 30-mile road from Hilo to the national park, you could make a last-chance stop at the *village* named Volcano (look for the sign), just off the bypass, about a mile outside the park border. There are two small places of business there, both selling flowers, groceries, and gas. The **Okamura Store** (Tel. 967-7210) also has a snack bar and even some table service for a short time at around midday. The **Kilauea Store** (Tel. 967-7555) is good for fresh-this-morning Saran-wrapped sandwiches.

Another food variation you might want to try anyway is to stop on the road at Mountain View, look up the **Mountain View Bakery** (Tel. 968-6353), and pick up a package of their famous rock cookies for nibbling throughout your park visit.

Be warned that if you leave the volcano area hungry—and are traveling toward Kailua-Kona—that you will have a very limited choice of places to eat on that long, long route. (See Naalehu, below.)

HONOKAA

The traditional wateringhole 40 miles north of Hilo is the **Hotel Honokaa Club** (Tel. 775-0678), in a tiny old hotel. It is certainly one of the most unexciting-looking restaurants we've seen in many a day. You might prefer to search out the modest **Tex Drive Inn** (Tel. 775-0598), on Highway 19 at the Honokaa School Intersection. They serve all three meals and feature some good Portuguese bean soup and *mahimahi* sandwiches. But Tex's *pièces de résistance* are his excellent, baked-fresh-daily *malasadas* (Portuguese doughnuts). These are all dough, too—none of your frothier air-filled type. Go early. They're sometimes gone by noon!

WAIMEA (KAMUELA)

There is one traditionally outstanding chuck wagon up here in cowboy country, the **Parker Ranch Broiler** (Tel. 885-7366) in the Parker Ranch Shopping Center: Rich, Victorian decor with booths and tables; oil paintings, red carpets, and pink tablecloths; plenty of prime beef from the surrounding range and fresh seafood from the surrounding ocean; cozy Colonel Sam's Cocktail Lounge adjoining. We'd skip the buffet, though, and order off the menu instead. Some readers have complained to us of slow service. The Paniolo Stew has always been very good; try the steak sandwiches at lunch.

At the moment, Waimea also has a genuine gourmet restaurant named **Edelweiss** (Tel. 885-6800) run by a German owner/chef who once cooked at the Mauna Lani and the Mauna Kea. Everyone's been raving about the veal, venison, and other European classic dishes for reasonable prices. But at this point, anyway, there are only 15 tables, and no reservations are taken. So you could drive all the way up here only to be disappointed when you can't get in. (The best bet is to arrive at 5:30 or 6, if you're serious about this.) Our advice is to recheck everything by phone on the day you might want to go. Harry Plate of Honolulu thought it was the best Swiss restaurant this side of Geneva. Look for the place on Highway 19—not 190—not far from the softball diamond. (Closed Mondays.)

Neither Edelweiss nor the Broiler serves breakfast, of course. If you spent the night in Waimea, you may want to head for the very modest but friendly and able **Kamuela Deli** (Tel. 885-4147), a drive-in on the highway next door to the Parker Ranch Center. Order through the window, take your plate and sit down, and listen to pidgin-speaking cowpokes at the next table talking over ranch problems. *Ono-ono!* (And in this case, that means yes-yes!) Building a good reputation, now, too, is **Great Wall Chopsui** (Tel. 885-7252). And another steak, ribs, and salad bar place currently in favor with local *paniolos* is the **Cattleman's Steakhouse** (Tel. 885-4077), not far from the Parker Ranch Center.

And onion soup? Strangely enough you may get a good bowl of that at **Wild Horse Pizza** near the police station.

KAWAIHAE

Kawaihae (pronounced "kah-why-*high*") reminds us of the letter written by a nineteenth-century Scotsman who landed at Kawaihae (then an important seaport) to travel to Hilo: "I went from Sky-High to High-Low with nothin' to eat but a bit o' paste on the end of me finger!"

Today you'll be hard put to find any *poi* on such a route, but you will find near Kawaihae some of Hawaii's most elegant tables at the **Mauna Kea Beach Hotel** (Tel. 882-7222). Most readers will be interested in the traditional buffet lunch with its assortment of gastronomic goodies on The Terrace from 11:30 A.M. until 2:30 P.M. Its flat rate may now be around $18. (The hotel practically pioneered the idea of the luncheon buffet, but lately we've had some reader reports saying that it is not quite the championship offering of days gone by.) Dress neatly or they won't let you in—at least cover-ups for women, no tank tops for men. Reservations advised. Four good restaurants are also open for evening dining, and a jacket is required for men in all but the Terrace. Parking is free with restaurant validation at lunch or dinner. (Watch out: No credit cards are accepted.)

Further down the coast, many say with conviction that the buffet lunch at the **Kona Village Resort** (Tel. 325-5555) now surpasses that of the Mauna Kea for around the same price or a little more. It begins at 12:30 P.M., and you should get there soon after that for the best choice. Admittance to the property is by advance reservation only.

CAPTAIN COOK

Yes, there is a restaurant in Captain Cook, at the **Manago Hotel** (Tel. 323-2642), a super-simple, old-fashioned frame false-front on the main drag. Meals are cheap enough—in the six dollar range, daytime or evening, according to our notes. Sometimes there's an excellent Japanese-style lunch, too. *Honolulu Advertiser* food writer Maile Yardley says Mrs. Manago's macaroni salad is fabulous.

NAALEHU

Halfway between Kailua and Hilo on the southern route, the **Naalehu Coffee Shop** (Tel. 929-7238) is okay, especially for local color. Also the **Naalehu Fruit Stand** opened up after our last swing through the village. You may find these two about the only places open between the volcano and Captain Cook.

KALAPANA

Directly across the road from the famous Kaimu Black Sands Beach on Highway 130 is the **Blacksand Beach Drive Inn & Gift Shop** (Tel.

765-7114). Besides the usual fare it serves Hawaiian plate lunches and baked goods with local fruits like papaya or banana bread.

Maybe a mile past this point is the **Kalapana Store and Drive In** (Tel. 965-9242), a neat and simple operation by go-getter Walter Yamaguchi, proprietor. Once when we were there, Mr. Y. was bubbling over the government tidal gauge installed in his antique Hawaiian well. You can either snack at his tables or pick up some goodies at the store and munch away at a picnic bench in the southern branch of the Volcanoes National Park a few miles farther along the road. Depending on the circumstances, you might find such a picnic your most memorable meal of all.

6. Sightseeing Hawaii—A Big Project on the Big Island

For 10 years, we began this section, as all other sections in the chapter, with a discussion of Hilo, the county seat. In this, the eleventh annual edition of this guide, however, we have changed things around a bit to start off with Kona, since more visitors now stay on this sunnier and drier side of the island than they do in Hilo. We still take things in a counter-clockwise direction around the island.

If you are one of the few who do make their first landing in Hilo, of course, you may turn the pages to deftly step into our little tour at that point. And, of course, if you land in Hilo and then make the immediate 30-mile run up to the volcano, you may leap over all our prior prose and turn immediately to the portion on Hawaii Volcanoes National Park.

We have divided our sightseeing section below now into seven parts: Kailua-Kona to Ka'u; the Volcano Area; the Puna Spur; Hilo; the Hamakua Coast to Waimea; the North Kohala Circle; and the Kohala (North Kona) Coast.

KAILUA-KONA TO KA'U

The Big Island's real resort town is **Kailua-Kona.** (Actually, its name is just Kailua, but "Kona" is often stuck on the end to avoid confusion with another prominent Kailua on the island of Oahu. And many here say "Kona"—which means the leeward, or west, side of the island—when they are talking specifically about the Kailua-to-Keauhou area.)

Despite some uncontrolled development here, Kailua remains a fairly attractive—if no longer rustic—coastline settlement, a haven for fishermen anxious to try out some of the world's finest marlin grounds, or for the young, single holidaymaker fishing for any kind of action. Interisland jets from Honolulu and even trunk airlines from the Mainland fly into its airport (see section 2), and it is becoming increasingly popular both as a primary destination itself and as a gateway to the Big Island.

Many think of Kailua as a two-mile stretch of street called Alii Drive, studded on one end by the "King Kam" hotel and bounded on the other by the Kona Hilton. Like Hilo, the Kailua-to-Keauhou area, about seven miles long, has several good hotels, restaurants, and bars. Unlike Hilo, it has much more dependable dry weather and convenient water activities.

One of the most prominent authentic historical sites in the village is the **Hulihee Palace** (Tel. 329-1877), next to the seawall on Alii Drive. (It's sometimes known as King Kalakaua's Summer Palace.) Built in 1838 of coral and lava, it was a royal retreat until 1916. Now furnished in Hawaiian monarchy (Victorian) period interiors, it is operated as a museum by the Daughters of Hawaii. Open 9 A.M. to 4 P.M. daily, but get there before 3 to get the interesting guided tour that makes it worth the price. (Admission $4 for adults, $1 for students, and 50 cents for children.)

Across the drive from the palace is the mission-built **Mokuaikaua Church,** which has remained almost unchanged since 1837. We enjoyed seeing (not eating!) the sausage fruit growing on a tree on the church grounds.

Be sure to walk out on the long **Kailua Wharf,** preferably at weigh-in time, between 4 and 5 P.M. daily, when the big fish are hoisted ashore from the charter boats. Nearby on the grounds of the Hotel King Kamehameha, Amfac Hotels and Honolulu's Bishop Museum have restored (in slightly reduced scale) the **Ahuena Heiau** and **Kamakahonu,** the final residence of Kamehameha the Great, where he spent the last years of his life and then died peacefully in 1819. This area was once a separate residential compound for the *alii,* and many who lived here are well-known personages in Hawaiian history.

Alii Drive becomes a narrow country road past the Hilton and winds its way along the shoreline. About halfway to Keauhou is **White Sands Beach,** also known as Magic Sands, and also as Disappearing Sands Beach, since it washes away from time to time, leaving only a lava shoreline. *Caution: Currents are dangerous here. Don't swim!*

Swimming is safer and more fun a little farther on at **Kahaluu Beach Park,** near the Keauhou Beach Hotel. (The last time we were there, there was a helpful man in a van who rented out snorkel stuff.) Be sure to see St. Peter's, known as the **Little Blue Church,** a tiny chapel with a blue tin roof built in 1880. Nearby is **Kona Gardens,** a historical and botanical park which we don't recommend.

At Keauhou Bay, there is an HVB marker pointing out the **Birthplace of Kamehameha III.** There's not much to see at the site, but the small boat harbor and the little beach adjoining are attractive.

The large structure over by the shoreline is the **Kona Surf Resort.** Next door is the Holua Tennis Stadium, site of the 1976 Avis Challenge Cup matches. (Free double-decker buses, designed for shoppers, run between this hotel and Kailua-Kona, by the way.)

From Keauhou Bay, you can take the side road up the hill past the Keauhou-Kona Golf Course and continue south, now on Route 11 (Kuakini Highway, or the Belt Highway).

Turn right just past Kealakekua on Route 160. On the way down the hill, you might stop at the **Mauna Kea Mill and Museum** (Tel. 328-2511), formerly the Sunset Coffee Mill, to see how Kona coffee is milled, although at times the place is mobbed with folks off the tour buses. Open 8 A.M. to 4:30 P.M. daily. At the bottom of the hill is the formerly active Hawaiian fishing village of Napoopoo (that has five syllables in it) and the historic **Kealakekua Bay** ("kay-allah-cake-*coo*-wah"), site of the visit and the tragic death of Captain Cook in 1779. The spot where Cook fell is indicated by a white monument on the distant shoreline. (It's virtually impossible to visit, except by boat.) The bay has now been made a marine preserve, and its clear waters are a popular snorkeling and scuba-diving spot. You can also see and walk upon the **Hikiau Heiau,** where Cook conducted a Christian burial service.

Instead of returning directly to the main road, try to stand the rough and bumpy four-mile road along the coast to Honaunau Bay and the City of Refuge National Historical Park. Well, that's what we still call it, although it has now been officially renamed **Pu'uhonua o Honaunau** (Tel. 328-2288), an unfortunate decision on somebody's part; but take note because it is that tongue twister that is used on all the highway directional signs. One of the most fascinating legacies from ancient Hawaii, this area was a religious sanctuary for criminals or prisoners of war. If they reached the sacred grounds ahead of their pursuers, they could escape death or other punishment no matter what they were accused of doing.

Today the well-preserved site has been completely restored, and is run by the federal government. Pick up a map/brochure from the Visitors Center and stroll through the shady coconut and pandanus groves by following numbered markers to the various structures and artifacts. There are occasional demonstrations of ancient game playing, wood carving, etc. The Visitors Center is open 7:30 A.M. to 5:30 P.M., but you can actually walk around the park until midnight—if you're not easily spooked. The City of Refuge is a must for any visitor to the Island of Hawaii.

About 2½ miles farther along Route 160 (one-half mile before Route 11), there is a side road on the left that leads, after about another mile, to St. Benedict's, the **Painted Church.** This old wooden structure was decorated around the turn of the century by its Belgian priest in order to bring to his hinterland congregation some idea of the glories of a European cathedral. The church was in danger of collapse until its restoration in 1985. It's a little hard to find, but charming when you do.

After you're back on Highway 11 southbound, check your gas gauge. It is at least 40 miles to the next station, or maybe 90 miles if it's Sunday.

If you're nervous and if the station at the corner of Highways 160 and 11 is closed, better drive the 10-mile route back north to Captain Cook.

On Route 11 southbound, you may be glad you rented a compact car (or wish you had). There are often sharp drop-offs from the pavement on the *makai* side of the narrow road, so watch carefully in any case.

As you cross the fingers of the **1950 Mauna Loa lava flow,** notice that the surface now supports life again, even if it is only represented by copious weeds and flowers. Earlier lava flows have been carved into house lots, and you'll see lots of fancy street names that represent real-estate projects based more on fast talking than fast action over the past decade or so.

About nine miles down the road is the turnoff to a five-mile bumpy road to the Hawaiian fishing village of **Milolii.** Allow two hours if you go. It's one of the few examples left of a slower pace of Island life. In a few years it may not exist at all; even since we were last there some subdivision has begun in the area, and the place is now less attractive.

If you're carrying the fixings for a picnic with you, you may want to turn in at the beautiful botanical grounds called **Manuka State Park,** about eight miles past the Milolii turnoff.

It's another 12 miles to the turnoff for **South Point,** a rough, 11-mile road to the southernmost point in the United States (all that hoopla back in Key West, Florida, notwithstanding). About halfway along, you may see a few giant wind machines. The 72-foot-diameter blades are attached to the largest such generators in the state, the first of a large group that will be a major wind farm. If you have a four-wheel-drive vehicle or hiking gear, and a good map, you can work your way another two or three miles along the waterline to **Green Sands Beach,** where the shoreline is colored by bits of volcanic olivine. ("Sand size" is as big as Hawaiian olivine gets, by the way. Those stones you see in jewelry stores come in from Arizona and Mexico!)

From that turnoff, Route 11 continues quickly into more verdant country. Suddenly you're in the settlement of Waiohinu, which boasts the Shirakawa family motel, the only place to stay in the Ka'u district, and, a few yards farther, **Mark Twain's Monkeypod Tree,** which he planted in 1866. (Just between us, the tree was blown over in 1957, and the one you now see sprang from the roots of the original Twain tree.)

The attractive hamlet of **Naalehu** ("nah-ah-*lay*-who") is the country's southernmost community, of course. For all its rusticity, there is a cosmopolitan flavor here. Proof that the Italians and the Filipinos get along well, for instance, are the side-by-side Little Sicily Service Station and the Luzon Liquor Store.

Continuing along the route, you may visit **Punaluu Black Sand Beach,** one of two well-known black beaches on the island. (The other is at

Kaimu in Puna.) The Seamountain Golf Course nearby is operated by C. Brewer & Co., one of the giant sugar firms of Hawaii. They've also opened a resort condo operation. On the same property is the Ka'u branch of the Aspen Institute for Humanistic Studies, an intellectual "think tank."

The last stop, if you stop, before the national park is the sugar mill town of **Pahala.** Take a left and drive down the main street to see as typical an example of a Hawaiian plantation town as exists any more. The weather-beaten, tin-roofed structures, some of them still on stilts, seem to live well with all the fresh flowers and shrubbery planted around them.

THE VOLCANO AREA

Entering the Hawaii Volcanoes National Park from the southern road, you'll run across three principal points before you get to the Visitor Center. You can backtrack to them later, if you want, but we'll take them in order here. Readers of this book who have come directly up from Hilo will just have to bear with us as we continue our counterclockwise route for the faithful who have been tagging along on our sightseeing circumnavigation. We're not going into exhaustive detail anyway, since the literature and maps you'll pick up from the National Park Service will saturate you with scientific information.

Just a mile or so inside the park boundary is the beginning of the **Footprints Trail** (which now may be relabeled the "Ka'u Desert Trail"). It leads to the preserved tracks made by members of a primitive Hawaiian army in 1790 when they unsuccessfully tried to escape a volcanic eruption. Read the exhibit at the beginning of the trail. The hike to the footprints is about two miles round trip, so allow about one hour. One example of the footprints is pointed out by a small shelter built over them. The others you'll have to look for in the same general area. How successful you are may depend on the whims of shifting sands.

Just past the **Namakani Paio Campground** cutoff is the Mauna Loa Strip Road, which leads first to the **Tree Molds.** These molds or holes were created when the ground beneath your feet was molten lava. The lava encircled the trunks of the ohia trees then growing here, creating a lasting impression. (Watch your step and hold onto your kiddies. Some of these are pretty deep!) A little farther along the same road is Kipuka Puaulu, better known as **Bird Park.** A *kipuka* is a piece of ground left alone by a lava flow. This particular fertile "island" has twenty species of trees in 100 acres. You may see these trees and perhaps several unusual birds while walking the circular one-mile, self-guided nature trail.

Back on Highway 11 for another two miles, you'll reach the badly marked cutoff to the **Visitor Center** (Tel. 967-7311), run by the rangers. Here you will get all your maps as well as up-to-date changes in park facilities. (Remember that the volcano and surroundings form a flexible environment, and roads have a way of being cut off by lava or earth cracks. These may force alterations in routes or even in the accessibility of certain areas.)

If you're lucky enough to come by when there is an eruption in progress, the rangers will tell you the best spot, if any, from which to observe it. The recent series of eruptions have been occurring in generally inaccessible areas, but if the lava fountaining is high enough, there will be places where you can see enough to get some appreciation for the event. Also be sure to get directions to the new **Thomas A. Jaggar Museum** in the former volcano observatory on the crater rim. It is scheduled to open in early 1987.

Just across the road from the Visitor Center is the **Volcano House,** a charming old inn. (See section 4.) The hotel is perched right on the edge of **Kilauea crater,** the immense, ever-steaming, two-mile-wide pit that is the awesome symbol of all activity in this area. (It's pronounced "kill-ow-*way*-ah.") Scientists prefer to call such a large feature a "caldera," instead of a crater, incidentally.

You may drive all the way around Kilauea. The Crater Rim Drive is about 11 miles in circumference. Many adjectives have been expended over the years trying to portray the vents, the steam, the smell of sulfur, the panoramas of black lava and deep rifts in the ground, but it can't be described. It may sound corny, but the volcano, whether erupting or not, must be experienced to be imagined.

If the weather's good, you may be able to see far in the distance the smooth-looking summit of the other volcano in the park, the 13,677-foot **Mauna Loa.** Although Kilauea fires itself up frequently, Mauna Loa is a reluctant dragon. After napping for twenty-five years, it erupted for a brief period in July 1975. Then it burst forth again in March 1984, putting on a spectacular show for 22 days. If you have a jeep and hiking gear, you may ascend to its huge caldera. See the rangers at the Visitor Center for advice on this and any other hiking trails, including some you may explore on the floor of Kilauea crater.

Meanwhile, there are several smaller craters to be seen in the immediate neighborhood of Kilauea. Foremost is the **Halemaumau Firepit** ("hahlay-*mao*-mao"), a crater *within* Kilauea, and said to be the current home of Pele, the Hawaiian goddess of the volcano. Nearby also is **Kilauea Iki crater** (*iki*—"eekey"—means little or junior, if you will) and **Keanakakoi crater** ("kay-ahna-cock-*coy*"), both of which have been fairly active in recent years.

One of our favorite walks is **Devastation Trail,** a mile hike through a former ohia tree forest that was killed by the 1959 eruption of Kilauea Iki. It seems almost like a walk on the moon.

Volcanic eruptions do not always come from the same crater. In fact, even with a dozen or so craters to choose from, an eruption may pick an entirely new and pristine area of real estate to open up and spew forth lava. At this writing, Kilauea has been in an active series of eruptions for the past four years, breaking out somewhere for several days nearly every month. As we indicated earlier, these eruptions generally have not been in its established crater, but in isolated forest areas inside and outside the park. And when you leave the Hawaii Volcanoes National Park, well, as we shall see, you haven't really left the volcanoes at all!

The dramatic **Chain of Craters Road,** first opened in 1965, then closed four years later by a series of lava flows that continued through 1974, reopened in 1979 along a somewhat different alignment. This new section of roadway allows access to many of the park's long-hidden assets and provides a route from the center of the national park direct to Kalapana and the Puna District—a longer but more stimulating ramble back to Hilo. (If you take this route from the volcano, the sights described in our next subsection on Puna will be encountered in reverse order.)

Along the road, keep an eye out for a sign pointing out **Mauna Ulu crater,** whose eruptions in the 1970s caused a lot of trouble hereabouts. There still remain traces of the old road, so you can see how it was permanently blocked by the lava. You might be able to discern how the hot, molten material streaked in fiery falls over the various *pali* (cliffs) and then wove its way to the shoreline and exploded into the ocean. The hardened lava to the left and right of the road is supposed to be completely undisturbed, since the road was built without allowing any construction equipment in any area outside the narrow right-of-way.

At the Mauna Ulu Crater parking lot is the beginning of the 7-mile trail leading eventually to the Napau Crater. From points along this trail, you can see the new **Pu'u O'o,** a cinder cone which has built itself up to at least 800 feet and where most of the fountaining has been occurring during the current eruption series over the past four years. This has been happening about once a month lately for periods of time less than 24 hours. If one of these eruptive phases happens to occur when you are in the park, this may be the place to go to see it—subject, of course, to instructions by park rangers. If you make the hike at any time, take at least water with you, wear sunglasses, a hat and rugged footwear, and stay on the trail. Don't set out late in the day, either. Hiking all the way to **Napau Crater,** where the eruptions actually began Jan. 3, 1983, will take at least three hours each way, and you will want to be back by dark.

If you leave the park on Route 11, it's only 30 miles to Hilo again. (If an eruption is on, you may be able to see Pu'u O'o from some locations, or at least reflections of the hot lava from the sky along this route between the park and Hilo.) You might want to turn right about 20 miles down the road for a 3-mile drive through the nut orchard to the **Mauna Loa Macadamia Nut Factory,** a fairly large operation by C. Brewer & Co. Recorded messages will tell you what they're doing down there on the cracking floor, etc. You'll get a handful of free samples, too, and are they ever delicious!

THE PUNA SPUR

The trip through the Puna District is too often spurned by visitors to the Island of Hawaii, but we find it just as interesting and almost as attractive as any other. Take Highway 130 at Keaau, travel the 11 miles to Pahoa, and then turn on Highway 132. At the proverbial fork in the road, the right tine (Pohoiki Road) will lead you almost immediately to the visitor center for the **Puna Geothermal Facility**. (Look for steam and sniff for sulfur.) This experimental station is the only place in the U.S. which is producing electricity using volcanic heat. The geothermal well taps the underground steam which turns a generator. A story board there will explain it in more detail. Unfortunately, visitors are currently not allowed inside the plant itself. Such facilities are somewhat controversial, partly because they apparently must be placed in areas likely to be overrun by future lava flows. Nevertheless, a major plant is now slated to be built nearby.

Back to the fork again, the left prong leads first to the **Lava Tree State Park.** It is populated by dozens of standing tree molds created during a volcanic eruption in 1790. The looser lava has eroded away, leaving only the hollow columns where the trees were. *Don't venture off the paths, for there are several dangerous earth cracks in this area.*

Continue on Route 132 to find the site of the village of **Kapoho,** which was slowly buried by a lava flow one day in January, 1960. (Everybody got out all right.) You're in the center of town at the crossroads, where there is nothing around you today but black lava, and an occasional piece of rusted corrugated metal which apparently was roofing material.

For a dramatic demonstration of what it means to be overrun by lava, however, continue along the dirt road toward the sea. First, take a left on the side road that runs up a little hill and see the **Kapoho Cemetery,** where just a few of the old headstones poke up from the lava flow. Then get back on the other dirt road again and take it oceanward to the very end and the **Kumukahi Lighthouse.** There the six-foot-deep flow inexplicably stopped after bowling over part of the fence and blistering some of the paint on the little building under the tower. It's an impressive exhibit of potential power. On the return, you may still see the barren cinder cone that spouted all the hot lava that fateful day.

Back at the Kapoho crossroads again, you can take the narrow and sometimes rough road (137) along the shoreline for 15 miles, past a couple of attractive beach parks. Some of the land along here is slated for property development despite the fact that vulcanologists say this part of the coast is sure to be overrun by lava flows sooner or later. (Big Islanders get very blasé about volcanoes and such!) The road rejoins Route 130 at the famous **Kaimu Black Sand Beach.**

Black sand beaches are formed when superheated lava flows into the ocean, causing violent explosions that throw off little drops of black glass. The waves then grind the lava glass down to sand.

This particular beach was created in about 1750 when lava entered the sea about a half mile to the northeast. For the past decade, it has been steadily shrinking in size, probably because the entire Puna Coast has been sinking into the sea ever since the 1975 earthquake—at least one inch per year. So have a good look at the beach while you can. But it is illegal to carry away the sand. (*Caution:* Don't swim here, either. There is no protective off-shore reef, and the current is tricky and dangerous. If you go barefoot, better wash the black stuff off in the little fresh-water pool beside the highway before getting back into your car.)

At **Kalapana,** you might be able to find the head of the 1977 lava flow. (Look for Keone Drive, which snuggles right up to the rough stuff.) The village was thought to be a goner until the magma stopped and cooled just 400 yards short of the settlement. Also saved was the little **Star of the Sea Painted Church,** which was directly in the path. As with most of the houses in Kalapana, the church's furniture was carted out as the lava approached, but the religious frescos along the walls and ceiling, painted just after the church was built in 1931, of course could not be removed. Later the pews were returned, and the artwork remains intact.

A little farther along the road there is a dirt road on the left to **Queen's Bath,** a natural freshwater pool in the rocks once ostensibly exclusive to Hawaiian royalty. It is now a favorite swimming hole for neighborhood youngsters—and visitors, too.

At the southern entrance to Hawaii Volcanoes National Park is the **Wahaula Visitor Center,** which includes a museum and sometimes crafts demonstrations, and the nearby **Wahaula Heiau,** one of the bloodiest sacrificial *heiaus* in Hawaiian history.

A mile or so inland and up the slope from this point is the crosshatch of streets making up the unlucky **Royal Gardens Subdivision.** The sparse-ly populated residential area was invaded by slow-moving lava flows several times during the eruption series that began in 1983 and that may not be over yet. It has destroyed some homes and cut off streets at odd angles and in strange places. If you decide to go up to have a look, be aware that the independent residents who live there without any public utilities tend to be a little sensitive about their misfortune, and probably don't conceive of their community as a tourist sight yet. Some visitors who have gone in reported they were asked to donate to a relief fund for those whose homes and property were destroyed.

Drive into the park, and you'll come to the **Chain of Craters Road.** (See the previous subsection on "The Volcano Area.")

If you return to Hilo on Route 130, somewhere on the *makai* side of this eight-mile Kaimu-to-Pahoa section of highway there may be a sign marked "scenic point." Pull over to have a look, although you may not see anything at first. But then a little whiff of steam suddenly appears above a rise, and then the smell of sulfur hits your nostrils for a moment. Then you may see that there, right in the middle of a vegetable patch, is a cinder cone—a little volcano, quietly waiting, and the advance guard of a potential beast you may have thought resided miles away up the mountain. It is enough to remind us that the Big Island breathes. It is an island that is still very much alive!

HILO—THE CITY OF "LIQUID SUNSHINE"

Rain is considered a naughty word in the Hawaii tourist industry, but the fact remains that Hilo is often soaking wet. Not counting the relative drought of the past year or so, the normal average annual rainfall is more than 136 inches, about five times as much as Kailua-Kona on the other side of Hawaii or Waikiki on Oahu. There once was some public-relations effort to call Hilo the "City of Rainbows." But a rainbow is caused when sunbeams strike raindrops, and to see a rainbow, you have to have the sun behind you and the rain somewhere out in front—not right on top of you. (No one's counted, but there could be more rainbows seen in Honolulu, where it doesn't rain nearly as much.)

If you wake up to the patter of little water drops, don't become discouraged. Have a nice breakfast and then get ready to go out anyway. By late morning, things are often drying out nicely. If so, life in the afternoon can be beautiful. Local boosters, too, are quite correct when they claim that the rain—Hilo's "blessing"—is responsible for much of the green and flowerful beauty that thrives in and around the city.

That gracefully curving avenue outside some Hilo hotels near the airport is **Banyan Drive,** with most of the banyan trees along it planted by visiting celebrities during the 1930s. There is a plaque by each tree, but some of the notables then are rather obscure today.

The east end of the drive skirts **Liliuokalani Gardens,** done up in Japanese style with lots of ornamental rocks and pagodas. A nearby footbridge leads to **Coconut Island** in Hilo Bay. When skies are clear, the bay is backgrounded by **Mauna Kea** (13,796 feet), the state's tallest peak, 25 miles away. Mauna Kea means "white mountain," and it is capped with snow in the winter months. It also wears six telescopes on its crown—some of the world's most sophisticated astronomical observatories—but you may need another telescope to see them from Hilo. (Three more telescopes are scheduled to be added.)

Banyan Drive heads into Lihiwai Street next to the **Suisan Fish Market** at the mouth of the Wailoa River. The market comes alive at 7:30 A.M. Monday through Saturday when the auction is held, with most of the bidding in pidgin. Worth seeing, hearing, and smelling (a clean, fresh fish fragrance), if you can get up that early.

Heading along Kamehameha Avenue toward downtown, the **Wailoa State Park** is on your left. This and lots of other open green space in the immediate area formed part of the business district before it was destroyed during the last tidal wave, or tsunami, which roared into Hilo Bay on Sunday afternoon, May 23, 1960. If possible, enter the park to see the **Wailoa Visitor Center** (Tel. 961-7360), the handsome octagonal structure with an information booth and changing cultural exhibits. (Closed Sundays.)

You can hardly go to Hilo without seeing one of its flower nurseries. One is **Orchids of Hawaii** (Tel. 935-6617) at 2801 Kilauea St. Here's one place to find out everything you always wanted to know about orchids, anthuriums, etc., but were too shy to ask. (Of course, everything's for sale there, too.) Open 8 A.M. to 4:30 P.M. (We haven't been to this new address, yet, but one reader complained that they seem less interested in having visitors than they did in their old downtown headquarters.)

Hilo Tropical Gardens (Tel. 935-4957), formerly Kong's Floraleigh Gardens, at 1477 Kalanianaole Ave., is well worth the charge—it's free. We also like the well-planned and well-displayed **Nani Mau Gardens** (Tel. 959-9442). There are scores of flowers, trees, and plants we didn't even know existed—things like the beefsteak plant, that really does look like lean red meat! It's a little hard to find—3.7 miles from Kamehameha Avenue on Route 11, then a left on Makalika Street for another half-mile or so. Well worth going out of your way for, but we only wish the admission were not $3 per person. (Open daily, 9 to 5.) Bruce Roberts of Morristown, Tenn., however, recommends **Akatsuka Orchid Gardens** (Tel. 967-7660) at Mile Marker 22 (Glenwood) on Route 11. (Admission free.) We haven't yet seen it.

Now this is not exactly an official "sight," but some newcomers who have wandered into **Hilo Dry Goods** at 188 Kamehameha Ave. say the old store with the hand-cranked cash register takes them back to an earlier day. The store has been at the same location—and in about the same condition—since 1920.

No history buff should miss the **Lyman Mission House and Museum** (Tel. 935-5021) at 276 Haili St., just off Kapiolani Street. The original building, constructed in 1839, belonged to the Rev. David Lyman. It has been carefully restored and is now operated together with the new building next door, which displays ethnic memorabilia from the different cultural groups in Hawaii's population. (Here we learned that the ancient Hawaiians used to carve out wooden cuspidors!) There is also a large collection of natural curiosities and other artifacts. (Open daily except Sunday 9 A.M. to 4 P.M.) Admission is now $3, but that includes a guided tour.

Nearby, just a little *makai* of the end of Kapiolani Street at 300 Waianuenue Ave., is the public library and its front-yard prize, the **Naha Stone.** A legend decreed that whoever could turn this stone would become king of all the islands. Despite the fact that the stone weighs an estimated 5,000 pounds, young Kamehameha I is said to have performed the feat. (A strong man from Missouri came to Hawaii in 1973 and showed how he did it. They wouldn't let him mess around with the real Naha Stone, but he raised a similar banana-shaped rock to its pivotal point and then swung it around. It was more a brain problem than one of brawn, he said.)

A little over a mile up the street in Wailuku River Park is **Rainbow Falls,** which sends a thundering torrent into the gorge below. The best time to see the falls is in the early morning. If the sun shines then, it may produce a rainbow in the mist at the bottom.

Farther up the stream about two miles is a point of interest called the **Boiling Pots.** It's not much if you insist on looking at the stream only from the parking lot area. If you want to hike down to the water, however, it's more exciting. In some ways, it's like the Seven Pools on Maui, but with more vigor as the series of falls spills from one pool into another. Some of the water flows beneath a level of old lava and then suddenly bubbles up, as if it were boiling.

Some brochures list a lot more Hilo "sights," but unless you have considerable time on your hands, we suggest moving on up the coast.

THE HAMAKUA COAST TO WAIMEA

Start early in the day, heading north from Hilo on Route 19—the Hawaii Belt Road. After about five miles you'll see a sign announcing a "scenic route." It's a short detour along a narrow road of flowers, birds, one-lane bridges, edible wild guavas, weather-beaten old churches, and crowing roosters. Take the road. It will rejoin the main highway in four miles anyway.

A fairly new attraction along that road now is the nonprofit **Hawaii**

Tropical Botanical Garden (Tel. 964-5233), headquartered at the former church (painted yellow) at Papaikou. For $6 you will be shuttled by minibus a mile away, where you can spend as much time as you like wandering through and looking at many tropical fruits, flowers, and plants in a 17-acre rain forest on Onomea Bay. Sorry, we still haven't been there, but reader reports have been complimentary.

Back on 19, at a settlement called Honomu, turn left on a five-mile road (No. 220) to **Akaka Falls State Park.** From the parking lot, a fairly easy half-hour walk along a paved path fragrant with ginger, orchids, and other flowers will bring you first to Kahuna Falls, which plunges a mere 100 feet, and then to Akaka Falls, which features a 442-foot vertical drop. It's lovely—well worth the drive and the hike. (On the way out, you might like to stop at the restored century-old Honomu Plantation Store.)

About 10 miles farther up the belt road is **Laupahoehoe Point.** View it from the side of the road, or, if you have a picnic packed, drive the one-mile curving road down to the park and dig in beside the crashing waves. There is a monument in this now-vacant settlement to twenty-four pupils and teachers who were lost here in the 1946 tidal wave.

Way up the coast about 25 miles is the cutoff on Route 24 through the creaky and antiquey village of **Honokaa** (population 1,600), which is formally or informally preserved in the Hawaii of the 1920s. It may also be a wetter town than Hilo. (In January 1979, it registered five *feet* of rain in five days.) You can take the side road *makai* (seaward) from Honokaa to the **Hawaiian Holiday Macadamia Nut Company** (Tel. 775-7743, open 8:30 A.M. to about 2:30 P.M.). This smaller operation is more commercial and hokey than the Keeau factory, but some like it better since it encourages a lot of different kinds of orders and offers more kinds of products. (We prefer the Mauna Loa brand of nut, but they're both good.) Anyway, if you've seen one macadamia-nut factory—whichever one—you've probably seen enough.

Continue on Highway 240 for another eight miles to the end of the road and the viewpoint for **Waipio Valley,** a dramatic green gouge out of the earth. The 2,000-foot gorge is one of the grandiose panoramas of the Islands, nearly comparable to that at the Nuuanu Pali on Oahu. It was once the home of an estimated 50,000 Hawaiians.

The road for conventional cars ends here. If you want to go down into the nearly deserted valley, you'll have to hike or have a four-wheel-drive vehicle *and know darn well how to operate it.* (Whatever you do, don't try to come to a complete stop on the steep road, going down or coming up.) It would be much safer to patronize the Waipio Valley Shuttle, a four-wheel-drive service, or to take other established tours. (See section 7.) (*Psst.* Not many know there's even a hotel down in the valley. It has no name and no electricity, but it does have a phone. See section 4.)

After returning through Honokaa, take either fork back to 19, the Belt Highway. The Tex Drive Inn is near the school, but for serious lunching continue for 15 minutes through the cattle country to the Parker Ranch Broiler or Edelweiss (see section 5 for both) in the ranch community of **Waimea.** There's always some confusion about the name of this village, since the U.S. Postal Service has decreed that one official Waimea in the state (on Kauai) is enough. Mail for the town is therefore addressed to **Kamuela.** (Actually, the post office for Kamuela is in a separate settlement a mile or two up the road.)

Kamuela is the Hawaiian name for Samuel, and it stands for Samuel Parker, grandson of John Parker, the founder of the **Parker Ranch.** Today it's the second largest single ranch in the U.S.A., consisting of about 250,000 acres. (Texas's King Ranch is 860,000 acres.) The Parker spread is headquartered right here in Waimea/Kamuela. Many of the white-faced Hereford cattle you see along the road belong to Parker's herd of some 30,000 head.

In Waimea, the traditional "point of interest" is the **John Palmer Parker Museum** (Tel. 885-7655) in the shopping center. The admission price is $2.50, and, frankly, we don't think it's worth it. One or two of the few exhibits are okay, and it's a highly polished presentation to be sure. But like many a large company history, it suffers from severe attacks of sycophancy, lack of objectivity, and confusing genealogical detail. It relies an awful lot on photographs, and the largest portrait in the museum is a three-times-life-size head shot of the current owner of the Parker Ranch, Richard Smart (whose mother was a Parker). The accompanying 15-minute slide-and-sound show was having considerable technical problems on our visit, but nobody in charge seemed to mind. All in all, we call it mildly interesting but wildly overpriced. (Closed Sundays.)

For around the same price, we prefer the more amateurish museum in the neighborhood, a few miles down the road virtually at the junction of Routes 19 and 250. The **Kamuela Museum** (Tel. 885-4724) winds throughout the home of Albert K. and Harriet K. M. Solomon (she's also a Parker descendant). The Solomons, interesting characters themselves, have the most incredible collection of hodgepodge from all periods of Hawaii—and from everywhere else, for that matter. It's not unlike traveling through your grandmother's attic, only much more so, and with nearly everything neatly labeled. (Ask the Solomons to show you and explain the "canoe breaker.") We should warn you that the museum has been officially for sale for the past two years, so anything could happen at any time. Keep your fingers crossed. The museum's very unprofessionalism has a certain naïve charm, and we've always liked it. (Open 8 A.M. to 5 P.M.)

If you're running short of time, take Highway 19 about 10 miles down the road directly to Kawaihae and skip this next small, seven-paragraph section. If it's still at least early afternoon, however, consider taking the 50- to 60-mile drive through the North Kohala District, described below.

THE NORTH KOHALA CIRCLE

Route 250 is the high road that heads directly through the Kohala mountains, reaching as high as 3,564 feet, and giving vast views of the coastline below. Midway along this breezy route through the 23,000-acre Kahua Ranch, you may catch a glimpse of the **Kahua Ranch Wind Farm**—180 steel towers, each with whirling 26-foot-diameter blades. (It produces up to 3.4 megawatts, enough power to satisfy the electrical needs of about 3,500 persons.) After about 20 miles, the pavement enters the village of **Hawi**, once an important sugar mill town, and now largely fallen into a state of more-or-less picturesque dilapidation.

Take Highway 270 to the right (east) for a couple of miles to the Kapaau Courthouse to see the **Original Kamehameha Statue.** Cast in Florence in 1880, it was lost at sea on its way to Honolulu. A replica was commissioned, and it is the one installed in front of the Judiciary Building in the capital. Then this original was recovered from the ocean and installed here near Kamehameha's birthplace. Surprisingly, it looks very different from the one at the Judiciary Building. The original is on a lower pedestal, for one thing, and painted in bright colors, and it has rather wild-looking eyes.

You'll pass several semi–ghost towns along the route. Ever since the Kohala Sugar Company shut down, the state government has been trying to pull this area back into solvency again, but with only marginal success.

Another six miles will bring you to the end of the road and a viewpoint for **Pololu Valley.** It's nice, but a definite second to Waipio. Fully equipped hikers might like to explore the valley below. The rest of us have to turn around and retrace our route the eight miles to Hawi.

From Hawi, continue on Highway 270 (some maps may still say 27), the Akoni Pule Highway. Dedicated culture-seekers can search out the hard-to-find thirteenth-century **Mo'okini Heiau** on a rough side road just off the Upolu Airport road near the airport. Human sacrifices were once taken here, and you may feel like a victim yourself if you have to make your way through mud. There may be an HVB warrior marker pointing out the place, now, and the reconstructed site could be worth the safari—at least on a dry day.

About seven miles farther is **Mahukona Beach Park,** an important and busy harbor in the days of the Hawaiian monarchy, and the adjoining **Lapakahi State Historical Park,** a project providing employment in this economically depressed area. The site is that of an ancient Hawaiian fishing village, and a brochure describes 23 points along a 1½-mile marked path.

In contrast to the lush mountains above, the return route cuts through desertlike rangelands and lava fields. But you haven't *really* seen lava fields. Not yet. Continue on 270 to Kawaihae, and rejoin Route 19 South.

THE KOHALA (NORTH KONA) COAST

The harbor of **Kawaihae,** once an important village, is still a significant commercial port, but the village part has all but withered away. Nearby (look for the sign) is the **Puukohola Heiau** (Tel. 882-7218), now a National Historic Site. Originally built around 1550, it was rebuilt by Kamehameha I and dedicated to his war god in 1791. It was to this ceremony that he invited the last remaining rival Big Island chief and then suddenly killed him there in cold blood. With this act, he consecrated his temple and began his island conquests at the same moment.

Almost next door to the *heiau* is **Spencer Beach Park,** one of the most popular beaches on the island. The sands are white, and fishing, swimming, snorkeling, body surfing, etc., are excellent. Tent carriers, this is a good place to put down stakes.

Another mile along the road is the turnoff for one of the country's most prestigious resorts, the **Westin Mauna Kea Hotel.** (See sections 4 and 5.) This may be the loveliest beach on the island, and in 1979 the United Airlines hotel bowed to political pressure and provided limited public access to it.

One more mile along the main highway is the entrance to **Hapuna Beach Park,** and this one features A-frame cabins that can be reserved from the state, hopefully still for under $10 a night. (See section 8.)

Also in the neighborhood, just down the road about three miles, is the village of Puako and the excellent **Puako Petroglyphs.** To find those Stone Age pictures, drive through the long, narrow village and look for the small hand-lettered sign that indicates a narrow path on your left, approximately opposite 152 Puako Dr. (If you miss it, come back from the end of the road about 200 yards.) Park on the road, walk through the gate, and follow the rocky path for 15 or 20 difficult minutes. There are lots of the mysterious carvings in at least three groups. These particular ones are thought to be some of the oldest petroglyphs in Hawaii, and anthropologists are still trying to draw meaning from them all. You'll see boats with sails, warriors with weapons, etc. If you have the equipment, petroglyph rubbings make terrific souvenirs. On stretched cloth, use chalk or charcoal pencils, not crayons or other waxy or oily substances, which can damage the originals.

You may observe that scant attention is called to petroglyph sites at any location in Hawaii. They are, of course, subject to defacing and vandalism, and there are some residents who understandably enough would like to delete all directions to any petroglyph fields. Don't take a chance on running into some petroglyphs somewhere else later. If possible, make this trip in the morning, when the day is cool and the shadows are long. This may be your only opportunity to ponder the undeciphered records of an ancient people.

If you have an urge to be a graffitist yourself, stifle it until you return to Route 19 south. Then, for about five miles, you may join the hundreds who have recently spelled out messages by placing lines of white coral stones against black lava fields along the highway. Some have reversed the technique, writing with black lava on the white fields of coral that were dredged from the sea nearby to use in the road construction. The vast black lava desert in this area was created when the volcano Hualalai last erupted, between 1800 and 1801.

This straight black road across 34 miles of sunbaked lava desert is the **Queen Kaahumanu Highway.** Designed to open up the area as a new "Gold Coast," the highway is of equal excitement to land developers and fun-seekers, for several previously hard-to-reach beaches and historic sites are now accessible along the shoreline. (The area is also being promoted as the "Kohala Coast," these days.) Another spectacular hotel along here is the **Mauna Lani Bay Hotel,** next to the Francis H. I'i Brown Golf Course. Then about five miles beyond Puako on 19 a turnoff to the right leads to the beautiful white-sand beach at **Anaehoomalu Bay.** No longer deserted, it now fronts the Sheraton Royal Waikoloa Hotel.

The beach itself, which also encloses an ancient fishpond, features hundreds of palm trees poking directly up through the sand. Almost unequaled in its type of splendor, Anaehoomalu Beach is reminiscent of Luquillo Beach in Puerto Rico. Several petroglyph fields and other historical sites are hidden nearby and are slated for special exhibition later. About the only defect of this green Eden on the edge of a desert is that it can be uncomfortably windy sometimes when the Waimeas are brisk.

If you cross Highway 19 and drive for about five miles on private pavement, you'll reach what Boise Cascade already has installed in the neighborhood, the **Waikoloa Village,** an uninspiring (at least to us) planned community with some townhouses, a very nice 18-hole golf course, tennis courts, and some riding stables. The road continues to connect with Route 190, the *old* Waimea-Kailua highway.

But unless we have a reason for heading Waikoloa way (like to attend the big April rodeo there), we'd skip the drive, turn south, and hammer down across the lava desert toward Kailua-Kona, about 20 more arrow-straight miles. (If you have to go to the bathroom—or to Honolulu—you can turn in at the **Ke-ahole Airport** in about half that distance.)

(Tel. 329-2955) in a large, glass-bottom boat decked out in the hokiest trappings imaginable. During the day, the 85-foot vessel sails out on several short one- and two-hour cruises for coral and fish viewing or snorkeling at rates from around $12 to $20. But Beans' best and most popular trips are the Sunset Dinner Sail at 5 P.M. and the Moonlight Dinner Sail at 8 P.M. For a tab of about $35, there's a full-course dinner, live entertainment, and a wide-open bar (no minors allowed). The original Captain Beans died not long ago, and his vessels were sold to a larger operation (Robert's Hawaii) which so far has been running it in the same way. Let's hope that continues.

For a more complete *daytime* cruise, however, we'd prefer the glass-bottom cruisers launched by **Hawaiian Cruises** (Tel. 329-6411) in either of the 96-foot craft *Captain Cook VII* or the new *Hawaiian Princess* (formerly the *Monterey Princess*). One or the other makes a three-hour cruise down the coast to the underwater marine preserve at Kealakekua Bay. The boat anchors near the Cook Monument so passengers can swim and snorkel in the clear water before the return trip. Price is now about $20 (half-fare for under-12s). Snorkeling equipment is provided free. There's no meal, but there is a bar and snack bar on board. The voyages leave Kailua at 8:45 A.M. and sometimes 1 P.M. This trip is usually dependable and good. Hawaiian Cruises has also begun a sunset dinner cruise in competition with the Beans operation, but we have had no report yet on its success.

Berthed down in Keauhou Bay, seven miles south, is the 50-foot trimaran sailing yacht **Fair Wind** (Tel. 322-2788), a convenient cruise choice for guests at the three Keauhou hotels. Half-day sail and snorkel tours (with lunch) go for around $40, at this writing. Some other kinds of trips are also available, and while we haven't sailed with them ourselves, we have received several favorable letters from Maverick readers.

Sunset and snorkel tours are also offered by a newer outfit, **Kamanu Charters** (Tel. 329-2021), which specializes in small groups. Half-day cruises run around $25.

(Boat trips designed principally for fishing or scuba diving will be described in the next section.)

8. Water Sports on the Big Island

"What this island needs is a good beach!" is the cry so often raised. Actually, the Big Island has several good beaches, although certainly not as many per mile of coastline as most others. Many are difficult to get to without an overland hike. Of the others, we have divided our picks into areas below.

Beaches in Hilo. Just one, we think, and that's **Reed's Bay Beach Park,**

a banyan-shaded cove of Hilo Bay near the defunct Hotel Royal Kalani. Facilities include rest rooms, showers, and drinking water. Calm-water fishing and swimming are okay.

Hamakua Coast. Not much of a beach at **Kolekole Beach Park,** although the popular Wailea shoreline is used for fishing and camping.

Kohala. About four miles past Hawi just on the other side of Niulii is **Keokea Beach Park,** which offers swimming on calm-water days. **Kapaa Beach Park** at Kapaa also has camping and other standard facilities (but no drinking water). Hiking, swimming, and fishing are popular, but skin diving is dangerous. And **Mahukona Beach Park** at Mahukona is located next to an abandoned village. There's good swimming, fishing, skin diving, boating, hiking, and camping.

Kawaihae Area. Just off Highway 250 a mile before Kawaihae Harbor is **Samuel M. Spencer Beach Park.** Swimming, skin diving, and fishing are all excellent at this popular white-sand beach. It's very crowded on the weekends, however. **Hapuna Beach Park** is also not far, about a mile past the Westin Mauna Kea Hotel going south. It's a beautiful beach, but in high wave conditions it features strong offshore currents and a dangerous shorebreak. During the winter, it's popular with body surfers, and it has lots of facilities including cabins that can be rented from the State Parks Division at about $10 nightly. (You can also swim at the hotel beach to the north, now that public access has been opened.) And **Anaehoomalu Bay,** about five miles down the road, now fronts the Sheraton Waikoloa Hotel. The palm-fringed beach is one of the loveliest on the island, and popular for swimming and skin diving.

The Kailua-Kona Area. Here the beaches are unimpressive. There is a tiny one in Kailua directly in front of the Hotel King Kamehameha. After that, about three miles down the coast, is **Disappearing Sands Beach,** also called White Sands and Magic Sands. Some local folks like to body surf here, but we say that whether the sand is in or out, the current is tricky and dangerous. **Kahaluu Beach Park,** near Keauhou Bay on Alii Drive, is the most decent beach in the immediate vicinity. Swimming and skin diving are fine.

Napoopoo Beach Park, with its black-sand beach, is better known as Kealakekua Bay. Skin diving is superb in this calm underwater park off Route 11, *makai* of Captain Cook. And **Hookena Beach Park** is located in an interesting beachside village about 23 miles south of Kailua. There is no drinking water or electricity, but plenty of good swimming, body surfing, fishing, and hiking. Tent and trailer camping, too.

Ka'u Area. Another beautiful camping, swimming, body surfing, and fishing site is on the famous black sand at **Punaluu Beach Park.** Some of the facilities may still be damaged from an earthquake some years ago, however.

Puna District. Not far from Kaimu Black Sand Beach (where you shouldn't swim) is the lovely **Harry K. Brown Beach Park** at Kalapana. Lots of park facilities are here, and swimming and fishing are popular and good.

SCUBA DIVING AND SNORKELING

Most of the Kona Coast is considered ideal for diving and viewing life beneath the sea. Visibility often extends to as far as 200 feet underwater, and there are many colorful fish and beautiful corals to be enjoyed. The best areas are at Kahaluu Beach Park, Keauhou Bay, Kealakekua Bay, and the City of Refuge (Pu'uhonua o Honaunau National Historical Park). Also the Koai'e Cove State Underwater Park is just offshore from Lapakahi State Historical Park (see section 6).

Professional instruction, equipment rental, and expeditions are available and abundant in Kona. For full-scale scuba-diving lessons, try the popular **Dive Makai Charters** (Tel. 329-2025), which has several program options. Lessons and all equipment run around $90. **Sea Paradise** (Tel. 322-2500) we know less about. If you just want to rent snorkel or scuba equipment, try **Ocean Sports Hawaii** (Tel. 329-8411), under Buzz's restaurant on Alii Drive, **Big Island Marine** (Tel. 329-3719) on Alapa Street, or **Jack's Diving Locker** (Tel. 329-7585) in the Kona Inn Shopping Village.

Headquartered down in Keauhou Bay, the attractive sailboat the **Fair Wind** (Tel. 322-2788), mentioned in our cruises discussion, also offers scuba-diving trips and instruction at comparable rates.

SPORT FISHING

Deep-sea fishing on the Kona Coast is world-famous, and records are made and broken here annually. Eager for marlin and similar deepwater denizens, anglers from everywhere converge on Kailua-Kona every summer for the Hawaiian International Billfish Tournament.

Kona charter boats have half-day, full-day, and now even two-day trips when they sail down the coast to South Point, the commercial fishing grounds.

For convenience, turn your fishing request over to either the **Kona Activities Center** (Tel. 329-3171), P.O. Box 1035, or the **Kona Charter Skippers Association** (Tel. 329-3600), P.O. Box 806, both at Kailua-Kona, HI 96740.

You can charter the captain, mate, and the entire boat with all necessary equipment for all day (eight hours) for about $400. Half-day trips run about $300. (If you come back with fish, the skipper and mate will expect a tip.) The bigger boats accommodate up to six passengers, so you can split the expense accordingly. There are also some trips sold by the seat—perhaps $100-$150 for all day.

9. Other Big Island Sports

The Keauhou-Kona area seems determined to become the *tennis* capital of the North Pacific, and it smashed a solid serve toward that goal in 1976 when the Avis Challenge Cup series opened in the new 2,500-seat Holua Stadium.

In the hotel next door is the **Kona Surf Racquet Club** (Tel. 322-9131): eight courts, three lighted; racket rentals, tennis balls, ball-throwing machine, and private lessons available. Rates are about $5 per hour per person.

In Kailua, the **Kona Hilton** (Tel. 329-3111) has four courts, and the **King Kamehameha Hotel** (Tel. 329-2911) has four courts, two lighted. Also there is one free lighted court at the **Kailua Playground** (which might become available at around midnight), and three unlighted courts in the **Kona Village Resort** that are free for folks on the register there.

In Hilo, there are four free lighted tennis courts at **Lincoln Park** (Kinoole and Ponahawai streets) and free unlighted ones and $5-per-hour lighted indoor ones at **Hoolulu Park** on Kalanikoa Street and at the **University of Hawaii-Hilo** campus at 333 West Lanikaula St.

In the hinterlands, there are 13—count 'em—13 courts in a spectacular 12-acre tennis park at the **Westin Mauna Kea Hotel,** but they are presently for guests only. The **Mauna Lani Bay Hotel** has 10, also reserved for guests. Two lighted courts are available at **Waikoloa Village** for $2 per person per hour. In Waimea, at the **Waimea Park,** there are two free lighted courts. And four courts are open now at the **Seamountain-Hawaii Resort** (Tel. 928-8010), next to the golf course in Ka'u. Guests at Colony One are free. Nonguests pay a modest charge.

GOLF LINKS ON THE LAVA

Now that horticulturists and architects have discovered the secret of growing golf courses on lava flows, spectacular greens and fairways have begun to carpet the Big Island, some of them ranking with the best in the world. On all these, we recommend you call ahead for starting times, any day of the week.

The **Westin Mauna Kea Golf Course** (Tel. 882-7222) is still the unofficial leader, designed by Robert Trent Jones, the prolific archon of golf architects. About 3½ miles south, the **Francis H. I'i Brown Golf Course** (Tel. 885-6655), with fairways sculpted between outcroppings of lava at the Mauna Lani Resort, has been getting rave reviews from everywhere. Two miles farther than that you'll find the **Waikoloa Village Golf Course** (Tel. 883-9621) inland, near the condominiums there. Then the newer **Waikoloa Beach Golf Club** (Tel. 885-6060) is next to the Sheraton down by the beach. Both Waikoloa courses are Robert Trent Jones Jr. creations.

An unusual set of links at the edge of a live volcano forms the **Volcano Golf and Country Club** (Tel. 967-7331) in the national park.

An attractive coastal course is the **Keauhou-Kona Golf Course** (Tel. 322-2595). Rates are around $25. The **Waikoloa Village Golf Course** (Tel. 883-9621) is located somewhat up-in-the-air in South Kohala. The **Seamountain Golf Course** (Tel. 928-8000) is the nucleus of a long-delayed resort down at Punaluu in Ka'u.

The county-operated **Hilo Municipal Course** (Tel. 959-7711) is also 18 holes and much less expensive. There are two 9-hole courses, the **Banyan Golf Center** (Tel. 935-7388) next to the hotels in Hilo, and the **Hamakua Country Club** (Tel. 775-7244) way up the coast at Honokaa.

RIDING IN COWBOY COUNTRY

You can rent horses through the **Mauna Kea Beach Hotel** (Tel. 882-7222) at Kamuela. The hourly rate, complete with a genuine *paniolo* guide, is about $15 per person. We enjoyed our own outing here not long ago. Also, the **Waikoloa Countryside Stables** (Tel. 883-9335) offers opportunities to ride over many wilderness trails for around the same price.

HUNTING ON HAWAII

Wild goats, feral sheep, bristling boar, and wild Vancouver bull—plus several game birds—may be stalked on the Big Island. Some kind of hunting is available the year around. The scenery in the hunting areas is terrific, and even if you don't bag something you'll have had an invigorating outing.

Game hunting on private lands is not state regulated, but you'll need a license in any case. That's $15 to the Division of Fish and Game, Hawaii Department of Land and Natural Resources. In Hilo, they're at 75 Aupuni St. (Tel. 961-7291), but there are also more than a dozen agents authorized to sell you a license.

The only hunting guide service we know of this year is **Hawaii Hunting Tours** (Tel. 776-1666), headquartered in Paauilo. Check with professional hunter Eugene Ramos about rates and supplies. Write P.O. Box 58, Paauilo, HI 96776.

SNOW SKIING? YES!

It seems that more is written about skiing on Hawaii every year as more people become intrigued with the idea of skiing in the tropics. But if you expect Mauna Kea to be another Aspen, you'll be very disappointed.

Skiing on Hawaii must be taken as a lark. There are no lifts or tows, and all skiing must be accomplished at a dizzying elevation of more than 11,000 feet, where altitude sickness, sunburns, and snow blindness are common. On the plus side, the runs are as long as three miles, with no trees and few rocks to worry about. The snow is either powder or, more likely, easily controllable corn. The ski patrol is sometimes on duty in case of accidents. Air temperatures vary between 30 and 65 degrees. The season runs vaguely from December through May, although skiable conditions have been known to persist long enough for a special Fourth of July ski meet!

You'll also need a four-wheel-drive vehicle and a free state permit, and we suggest avoiding the slopes on a weekend, when the road to the summit can be crowded and the thin air has been known to increase driver irritability. If you're determined to try it, we think the best thing to do is to turn the whole project over to Hawaii's ski guru, Dick Tillson, owner/operator of **Ski Shop Hawaii** (Tel. 885-4188), whom you may write at Kamuela, HI 96743. All-inclusive, per-person rates will probably be around $130 a day, with all equipment included—including spare oxygen. (Tillson also has another branch of his shop at 830 Ala Moana Blvd. in Honolulu, P.O. Box 8237, Honolulu, HI 96815, Tel. 946-4506. However he often closes down both shops and cancels the telephone in the summertime.) Sexagenarian Tillson, the "old man of the mountain," also runs all the ski meets on Mauna Kea. Tell him we sent you!

10. Big Island Shopping—from Bamboo to Nuts

In Kailua-Kona, the *alii* of shopping centers is the 30,000-square-foot, self-contained mall at the King Kamehameha Hotel. You'll find there a link in Honolulu's classy **Liberty House** chain, and a branch of **Andrade's,** this one specializing in women's and children's apparel. You'll see a good supply of locally made jewelry in the **Jewel Palace** and a nice selection of canvas tote bags at **Traveler's Choice.** Even flowers are made out of shells at **The Shellery.** But the best Niihau shell *leis* seem to be sold at **Traders.** They begin at $175. Some beautiful Chinese china and decorative tiles are featured at the **Orient Gift Shop.** We liked the delicate Filipino baskets and other unusual things at **Gifts for All Seasons,** too. And at **Bri'oni,** we saw some modern glass sculpture displayed along with modern fashions. For some reason there are separate entrances for those interested in men's or women's garments. The glass worker is also on the premises, but not on display.

Most of Kailua's shops are tucked into greater or lesser arcades or plazas that have narrow openings onto the main drag. Some are attractive. Most are a hodgepodge. It's easy to get lost and darned hard to tell someone how to find something. Street addresses mean very little in this higgledy-piggledy setup. There could be a dozen or two stores at "75-5699 Alii Drive," for example.

We saw some unusual clothes for both sexes at the **Butterfly Boutique** in the Seaside Mall, across from the King Kam Hotel. Some are locally made.

Old-timers shed a tear today for the more authentic ancient ambience gone with the demise of Emma's General Store in the commercial center of Kailua. Just across from Emma's Market Place (yes, they named that after the old store) is a shop called the **Sandal Basket,** which seems to sell as many hats as sandals or baskets.

Past the church in front of the Kona Plaza Shopping Arcade is the **Coral Factory.** Prices may run a little higher here, but the atmosphere is attractive, the products are well displayed, and the clerks are helpful. In the arcade itself, **Neptune's Garden** for years has displayed a good collection of shell craft and the like. The **Middle Earth Bookshoppe** has moved its well-stocked shelves to a site nearby, but may still be too busy to put up its shingle.

Next door, the World Square Arcade presents an interesting semicircular browse. (It's to this site that the free red London bus carts you from hotels in Keauhou.) We were drawn to the **Smuggler's Loft**—partly because of its nautical brass items, but what we really found interesting were the genuine Big Island mounted and polished boars' tusks for around $85 to $225. (Friendly Jackie Gour will tell you all about them.)

Across the street, the Kona Inn Shopping Village contains pretty much the same kind of products as elsewhere on the street. We did like the opals and emerald jewelry we saw at Jim Bill's **Gemfire,** however. Gemologist Colleen Johansen may be there to explain them all. How about an eelskin lamp? You'll find that at **Exotic Skins** in the same area. There Muriel Pavao also spreads out some rare coins and antiques.

Often overlooked is the less-showy Kona Coast Shopping Center, just up Route 190, where you'll find the supermarkets—and many better prices. **Bell, Book and Candle** (Tel. 329-1441) is up there, now, still offering a good selection of Hawaiian books and recordings plus lots of greeting cards and gifts in expanded quarters.

South of Kailua, now, the new **Keauhou Shopping Village** is open, but we haven't been in personally. All in all, remember that Kailua's and

Keauhou's shops have a way of changing before our perishable research can find its way into print. As in Lahaina, many of Kona's most intriguing stores will be temporary—ambitious boutiques and art huts selling something new, clever, and cute, springing up now here, then there, and later perhaps even moving on to another island when the owners seek new inspiration—"Here today, gone to Maui!" is a favorite expression around here.

Over in Hilo, a fancy new air conditioned shopping center, the **Prince Kuhio Plaza**, has opened on the Volcano Highway at Puainako Street. Here you'll find your Sears, your Liberty House, your Woolworths, etc., along with movie theaters, drug stores, and fast-food restaurants.

In the Banyan Drive area, we were intrigued by the joyful jumble of good and bad stuff in the **Polynesian Market Place** in the Hilo Bay Hotel. It sells just about every kind of curio ever made in Hawaii—or anyplace else. Some things are very inexpensive. You'll find more quality items, however, at the shops next door in the Naniloa Surf Hotel.

Midtown Hilo, also called Kaiko'o, is generally not so interesting for visitors, although the Hilo Mall Shopping Center is there, equipped with such standard places as Penney's and branches of Honolulu establishments. More isolated stores in Hilo include the **Hawaiian Handicraft Shop** (Tel. 935-5587) at 760 Kilauea St., across from the mall, where you may sometimes watch the woodcarver at work. Also, see if you can resist **The Most Irresistible Shop in Hilo** on Keawe Street near the Mun Cheong Lau restaurant. TMISIH specializes in little things—soaps, stationery, hand-made dolls, and, as they say in the islands "wat-evah." And some clever sweets—like maybe candy *sushi*—are sold at **The Chocolate Bar** from its addresses at 98 Keawe St. and in the Prince Kuhio Plaza.

A late-late everything store? Like on a Sunday night when everything's closed, and you want a newspaper or maybe a box of school clay, or perhaps an old Nixon/Agnew button? Try the **Hawaii Bargain Store,** at 278 Kilauea Ave.

You'll recall that Hilo is the center of the anthurium and orchid industry. For orchids especially, check out **Orchids of Hawaii** (Tel. 959-3581) at 2801 Kilauea Ave. Several flower farms are dependable, notably the **Hirose Nursery** (Tel. 959-4561) on Highway 11, just out of town. We once bought some anthuriums here, and were very impressed with the friendliness and efficiency we encountered. Readers have written more recently to echo our views. Tell 'em we sent you.

For books, you will enjoy browsing the complete stock in the **Book Gallery** (Tel. 935-2447), run by Steve and Frances Reed in the Kaiko'o Mall in Hilo. Also browse through **Basically Books** at 169 Keawe St. downtown. You might run across a pleasant surprise at the **Serendipity**

Bookshop (Tel. 959-5481), 2100 Kanoelehua Ave. and now **Waldenbooks** has opened a branch in the Prince Kuhio Plaza.

Macadamia nuts? You can buy them anywhere, so there's really no need to make a special trip to either of the two competing factories. Our personal preference for consistently good-quality nuts is the **Mauna Loa** brand, the large C. Brewer operation. You can visit the factory in Keaau (Tel. 966-9301), but they sell the nuts there at the suggested retail price, and there's not much selection of different kinds of products. The mechanical operation is well explained, however.

The other brand, **Hawaiian Holiday,** is produced with more pizzazz by a family factory up in Honokaa (Tel. 775-7743). Instead of just the nuts and nut brittle, they've combined their macadamias with coconut chips, Maui onions, hickory-smoked this and that, and all kinds of candies in every form possible to make scores of things to choose from. The factory itself is smaller, more human size, and the country store they've tacked on and gussied up to sell the nuts from is, well, nutty but fun. Both will arrange mail orders to the Mainland (air or surface).

11. Big Island Big Nights on the Town

On the Kona Coast, now, there's a good luau/Polynesian extravaganza for folks who've not yet seen a big luau/Polynesian extravaganza at the **King Kamehameha Hotel** (Tel. 329-2911) in Kailua-Kona. However, the most delicious and authentic luau on the island this year is probably the Friday-night-only **Kona Village Luau** (Tel. 325-5555). You must reserve ahead or you can't get in the gate, and you'll need a car to make the 15-mile trip up the coast from Kailua. Some other hotels have luaus on an irregular basis. Also complimentary Hawaiian shows are given for evening patrons at **Cousin Kimo's Restaurant** in the Kona Bay Hotel.

The premier Kona discotheque may be the **Poi Pounder** in the Kona Surf Hotel, which pounds until 2 A.M. On the same property, the **Puka Bar** has been tamed into a lovely lava-rock drinking den with more modest entertainment.

Over in Hilo, there is one excellent, dependable showroom, and it's at the Naniloa Surf Hotel (Tel. 935-0831). The well-designed, ground-floor **Crown Room** seats a multitude of 400, giving virtually all an excellent view of the stage, and usually serves a full sit-down dinner (no buffet) for about $25 or $30. It brings in top acts from Waikiki, and sometimes even from the Mainland.

Also in the Naniloa Surf is the **Hoomalimali Bar,** where there is usually a lounge act like Boyson, Stan, and Mary Lou Brown, a talented Hilo trio. This is also a favorite meeting place for the more mature (over 25) crowd. The teenies and teenies-plus seem to discover each other's mysteries these days at **Club CJs** just across Banyan Drive near the golf course.

You might look for the versatile falsetto artist Bunny Brown and his group, who could still be playing in the **Menehune Land Lounge** in the Hilo Hawaiian Hotel (Tel. 935-9361). And a locally favored establishment outside the hotels is the **Green Door** (Tel. 935-6388), usually featuring some kind of entertainment. Stay alert; you may discover the drinks are more reasonable than some of your fellow customers. It's on the Kilauea Street side of the Kaiko'o Mall, and you'll know the place... well... by its green door.

12. Big Island Address List

Bakery— Mountain View Bakery (famous cookies), Mountain View. Tel. 968-6353.

Barber— Sel's Barber Shop, 145 Mamo St., Hilo. Tel. 935-1771.

Beauty salon— Kona Surf Beauty Salon, Kona Surf Resort, Keauhou. Tel. 322-9100.

Camping equipment rental— Kona Rent All, 74-5602 Alapa St., Kailua. Tel. 329-1644.

Chamber of Commerce— Hawaii Island Chamber of Commerce, 180 Kinoole St., Hilo. Tel. 935-7178.

Dry cleaners— Kona Dry Cleaning, 75-5705 Kuakini Hwy., Kailua. Tel. 329-8115. Hilo Quality Cleaners, 865 Kinoole St., Hilo. Tel. 935-1620.

Fire department— Emergency Tel. 961-6022.

Hawaii Visitors Bureau— Marlin Plaza, Kailua. Tel. 329-7787. 180 Kinoole St., Hilo. Tel. 961-5797.

Health-food stores— Aloha Village Store, Kainaliu, Kona. Tel. 322-9941. Hilo Natural Foods, 306 Kilauea Ave. Tel. 935-7002.

Hospitals— Kona Hospital, Kealakekua. Tel. 322-9311. Hilo Hospital, 1190 Waianuenue Ave. Tel. 961-4211.

Laundromats— Kaiko'o Coin Laundry, 401 Kilauea Ave., Hilo. Tel. 961-6490. Hele Mai Laundromat, Kailua. Tel. 329-3494.

Pharmacies— Long's Drug Stores, 555 Kilauea Ave., Hilo. Tel. 935-3357. Pay'n Save Drug Store, Kona Coast Shopping Center, Kailua. Tel. 329-3577.

Police— Emergency Tel. 935-3311.

Supermarket— Safeway, Kuhio Plaza, Hilo.

Volcanic activity— 24-hour recorded information, Tel. 967-7977.

Appendix

Now that there is Wide Area Telephone Service (WATS) to Hawaii, you can dial several numbers in the Island State toll-free from other parts of the United States and Canada. To use these numbers, you must dial the code "800" first. *This should not be confused with "808,"* the standard area code for all regular Hawaii telephone numbers. Through an unfortunate coincidence, it is very similar.

Keep in mind that many of these numbers will not work from certain areas, and that several Hawaii hotels and other facilities still do not have toll-free 800 numbers. Also, certain chains encourage reservations through other branches of their operations in your local area, and even some 800 numbers do not connect you direct to Hawaii, but to some other central reservations facility on the Mainland. Most genuine Hawaiian WATS numbers—which will be answered by someone actually in Hawaii—begin with "367." (Until last year, they all did, but a few new prefixes are now being used. Nevertheless, any "367" number is apparently still assigned to a company in Hawaii.) With a few exceptions, such as with rental cars, we have tended to eliminate from our list any 800 numbers which we believe will not be answered in Hawaii on the theory that the people you talk to on the Mainland generally won't be as familiar with the facilities as the staff on the scene.

Some of the hotels, rental-car firms, and others who answer these toll-free numbers are expecting calls mainly from travel agents. However, if you are an individual traveler making your own arrangements, here is a chance to nail down exactly the kind of accommodation or vehicle you want. Most of these places will be glad to deal with you direct.

Travel agents, too, will find these 800 numbers useful. By calling them, they can get instant free feedback on their requests. Of course all such bookings are tentative, and neither individual traveler nor agent will have confirmed reservations until any required advance deposits have been made.

In all cases, please tell 'em we sent you.

TOLL-FREE NUMBERS FOR SOME HAWAII HOTELS AND CONDOS

(Remember to dial 800 first—from some areas, 1-800. Note that many hotels associated with each other share the same number, so be sure you know exactly which place you're booking into.)

451

Honolulu, Oahu, and Multi-Island

Ala Moana Americana. 228-3278
Amfac Resorts. 227-4700 (California 622-0838)
Aston Hotels & Resorts. 367-5124
Colony Resorts. 367-6046 (Canada, 263-8189)
Colony Surf (East and West). 367-6046
Coral Reef. 367-5124 (Canada, 663-3602)
Coral Seas. 367-5170 (U.S. only)
Diamond Head Beach. See Colony Resorts.
Great American Management. 367-2363.
Halekulani. 367-2343
Hawaiian King Hotel. 367-7042
Hawaiian Pacific Resorts. 367-5004 (Canada, 663-1118)
Hawaiian Regent. 367-5370
Hawaiiana Resorts. 367-7040
Holiday Inn—Waikiki Beach. 367-8047, Ext. 2570
Hotel Corporation of the Pacific. 367-5124
Hukilau Sand & Seaside Hotels. 367-7000
Hyatt Regency Waikiki. 228-9000
InterIsland Resorts. 367-5360
Kahala Hilton. 367-2525
Miramar. 367-2303 (California 622-0847)
Moana. See Sheraton hotels.
Outrigger, Outrigger East, Outrigger Surf, Outrigger West, Waikiki Village, Waikiki Surf, and Reef Hotel, Reef Lanais, etc. 367-5170 (Canada 826-6786)
Pacific Beach and Pagoda hotels. 367-6060
Princess Kaiulani. See Sheraton hotels.
Quality Inn Waikiki. 922-4671.
Queen Kapiolani. 367-5004
Reef Hotels—Edgewater, Reef, Reef Towers, Waikiki Tower. 367-5170 (Canada, 826-6786)
Royal Hawaiian. See Sheraton hotels.
Sheraton hotels. 334-8484 (Eastern Canada 268-9393, Western Canada, 268-9330)
Surfrider. See Sheraton hotels.
Waikiki Beachcomber. 227-4700 (California 622-0838)
Waikiki Grand. 367-5314
Waikiki Resort. 367-5116
Waikiki Surf. See Outrigger.
Waikiki Surfside. 367-5124
Waikiki Village. 367-5170
Waikikian. 367-5124
Westin Ilikai. 228-3000

Kauai Hotels

Coco Palms Resort. 542-2626
Coral Reef. 843-4659
Hanalei Bay Resort. 367-8047, Ext. 251
Kauai BeachBoy. 227-4700 (California 622-0838)
Kauai Resort. 367-5004
Kauai Sands. 367-7000
Kiahuna Plantation. 367-7052
Princeville—Makai Club Cottages, etc. 367-7090
Sheraton Kauai, Sheraton Coconut Beach, Sheraton Princeville. See Oahu, Sheraton hotels.
Waiohai Resort. 227-4700 (California 633-0838)

Maui Hotels

Coconut Inn. 367-8006
Hotel Hana-Maui. 367-5224
Hyatt Regency Maui. 228-9000
Kaanapali Beach. 227-4700 (California 622-0838)
Kamaole Sands. 367-6046
Kapalua Bay Resort. 367-8000
Lahaina Shores. 367-2972
Maui Beach. 367-5004 (U.S. only)
Maui Connection. 628-4776
Maui 800. 367-5224
Maui Inter-Continental Wailea. 367-2960
Maui Lu Resort. 367-5244
Maui Prince. 321-6284
Maui Sands and Hukilau. 367-5037
Napili Kai Beach Club. 367-5030 (Canada, 263-8183)
Noelani. 367-6030
Papakea Beach Resort. 367-5637
Royal Lahaina Resort. 227-4700 (California 622-0838)
Sheraton Maui. See Oahu, Sheraton hotels.
Stouffer's Wailea Beach. 468-3571 (Canada, 265-4870)
TraveLodge at Lahaina. 255-3050 (Canada, 261-3330)

Molokai and Lanai Hotels

Hotel Lanai. 367-8047, Ext. 448
Hotel Molokai. 367-8047
Ke Nani Kai. 367-7040
Molokai Shores. 367-7042
Paniolo Hale. 367-2984
Pau Hana Inn. 367-8047
Sheraton Molokai. See Oahu, Sheraton hotels.
Wavecrest. 367-2980

Big Island Hotels

Hilo Bay (Uncle Billy Kimi's). 367-5102
Hilo Hawaiian. 367-5004 (Canada, 663-1118)
Hilo Hukilau. 367-7000
King Kamehameha. 227-4700 (California 622-0838)

Kona Bay. 367-5102
Kona Lagoon. 367-5004
Kona Hukilau. 367-7000
Kona Seaside. 367-7000
Kona Village Resort. 367-5290

Mauna Kea Beach. 228-3000
Mauna Lani Bay. 367-2323
Naniloa. 367-5360
Volcano House. See Oahu, Sheraton hotels.

TOLL-FREE NUMBERS FOR SOME CAR-RENTAL FIRMS

(Dial 800 first. Note that some companies operate on all islands, some on only one island. Several numbers below are Mainland offices.)

Alamo. 327-9633
Aloha Funway Rentals. 367-2686
American International. 527-0160
Avis. 331-1212 (Oklahoma 482-4554, Canada 268-2310)
Budget. 527-0707
Dollar Rent-A-Car. 367-7006
Hertz. 654-8200

Holiday Rent-A-Car. 367-2631
National Car Rental. 328-4300
Rent-A-Wreck. 367-5231
Sears Rent-A-Car. See Budget above.
Thrifty Rent-A-Car. 367-2277
Tropical Rent-A-Car. 367-5140 (Canada, 663-9017)
United Car Rental System. 367-8100.

MISCELLANEOUS FIRMS WITH TOLL-FREE 800 NUMBERS

Akamai Tours. 922-6485
Aloha Airlines. 367-5250 (Canada, 663-9471)
Aloha Lei Greeters. 367-5255
American Express Travel Service, Hawaii. 367-2333
American Hawaii Cruises. 227-3666 (California 622-0666)
Central Pacific Divers. 821-6670 (Canada, 262-6670)
Charley's Hawaii Tours. 367-5200
Chuck Machado Luau. 367-5255
Destination Molokai Association. 367-4753 (Canada, 423-8733, Ext. 447)
Greeters of Hawaii. 367-2669
Harrington, Al, Show. 367-2345
Hawaiian Airlines. 367-5320 (Canada, 663-3389)
Hawaiian Holiday Macadamia Nuts. 367-5150
Hawaiian Holidays Tours. 367-5040
Hawaiian Pacific Helicopters. 367-8047, Ext. 142

Hokunani Cruises. 367-5270
Island Odysseys (Trek Hawaii). 367-5696
Kalo's South Seas Review. 367-6077
Kenai Helicopters. 367-2603
Kona Activities Center. 367-5288
Kona Charter Skippers Assn. 367-8047, Ext. 360
Lahaina Divers. 367-8047, Ext. 102
Lahaina, Kaanapali & Pacific R.R., 367-4753
Maui Helicopters. 367-8003
Mid Pacific Airlines. 367-7010
Ocean Activities Center. 367-8047, Ext. 448
Polynesian Cultural Center. 367-7060
Princeville Airways. 367-7090
Society of Seven. 367-5170
South Sea Helicopters. 367-2914
Spirit of Windjammer Cruises. 367-4753
Trade Wind Tours. 367-5333
Windjammer Cruises. 367-5000
Windsurfing Hawaii. 367-5945

Index

455

Please tell us about your trip to Hawaii.
(This page can be folded to make an envelope.)

Cut along this line.

Cut along this line.

re: 1987 edition Hawaii

Place
first class
postage
here

Bob and Sara Bone
The Maverick Guides
Pelican Publishing Company
1101 Monroe Street
P.O. Box 189
Gretna, Louisiana 70053

TRAVEL NOTES

TRAVEL NOTES

TRAVEL NOTES

SEE HAWAII—With the Video Travel Advisor!

The perfect companion to the *Maverick Guide to Hawaii*, these videotapes give you an honest visual and verbal tour of *your* destination.

Whether you're bound for Oahu or one of the neighbor islands, the Video Travel Advisor provides the *kamaaina* [native] perspective you need to make informed decisions. Climate, culture, nightlife, lodging, restaurants, and recreational activities are all evaluated, in full color.

Each videotape retails for $19.95, or $37.90 for both. Enjoy the beauty of Hawaii with *Oahu* and *The Neighbor Islands!*

_____

Please send me:

_____ copies of *Oahu* @ $19.95 each (plus $2.00 for shipping and handling for one tape and 50¢ for additional tapes).

_____ copies of *The Neighbor Islands* @ $19.95 each (plus $2.00 for shipping and handling for one tape and 50¢ for each additional tapes).

_____ copies of the set, *Oahu* and *The Neighbor Islands* @ $37.90 (plus $2.50 for shipping and handling for each set ordered).

Name _____

Address _____

City/State _____ Zip_____

PELICAN PUBLISHING COMPANY
P.O. Box 189
Gretna, LA 70053
(504) 368-1175